1992

SOFTWARE SUCCESS™

REFERENCE BOOK

BY DAVID H. BOWEN

ISBN 0-9625967-1-X

Published By Software Success
David H. Bowen
Publisher
PO Box 9006
San Jose, CA 95157-0006
(408) 446-2504
FAX (408) 255-1098

Printed in the United States of America

First Printing, 1992

Table of Contents

Chapter I. Promotion

Table of Contents

Table of Contents

Chapter II. Lead Generation

Table of Contents

Table of Contents

Chapter III. Pricing

Table of Contents

Chapter IV. Distribution

Table of Contents

Table of Contents

Table of Contents

Table of Contents

Chapter VI. Customer Support & Technical Issues

Table of Contents

Chapter VII. Feature Articles and Case Studies

Chapter VIII. Sales Cycle

Chapter IX. Index

1992
Software   Success
Reference   Book

Chapter I
Promotion

A. Promotion Survey (Oct - 1991)

Our promotion survey indicates that it will probably be a busy autumn for CEOs and marketing departments. Many companies are axing their agency accounts and heaping more responsibility for promotion upon their presidents and marketing communications people in an apparent attempt to cut costs and gain more control over their marketing efforts.

Furthermore, our survey shows that many software companies could better exploit cheaper ways of generating publicity. For example, very few companies develop long-term working relationships with the press, despite the benefits of such relationships.

1. Company Revenue

We received 125 responses to this survey, and the responding companies had lower revenues than those who've answered our previous surveys. This leads me to wonder whether smaller companies are more resourceful in using promotional opportunities than larger companies. Do small companies have to be shrewd self-promoters because every dollar they spend has to count? Or is it that larger companies, facing tough economic conditions, have decided to cut their promotion budgets and coast upon their more established, easily recognized trade names to get themselves through troubled times, a luxury that small, unknown companies can't afford? If you're Oracle, in other words, you can probably coast on your name for a little while. Perhaps both factors had an effect on the numbers. Comparing this year's results with last year's, we find a decided drop in the company revenue of respondents:

Company Revenue	Percent of Respondents This Year	Percent of Respondents Last Year
less than $250K	20.0	10.3
$250K-$500K	15.2	5.1
$500K-$1M	18.4	17.9
$1M-$2M	24.0	33.3
$2M-$5M	14.4	15.4
greater than $5M	7.2	12.8

2. Computer Type

The survey also shows that LAN and Macintosh products have greatly increased since last year, when we didn't specifically ask about Macintosh products, and the reported number of LAN products was roughly half of what it is today. This change is especially significant when one compares this year's responses to those of last year's promotion survey. The following table demonstrates this marked increase:

Computer Types Supported	Last Year	This Year
PC	59.2%	59.0%
LAN	31.2%	17.9%
Macintosh	15.2%	NA
Workstation	12.8%	NA
Multi-user PC	21.6%	NA
Mnicomputer	24.8%	15.4%
Mainframe	10.4%	15.4%

Last year, respondents sold software that ran on an average of 1.1 machines. This year, the average was 1.75 per respondent. This means that last year, 10% of the companies offered their product on a second computer type, but 75% of companies answering the survey this year support their products on more than one computer platform.

Of course, we have included more computer types in our survey this year, but it is also true that many companies are porting their products to several platforms. This strategy is a wise one for most companies; once a company has established itself in a market, it should serve as much of that market as possible. If supporting multiple platforms increases your product's available market, porting may be a better tactic than modifying the product for a different target market.

Considering that the U.S. economy is growing at a rate of less than five percent, software companies are doing unbelievably well.

Now that software tools and database software have made portability much more affordable, I think we'll see many products running on diverse platforms.

Portability, in other words, is finally an option even (perhaps especially) for companies that don't have huge staffs of programmers. Why didn't this happen earlier? I think that this is one of those concepts that the press turned into a buzzword years ago, but hardware-dependent code, poor tools, and programmers inexperienced in developing software for multiple platforms made the concept much more difficult to actually implement than people anticipated. The press went on to other, more exciting issues, but the software companies jumped into the trenches and dug themselves in. They took a few hits along the way (What developer doesn't have horror stories about "Our First Port?"), but they kept working at it, and today, five or ten years later, the concept has become a reality for most companies. The result is that software companies can support more platforms. I believe that this demonstrates a fundamental shift in how software companies think of their market.

3. Expected Revenue Growth Rate

The median companies that responded to this survey are expecting to grow 20% to 30% this year. Considering that the U.S. economy is growing at a rate of less than five percent, software companies are doing unbelievably well:

Expected Growth Rate	% Responding
0%-20% decrease	4.0%
No change	8.0%
Less than a 10% increase	13.6%
10%-20% increase	25.6%
20%-30% increase	20.0%
30%-50% increase	16.8%
Greater than a 50% increase	11.2%

4. Marketing Budget (including salaries)

The median marketing budget is 10% to 15% of revenue, which appears to be slightly higher than the 10% average we found in the operating expenses survey. The following table details the marketing budgets as a percentage of total revenues:

Marketing Budget	% Responding
0%	1.6
1%-5%	21.6
5%-10%	18.4
10%-15%	17.6
15%-20%	15.2
>20%	20.8

5. How much of the marketing budget goes to Promotion?

Marketing budgets are allocated to promotion and lead generation, where lead generation is distinguished from promotion by its short-term orientation. Companies usually allocate 25% to 50% of their marketing budget to promotion, which is significant, considering the high growth rates companies expect to sustain and the demands that this puts on the lead generation budget.

% Allocated to Promotion	% Responding
100	3.2
75-100	7.2
50-75	20.8
25-50	25.6
0-25	32.0
0	4.0

6. Responsibility for Promotion

Marketing departments and CEOs usually share responsibility for promotion, but presidents are playing a much more active role in promotion than they did last year. This year, presidents at 39% of the responding companies had primary responsibility for marketing. In comparison, 20% of the presidents had primary responsibility last year. Marketing communications specialists have also gained responsibility since last year, when they had primary responsibility for promotion only 5% of the time.

While press releases are the backbone of most PR departments, 20% of responding companies have never sent out a single press release.

Chapter I. Promotion

Agencies have become less popular than last year, when they, too, had primary responsibility at 5% of the firms that responded and secondary responsibility at 15%. These changes seem to support the perception that in tough times, CEOs take on greater responsibility at their companies, often in an effort to rein in the cost of extraneous expenses such as agencies. The following table documents this trend:

Person Responsible	Primary (%)	Secondary (%)
Marketing	39.2	25.6
President	39.2	28.0
Marketing Com.	16.0	8.0
Agency	1.6	5.6
Sales	9.6	22.4

7. Outside PR Resources

Most of the companies didn't use any outside personnel (49.6%). About 26% of responding companies used "freelance" people, and 18.4% used an agency. An additional 5.6% used other human resources. Several people mentioned that their printer or typesetter helped them with their promotional materials.

8. Usage of Promotional Techniques

Press Release Usage

While press releases are the backbone of most PR programs, 20% of the companies have never sent out a single press announcement.

Trade Show Usage

Trade shows are the most popular promotional technique and are viewed as tops in effectiveness. Only 8.8% of responding companies have never gone to a trade show.

Newsletter Usage

Newsletter usage ranks second among the available techniques and third in effectiveness. This year, 15% more companies than last year reported that they had published at least one newsletter.

Display Advertising Usage

Display advertising ranked third. I was surprised that 10% more companies were using it this year

than last. I would have thought that few companies could afford promotional advertising.

Companies are making the editorial circuit more regularly than they did last year, but I'm worried about the 33%, or one-third, who never talk to editors.

Article Usage

Relatively few companies make regular use of articles, but a majority of companies occasionally place articles. Although it would be nice to have a constant stream of articles published, it takes sustained effort. Still, even a few articles can provide effective materials to include in follow-up mailings to your prospects.

Press Kit Usage

More than half the companies have never used a press kit, but 20% use them regularly. I think the low usage is related to the small percentage of companies that regularly talk to editors.

Talking to Editors–Usage

Despite the adage that "talk is cheap," only 16% talk to editors on a regular basis, but 39% do so occasionally. Still, companies are making the editorial circuit more regularly than they did last year, but I'm worried about the 33%, or one-third, who never talk to editors.

Press Tour Usage

Almost 25% of the responding companies have conducted at least one press tour. I am impressed with this commitment because it's so expensive to arrange and conduct press tours. They are a major investment.

Seminar Usage

Seminars are quite popular as a promotional technique, though they are used much less for lead generation.

Usage of Promotional Techniques

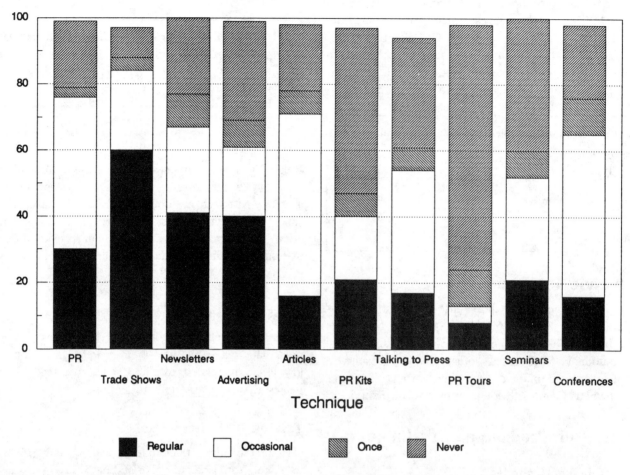

Technique

Regular ☐ Occasional ▨ Once ▨ Never

Speaking at Conferences–Usage

Speaking at conferences is a very popular promotional technique. About 48% of the companies do this occasionally, but only 16% do it regularly. Like placing articles, speaking at conferences regularly is a lot of work, but it's a good technique even if used in moderation.

Several of my clients focus their entire promotional program on speaking at conferences; they find it to be a highly successful strategy. The presidents of these companies really enjoy speaking at conferences and talking to the organizers. Again, the personality of the president heavily influences which promotional techniques a company emphasizes.

9. Effectiveness of Promotional Techniques

Press Releases–Effectiveness

Most companies rate press releases as "good" or "fair." I think that they deserve more credit than they get, but their effect is almost impossible to quantify. And of course, there are ho-hum press releases, and there are interesting press releases, and your release had better be interesting and targeted to the right publications if you want the news to see print.

Trade shows got top marks for effectiveness, even better than last year. The number of companies that rated trade shows as poor dropped from 17.9% last year to 8.8% this year.

Effectiveness of Promotional Techniques

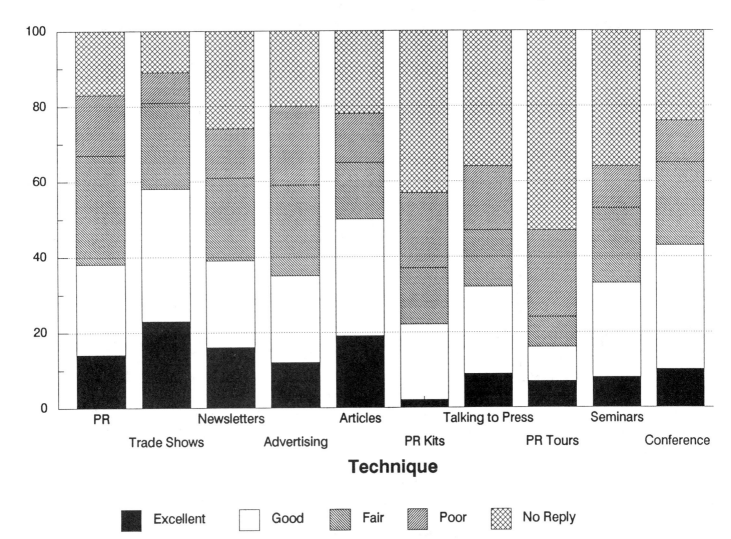

Technique

Legend: Excellent | Good | Fair | Poor | No Reply

Editors are chronically overworked; an editor of an MIS publication once told me that she used to get two full postal tubs of mail–those big, white, corrugated plastic things you see in mailrooms–every week. She said that many of the releases were addressed to people who hadn't worked at the magazine for years, or they were obviously inappropriate for her magazine. So, use your judgement, develop good mailing lists, and follow up with phone calls for best results.

Trade Shows–Effectiveness

Trade shows got top marks for effectiveness, even better than last year. The number of companies that rated trade shows as poor dropped from 17.9% last year to 8.8% this year. Considering the high cost of attending trade shows, it's good to see that their effectivness seems to be increasing.

Newsletters–Effectiveness

While newsletters rank third in effectiveness, a number of companies consider them poor promotional tools. Of course, many companies only publish newsletters sporadically, which hurts their corporate image, giving the impression that the company is either a little flaky or perhaps more interested in self-promotion than legitimate editorial coverage of topics relevant to their products' users.

Chapter I. Promotion

Display Advertising–Effectiveness

Companies rated display advertising as much more effective this year than last; such advertising enjoyed a larger increase in rated effectiveness than any other technique. But considering the high cost of display ads, I am still concerned that 20% of the companies rated them as poor.

Articles–Effectiveness

Articles rank second in effectiveness. Once you have the reprints of the articles, you can use them to help close sales, but a surprising number of companies felt that articles were poor vehicles to promote products. I have an alternative theory: This attitude might merely reflect anxiety about seeing your company's name in print. I have talked to people who were upset about one mildly critical paragraph in a four-page article. I thought that the overall article was very positive, but the people at the company felt that they had been slammed. In this particular case, the phone rang off the hook, so the prospects must have shared my impression.

A reviews editor recently confirmed my impression that executives are often overly sensitive about what is written about their companies. In the late 1980s, the editor had done a review of C compilers that had stated that, for most types of code development, Company A's compiler was probably the best of the thirteen (!) compilers reviewed, but for some special uses, Company B's compiler was probably better and was certainly cheaper. You can imagine how flabbergasted she was when she, the editor-in-chief, and the publisher all received vague but vociferous complaints from Company A that the review had "the wrong tone," and therefore was not a good review.

"I was used to getting calls about negative reviews," she said, "but this is the first time the winner had called to gripe." Company A got the reputation of being "a whining sore winner." Company B, on the other hand, was overjoyed that it had in some sense tied or beaten the leader, if only in one area. Company B then wrote a polite letter thanking the editor for including Company B in the review. Thus, Company B earned the respect of everyone on the editorial staff. Which company would you rather be?

Press Kits–Effectiveness

Press kits received poor effectiveness ratings, but they did better than last year. (Press kits are folders or binders filled with background information about your company and its products, press releases, and occasionally, photos or slides of the product.)

Talking to Editors–Effectiveness

More companies are talking to editors this year, but more of them feel that it isn't working. I think that perhaps some of these companies are talking to the right editors, but they are using the wrong people to do it. If you aren't comfortable with the press, don't force it. See if you can find someone in your company whom you trust and who would enjoy talking with editors. Chances are they will be more effective than someone who doesn't like contact with the press.

If editors have been following your company long enough to know that it's fundamentally sound, a single bad quarter or negative review probably won't result in a slew of negative articles.

Also, it is important to develop good relationships with editors when things are going well for your company. If you ignore them when times are good, your chances of managing stories during negative times are slim. But if editors have been following your company long enough to know that it's fundamentally sound, a single bad quarter or negative review probably won't result in a slew of negative articles. And if editors with whom you've been working do have to write bad things about your company, they'll probably go out of their way to get your company's side of the story.

Press Tours–Effectiveness

Press tours received the worst rating of any technique, with twice as many companies commenting on their effectiveness (or lack thereof) as the number of companies who said they actually used press tours. Either many people have tried press tours before and believe they got burned, or many of the people who perceive that press tours are ineffective haven't tried them. (Maybe we need a name for this phenomenon. How about the "Green Eggs and Ham" Syndrome? In other words, don't knock it if you haven't tried it.)

Seminars–Effectiveness

Seminars rated "good" to "fair" in effectiveness. If you can draw people into a promotional seminar cheaply, this might be a reasonable thing to try.

Speak at a Conference–Effectiveness

Speaking at a conference is "good" or "fair." Conferences are much like seminars, except that someone else arranges for people to attend.

10. Change in Usage of Promotional Techniques

Press Releases–Change in Usage

Press releases enjoyed an increase in use that was second only to that of articles. Considering the low cost of press releases, I am pleased that so many companies are discovering their value. It is also worth noting that very few firms are decreasing their use of press releases.

Trade Shows–Change in Usage

The jury seems to be split on trade shows. A significant number of companies are increasing their usage of trade shows, but at the same time, a surprising number of companies are decreasing it. This year, 2.8

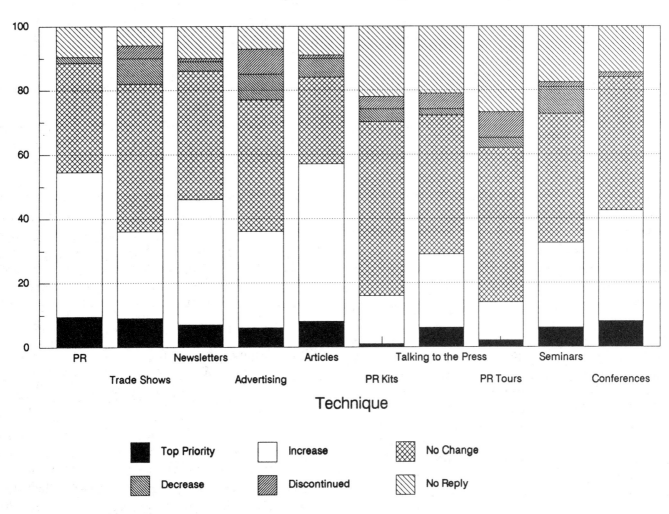

Changes in Usage

Chapter I. Promotion

times more companies say they increased their use of trade shows than say they didn't. Last year, 1.6 times more companies increased their attendance of trade shows than decreased it.

Newsletters—Change in Usage

Newsletter usage continues to increase significantly, and the change in usage is even more positive than last year. Considering the low cost of publishing a simple newsletter and the customer relations benefits, I am pleased that companies are increasing their use of newsletters.

Display Advertising—Change in Usage

Companies are also split on the use of display advertising. While many companies are increasing their use of this type of promotion, a non-trivial number of companies are discontinuing or decreasing their usage of display advertising for promotion.

Articles—Change in Usage

Articles are also being used by more companies. Nine times more companies are increasing their use of articles than are decreasing it. Still, 5.6% of the responding companies are decreasing their use of articles.

Press Kits—Change in Usage

Half as many companies are decreasing their usage of press kits as are increasing it. I would like to hear from those of you who are decreasing your usage to understand why. Did you just not get good enough results for the effort that you invested, or did you get negative results?

I suspect that several common practices contribute to the ineffectiveness of some press kits. My editor friend was harsh on those who send press releases to "every editor who has had this job since the dawn of time," and she goes "positively ballistic" when she gets multiple, slick, expensive press kits at the same time from the same company.

"It really upsets me to see small and mid-sized companies throwing away money they can't afford on this stuff, and they send it to people who are long gone or to magazines that don't even cover their market," she says. Her advice? "Most small to mid-size companies should have a press kit mailing list

of publications that has no more than 100 names, including user-group newsletters. If your list is small and focused, your marketing or public relations people should be able to look at it and tell whether it's current."

Another tactic often used to limit the number of press kits is to mention in press releases that kits are available on request. This technique really cuts down on waste.

Talking to Editors—Change in Usage

There has been a moderate increase in companies that talk to editors, but 4% of the companies have discontinued talking to the press. What happened, guys?

Press tours—Change in Usage

Twelve percent of the companies are increasing their usage of press tours (planning their first press tour?), and 6.4% are discontinuing them altogether. Did you fail to see a payback? Or did you do one last year and decide that you don't need to do another one this year?

I worked with several companies who launched their promotional programs with a press tour. Once they had made the initial contacts with many editors, they were able to maintain the relationships over the phone and by arranging individual meetings at trade shows and other talks.

Seminars—Change in Usage

The change in the use of seminars was positive. It seems that more companies are offering educational seminars, especially in new applications areas. Everyone is looking for an edge, especially in recessionary times.

Speaking at Conferences—Change in Usage

This technique shows the greatest net increase in usage because only 1.6% of the companies are decreasing their use of speeches at conferences. I think that this reflects the same demand for education that is increasing seminar usage.

Newsletter frequency

Most newsletters are published quarterly, but 8.8% of the respondents have only done one issue of their newsletter, which is a much larger percentage of "one-shot wonders" than I would like to see. Most customers see such one-time newsletters as what they often are: thinly disguised advertising mailers. Hopefully, these companies will follow up with subsequent newsletters and increase awareness and understanding of their products among customers, prospects, and the press.

Newsletter Frequency	This Year	Last Year
Once	8.8%	2.6%
Annually	6.4%	NA
Every six months	16.0%	10.3%
Quarterly	40.0%	38.5%
Montly	2.4%	2.6%
Other	11.2%	7.7%

Representatives of some companies said that they publish a newsletter only when they have something to say. Such reasoning makes some sense, but I think that it is much better to have a regular, periodic presence.

11. Promotion Budget as a Percentage of Revenue by Computer type

Last year, we found that none of the mainframe and minicomputer companies were spending more than 15% of their revenues on promotion. This year, we asked about the marketing budget (including salaries) as a percent of revenue. We found some differences by computer type, but they aren't as significant as last year. This may be due in part to the fact that we have a larger sample this year, but I believe that many mainframe and minicomputer software vendors who subscribe to *Software Success* are learning that a little marketing savvy can help their business. This is especially true if few of your competitors do any active marketing.

12. Promotion Budgets: Getting Bigger?

The following chart shows the percentage of companies spending more than 15% of revenues on promotion:

Type of Product	Percent of This Year's Respondents	Percent of Last Year's Respondents
PC	42.6%	16
LAN	33.4%	25
Macintosh	42.9%	NA
Workstation	18.8%	NA
Multi-User PC	22.2%	NA
Minicomputer	32.2%	0
Mainframe	15.4%	0

I believe a second trend is causing these marketing increases. The level of competition in almost all markets has been increasing for the last several years, and it appears that competitive stress is continuing to accelerate, and marketing is much more important in a competitive environment. If you are the only company in a market, and your customers buy your product based on its technical merits, sophisticated marketing isn't really necessary.

On the other hand, if you are in a commodity market where there are many perfectly adequate substitutes for your product, marketing is necessary for success. Anyone in a commodity market who doesn't market aggressively will not do well. I expect that the software companies who learn to market will survive and thrive. It is going to be very difficult to continue to find market niches where technical excellence alone is sufficient for success. In many markets, technical excellence is necessary, but it just isn't enough anymore.

Different Markets, Different Strategies

All of these markets are quite competitive. The Macintosh-oriented companies make especially good use of press releases. I think that this is due to the nature of the Macintosh market. Because Apple developed its now famous user-interface guidelines and encouraged small outfits to write any software they liked, so long as it conformed to those guidelines, many small companies grew up around the industry. Therefore, the Macintosh magazines usually encourage small companies to send in press releases. Interestingly, the Macintosh-oriented companies use image ads (display advertising) far less frequently than other types of companies surveyed. None of the Macintosh-oriented companies regularly use press tours. This might just be a fluke arising from the

Computer Type	Press Release	Trade Show	News-letters	Image Ads	Articles	Press Kits	Talk to Press	Press Tour	Seminars	Talk at Conf
PC	30.7	62.2	39.5	39.2	17.3	24.0	16.2	8.1	24.3	21.3
LAN	25.6	64.1	46.3	48.7	17.9	23.1	15.4	7.7	23.0	23.1
MAC	42.1	52.6	36.8	15.8	15.0	26.3	21.1	0	5.3	10.5
Work station	31.3	50.0	56.3	25.0	6.3	18.8	18.8	12.5	25.0	18.8
Multi-User PC	22.2	59.3	39.3	37.0	14.8	18.5	14.5	11.1	35.7	22.2
Mini-Computer	25.8	51.6	54.8	48.4	12.9	12.5	12.9	12.5	25.8	9.7
Main-frame	23.1	61.5	61.5	38.5	7.7	7.7	7.7	7.7	14.3	30.8

small sample of Macintosh-oriented companies, but companies that produce software for the Macintosh talk to the press a little more often than PC and LAN oriented companies, which use seminars and conferences more frequently.

13. Regular Usage of Promotional Techniques by Computer Type

Companies that sell software for multi-user PC environments are almost identical in profile to companies whose software runs on stand-alone PCs, but they stand out because of their greater use of seminars. This is probably because they are establishing themselves as industry experts in their target market. They also use fewer press releases, probably because fewer magazines are interested in their press releases. Most multi-user PC products are aimed at vertical markets that may have one or two trade magazines. While these magazines might print your press release or review your product, the hundreds of general-purpose PC magazines probably would have no interest in such an announcement.

Workstation- and Minicomputer-related Companies

It seems to me that workstation software companies have some characteristics of both PC-oriented com-

panies and minicomputer-related firms. They use fewer press releases and trade shows in their marketing efforts, but they make higher use of newsletters. My experience has shown that minicomputer companies focus on supporting their customers. The president of a minicomputer company told me, "We put our marketing into customer support. If we take care of our customers, they will take care of us." While this is a great concept, I think that their spurning of other marketing tools will hurt them in the long run because such a policy doesn't proactively bring in enough new customers. And of course, without a sufficient number of new customers, it's impossible to expand the business.

The workstation software companies publish few articles, but both they and the minicomputer companies talk to the press and go on press tours. They also teach seminars. The workstation companies talk at conferences, and the minicomputer companies don't. Vendors of mainframe software, on the other hand, often go to conferences where the main topic is applications development. Thus, IBM can be seen at conferences discussing statistical computing or financial analysis, and Oracle goes to conferences where users of its product are expected to speak about their innovative applications that run under Oracle software.

Chapter I. Promotion

Mainframe Software Companies

Mainframe software companies rarely use press releases and articles. There are few magazines that cater to the mainframe marketplace. They also do little to work with the press. They make very high use of newsletters because many of them are focusing on cultivating their customer base. I was surprised that so many of them speak at conferences. I wonder what conferences they are speaking at? A reporter I know says that companies such as IBM, Oracle, and DEC often speak at trade conferences that center around applications development. For instance, IBM representatives often give talks at conferences on object-oriented development or statistical computing. They also send representatives to mathematical conferences. I would be interested to hear about this from anyone.

B. Miscellaneous (1991)

1. Competitive Analysis (Feb)

Dear Dave:

After reading Software Success, I thought your readers may be interested in knowing about the services of Local Knowledge. We provide comprehensive business intelligence for hardware and software vendors in the computer and telecommunications industries.

The six types of business intelligence are:

Market intelligence: the development of an accurate picture of the market for products and services. It answers general questions such as the overall potential of the market and what issues are keeping buyers awake at night.

Competitor intelligence: the gathering of specific data on competitor's activities such as pricing, cost and strategy. This goes beyond putting together feature - function - benefit matrixes of a competitors' products. It means gaining intimate knowledge of a competitor's costs, and pricing, and strategies and tactics.

Product intelligence: the ongoing understanding of new and old products in the marketplace.

Customer intelligence: the identification of major consumers for certain products and understanding their behavior. This form of intelligence answers these questions about customers: Who are they? Where are they? What industries, companies, departments? What keeps them awake at night?

Technological intelligence: keeping up to date on research and development. In the software industry, this form of intelligence is essential. It seeks to determine emerging industry technology standards, identify what competitors have on their drawing boards and what is planned for future product introductions.

Environmental intelligence: understands the social, political and cultural environments in which a vendor and its industry operates.

Dave, thanks for the opportunity to share this with your readers. I'd be happy to answer any questions you or your readers may have about Local Knowledge,

Regards,
Kevin Cronin
(415) 837-7464

2. Justifying Promotion (Aug)

A new newsletter, Great Publicity and Promotions Strategies, by Daniel Janal had an interesting article on how to justify promotion. In his April 1991 issue, Janal interviewed Holly Hartz, director of public relations at Electronic Arts (EA). According to Hartz, EA "correlates the amount of editorial coverage to the amount of money the company would have to spend to buy an equivalent amount of advertising."

I like this approach and urge you to try it to see how much "free advertising" your PR program is generating. When money is tight, there is a real temptation to drop PR. Perhaps EA's approach will help your company avoid making this mistake.

Dan Janal also has a book (How to Publicize High Tech Products and Services) and seminars on International Publicity. His seminar will be presented two times: August 23, and September 27 in Silicon Valley area hotels. For more information call (408) 496-6744 or (408) 241-6834.

3. Recession Strategies (Aug)

The following is a good list of "budget stretchers" provided by Tom Eisenhart in his article, "When the screws get tightened ... How to stretch a marketing budget that's been scaled back." (Business Marketing Magazine, January 1991)

1. Don't redesign your ads unless necessary.
2. Narrow the list of publications you advertise in.
3. Pump up your PR budget.
4. Boost Co-op ad programs.
5. Use publications research & merchandising services.
6. Closely monitor vendors' production costs.
7. Hire free-lancers.
8. Coordinate promotional materials to cut printing costs.

Another resource is "Recession Proof Business Strategies", a special report by Robert W. Bly. The following list from his booklet contains "14 Winning methods to sell any product or service in a down economy." :

1. Reactivate dormant accounts.
2. Reactivate old leads.
3. Help existing clients or customers create new assignments or sales for you.
4. Give a superior level of service to your clients and customers.
5. Quote reasonable, affordable fees and prices in bid situations.
6. Use low-cost, "add-ons" to generate additional revenue.
7. Avoid being a prima donna.
8. Postpone any planned fee increases.
9. Downgrade slightly your acceptable client or customer profile.
10. Plan an aggressive new-business marketing campaign.
11. Repackage your services to accommodate smaller clients or customers and reduced budgets.
12. Add value to your existing service.
13. Keep busy with ancillary assignments or accounts.
14. Be positive

This booklet is available for $6 (add $1 for Canadian orders).

To order, contact:
Robert W. Bly
TEL (201) 599-2277
FAX (201) 599-2276

4. Media Directories (Aug)

Dear Dave,

I recommend three directories for detailed information about the computer and software press: Computer Media Directory, NewsFaces, and MediaMap. These directories differ in their depth and, correspondingly, their price. Here's a thumbnail description of each:

Computer Media Directory is by far the least expensive source of information focusing on high-tech publications. A single issue of the directory costs only $89.95, although the company prefers to sell an annual subscription (two directories, plus periodic updates) for $169.95. The directory lists information on over 500 publications, including high-tech and general business publications. Analysts and free-lance writers are included. The Computer Media Directory lists the type of products and news each publication covers, and lists each editor's area of responsibility. As a bonus, a brief summary of the editorial calendars of the top 100 computer publications is included.

NewsFaces in High Technology is the median-priceddirectory in the group, at $765, for the four-volume set. An editorial calendar directory is also available for $495. The added cost of NewsFaces over Computer Media Directory brings much added information: NewsFaces interviews one or more editors on each major publication and helps you "get inside the heads" of these editors so that you can send press releases or propose articles or product reviews that they will embrace. NewsFaces covers over 250 publications, including all the important ones in the computer and software fields. I particularly like the section describing editors' "pet peeves." As important as understanding what turns editors on is understanding what turns them off. NewsFaces does an excellent job in this area.

MediaMap is the most expensive directory in the group, costing $1,995 for an annual subscription to its Computer Industry Service that includes four large quarterly directories, semi-annual editorial calendar planners and a monthly newsletter. Although MediaMap doesn't cover as many publications as either Computer Media Directory or News-Faces, its coverage includes a variety of different media (MediaMap covers approximately 180

Chapter I. Promotion

zines, newspapers, newsletters, syndicated columnists, radio/TV media, users groups, and independent research organizations.) The information is comprehensive and extremely useful — especially to marketing communications folks. In addition to interviews with key editors (a la NewsFaces), MediaMap analyzes each major section of the publication and suggests ways to gain attention and coverage. MediaMap has been described as the Cadillac of media sources, and that description is appropriate.

All three directories are available on disk (IBM and Mac formats), ranging from comma-delimited data files to complete menu-driven systems. (NewsFaces' PR Power product, in particular, is most impressive!) For more information contact:

> Computer Media Directory, c/o DeskTop Innovation Inc., 742 Gilman St., Berkeley, CA 94710
> TEL (415) 525-4691, FAX (415) 525-2501
> MediaMap , 130 The Great Road, Bedford, MA 01730
> TEL (617) 275-5560, FAX (617) 275-4999
> NewsFaces, Power Information, Inc., 996 Minnesota Ave, Ste 205, San Jose, CA 95125
> TEL (408) 995-6660, FAX (408) 995-6675

This information is derived from my all-day seminar/workshop, *"Inside Scoop: Working with the Trade Press to Your Advantage"*, which will be presented in Costa Mesa, CA (Sept 12), San Jose, CA (Sept 17 and 19), Seattle, WA (Sept 24), and Austin, TX (Oct 1). Readers of Software Success can attend *Inside Scoop* at a $100 savings from the regular price of $395 for the all day seminar. For more information, call me.

Sincerely,
Jerry Werner, President
Communications Alchemy, Inc.
TEL & FAX (512) 219-1966

Dear Jerry,

Thanks for the information. I suspect that most readers will start with the cheapest list, and will consider the others as their approach matures. I bought a list of 644 Computer Magazine Editors from DP Directory for only $150. Their number is (203) 659-1065. I have been pleased with my results using this list. The first step is to start sending out your press re-

leases. Then you can start to really work with the magazines. If you are serious about getting articles in the trade press, even the most expensive directory is cheap if you get results.

Dave

5. Company Brochure (Sept)

Dear Dave,

I am a new subscriber to your newsletter and have enjoyed your approach and insight into the software industry. I have been reviewing techniques of promotion and lead generation suggested in your recent newsletter on promotion and in your annual reference guides.

What seems to fit my company the best is a company brochure. I would appreciate your insight on developing a company brochure. What type of format has worked best for your clients in the past? What information should be included? What type of reply device (should I use) if any?

Let me give you a brief overview of my company to assist you in your recommendations. I have been in operation for 4 years. At present, 60% of my income comes from supporting and modifying software from companies which are no longer in business, 30% from custom programming and 10% from hardware sales. I currently am specializing in software for non-profit organizations and book publishers. The work I have done in these areas also lends itself to distribution and inventory control functions. I am in the process of rewriting and updating my software in these areas, but would like to expand my client base for custom programming and support which is why I thought a company brochure would be appropriate.

I look forward to receiving your input on this subject. Thank you for your time.

Sincerely,
Matthew A Harting
President
Progressive Software Solutions
(918) 252-9769

Dear Matt,

As we discussed, I think of a company brochure in your type of situation as a personal sales call written down on paper. Think about the subjects that you talk about when you visit a prospective client:

* Your company

* Your technical capabilities

* Background of individuals

* Examples of projects

* Customer testimonials

My best advice is to start simple and print something with desktop publishing that you can get printed inexpensively in small quantities. (11" X 17" sheets can be folded to make a simple four page brochure).

Print up 50 copies of the prototype brochure. Ask you clients to comment on it. Give it to prospects after you have met with them and ask for their feedback. My experience is that if you keep it cheap you can make the changes and end up with a much better story before you cast it in stone.

The next thing we talked about was using direct mail to solicit prospects for your custom programming and support. You were assuming that you would send the brochure to everyone and you would provide them with a mechanism to respond. I suggested a reply card.

I suggested that you might be better off not to include the brochure in the mailing. Write a mini-article on some topic of interest to your prospects. Let them request the mini-article and then send them your brochure. At that point you can follow up with a call to make sure that they received the mini-article. In this call, I suggested that you could try to sell them on a "free technical meeting, no salesman will attend". This is true since you don't have a sales person on your staff, and I believe that prospects will be much more willing to set up a technical meeting to discuss their requirements and possible approaches.

I was pleased that this felt like a reasonable approach to you and look forward to hearing how well it works.

Thanks,
Dave

6. Promoting via Trade Associations (Sept)

Dear Dave,

Enclosed is our response to your recent promotion survey. I wanted to share with you our unique strategy for promoting our software products through trade associations. It may work for some of your readers.

LeaseTek is the leading provider of PC and PC-based LAN software system for vehicle and equipment lease portfolio management. We are a software developer and distributor in a niche market. Our prospects are members of one or more leasing industry associations. We establish credibility and awareness by actively participating in these associations as associate members. Below is our formula:

1. Send press kits to the chairman and to the association headquarters. This acts as a formal introduction to our software product and services.

2. Attend an association conference. Before investing in a booth, go to a conference to research the association's membership and activity. Ask the critical question: "Is this a match? Can our software satisfy their system needs?"

    Meet with the "players," i.e. the board chairman, committee members, and headquarter staff members. If you can, find out what software they recommend to their members. Which of your competitors is exhibiting and sponsoring conference events?

3. Offer our services to the association. For example:

a. Our "experts" as speakers at their conferences or seminars.

b. Our programming experience. Maybe work with them to develop a free disk for the association membership.

c. Space in our newsletter. They can publish their association news, i.e. dates of upcoming conferences.

d. Our services as a writer for an article to be published in their magazine.

4. If there is a match, consider advertising and exhibiting at their conference or seminar. Con-

tributing money to most associations is the most appreciated sign of support.

5. **Promote the association. Do our customers belong? If not, try to enlist them and make sure the association knows that we referred them.**

6. **Maintain the relationship.**

a. **Send news releases about your updates and company news.**

b. **Constantly brainstorm to develop new avenues for the relationship.**

Also, we constantly revisit our leads and sales reports to insure that we are receiving something in return for the effort mentioned above. We also review the actual association membership to verify that the audience has not changed.

I hope these tips help. We really enjoy your newsletter. If you have any questions, feel free to call.

Sincerely,
Michele P Quinn
Director of Communications
LeaseTek
TEL (412) 829-3080
FAX (412) 829-0840

Dear Michele,

Thanks for the letter. I am impressed with your methodical approach. I see too many cases of companies who start out working with an association to help promote their software, but then don't follow through. They make some scattered efforts, and then drop everything. They lose money on this uncoordinated effort, but even worse, they look disorganized and unprofessional to the association and its members. Bad publicity can come out of these aborted efforts.

I am very pleased that you mentioned the follow up to insure that you are getting the return on your investment. The program that you have laid out requires a significant investment. Associations can change and your effectiveness can change.

I was impressed that you listed the three associations that you are a member of on the bottom of your letterhead. This helps to promote the associations, and it increases your credibility by association.

You mentioned that you had included a brochure and a free disk for the association membership. It includes directory information from two of your associations. Your software allows association members to search the data base looking for funding sources that match their selection criteria. They can also update the information in the data base. I really like this as a marketing/promotion tool. I am sure that this free disk creates a very positive impression with the association members. Bravo!!!

I also liked your company brochure. It was very simple and classy. It is 6 pages (3 panels) and four color. I particularly liked the fact that you had 6 questions on one panel and you had 6 corresponding testimonials on an adjacent panel.

Thank you for sharing your experience. I would be interested to hear from others who have worked with associations or other adjunct organizations.

Thanks,
Dave

7. Product Positioning (Sept)

Dear Dave,

As a new subscriber to Software Success, it is obvious that I am joining a legion of Dave fans. I have a question about Promotion to ask you and a suggestion to address a question raised by another reader.

First the question. We produce PC-based software product called KnowledgeSEEKER. It is so unique that it doesn't fit into any of the traditional product categories. As such, we are running into "review roadblocks" where trade magazine editors prefer to do comparative reviews.

We describe KnowledgeSEEKER as Decision Making Software. It links into any database, uses statistics and AI techniques to look for trends and patterns that will maximize or minimize any success factor of your choosing. It graphically presents this information in the form of a decision tree. We use it to analyze our customer/prospect base and determine the characteristics of the person most likely to respond to a specific promotional technique so we can target our market more closely. It is used by banks to predict the high credit risk applicant, by

doctors to look for patterns in symptoms to help with disease diagnosis, and even by farmers who want to analyze what factors contribute to high or low milk production in dairy cows.

We have seen what a product review can do for us in terms of generating leads and sales (Byte Feb 1991–358 leads, 42 sales), but this lack of categorization remains a problem. Should we continue to stand on our new category foot, or should we agree to be slotted into a category that we overlap, where our uniqueness (and value) may be overlooked?

By the way, KnowledgeSEEKER is ideal for survey analysis and if you used it to do your survey analysis, the attached question of presenting accurate and valuable response categories becomes moot. If you simply allow the user to respond with the actual value, KnowledgeSEEKER will, among other things, determine the most statistically relevant ranges. If you'd like to try KnowledgeSEEKER, please give me a call.

Looking forward to hearing from you,

Lynda Partner
Director of Marketing
FirstMark Technologies Ltd
TEL (613) 723-8020

Dear Lynda,

Thanks for the offer of your software. I will try to use it to analyze results in a later issue.

On your question of the category for the product reviews, I would take any category that the magazines offer. I am sure that they will review you with statistical analysis packages, and I agree that you are different. You should focus on informing the reviewer of your capabilities and the best way to use your product. Hopefully, they will highlight your product in a sidebar article. I have seen a number of reviews where they were comparing apples and oranges and the differences were pretty clear.

Right now the PR will really help, and I would try to minimize any risk by working with the reviewer.

Good Luck!
Dave

8. Software Product vs. Total Implementation (Oct)

Dear Dave:

We develop and sell software for multi-user systems. Our product sells for about $250,000 per installation. The software is used by large manufacturing companies to track pollution and prepare reports for the Environmental Protection Agency (EPA) at sites throughout the United States.

Each user needs significant assistance from us during start-up. This includes training, data entry, minor customization, and integration services. We have had a very difficult time convincing our users of the importance of a total implementation strategy that includes these services. After attempting (and failing) to implement the software on their own, they usually recognize the need for additional services and are annoyed at the possibility of spending additional money to make the software really work.

How can we impress upon our prospects the importance of a total implementation strategy without scaring the prospects away?

Sincerely,
William C. Hope
General Manager
ERM Computer Services
TEL (215) 524-3600

Dear Bill,

As we discussed on the phone, the reality is that your good customers often spend three to five times the cost of the software to fully implement your system. This is fairly common for complex applications that have an impact throughout large organizations. Smart customers are beginning to understand that they get more value by investing more in the implementation. Just buying the hardware and software does not guarantee that the system will be implemented and that the customer will benefit. I have seen other situations in which customers had the internal resources to implement the applications, but your experience has shown that very few of them are capable of doing it alone.

Chapter I. Promotion

If you can convince a prospect that they really want the full applications implementation (FAI), they won't even consider your software-only competitors.

Your biggest concern is that your company is committed to supporting your customers with full implementations, but your competitors are just selling software. They are telling their prospects (and yours) that all they need is the software. You are concerned that when you tell the prospects how big the job is, they will think that the problem is your software. People don't want to believe that it takes so much work to implement such applications.

While I realize that this can be a problem, it can also be a major competitive advantage. If you can convince a prospect that they really want the full applications implementation (FAI), they won't even consider your software-only competitors. These are two very different "products," and it is very easy to differentiate them. Now the challenge is to sell the FAI.

The first step is to document the success stories of customers who bought into the concept of FAI and received a good return on investment from the much greater cost of implementing the FAI. Once you get these success stories, you can distribute them to your prospects. Eventually, you might be able to get articles published in magazines, providing further support for the FAI.

I liked your idea of packaging your add-on services into mini-products, making it much easier for people to spend money on them. We discussed small brochures for these add-on service packages. You can include testimonials and your customers' success stories in these brochures.

Once you get this level of documentation and support, you should be well positioned to handle the competitive situations. If your prospects are considering the software-only solution (SOS), have them talk to customers who have successfully implemented your FAI. If one of your competitors is selling the SOS as a much better solution, tell the prospect to ask the competitor for reference accounts. From what you say, it is very unlikely that the customers will get the results they want without the full implementation.

We also talked about a question-and-answer interview with a customer who had originally tried to implement an SOS and then decided to buy the FAI. It sounded as if you could address the key issues in two pages. This could be a very effective tool in selling FAIs.

If one of your customers decides to proceed with the SOS, you should talk to the decision maker. You should explain very clearly exactly what type of support comes with the software and how much the customer will have to pay for additional support.

If you act as a consultant and an adviser from the beginning, you may be able to influence prospects' decisions. Interestingly, once you get MIS departments involved in the discussion, they understand reality. They, in turn, can help you convince users of the long-term value of the FAI.

If you can implement these programs, I think you'll have a good chance to increase your sales and manage your competition.

Good luck!
Dave

C. Promotional Activities Survey (1990)

1. Company Revenue

In general, the companies who use promotional methods are larger than the average Software Success subscriber firm. I believe that this reflects the fact that promotion is a sophisticated activity which takes time to achieve payback. Larger and more established companies are much more likely to use promotional methods. It also appears that companies who are sophisticated enough to use promotion effectively are much more likely to grow larger.

COMPANY REVENUE	%RESP
<250K	10.3
$250K - $500K	5.1
$500K - $1M	17.9
$1M - $2M	33.3
$2M - $5M	15.4
>$5M	12.8

2. Computer Type

This survey had slightly fewer PC and mini companies and more mainframe companies than prior surveys. It also looks like the focus on LANs relative to PCs is increasing.

COMPUTER TYPE	% RESP
PC	59.0
LAN	17.9
Mini	15.4
Mainframe	15.4

3. Market Size

The companies who responded to this survey are generally selling to larger markets than those who answered the distribution survey. This may reflect the fact that promotion is more compelling and more effective in larger markets. This isn't to say that you can't promote products or services in a small market, it is just easier in larger markets.

MARKET SIZE	% RESP
500	10.3
500 - 1K	7.7
1K - 10K	20.5
10K - 25K	7.7
25K - 100K	12.8
100K	15.4

4. Promotional Budget

Ten to fifteen percent of revenue is the most likely level for the promotional budget. Many companies spend less, but few spend more than this. (See the graph on the next page for more detail.)

This is higher than I would have expected. I wonder how many of the respondents included all marketing budget items including lead generation. I suspect that a number of the companies in the ten to fifteen percent range were including their lead generation budget. Some of their comments indicated that they were unable to distinguish between these two types of marketing programs.

I would expect a software company to spend fifteen to twenty percent of revenue on marketing if personnel expenses are included. I would expect pure promotion to be under five percent because most promotion is inexpensive. Lead generation would range from ten to fifteen percent and salaries might be five percent. This balance will depend in large part on the company's evolution. Early on, I would focus on hard lead generation and free publicity. Over time, more money will go into salary and more long-term projects.

5. Effectiveness

We didn't get a lot of feedback on the effectiveness of different groups performing promotion.

Agency Effectiveness

Only 18 percent of the respondents answered this question and most of them felt that their agency was good.

Freelance Effectiveness

Only five percent of the respondents answered this question and they felt "good" or "OK" about the freelancers who had helped with promotion.

Promotion as a Percentage of Revenue

Percentage of Respondents

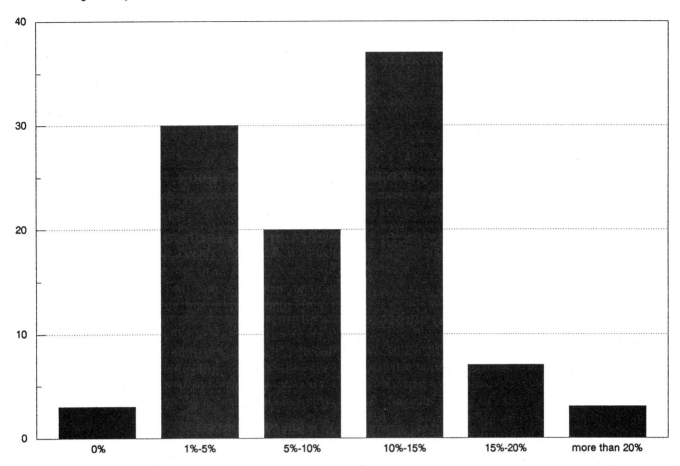

Promotion as a Percentage of Revenue

Communications Manager

Ten percent of the respondents answered this question and most of them felt good about the communications manager.

President

Forty-three percent of the respondents commented on this question and most of them felt that the president was "OK." This supports my experience. While the president has the knowledge and the background to do a great job of promotion, they have far too many demands on their time to do a good job.

Marketing

64 percent of the respondents answered about marketing. "Good" was the top answer and "OK" was a distant second. This is the type of project at which a marketing department can excel.

Sales

Twenty-five percent of the respondents ranked sales as either "OK" or "good" (even). This was higher than I expected, but many sales people like marketing and do well at it.

6. Responsibility

Marketing is most likely to have primary responsibility for promotion, with the president second. (See the graph on the next page.) In most companies, the president starts off with responsibility for marketing and promotion. At some point, it becomes clear that the company needs a stronger

Primary Responsibility for Promotion

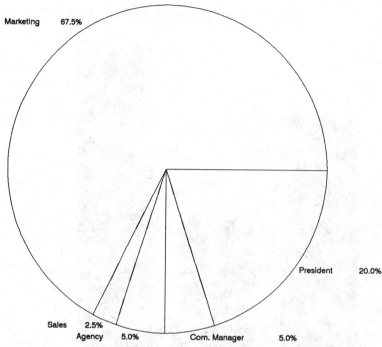

Marketing 67.5%

President 20.0%

Sales 2.5%
Agency 5.0%
Com. Manager 5.0%

Primary Responsibility for Promotion

marketing effort and that this will require someone dedicated to marketing.

In many cases this is an entry person with a marketing education and a strong motivation to learn, but little practical experience. I have seen a number of cases where a good marketing coordinator can be very effective. The president and the company know what they want to do, they just need someone to get it done.

7. Secondary Responsibility

	% RESP
Agency	14.7
Freelance	5.9
Com Mgr	8.8
President	32.4
Marketing	2.9
Sales	26.5
Other	8.8

As you can see, the president is the top choice to have secondary responsibility for promotion. This is usually the case if he or she has passed the responsibility down to marketing. If the president is

marketing and/or customer oriented, I believe he or she must remain involved at least secondarily in promotion.

Sales is the next most likely group to have secondary responsibility. This is quite common if the president has a technical background. In this situation, there is often a strong sales manager who provides sales and customer input to the marketing programs.

I was surprised at the number of firms who have an agency or freelance person with secondary responsibility. Last year we found that only 3.2 percent of the firms made an agency fully responsible. This figure has increased to 5.1 percent. While the difference is not statistically significant, it does indicate that companies are making greater use of outsiders in a secondary role. I believe that this can help augment internal resources.

8. Usage of Promotional Techniques
Press Releases

Press releases are very common and 35 percent of the companies make regular use of them. They are almost mandatory if you are serious about being in business. Given the very low cost and the high potential return, I urge everyone to make regular use of press releases.

Trade Shows

Trade shows are even more popular than press releases. I was surprised that 56 percent of the respondents make regular use of trade shows. This was much higher than I would have guessed, but in many industries there is at least one trade show that is mandatory.

Company Brochure

I think that most people answered this based on having a product brochure. Most companies I talk to don't have a general company brochure that isn't product specific. Only larger and more established companies can afford a non-product brochure which sells the company.

Mandatory Requirements

Almost everyone in our survey (80 percent plus) made use of press releases, trade shows, and company brochures.

Newsletter

I was very impressed that 46 percent of the respondents make regular usage of a newsletter. It sounds like some of the Software Success Readers are implementing some of the ideas I have been suggesting.

Image Ads

Only 30 percent of the companies are doing image advertising on a regular basis, but another 25 percent are doing it occasionally.

Articles

Only ten percent of the companies make regular usage of articles, but another 48 percent make

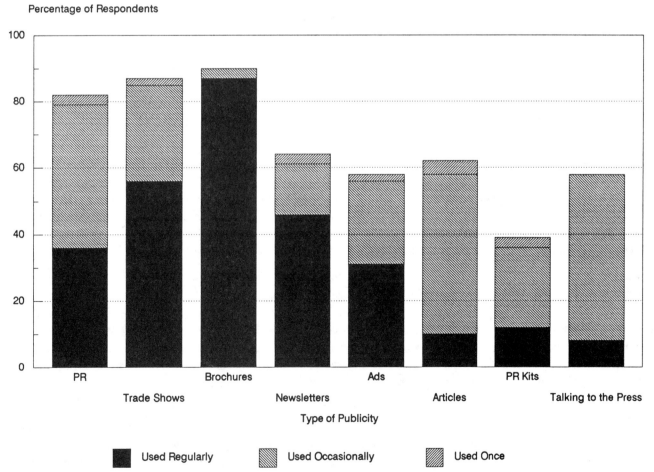

Usage of Promotional Techniques

Usage of Promotional Techniques

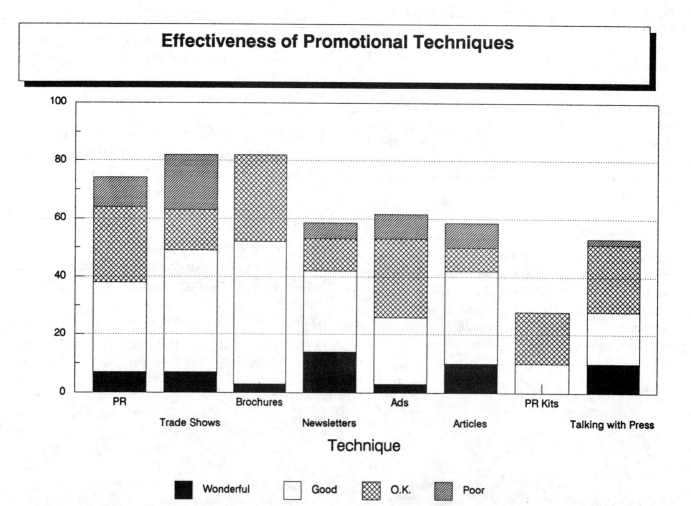

Effectiveness of Promotional Techniques

Effectiveness   of   Promotional   Techniques

occasional usage of articles. Given the lead times for articles and the limited opportunities for articles, occasional publication of articles can represent a significant investment and can offer a good return. I have clients who get two or three articles a year which may generate half their annual leads.

It would be nice to get more articles, but you need to think about how many slots are available. If there are two monthly magazines in your market, you have a maximum of 24 available slots. Getting one of these magazines to carry 2 or 3 of your articles is quite an accomplishment when you consider the percent of their slots they are allocating to you.

Press Kits

Only 40 percent of the respondents use a press kit, but they can be quite effective if you meet with the press. This is especially true if you meet the press at

trade shows. I have found that offering to mail your press kit to the editor's office when you meet them at the trade show can be very effective. He or she will probably want a copy to read and come back with more questions. If you mail it to their office, it saves the editor from having to pack it back on the plane

Talking to the Press

Slightly more than half the companies talk to the press, and less than ten percent of the companies talk to the press on a regular basis. If you put yourself in this ten percent, you will have a serious advantage over your competitors who don't.

I have found that if you approach the press with the attitude that they owe you coverage, you will have problems. They will be offended. On the other hand, if you offer help, the press will respond in kind.

9. Effectiveness of Promotional Techniques

Press Release

Press releases were generally rated either "OK" or "good." It is rare that they were rated "poor" or "wonderful." In most cases, it is difficult to attribute specific results to press releases. In spite of the difficulty tracking the results, I believe they are very effective.

Trade Shows

While a lot of companies were happy with trade shows, I am concerned with the number of companies who felt that trade shows had poor effectiveness (17.9 percent). This is the worst of any of the techniques in this survey. On the other hand, 7.7 percent felt that they were wonderful. Given the high cost and effort to attend trade shows, you deserve good results.

Company Brochures

Company brochures were rated as either "good" or "OK." They were not rated "poor."

Newsletters

Newsletters have the highest "wonderful" rating of any technique. This matches my experience. I suspect that the "poor" ratings were from companies who tried one newsletter, and never published another.

Image Ads

Image ads have a low "wonderful" rating given their high cost. Other than trade shows, most of the other alternatives have low cash costs. The advantage of image ads is that once they are done, you just mail checks to the magazines. The other alternatives usually require less money, but more labor. Most software companies are short on money and long on talent, so the other alternatives are usually more appropriate.

Articles

Articles have a good "wonderful" rating and have been good for a number of other companies. I wonder about the "poor" experience with articles. I have seen cases where a magazine writes an article about a company, which is less than flattering. This can be negative promotion and can be viewed as having poor effectiveness. On the other hand, if you are paying someone to write an article about one of your customers, you should be able to ensure that you look good. If you don't, don't submit the article.

Press Kit

Press kits are "good" or "OK." I see them as part of talking to the press. If you are going to talk to the press, you really should have a press kit to hand them. It doesn't have to be fancy, but you should give it some advance thought.

Talking to the Press

Talking to the press has one of the better "wonderful" ratings. I find this especially significant given the low cost for this alternative. At most you might spend a couple of hours a month talking to the press. You already know your market, so you don't have to prepare for these conversations. This gives many companies a very high return on investment.

There were several companies who had poor experiences with talking to the press. There are a number of things that can cause this. You can have the wrong person talk to the press. They may not be comfortable or diplomatic. Another situation is when the press hears that you have a problem, and they come after you. While this is a difficult situation, not talking to the press isn't the answer. Exxon tried that and they really made matters much worse for themselves.

My feeling is that if you have established a dialogue with the press and a problem comes up, that you will handle it much better. The press will also be much more likely to call you first and give you the benefit of the doubt if they already know you.

10. Newsletters

Frequency

Quarterly was the most popular frequency for newsletters. It is the frequency that I recommend to my clients. It is frequent enough to be effective in maintaining customer and prospect contact, but it keeps the work down to a manageable level.

FREQUENCY	% RESP
Once	2.6
6 months	10.3
Quarterly	38.5
Monthly	2.6
Irregular	7.7

Who Writes the Newsletter?

Almost everyone writes their own newsletter. (59 percent of the 61.5 percent who answered these newsletter questions.) Only 2.6 percent of the companies used contract writers. I believe that this is so low because most companies have people who can write well. For companies with limited funds, the principals can write the newsletter and keep the money themselves.

Hiring an Agency

Having an agency write a newsletter can be a very expensive proposition. First they will need time to research the topics and to interview people, and review the drafts with your staff. Given this combination of training and approval, the agency can invest a surprising number of hours in your newsletter.

The other factor with most agencies is that they want to produce a very nice looking NL which will look good in their portfolio. They would rather have one great newsletter which no one ever matched, rather than a modest one which improved with each issue.

This desire for excellence increases both the creative time and the printing cost. In the extreme, I saw one case where the company paid $5,000 to the agency for the creative work and $15,000 for printing 5,000 copies. They had a great newsletter, but it was a long time before they did another. I believe that they would have been much better off with a simple four-page Mac-based newsletter written by the marketing staff. They might have had some weekend work, but it wouldn't have cost $5,000. The printing costs might have been $1,000 if they had limited themselves to two-color printing.

It is very easy to improve the quality of a newsletter, but it is very painful to take a step back once you have set a new standard. Newsletters are a forum to communicate with your customers, and prospects who have expressed an interest in your company and your product. While I wouldn't suggest that you send out something that would embarrass your company, you can put together a very nice newsletter with desktop publishing and print it cheaply.

11. Why use Promotion?

The real reason that most companies use promotion is to generate leads and sales. Eventually it leads to this, but most promotional techniques are indirect. That is, the greatest benefit of an article may not be the people who call you because they saw the article. It may be the people who respond to your next mailing because they are more comfortable with your company after seeing the article. I truly believe this, but proving it is very difficult. Over time you might find that your cost per lead declines. Is it because you have gotten smarter about lead generation or because your investment in promotion is really paying off?

Finding new accounts can be a very strong reason to use promotional materials. In many industries, a significant percentage of the target market aren't on the available lists. This can be especially true if they are small companies which haven't been in business for a long time. If you have this situation, promotional items might find their way to these new accounts. One of the really nice aspects of this type of new account is that they are less likely to know all of your competitors.

Another new account scenario is where you are dealing with mature accounts who are very careful about who they put on their approved vendor list. While direct mail and other lead generation techniques can help this situation, they can be very slow. Promotion, on the other hand, can give you the instant seal of approval. Even the most sophisticated prospects will think that you were endorsed by the magazine when they read an article about one of your customers talking about how great your product is. They do this on an emotional level even when they know that you paid to have the article written. Amazing, but it works. Finally, it is fairly easy to verify that promotion is opening new accounts for you.

The strategic rationale for promotion was very low. I wish it was higher.

I like the "lets invest in promotion, get lots of exposure so that we can sell the company" approach. My experience is that companies with a high promotion rating are much more likely to be approached by buyers. On the other hand, sophisticated buyers will

Chapter I.   Promotion

do enough due diligence to ensure that there is real content before they buy.

	% RESP
Leads	66.7
Sales	43.6
New accounts	28.2
Strategic	5.1
Sell Company	10.3

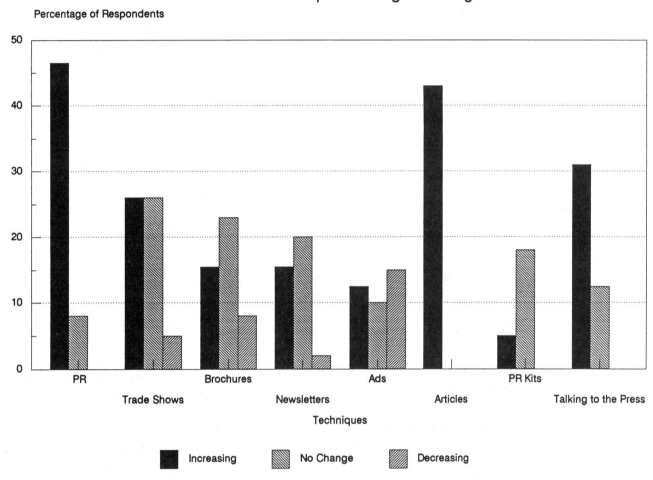

Promotional Techniques - Changes in Usage

12. Primary Promotional Technique

The chart on the prior page lists the responses. As you can see, the responses add up to 158 percent since people indicated more than one primary promotional technique.

The top three: press releases, trade shows, and company brochures continue to be the most popular.

The other four: newsletters, image ads, articles, and talking to the press are roughly equal in popularity.

One of the nice things about promotional programs is that they are independent. Initially, you might decide to send press releases, go to the big industry trade show, and have a company brochure. These three are mandatory, so you don't have a lot of flexibility. After that, you can select the ones that you think will be most effective and that sound the most fun. If you have a large customer base, and you sell more product to this base, a newsletter might be very effective. If you have the budget and would like to see your company name in lights, you might opt for image ads. If the trade magazines are especially hungry for articles, you might be pulled into this. Finally, if someone in your company loves to talk, he or she might be a good person to handle this.

13. Changes in Usage of Promotional Techniques

Press Releases

Of the companies which responded, 46.2 percent are increasing their usage of press releases and none are decreasing it.

Trade Shows

The percentage of companies increasing their trade show usage is 25.6 percent. The same amount aren't changing it. This is a more positive toward trade shows than I have observed in my consulting work.

Company Brochures

The results here are mixed. It appears to me that a number of companies have made a major investment in their first real brochure. They did it to achieve credibility, but now that they have it, they wonder if they might have saved a little money.

Newsletters

Again the results are mixed. A few companies are increasing their usage of newsletters, but it isn't a stampede.

Image Ads

More companies are decreasing their usage of image ads than are increasing their usage. This is the only technique for which this is true. I believe that most companies are finding that you can work smarter with less money to gain more visibility.

Articles

Everyone who replied is increasing their effort to publish articles. This really pleases me.

Press Kit

Only a few companies are making an investment in this area.

Talking to the Press

I was surprised and pleased that 30 percent of the companies were increasing their investment in talking to the press. I believe that these companies will have a significant long-term advantage in terms of visibility. Talking to the press helps get your press releases and articles published, so there are a number of positive secondary benefits from talking to the press.

14. Agency You Would Recommend

Only two companies recommended an agency. Out of 39 respondents this is only 5 percent. I am afraid that my experience is that agencies don't work well for most small software companies. I would be happy to talk to companies who have other agencies to recommend.

The two recommendations are:
Pitcock Group,
(219) 233-8606
Larwin Livers Ad Agency
(215) 657-1515

15. Promotion Budget as a Percentage of Revenue

The LAN companies are clearly spending the most on promotion. This makes sense since they are in a new market which is getting a great deal of attention. The PC companies are still spending a lot on promotion. The mini and mainframe companies are spending significantly less.

	0%	1%-5%	5%-10%	10%-15%	15%-20%	20%
PC	5%	16%	21%	42%	11%	5%
LAN	0%	0%	0%	75%	25%	0%
Mini	0%	40%	20%	40%	0%	0%
Mainframe	0%	67%	17%	17%	0%	0%

16. Primary Promotional Technique by Computer Type

PC and LAN companies are making heavy usage of brochures, which is appropriate for young companies. LAN companies are making heavy use of almost all of the techniques. I was especially impressed that 29 percent of the LAN companies are talking to the press. The mainframe companies make very little use of promotional materials and the mini companies focus on press releases, trade shows and newsletters. I see this as a function of a mature business with established trade shows, good magazines, and loyal customer bases. I am surprised that the mini companies don't talk to the press.

	Press Rel.	Trade Show	Brochure	Newsletter	Image Ads	Article	Press Kit	Talk to Press
PC	17%	26%	43%	13%	13%	13%	4%	13%
LAN	29%	29%	29%	14%	29%	29%	14%	29%
Mini	33%	33%	17%	33%	17%	17%	0%	0%
Mainframe	17%	17%	0%	17%	17%	0%	0%	0%

17. Increasing Use of Promotional Technique by Computer Type

Even though the LAN companies are doing more than anyone else, they are increasing their usage of all the techniques except image ads. They are the only type of company dramatically increasing their investment in newsletters. The PC, mainframe and mini companies are using more press releases and more articles. They are also committed to talking more to the press. These three are also investing more in image ads.

	Press Rel.	Trade Show	Brochure	Newsletter	Image Ads	Article	Press Kit	Talk to Press
PC	39%	17%	17%	9%	13%	30%	4%	26%
LAN	57%	43%	43%	29%	0%	43%	0%	14%
Mini	50%	17%	17%	17%	17%	50%	0%	33%
Mainframe	50%	33%	17%	0%	17%	83%	33%	50%

18. Promotion References

NewsTrack is a public relations media and client contact program, covering management, tracking, reporting and billing. $495

The Right Brain Inc.
420 N. 5th StMinneapolis, MN 55401
(612) 334-5620

Chapter I. Promotion

MediaMap is a database of business, high-tech and computer media, plus public relations reference books. The price is $1,495 per year, which includes three quarterly updates of diskettes and books

Cambridge Communications, Inc.
130 The Great RoadBedford, MA 01730
(617) 275-5560

Print Design and Production includes research on eye tracking studies conducted by Perception Research Services Inc.

Centennial Printing Corp
PO Box 553
King of Prussia, PA 19406

Advertising and Marketing Checklists offers 77 checklists for busy advertising and marketing professionals who know the business but welcome the structure of lists and brief pointers.

By Ron Kaatz
NTC Business Books
Lincolnwood, IL
(312) 679-5500
175pp $17.95

Adweek Portfolio of Marketing & Promotion Resources is a collection of companies specializing in services ranging from individual promotion projects to full-service marketing and promotion services.

Adweek Portfolios
49 East 21st St.
9th Floor
New York, NY 10010
212) 995-7268

Advertising Ratios & Budgets is a study containing historical advertising spending for 1988, estimates of ad budgets for 1989, and a forecast of spending for 1990 for over 5,700 companies. Included also are each firm's advertising to gross profit ratios, advertising to sales ratio, plus advertising and sales growth rates and over 400 industry summaries.

More than 600 computer, telecommunications and electronics firms are covered by the study, including 115 software companies. The price is $295.

Schonfeld & Assoc, Inc.
2530 Crawford Ave.
Evanston, IL 60201
(312) 869-5556

The Levinson Letter includes "action ideas for better marketing communications".

Ivan Levinson & Associates
44 Montgomery St, #500
San Francisco, CA 94104
(415) 955-2737

Newspaper Advertising is a booklet to help you with your ads.

ASAP
1223 St. Francis Dr., Suite B
Santa Fe, NM 87501

Power Packed PR Ideas that Work is a 50 page booklet containing articles on PR.

Communications Briefings
140 South Broadway
Pitman, NJ 08071
(609) 589-3503

Standard Periodical Directory lists over 70,000 U.S. and Canadian publications. 1,600 pages are arranged by interest, category, circulation size, names and phone numbers of Circulation Directors, Publishers, Advertising Directors, and a full description of publications including paid vs controlled and trade vs consumer. $325

Oxbride Communications
150 Fifth Avenue, Rm 301
New York, NY 10011

Public Relations Writing is a step-by-step, 349 page, "how-to" manual. It covers:

1. How to Plan Message Media Development
2. Uncontrolled Media
3. Controlled Media

By Kerry Tucker and Doris Derelian; $24.33

Order 15-day trial copy from:

Steven T. Landis
Prentice Hall
College Mail Order Sales Department
Englewood Cliffs, NJ 07632
(201) 767-5937

Advertising Compliance Handbook examines the increasingly complex issue of claim substantiation in developing advertising copy and meeting competitive challenges. (No price given.)

Practicing Law Institute
810 Seventh Ave

New York, NY 10019

(212) 765-5700

Designing Effective Manuals is a two-day workshop for writers and managers involved in creating manuals.

Comtech

710 Kipling, Suite 400

Denver, CO 80215

(303) 232-7586

Editors on Disk developed lists of computer magazines, newspapers, user groups, computer stores, etc. All names are available either as labels or on disk.

DP Directory, Inc.

525 Goodale Hill Road

Glastonbury, CT 06033

(203) 659-1065

Space Trak Reports can provide you with the ad schedules of every one of your competitors. You can learn their schedules, the sizes of ads placed, etc. They track 70,000 companies in 300 magazines and 50 market areas.

Space Analysis Systems

2300 Computer Ave, H38

Willow Grove, PA 19090

(215) 784-0404

Complete guide to Creating a Successful Brochure is a 134- page book which covers all the aspects of creating a brochure. $29.95

By Karen Gedney and Patrick Fultz

131 Heartland Blvd

PO Box W

Brentwood, NY 11717

(516) 254-2000

Namer Software is a $150 PC program for creating company, product and service names.

The Salinon Corp.

7424 Greenville Ave

Suite 115

Dallas, TX 75231

(214) 722-0054

How to Improve your Business-to-Business Print Advertising is a 27 page booklet on effective advertising. It includes some research and guidelines and rules.

By Jack Edmonston

Vice President, Research

CW Communications, Inc.

375 Cochituate Rd., Rt 30

Framingham, MA 01701

(617) 879-0700

Media Kit Information is available in Standard Rates and Data Services (SRDS). It should be available through your local library.

Business Publications Rates and Data

3004 Glenview Rd.

Wilmette, IL 60009

Electronic Media Directories

Gebbie's Disk Media Directory

(212) 255-7560

download data

PR 6-in-1

(212) 687-8600

$1,000 + $200/person

PR Flash

(800) 624-5893

$149.95

+ $100/year for updates

Personal Computer Publicity Book

(213) 399-7938

No specific info

Targeter

(212) 279-4800

$12,000

D. Questions and Answers (1990)

1. Press Release Mailings

We would like to mail a press release, but we don't know the best way to get a list.

There are two lists that you need to develop. The first is the targeted list of editors and writers who are interested in your product area. You can start with the magazines that you and your customers read. Again, ask your customers what magazines they read if you aren't sure. Then contact the magazines and ask for both the editorial contact and a media kit. Another step to expand the short list is to do a search of one of the on-line databases of magazines articles which mention topics relevant to your product. (I use Dialogue in Palo Alto.) You can find

Chapter I. Promotion

product. (I use Dialogue in Palo Alto.) You can find magazines and writers who are interested in your subject.

I would do such a search and then get information on all the magazines. I would also try to get the address and phone numbers for all of the writers.

Some magazines may give out this information for writers who have been published in their magazines. Others will forward mail to the writers. One other group that might be relevant is market research analysts who write reports on your market area. If you conduct a consistent campaign of this type, you should be able to develop the 50-name list of key influencers.

You might check the June issue for some PR list vendors. The next thing that you need is the big list. There are any number of lists of 700 computer magazine editors, or 1,000 business magazine editors, or 50 editors in construction, and so forth. You might be able to get such a list from a local PR firm, or from companies who publish books of all magazines.

Another alternative is DP Directory (I just bought their list). They have a number of PR lists:

* 612 computer magazines
* 1,152 computer news columnists
* 263 IBM PC user groups
* 718 Apple/Mac user groups
* 123 shareware groups
* 312 PC magazines - all names
* 1,623 PC stores
* 956 business magazines
* 309 education magazines
* 356 agricultural magazines

Newspapers

* 1,706 Managing Editors
* 1,595 Business Editors
* 1,288 Medical Editors
* 1,293 Farm Editors
* 1,493 Education Editors
* 1,091 Travel Editors
* 1,597 Sports Editors

DP Directory, Inc.
525 Goodale Hill Rd
Glastonbury, CT 06033
(203) 659-1065

Another alternative is to use a directory of magazines to get more information on possible magazines. The directory that I bought is "The National Directory of Magazines" which is published by Oxbridge Communications (800) 955-0231. You should be able to find this and other similar directories at your local public or university library.

My advice is to get a big list (of reasonably relevant names) and mail to them. I am commonly asked how 700 editors can be interested in my press release (I mail to my house list of 130 editors plus the big list of 700). My answer is that my entire press release mailing costs me about $400 and I typically get 10 to 20 mentions for one of my press releases. Many of them are from my short list, but maybe half of them are from magazines I have never heard of. I include a letter with my press release offering a free subscription to my newsletter to the editors. They respond and my short list grows. As a vendor, you can offer to be an industry source, or you might have a booklet on your product area.

One of my favorite ideas for an initial press release for a new software company is to write a ten-page booklet on how to automate a car wash or some other relevant topic. This booklet shouldn't be on your products in particular. You then send out a press release announcing that this booklet is available. You also offer a copy of the booklet to the editors. When they respond, you can add them to your short list.

As you can see, PR is a numbers game and you have to push the numbers. You will send press releases to magazines who don't care, but if you keep in mind that magazines publish news and information, you can make your press releases more interesting and they will be more likely to get published.

If you send out a press release and no one publishes it, you might have someone call up some of the editors and ask them why they didn't pick it up. Was in boring? Do they have too many press releases of this type? Are they uninterested in this topic? Ask them about topics of interest to them. If you have someone with a small ego and a good phone presence make these calls, you may really learn something that will help you succeed. If you stick with it, I am sure that the rewards will be worth the effort.

Good luck!

2. Working with Creative People

Dear Dave:

I wanted to drop you a note to let you know how much I have gotten out of reading your newsletter for these past two years. The surveys are a most helpful way for me to find out how other people are making decisions about their future. Often, we find that your other readers have the same concerns that we do - and have gone about addressing them in much the same way as we have.

Your article on promotion was most informative. I must differ with one point, however. If others' experience is the same as mine, you will find that many of us who do not work in a formal relationship with an agency do work with those who function in the same way as an agency. I have been with this firm since 1984. It was founded in 1981 as Mount Castor Industries, Inc. In 1988, I purchased the company upon the retirement of Mount Castor's owners.

Until 1985, Mount Castor was represented by a New York ad agency. We felt that the agency treated us as a poor country cousin because of the relatively small amount of income they derived from our account. We also felt a certain "attitude" from their creative people. To make a long story short, we terminated Communique in 1985 and tried to do things on our own. This resulted in a disastrous campaign in 1985-1986.

We then discovered that one of the local commercial printing firms had developed quite a reputation as a quasi-ad agency. Their creative people included several individuals who worked for large agencies in New York and Boston. These people migrated to Cape Cod to get out of the big city rat race and landed at this printing company. While their primary function is to support the printing business, they have developed a well-earned reputation as creative experts. They do all of our direct mail pieces, magazine ads and catalogs. I have enclosed a sample of their direct mail pieces (both of which drew 4 to 4.5 percent responses this year) and a copy of the catalog they did for me.

The creative people come up with a slogan and graphic for a campaign (used in direct mail and magazine ads) and then I adjust my copy to link up with the slogan. The catalog is a lot of work and has deteriorated in appearance a bit over the past year (as we doubled our product offerings). We are currently re-designing it to include more graphics and some black and white photography for the inner pages.

I guess the point I'm trying to make here is that it might be a bit misleading to draw the conclusion that a CEO or Marketing Coordinator is bearing as much responsibility for promotion as they might have indicated in the survey, since they are most likely working with third parties. The other point is that, while most of us are not using agencies, perhaps many of us have equivalent resources at our disposal.

At any rate, keep up the good work with your publication. I really look forward to sharing a cup of coffee with you and Software Success each month.

Robert W. Fellows
Surfside Software, Inc.

Dear Robert:

Thanks for the letter. Your experience matches mine. I don't really know of a case where a small software company and an ad agency have really worked well together. I believe that it just isn't a fit. On the other hand, I have had excellent success working with freelance creative people. I find that their rates are significantly lower because they aren't carrying a high overhead burden. While this is nice, the thing that I really like is that I am dealing directly with the creative person who is doing my work. In almost all cases, they are doing all my creative work so the results are much better. In some cases, I am paying high rates for these freelance individuals, but I am getting some of the best creative talent around. I have also found some very good creative people who are associated with printers and lettershops. If people ask around, I am sure that they will find their own pockets of local talent.

I would also like to compliment you on the quality of your materials. Your flyers and catalog look very good and the results that you have gotten reflect their effectiveness. Thanks for the letter. I hope that your letter will encourage others to share their experience.

3. Magazine Discounts

What is the common practice as far as getting discounts from magazines?

As with most things, discounts with magazines are negotiable. Some magazines will not discount, but others will discount dramatically.

There are several points in time when it is appropriate to negotiate with the magazines.

New Magazine
This is the time when you should negotiate the hardest. You are taking the most risk, and the magazine needs your business the most. I have been able to negotiate $/lead deals with new magazines where the price paid depends upon how many leads the ad generates.

Try a Different Magazine
If you are approached by a different magazine, and you have a magazine that you are happy with, you can demand that the new magazine make it worth your while to test with them. If you stick to your guns, you can test the different magazine at a very low cost. Make sure that if it fails, you minimize your exposure.

New Year Budget
When you are doing your marketing budget for a new year, you can talk to the magazines about how much of a discount they are willing to give you to commit more of your budget to them. Occasionally, they will be willing to cut you a very nice deal.

Conclusion
Some magazines don't discount off the rate card, and get offended that you asked, but I view that as their problem. Get what you can.

4. Ad Agency for Software Companies

Dear Dave:

I received your promotional literature on Software Success. Your table of contents would seem to leave no stone unturned!

One of the headings, "Ad Agencies for Software Companies," was intriguing to me. If it is a listing of such agencies, I would like you to know more about Johnson Direct so that we might be among that list.

Enclosed is a small brochure and a copy of a letter we sent to software entrepreneurs recently. Jim Johnson advises his clients from his own wide range of experience in the computer industry, and his background as a clinical psychologist gives him a particular understanding of human nature. Since we're so close, I'd like to meet with you to show what we've done for our clients in the software industry.

Sincerely,

Christine   Hopf-Lovette
Account   Supervisor
Johnson   Direct
(415) 321-3777

P.S. - Our current clients include: Advanced Software, Antic, Bravo, Delta Technologies, Envisions/Logitech, Falcon Microsystems, Flinder Software Laboratories, Frontline Systems, IMSI, Kyocera Unision, Maze Computer Group, Megasoft, Nashoba Systems, Neuralytic Systems, Softstream Technologies, Systems Plus, Tech Resources, and WordTech Systems.

Dear Christine:

Thanks for the letter. Your client list is impressive. I thought that I would highlight the points in your Software Executive letter that you included.

You mentioned three uses of direct mail for software companies (the following is directly from your letter).

Sell your software directly to the eight million computer users who routinely buy through direct mail. A significant benefit is that you automatically acquire a dependable customer base you can use again and again for selling future products.

Mail specially priced upgrade offers to your current customers. A few smart companies are now using this guaranteed formula for easy profits, offering product upgrades two and three times a year to double sales - and triple their profits!

Offer add-ons, for yet another effective way to boost sales, earn money and gain customer satisfaction. This may not yield the spectacular profits of the first two strategies, but it is an excellent method for obtaining ready cash.

I agree that these are all programs which can be adapted to any software company to improve the bottom line. If any of my readers are looking for an outside resource, it appears that your firm is uniquely positioned to help them.

In your company brochure you listed the services that you offer:

* Professional Staff
* Account Service
* Creative Platform
* Direct Mail Letters
* Mailing Lists
* Graphic Design
* Printing and Mailing Services
* Analysis and Review

Sincerely,
Dave

5. Specialized Service Marketing

We offer a specialized product/service converting large volumes of word processing documents from Wang to PC formats.

Our prospects are easy to identify (Wang owners), but it is impossible to predict when they will decide to make the move.

We have found that small classified ads allow people to find us, but direct mail campaigns have been very slow to pay off. What do you suggest?

The first step is to get some publicity. An article on one customer's experience with your product/service would be a first step. Next, I would send out a mailing offering a copy of the article to any Wang user who was interested. I might do this every time I got an article published. The companies who responded would warrant more active follow-up. Perhaps you could send a monthly letter.

E. Trade Show Survey (1990)

1. Record High Survey Response

The Trade Show survey had 85 responses, which is an all-time high. This reflects the increasing readership, but I believe that it also demonstrates the high level of interest in trade shows.

The revenue of the respondents was much like the July Lead Generation issue. The median revenue was $1 million.

I added "workstation" to the question regarding Computer Type and I was surprised at how many workstation vendors we have. The other percentages were very similar to the other recent surveys.

COMPUTER TYPE	% RESP
PC	64.7%
LAN	11.8%
Mini	16.5%
Workstation	14.1%
Mainframe	12.9%

The only other significant change was a decline in the number of LAN vendors. Perhaps a number of the workstation vendors had previously registered under LAN.

2. Market Size

The companies who responded to this trade show survey have significantly larger markets than the average Software Success reader. In particular, I have compared this with the July Lead Generation responses.

It is very clear that if your market has more than 10,000 prospects you might be able to find effective trade shows. This is a necessary condition. You still have to find a good show to make this work.

Most of the mainframe vendors with which I work are selling to large IBM mainframe sites. The NCC was the last real mainframe show and it ceased to operate. I think that these statistics show why. There are only 5,000 (MVS) large IBM mainframe sites and there are another 5,000 smaller sites (VSE).

If you compare these numbers with the fact that the people interested in trade shows operate in larger markets, it makes sense that there are no IBM mainframe trade shows. I suspect that the trade show industry understands this aspect of their business much better than we do.

One final note is that you should really research shows before you go. Get all the information you can about the target audience. I would take their descriptions with a grain of salt. I have had several clients go to shows which they thought were targeted to their market only to find a much more diverse audience. In these cases, they ended up talking to too many non-prospects and wasting their time and energy.

One line of questioning that you can pursue is to ask which lists and magazines the trade show vendor is using to promote the trade show. Look at the promotional material. If you follow this line, at least you know who they want to get to the show. At the very least, make sure that this matches your target market.

A second line of research is to call companies who were at the show last year and are planning to go this year. If your competitors were there last year and plan to be there this year, you have an easy decision. (You have to go to keep up with the Joneses.)

Even if none of your direct competitors have attended the show, it still could be a good place to attend. Call the companies who sell to a market as close to yours as possible. Ask them about the audience, how it worked for them, and so forth. Tell them about your product and your market and ask them if they think you should attend. I find that most marketing and sales people enjoy this type of conversation and that they will give you invaluable advice. If the show passes all of these filters, go and keep your eyes open.

3. Product Price

The price of the product doesn't seem to be a real factor. The price spread is:

PRICE	% RESP
No reply	11.8%
$1K	27.1%
$1K - $10K	34.1%
$10K	34.1%

4. Number of Shows

The chart above shows the number of shows. As you can see, most firms only go to one or two shows. Companies who go to regional shows have a slight tendency to attend more shows. I have talked to several firms who view regional shows as key to their marketing strategy, and they go to nine or more.

I was surprised that the companies who attended local shows tended to attend fewer. I suspect that these companies were making use of a local show to do some inexpensive PR and marketing. National shows were more popular than regional shows, which were more popular than local shows.

Percent of companies attending by type of show.

TYPE OF SHOW	% RESP
National	81.2%
Regional	65.3%
Local	29.4%

My experience is that it is as much work to attend a national show as a regional one and that the national show almost always offers better exposure. You might have to pay a little more for the exhibit space and the airfare, but these costs are a small part of your total investment in the show. Comdex is a good example of this. The fall Comdex at Las Vegas is the show to do if you are only doing one. While I understand that the other regional shows are improving, my experience is that they offer far less in both quantity and quality of prospects. The only counter example is industries where the prospects don't want to spend the money to travel to a national show. In these industries the regional shows may be the only viable alternative.

5. Cost of Attending a National Show

Very few companies can go to a national show for less than $1,000, but most of them spend less than $10,000. A few spend $10,000 to $25,000, but very few spend over $25,000. (See the pie chart below.)

I think that this is critical to success with trade shows. If the people are willing to hold down expenses, trade shows can be cost-effective.

I intended that this question cover out-of-pocket expenses, and I believe that this is how it appeared that most people answered the question.

The people cost of trade shows can be considerable. Let's say you send four people to a show and they all make $52,000 per year, or $1,000 per week. You have another $4,000 for the week they were at the show and another $4,000 or more in getting ready for the show.

Number of Trade Shows

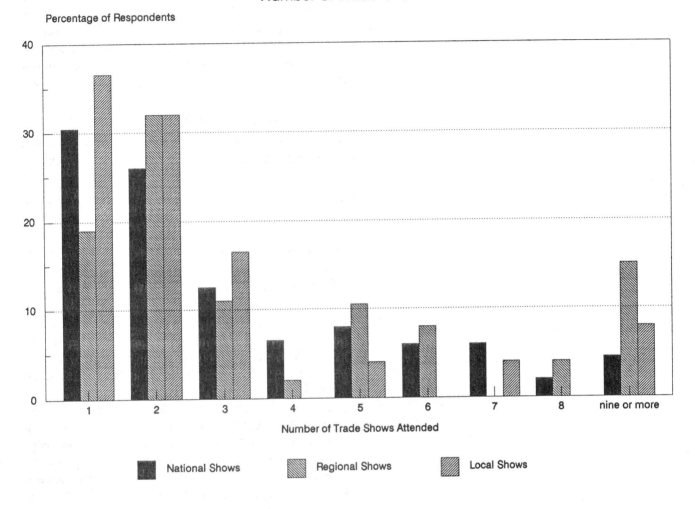

Percentage of Respondents

Number of Trade Shows Attended

National Shows   Regional Shows   Local Shows

When I have looked at it, these hidden expenses make trade shows a lot more expensive than the out-of-pocket expenses would indicate. If you consider the opportunity cost of having your best sales and marketing people off at the show, your costs will be even higher.

6. Comparing the Cost of National, Regional & Local Shows

If you look at the table on the next page, it is very clear that companies spend less for local and regional shows.

Companies often spend up to $10,000 with regional shows, but very few spend more. I suspect that it is difficult to spend less than $1,000 if you have to travel and pay for a hotel.

Most companies spend less than $1,000 with local shows. I have talked to a number of clients who have pulled back their investment in local shows.

They found that it wasn't worthwhile to send some-one from headquarters to a local show. Usually they have their person in the city where the local show is cover it. This might be a dealer, or a remote sales person. If the ground rules are to use the local per-son for the local show, you can hold the costs down under $1,000.

Cost of Attending a National Trade Show

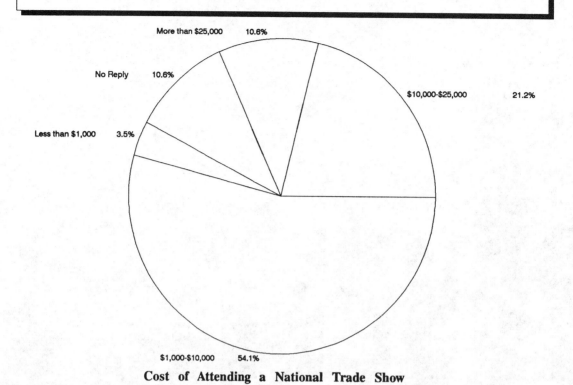

Cost of Attending a National Trade Show

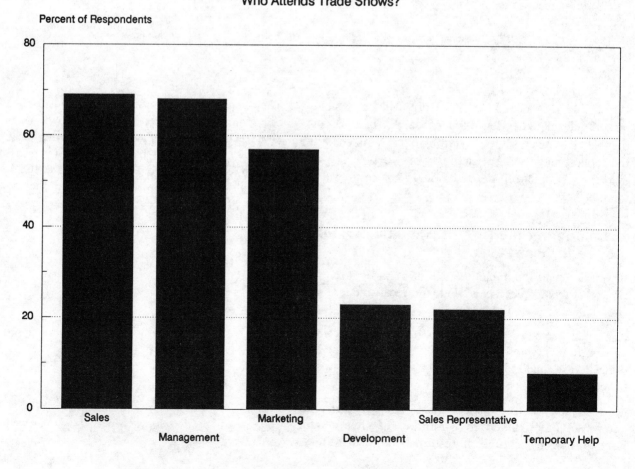

Who Attends Trade Shows?

Chapter I. Promotion

Table IV - Cost of Attending Shows

Cost of Attending a Show	(% of Respondents		
	National	Regional	Local
No Reply	10.6%	34.1%	54.1%
<$1K	3.5%	12.9%	30.6%
$1K-$10K	54.1%	45.9%	30.6%

Market Size	Lead Generation Survey	Trade Show Survey
<1K	17.5%	8.4%
1K - 10K	27.4%	19.7%
10K	5.0%	71.8%

7. One Time Cost per Exhibit

COST	% RESP
No reply	12.9%
$500 - $1K	20.0%
$1K - $5K	49.4%
$5K - $10K	3.5%
$10K - $25K	8.2%
$25K	3.5%
$500	4.7%

The median expense for an exhibit is $1,000 to $5,000, which will get you a nice off-the-shelf exhibit. It won't get you the fancy custom exhibits that are so nice. They run $25,000, and less than 3.5 percent of the respondents take this approach. This is consistent with the hold-down-the-costs philosophy that is coming through these surveys.

8. Who Attends Trade Shows?

If you look at the chart on the prior page, you will see that most companies send their sales people and managers. Marketing is a reasonable third, and everything else is dramatically lower.

I found it interesting that 21 percent of the companies send their reps. This corresponds to the 30 percent who use local shows. While I can't prove it, I would bet that a lot of companies have found that local shows can be very good for their dealers/reps,

but they can't afford to send corporate people to these local shows.

I expected to see more developers attending shows. Much of my experience with trade shows is with very small PC software companies going to Fall Comdex. In several of these cases, it was critical for the lead developer to be present at the show. We used the show to discuss the custom requirements for some very large customers.

It was also important to establish technical credibility when we were talking to the large chains. They wanted to be sure that we could convince them that we could make the modifications and extensions to the product that would be required over time. Finally, I believe that it is really important for developers to meet the customers, and learn first hand who is using their product and what they are trying to do with it.

The number of firms reporting that they use temporary help seemed lower than I expected based on my experience at trade shows. Smaller firms with technical products don't feel that a temp can learn enough to be effective communicating with their prospects. My experience with shows is that you can train newcomers to handle the first-level contact.

When I have worked a booth, we typically had someone who pulled people in with the question. You ask the question to find out if the prospects are qualified and to see if you can pull them in. In one case, we were demonstrating the first PC backup software at Comdex. Our question was "When was the last time that you had to deal with a hard disk crash?" It was simple to deliver, and if they had experienced one with a customer (these were dealers) in the last week, they were pulled in. The catcher

Chapter I. Promotion

would ask them if they would like to see a demo of a product which could backup all the data on their customer's disks so they wouldn't have to spend hours of tech support time recovering customer data.

The second person handled the demo (which was 30 to 60 seconds long), and handled the first-level questions. They handed out the materials and tried to sell the show special. We had two people at the second position. One would demo and then take their group aside and try to close the sale. They alternated positions and we had great results.

While I haven't hired a temporary person to be the catcher, I don't see any reason it wouldn't work. If you watch the booths for the larger companies, you will see that many of them have temporary workers in this catcher role. They are dressed in business suits and look very professional, but if you ask them you will find they were just hired for the show.

This keeps their sales people selling. The one reason that I would consider it is that I found that the sales people got very bored with the catcher role. I would be interested to learn about experiences others have had with this approach. Finally, it is probably a lot cheaper to hire a local temp than to send someone from headquarters.

9. Why Do Companies Attend Trade Shows?

The answer is leads and PR, with leads only slightly ahead. (See chart on the next page.) Everything else is clearly in second tier.

In my mind, networking is part of PR. Therefore, I would have rated it higher. Meeting the editors and writers at a show is a unique opportunity. I guess that most of the respondents classified this as PR.

I was surprised that Sales was so low. When I ask companies about why they attend, in most cases they point to the contacts that they made at the show that turned into sales. In most of these cases, they didn't make the sale at the show, but it was fairly directly linked to being at the show. Thus, this is probably classified as lead generation.

Selling at a show is very difficult for a number of reasons. The first is that many shows frown on vendors selling on the show floor. They feel that it gives the show a carnival atmosphere. Even if you are al-

lowed to sell, very few products can be sold to the people who attend a show. This is especially true with complex sales which involve a number of employees and levels of management.

Showing the flag is required when there is one big annual show, and everyone has to go. You can also generate leads and get PR, but in this type of situation you would be forced to attend even if you didn't generate leads and PR. This has been very important to several of my more mature clients. It is especially true when you are the market leader.

Introducing a product at a trade show can be a great way to jump start your marketing. If you have a hot new product, and you have a good show to go to, you can have a great launch. For may of my clients, this is the one reason that they would consider going to a show.

Why Do You Attend Trade Shows?

I suspect that the only reason that it isn't more popular is that new product introductions don't occur all that often. Most products have a five to ten year product life so most of the time we are flogging a mature product, not introducing a hot new one.

The other probable reason is that most companies with hot new products don't have marketing people. In most of the cases that I have seen, they have a CEO President and a sales person. If you ask these people why they are taking their new product to the show, the CEO will say to get PR/exposure (visibility for his baby), and the sales person will say leads (to get sales).

Almost no one goes to shows for fun. Really? I know that they are really hard work, but it is a real rush to show your product to a steady stream of live prospects. People gather information in different ways.

Some people talk to people in person, others talk on the phone while others read and analyze. One of my theories is that the face-to-face people really like trade shows because they provide that direct contact. Others prefer telesales, while some of us love the hard quantified results that direct mail provides.

38 Software Success® 1992 Reference Book

Why do you attend trade Shows?

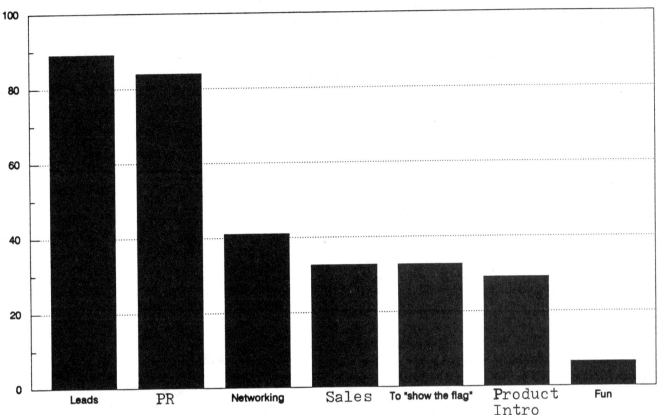

Percentage

MORE LEADS	% RESP
Yes	29.4%
No	27.1%
Maybe	35.3%
Don't care	8.2%

Do you believe that you could invest the same money in hard lead generation and generate more leads?

To be honest, I expected fewer people to acknowledge that hard lead generation might generate more leads. The "don't care" people are going to shows for the PR, while the "no" people are sure that they are effectively generating leads.

The "yes" and "maybe" people have the really interesting dilemma. How much is the PR really worth? In theory, you should determine how much it would cost you to generate the PR via alternative programs. Then you could allocate this part of the cost of going to the show to PR. The remainder would be the lead generating budget, and you could determine the effective cost-per-lead for this lead generation budget.

I realize that this sounds like an academic exercise, but I feel that it is very practical. When you are spending $10,000 to go to a show, we could assume that $5,000 of this is for PR and the remainder is for leads. $5,000 will buy you a lot of PR, and the other $5,000 will generate some really good leads. If you are in this "yes/maybe" camp, I urge you to step back and look at the alternatives.

10. Trade Show Usage

CHANGE	% RESP
No reply	2.4%
Increasing	29.4%
No Change	49.4%
Decreasing	18.8%

"No change" is the most popular answer, but 1.56 times more firms are increasing their usage of trade shows than are decreasing it.

What I didn't ask was how trade shows as a percentage of their marketing budget is changing. Since most of our readers are in high growth companies,

Chapter I. Promotion

no change means that their marketing budgets are growing rapidly. I must admit that I am letting my biases show through here. I believe that trade shows can be very effective given the right factors, but there isn't much room for error. If you have a very good targeted show, you can really benefit from going to the show if you have your act together. By that I mean that you have to have good product materials and demo for the show.

11. Cost of Attending a National Show as a Function of Company Revenue

If you look at the table on the below, it is very clear that the amount that companies spend on national trade shows is very much a function of company revenue. Companies under $2 million rarely spend more than $10,000 to go to a show. Companies in the $2 million to $5 million range are likely to spend $10,000 to $25,000, and companies over $5 million spend over $25,000.

As you may recall, in the salary survey issue we found that the compensation for CEOs increased dramatically once their company got over $2 million in sales. I think the problem is that there are a number of fixed costs that can really strain a company with $1 million in revenues. Things really loosen up once the revenues get to $2 million. Most of the companies in the $2 million to $5 million range spend $10,000 to $25,000. When companies get over $5 million they tend to spend over $25,000.

I really like these results. I believe they provide some practical guidelines on what companies should plan to spend on trade shows as they grow.

12. Number of Shows by Market Size

Companies with markets of less than 1,000 prospects don't go to more than two shows. I suspect that in markets this small there aren't more than two shows.

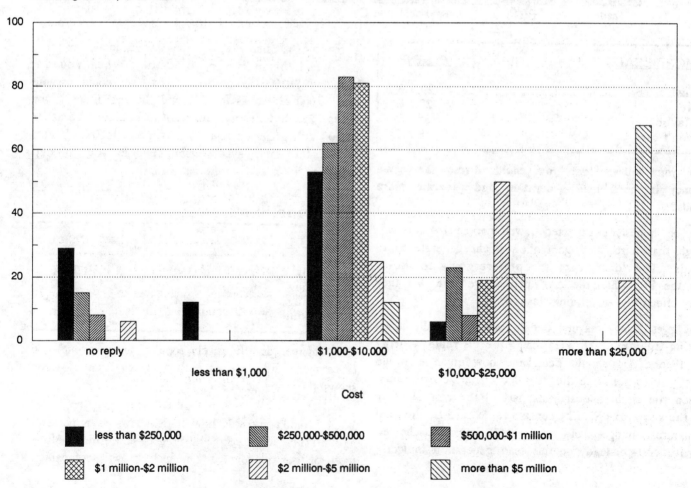

Cost of Attending Trade Shows vs. Revenue

Companies with more prospects go to three or more shows over 30 percent of the time.

Isn't Comdex a PC show? Not really. It is a dealer show. Large end users who have internal dealerships also attend. It turns out that most of the dealers are interested in PCs, but LAN and workstation vendors might have a very good audience at Comdex.

I also looked at how many shows companies went to based on their revenues and there was very little difference. It looks like companies figure out that there are a certain number of key shows to attend.

13. Number of Shows by Computer Type

Looking at the percentage of the firms who go to three or more shows, there isn't much difference by hardware platform.

PLATFORM	% RESP
PC	25.4%
LAN	30.0%
Mini	21.5%
Workstation	33.0%
Mainframe	45.0%

This is as it should be. Most trade shows are for end users, rather than hardware platforms. They are targeted toward a market. The large generic hardware oriented shows are a thing of the past. I suspect that the disappointment with the attendance at the MAC Expo last spring was part of this trend. Even when they are very small, they try to attend all the relevant shows. They do this by working very hard to hold down their costs. As revenues grow, companies spend more money on the shows that they attend rather than attending more shows.

14. Trend in Trade Show Usage as a Function of the Lead Generation Capability of Trade Shows

If you recall, we asked people if they felt they could generate more leads with hard lead generation instead of trade shows. A very significant number of respondents felt that they could generate more leads by taking the same dollars and putting them into

hard lead generation. It turns out that the attitude on lead generation has a profound impact on the trend in increasing or decreasing trade show usage. (I realize that this is intuitively correct, but it means that when it gets down to brass tacks, most companies are truly looking to trade shows to generate leads.)

The overall factor was that companies were increasing their trade show usage 1.56 times more often than they were decreasing it. If you look at it by the lead generation quality, the differences are much more pronounced.

MORE LEADS	% RESP
Yes	0.66
No	5.00
Maybe	1.10
Don't care	infinite

When companies believe they can generate more leads via hard lead generation, they cut down on trade shows. In practice, they take the trade show budget and divert it into hard lead generation. This is as it should be.

On the other hand, if trade shows are generating more leads, companies are increasing their usage of trade shows. You put your money into the programs that work.

Trend in Usage

More Leads	Decrease	Increase	No Change
Yes	16.0%	56.0%	24.0%
No	43.5%	47.8%	8.7%
Maybe	30.0%	40.0%	26.7%
Don't care	28.6%	71.4%	0%

F. Trade Show Research (1990)

This section summarizes various market research statistics that I have compiled from recent articles.

1. Successful Meetings

Getting the Most from Your Exhibitor Dollars
By Richard Murphy
August 1990

"Companies spent $21 billion at more than 9,000 trade shows in 1989...

One out of three exhibitors does not set quantifiable objectives for each show.

Most exhibitors (56 percent) don't train the People staffing their booths.

Some 78 percent don't promote their exhibit prior to the show.

A vast majority (83 percent) don't analyze a show's value based on return on investment....

As many as 80 percent of the leads are never pursued, and whatever follow-up there is often occurs so long after the show that the chances of making a sale are virtually nil."

This is a pretty sad litany. If you make use of trade shows I urge you to see how many of these items you are doing right. The good news is that if you do it right, you will have a real advantage over your competitors who are closer to the norm.

2. Trade Shows Poised for 1990s Growth

Business Marketing
By Richard K. Swandby, Jonathan M. Cox, and Ian K. Sequeira

"The average attendees spent an average of 7.3 hours viewing the exhibits over an average of two days...

Attendees stopped to talk or acquire literature at an average of 26 exhibits each day...

If we deduct an estimated one quarter of the attendees' time for walking, eating, talking or resting, the average time spent at each exhibit drops to about 13 minutes...

Traffic density declined over the past decade. The decline in traffic density occurred because show attendance did not keep up with exhibit space sales."

My experience is that people spend more time walking the aisles and just looking than 25 percent. I think you have significantly less than 13 minutes to deal with.

The decline in traffic density concerns me. One of the factors you might calculate for shows where you have exhibited is the number of attendees divided by the square feet of exhibit space at the show. See if this factor is increasing or decreasing. (Traffic density adds in how many hours the average attendee

spends on the show floor per day. I have just assumed that this is unchanged.)

Reaching the Unknown Prospect
March 1990
Direct Marketing

"An average of 83 percent of trade show visitors have not been called on in the last year by sales personnel. Computers were the highest industry with 91 percent not being called on, and software was third at 87 percent."

3. Influence Buying Decisions Business Marketing

Business Marketing
By Kate Bertrand
March 1990

"Dallas-based consultants B.R. Blackmarr & Associates conducted the mail survey for the Trade Show Bureau under a grant from Skyline Displays, Burnsville, Minn. More than 40 percent of the respondents were final purchasing decision makers, and another 25 percent were influencers."

The factors for people to attend computer trade shows are shown below. (On this scale, a rating of 5 represents the greatest importance).

The lowest interest reason was to purchase products, at 1.9.

I also think that people go to trade shows to see things they can't get through the mail. The average trade show attendee is spending $1,300 to attend the show, so they want to have something to show for their effort and expense.

Why People Attend Trade Shows

Trade show usage vs. more leads via hard lead generation

4.0 New Product Introduction
3.8 Interest in Specific Exhibitors
3.7 To Meet Other Industry Professionals
3.0 To Gather Information for Purchase

4. CEO Attendance at Trade Shows Doubles

Sales & Marketing News
November/December 1989

Chapter I. Promotion

This was from a survey by Allen Konopacki, President, **Incomm International**

It is available from:
Jim Monahan
Monahan & Associates
9933 Lawler Ave
Skokie, IL 60077
(312) 675-9060

5. Demos

If your demo lasts more than a minute, and new people have to wait for it to start, you could lose 58 percent of the attendees. (See box below.)

March 1989

> **Amount of Time a Visitor Will Wait for a Sales Rep in the Booth**
> 6% Will Not Wait
> 11% Will Wait 30 Seconds
> 41% Will Wait Over One Minute
> 28% Will Wait Three Minutes
> 14% Will Wait Five Minutes
> **Incomm International Tradeshow Week - 2/27/90**

6. The Higher Cost of Exhibiting

The Trade Show Bureau reports that you could estimate your expenses for a trade show by starting with the space charge.

"...for every $100 that you spend on space, the total direct cost of participation will be just under $417. Expenses for booth personnel are more difficult to estimate, but the bureau says you should expect to spend a third again on salaries and travel, bringing the total to $554 for every $100 of rental space."

This seems a bit high to me. I am working with a client who is considering attending a show where the space charge is $2,900. I can't image that we would spend $16,066 to attend this show.

Another way to look at this number is to divide our $10,000 total expenditure by 5.54 to calculate the comparable space charge of $1,800. While this might be reasonable for smaller shows, most of the shows I have seen are charging more than this. I suspect that software companies are doing a good job of holding down their other expenses.

7. Top Reasons Other than Size for Remembering an Exhibit

Trade Show Bureau
1660 Lincoln Street, Suite 2080
Denver, CO 80264
(303) 860-7626

This eight-page study that includes a set of two 35mm color slides can be obtained for $10. The reasons for remembering an exhibit were:

> 39% Interested in Products
> 25% Live Demonstration
> 14% Exhibit Color/ Design
> 10% Booth Staff
> 8% Obtain Literature
> 4% Well-Known Company

G. Trade Show References (1990)

1. Trade Show Report

Is a report published by MediaMap of Bedford Mass (617) 275-5560. As reported in **Marketing Computers** (July 1990) and **Sales/Marketing Briefs**:

"This is a 400-page quarterly report for the computer industry which covers nearly 200 shows worldwide. The price is $795, but there is an introductory price of $595."

2. 1990 Trade Show Book Available

This book was published by **Tradeshow Week** (213) 826-5696. It covers nearly 4,000 trade and consumer expositions. It costs $250.

If you are looking for non-computer trade shows, this might turn up just the show you have been looking for.

3. The 1990 Tradeshow & Exhibits Schedule

Has 11,000 listings. It is 400 pages and covers 82 industries. It costs $105 and can be ordered by calling (800) 234-4553.

It covers:

* Where and when important events will be held;
* What the expected attendance and exhibit space usage will be; and
* Who show managers are and how to contact them.

4. Aisle View

745 Marquette Bank Bldg
PO Box 351
Rochester, MN 55903

This monthly newsletter for small exhibitors and novice exhibit managers costs $38 per year.

"In every issue you discover new ways to..

* Select the right shows, and the best space
* Create traffic-stopping promotions
* Reduce costs on displays and graphics
* Increase sales leads from shows
* Train and motivate booth staffers
* Compete successfully against big budget leaders

If you are serious about trade shows, I would recommend that you take a look at this newsletter.

5. Solving the Exhibition Maze

Suite 2080
Denver, CO 80264
(303) 860-7626

This eight-page study that includes a set of two 35mm color slides can be obtained for $10.

$199.95 training video which provides a scenario of a company contemplating its first trade show.

Carol Davis-Beach
Events Management Media
1559-55 Bay St
Taunton, MA 02780
(508) 880-3233

6. Exhibit Better

Is published by Skyline Displays, 612-894-3240. It includes over 750 pages of workbooks, reprints, worksheets, more than two hours of videotapes, and a 38 minute audio tape. Designed and written by Diane Weintraub, President of Communique Exhibitor Education. You will learn how to:

> * Determine the Best Shows
> * Design Effective Exhibits
> * Select Exhibit Space
> * Plan Persuasive Promotions
> * Profit from Lead Management
> * Record Objectives and Results
> * Make Justifiable Budgets
> * Prepare Detailed Planning
> * Increase Booth Traffic
> * Prepare Detailed Planning
> * Increase Booth

If you are new to trade shows, it sure looks like this would be a good investment. When you think about how much you spend on trade shows, it sure makes sense to spend some time and money to be more effective.

7. Trade Show Guides are available for $5 each from:

The Trade Show Bureau
PO Box 797
8 Beach Road
East Orleans, MA 02643
(508) 240-0177

*Tradeshow Marketing and Sales, Volume 1 (24 pages), a system for effective selling.

*Tradeshow Marketing and Sales, Volume 2 (16 pages), a guide to the marketing potential of the medium.

Prepared for the bureau by Fred Kitzing, owner of a tradeshow marketing agency, the booklets walk exhibitors through practical methods.

Mentioned in **Successful Meetings**, December 1989.

8. Exhibit Staffer Training

Giltspur offers half and full day courses customized to your company's requirements.

(800) 727-0069

9. Trade Show Seminar

Endorsed by the Trade Show Bureau, and produced by the Interface Group. The topics include:

* Trade shows and your marketing plan

* Optimizing your exhibit space for maximum results

Table IV - Selecting Promotions

Media	Image	Leads	Appt	Sales	Intro	Press
Contest		X			X	
Telemarket			X	X		
Direct Mail	X	X	X		X	
Giveaways		X			X	
Hotel	X				X	
Signs	X	X			X	
Show ads	X	X		X	X	
Billboards	X				X	
Trade pub ads	X			X	X	
Press briefing	X				X	X
Press release	X				X	X
Photo opportunity	X				X	X

* Promotional techniques that will work for you

* Boothmanship - proven ways to produce more qualified leads

* Post show - getting results with minimum effort

* Management tools for the multi-show mix

The fee is only $249.
(617) 449-9155

10. Trade Show Tips

You can get a free booklet from **Expoconsul International**, Princeton, N.J. explaining how to get the most out of the publicity opportunities at trade shows.

Expoconsul
(609) 987-9400

11. Exhibitor Magazine

When you subscribe to this magazine you get:

* Buyer's guide to exhibits

* Exhibit Manager's Salary Survey.

* Exhibit Planning Guide

Lee Knight Publisher and Editor
Exhibitor Magazine
(507) 289-6556

12. Selecting Promotions

The article in Exhibitor, August 1990 had the table below. The goals are:

* **Image Awareness**

* **Lead Generation**

* **Appointments**

* **Book Sales**

* **Product Introduction**

* **Press Exposure**

The promotional activities at the top of the list are the most active while those at the bottom are more passive.

When you look at this list it becomes very apparent how many alternatives there are, and how they might help accomplish these different goals.

This should reinforce why it is so important to define your objectives before you attend a show. Once you have done this, you can rate the programs based on your objectives.

H. General Promotion (1989)

In discussing ways that software companies promote themselves and their products, we have found it useful to divide these activities into two categories: promotion and lead generation. There are some important distinctions between these two activities that we would like to highlight.

Promotion is the soft side of marketing. It is comprised of activities that take the longer view. While these activities may generate leads, lead generation isn't the primary objective or benefit. Included in the promotional category are the following:

* Public   Relations
* Image   Advertising
* Trade   Shows
* Self   Promotion

Public Relations
Public Relations is a major component of Promotion. It includes: Press Releases, Press tours, obtaining (favorable) product reviews, generating articles about your product in the trade press, and more.

Image   Advertising
Image advertising is designed to establish your company and position your product(s), rather than directly sell your product.

Trade Shows
Trade Shows can be, depending upon your products and industry, a very effective means of promotion.

Self Promotion
There is also a category of self-promotion which can be both very effective and very inexpensive. Items in this category include:

* Newsletters
* Events   Sponsorship
* Seminars
* Speaking at trade shows

1. Why use promotion?

We are often asked, "why should we spend our hard dollars on soft promotional efforts?, when we can put them into direct lead generation programs which will result in near-term sales". There was an article by John R. Graham in the December 7th issue of Sales and Marketing Executive Report which listed 12 reasons to invest in this type of strategic marketing programs (note that he uses marketing where we would use promotion):

1. **Marketing establishes your firm as a permanent player .**
2. **Marketing gives you a level playing field.**
3. **Marketing helps avoid a 'crisis-to-crisis' business   environment.**
4. **Marketing eliminates the need for 'sales pushes'.**
5. **Marketing builds enduring relationships with customers.**
6. **Marketing lets you focus on the customer.**
7. **Marketing gives you control over your company's   image.**
8. **Marketing aids in customer retention.**
9. **Marketing helps you sell more to your present customers.**
10. **Marketing lets you attract the right customers.**
11 **.Marketing helps you avoid wasting money.**
12. **Most important of all, marketing allows you to devote your efforts to your real business.**

These are all long term investments to make the sales easier. We realize that it takes an act of faith to invest for six months to a year before you see any return on your investment, but there is a lot of evidence that companies who invest in promotion end up with a better long-term business. We should also point out that many of the self-promotion programs require very little money. They take time and energy, but you can get good results without a big budget. If you don't have the money to spare, we strongly urge you to look for inexpensive promotional programs to start now.

2. Marketing Expenditures

Q: **Several of readers responded to our estimates of reasonable levels of investment in marketing. The following quote is typical: "We liked this issue of the newsletter. Very useful, but we spend much more on marketing than you show. We think it pays off. Why do you think our numbers are higher than your published numbers?"**

Chapter I. Promotion

A: There is a great deal of uncertainty in the definitions of marketing expenses. We have seen many companies which shift marketing and administrative budgets back and forth. Another reason is that small companies are often forced to spend more because there are so many fixed costs. In our experience larger companies spend less, percentage wise, because they spend so much more in absolute dollars. These companies also tend to have higher management and administrative budgets. In many cases these management and administrative costs are really marketing related.

Our operating expense guidelines are just that:guidelines. The most important element in any marketing program is success. If you think that higher expense level pays off, keep going.

I. Promotional Activities Survey (1989)

Earlier this year we enclosed a survey on promotional activities within our subscriber companies. Many of the questions were similar to the questions that we asked in our Subscriber Survey (reported in the June '89 issue). Since the results validated the previously published results, we won't discuss issues such as Company Type, Revenues, Marketing Budget, Number of employees, etc.

1. Market Size

We were surprised at how few companies answered this question, and how small most of the companies saw their market. We believe that the reason that so few companies answered this question is that as an industry we aren't sophisticated in how we see ourselves. In more mature industries, everyone can tell you the statistics on their markets.

The second factor is the very tight focus most companies have. They see their market in terms of products which are technically comparable with theirs. We believe that the market needs to be seen from the customer's point of view.

We will give an example for our consulting business. If we were to take a narrow view of our total marketplace, we would say that there are only a handful of software marketing consultants. All of these con-sultants together probably generate less that $2M or $3M in annual revenues. But this narrow view ignores the other people who provide similar services: ad agencies, general management consultants, etc.

Interpreted more broadly, the total market is more like $30M to $40M. There are over 7,500 software companies and they probably spend $5K per year on average on outside marketing and management consulting. That's quite a difference from a "tiny" $2-3M market!

We suspect that most of our respondents gave a lower estimate for their own situation. This is important for several reasons. First of all, if you focus on a small-sized market, you may be leaving real opportunity on the table. If you take a very limited perspective, it is easy to conclude that you can only make sales at the expense of your direct competitors — a difficult task.

Successful companies see their market in larger terms and find ways to meet the larger needs. This allows them to grow quickly by tapping into these other markets.

Item	Value
No Reply	58.1%
<$1M	3.2%
$1M-$10M	22.6%
$10M-$100M	6.5%
$100M-$500M	3.2%
$500M-$1B	3.2%
>$1B	3.2%

Table 1 — Market Size/Annual Revenues

2. Promotion Responsibility

We were surprised at the number of medium sized firms where the president was responsible for promotion. Given all of the other demands on the president's time, it is very difficult for them to give promotion the consistent attention that it requires. We would be very interested in hearing comments on the pros and cons of having a marketing executive responsible for promotion.

We weren't surprised at the low number of Marketing Communications Managers. Given the fact that most of the companies had only one or two people in Marketing, it isn't surprising that they didn't have one person dedicated to Marketing Communications.

Item	Value
President	51.6%
Mktg Exec	54.4%
Mar Com Mgr	6.5%
Outside Agency	3.2%

Table 2 — Promotional Responsibility

Promotional Techniques Used

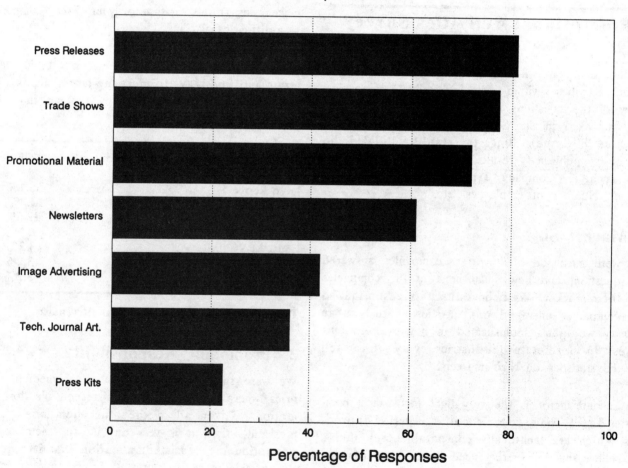

Figure 1 — Promotional Techniques Used

3. Promotional Techniques

PR was the most popular from of promotion. Press Releases, the most ubiquitous form of PR, are inexpensive, are easy to do, and can be very effective. We were surprised at the popularity of trade shows. As you will see later on in this issue, software companies are using regional and local trade shows to gain visibility when they have limited funds. Promotional material is almost mandatory. If you don't have a package, with product literature, are you really in business?

We were surprised at the number of companies who have newsletters. We suspect that the newsletters aren't as frequent as the companies might like, but they are a good first step. Image advertising is often tied in with the company's lead generation strategy since it is difficult to justify image advertising purely on the basis of promotion. Technical journal articles were surprisingly uncommon as were press kits.

4. Who Does the Promotion?

Item	Value
In house	93.5%
Agency	32.3%
Freelancer	25.8%

Table 3 — Who does the Promotion?

We were surprised at the number of firms who used agencies. Typically these were the larger firms. Free lancers can be a very effective way to stretch a limited marketing budget.

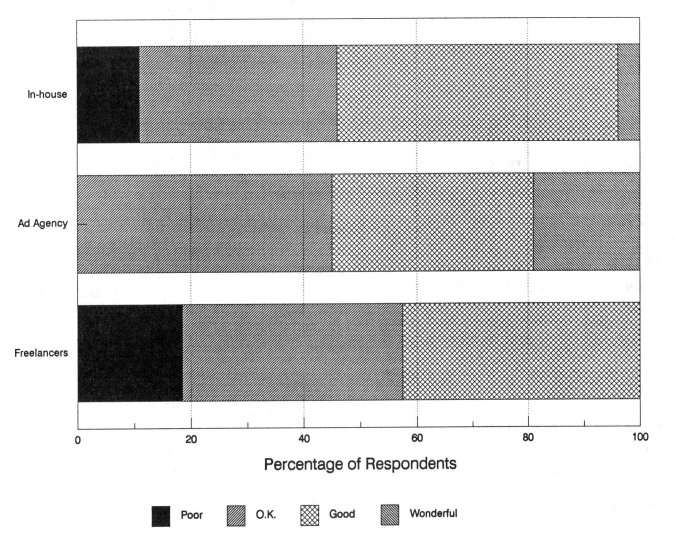

Promotional Effectiveness by Practitioner

Figure 2 — Promotional Effectiveness by Practitioner

Chapter I. Promotion

Promotional Effectiveness by Method

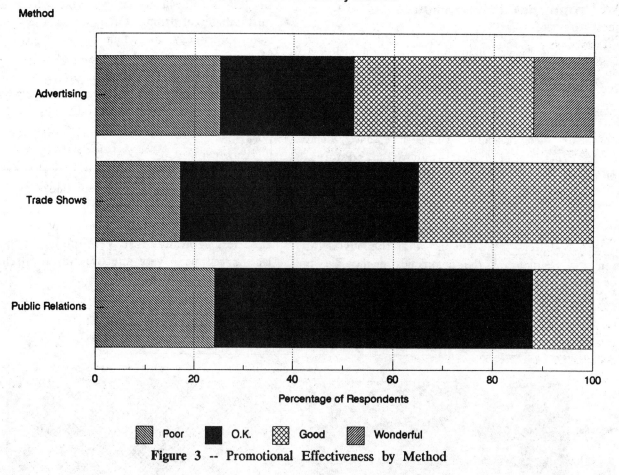

Method

Figure 3 -- Promotional Effectiveness by Method

5. Promotional Effectiveness

There were a number of questions in the survey designed to find out the effectiveness of both promotional practitioners, and of promotional methods.

In-House Staff

As you might expect, most respondents felt that their in-house promotional staff was at least "Good". If they aren't good, you must replace them or face business failure. While most of the in-house efforts were competent, they weren't any better than that; very few in-house promotional staffs were rated as "Wonderful!"

Ad Agencies

Image advertising and promotion are a natural for ad agencies. Promotional materials, too, use many of the same creative resources that agencies use to build their bread-and-butter existence. On the whole, ad agencies got the best rating from our respondents. Many were OK, some were GOOD,

and a surprisingly high percentage were rated "Wonderful!". There were no "Poor" agency ratings. (Perhaps they all got fired.)

Free-Lance Outsiders

Our respondents were less happy with the efforts of free-lance outsiders. In addition to the raw statistics, we received a number of negative comments from people who no longer use free lance promotional consultants. As we've discussed in previous issues, you must closely manage the efforts of free-lance consultants to be sure of effective results: you too will be unhappy if you don't.

6. Public Relations

While PR is the most highly used method of promotion, it was the least highly regarded among our respondents: more people rated PR "Poor" or "OK" than any other method.

Chapter I. Promotion

We believe that this response is misleading since most companies don't have a method to measure the effectiveness of their PR. Without any real effectiveness measures and because it is relatively inexpensive, it's easy to simply rate PR as being "OK".

This brings us to one of our continuing themes: You must measure the results of your promotional and lead-generation activities to know how you are doing. Pick a number of trade-press mentions that you want to achieve with a given Press Release, for instance. (Pick this number before you send out the release.) Then count the number of actual mentions or reprints as they happen. Compare the actual results you achieved with your expectations. Did you have a positive or negative variance? Were your pre-release expectations unrealistically high or low? Was the release itself more or less effective than it could have been? A hard-nosed insistence on quantitative measures will pay big dividends as you accumulate experience and face an ever-widening field of promotional and lead-generation opportunities.

7. Trade Shows

While we haven't seen any statistics, we suspect that software companies spend more money on trade shows than do other companies of a similar size. Most of our respondents exhibit in three or fewer trade shows, but a few are "on the road" full-time. Some companies exhibit at only nationally-known events like Comdex, while others like to exhibit in regional or vertical market shows with a more limited audience. In general, regional shows seemed to be more effective with our respondents (perhaps because they were less expensive) than national shows.

The cost per trade show was reported to be from $10-15K per show. This seems low to us but may only include the cost for exhibit space. There is one

Item	Value
No Reply	29.0%
1	9.7%
2	19.4%
3	22.6%
4 to 7	12.9%
8 or more	6.5%

Table 4 — Number of Trade Shows

unusual fact reported by our respondents — there is no economy of scale in trade shows:The companies who exhibit at a lot of shows spend even more money per show than the average.

Trade shows are seen as being a good, effective promotional method. They had the lowest "Poor" rating of any promotional method and had a higher "Good" rating. You are unlikely to hit a marketing home-run by exhibiting at trade shows, however: nobody rated trade shows as "Wonderful!"

8. Advertising

On the whole, advertising received better ratings than any other method. The distribution of responses was bi-modal; our respondents either liked it very much or didn't like it at all. This method received higher ratings for both "Poor" and "Wonderful!" than either of other two promotional methods.

J. Managing Your Promotions? (1989)

One of the real issues with technically oriented companies is who should manage the advertising and promotional efforts. In many cases the senior managers are technically oriented and are uncomfortable with the 'fuzzy' nature of advertising work and the unpredictability of promotions and marketing. Because they aren't confident in their own abilities in this area they tend to delegate these responsibilities. There are a couple common scenarios which we see:

1. Hire a big agency

In this scenario the CEO decides to play it safe and go with a big agency. When the software company in question interview agencies, a large advertising agency often comes off very impressively. The senior partners in a large agency are quite skilled at selling the agency — it doesn't take much to dazzle an innocent 'techie'. "They may cost a little more," muses the software CEO, "but if we can get their experience and expertise it will be well worth it."

Once the agency contract is signed, the small software company typically is handed off to a junior account manager. Senior agency management is supposed to be overseeing the effort, but since software companies tend to be a very low dollar account, agency management focuses on their major accounts.

Typically, the results with the junior account manager are disappointing. There is usually a series of crises where the client insists on more senior manager involvement. Eventually the software company leaves the large agency because they aren't getting the control that they want. But they leave behind a substantial amount of money.

It has been our experience that you need to work with the talent that attracted you in the first place — not handed off to a junior person with the assurance that management is 'looking in.' If you cannot get a guarantee that the person that you want will actually be running your account, move on.

2. Hire your own advertising manager

The CEO decides to hire a full-time junior person to manage the advertising and promotional effort. "This will cost less than the agencies," the CEO thinks, "and there should be much more control because the person works for us." This scenario can work as long as management realizes that they have to supervise the in-house advertising manager. If you totally delegate all advertising and promotional decisions to a junior person, don't be surprised if their results are disappointing.

3. Hire a small agency

This is an alternative where middle managers in a large agency have left to form their own firm. The real advantage with these smaller agencies is that the principals work on your projects. They don't delegate them to junior account managers because their firm isn't large enough to have junior account managers. The other reason is that the founders of these smaller agencies often decided that they would rather do the work themselves than delegate it and do more marketing. If you can find a smaller agency where you can get the direct attention of a principal you respect, you might get the best results. The common theme in all of these scenarios is that management must make the commitment to 'get smart about promotion'.

4. Measures of promotional effectiveness

There was a study of promotional effectiveness written by John Yokum, President of Checkmate Marketing Resources, a promotional consulting firm in Toronto (no phone number). The article, Facts: The Final Frontier of Promotion, appeared in the November 14, 1988 issue of Promote. Checkmate Marketing built a promotional research model to attempt to predict the business impact of a promotion. His model has "consistently predicted actual business gains within plus or minus 10 percent". The next step was to test junior managers, account managers, and senior managers (client/ agency). While the junior managers identified the best promotion, they were unable to identify the real dogs. The account managers were even worse. They were even more bullish than the junior managers.

5. Experience Counts!

The senior managers (both client and agency) were much more accurate. The moral of the story seems to be that if you can involve senior managers you can dramatically improve the quality of your promotions. Don't leave your advertising and promotion to amateurs.

K. Trade Shows (1989)

We receive a number of questions regarding trade shows each month. Many software executives feel that their company must go to one or more shows, yet the feel that somehow they are wasting their money. They also are concerned about the impact on their sales and marketing staff. These are very reasonable concerns, indeed. One week-long trade show might cost you one month of sales when you consider the preparation time, the time at the show, and the post show follow up and recovery.

Yet you cannot ignore the value of trade shows. Annually one or more software companies exhibits a product that excites interest at a show (typically Comdex) and their sales 'take off.' The benefits of a good trade show goes well beyond having an occasional company hit the jackpot — many companies have found that their best and most lasting customers were unearthed at a trade show.

Chapter I. Promotion

This article, then, analyses the pros and cons of exhibiting at trade shows. In addition to depending upon our own experience, we have uncovered a number of papers and magazine pieces on this subject: a list of references can be found at the end of this article.

1. Should you go?

Are trade shows part of your marketing & lead-generation strategies? Should they be? Some software companies use trade shows almost exclusively, others eschew them. We think that this is the most important decision you can make regarding trade shows.

Reasons for:

There are a number of reasons that you can decide to exhibit at a show:

1. Launch a new product. Every year a number of companies use the trade show season as an excuse to kick off the sales cycle of their new products. Although there is some possibility of getting lost in the crush of other announcements, skillful PR can start a media blitz that can pay big sales dividends.

2. Begin a promotion/push for an existing product. Existing products can be successfully promoted at trade shows. You'll need a new wrinkle, however, to attract attention. A new release and/or new features work best, but even a price promotion may be sufficient to gain notice.

3. Generate leads. Nothing is better than a batch of fresh new prospects (except a batch of fresh new customers!)

4. Meet dealers and distributors. If you use distribution (or want to use distribution, or think you want to use distribution) trade shows, especially Comdex, are excellent.

5. Be seen. Sometimes exhibiting in the proper show is mandatory just to show 'em you're still in business.

Reasons Against

Likewise there are a number of reasons not to attend:

1. You can't afford it. Even the smallest, cheapest show will cost far more than you think; when all the costs are added in, a 10 by 10 booth at Comdex will end up costing a minimum of $10,000.

2. You can't afford the resources. Doing a show right will be a real drain on your marketing and sales organization, especially the first one.

3. You don't have enough time. If you've made you mind up just today to attend the WhoozisExpo, you may simply not have enough to procure a booth, get brochures, schedule personnel, etc.

4. It doesn't work for you. This is perhaps the most compelling reason of all. Some companies and/or products can't be sold or marketed effectively at a trade show. Maybe you haven't been able to identify the 'right' show. Maybe your market is too narrow. Whatever the reason, if trade shows don't work, then don't go.

Before you make up your mind to exhibit in a show, carefully weigh the costs and list the anticipated benefits. Formulate, if you can, measures of success:

* How many Contacts/Leads?

* How many customers?

* What kinds of new contacts?

Show Size Grows

There are some trends in trade shows that might influence your decision on whether you should go to a trade show. There was an article in May 1988 Business Marketing on "Show Size Grows; Audience Quality Stays High", Jonathan M. Cox a VP of Exhibit Surveys Inc. of Red Bank, NJ. This article is based on 55 surveys of different shows. They selected a sample of 800 to 1,500 show attendees. They get a 25% to 60% response by including an incentive and a personalized cover letter.

Chapter I. Promotion

"According to an analysis published Feb. 8 by Tradeshow Week, professional attendance ... increased 9.9% for all of 1987. Net square feet of space sold increased by 6.9%, and the number of exhibiting companies was up 8.9% during the year." More of your prospects are going to shows and more of your competitors are exhibiting (with smaller than average space).

"The Net Buying Influences for 1987 was 85%, which is up slightly from 83% in 1986. Net Buying Influences is the percentage of the show audience that has the final say, specifies, or recommends for purchase one or more of the types of products/services exhibited." This means that the audience quality is holding up.

We were surprised that only 10% of visitors to an exhibit had been "called on by a salesperson from that company within 12 months before a show." This means that you are creating a lot of first impressions when you exhibit.

Keep it short 'n sweet

They also found that visitors only spend 17 minutes at each exhibit. This is higher than we have experienced at shows like Comdex, but it seems about right for smaller shows. They suggest that you limit your demos or presentations to 10 minutes so that you can have time to talk with your visitors. We would try to keep it even shorter at the big shows where everyone is struggling to cover the show and uncover all of the exhibits they might be interested in.

This increase in show activity is causing companies to re-evaluate their trade show plans. At the same time, we have talked to many companies who have exhibited widely in the past and are reconsidering their plans in light of their other alternatives.

Setting Objectives

Once you have decided to go to a show, you must set your objectives. Caterpillar[1] has a checklist that they review for every show that they are planning on attending:

Will we promote new products, or reinforce existing products?

What will be the role of product support and other customer services at the exhibit?

What is the best way to insure that we yield the maximum number of qualified sales leads?

What role should the show play in enhancing Caterpillar's corporate image?

Which staff members will assure the most effective sales coverage of new prospects and reinforce ties with long standing customers?"

While you may not have the staff that Caterpillar does, we think that these are good basic questions that everyone should answer before going to a show.

Keith Clark[2] has had a strategy of using trade shows primarily for promotion. This is due in part to their industry. They sell office products with a date on them (calendars, appointment books, etc.) which are ordered in the spring, and their major show takes place in the fall. Since Keith Clark's customers aren't ready to write orders in the fall, they have evolved five goals:

1. **Promoting new products.**
2. **Penetrating new markets (distribution).**
3. **Increase name recognition.**
4. **Researching the market.**
5. **Improve public relations.**
6. **Prepare written objectives**

Writing down your objectives seem like a lot of work, but we think that it is a crucial step. You must know what your real objectives are for attending a show, and preparing a written list will give you an excellent opportunity for analysis and introspection. Be honest with yourself — if what you want is a little fame and fortune for your company (or yourself) go for it!! But be sure to critically examine each of your trade show objectives in light of your company's overall marketing needs.

2. Which Show is the Right One?

Caterpillar [1] seeks shows that appeal to specific market segments. They analyze the exposition demographics to see how the show fits one of their target markets. They also look at information about audience quality, buying influences and buying plans. Once they have selected a show they must insure that they get the most out of that show.

Talk to Show Managers

The choice of which show may be obvious if there is only one major trade show for your market, but we advise you to do your home work. Talk to the show managers about the audience, and who attends and exhibits. They should have hard statistics on this. We would also talk to them about subjective issues like, why people attend.

Interview other companies

Call up other similar companies who exhibited. Ask them what their objectives were and how they felt about the show. Tell them what your objectives are and ask them for their reaction. Would they attend this show if they were you? We continue to be impressed at how helpful most people are. With all of this input you should be able to decide which trade show to try first.

3. Planning for the show

At this stage you have to make your plans for the show. You need to consider what size exhibit you want, what you what to show, how you want to show it, etc. Let your defined objectives help guide you to the right answers for your company and market.

Planning a Stunt

One of the items that you might consider is putting on a promotional stunt. By this we mean staging some kind of event that makes show-goers seek out your exhibit. While you are considering what you can do, we urge you to remember that this is show business — be outrageous!! As technical professionals we tend to be dour and serious about our products. Lighten up! Try to think of something fun and interesting to pack 'em in.

Keith Clark felt that in order to meet their objectives they needed to attract customers and qualified prospects to their booth in large numbers. For the past three years, they have used a well-known cartoonist who is identified with their new premium line. He autographs free copies of his cartoons which they distribute along with samples. This approach has been very successful.

Visitors to the Keith Clark booth are willing to stand in a long line while awaiting their turn at the cartoonist. This gives the Keith Clark sales reps a chance to talk with the visitors, and to seek out the active prospects among the waiting throng. Interestingly enough, the illustrator has out-drawn Miss America (who was present at another vendor's booth)!!

Evaluating the results

Evaluating the payoff from this type of giveaway is difficult. We really like the fact that there is a sold product tie-in. They get face-to-face with 2,000 retailers at the show. They value these sales calls at $80 each so they feel that they are getting $160K in marketing value. They believe that the show is worth more than $160K in trade journal advertising which is another alternative. Finally, their sales have been increasing by over 100% over the last three years, and that is the real proof of the pudding.

We think that there are several lessons from this experience. The first is that trade shows are theater, but people want relevant theater. We would have guessed that Miss America would out-draw a cartoonist, but that isn't the case. We believe that people at a trade show want to feel that they are spending their time productively. They want to learn as well as being entertained. Keith Clark has learned how to mix these two ingredients. The next time you are planning for a trade show, spend some time brainstorming about how you are going to draw and educate your visitors.

Another approach

We came across another article3 about a small startup company (under $1 million) that used trade shows as its major marketing push to break into the market with "one product, no money, and little awareness" — exactly like a typical small software company! The company, Lamourn Limited, sells an

Aerobait bait container which keeps live fishing bait cool and increases the oxygen supply with a battery powered aerator. They had decided to use trade shows as the centerpiece of their long term strategy. They felt that they needed to exhibit for three to five years to get the most out of their investment. You can improve your booth position every year.

Planning yields results

Lamourn's priorities at their initial show were to sign up manufacturers reps and distributors as part of a 'push' strategy. They signed up 70% of the distributors they needed and 85% of the manufacturers reps. They attribute their success to their planning. The planning list that they followed was as follows:

Select the right trade show

Develop a critical path plan

Prepare unified sales materials

Generate effective booth graphics

Send out a pre-show mailing

Follow-up with a post-show mailing

Run media ads for show

Have literature for show

Generate press releases for show

Have and use lead tracking forms

Train the booth staff thoroughly

Hold press briefings at the show

Follow-up with the leads from the show

When Lamourn went to their first big show they rented a 10' X 10' booth. They took pictures of their product and blew them up. This helped generate the booth traffic they were looking for. They also helped themselves by sending out pre-show promotions and mailers to a rented prospect list. It is inter-

esting to note that their pre-show promotions and mailings cost $5,000 versus $1,700 for the exhibit space itself!

At the show they handed out a simple specialty item — a letter opener with their 800 IN-WATS phone number on it. They also had a Sales Manager standing by to write orders at the show. Since the show was in Las Vegas, he operated a spin-a-wheel which would give buyers 1, 2, 5, or 10 percent discounts. They also used their reps to work with the major distributors and the chains.

While some of the things that worked for Lambourn may not work for you, we believe that their passion and energy in pursuing trade shows is key to their success. Trade shows can be a real factor in your marketing mix, but you have to be prepared to make the investment if you want to get the results (no pain, no gain).

4. Follow-up

Like every other marketing activity, the impact of trade shows is magnified by a rigorous, prompt follow-up. Nothing is more frustrating and off-putting to a potential customer than to request literature or a sales call and not receive it for six weeks! At this writing (late January) we are still waiting for some literature to arrive at our offices from fall Comdex (in November).

Include after-show tracking of leads and results in your basic trade show plans. Send out the literature within one week of show termination. Call all those that requested a call within the first few days. Perform the post-show telemarketing (if that's in your plans) within one month of the show's conclusion.

Performance Analysis

Caterpillar was faced with an extreme set of problems. Because of the variety and quantity of shows at which they exhibit, few staff members work at more than a couple shows per year. These personnel have the in-depth skills to sell equipment in their specialty, but they weren't trained to work at trade shows. In particular they didn't have the experience to perform several important trade-show functions:

Engage and qualify new prospects.

Handle big crowds.

Weed out the 'tire-kickers'.

Because of these concerns, Caterpillar hired Exhibit Surveys of Red Bank, NJ to conduct research among visitors at six shows. Exhibit Surveys found that Caterpillar had created a good impression with their displays and their products, but their sales people got poor grades. This was illustrated by the fact: the 82% of show-goers rated the typical exhibit-floor salespeople as 'good'; by contrast Caterpillar's rating was a rather poor 79% approval. In addition almost 10% of those interviewed rated Caterpillar's sales people as 'poor' — three times the average for all exhibitors. These results indicated that they needed to improve show worker training.

Trading Surveys

Again, while it may not be reasonable to hire an outside firm to survey your visitors. You might, however, be able to conduct your own survey. We think that you would get best results if it was conducted by someone who wasn't identified with your booth. Perhaps you could conduct surveys for another exhibitor in exchange for them surveying people who had walked by your exhibit.

Caterpillar hired Diane Weintraub President of Communique, Englewood, NJ, a recognized authority on improving trade show effectiveness. After interviewing the show workers she recommended that they develop a pocket-sized guide for show sales people. It covered why they attended shows, and why the sales people are important. It also gave a profile of the shows and summarized show selling techniques.

They also developed a video tape training program. The tape covered:
1. How to engage and qualify a visitor.
2. Product discussion and conferencing.
3. What not to do?
4. Booth layout and traffic flow.

In a small company, you should discuss all of these items with everyone who is going to the show. We would review all of the items that Caterpillar cov-

ered and make sure that you cover them with your people.

5. References & Resources

1. Caterpillar Tractor — There was an article in the June 1988 issue of Business Marketing on "Training Trade Show Salespeople: How Caterpillar Does it", by J. Edward Roberts. Roberts is the Manager of Conventions and Exhibits for Caterpillar. Since they now exhibit at more than 45 conventions and expositions each year, Roberts has extensive experience with trade shows.

2. Keith Clark — There was another article in the September issue of Business Marketing by Micheal Kinnick, the Director of Marketing of Keith Clark, a Sidney, NY based office products manufacturer, "Don't Exhibit Just to Sell - The value of a trade show can go well beyond the number of orders you write.".

3. Lamourn Ltd. — The article was "A small fish makes a splash in the big pond", and it was in the September 1988 issue of Sales & Marketing Management.

Other Resources

If you are serious about trade shows you might consider the following resources:

Exhibitor magazine. $90 for 12 issues including 3-free Exhibit Management and Planning Guides. "America's leading magazine for those who plan, implement or execute any part of their company's trade show exhibiting program!" Their address: Exhibitor Magazine; 745 Marguette Bank Bldg.; P.O. Box 351; Rochester, MN 55903.

Trade Show Book There is now available a 245-page book, How to Participate Profitably in Trade Shows. It costs $75.50 plus postage, handling and sales tax. According to the publisher, XYZ Publishing Corp, the book "shows you how to decide which of the 8,000 trade shows to participate in. How to work exhibiting into your marketing plan for maximum sales success. How to "show and tell' your product and/or service in a dramatic way. How to use inexpensive advertising methods to stir up interest in your exhibit. How to put your exhibit to additional money-making uses. And, how to evaluate your exhibit's effectiveness in order to make it more profitable." If you are interested in ordering the book, the publisher can be reached at (805) 687-3137. Call between 9 to 3 PM (PST).

L. Advertising Effectiveness (1989)

We recently ran across a unique study that measured the effectiveness of advertising. The study is entitled Summary of the Findings: The Impact of Business Publications on Sales and Profits. It was produced by The Association of Business Publishers. Information on ordering study reprints is contained at the end of this article.

Although the products studied were not computer or software-oriented, the study addresses some age-old unknowns about advertising:

How much advertising is the right amount?

Is advertising profitable?

How long will it take to show results?

Do color ads deliver increased results?

Since this study was commissioned by a bunch of business magazines, you probably won't be startled by their startling conclusion: business advertising works!

They studied several different products for twelve months in appropriate trade publications. The products they were testing received no other advertising or promotion. They then ran different ads to create low, medium and heavy advertising 'cells'. Awareness, recall, sales inquiries, product sales and profits were measured for each cell. The study went on for many pages explaining conclusions that could be drawn. In short, however, the major findings were as follows:

1. More Advertising Means More Sales

2. More Advertising Results in Higher Profits

3. More Advertising Increases Sales leads

4. It takes four to six months to see the results of an advertising program.

5. Four-Color advertising can dramatically increase sales.

6. An advertising campaign keeps working for a full year ... and more.

7. More advertising helps build a dealer network.

8. It pays to advertise to both dealers and end users.

9. Business Publication Advertising Works - no matter what the product or the price point.

1. Observations

You don't have to be a rocket scientist to realize that this test might not have been entirely unbiased. (It was funded, don't you remember, by the Association of Business Publishers.) Nonetheless there some interesting observation that can be gleaned from a careful study of the results:

A. Don't be wishy-washy — The studied compared low, medium, and high advertising 'cells'. The in general the low cell boosted sales by 260%, the high cell boosted sales by 670%, but the medium cell showed only a 265% increase in sales. Although the study did not report on how much money was spent to achieve each cell, it's clear that the medium course would be ineffective: spend little, or spend a lot, but don't be wishy-washy.

B. Advertising has a longer time cycle than you think — by this we mean that it takes longer for advertising to pay off than you expect, and the benefits will continue to accumulate for much longer that you think. There's another way to say this: you'll spend more and spend longer for a planned result, but the results will be far longer lasting than you'd otherwise imagine.

2. Reference

This is a unique study. They spent $390K and attracted 45 sponsors. You can buy the study, if you're of a mind, by contacting the Association of Business Publishers, 205 East 42nd St, New York City 10017. The a full-color summary of the study, with graphs, costs just $8.50. An addendum that contains fact sheets costs another $8.50.

3. Finding an Agency

Q. How can we locate and evaluate advertising agencies and/ or free lancers? Once we find them, how do we use them properly?

A. The hiring part is just like hiring a new employee except that potential employees don't have listings in the Yellow Pages. Think of it as interviewing to fill a position.

4. Hiring outside advertising assistance

The first step is to locate a reasonable number of candidates. Start by asking your friends. Look in those Yellow Pages. Call up other companies in town who have nice looking marketing materials. Call the President or VP of Marketing at these other companies. If all else fails, run an ad. Develop a list of ten to twenty agencies and/ or free-lancers. (The decision on looking in the phone book or running an ad will depend upon how many names you get from references.) The phone book is probably a good way to find the agencies while the ad will be more likely to turn up free-lancers.

Once you have your list you should narrow it down to the top five or six. You might want three agencies and three free lancers if you aren't sure which way you want to go. Now that you are down to the short list, proceed to interview them. Develop a list of questions and send it to them before the interview. "What other software companies have you worked for? Have you ever done high-tech? What size accounts do you have? What does an ideal client look like? How much money do you need to work well?" If you need a direct mailer, ask them for examples of what they have done. Ask the agencies who will be on your account. Make sure that is very clear. This isn't an issue with the free-lancers. With the free-lancers, you must be sure that they have enough time to service your account.

Appoint one person to select the agency or free-lancer. Select someone in your company to whom this decision will be really important. Give the selection responsibility to the person who will have to manage the selected agency. If your marketing manager can't stand your agency head, it won't work out. Costs will be an issue. Look at what they have developed for others. Check on their references.

5. Working with an Agency

Once you have selected someone, start them with a probationary project. Work with them to identify what you want done, what it should cost, and how long it should take. (You should do this with all outside contractors.) It keeps them honest and it allows you to objectively monitor them. We have seen too many cases where the company has been sloppy in specifying just what needs to be done, the agency has drifted along with little direction but manages to run up really big bills with little to show for it. The software company wakes up to the fact that they are wasting their money and they fire the agency in a fit of anger. While the agency should have managed the company better, it is really the company's fault and the company's problem. If you accept responsibility for managing your agency relationship, you will gain a clear understanding of what you are getting for your money. If the agency falls down on the job, you can quickly bring it to their attention and demand that they fix it. If they fail to remedy within the agreed time frame, you can fire them and hire a new agency.

M. Ad Agencies: Do you need one? (1989)

In every software company's life the question of retaining an ad agency inevitably arises. You find yourself asking questions about agencies: What compensation do they expect? Are they knowledgeable about software? Will they understand our product? Do they know our market? The first question to ask is the most important one — Do we really need an agency at all?

This point was brought forth by Ralph Blois in the October 1988 issue of Sales & Marketing Management. His article neatly lays out the alternatives, when to use an agency, and when not to.

The Alternatives

Blois has over thirty years experience in the advertising business and he asserts that there are only three basic choices:

Don't advertise — Depending upon your market and market position, this may be a viable alternative for some software companies.

Hire an agency

Do it yourself — This usually involves setting up an in-house agency or contracting for a variety of outside services.

1. When to use an agency

A. *If you need an outside viewpoint.* You may be too close to the situation for an unbiased evaluation of your advertising needs. "You may get knowledge-able advise from an agency," notes Blois, "but you can also do this by asking your prospects, sales force, and others."

B. *You have no professional advertising person on staff and feel that you can not afford to hire one.*

C. *You have a tight cash flow problem and can't do everything in-house.* The time difference between paying an agency's invoice and footing the cost of in-house employees doesn't seem to be worth the effort, in our opinion.

D. *The agency can save funds on media buying.* Agencies often know about or can elicit 'special offers' that you might not otherwise receive.

2. When to do it yourself

A. When you want to reduce costs without sacrificing quality. "In-house professionals can usually offset overhead expenses by eliminating agency markup and earning the agency commission," says Blois.

B. You want to gain total control of your advertising. You may need to produce specialty ads, have a demanding time-table, or have some other situation that demands total control and supervision of the complete situation.

C. Your budget is too small to interest an outside agency. Even the hungriest of agencies want to receive at least $3-5k per month in commissions to provide even minimal services. If they are being paid out of media placements, a $3k commission requires $20k in monthly billing — a big nut for a small software company.

D. You want a larger talent pool. If you have your own in-house agency, you can select from among hundreds of freelance designers, graphics people, copywriters, etc.

E. You are already doing most of the work.

F. You want to capitalize on your expertise in a very specialized market. Many smaller software companies work in a narrow niche that requires specialized advertising skills. If this is the case for you, you may be better off hiring and educating a permanent staff rather than depending on an agency.

3. Ad agencies for Software Companies

Our experience is that small software companies are better off to do it themselves for several reasons. First, the budget for a small software company is typically too small to interest an outside agency. As we mentioned above, most agencies require a minimum retainer of $3K to $5K per month before you start paying for projects. Given these costs, you are faced with a dilemma of limiting your marketing or running up your tab at the agency. There is another fact that may not come as a surprise — as a small account you won't receive the services of top talent that attracted you to the agency in the first place.

The final difficulty is finding agencies who understand the software business in general and your market in particular. Software companies often need fact-filled, wordy ads to explain a new product or feature to a technical audience. Agencies sometimes ignore this need and go for visually stunning, 'pretty' ads. The worst example in our memory concerned an agency-prepared ad for a new software product. It was beautiful. The company in question really pushed the ad, spending over $1 million running the ad. The agency won awards for the ad. The software company sold no copies of the product. Zippo. Although this is an extreme example, you need to remain aware that the goals of an ad agency may be different from yours. Don't let an agency pressure you into meeting their needs and not yours.

4. Setting Up an In-House Agency

You can establish an in-house agency and retain the 15% placement commission for yourself. You aren't totally on your own if you decide to do it yourself. If you are going to be doing a lot of advertising, hire an experienced advertising pro to head up the effort. Use freelance people and boutiques to contract specific tasks. It's a lot like being your own construction contractor: you can find specialists for every phase of your needs. Don't be afraid to use outside copywriters to put just the right 'punch' in your ads. There is a nice part about this approach that is often overlooked: you will have more control over your costs and will be able to set your own timetable.

We are interested in success stories with using agencies and doing it yourself. Please call or write if you have something to contribute in this area.

5. The Value of a PR Agency

Q. We have been using a PR agency, but we aren't sure how to determine their value to us. How would you approach this?

A. Our first question that we would ask is "What were you doing in the area of PR before you hired the agency?" In many cases, companies weren't doing anything at all, so one major benefit of hiring a PR agency is that it forced you to make an investment in PR. In general, we see two major types of dissatisfaction with PR agencies.

High Cost — This is usually a combination of, "We aren't getting the value for our money, and we could do it cheaper ourselves."

Low Quality — If you aren't happy with the quality of their PR effort, don't settle. Demand the level of quality that you expect.

Managing the Cost

In many cases, software companies haven't set specific objectives for their PR agency. Unless you established your expectations, it is very difficult to determine if you did OK. If you are in this situation, we would advise you to sit down and try to recreate targets for the agency. Involve the agency in this discussion. Establish objectives for the immediate future so that you can begin to track the specific achievements of your agency.

If you set objectives and your agency is meeting those objectives, and they still cost too much, you have a more difficult problem. You need to either revalue the PR that you do receive — appreciate it more, or abandon the PR effort. The value of PR is difficult to quantify because it is very elusive. Sometimes it takes a long time to ascertain the payback. We would urge you to give it a year before you drop your agency. Let them know that you are trying to convince yourself that it really is paying off. Involve them in gathering the data to help make this decision. At the same time you might talk to other similar non-competitive companies who are in your market. See what their experience with PR is. We have found that the value of PR varies dramatically by market. In some markets there is an active trade press which is very influential. In others there are no targeted magazines, and the larger mass market magazines aren't interested in your market.

Internal PR

The alternative to do more of your own PR internally depends on both quality and cost. We have talked to agencies which use a "blended rate" of $100 per hour. That is OK for the creative types, but it is pretty expensive for a technical writer to write press releases.

If you identify a task which you believe you can do better and cheaper yourself, the first step is to really understand what your agency is doing for you in this area. What guidance and support are your personnel providing the agency people? Make sure that you understand the process before you make changes. In a number of cases, we have found that the agency wasn't given clear directions. They thought that the company wanted company oriented image releases while the company really wanted semi-technical releases which would generate leads.

Once you are all playing from the same game card, you can fairly evaluate the cost effectiveness of using the agency.

If you feel OK about the quality, but are unhappy about the cost, haggle. Let your account rep know how you feel, and see if they aren't willing to adjust this fee. In some cases, it really is much more cost-effective to do some of these tasks internally. Just make sure that you have the discipline to get them done as planned. Make sure that they aren't cheaper because they don't get done.

Keeping up the Quality

The second issue where you aren't happy with the quality. We feel that this is an area where you shouldn't compromise. PR agencies are expensive and PR is a sharp sword. Good PR can be very positive and bad PR can really damage your reputation.

The first question to ask is "Does anyone at the agency have the experience and skills to do a good job for us?" If the answer to that question is "No", you must find another way to get your PR done. Meet with your agency, review your contract and work it out.

A more common situation is that the senior person who sold you has the experience who do an excellent job, but your work has been passed down to a junior person who is learning at your expense. In retrospect, you probably should have pinned down these details before you signed a contract with the agency. (Remember this if you haven't hired an agency.) Even if you didn't get this in writing, you can meet with the senior person and raise the issue. Tell them that you are unhappy and that you will take your business elsewhere unless they remedy the problem. Ask them what they are going to do to make you happy. In far too many cases that we have seen, software companies don't spend the money to keep the senior people in medium to large firms involved. We often find that small software companies are better off with smaller firms or free-lancers because you can get the primary attention of the principals in these organizations.

N. Specialty Advertising (1989)

'Rocket' Ray Jutkins, a well-known authority on direct mail advertising, (he's part owner of an ad agency specializing in direct mail) wrote an article, "Defining Advertising Specialties and Premiums" in the November 1988 issue of Target Marketing.

The article was interesting because it took some time to cover a marketing/advertising niche that is very often overlooked by technological companies — software companies in particular.

1. Ad Specialties

Advertising specialties, according to Rocket Ray, have these characteristics:

A useful idea

Has a small or nominal value

Has a message — It brings with it, some message, usually very specific, as part of a total marketing program

Name included — Includes the name and logo of the distributing company.

No Strings — It is offered with absolutely no strings attached - you receive it because your are who you are, you don't have to do anything to get it.

2. Premiums

Premiums are a little different:

Very Useful — as opposed to the perhaps marginally useful doodads offered above, premiums are usually generally quite useful — something you'd almost pay real money for.

High Quality — Premiums are usually also of a higher quality.

Subtle Message — Many times premiums offer a message, not with the premium itself, but with the product or service being promoted by the premium.

Chapter I. Promotion

Strings Attached — They are available with strings attached... strings that say if you do this, such as buy this product within the next 30 days, we'll give you a nice gift, i.e., you make a buying decision and you gain a bonus - the premium.

Benefits

Specialty advertising and premiums offer four key strengths:

1. They target a specific audience.

2. They are an item of lasting value.

3. They can serve as a motivational tool.

4. They communicate a specific message.

3. Objectives of Specialty/Premium Advertising

The possible objectives include:

Introducing new products.

Increase trade show attendance.

Increasing sales of existing products.

Examples

One enterprising mainframe software company offered a specially imprinted coffee cup to all qualified leads. All the respondent needed to do was to send in the postage paid card to receive the cup. This little gimmick cut the cost per lead from $150/lead to $8/lead!

Software Success offers a premium to new subscribers — reprints on 23 articles on how to manage a software business.

4. Premium Checklist

Martin Gross had an article in the December 1, 1988 issue of Direct Mail News titled, "Placing a Premium on Offering Assistance". In it he had a list of questions to consider when building a premium offer:

Can the premium be produced internally and easily? If not, is it so helpful - and exclusive - that it will pre-empt the market and be eagerly welcomed by prospects who will give me all the credit.

Does the premium reflect my product or service?

Does the premium fill a need?

Will the premium disappoint prospects? Am I over-selling it?

Does the premium overshadow my product or service?

Can the premium become a revenue source later on? For instance, first giving away reprints.... and then charging for them at some later date?

Would I want the premium in my own home or business?

How long before my competitors copy my idea? Can it be made exclusive?

Can I handle a heavy demand for the premium?

Have I remembered to test all promotions with and without the premium?"

We think that this is a great checklist for anyone considering offering a premim.

5. Perception of Specialty Advertisers

There is an ongoing debate over whether specialty advertising, premiums, and coupons cheapen a product's image. There was an article in Adweek's Promote December 12, 1988 issue titled, "Study Redeems Coupons' Value".

A national mail survey of 654 households run by Frankel & Co., Chicago, concludes that 47% of all U.S. households have a more favorable opinion of brands that offer promotional discounts and only 3% feel unfavorable toward these brands. The rest are neutral.

While this isn't a survey of business buyers, these attitudes should carry over to the business to business market.

We were surprised that 97% of the households had used coupons in the prior 30 days. 13% of the people found promotions to be an incentive to try new products, and 12% liked them to save money. A premium may be the incentive that prospects need to try your product.

6. Profitability

The profitability of specialty advertising was covered in an article in the December issue of Sales & Marketing Management. They quote a study by James S. Gould, a professor of marketing at Pace University in White Plains, N.Y.

"Promotions using specialty items will result in higher profits per sale and total dollar sales than those that do not. The cost per sale may increase, but this cost is offset by higher sales and profits."

He also compared responses when 'flat' vs. 'round' specialty items were used. The findings were: Bulkier items will result in higher profits per sale and total dollars.

"A promotion that sends the specialty item outright will result in higher sales and profits than one that promises an item on request - or by order. Cost per sale is lower for the promotion that provides only the promise." All of this research indicates that specialty items can help give your lead generation a boost.

7. Planning a Specialty Advertising Campaign

There are a number of steps to take in devising a specialty marketing plan. This topic was covered in an article in the September 1988 issue of Direct Marketing, entitled "Lo-Tech Marketing". They list the steps necessary to develop a specialty marketing campaign. The steps are:

1. **Define a specific objective.**
2. **Identify the audience to be reached.**
3. **Determine a workable distribution plan.**
4. **Create a central theme for the promotion.**

5. **Develop a message to support that theme.**

6. Select an appropriate advertising specialty, preferably one that bears a natural relationship to the service, advertising, or theme."

Large number of specialty items

Picking a specialty item won't be easy because there are over 15,000 different types of items available.

Value of Specialty Advertising

A study done in 1982 by Schrieber & Associates showed that nearly 40% of all persons receiving advertising specialty items could recall the name of the advertiser as long as six months later. This is longer and higher retention than you are likely to get with ordinary advertising. A study done by Gould/Pace University in NY found that inclusion of specialty advertising in a direct mail solicitation not only generates a greater response, but also dollar purchases per sale can be as much as 321% greater than those produced by direct mail alone.

The examples in the article include:

1. A network of 13 trade publications launched a direct mail campaign to 300 national consumer product companies and their advertising agencies. The program included a series of mailings with a 'pen with invisible ink' and a 'plastic jar with scented potpourri'. "The promotion contributed to an almost 95 percent increase in the number of advertising pages by year end, despite a recent ad rate increase by the magazines."

2. A company with a safe cleaner/ degreaser offered card deck respondents an imprinted micro instrument. The company claimed that inquires were up 700 percent and sales were up 264 percent.

3. Another company had had trouble attracting executives to a reception at an annual industry trade show. They mailed the executives earphones and offered them the radio if they attended the reception. They produced an overflow crowd.

4. A bank was opening a new branch. They sent out T-shirts, and gave coffee cups to the first 200

new accounts. They exceeded their new account goals in two of the three months.

5. A self storage firm mailed balloons which had to be blown up before the recipients could read the message, "Present this balloon inflated to receive a free gift." "The grand opening was a success, with nearly 50 percent of the balloons brought in to the festivities." More importantly the initial rentals were "well above what the firm had predicted for early sales".

Planning Yields Results

As you can see the possible variety of specialty promotions is almost unlimited. We believe that the success of specialty programs depends upon very careful planning. Depending upon your interest, we have a number of other examples of specialty marketing success. We would suggest that you go back to the list of questions earlier in this article. Take the time before you embark on a specialty promotion. They can be very expensive and can backfire if you aren't careful. We believe that specialty advertising is like playing with explosives. If you use it well, it can be very powerful.

O. Public Relations (1989)

1. Exploiting Technology

Q. My software company has written its software utilizing some really advanced, state-of-the-art technology. How can we exploit this with seminars?

A. If you really have state-of-the-art technology, you have a strong drawing card for a quasi educational seminar. People love to learn about a hot new technology. There are a number of audiences who might attend such a seminar:

* The Press

* Prospects

* Technologists

You can undertake such a seminar to generate publicity, get R & D feedback, or to generate sales leads. Your primary objective will influence the best approach.

PR Generation

If your objective is to generate PR, you should use your seminar as the cornerstone of a PR road-show. Make sure that you have time in your schedule to have private meetings with key members of the press. You might start by listing the cities you need to visit to meet with the magazine editors and reviewers who are important in your market. Then schedule your seminars to optimize your exposure to the press.

Lead Generation

If you want to generate leads, you might try targeted marketing like direct mail or telemarketing to get prospects to attend your seminars. Usually advertising your seminar isn't effective unless you are planning a nationwide seminar series.

Technology Recognition

If you want to get the technologists you should advertise your seminar in technical magazines and newspapers. You might also consider advertising in the local newspaper just prior to your seminar. If you want to get other software developers to attend, you can simply mail invitations to them.

Another area which is critical to the success of your seminar is to ensure that your seminar content is appropriate for your audience and your objective. If your objective really is to educate people, make sure that you don't oversell. While everyone expects a modest sales pitch, if you lay it on too hot and heavy you can really turn your audience off.

2. XTree Amnesty Program

Q. I heard that XTree is offering an amnesty program. How does it work?

A. XTree ran ads which for a limited time offered users with unauthorized XTree copies the opportunity to pay $20 and become a legal registered user complete with the 52-page user's manual. The new customers can even qualify for free technical support, and discount deals on more recent versions of XTree (XTree Pro, etc.). They ended their ad with the warning that once this amnesty program expired, they would prosecute known offenders.

This program has generated a great deal of good publicity for XTree. From my point of view, the real genius in this program involves giving away the old version of their program which currently sells for about $40. With this amnesty program they are making money selling these copies directly to previously unauthorized users. In addition, they have the opportunity to sell these users a more recent version of the product. This appears to be a very good use of an old product. In particular, I would prefer that people buy my old product for $20 instead of buying a competitor's product. It will be interesting to see how well this works out for XTree.

P. Startup Advertising Budget (1989)

Q Could you tell me more on advertising for small software companies - perhaps an idea of how you would spend $50,000 to $75,000 for the first six months for a startup company. Where would you spend the money: 1/2 page ads in leading magazines or small classified ads in the classified sections (back of the book), etc?

A. We don't really have enough information to advise you, but we can discuss some of the issues which you need to examine.

The first question that you must answer is, "What is your marketing objective." We can already hear you yelling, "sales!". That is not good enough. Can you expect to sell your product from your ad, or do you anticipate a two-step sale where you send them information to convince the prospect to buy? Are you trying to generate leads or sales from your advertising?

1. Generating Sales

If you are trying to generate sales from your advertising, you need lots of information in your ad. You'll need large layouts and lots of space to convince the reader to buy. Since your budget won't allow for really large, repeated ads in major magazines, you should think of alternative, lower cost, methods of full-information advertising. Investigate software catalogs, cooperative mailings with other software firms, industry-specific limited-circulation magazines, etc.

2. Generating Leads

Going for a direct sale eliminates one inexpensive but often effective form of advertising: classified ads. If you are trying to generate leads, classified ads can be very effective.

3. Preparing Collateral Materials

If you decide to go the two step path (generate leads to which you send a response package and then they buy) you will need much better product marketing materials. Typically this type of package requires a product brochure, price list, and references. If you don't have a good product brochure and other product marketing materials the lead generating advertising could be very disappointing. You could generate lots of leads and turn very few of them into sales because your product marketing materials weren't up to the task.

Developing a very good product brochure can cost $10,000 to $25,000 including printing costs, design work, art-work, etc. It also can take several months to complete if you have to create all the text from scratch.

4. Doing without a Brochure

If you don't have a brochure, and don't have the time and money to produce one, try to short-cut the process by reproducing large ads which are long on content. Chances are this is the state of your current product brochure. "Since we don't have any more information lets see if we can sell with what we have."

5. FAX as Advertising

Here's a thought that might prove interesting: Try FAXing your ad to your generated leads. While we haven't actually tried this approach, it has the promise of increasing the impact of your material and shortening the sales cycle. (Did you ever put off reviewing some requested literature? Probably yes. Have you ever refused to read a fax? Probably not.) There are a number of states which are considering outlawing junk FAX so you might wait before you try this.

6. Developing a Brochure

At the same time, I would start developing my product brochure. Record all the questions you are getting from people who read your ad. Solicit testimonials from your customers. Start writing. This is a time-consuming effort for your staff.

As an interim effort, you might produce a black and white brochure with the most common questions and more detail on your product. You can do this very cheaply with desktop publishing software. It gives you some information to send out to the people who insist on a brochure.

There is another benefit with this developmental stage. It gives you time to work out what your prospects really need. All too often we see companies who hire an agency to develop a brochure. The agency often develops a really pretty brochure which does a lousy job converting leads into sales. The company really didn't understand what was required. You can't blame this on the agency. If you don't know what you have to communicate, an agency can't help you.

7. Measuring Results

Track the results of your ads very carefully. Chances are you have spent $10,000 to $15,000 of your war chest. If you aren't getting your money back on the direct advertising dollars, stop ASAP. While it may take a couple weeks for the responses from an ad in a weekly magazine to come in, 90% of the responses should be in by the time the next issue hits the street. Advertising should be 10% of revenue or less for established companies. This means generating 10 dollars in revenue for every dollar spent on advertising. As a startup, you won't reach this level for quite a while.

If you aren't at least starting at 1 to 1 (generating one dollar in sales for every dollar spend on advertising), you should rethink your advertising. If you are at least doing 1 to 1, the advertising is replenishing the war chest. It may not be paying your rent, but at least it is carrying its own weight.

One common assumption is that advertising is cumulative; your return on advertising should increase over time. There are many studies which support

this (reference the February 1989 issue), but we have observed one phenomenon which you should watch out for where sales actually slump.

8. Fast Track Sales

Sometimes new products will show a slow-down in response after the first month or two once you have skimmed off the true pioneers. There is a significant group of trend-setters which will order any interesting software that they see advertised. They want to be the first kid on their block to buy one. On the success path, if they like it they will tell a friend who tells a friend, etc. This is the basic trend you are trying to get going.

There are a couple of scenarios which can result in the dip in responses. The first and most obvious one is if people don't like your product the negative word of mouth can be devastating. The next scenario is one where there is a very small population of trend-setters; there is a significant delay in getting the middle-of-the-road customers to buy. They may be very busy, or it may take the trend setters significant time to really evaluate your product.

9. Continuing to Measure Results

Assuming that you are now in month two, and that your advertising is a least break-even and is improving with every ad, you have to decide how to improve your marketing program. We strongly urge you to plot the results of all of your ads to detect early trends. Please collect the data and look at it. You are risking your business, and not making the time to analyze your results can be very expensive. If your ads are beginning to turn down, you can waste $10,000 by not paying attention.

Talk to your customers about your ads. Ask them what magazines they read. Test other magazines on a careful, limited basis. You can also test other ad sizes.

Do penetration (what percent of your target market sees the ad) and effectiveness (what percent responds) comparisons. If you started by running classified ads, correlate any new advertising with the classified. How does their sales multiplier (revenue divided by cost) compare with your 1/2 page ads?. Try a 1/3 page and a 1/4 page ad. Look at what other similar companies are trying. Call them up and compare notes. Ask your space rep for his ideas. This is an art not a science, but you can improve your situation by analyzing your results and testing alternatives. If you stay on top of the results, you should be best positioned to optimize your return and grow your business. Good luck.

Q. Display Advertising (1989)

1. Getting Big Quick

Q. What is an effective advertising strategy for a small company which wants to get big quick?

A. You want your prospects to perceive you as a big company which just happens to be small at present. To do this, you should examine the advertising for other good sized companies in your market. Identify the companies who are where you would like to be two years from now. Study their style and see if it is one you would like to copy. Usually, there is a clear market leader that you should emulate.

We should warn you that adopting the approach of a much larger company can be quite expensive. There are also cases where their approach is inappropriate. For example, they may run seminars to exploit their regional offices. Seminars can be very difficult if you don't have a local presence. Work through the entire marketing strategy to make sure that you have all the required pieces.

1992
Software   Success
Reference   Book

Chapter II
Lead   Generation

A. Direct Mail Survey (May 1991)

This survey had 179 responses, which is very good. It isn't a record, but this is quite good when you consider that direct mail was a primary lead source for only 26.5% of the respondents in last year's Lead Generation Survey.

1. Demographics

The company revenue profile was very close to earlier surveys. We had slightly more companies in the $100 to $10K price range where direct mail is most effective. There were also slightly fewer companies under $100 and over $10K, but none of these differences are really dramatic.

Product Price	This Survey	Competition Survey
Not indicated	1.1%	8.3%
< $100	7.4%	9.3%
$100-$500	16.0%	14.5%
$500-$1K	16.0%	9.3%
$1K-$10K	36.0%	31.1%
> $10K	24.6%	30.6%

2. Computer Type

This was the first survey where we included the Mac as a specific computer type. We had more PC companies and fewer LAN and Minicomputer respondents than in the past. I wonder if some of the Mac companies had previously responded as LAN companies since many Mac products operate on LANs.

Computer Type	This Survey	Competitive Survey
PC	70.9%	59.6%
Mac	7.4%	NA
LAN	10.9%	20.2%
Minicomputer	9.7%	16.6%
Workstation	9.1%	10.4%
Mainframe	8.0%	6.7%

3. Number of Prospects

More companies in this survey tend to have markets with less than 10K prospects compared with last year's lead generation survey. There was a dramatic drop in the number of companies with 10K to 100K prospects.

Number of Prospects	This year's Survey	Lead Generation
< 1K	14.9%	14.3%
1K-10K	39.4%	22.4%
10K-100K	18.9%	30.6%
> 100K	12.0%	14.3%

4. Number of leads per month

The total number of leads per month closely matches last year's lead generation survey. Once again the median number of leads appears to be close to 50.

Number of Leads per Month	% Respondents
< 10	10.3%
10-25	24.6%
25-50	19.4%
50-100	13.1%
100-250	13.7%
250-500	8.6%
500-1K	1.1%
> 1K	7.4%

5. Leads per sales person

The median number of leads per sales person was only 10 to 25, but 30% of the respondents for this question said they were actually giving their sales people less than 10 leads per month. The median and mode (most likely answer) target was the 10 to 25 range.

I continue to be surprised at how few leads, as an industry, we provide our sales people. Typically, 5% to 10% of leads may buy within a year. If this ratio applies, the 10 to 25 leads a month is probably only one or two sales per month. If you multiply this by the median product price of $1K to $5K, we are giving our sales people less than $10K per month in marketing initiated sales. Comparing this with monthly quotas of $20K to $60K it shouldn't be a big surprise that most software sales people aren't making quota.

6. % Leads Generated by Direct mail

The people who responded to this survey are making direct mail work for them. Last year in our lead generation survey, we found that only 10.2% of the companies generated more than 25% of their leads by direct mail. In this survey 49.8% of the respondents generated over 25% of their leads by direct mail.

% Leads by Direct Mail	% Respondents
Not indicated	4.6%
0%	17.1%
<10%	21.1%
10%-25%	13.1%
25%-50%	20.6%
50%-75%	16.6%
>75%	12.6%

I am pleased with this result since it is much more consistent with my consulting experience. I have a high percentage of clients who are generating over 75% of their leads by direct mail.

7. Satisfaction with Direct Mail

Most people who responded to this survey feel good about direct mail. You would expect those who don't feel good about direct mail have stopped using it and would have been less likely to respond to this survey.

Satisfaction with Direct Mail	% Respondents
Not indicated	8.0%
Wonderful	13.7%
Good	31.4%
OK	21.7%
Poor	17.1%
Don't Know	17.1%

8. Other Lead generation programs

The people who responded to this survey make much more use of other lead generation programs than we have seen in the past. I am afraid that it is a little misleading to compare these results with those from last year's lead generation survey. This year I asked, "Other lead generation programs used", and last year I asked "Primary lead generation programs". Thus, I doubt you can look at the absolute value of the responses since we got many more responses this year than last. This is exactly what you would expect. On the other hand, the relative responses are interesting.

Programs Used	This Year	Last Year
Advertising	70.9%	40.8%
PR	44.6%	42.9%
Dealers	26.9%	16.3%
Trade shows	72.0%	38.8%
Card decks	19.4%	8.2%
Telemarketing	33.7%	12.2%
Referrals	74.3%	42.9%
Seminars	30.3%	2.0%
Hardware Vendor	24.0%	4.1%

Advertising was even more popular this time. I suspect that a number of companies using direct mail as a primary lead generation program, make secondary use of advertising. Classified ads can help support your direct mail if you mail to the subscriber list of the magazines which carry your ad.

Dealers were slightly more popular with the respondents to this survey. I believe that this reflects the fact that middle price range products do better with dealers.

Trade shows are also extremely popular with this group of respondents. (I wonder if these are the same people who responded to the trade show survey?)

Card decks were twice as popular as last year. I think that card decks can be an effective add on for products which do well with direct mail. Card decks rarely are a primary lead generation program, but they can add another component. This is especially true when you can advertise in a magazine, mail to its subscriber list, and have a card in its card deck.

Telemarketing was dramatically higher. I expected it to be lower because I've found that most companies using telemarketing usually use it exclusively.

Referrals were higher but I expected this. Everyone generates some leads from referrals even if referrals aren't part of the primary lead generation program.

Seminars were quite popular. This was the first time seminars have shown this level of popularity. This is an interesting development. (Please send me some feedback on this.)

The hardware vendors were also moderately popular. This is another program which can generate some good leads, but rarely as a primary lead generation program.

9. Changes In direct mail usage

7.7 times more companies are increasing their usage of direct mail as are decreasing it. This is very positive. The same ratio was 1.56 for trade shows in last year's survey. This supports my experience that direct mail is growing faster than trade shows. The "Plan to start" group is also increasing their usage of direct mail so the interest in direct mail is even higher than the factor above.

Direct Mail Usage%	% Respondents
Not indicated	2.9%
Increasing	48.6%
No change	29.1%
Decreasing	6.3%
Plan to start	12.6%

10. Reason for change

People decrease their usage of direct mail if it isn't cost effective or if they have a better alternative. They increase their usage if direct mail is more effective. People do more of what works.

Reaason for Change%	% Respondents
Not indicated	31.4%
Too much work	2.3%
Not cost effective	9.1%
Bettter alternative	8.6%
Direct mail better	50.3%

11. Direct mail resources used

A good number of people don't use any outside resources. I was surprised at the number of people who use graphic artists. I didn't think that it would

be this high in the age of desktop publishing. I thought more people would make use of lettershops. The usage of ad agencies was just a little higher than I expected. It was 14.7% last year. I find that most software companies can write pretty well and they don't feel they can afford to pay a copywriter to learn about their market. I also find that many founders are very concerned that a copywriter will be too aggressive and cheapen the company and the product. Don't worry about this. It's your product and you have the final word.

List brokers can help you find additional lists and receive a commission from the list owner. If you can get a good broker looking for lists, it can help extend your reach.

DM Resources Used	% Respondents
Not indicated	12.6%
None	34.3%
Ad Agency	16.0%
Copywriter	9.1%
Graphic artist	32.0%
Lettershop	20.0%
List broker	21.7%

12. Cost per lead — company average

If you look at the graph on the top of the next page, you can see that the median average cost per lead is $25 to $50. The median direct mail cost per lead is $10 to $25 which is lower than the average. A significant number of the companies reported direct mail cost per leads under $10. You have to have quite inexpensive mailings with good response rates to keep the cost per lead under $10. If your mailing costs $0.30 including postage, printing, labels and the lettershop, a 1% response rate would be $30 per lead and a 5% response rate would be $6 per lead.

While I have worked with companies with these types of numbers, my experience is that many of my clients' costs per lead are higher.

For lead generation programs other than direct mail, the cost per lead is higher. Only half the respondents answered this question, but I believe this is usually true. Direct mail is usually the hard core lead generation program. There is little promotional component to direct mail. It is focused on generating leads and it does a good job of this task. At the same

Average Cost per Lead

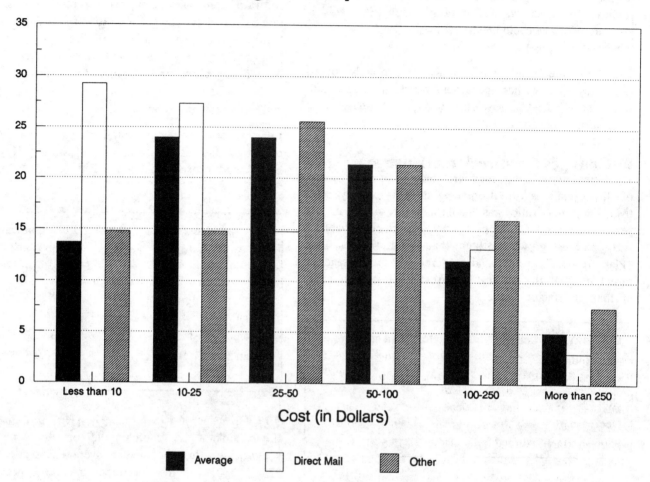

time, you might use display advertising or trade shows to generate some additional leads. These programs probably will be more expensive to generate leads, but they will also help promote your company image. I also believe that these promotional programs help the hard core lead generation programs, over time, as your visibility increases. For all of these reasons, I would happily pay a little more for leads from these other programs than I pay for direct mail, as long as direct mail is the primary lead program.

13. Cost effectiveness of Direct Mail

If you look at the table on the next column, you will see that our respondents were pragmatically positive about the cost effectiveness of direct mail. The median response indicated direct mail as good and very few people felt that it was poor. This may be biased by the tendency of people who have a really negative attitude about direct mail to stop using direct mail and to refuse to complete a questionnaire on direct mail. (This is the old, "If you can't say anything nice, don't say anything at all.") I was surprised that 15% of the respondents felt direct mail had poor effectiveness and yet only 6.3% were decreasing their usage of direct mail.

Cost effectiveness	% Respondents
Much better	31%
Good	34%
OK	17%
Poor	15%

One explanation for some respondents feeling direct mail had poor effectiveness, but not decreasing their usage of it, may be that they believe that direct mail is very much an incremental experience. Each time you send out direct mail, you learn something which will make your next mailing more effective. When we look back at our mailings from a few years ago, we are embarrassed. Could we have sent out anything that amateurish? The answer is yes, but that was part of the experience which has helped us get to this level. Another factor may be that far too many people don't really analyze the cost effectiveness of their direct mail. If you don't analyze it, you don't have a basis for change.

I noticed one thing in reading through the surveys. A number of the companies who felt that direct mail wasn't cost effective were "doing it all" themselves (e.g. copywriting, design, lettershop, etc.). This is something I also had to deal with in my consulting practice. Using outside resources can help reduce the costs of doing direct mail (lettershops in particular can do mailings much cheaper than imposing on everyone in your company to periodically spend hours applying labels and licking stamps.)

14. Monthly direct mail budget

The median budget for direct mail is $500 to $1K per month which is one reason that direct mail is so popular. Anyone with a PC and a prospect data base can send out a couple hundred to a couple thousand letters per month.

Monthly Direct Mail Budget	% Respondents
Not indicated	32.0%
None	16.6%
< $100	1.7%
$100-$500	10.3%
$500-$1K	14.9%
$1K-$2K	6.3%
$2K-$5K	8.6%
$5K-$10K	7.4%
$10K-$25K	3.4%
> $235K	1.7%

15. Sources of Lists

House lists were most popular and compiled lists were a close second. I would have expected magazine lists to be used more often. My experience with trade show lists is mixed if the mailer doesn't have exposure at the trade show. I was pleasantly surprised that a fair number of people were using other vendors' lists. I see a fair number of vendors who are trading lists and this can be quite effective.

Sources of Lists	% Respondents
Not indicated	30.9%
House list	49.1%
Compiled	42.9%
Magazines	28.0%
Trade shows	30.3%
Other vendors	16.6%

16. Lettershop usage

I was really surprised at how many people never use a lettershop. Given the labor intensive nature of assembling mailings, I think that this is an obvious thing to farm out. In my own business, we now use outside people for all mailings over 500 pieces. We use a lettershop associated with our printer for our large mailings, and we have some individuals help us with smaller mailings of 500 to 1K pieces.

Lettershop usage	% Respondents
Not indicated	33.7%
Never	36.6%
Over 10K	5.1%
Over 1K	12.6%
Over 100	8.6%
Always	4.6%

17. House List

At least everyone has computerized their house list. Some companies have a bare minimum house list consisting only of customers who've actually bought something. If you don't at least do this you are giving up the possibility of selling more products to your customer base.

The next level is to put your prospects into your data base and use periodic marketing letters to help sell them. I have seen a number of cases where sales took full responsibility for contact with the prospects. Sales said they would make calls to move the prospects along. The reality is that phone calls take a lot of time and energy and in spite of the best intentions, it is very difficult for sales to maintain adequate contact with the prospects. The sales people focus on the "hot" prospects and try to close these sales first (as they should). My experience is that a well planned campaign of marketing letters can double or triple the lead to sale conversion rate. These letters should urge the prospect to call or request a call by filling out a reply form. If the prospect shows this additional interest, it is very appropriate for the sales person to then call the prospect.

The most active level is to use marketing to pull in soft leads who can be put into the house list and marketed to over time. You might use press releases, classified ads, card decks, etc. to generate a high volume of these lower quality leads. If you have an automatic marketing letter follow up, you can generate some hot leads for sales.

Using House list	% Respondents
Not indicated	29.7%
Not computerized	1.7%
Customers only	16.0%
Prospects + Customers	39.4%
Marketing build the list	35.4%

18. House list as % of Market

When you start off with your first mailing, you might get a 1% response or as high as 4%. If you mail to your entire market, your house list at that point would be 1% to 4% of your market. Over a couple of years you might have 10% to 25% of the market in your list depending upon how many times you mailed and your response rate. As you can see, this was the most popular range.

If you want to get a much larger percentage of the target market in your house list, you will have to aggressively use marketing to build your house list. (35% of our respondents in the previous question said that they were doing this.) Even if there are good lists available for your market, there are advantages to building your list. The first is that you don't have to pay list rental fees. While this is nice, don't forget that you will have to maintain your data base by periodic merge/purge and updates to keep all the information current. In our experience, we have found that up to 10% of all businesses move yearly and that contact names also change frequently. Don't forget to use any non-deliverable pieces which are returned, to delete invalid addresses, change the names and addresses of people currently in your data base, and add new names to your list.

I would suggest that you use "Address Correction Requested" on your third class mailings. This will get you the change of addresses back for a fee (they are free if you mail first class). You also can mail your mailing list on disk or tape to a NCOA (National Change of Address) service bureau and have your file cleaned. The service bureau will delete all the non deliverable names (NIXIES) and will make the change of address corrections. You can get these records on disk or tape and then update your data base. There is a fixed fee of around $1K so this begins to make real sense with 50K names and might make sense at lower levels depending upon the quality and volatility of your list.

If you can buy good compiled lists you might find companies who will sell you the names on disk. Some people make the names available for one year of unlimited use (rental), and others let you use the names forever. Don't forget that you are picking up responsibility for the list maintenance. If you are lucky and there are a number of lists available on disk, you should be able to build a house list containing up to 50% of your target market.

I think it is useful to have an extensive house list because there are often a number of smaller targeted mailings you may want to make without buying labels. For example, I do a monthly mailing in the San Jose area for my seminar. Since I am already doing the list maintenance for my big mailings, these labels are almost free. (My lettershop prints cheshire labels from my disk.)

House list		
% of Market	%	Respondents
Not indicated		38.3%
0%		0.6%
<10%		24.0%
10-25%		19.4%
25-50%		8.6%
50-75%		5.7%
>75%		3.4%

Sometimes companies have no choice but to build a house list. If there are no direct lists for your target market, you can either mail to lists which have a low percentage of qualified prospects or you can develop your own qualified list. For example, if you sell to left handed carpenters, chances are that you can't buy a list with your market. You can mail to carpenters and know that 80% of the people on the list are right handed (I don't have a clue what percent of people are left handed, but I hope you get the point.) It will take a marketing investment to develop this list, but once you have it, you will have a major advantage.

This may not be as far fetched as my example made it sound. I have had several clients who were selling vertical market packages to mature markets and they were focused on the replacement market. They wanted to find companies in their market who had already purchased computers and software and were looking to replace their software. No one has this type of list. We decided to develop a house list with the hardware and software installed and the dates they were installed. This data base became a major corporate asset. Before we had this list we felt that some significant percentage of our direct mail was wasted on lower probability prospects. We tried to manage this by mailing to larger companies who

were more likely to have installed systems, but we were missing the small prospects with installed systems.

19. Postage

I am not surprised that so many people only mail first class. I have talked to a large number of Software company CEO's who would never consider mailing third class. They feel that third class mailings are junk mail and are worried that using third class will taint their company reputation.

Another reason that some companies are reluctant to mail third class, is that they are doing their own mailings in house and they don't have the expertise to submit third class mailings. There are expenses to get a third class permit and you have to read and understand the postal regulations to mail third class. This isn't difficult, it is just a hassle. Earlier in the survey we found that only 20% of the respondents used a lettershop, so some of the companies who are mailing third class are doing so themselves.

Postage used	% Respondents
Not indicated	29.2%
Always First Class	30.9%
Tested 1st Better	9.1%
Tested 3rd Better	5.1%
Always Third Class	12.0%
Mixed	13.7%

Another reason that people don't mail third class is that there are a number of studies showing that 10% to 15% of correctly addressed direct mail packages mailed third class mail are not delivered. It is very easy to react emotionally to the revelation that the post office is trashing your precious direct mail. Once you get over that shock, I would like to show you how the difference in the cost of your mailer affects the impact of the non-delivery of third class mail. I will calculate the cost per delivered mailing for a couple of different package prices.

There are also a number of studies which indicate that if your mailing looks important (like First Class mail) that it will get First Class treatment. I have done some tests which showed that third class postage stamps performed as well or better than first class postage stamps.

```
$1.00 Package + Postage
    First class =$1.29 per delivered package
    Third class =$1.20/ 85% =$1.41
First class is cheaper for the $1.00 package.

$0.15 Package + Postage
    First class =$0.44
    Third class =$0.35/ 85% =$0.41
Third class is cheaper for the $0.15 package.

$0.30 Package + Postage
    First class =$0.59
    Third Class =$0.50/ 85% =$0.59
This is the same if 15% of the third class mail
isn't delivered.
```

This also suggests that you should consider how your mailing looks. If it looks like junk mail, all of the various gatekeepers (the postal employees, mail room workers, secretaries, etc) will be more likely to toss your mailing into the trash. Getting through this gauntlet will have a major impact on the success of your mailings, and I believe that using third class stamps allows you to maintain a top level image while getting the cheapest delivery.

Most of my clients end up with a mix of first and third class mailings. They use third class mailings for the large volume low cost mailings where third class is clearly cost effective. Third class is also especially effective for mailings over 1oz. and under 3 ozs. since the first class cost goes up significantly. On the other hand, smaller mailings to targeted groups are often sent first class. This is especially common if it is important that everyone on the list get the mailing. If this is the case, you should use first class.

20. Most effective direct mail package

Letter mailers are the most popular type of direct mail package. This is also very close to the number of people who only mail first class. First class letter mailings can be very nice. You can laser print personalized letters and insert them in window envelopes with a reply envelope for only $0.10 to $0.15 for your printing. Your lettershop cost might be $0.06 so you can get the entire mailing into the mail

for $0.50 (Printing ($0.15) + lettershop ($0.06) + Postage ($0.29)). These mailings are easy to do, look nice and can be a very easy way to start with direct mail.

Self mailers don't require an envelope and can range from single sheets of paper folded once or twice up to 16 page (or more) flyers complete with an order envelope and order form. These are easy to design, especially in the simpler formats.

One advantage of a self mailer, if you stay within the constraints of your printer, is a reduction of the lettershop charges. Your printer assembles your mailing for you with machines instead of having people do it in a lettershop. For this reason, you should look at the combined cost for the printing plus lettershop when you are comparing different types of mailings. Lettershop costs become especially significant when you are dealing with larger packages.

The larger packages are often "everything but the kitchen sink" mailings. I was surprised that these were so popular, but I have seen a number of mailings to very technical audiences which contained a great deal of material. I worry that so much material might confuse the prospect, so make sure it is clear and organized. It is very important to clearly think about the objective for a direct mail piece. If you want to close a one step sale and get them to send money, you may have to put in more information. On the other hand, if you just want to get inquiries, double post cards and card decks may be more appropriate.

Most effective Direct mail piece	% Respondents
Not indicated	45.7%
Letter	26.9%
Self mailer	10.9%
Larger package	10.9%
Double post card	5.1%
Card deck	3.4%

21. Number of major mailings per year

I was surprised that the median and the mode (most likely) number of major mailings was 5 to 6 per year. I thought that three or four major mailings would have been more common. A number of readers asked what I meant by a "major mailing", so this confusion may have made the numbers a little higher. To me, a major mailing is one to a large part of your target market. In my business I make four such mailings per year. If you are mailing six times a year to one list, you are hitting them every two months, which is probably the maximum effective frequency. In my business, it takes 8 to 12 weeks to complete a mailing in terms of responses. So we do our mailings quarterly to keep the workload down and to minimize overlap. On the other hand, if you are mailing to two lists and alternating the lists, you might reduce your costs by printing the same piece for both lists and then mailing them at different times.

Number of major Mailings per year	% Respondents
Not indicated	34.3%
None	6.9%
1	3.4%
2	9.7%
3	8.0%
4	8.6%
5-6	12.0%
7-11	9.1%
>12	8.6%

I have read a number of studies analyzing responsiveness by month of the year, but I am not 100% convinced that these studies are very useful for marketing software products. I believe that there may be a couple of periods where it is best NOT to mail (March-tax season, August-vacations and December-holidays). However, if everyone mails in January, May and September (as the direct mail professionals suggest), I suspect much of the advantage may be offset by the increased traffic from all the other mailings in these key periods.

22. Personalized Letters

A sticky label on an envelope is the cheapest approach and it is also the most popular. Printing directly on the envelope is popular with the top quality/First Class crowd. If you have an envelope feeder for a laser jet you can do this at reasonable cost even though it takes a lot of time to baby sit the printer and envelope feeder. I was a bit surprised that so many people used cheshire labels on personalized letters. My favorite approach is window enve-

lopes. I think that they look nice and the lettershop cost is low since the lettershop doesn't have to verify that the name on the letter matches the name on the label on the envelope.

Personalize letter	% Respondents
Not indicated	66.9%
NA	8.0%
Envelope	13.1%
Window envelope	7.4%
Sticky label	24.6%
Cheshire label	7.4%

23. Mailing list requirements

Names are the most common requirement for mailing lists. I share this preference, but I have mailed to lists without names and received exceptional responses a couple of times. (These are the exceptions that prove the rule.) Demographic requirements (SIC code, company size, etc) are second. This is very important to me. If you know that your target market fits certain demographic criteria, you can significantly improve your response rate and your return on investment by limiting your list to your target market.

Limiting yourself to lists that are available on tape or disk can keep you from mailing to some otherwise very good lists. I have one client who wanted to send a personalized letter with a window envelope mailing to a list that wasn't available on disk. We printed the letters with spot marks to show where the address label should be applied to the letter and used a generic salutation. The labels were applied and the letters were then inserted in the window envelopes. This wasn't quite as good as a truly personalized letter, but the list was great and the results were wonderful.

Mailing list requirements	% Respondents
Not indicated	72.6%
Demographic	12.6%
Cheshire labels	7.4%
Names	16.0%
Disk/tape	9.7%
Phone verified	4.6%

I wonder why some people require that the list be available on cheshire labels. (Cheshire labels are printed on plain continuous form paper and special machines cut the paper and glue it to the mailer or envelope.) Cheshire labels are the most common mailing label for large lettershops which handle high volume mailings. The cost for applying one up "sticky labels" is significantly higher than for applying cheshire labels. Thus, if you are really worried about holding down the cost of your mailing, getting cheshire labels might be important. I find that the small specialty lists are usually the ones that aren't available on cheshire labels. Usually, these lists cost more per thousand, but I have found that they often pull better because they are better targeted or they contain names that aren't on the large standard lists. In this situation, I have found that the cost per lead for these specialty lists is excellent, even when I factor in the additional costs for the list and for applying the sticky labels.

Phone verification is nice to have, but many of the available lists are not phone verified. I don't think its critical to avoid a list simply because it isn't phone verified.

I hope that these survey results help guide your direct mail program. I believe that it helps to know what most software companies are doing in direct mail. You shouldn't avoid experimenting with your direct mail programs, but proceed with caution.

B. Miscellaneous (1991)

1. MicroBiz Catalog (Jan)

Dear David:

We are a new subscriber to Software Success, and I wanted to tell you how interesting I found this issue on trade shows. We have been looking for a source for trade show listings for some time, I welcome your suggestions.

As a small software company (currently $ volume 5 million) and one that is rapidly growing (average growth is 300 percent per year for 5 years now) we are constantly faced with a number of challenges. These challenges include cash flow management, maintaining a good technical support department, and so on. Your publication is both timely and relevant.

If you need volunteers for information, I would be delighted to spend some time on the phone with you. Feel free to use our 800 number to call. We may be able to help some of your other readers get low cost advertising. I have taken the liberty of enclosing our newest marketing piece, and one of our mascots (very user friendly).

As I see it, the marketplace is almost completely closed for small software companies with limited advertising budgets. You can't get into Ingram or other large distributors. If you don't have a potential market of at least a million customers, you are probably going to be stuck doing your own marketing.

Something that we may be able to offer your readers is advertising exposure in exchange for merchandise. The concept is obviously not new, however we are willing to take more risks than most catalogs. Additionally we have an already established base of 3000 dealers throughout the US and Canada, into whose hands we can put literature. Our catalog, now done twice yearly, is sent to over 600,000 people each time. We are always looking for new products.

I hope to hear from you.

Very truly,
Craig L Aberle, President
MicroBiz ,
(914) 425-9500/ (914) 425-4598 FAX

2. CD ROM Yellow Pages (Jan)

Dear Craig:

Thanks for the letter and the your cute mascot. I think that catalogs are evolving as an alternative distribution channel for low priced PC products.

Your catalog is a very nice and is 48 pages with 4 color. The sections are:

* **Business**
* **Financial**
* **Hardware**
* **Productivity**
* **Education**
* **Word processing**
* **Spreadsheets**
* **Point of Sale**

Looking through your catalog I realized that you are a software company that has developed your catalog to sell your own products as well as other products. It appeared to me that there were three categories of products in your catalog:

1. Your own products
2. Standard distributor products
3. Specialty products from small companies

A number of the small company products had full page four color ads as well as smaller ads.

I think that anyone who has a PC product which can sell to a mass market should investigate selling through catalogs like yours. I have a client who sells through catalogs and we have found that it is important to analyze the overall discount rate. This discount rate can be high when you include the free product for the ad in addition to the more standard discount on the product sold through the catalog. I am not saying this to discourage anyone since I believe that the catalog vendor should be rewarded to taking the risk. From the publisher's point of view these are probably incremental sales which generate contribution margin. They are also generating some momentum and increasing the size of the customer base.

I would be very interested to talk to people who have used catalogs to get their sales moving.

Thanks again.
Dave

Dear Dave:

After speaking with one of your employees, it was suggested, I put down on paper, what we are proposing. We are putting together a CD-ROM "Try Before You Buy Software Yellow Pages". As I explained, this CD-ROM will feature software demo disks from various vendors. We will distribute the CD-ROM to thousands of people who will be able to view what software is available in the market today for their application. There is no charge for this. Our profit will be made in publishing and distributing the CD-ROMs. We have been in the PC manufacturing business since 1984.

All orders for your software will be taken directly by your company or from your various distributors nationwide. We are not involved in this at all. Our only involvement is publishing and distributing the CD-ROM disk.

Any company participating in the first issue of our "Software Yellow Pages" will be grandfathered in and will be featured in all future issues at no charge. We do however have the right not to publish software if we deem it in poor taste or we have reason to believe that it is misrepresentative of the product.

Some of the companies who are participating include Borland, Software Link, Autodesk, PeachTree, to name a few. Should you want to take advantage of our first issue, please be sure to send us a letter granting permission that we include your company as well as any demo disks or promotional materials you would like to include. The decision to include the printed material on the CD-ROM will be based on clarity, availability of space and time constraints. Consideration will be given on a first come first serve basis. Please also include what category or categories you would like your product to be listed under. Please distribute this information to any of your other divisions, as we would like to include as many of your products as we can.

Our deadline for the first issue is December 12, 1990 (note this was faxed to me on December 5, 1990). Feel free to contact me or Charles Papir, Marketing Manager regarding additional information.

Sincerely,
Beth N. Roscoe, President
CCI Computer Products,
(305) 824-9000

Dear Beth:

I am sorry that I didn't learn about your "Software Yellow Pages" in time for my subscribers to take advantage of your first issue offer. I hope that you will agree to extend this offer if they respond in time for your next quarterly edition. (I called them and was told they were expecting to publish the yellow pages quarterly.)

I hope that this idea works, but I have several concerns. The first is who will pay for a CD-ROM filled with demo disks. You can get your very own demo disk and brochure form a high percentage of software companies for free. I can see that dealers might like to have magic machine with lots of demos that might sell lots of software, but will they pay for a CD-ROM player and pay for the disk?

My next concern is the users, I find that many companies have trouble getting prospects to look at a demo disk. If it is too hard, they won't make the effort to learn enough to evaluate the product. If it is too easy, they feel insulted and don't feel that they learned anything. I have concluded that we are asking a buyer to sit down and do something difficult so that they can spend money. This is a lot to ask.

This sounds like an interesting opportunity. If the major software companies put some effort (money) behind this and get wide distribution for the CD-ROMs, this could be really great.

I see any number of people trying to solve our distribution problem. "How do we get information out there so that consumers can buy low priced software?"

Thanks for the information.
Dave

3. Concerns about Wild and Crazy Ideas (Jan)

It is very clear to me that we have a structural problem in our business. It is almost impossible to get a new product into mass market distribution unless you have lots of capital for a massive advertising campaign. It also helps to have a world class product.

Lots of very smart people are aware of this problem, and many of them are proposing some very creative solutions. Some of these are so creative that they make me nervous. I would like to describe one that I recently learned about.

This is going to be a new company. They have two basic concepts. The first is that they will have a catalog where people can download from a BBS. They will pay for the software via a 900 number. They will feature a deal on 9600 baud modems so that people can minimize the connect time.

The second concept is that people will receive credits for introducing people to this company. They will receive a commission on everything their friends buy.

The people that were putting this company together were looking very hard for products to put in their catalog. I was concerned about how people would feel about buying software (at full retail) and not getting a physical package. When people download shareware from a bulletin board, they realize that they won't get the package until the register the

package. Paying full retail for a product and not getting the manual concerned me.

I was also concerned about how many people (general consumers) were really comfortable downloading software. It isn't clear that people will buy software based on the recommendations of friends and acquaintances, but that might work for general purpose software. My final concern was with the 900 number as a billing mechanism.

My point is that there are lots of innovative proposals, and you should take great care to protect yourself. It is difficult to sell software, and I have seen a number of these new schemes fail over the years. I believe that you should allocate 10 percent to 20 percent of your marketing budget to experimentation so don't close your mind. Just make sure that your manage your risks and evaluate these new concepts carefully.

Good Luck,
Dave

4. Videotapes (Feb)

Dear Dave:

I'm a recent subscriber and I'm very happy with Software Success. It's focused, has variety and is "real world." I have two questions I hope you can address.

Question 1:

My company is producing a video for our software product. Our product sells for between $600 and $1,000. Our primary source of leads for our direct sales are from magazine advertising. We receive around 300 leads per month. I want to use this video to shorten the sales cycle. My concern is how to deliver the video. I certainly don't want to send one out to unqualified leads. I've thought about having them call in for the free video. That way we could qualify them over the phone. That's how our competition delivers their video. I wonder about the idea of charging say $5 or $10 (refundable upon purchase)? I would appreciate your feedback.

Question 2:

Same product, same price. I'm trying to get resellers to carry our product. The most difficult part is getting them to listen to us. We have a good story and a good product but we can't break through the noise. I understand they are continually assaulted by developers to carry their product. The resellers who carry our product now are very happy with both the product and our support. How can I get the others to listen? I've been thinking about a video aimed at the resellers but at $10,000 I think it's a little risky! Our goal is to sell 80% of our product through the resellers and 20% direct.

Sincerely,
Janice Conte
Marketing   Manage
CIMLogic
(603) 881-9918

Dear Janice:

My immediate answer to your first question is that your competitive situation limits your options. You must make your video at least as available as the competitor. Preferably, your video should be more available. (By "available" I mean easy for the prospect to get.) For this reason, I would be very uncomfortable charging for the video when your competitor is giving it away for answering some qualifying   question.

If you didn't have the precedent set by your competitor, I would still hesitate to charge for the video. I forgot to include the question on whether people were charging for their demo disks and video tapes on the survey, but it seems to me that this is declining. The real issue is that we as marketers want to get our material in as many qualified hands as possible.

Initially, when demo disks and video tapes were unique, people were easily able to charge for them. The fact that marketing materials became a profit center was a very pleasant surprise. Even though we were experiencing some very pleasant emotions at this stage, we all knew that we weren't going to cover the payroll by selling demo disks and video tapes. We began to get calls from good prospects who didn't want to pay and we began to make exceptions. At this point, managing who has to pay and who gets the demo for free becomes uncomfortable. It is also a concern that good prospects aren't getting the demo disk or video tape because we have made it unnecessarily difficult.

The other side of this issue is that people will respond to an offer of a demo disk or video tape to get the media. You can generate a large quantity of totally unqualified and uninterested leads. You are spending money sending them your mailing package and then following up. This is especially demoralizing in a small company where cash is tight. I had one client who sold a vertical market package. Historically, they had sold their demo system for $50 and had offered this as a credit toward the purchase of the whole system which sold for $2,000. The demo system was a limited function system complete with documentation so they didn't have to re-ship the documentation when a demo prospect purchased the product. Thus it really made sense to give them the credit when the purchased the full system.

My recollection was that the sales people ended up authorizing free demo systems ten percent of the time. Even though there was some ambiguity in the situation, they felt comfortable dealing with it. The other factor was that almost all of the vendors in this market were selling demo systems for a similar amount of money. The most common time that we ended up giving away the demo was when we were late to get into a competitive evaluation. The prospect had already paid for three or four demos and had almost decided on one of them. It was easy for the prospect to say, "I have already spent over $200 on demo systems, and I like XYZ. Why should I spend more money just to take a look at yours when I think that I am going to end up buying XYZ?"

Our first demo special offered a free demo system for a limited time. We got a great response, but they were totally unqualified. The sales people spent a great deal of time calling these prospects and very few of them ended up turning into real business. I am sure that some people just wanted the nine disks, and others might have had an illegal copy of the software and wanted to get a full set of documentation. (Note: This last idea is just one that I had and I don't recall that it was supported by the evidence at the time. I just recall that there were a number of respondents who were very eager to get off the phone with our sales people.) Whatever the reason, we incurred the extra cost for the demo systems, and the phone calls; and we didn't generate significantly more business than we normally would have expected in that period of time.

The next promotion was to offer the demo system at half price ($25) to qualified prospects (e.g. ones who had talked to a sales person and said they were in the market for this type of system). This was promoted as a limited time offer so we did generate a good response rate. It wasn't as high as the free demo disk, but it was quite a bit higher than the normal response. The good news was that the phone qualification screened out the disk collectors. It also helped the sales people to be giving the prospect a deal. The sales people felt that the prospects were a little friendlier than usual since we were giving them a gift.

From an economics point of view, we should offer demo disks until our marginal cost is equal to our marginal revenue. Thus, in theory, we should be happy to give demo disks to successive populations until our purchase rate covers the cost of the demo disks. For example if the demo disk costs ten percent of the purchase price, we would be happy as long as ten percent of the demo disk recipients purchased the full product. Before the accountants get in an uproar, I should note that the accountants would want you to include overhead allocations and all the labor to ship the demo disk, follow up on the demo disk, and any sales effort. Even if you try to factor in all of these costs, the economics will indicate that you should take more risk (e.g. send your demo disks to less qualified prospects) than "feels right."

I think that there are a couple factors in the "feels right" equation. The first is that your sales capacity at any point in time is limited, and if your sales people are chasing very low probability demo leads, they aren't selling the really good prospects. It is also very discouraging to your sales people to encounter the extremely low closure rates that this strategy generates.

Finally, the sales people are likely to generate lower sales per month (and thus lower commission) if they spend too much time calling the low quality demos. It might make sense to encourage less qualified prospects to request the demo, get the qualifying information before the demo is sent, and then using automatic letters to do the early selling to these demo prospects. If they call in, they are clearly worth the sales person's time, but it might not make sense for the sales people to call out to everyone who requests

a demo. I would be interested to hear how others have dealt with this issue.

Your second question is more difficult for me. Getting resellers to carry a product in today's world is a real challenge. I agree that it doesn't feel comfortable to spend $10,000 on a video aimed at the resellers. That is a lot of money and I am not sure what the return would be. The really big companies can afford this type of marketing program, but I don't see it from the smaller firms.

One way to think about it is what are the other ways to spend your $10,000 that might generate more resellers and more sales. I will list a couple.

1. **Offer free end user videos to resellers.**
2. **Visit resellers and show them your product and your video.**
3. **Run ads to generate more prospect leads that you turn over to resellers.**
4. **Run ads to generate more reseller interest.**

While I don't know which one of these is best, I am pretty sure that they are better than spending $10,000 on a reseller video.

I hope that this helps.

Dave

5. Direct Mail That Works (Mar)

Dear Dave:

We have been mailing to the same market for six years and have watched our response rate erode as familiarity and name recognition grew. Most mailings now have less than two percent response. However these two did much better:

The first is the old bulky envelope which always entices one to open it and then review the contents. It was mailed in an envelope without our logo to further deter any preconceived notions about what was in it. Response was nearly four percent.

The other is an offer of a free booklet with information that everyone can use on making money and surviving in their business. Obviously, the key to survival, as found in the booklet, is buying a computer system. Response on this was a little over three percent.

Though these response rates are not that outstanding, they represent a big improvement. Ours is definitely not a virgin market, and we are the main players in the game. Thus, I was pleased with these results.

I look forward to reading about other successful efforts from among your readers.

Yours very truly,
Howard W. Worrell, Jr., President
Direct Systems, Inc.
(804) 320-2040

Dear Howard:

Thanks for the letter and your samples. While I appreciate the fact that your 2 percent response rate is lower than your previous results, it is still pretty good. I have clients who are suffering with response rates of 0.5 percent or even lower. They have successful business, it is just difficult to generate leads.

Nonetheless, I applaud your efforts to improve your response rates. The "old bulky envelope without an external logo" is something that I have read about and heard from commercial direct marketing people. I should mention that the original "old bulky envelope" campaign included a disposable razor. The tag line was "Keep the close shave at home and not at your agency." I believe that you need some minimal logical link between this type of premium/gimmick and your appeal. It doesn't have to be a big one, but I would worry about a bulky mailing with no link. I don't know if anyone has tested this particular situation, but I would be reluctant to be the first to try an unlinked bulky item.

I also want to mention that your envelope without the logo had your post office box so it could be returned to you. Your return address was located on the upper left corner of the front of the envelope (the traditional location). I have also heard of people who place the return address on the flap on the back of the envelope. This was supposed to make it easier for them to open.

Your booklet is "A Bay Head Marketing Report." I believe that this gives the booklet much more credibility. There was a case that I reported on earlier in the newsletter where a founder had written a book. This was a very effective lead generator. I believe that this is due to the fact that the author was known in his industry. In your offer of the booklet, you say, "Commissioned for Direct Systems by the Bay Head

Marketing Group." One final comment is that the booklet is a nice little 32-page 5-1/2 X 8-1/2 inch document. It isn't fancy, but it does look nice. I think that this is important. If you give your prospects something which isn't professional, this exercise ends up backfiring. It doesn't have to be fancy, just professional.

One final thought. I am really pleased that you have been trying some new and different things. I have seen far too many small software companies who are so very conservative in their marketing. I believe that part of this is the fact that the founders identify with the company, and they feel that the marketing reflects on them personally. They are concerned that mailings which are somewhat glitzy (shoddy?), will damage their reputation. My experience is that you can do innovative things without looking tacky. I am really pleased that you have been rewarded for your innovation.

Dave

6. Another Video (Mar)

Dear Dave:

I would appreciate your comments. This video is a response piece for qualified prospects from our direct mail program. We have a 7.6 percent initial response rate thus far.

Ron Workman
Product Marketing Vice President
Ready Systems
(408) 736-2600

Dear Ron:

I like your approach. If a four dollar video can double your response rate, it is a great deal. It can also raise your level of professionalism. My one concern with your video was that the initial segment was directed to the managers. It described the product, "A future where real-time engineers can evaluate a wide variety of design alternatives and still beat your competition to market." I believe that this is very important when you are marketing a product which is establishing a new category. Managers like to know what box to put it in, and your video did a very good job of this. I learned more from watching the first five minutes of your video about your product than I did from reading your brochure for ten minutes.

The next segment was much more of a demo. You showed screens, commands, and how you actually use the product. There was no warning that I was entering the "techie zone." I was bothered by the lack of closure on the first segment and wasn't interested in the technical part. I think that your video would be more effective if you wrapped up the first segment by restating the benefits and then announcing that the next part would be the technical overview of the product and that it would last ten minutes. By giving me that information, you have given me permission to turn the tape off and hand it to my technical evaluator.

I think that it is important to focus on the specific steps that we want people to take when they review our marketing materials. When the manager reviews the tape, we want them to pass it to the technical evaluator. If that is what we want, let's tell them what to do. After the technical evaluator reviews the demo section, we want them to recommend that they call us to arrange for a trial.

I don't mean to be too critical. The tape was very nice, and the production was professional. I think that if you refine the sales story in the tape that you will increase your tape to sales conversion rate. Once you get a 7.6 percent response rate, this the next challenge.

Good luck.
Dave

7. Business Software Database (Mar)

Dear Mr. Bowen:

As a follow up to our telephone conversation of a few days ago, I am enclosing brochures which describe Business Software Database. I have been working in the computer and software business for more than 20 years. When I started, computers were part of the data processing function and most professionals had no exposure to the use of computers. In the early 1980's, the data service which I founded became a DEC OEM and we started to sell turnkey systems using the early PDP-11 business computers. In those days I struggled to locate software which would allow managers to computerize some tasks.

Finding software was very difficult and most of the systems we sold required custom programming.

About that time I started collecting information about available software for minicomputers and this led to the publication of our first edition of Business Software Database 1983. The first edition was called *Small Systems Services and Software Sourcebook*. We have come a long way since that time and Business Software Database is now offered as an online database through commercial database vendors.

Directory product listings are available to software producers at no charge. Software producers should contact us and request that they be sent a listing application form. This is a standardized form so that the information appearing in the database can easily be searched and compared.

Sincerely,
Ruth K. Koolish
Information Sources, Inc
(415) 525-6220

Dear Ruth:

Thanks for the information. Given the fact that your directory is free, everyone should get a listing.

Dave

8. CD-ROM Pro and Con (Mar)

Pro

Dear David:

It was nice chatting with you today regarding our CD-ROM Yellow Pages. Once again, thank you for publishing our letter. As we discussed, our deadline has been extended due to the holidays. To date we have over 100 software vendors participating. There will be no charge to vendors who appear in our first issue. Our profit will be made in the sale of this publication.

Distribution of this CD-ROM will be primarily through various distributors. It will be sold to end-users as well as retail software stores, distributors and given to trade journals for review. Should this CD venture be successful, we believe a distribution of 10,000 per quarter will be realistic.

Feel free to contact Mr. Charles Papir or myself for any additional information.

Sincerely,
Beth N. Roscoe, President
CCI Computer Products,
(305) 824-9000

Con

Dear Dave:

Thanks for the quick response in getting out my first issue of Software Success. I am very impressed. This is what industry newsletters should be. Now I want back issues.

Since 1980, I have been involved in marketing interactive video technology (Sony) and since 1983, designing, integrating and consulting on videodisc recording systems (Panasonic) for presentation, industrial, scientific and medical uses. In 1987, I moved the business to Palo Alto and decided to specialize in Macintosh systems for our projects, making us a much bigger (and more productive) frog in a smaller pond.

During the last year we have begun exploring the horizontal market with a general purpose database product aimed at videodisc recording users. We are using Panasonic as a marketing partner, but your January issue has given me several good ideas already. In particular, we are using a $995 runtime as the trojan horse for the $2,500 "developer version" and additional customization.

The real reason for this note is actually to respond to the Q & A on CD-ROM "Yellow Pages" in the January issue. As a person involved with both videodisc and CD-ROM since the beginning, I have seen dozens of such schemes come and go. Some have gotten a first issue out, but none have survived much longer. There are many reasons for the failures, but the CD-ROM provides a particularly clear example of hardware infatuation.

As I have contended for many years, the CD-ROM is just too slow to use as any kind of interactive peripheral except for large data bases. Enthusiasm for the product among expert computer users is essentially nil and the installed base is growing very slowly.

Now let's look at the business objective of selling software: As you correctly point out, many users

don't like (poorly designed) demos. In fact, a well designed interactive video demonstration would be more effective in most cases. Consumer videodisc machines (which also play CD music) are available for about half the cost of a CD-ROM drive and are fully capable of random access to individual segments. The consumer, industrial, and educational installed base is larger and growing much faster than CD-ROM.

Even an indexed videotape (100 percent installed base) would be far more efficient than CD-ROM at getting software in front of customers.

This is a classic example of limiting the business success by tying the business plan to an inappropriate distribution technology. But not to worry - Philips, Intel, Microsoft and many others who should know better have made the same mistake. I would be interested in contributing to your newsletter in any way that might be appropriate. Keep up the good work.

Best Wishes,
Mark Heyer
HeyerTech, Inc.
(415) 325-8522

I appreciate both of these letters. I hope that CCI succeeds in establishing a new information and communications medium. The entire industry is crying out for a better way to get information on their products to their prospects. There have been a number of efforts in this area, and none of them have really been successful. I hope that this one works.

I also have concern about CD-ROM technology. CD-ROMs are a possible alternative to cartridges for home game machines (Nintendo and Sega). One machine in Japan has been very successful with a role playing game for pre-teen girls. In discussing using this same technology for games in the United States, there was great concern about how slow the machine was. Why it was so successful in this one application is a mystery to me.

This is clearly a risky new technology area and you should approach it with caution. I don't know what the odds of success are, but they aren't high. On the other hand, if one of these new approaches works, it could be a real boon to the industry.

One of things that appealed to me about the CCI yellow pages is that they didn't cost anything. To make matters even nicer, everyone who is in the first issue is grandfathered and gets all future issues at no charge. This is a no-risk deal. If they had been charging money to be in this first issue, I probably wouldn't have been inclined to recommend it. I think that you have to consider some of Mark's concerns, but if you manage your risk you might get an unexpected return.

Dave

9. Business Line BBS (Mar)

Dear Software Author:

If you are writing software targeted for the Small Business community I would like to extend an offer for you to distribute your programs or Demo programs on the Business Line BBS.

The Business Line BBS has been up and running since October 1990. Since that time we have received over 5,000 calls. The main purpose of the system is to provide information, products and dialogue to Small Businesses, Entrepreneurs, and those looking into such endeavors. The system is available to the public at no cost. Support for the system comes totally from individuals, organizations and companies who believe in the small business enterprise.

If your market is small business owners, then the Business Line - BBS is the advertising and distribution vehicle for you.

I have enclosed a rate card outlining the fees and procedures to get your programs distributed by the Business Line - BBS. Our rates are economical, but instead of thinking of it as a cost think of it as an investment in the Business Line - BBS and the small business community. If you have any questions please give me a call at (404) 619-0733.

Best Regards,
Michael Deen
Systems Administrator
Business Line - BBS

Rates:

Software Distribution - $0.20 per Kbyte per year
Catalogs (text, binary) - $0.75 per Kbyte per year
Directory listings - $25.00/per year

Business Line BBS
PO Box 769021
Roswell, GA 30076

Dear Michael,

Thanks for the letter. This seems like an opportunity for companies marketing to small business.

Dave

10. Advertising Repetition (Mar)

This is one of those topics that is of interest to all of us. I saw this article and thought I would share it with you.

The original work on memory was conducted in 1885 by Herman Ebbinghaus in Leipzig. Herman found that people forget half of what they read within a week, and eighty percent or more after three weeks. "You've got to keep building awareness or you will lose it."

If your ads run less than once a month in any publication you are almost starting over. This makes me feel bad since I advertise in monthly magazines.

In 1977, Dr. Edward Strong of Tulane University reported his research in the Journal of Advertising Research (December 1977). His control was 13 ads per year (every four weeks). His first conclusion was, "The effect of two exposures close together is greater than the effect of the two separated in time from each other."

Thirteen ads over 52 weeks produced an annual recall of 27.1 percent. Bunching the same thirteen exposures together increased the exposure to 31.3 percent. This is average annual recall. The optimal schedule (of 13 exposures) is to start with four, nine weeks off, three on, nine off, and then three groups of two spaced evenly over the remainder of the year.

Jack Edmonston on Magazine Marketing
"The First Three Rules of Advertising:
Repetition, Repetition, and Repetition"
Magazine Week
December 31, 1990 - January 11, 1991

If you advertise in a weekly magazine, you might try this pattern. I must admit that it makes me uncomfortable, but the potential increase in annual recall is appealing. If you advertise in monthly magazines, it sounds like every issue is a must.

11. What Should I do about Advertising in a Recession? (Mar)

This is another hot topic that I get asked about a lot. Jack Edmonston covered this in the December 17 - 21, 1990 issue (see prior reference). Cahners Publishing sponsored a study several years ago. It was conducted by the Strategic Planning Institute of Cambridge, Massachusetts.

"By looking at proprietary data from nearly 2,000 individual businesses that was submitted to SPI by its corporate members, they were able to show that companies that increased their advertising by more than 28 percent during recessionary times enjoyed, on average, market share gains that were nearly double those experienced by similar companies that did not increase advertising that much."

"Not only that, but this market share increase was accomplished without any loss of profitability, even when the increased advertising costs are taken into account."

I would be interested in hearing about how many of you are increasing your promotion and lead generation in the face of the recession. I would welcome your calls. Perhaps I could interview those of you who call and combine these interviews into an article. I look forward to those of you who are putting it on the line in 1991 to increase your market share in the future.

Dave

12. Multiple Mailings (Apr)

Dear Dave:

I've been a subscriber for several months now. Please accept my compliments on a very useful publication. However, I think you may be "preaching to the choir" a bit as far as your own direct mail efforts go. I think the enclosed solicitation is the second or third I've received since I became a subscriber.

The repeated pitches don't annoy me, but I would think they represent a substantial cost to you since I'm already sold. Surely, dropping "converts" from your prospect list after you've already sold them would be more cost-effective than sending out offers again and again to people who are already subscribers.

Please don't think me overly critical. I enjoy your publication immensely and have found it very use-

ful. I only point out the apparent oversight because if I'm on both your prospect and subscriber lists, I suspect that a number of other subscribers are as well. It seems logical that a little list housekeeping would allow you to save some money here.

Sincerely,
Bob McDermott
Specialized Software Solutions

Dear Bob:

I appreciate your letter. It turns out that I have two problems as far as sending mailings to people who already subscribe.

The first is that I am buying names from magazines and other outside lists. I investigated getting the names on mag tape and merge-purging them. This would also eliminate multiple mailings to people (subscribers or not). I even found a service bureau to do this. The bad news is that only 1/3 of the lists that I am using are available in machine-readable format.

My other problem is my house list, which includes a number of lists that I have purchased for one year and perpetual use. I have purchased some merge-purge software to eliminate duplicates. Hopefully, I can solve this problem.

I hope that you find this interesting and appreciate the fact that I am making an effort not to waste money and kill extra trees.

One final thought is this: If I end up sending you duplicate mailings in the future from outside lists, please pass them along to friends and acquaintances. We both might benefit! Thanks!

Dave

13. Lead Tracking Parameters (May)

Dear Dave,

Our company has entered the retail software distribution channel fairly recently with a new product, IdeaFisher. We have been receiving a great deal of publicity and many inquiry calls as a result. Since we are not yet capable of being fully dependent on resellers, we sometimes sell direct at our list price of $595. Thus, it still behooves us to cultivate potential customers with follow-ups, etc.

Chapter II. Lead Generation

This brings me to my question. When attending your Software Success Seminar, we spent a lot of time discussing lead generation and conversion to sale. Since then, the importance of being able to track everything about leads and customers has become almost an obsession with me. I have just spent many hours deciding how we should configure the new D-Base software we just acquired to help us utilize our lead base more effectively. Would you mind sharing some ideas with myself and your other readers.

I'm particularly interested in the different search fields you would recommend we set up and what questions we should try to get leads to answer when we speak with them.

Thanks in advance for your help.

Sincerely,
Matt Engen
Marketing Coordinator
Fisher Idea System, Inc.
(714) 474-8111

Dear Matt,

My experience is you can ask people 3 or 4 questions at most, when they are calling in to inquire about your product. I have seen far too many cases where companies had a three page questionnaire that never was completed. You have to keep it short and sweet if you want to get it complete.

The next consideration is that you want to focus on questions that are easy for people to answer and that will result in real changes in your behavior. There are lots of great questions that you can't really use the answers to. For example, you might wonder how creative your people really are. This is an impossible question to answer and even if they do answer, I don't have a clue about what I would do with their answers.

One practical question is, where did you learn about our product? Which magazine or press release? This is fairly easy for people to answer and you can (and should) use it as a way to determine which ads are generating the most leads.

The next set of questions really focus on the selection criteria that the appropriate lists might have available. You need to think about your preconceived profile for a good prospect. Lets say that they work for a large company (lots of money), or they work for an ad agency, and they have a managerial position. If I was going to limit my mailings to large companies, the company revenue question would be very useful. Asking people if they worked for an ad agency could give you a clue if mailing to an ad agency list (or advertising in a magazine read by the trade) would pay off. Job title selects are also available with most lists. I would pick the actual job titles available for the magazines you are in. This way you don't have to translate job titles you've chosen into the ones used by the magazines.

This might be my start. A month from now I might find that ad agencies are a dead end, but engineering consulting firms are great. At that point I would change my questions, and hopefully could change my data base selection criteria. This is one of those exercises that evolves as you feel your way along. If you keep focusing on the decisions that you are trying to make, and getting information to help those decisions, your marketing will improve with experience.

14. Win $100 — An Innovative Approach to Lead Generation (Aug)

Dear Dave,

I sell funeral home software. There are 20,000 funeral homes in the US and we have used card decks in the past to generate leads. Typically we have generated 30 to 40 leads from a 20,000 circulation card deck. After reading Software Success, I was trying to come up with a premium offer to improve my response rate. I decided to offer people a chance to win $100 if they filled out a survey. We asked them the five questions that our sales people had been asking on the first cold call. The card says, "One card drawn at random will be awarded a check for $100." At the same time, we stopped providing postage.

The results so far have been great. In the first week of responses we have received over 40 completed surveys. It looks as though we will end up with at least twice as many responses as our prior efforts. It also seems like these are more qualified responses based on the follow-up calls our sales people have been making.

I thought your other readers would like to know about this.

Sincerely,
Frank Cooke
Association Computer Services
(317) 545-0500

Dear Frank,

I really appreciate your sharing this with me and the readers of Software Success. I would never have guessed that a chance at $100 would have such a dramatic impact on your responses. If you end up with 80 responses, your premium is still costing you less than $2 each, which is comparable with the typical premium item.

I talked to another subscriber who offers coffee cups as a premium and who received 300 responses to his first card offering the cup.

Both of these cases support the power of premiums, but I must admit I never would have guessed people would respond to a chance to win $100. I always throw away ads that say "listen to our condo pitch and win a TV". I guess I just don't trust the people selling condos and your prospects trust you.

This is a great example of why people should experiment.

I look forward to hearing from you once the results of this program are in. The real question is, are you going to end up with more business out of these leads?

Thanks and Good Luck!
Dave

Note to Readers

We spoke to Frank and so far he's received over 100 responses on this deck!

15. Survey Scanning Service (Aug)

Dear Dave,

We enjoy **Software Success** very much and look forward to each new issue. We certainly recognize ourselves in many of the problems you address, and are striving to implement some of the insights you and your readers provide.

We were very much interested in the new survey form included in the May 1991 issue, because it comes so close to services of our own.

I've enclosed another version of your survey form, composed by us as an example of our MainSail data scan services. The primary difference between the form you published and the form sampled here is that ours is scannable , meaning that we can scan response sheets directly into the computer at the rate of 2000 sheets an hour, eliminating both the hours and error of keyboard time.

We can design one page questionnaires complete with scanner interface requirements within an hour or two, depending on the complexity of layout, and response type. We can provide camera ready master or up to 250 copies within four hours of form approval, or thousands of copies within 24 hours, exclusive of shipping times.

Computer analysis of data can be provided by us, or the data can be shipped via diskette or modem in ASCI or DBF formats to the customer for in-house analysis on his own software.

Also of possible interest to your readers is our ability to develop custom forms and scanning interfaces for capturing data for their software products. Nearly four years ago we developed this type of automated data entry interface for our highly specialized production/tracking software and achieved recognition as the leader in our target market because of our dramatically unique capabilities to save time while simultaneously improving accuracy. The sales of forms and scanners certainly hasn't hurt our revenue flow either.

We'd certainly welcome the opportunity to help anyone interested in these capabilities. Thank you for your time; we're looking forward to more of **Software Success**.

Sincerely,
John A Erwin
President
J.A. Erwin and Associates
TEL (704) 299-3050
FAX (704) 299-3053

Dear John,

Thanks for your letter. A person can manually enter around 50 surveys per hour. With less than 200 surveys it probably doesn't make sense to automate the process.

However, any subscribers who are conducting surveys with large numbers of responses should consider automating the process.

Dave

16. Face-to-Face Business — Still the Best Way Outside the U.S. (Aug)

Dear Dave,

You shouldn't be surprised that business is "still" done face-to-face in other countries. There are reasons for doing so which will not go away quickly! One is geography — from Houston, I can be quite effective cold-calling around Dallas looking for new business, but a Parisian salesperson won't get anywhere cold-calling London, and will spend a fortune. I think another big reason is the relative lack of competitiveness. A European customer is more likely to stick to an underperforming vendor when an American would think "there MUST be somebody better than THIS". Foreign vendors spend more time cultivating their existing base (in person) than fighting for new business against high levels of loyalty. I know this comment is subjective and I would be interested to know whether other readers agree? And then again, there is a cultural difference we forget about: Europeans were not brought up with a "children's phone" and free local calls.

Sincerely,
Toby D. Atkinson
Director of Marketing
Informed Management Environments
TEL (713) 869-4630
FAX (713) 869-8792

Dear Toby,

The changing style of business is controlled by many factors. Some of these are economic and others are cultural. The cost of doing business outside of the US can be much higher than we are used to here in the US. The more it costs to do business remotely, the greater the local advantage. In Canada, phone calls cost 4 times as much as in the US and airfare is 2 to 3 times the comparable US airfare. I even had one case where I was paying 35% as much as my Canadian client for a round trip ticket on a Canadian airline. The only difference was that I was buying my ticket here in the US and he was buying his in Canada. I wonder how these economic factors will change in Europe after 1992.

The cultural factors seem to lag the economic factors. Thus, it seems to me that as long as the remote competitors are paying an expensive burden for marketing long distance, customers will buy from local companies. People like to buy from local companies, but they will buy remote with the proper incentive. Part of the incentive is economic, but there are also other risk factors.

In the early days of personal computers, everyone bought from local dealers who really understood these new computers. There was very little discounting because people purchased based on the knowledge of the dealer. Within a year of the Apple II being introduced, I bought my first Apple II mail order at 35% off list price. When the IBM PC was introduced, corporate America continued to buy from local dealers. Businessland focused on selling to corporate America by offering superior service at a premium price. Dell Computer offered technically superior computers, and great technical support. The shift to buying PC's by mail order was partly responsible for BusinessLand's failure and Dell's success.

I have seen a number of shifts of this type. I urge you to keep an open mind and carefully watch how your prospects are buying. I predict that the style of doing business in Europe will change if the costs of remote marketing change.

Thanks for the input!
Dave

17. 900 Numbers (Aug)

Dear Dave,

In your last few issues, you have discussed the problem of 900 number service lines. A solution available to many software developers is a shared 900 support line provided with the software developer's office management system sold by S.L.A.M. Software. Companies using the program can provide support for their own software users by having them call the shared 900 line. The 900 number operator redirects the call to the appropriate company handling the program support. You designate where the phone calls should be routed. While you provide support to your users, you earn approximately 50 cents per minute. Your user pays

$2.00 for the first minute and $1.50 for each additional minute. The only cost you encounter is the initial cost of Developer's Assistant — $129.00.

Incidentally, this benefit is only one minor facet of their system. Reach S.L.A.M. Software by calling 512-834-8927 or write to them at Dept. 176, PO Box 9802, Austin, TX 78766.

Sincerely,
D. Roger Maves
President
Compumax
TEL (303) 427-9234

Dear Roger,

Thanks for the letter. The shared 900 number is an interesting concept. As I was writing this article, a client called me with some costs for getting your own 900 number. The costs that he found were:

$0.30	MCI or Sprint/minute
$0.20	$2.00/min - 10% commission based on the gorss amount billed
$0.15	800# route from out of state service company
$0.55	per minute

There are also fixed monthly service fees to the long distance provider (MCI or Sprint) and the service bureau. While these costs vary depending upon the the level of service, my client felt that this would be at least $1K per month. The prorated cost per minute of these fixed fees depends upon the minutes per month that you bill. If you have two people providing 900 support full time, they might bill 10K minutes per month. This would give you $0.10 per minute for the fixed fees. The effective cost per minute could go much higher if your demand is lower. It looks like your overhead cost per minute won't go below $0.60 per minute. If you can bill $2.00 per minute, and you have high volume, your overhead cost is 30% ($0.60/$2.00). I have talked to several companies who are using 900 numbers for providing support and they say that they are receiving only 50% of the revenue.

Within this context, the shared 900 line is a low cost way for small software companies to start offering 900 support. Getting 33% of the revenue isn't great, but you would have to generate a high level of calls to even net 33% of the revenue.

I expect that this technology will evolve, but the costs are really going to have to come down if it is going to become widespread. If the overhead gets down to 10% to 20% from the current 50% or more, I think that this technology might gain widespread acceptance.

Dave

18. Mailing Lists (Sept)

Dear Dave,

We are a small company whose primary product is a health claims and billing system that runs on NOVELL local area networks. We sell or lease the package and also sell our maintenance service. Currently, we have 26 customers in locations across the country. These companies are split between third party administrators and self-insured companies that administer their own health claims (such as Dr. Pepper Company, Tifton Aluminum, Tesoro Petroleum and several self-insured hospitals).

Recently, we were developing a system for a medical research firm which I was largely responsible for. That firm lost its major investor, so they have put further system development on the back burner indefinitely. As a result, I have been shifted to the Health Claims marketing area. To be frank, this is a new experience for me and I am having difficulty approaching it properly.

I am looking for references to third party administrators or self-insured companies. We purchased a mailing list for third party administrators, but discovered that it was so woefully inaccurate and out-of-date that it was essentially worthless. My forays to the library have not been very productive.

Do you have any suggestions on other ways of gathering the needed information?

Sincerely,
Ron Blackburn
Minimax Systems, Inc.
TEL (918) 582-5822

P.S. I thought your article "Source Code Pricing" in the June 1991 issue was very informative. We have a customer that wants to purchase the source code to our programs. Originally, we said no because of the seemingly never-ending loopholes in contracts. We feel that the advice that was given to Mr. Cartier can also help us. Thank you.

Dear Ron,

I am pleased that the "Source Code Pricing" article was useful. This is an issue that a number of people seem to be dealing with.

My first advice is that you need to get a list broker. List brokers find lists for people. They are paid a commission by the owners of the list so it doesn't cost you anything to work with them. They have access to computerized data bases of lists and can quickly get information on a wide variety of lists that are available.

The two brokers that we work with are:

L.I.S.T.
Glenn Freedman
TEL (516) 482-2345
FAX (516) 487-9584

NameFinders
Ken Brown
TEL (415) 553-4177
FAX (415) 553-8677

You can also find names of list brokers in the yellow pages of your phone book.

Even if you are working with a list broker, I urge you to keep your eyes open and ask people about availability of lists. Even with two very capable list brokers I manage to find several new lists every month that they haven't yet identified. It isn't that they aren't doing their job. Some of the best lists available aren't yet listed in the computerized data bases. Instead, you may talk to a sales rep who tells you about a magazine that turns out to have a great list. Seek and ye shall find!

Good luck!
Dave

19. Survey Return Rates (Oct)

The *Journal of Services Marketing* had an interesting article titled "Another Note on Survey Return Rates," (Vol. 5, No. 2, Spring 1991). Since registration cards are a survey of sorts, I thought that it might be germane.

"8 1/2 X 11 inch paper provided higher response rates than 8 1/2 X 14."

"Adding a second page didn't affect the response rate."

"Stamped envelopes had a significantly higher response rate than the reply-permit group."

"The promise of a contribution to a charity did not produce significantly higher return rates than the no-incentive group. However, a cash incentive did provide a higher return rate than the control group."

"Response rates were significantly increased by the use of a twenty-five cent premium, but not affected by free book premiums."

"The twenty-five cent incentive still (16 years later) produces a significant increase in return rates."

"A non-monetary incentive (ballpoint pen) had a negative effect on response quality."

This research would indicate that including money with your registration card might be the most effective way of increasing your response rate. You might test quarters and dollar bills.

"A signature on the cover letter increased survey response rates. (Maybe you should include a signed cover letter with a survey asking them to complete the registration card and explaining why you want them to register.)"

"The authors concluded that the importance of the monetary incentive stems primarily from the psychological impact of receiving money, as opposed to the monetary value itself."

Observation: This research would indicate that including money with your registration card might be the most effective way of increasing your response rate. You might test quarters and dollar bills.

20. Mailing Lists (Oct)

Dear Mr. Bowen,

I talked to you last week about the possibility of renting names from your mailing list to help me sell my C programming library software product. I still think your list will be an excellent marketing resource for me, but I think I need to work another list I compiled myself a little more and try to generate sales to pay for new marketing efforts before I get going with your list.

Incidentally, do you rent names on a one-time basis only, or on a permanent basis? I just received a mailing from a company that sells a list of 4,000 software companies, "Serious PC Software Developers," for about $149, and the list license is for permanent use by a single company. I talked to them, and they said that they saw a real need for multiuse rental for software marketers because several contacts are usually required before purchase is elicited from a significant portion of the list when a product that costs more than $100 is marketed. A one-time use list must be rented several times in order for its use to be effective.

I experienced this myself. I rented 5,000 names from a programming magazine's mailing list in June and sent out a mailing. I did receive a fair response rate, but to date, no sales of my $429 product have resulted from the mailing. Although I really need to go back and work the 5,000 names again (and even a third or fourth time if necessary), I just can't afford to rent the same list again. So the initial mailing, which took a significant portion of my start-up advertising resources, was useless, and I feel I wasted my money (even though the list is probably an acceptable list). It was a learning experience. But, if people would sell their lists for perpetual use, I would not consider it to have been, for the time being at least, a waste of money and a significant loss of advertising abilities.

If this magazine's list license allowed perpetual use, I would purchase more names from their list. However, under the circumstances, I definitely can't justify (or afford) purchasing more names from the list, even duplicate names, until I have made more sales. Something of a catch-22, since I need to do mailings to increase sales. Of course, I am also considering other types of advertisements.

I know that one-time rental is the norm for the list rental industry, but most lists are rented to sell inexpensive (under $100, if not under $40) products. I don't think one-time rental works as well for list renters whose product costs more than $100, and if you do rent for one-time use only, you might consider changing that policy.

Of course, since you are a marketing expert, you may well have a different and more accurate view of things than I. Anyway, thanks again for speaking with me last week.

Sincerely,
Anonymous

Dear Anonymous,

I feel that you haven't come to terms with your real problem. You did a mailing in June and you still haven't made any sales of your $429 product by September. There is something dramatically wrong with your product or your marketing materials. I would focus on this as my top priority if I were you.

There are lists which are available on a perpetual basis for a one-time fee. If you can find such a list, which targets your market, and has high quality names, it could be a very good tool. Most of these lists are compiled lists and are of generally lower quality than rental lists.

We have purchased some of these compiled lists, and their non-delivery rate has been as high as 20%. Non-delivery rates on rental lists are typically less than 4% for software companies. If you buy bargain names, and 20% of them are bad, then these are actually expensive names.

My own experience has taught me to buy the best lists possible. I include the cost of the list rental when I determine my return from my mailings, but some of my most expensive lists are among my best performers. If your mailing cost is fifty cents per letter with printing, postage and the one time rental of the name, your list rental is 20 to 30% of your cost, but it can more than compensate with better delivery rates and response rates.

Non-delivery rates on rental lists are typically less than 4% for software companies. If you buy bargain names, and 20% of them are bad, then these are actually expensive names.

The other factor to consider is the cost of maintaining the list. Companies who rent their lists have to keep them current, correct the addresses, and delete the companies who are no longer in business. This is a hidden cost that you are incurring when you buy names for perpetual use.

Since 10% of all companies move each year, a perpetual-use list will soon have a significant number of bad addresses. Unless you mail to these people fairly often (once a quarter, maybe) and use first-class postage to get forwarding and mail-return services, it won't be long until your list is almost useless.

Instead of buying the whole list, test a small part. That way, you'll only have to spend a little money to see if your marketing materials are going to work for you.

I am pleased that you are interested in learning about mailing lists, and I wish you good luck in marketing your product.

Dave

21. Do audio-cassettes really convince anyone to buy software? (Nov)

Dear Dave,

My company develops and markets software products for mid-range computers. During the coming year, we hope to get our products reviewed in different trade journals. I am looking for ways to increase the positive impact of these reviews beyond what we have achieved before by using reprints of the reviews. One idea that I am considering is getting approval from publishers to create audio-cassettes of favorable reviews. I think it might be convenient for some buyers to learn about our product by listening to the tape while driving. Have you or any of your clients tried this? If so, what was the result?

**Sincerely,
Anonymous**

Dear Anonymous,

Many of my clients have considered creating an audiotape, but only one has actually produced one and offered it to prospects. This company had created a product that used new technology and was selling it to a vertical market. The product had new, very powerful features, but it required the prospects to think about their businesses in a slightly unusual way.

The company showed its product to industry opinion leaders and gurus, and one well-known industry spokesperson became so excited about the potential of the new capabilities of the product that he offered to help promote the product for free.

The new spokesman had been an actor earlier in life and had a fantastic voice. The company had him produce a professional-quality, highly effective audio-tape.

Based on this success, the company wondered whether it should also have made a videotape. Nonetheless, this audio-tape proved to be very effective in generating leads, and it seemed to help turn listeners into serious prospects.

Other clients who have considered audio-tapes and then decided against them have faced a number of the following questions:

1. Will prospects make an effort to play the audio-tapes in their cars? Many people won't look at a videotape or a demonstration disk, and audio-tapes often face the same psychological barrier. Prospects must be well-motivated to overcome such an obstacle, and in many cases, the tape, disk, or cassette actually becomes an impediment to proceeding with the sale. Thus, your attempt to expedite the sale can actually become a stumbling block.

2. Do you really have enough information to make the tape interesting? The last thing you want is for prospects to spend time listening to the tape and then feel they haven't learned anything. Many of the shallow "story board" demo disks fail for the same reason: they contain less information than a simple brochure, and prospects are upset that you wasted their time.

3. Does the speaker have a pleasant voice, or, if you're considering a videotape, a good camera presence: The homemade commercials on late-night TV that feature car dealers and their families are often

painfully embarrassing. The audio-tape that I discussed earlier succeeded, in part, because the guru had taken voice training. You need to create a professional product, and you must insure that all aspects of it are of high quality.

4. Can you communicate your message using only the spoken word? Many marketing messages require both auditory and visual stimulation, making video-tapes more appropriate. How strong will your message be without any visual reinforcement?

As you might have guessed, I feel that an audio-tape is a risky marketing technique. A number of conditions must be met before you even consider it. Conversely, many factors may eliminate it from your consideration. Please be careful.

Thanks,
Dave

Postscript: I am relieved that the writer of this letter decided to drop the idea. I am interested in hearing from anyone who has created audio-tapes. Did they help your marketing efforts?

22. Marketing with Newsletters (Nov)

Dear David,

As computer hardware and software marketers have been avid users of newsletters, I thought you may be interested in seeing a press kit and review copy of my book, Marketing with Newsletters. Examples in the book include publications from SCO, Aldus, Arnet, Quark, Digital, Informix, Northern Telecom and XYQuest.

While running a newsletter consulting service, I realized that businesses of all sizes need more information on the subject. Although lots of material exists explaining how to create materials such as brochures, no single book has ever been dedicated solely to using newsletters as a marketing tool.

I hope that you find the book of interest to your readers.

Sincerely,

Elaine Floyd
EF Communications
5721 Magazine St, Ste. 170
New Orleans, LA 70115
Telephone: (800) 247-6553
(504) 283-6305

(The 265-page, soft-cover book is available by mail from EF Communications for $27.95, which includes a $3 charge for shipping and handling.)

Dear Elaine,

I think that anyone who is publishing a customer newsletter or considering one could profit from reading your book, and I am including the following highlights from your press release:

"In each chapter, my goal is to give marketers practical advice they can use immediately," says Floyd. "While the book is packed with information, I tried to keep the style light-hearted and fun to read. Every page has a little treat (such as) newsletter examples, cartoons, testimonials, subheads, checklists...something to keep reading painless."

"Readers learn how to stretch their newsletters' budgets, leverage time by using subcontractors, develop a targeted mailing list, survey readers, and coordinate the newsletter with other marketing projects. The book includes such tips as how to motivate people to immediately read the newsletter; choosing between 20 different types of newsletter articles; the fastest ways to collect high-quality news; and nine different ways to spur readers to respond."

"An entire chapter is devoted to designing and conducting readership surveys. The chapter includes information on choosing between written and telephone surveys, a list of 23 sample questions, and 14 different suggestions for increasing response rate."

Thanks for the information.

Dave

C. Case Studies (1991)

1. Following Up on Leads (Aug)

One of my clients markets products in the $10K price range to large customers, with the sales people each averaging $33K per month in sales. To generate leads, letters were sent to prospects and then two weeks later the sales people called each of these prospects. 2% of the prospects responded before the follow-up calls were made. Another 6% expressed interest after the follow-up call, bringing the total response rate to 8%.

The company was very pleased with the 8% response rate, but after awhile the sales activity began slowing down. The first step in the sales cycle had been to have the prospect trial the product, and even trial activity was down. Management wondered why they were getting these very good marketing/sales responses, but seeing a decrease in trials.

The market for my client's company was very large (5K to 10K prospects), and the lead generation letters were being sent in small batches of 100. At this low volume, the letters were costing $1.00 each and the cost per lead was $50/lead with the 2% response rate.

I was pushing to increase the size of the mailings to lower the cost per piece to $0.50 and hopefully lower the cost per lead to $25 (assuming that the response rate didn't decline). I felt the company would benefit by generating more leads for the sales people to follow up on. This is the classic "mail/phone/mail" strategy in which the sales people make follow up calls only to people who have responded. Additional information is then sent to the prospects who show interest during the follow-up call.

Now that this strategy is in place, the sales people really like taking control of their lives and generating a 6% response rate on their own. Since they have generated these additional leads, they have more ownership in them and feel more comfortable following up.

At first, I was concerned that the phone leads might turn out to be less qualified than the mail leads. (Some of the prospects had feigned interest just to get the sales person off the phone.) I have seen sales people push very hard to get prospects to agree to take literature which they really don't need.

The following analysis better explains the cost of having the sales people make the follow up calls. A sales person could make about 50 calls per day. To generate the 6 leads, it took 300 calls or 6 full days of one sales person's time. The low assessment of the cost per day would be to take the $2K monthly base salary of the sales person and divide it by 20 days in the month. This is a cost of $100 per day, with the sales person generating one lead per day. Marketing could do this for $50, and could lower it to $25 with larger mailings.

Looking at the cost of these sales generated leads in more detail, they are higher if you look at some other factors. If you double these costs to cover the other costs (benefits, rent, phone expenses, sick leave, etc) your cost is probably at least $200 per day. Plus, you have the opportunity cost of the sales person not selling. To get this cost, divide their actual monthly sales of $33K by 20 days per month for $1.65K per day in expected sales. Thus, every day that you have a senior sales person making follow-up calls to the mailing, it costs you $1.65K in lost sales just to generate one lead. This analysis convinced the company to do more mailings to generate more leads. The sales people then followed up on only those leads who'd responded. Because these leads were better quality, more of them converted to sales.

Since this strategy's been in place, the cost per lead is down to $6 (formerly $50!), and the salespeople are now averaging $55K/month in sales (up nearly 67% from their previous $33K/month average).

2. Ownership of Leads (Aug)

With another client, we did a detailed study of the conversion rate of various types of leads to sales. The conventional wisdom within the company was that sales generated leads were best. The sales people felt these were good leads because they had brought these leads in by personal effort. They felt a closeness to these leads and a feeling of "ownership". Display advertising leads were considered second best, and card deck leads were at the bottom of the list. The card deck leads were perceived as low quality because the salespeople had put no personal effort into bringing them in.

When we analyzed the percentage of leads that actually bought, the card decks were the best on both the percentage of leads that bought and the cost per sale. It appeared that people who responded to the card decks were serious buyers, and we did well. The bad news is that the card deck leads took their time evaluating the various alternatives and they didn't buy quickly.

For the most part, the sales people hated these card deck leads. Only one sales person liked them, and was making a lot of cold calls. He far preferred to call someone who had expressed interest through the card deck than someone who was really a cold lead. He had very low ego involvement with the leads and was grateful for the card deck leads since they made him more effective.

This issue of ownership and involvement with leads is very important. Marketing can generate all sorts of

Chapter II. Lead Generation

leads, but if the sales people don't feel a "bond" with them, then the chances of ending up with a sale is far reduced. Sadly, this is a self fulfilling prophecy. Sales people decide that these are lousy leads, they don't follow up with as much vigor, and they end up with fewer sales.

I like to take the approach of reviewing the numbers and the alternatives with the sales people. I tell them, "The company has budgeted $X/month for you to do lead generation. Lets' decide the best way to spend your lead generation money." Then I try to implement some of the sales peoples' suggestions and let them experience the implications of their own ideas.

In the case regarding the card deck leads, the sales department decided that they wanted to cut back on the card decks. They did so with the commitment to make cold calls to replace the card deck leads. Once the card deck leads slowed down, the sales people began to complain about not having enough leads to follow up. At that point, they finally understood the value of the card deck leads.

The best way I can sum this up is to think of it as similar to dating back in high school. Your odds of success are much better if you go after the ones who've already expressed interest.

D. Generation Survey (1990)

1. Company Revenue

The companies who responded to this survey were larger than the typical Software Success survey respondents. I believe this is due to the fact that lead generation is an activity which is characteristic of somewhat larger and more sophisticated companies.

REPLY	% RESP
<$250K	16.3%
$250K-$500K	8.2%
$500K-$1M	24.5%
$1M-$2M	28.6%
$2M-$5M	12.2%
>$5M	6.1%

2. Computer Type

PCs were dominant in this survey, but LANs are becoming more important.

REPLY	% RESP
PC	71.4%
LAN	22.4%
Mini	16.3%
Mainframe	16.3%

3. Distribution

Everyone in the survey sells direct, but there was much more indirect selling (using dealers and distributors) and OEM distribution.

REPLY	% RESP
Direct	100%
Indirect	51%
OEM	22%

Direct sales also dominate the marketing mix for most companies. Indirect sales are less important,

but I was surprised at the number of firms generating significant sales indirectly. I was also pleasantly surprised that fourteen percent of the companies were generating OEM sales.

4. Market Size

There was quite an even distribution of market size in this survey.

REPLY	% RESP
<500K	8.2%
500-1K	6.1%
1K-10K	22.4%
10K-25K	12.2%
25K-100K	18.4%
>100K	14.3%

5. Number of Leads per Month

The median leads per month is about 50, which seems pretty low to me.

REPLY	% RESP
0-10	10.2%
10-25	26.5%
25-50	10.2%
50-100	16.3%
100-250	12.2%
250+	20.4%

6. Percentage of Sales by Distribution Method

REPLY	DIRECT	INDIRECT	OEM
0%	2%	49%	78%
10%	4%	16%	8%
10%-25%	4%	4%	0%
25%-50%	16%	14%	15%
50%-75%	12%	10%	0%
>75%	61%	6%	0%

7. Lead-to-Sale Conversion
How many leads actually become sales?

The median conversion rate of leads to sales within a year is five to ten percent. On the other hand, there is wide variation in the conversion rate.

I should point out that a very high conversion rate of leads into sales isn't necessarily good. I have seen situations where thirty percent of the leads were hounded into buying.

This high conversion rate was just evidence that this company didn't have enough leads and the sales people were working and reworking the leads they had.

The company became much more profitable when it started to generate more leads and to get more sales out of the sales people.

The one thing that is really important is the trend in the conversion rate. One of the first signs that a market is changing is a decline in the lead-to-sale conversion rate.

On the other hand, an improving conversion rate is usually solid evidence that a company is marketing and selling better to its leads.

I was really pleased that most of the companies who replied to the survey are aware of their lead-to-sale conversion ratio. This is one of the critical numbers that every good marketing person should know.

8. Annual Sales Quota

There is a wide variation in the sales quota. I believe that some of the "over $800,000" answers are for the entire company.

A couple of these companies have one sales person. Everyone in the company sells, but they have only one sales person.

REPLY	% RESP
$100K	8.2%
$100K-$200K	10.2%
$200K-$400K	8.2%
$400K-$600K	14.3%
$600K-$800K	14.3%
$800K	30.6%

9. Who is Responsible?
Who actually handles the lead generation program?

As you can see, marketing is the group that is most often responsible for lead generation. This is as it should be. Fewer presidents are responsible for lead generation than we found last year. I am very pleased that this is true because it is impossible for any president to devote the required consistent attention to lead generation with all of his or her other duties. Successful lead generation programs require a great deal of leg work and follow-up by a dedicated person.

Sales is the other group which is often responsible for lead generation. I have found that this solution suffers from some of the same lack of attention and inconsistency that occurs when the president is responsible for generating leads.

With sales people, they start to work a batch of leads and they stop generating new leads. In a month or two, their sales pipeline is dry and they are in a panic to generate new leads. Having one person who is responsible for generating leads is a major step in alleviating this problem.

10. Primary Lead Source

REPLY	% RESP
Referrals	42.9%
PR/ Articles	42.9%
Trade Shows	38.8%
Display Ads	40.8%
Direct Mail	26.5%
Card Decks	8.2%
Telemarketing	12.2%
Seminars	2.0%
Dealers	16.3%
Hardware Vendors	4.1%
Directories	10.2%

The first thing you will notice is that these numbers total more than 100 percent. In fact, on average, the companies identified two lead sources as primary.

Many companies identified referrals as a primary lead source. I believe this is due in part to the very positive emotional association with referral leads.

I was surprised that PR/Articles were this highly rated.

Trade Shows, Display Ads, and Direct Mail are the big three lead generation approaches. I would have thought that Direct Mail would have been rated higher.

Card decks aren't highly regarded. I know a number of firms who use them as a key part of their lead generation program, but very few people "love" them.

Telemarketing was much higher than last year. This may reflect the growing trend toward focusing on your target market. If you have a very well-defined market and a strong sales pitch, telemarketing can do well.

Seminars are the least popular lead generation technique. As I talk to companies who are using seminars successfully, there seem to be a couple of common factors:

1. They are large companies who can afford to invest $250,000 or more in a seminar series, or they have a strategic alliance with a big brother who can help foot the bill.

2. They have lots of sales leads, and sales which are in the pipeline. They typically use the seminars to help move the sale along. By and large they aren't drawing cold prospects into the seminar.

3. They are very interested in enhancing their reputation with their customers and prospects. Thus they often view their seminars as a public relations activity.

Dealers were more popular than I would have expected.

Hardware Vendors aren't very successful as a primary lead source. This matches my experience with small companies investing huge amounts of time with hardware vendors to no avail.

Directories were significant to a number of firms. I was pleased to see this since I felt badly that so many firms weren't using directories in last year's survey.

11. Referrals

Referrals are used as a primary lead source by 42.9 percent of the companies.

In my experience, it is very difficult for a company to generate more than ten percent of its leads via referrals if it has an active lead generation program. Either the respondents are very successful in encouraging referrals or they aren't generating many other leads.

Percent of Leads

REPLY	% RESP
0%	14.3%
<10%	34.7%
<25%	22.4%
>50%	16.3%
>50%	2.0%

It appears that one explanation for the high level of leads from referrals is the corresponding high level of effort spent on encouraging referrals. I would really be interested to learn what readers have done to generate referral leads and how well it has paid off.

LEVEL OF EFFORT	% RESP
High	14.3%
Medium	20.4%
Low	36.7%

It appears that this high level of investment in referrals extends to the budget. Twenty percent of the companies spend less than ten percent of their budget, but they are spending money.

PERCENT OF BUDGET	% RESP
0%	44.9%
10%	20.4%
50%	2.0%

Most companies are increasing their investment in encouraging referrals. In fact thirteen times as many companies are increasing their effort than are

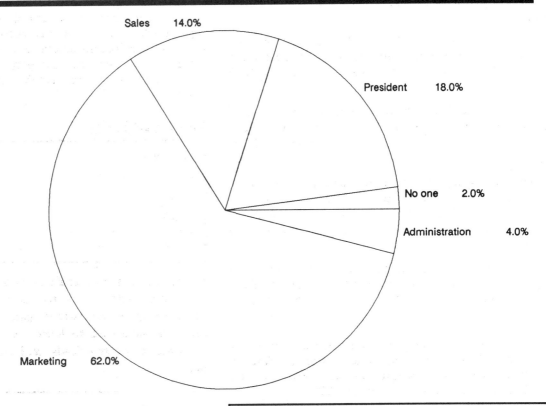

Who is Responsible for Lead Generation?

Sales 14.0%
President 18.0%
No one 2.0%
Administration 4.0%
Marketing 62.0%

decreasing their effort. This represents the second highest ratio we found in this survey.

TREND	% RESP
More effort	26.5%
No change	20.4%
Less effort	2.0%

12. PR/Articles

PR and Articles are almost as popular as referrals (42.9 percent).

While most of the companies generate less than ten percent of their leads this way, it is possible to generate more leads with articles.

PERCENT OF LEADS	% RESP
0%	24.5%
<10%	36.7%
<25%	18.4%
<50%	8.2%
>50%	2.0%

I was pleased at the number of companies who are expending a high level of effort in PR. iven the long-term cumulative effect of PR, these companies are investing in their future.

LEVEL OF EFFORT	% RESP
High	24.5%
Medium	18.4%
Low	22.4%

Companies are also making a budgetary investment in PR. For most companies it is less than ten percent of their budget, but they are generating more than ten percent of their leads with PR. When I have analyzed it for clients, PR can have one of the best cost-per-lead rates of any alternative.

PERCENT OF BUDGET	% RESP
0%	32.7%
<10%	26.5%
<25%	4.1%
<50%	8.2%

Companies are increasing their investment in PR. Fourteen times more companies are increasing their effort here than are decreasing it. This is the highest ratio in the survey.

TREND IN USAGE	% RESP
Increasing	28.6%
No change	16.3%
Decreasing	2.0%

13. Trade Shows

A total of 38.8 percent of the companies depend upon trade shows as a primary lead source. This was one of the highest percentages in the survey. Trade shows can generate a lot of leads. They can be the primary lead source for certain companies. This depends upon the existence of appropriate trade shows.

PERCENT OF LEADS	% RESP
0%	24.5%
<10%	22.4%
<25%	18.4%
<50%	14.3%
>50%	6.1%

Trade shows require a great deal of effort. If you are going to use trade shows, you must make the investment to be able to go to shows efficiently.

LEVEL OF EFFORT	% RESP
High	40.8%
Medium	10.2%
Low	10.2%

My experience is that trade shows are generally an expensive way to generate leads. I have had several clients who have moved from trade shows to direct mail and have been able to generate more and better leads with the same budget. In one case, the client bought the mailing list of the trade show attendees and mailed to them before and after the show. This turned out to be very effective.

The one indication that this might be true for the companies in the survey comes from comparing what percent of the budget goes to trade shows and what percent of the leads come from trade shows. A total of 12.2 percent of the companies spend over 50 percent of their budget on trade shows, but only 6.1 percent of the companies generate over 50 percent of their leads from trade shows. This at least indicates that some companies are spending more on trade shows than they are getting back in leads.

I feel like I should have an aside on behalf of trade shows. There are a number of companies who believe very strongly in trade shows. They will argue that in addition to the leads that they are getting PR and exposure that they could get no other way. I believe that there are a number of necessary conditions for trade shows to make sense.

1. **There must be some very good targeted shows.**

2. **The principals must be outgoing and enjoy mixing with people in a public setting.**

3. **The principals must be willing to travel cheaply and work to hold down expenses.**

PERCENT OF BUDGET	% RESP
0%	22.4%
<10%	8.2%
<25%	12.2%
<50%	14.3%
>50%	12.2%

While more companies are increasing their investment in trade shows, a significant number are decreasing their trade show effort. Only two times more companies are increasing their investment than are decreasing it.

CHANGE IN EFFORT	% RESP
Increasing	12.2%
No change	28.6%
Decreasing	6.1%

14. Display Advertising

Display advertising is the primary lead source of 40.8 percent of the companies. If you have a low priced product in a mass market, display advertising might be your only realistic lead generation alternative. In particular, if your price is too low, trade shows and direct mail may not be cost effective.

The graph entitled Leads by Primary Lead Source compares the leads for each major lead alternative. Display advertising stands out because it generates over 50 percent of the leads in 14 percent of the companies surveyed. Nothing else even comes close.

PERCENT OF LEADS	% RESP
0%	18.4%
<10%	22.4%
<25%	14.3%
<50%	10.2%
>50%	14.3%

For the most part, display advertising takes medium effort. It is hard work to generate a good ad and work with your copywriter and graphic artist, but once the ad is done, all you have to do is send money.

LEVEL OF EFFORT	% RESP
High	18.4%
Medium	32.7%
Low	8.2%

Display advertising is expensive, and in many cases there are more cost effective ways to generate leads. If you compare the budgets and the leads you will see that 18.4 percent of the companies spend over 50 percent of their budgets on display advertising, but

only 14.3 percent generate over 50 percent of their leads.

The advocates of display advertising will argue that part of this is a premium that you pay for the PR exposure. I guess that I would rather spend a lesser amount of money on press releases and articles for the pure PR and put my lead generation dollars into the programs that will generate leads most cost effectively.

Somehow this dual purpose argument reminds me of life insurance salesmen who are selling whole life policies. I would rather buy the term life insurance that I need and then make my investments. This is probably the reason I am biased against trade shows and display advertising since they are justified as being both lead generation and promotion.

PERCENT OF BUDGET	% RESP
0%	16.3%
<10%	4.1%
<25%	10.2%
<50%	14.3%
>50%	18.4%

The trend toward display advertising is tempered by companies who are decreasing their investment. At 2.4 times more increasing over ones decreasing, it is better than trade shows, but it still isn't very good.

TREND IN EFFORT	% RESP
Increasing	20.4%
No Change	16.3%
Decreasing	8.2%

15. Direct Mail

Direct mail is the primary lead source for 26.5 percent of the companies. According to this survey, it is difficult to generate more than 25 percent of your leads via direct mail. In my consulting, I see more companies generating closer to 50 percent of their leads via direct mail than were reported in this survey.

PERCENT OF LEAD	% RESP
0%	32.7%
<10%	24.5%
<25%	14.3%
<50%	6.1%
>50%	4.1%

PERCENT OF BUDGET	% RESP
0%	30.6%
<10%	16.3%
<25%	12.2%
<50%	4.1%
>50%	4.1%

Direct mail can require a great deal of effort. This is especially true when you are first using it. I strongly advise you to use a lettershop to stuff your envelopes. For smaller mailings, you can find local groups or individuals who will perform these services very cost-effectively. I have seen a number of companies which were totally disrupted by their one and only mailing.

LEVEL OF EFFORT	% RESP
High	16.3%
Medium	16.3%
Low	14.3%

By and large, direct mail can be cost effective. It is easy to track the responses and kill direct mail programs which aren't cost effective. You will notice that the same number of people spend over 50 percent of their budget as get over 50 percent of their leads using direct mail.

At the other end of the spectrum, it appears that some of the firms who are making a modest investment in direct mail aren't getting a good return on their investment. A total of 24.5 percent of the companies get less than 10 percent of their leads from direct mail, but only 16.3 percent of the companies spend less than 10 percent of their budget on direct mail.

I think several factors are at work. The first is that there are real economies of scale in printing and very small mailings can be expensive. The second factor is that direct mail is a classical trial and error process. My initial mailings had a cost per lead of $300 or more. Over time, I was able to get this down to $15 per lead. A ten times improvement in cost per lead with direct mail over time is common in my experience.

The trend toward direct mail is the strongest of the major programs (six times more increasing than decreasing where trade shows were two times and display advertising was 2.4 times).

TREND TOWARD DM	% RESP
Increasing	24.5%
No Change	4.1%
Decreasing	4.1%

16. Card Decks

Card decks aren't very popular, and most of the companies who use them generate less than ten percent of their leads via card decks. Card decks are the primary lead generation approach in only two percent of the companies.

PERCENT OF LEADS	% RESP
0%	51.0%
<10%	16.3%
<25%	2.0%
<50%	2.0%

Given the low level of leads that companies generate with card decks, it is nice that they require a low level of effort.

LEVEL OF EFFORT	% RESP
High	2.0%
Medium	4.1%
Low	20.4%

Companies also don't spend much money on card decks.

PERCENT OF BUDGET	% RESP
0%	49.0%
<10%	8.2%
<50%	2.0%

There are as many companies decreasing their usage of card decks as there are companies increasing their usage of card decks. Thus, relative to the other programs, card deck usage is declining.

TRENDS IN USAGE	% RESP
Increasing	8.2%
No Change	4.1%
Decreasing	8.2%

17. Telemarketing

Telemarketing was the primary lead generation technique in only 12.2 percent of the companies. Very few companies generate more than ten percent of their leads with telemarketing.

PERCENT OF LEADS	% RESP
0%	51.0%
<10%	12.2%
<25%	4.1%
>50%	6.1%

It is nice to see that the 6.1 percent who are making a high investment in telemarketing as a primary lead source are generating over fifty percent of their leads via telemarketing.

These same companies are expending a high level of effort on telemarketing. I was pleased to see that ten percent of the companies were investing a low level of effort in telemarketing. It can be a very nice part of your lead generation mix in the right situation.

LEVEL OF EFFORT	% RESP
High	6.1%
Medium	2.0%
Low	10.2%

Companies generate more leads as a percentage than they spend their budget as a percentage. Thus it appears that telemarketing is a cost effective way to generate leads.

PERCENT OF BUDGET	% RESP
0%	46.9%
<10%	10.2%
>50%	4.1%

The trend toward telemarketing is fairly strong (the number of companies increasing is three times larger than those who are decreasing.)

TREND IN USAGE	% RESP
Increasing	12.2%
No Change	4.1%
Decreasing	4.1%

18. Seminars

Seminars were the primary lead program for only 2.0 percent of the companies. Very few companies generated more than ten percent of their leads via seminars, and no one generated more than 25 percent of their leads via seminars.

PERCENT OF LEADS	% RESP
0%	55.1%
<10%	10.2%
<25%	2.0%

The same two percent who generated more than ten percent of their leads but less than 25 percent expended medium effort. No one spent high effort on seminars.

LEVEL OF EFFORT	% RESP
Medium	2.0%
Low	12.2%

It appears that seminars are a good investment since companies spent less money on them than they obtained as a percentage of leads.

PERCENT OF BUDGET	% RESP
0%	59.2%
<10%	6.1%

Companies are increasing their investment in seminars five times more often than they are decreasing it. (The cynic would point out that so few people are using seminars that it would be tough for very many of them to decrease their usage.)

TREND IN USAGE	% RESP
Increasing	10.2%
No Change	2.0%
Decreasing	2.0%

19. Dealers

I was surprised that 16.3 percent of the companies viewed their dealers as a primary lead source. Most dealers want leads from the vendor.

I see a few cases where a dealer is strong in a local market where they generate their own leads. I have also seen cases where "dealers" were really marketing companies for development companies.

The reality of the situation is that it is difficult to generate more than ten percent of your leads through dealers. The surprise is that some companies generated up to fifty percent of their leads via dealers.

PERCENT OF LEADS	% RESP
0%	44.9%
<10%	20.4%
<25%	6.1%
<50%	8.2%

It isn't surprising that most of the companies generating over ten percent of their leads expended low effort. I was impressed that a number of companies were able to generate less than ten percent of their leads with low effort.

LEVEL OF EFFORT	% RESP
High	12.2%
Medium	8.2%
Low	14.3%

Generating leads via dealers does not take much budget.

PERCENT OF BUDGET	% RESP
0%	46.9%
<10%	16.3%
<25%	2.0%
<50%	2.0%

The practice of using dealers to generate leads is on the upswing. Eight times more companies are increasing their effort with dealers than are decreasing it. I would not have predicted this.

TREND IN USAGE	% RESP
Increasing	16.3%
No Change	8.2%
Decreasing	2.0%

20. Hardware Vendors

Software companies have been pretty badly burned by the siren songs of the hardware vendors. Only 4.1 percent of the software companies view hardware companies as a primary lead source.

On the other hand, a few companies are generating some leads with the hardware companies.

Chapter II. Lead Generation

Percentage of Leads by Primary Lead Source

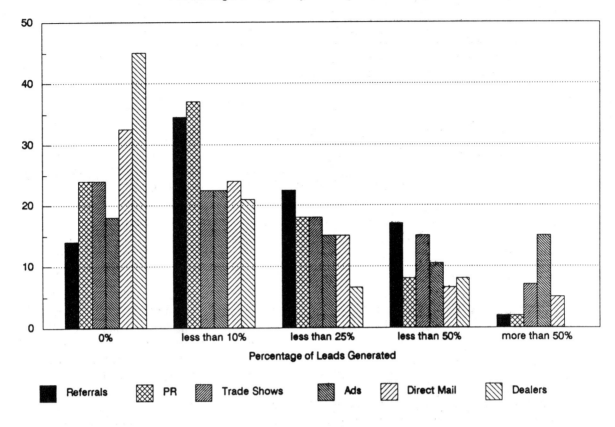

Percentage of Leads Generated

Referrals   PR   Trade Shows   Ads   Direct Mail   Dealers

PERCENT OF LEADS	% RESP
0%	59.2%
<10%	8.2%
<25%	2.0%

A company can easily put a high degree of effort into working with hardware vendors. Some of the companies putting in high effort are generating less than ten percent of their leads via hardware vendors.

LEVEL OF EFFORT	% RESP
High	4.1%
Medium	4.1%
Low	8.2%

Companies don't invest a lot of money in working with hardware companies if one doesn't count the salaries and the opportunity costs of the key people who are training and selling the hardware companies.

PERCENT OF BUDGET	% RESP
0%	63.3%
<10%	4.1%

Hardware vendors have a ratio of one to one (increasing effort versus decreasing effort). Far too many companies have been burned, and they are pulling back.

TREND IN USAGE	% RESP
Increasing	4.1%
No Change	6.1%
Decreasing	4.1%

21. Directories

Directories were the primary lead source for 10.2 percent of the companies. This is quite high. I have received calls from a number of subscribers looking for lists of free directories. Does anyone know of such a directory of directories? Many companies generate less than ten percent of their leads with directories, which is quite a nice return for such a low cost lead generation technique.

PERCENT OF LEADS	% RESP
0%	44.9%
<10%	24.5%
<50%	2.0%

ew companies felt that they had invested high or medium effort in directories. I feel that every company needs this type of short write-up on their company and products. You should have it, even if you aren't going to submit it to directories. Thus I wouldn't count the effort to create a directory write-up against the directory. I view it as a basic marketing task that needs to be done.

LEVEL OF EFFORT	% RESP
High	6.1%
Medium	6.1%
Low	22.4%

I have received a number of calls asking about good directories in which to be listed. I would appreciate hearing about any good ones that you have found. My best advice is to ask your customers what directories they use. You could just send a letter to your customers and ask. Directories don't take a lot of money.

Percentage of Leads by Primary Lead Source

PERCENT OF BUDGET	% RESP
0%	46.9%
<10%	16.3%

There is a modest increase in directory usage. It has increased twice as much as it has decreased. I hope that this really means that everyone who is interested is already using them, they just didn't bother to answer this question.

TREND IN USAGE	% RESP
Increasing	4.1%
No Change	18.4%
Decreasing	2.0%

22. Percent of Leads

The graph on the next page shows the distribution of percent of leads for the six top lead generation programs. I believe that this is an interesting way to compare the capabilities of different types of programs.

References

I expected that most companies would generate less than ten percent of their leads via references, but I was very impressed at how many generated 25 percent and 50 percent with references. I worry that they could be doing much better if they generated more leads from other sources and reduced the percentage for references, but I remain impressed.

Public Relations

Again, most firms generate less than ten percent of their leads via PR. I was disappointed that 25 percent generated no leads via PR. A significant number of firms generated up to 25 percent of their leads via PR, but very few generated more than that.

Trade Shows

Almost as many firms generated up to 25 percent of their leads via trade shows as generated less than ten percent. I think that this means that if you are going to use trade shows, you have to make a serious investment. Once you are set up to go to one show, it just makes sense to take it to the others. Thus it is quite reasonable to generate up to 50 percent of your leads with trade shows. The other side of this is that it may be dangerous to dabble with trade shows. If you don't know what you are doing, you might generate very few leads and expend a great deal of effort.

Display Advertising

Display advertising is much like trade shows. If you are going to do it, you should do it right. You can generate a lot of leads with display advertising. In fact display advertising was the only media which

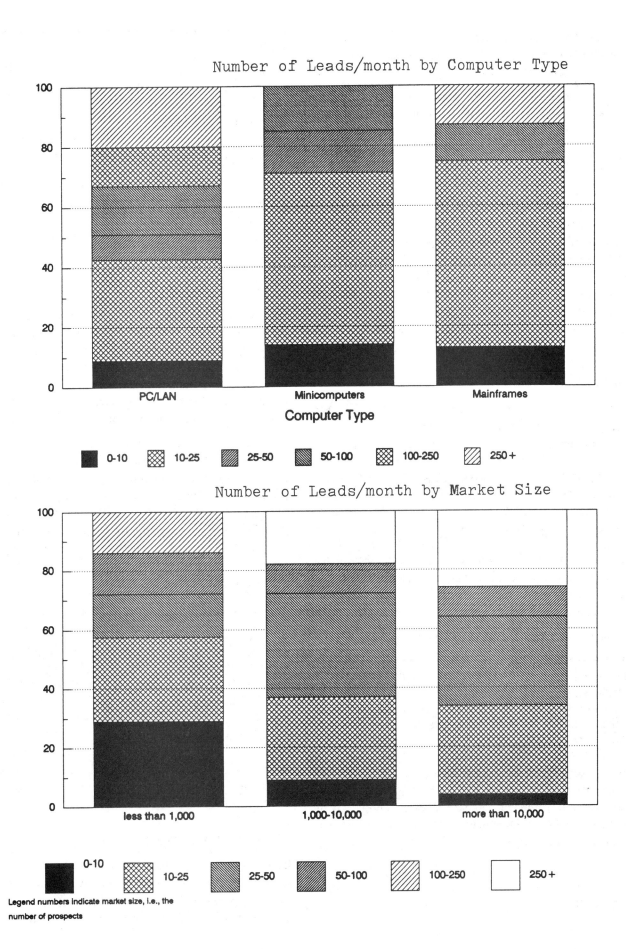

Number of Leads/month by Computer Type

Number of Leads/month by Market Size

Legend numbers indicate market size, i.e., the
number of prospects

was able to generate over 50 percent of the leads for a significant number of companies.

In certain markets, display advertising may be the only option, and it can work very well. My feeling is that a mass market for a low-priced product is ideal for display advertising.

Direct Mail

A very significant number of companies generate no leads via direct mail. Most of the companies who use direct mail generate less than ten percent of their leads via direct mail. A moderate number generate up to 25 percent, but it really drops off above that. Direct mail is hard work and very few companies can push the numbers with direct mail to generate almost all of their leads. I guess I expected to see more than five percent of the companies generate over 50 percent of their leads with direct mail.

Dealers

Dealers are even more difficult and less popular than direct mail. Almost half the companies generate no leads via dealers, and no one generated over 50 percent of their leads via dealers. It is possible to generate ten percent of your leads with dealers, but you shouldn't expect much more.

23. Number of Leads by Market Size

The graph on the previous page (bottom) shows that there is some correlation between the size of the market and how many leads companies generate each month.

In small markets (fewer than 1,000 prospects) it is difficult to generate more than 250 leads, but almost 15 percent of the companies report this. I suspect that many of these companies are really operating in larger markets than they realize. See the article later in this issue on working with lists to determine how large your market really is. As you would expect, the percentage of firms generating more than 250 leads increases for larger markets. Over 20 percent of the companies with markets over 10,000 prospects generate more than 250 leads a month. Over half of the firms in these large markets generate more than 50 leads a month.

When companies are dealing with very small markets (fewer than 1,000 prospects), half of them generate less than 25 leads a month.

Even 25 leads a month is incredible penetration if you look at a yearly exposure. At this rate you might generate 300 leads which could be 30 percent of your available market. In this type of small market, building up your house list can be a real marketing strategy. I have seen cases where the mailing list has become a strategic asset for this type of company. Once you have the list, and the reputation with your market, you can sell additional products to your prospects.

The median number of monthly leads for the mid market (1,000 to 10,000 prospects) is 25 to 50 leads a month. It is 50 to 100 leads a month for the larger markets (over 10,000 prospects). Thus it appears that the median level of lead activity is doubling with an increase of five to ten in the size of the market. Thus companies with smaller markets are working their markets more intensively than companies with larger markets. In part, this is due to the fact that smaller markets are usually more focused and thus more receptive to a product designed for that small market. Thus, smaller markets should be more responsive in general than larger markets.

Because of this higher level of responsiveness and the limited size of narrow markets, it usually makes sense to market more intensively to these smaller markets. Thus, you might mail once a month or once every other month to everyone in your market if there are only 500 to 1,000 available prospects. On the other hand, if you have 100,000 names you might mail once a year to everyone. You might do this because the cost of mailing 100,000 pieces is high. Also, you might want to allow people to cool off so you get as good a response rate as possible.

With smaller markets, where you want to mail more frequently, it might make sense to buy names on disk for unlimited use. This may only cost 1.5 to 3 times the one time use fee so you can save money if you are mailing five to ten times a year. If you buy names and include them in your house list, don't forget to get the address corrections so that you can keep your list current.

24. Number of Leads by Computer Type

As you can see in the graph on the previous page, (top), PC companies generate a lot of leads. The median number of leads for PC companies is 25 to 50, but a surprising number (20 percent) generate over

250 leads a month. I think that this level of activity is due in part to the fact that PC companies are generally in larger markets since so many PCs have been installed.

This market size correlation may partly explain why PC companies generate so many leads, but I believe that it is also due to the higher level of competition and sophistication in the PC marketplace. Minicomputer software companies generate significantly fewer leads than the PC companies. Almost 70 percent of them generate 25 or fewer leads a month. This is probably due in part to the fact that many of the minicomputer software companies are in medium sized vertical markets (less than 10,000 prospects), but when you compare the minicomputer leads with the 1,000 to 10,000 prospect leads, you will see that the mini computer companies generate fewer leads.

I happen to believe that the real reason for the low level of lead activity with minicomputer software companies is that many of them were founded ten to fifteen years ago. They were reselling expensive hardware and the price of their software was almost as expensive.

It was common in that era for the typical hardware/software sale to be greater than $100,000 with over $50,000 in gross margin. With these numbers, you don't need a lot of volume to do quite well. The hardware vendors were also pretty good about working with their OEMs or VARs.

In the 80s when the PCs began to drive the price of minicomputer systems down, these OEMs began to experience severe pressure. Not only did the price of the hardware drop (along with the margins), but they began to get substantial price pressure from new PC software companies who were selling newer, sexier software at much lower prices.

Initially, the minicomputer companies were able to hold off the PC companies based on fundamental capabilities, but over time the PC companies enhanced their products so that they were better or equal to the minicomputer products. In the end, many of the minicomputer software product prices declined and the margins to these companies declined. I have seen a number of cases where this type of company has faced declining revenues and lower margins because of this price pressure.

The solution was to generate more leads and sell more units to maintain the same gross margin. This involves changing the company culture because generating a higher level of leads and sales is less personal and more by the numbers. This can be a very uncomfortable transition for a mature company, but without this change many of these minicomputer OEMs and VARs have quietly gone out of business.

The mainframe companies are similar to the minicomputer companies in that most of them generate fewer than 25 leads a month. This can be okay if you are selling a $20,000 product.

Let's assume that 20 percent of the leads will trial your product. (You only have 25 leads a month, so you can really work on them.) Therefore, you have five trials a month. With this level of activity, and an excellent product you might close 60 percent of the trials for three sales a month. This would generate $60,000 a month in new sales, and over time the annual sales might approach $1 million.

The other group of mainframe companies generate over 100 leads month (these are 25 percent of the software companies). These companies are the serious marketing companies who are generating leads for their sales people.

25. Primary Lead Source by Computer Type

The graph on the next page shows the frequency of using the most common lead sources as primary lead sources. I normalized these answers to the people who provided this information. Thus the most popular lead source is 100 percent. The PC companies tend to use most of the primary lead sources. Direct mail is the least used, but over 70 percent of the PC companies use direct mail.

I think that the references are less than 100 percent since a number of the companies are marketing new products which don't have an established reference base yet.

Trade shows are very high. I believe that this is due to the fact that there are so many trade shows. They range all the way from the Fall Comdex in Las Vegas to local shows with a retail slant.

The LAN companies are doing less than the PC companies, but they are following much the same pattern. I believe that the lower utilization for LAN

As the Primary Lead Source

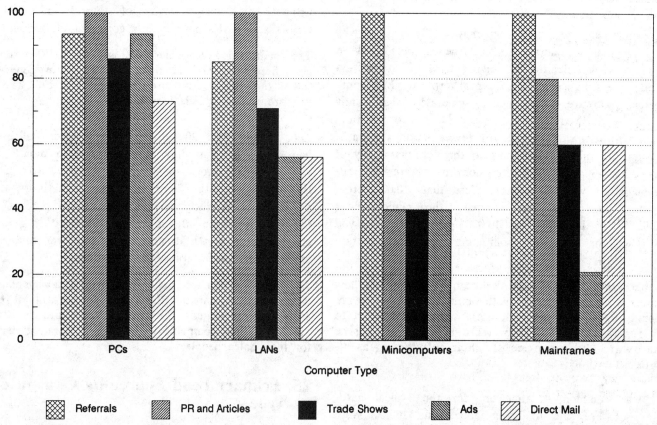

Percentage of Respondents

Computer Type

Referrals   PR and Articles   Trade Shows   Ads   Direct Mail

companies is due in large part to the fact that they are introducing new products so they haven't had the time or money to fully exploit the available alternatives.

The minicomputer companies are living off their installed bases. Less than 40 percent do anything other than generating leads via references. None of them used direct mail. While I am sure that few of them use direct mail, I believe that this showing was due to the small sample size of minicomputer companies who answered this question (ten).

The mainframe companies make very high use of references, and they make moderate use of PR/-Articles, Trade shows, and Direct Mail. I assume that most of the trade show attendance is at industry specific shows since their isn't an active mainframe trade show analogous to Comdex for the PC companies.

Display advertising was very low for the mainframe companies. This was lower than I would have guessed because there are several magazines which cater to MIS/DP companies which have moderately priced advertising.

E. Questions and Answers (1990)

1. Exploring New Ways to Utilize Mailing Lists

There are a number of reasons why your market may be larger than you think. The first is that even if there are only 1,000 companies that you can sell to, there might be four or five people in each of those companies who might buy your product. Thus, your market really is 4,000 to 5,000 prospects.

The next possibility is that you may be misled by the available lists. For example, in one market that a client was working with, there were a half dozen lists available. These lists each had 5,000 to 10,000 names. My client then assumed that his market was

Chapter II. Lead Generation

really 10,000 prospects maximum. (He also realized that there might be multiple people in each firm, but this is the first factor that we discussed.) My client was very comfortable with this assumption, but it was wrong.

We did a mailing where we merged/purged two of the lists. Much to our surprise, we found only a 15 percent overlap between the two lists. In other words, 15 percent of the names in the combined list of almost 20,000 names (or 3,000 names) were duplicates. The total raw names gathered from all available lists was close to 40,000. If 20 percent of these names are duplicates, my client still has 32,000 prospects which is much larger than he had ever thought.

The quality of this list is probably a little less than using the largest list because the merge/purge process will miss some true duplicates. The reasons for this include companies operating under different names and people with different spellings of their name. Modern merge/ purge software is pretty sophisticated, but I am sure that it will miss some of these invisible duplicates.

You might also assume that you are getting two names on average from the same company so that the 32,000 names really represent 16,000 companies. When you do the merge/purge you have to specify if you want to purge duplicate companies at any location, duplicate companies at the same location, or duplicate people at the same company.

My feeling is that if you can sell to more than one person within the company, that is that multiple people can make the buying decision, that you are better off to only eliminate duplicate people. This avoids people getting multiple copies of your mailing, which I find to be distressing.

Many lists will provide you with the "top guy" at the company or location. If you eliminate duplicate people you may send to the new CEO as well as to the former CEO, but I don't see what you can do about that type of problem.

I see a lot of companies and people who worry excessively about the quality of their mailing list. In many situations there are one or two lists which are clearly the best. These lists are the best maintained and so forth. Usually there are other lists available which aren't as clean as the primary lists.

Many companies shy away from using these lists because they feel that they aren't as good. They might not have the demographic data or company size that the primary list has. In other cases, the actual quality of the information may be lower.

It turns out that these secondary lists have one very powerful advantage, the people on them haven't been bombarded by everyone in your industry since the beginning of time. One factor that can reduce the responsiveness of the primary lists is the collective wear out effect. If you are on a primary list you might get 100 pieces of mail a week from vendors. This barrage of mail will certainly reduce your attention to any given mailing.

On the other hand, if you are in the same position, but you aren't on the primary list you might only get occasional mailings from the secondary lists.

I have seen a number of cases where mailings to these secondary lists out-pull the mailings to the primary lists. To be fair, I have also seen cases where apparently attractive secondary lists were a total disaster. Use discretion in testing additional lists, but please do test them.

If you have a mailing that makes money and you can triple the available lists, you can make more money by mailing more. You may decide to only double the rate of your mailings rather than triple it. This will allow you to reduce the overutilization of your best lists since you are mailing to the new lists in the intervening months. It may even increase the responsiveness of your primary list.

Another factor which might help your cost per lead is that with larger print runs, your unit cost for printing might drop significantly.

How big is your market? With a little research and testing, you may be surprised at the answer. You may also be quite pleased with the number of new leads you generate.

2. Impersonal Lead Generation

Dear Dave:

I sell a technical product to programmers, and I use classified ads to generate leads. Last year we were generating a lot of leads and I thought I would try using an 800 number to reduce some of the phone load. We identified the 800 number as information, and continued to list our regular number for technical information. We received a dramatic increase in the number of leads. It appears that a good number of people were intimidated by calling our number, and that the 800 number was less

intimidating. Whatever the reason, we got more calls. I just thought you would like to know.

Bob Winsor
General Programming

Dear Bob:

I was as surprised as you were by your increase in leads. I have worked with companies who implemented an 800 number because they wanted to facilitate off-hours calls. We thought that a 24-hour 800 number would generate additional leads on nights and weekends. We picked up another ten percent in leads which seemed to correspond to the off-hours calls.

I guess the lesson is that we have to figure out all the possible things that may be slowing our prospects down. Once we have the list of barriers, we have to work to lower them one by one. Your experience is an excellent example of an apparently minor change having a major effect. Thanks for the input.

Dave

3. Lead Pooling

The following article discussed the concept of "prospect pooling". This was the best description of a concept that I have been pushing for over the last years. The basic concept is to hit all names of all leads ("good, bad, and indifferent inquirers/requestors in one mishmash pool"). This is contrary to the conventional wisdom is that you should try to discriminate between the "good" and the "bad" leads. The problem is that "In a well-intended attempt to avoid spending promotional bucks on "bad" prospects, these nervous Nellie direct marketing advertisers also rid themselves of scads of "maybe" prospects."

Shell feels that you should mail to your prospect pool at least once every six weeks, and he feels that monthly will be even better. Time and time again, he stresses that you should keep it simple to hold down your costs and generate quality leads as cost effectively as possible.

He had an interesting approach to deciding when to stop mailing to a segment. When the segment's response is half the mean response he feels that it is time to stop mailing to the segment. He also suggests that you segment your leads by the age of the respondents. You might also might try including the source along with age.

One final note that he suggested was to take great care to purge duplicate names. Given the numbers game that you are playing, duplicate names can be expensive.

"In summary, the prospect pooling concept has worked wonders for a wide range of consumer and business mailers. It's not very difficult to get started. And the technique's immediate potential as a sales building tool justifies giving it at least a try." I agree, and would like to hear from those of you who have tried this.

Reference: "The Good, the Bad, and the Indifferent" By Shell R. Alpert, August 1990, Business Marketing.

4. Lead Follow-up

Why should we follow up on cold leads? Our sales people call all the good leads and work the hot ones. They don't feel that the others are worth the effort. Why do you keep harping on this?

As you point out, this is one of my sore points. I see companies spending a hundred dollars per lead or more, and they have their sales people skim the cream. The sales people view anyone who is about to buy as hot, and they lump all the others into cold category. I feel this is very wasteful.

My experience with my own marketing and that of my clients is that if you spend another $5 for ten follow-up letters, you might double your response. Thus, if I paid $100 for the first lead, the second lead would cost $5, which almost cuts the cost per lead in half. The concept is that the people who responded are much more likely to buy than the cold list and as such, they are much more worth cultivating. The debate over whether or not to follow up on these leads can become somewhat emotional.

5. Marketing to Multiple People in Large Organizations

We sell a product to large companies which has a major impact on operations. Initially, there are a number of people involved in the evaluation process. What is the best way to use direct mail in this situation?

The simple answer is to mail to anyone who could possibly care about your product. If you can get names for multiple players, you might just mail them all the same pitch. This works, even if it isn't very smart.

Chapter II. Lead Generation

The next step is to develop a sequence of letters which are personalized and refer to the other individuals in their organization. For example, you might mail the first letter to the plant manager and the second letter to the CFO. The second letter would mention that you had offered the plant manager a chance to cut costs by 20 percent and you thought the CFO might be interested in learning more about this solution.

The good news is that you can generate more activity by stirring things up. The bad news is that you will get calls from some of the people who are stirred up. If your sales people have the skills, many of these irate calls can be turned into sales. The plant manager got upset because there was a real need, and they didn't pursue it.

An article in Journal of Direct Marketing, Volume 3 Number 2, Spring 1989, entitled "A Method for Inducing Response Rates in Business-to-Business Direct Marketing Campaigns," by Mary Beth Pinto, investigates the effects of a combination of direct telephone interaction and mail survey methods for improving customer response rates. Furthermore, this article examines the role of a "significant other" in the organization and the impact of this individual's endorsement on the cooperation and response rate from multiple organizational members.

The first area they looked at was "snowballing." This is a procedure in which the researcher contacts one member of the organization and asks them to provide the names of others involved in the particular topic of interest. While I have seen this used to great effect once the prospect had requested information, I was surprised that it had been effective to call the CEO and ask for members of his management team involved in a topic.

The first step of this study was to call 122 hospitals to identify the key person and the project members who would be interested in the topic. The researchers were able to get 299 names from 73 of the hospitals.

They mailed 299 questionnaires and two reminder letters to individuals who hadn't responded. The reminder letters were also sent to the other project members. The final mailing included another copy of the questionnaire.

An amazing 85 percent of the organizations provided usable returns from all the project members!! The questionnaires were both mailed to the individuals and distributed by the key person. While the result wasn't dramatic, direct mail was more effective than having the person distribute the surveys.

The researchers felt that the quality of the contact person was responsible for the response rate. I was surprised at the effort required to make the initial phone contact. "In some cases, it required up to 14 telephone calls to initially reach the phone person." Even with this level of persistence, the researchers were unable to contact 26 percent of the key people. Once the contact was made, developing the rapport and identifying others seemed to proceed predictably.

I wonder where this approach would be justified given its combination of high up-front costs and incredible response rates. If you are dealing with a limited market and complex sales, it would be imperative that you get as much mileage out of each potential site as possible. If you have such a situation and you decide to test this approach, I would appreciate hearing how well it works.

6. Product on Evaluation

We get lots of requests to provide evaluation copies of our software. What should we do?

It is conventional to provide an evaluation copy of software. The exact format for the evaluation depends upon the price range, the hardware platform, the customer set, and the application type.

In mainframe software which is typically sold to Fortune 1000 companies, most vendors offer a free trial. They get the prospect to sign a trial agreement which protects the vendor's legal rights, and then send them a full version of the product. Trials typically are set at 30 days but often stretch into 60 and 90 days. The vendors are protected by both the legal agreement and the type of customer. I know of very few cases where Fortune 1000 companies steal mainframe software. It is just too visible.

With PC software to the Fortune 1000, you are talking many copies so that the dollar amounts of the sale are much like a mainframe sale. Typically the vendor provides a handful of copies for the evaluators. Sometimes these are provided through dealers and are marked, "evaluation copy not for resale". The tacit understanding is that the evaluators won't use the packages to do real work. If they end up with a real application, they will buy single copies even if their company decides not to purchase many copies.

The next level is selling to smaller companies. These companies are a bit more of a risk in that the money is more important to them, and there is less visibility. Sometimes, I have seen companies send evaluation copies, but they have insisted on the trial agreement being signed by an officer of the corporation. This increases the protection.

More often, the vendor visits the vendor and either demonstrates the software on their own PC which they take when they leave, or they install it on the customer machine. If they leave it on the customer machine, they need a trial agreement like the mainframe agreements. In many cases, the vendor returns and de-installs the software if the prospect decides not to become a customer.

Individuals are the most difficult situation. When you start dealing with small dollar amounts, it isn't economic for the vendor to sue the prospect for stealing the software. Individuals are also much more difficult to sue than companies. For these reasons, very few companies send evaluation copies to individuals. The only exception that I recall was sophisticated software for private investors which sold in the $5,000 to $10,000 range. I believe that it was the combination of a reasonable price, high net worth individuals, and the importance of their reputation to these individuals which made a difference in this case.

In most other cases, companies send either a screen display demo or a full demo with disabled functionality. The display demo allows you to see the screens. In many cases it is much like a brochure. I am unsure that it really works much better than a brochure, but some people have had good luck with this type of demo.

The full product with limited functionality, involves some risk to the vendor. If the customer is a hacker or has a hacker friend they can usually remove the limitations. I don't view this as a real issue. If people want to steal, they will. In the current world of no copy protection, they can make backup copies from a customer and copy the documentation. My real concern with this type of demo is the amount of time and energy for the prospect to really use the demo. It is very easy for the prospect to get confused and give up.

The challenge is to give the prospect the information they need to make the purchase decision. You are trying to lower their risk. A money back guarantee

is another way to do the same thing. I feel very strongly that you should offer a money back guarantee. If you provide on site installation and training this is more difficult, but you can't afford to have unhappy customers. My experience is that if you offer a customer a choice of their money back or to continue to work with you to solve the problem.

7. Choosing the Best Media

We use direct mail, card decks, display ads, and classified ads to generate leads. How should we compare the quality of these leads and determine which media is the best deal?

This is a real issue which is difficult to come up with black and white answers. The first point is that what you really want to know is your cost per sale by media. If you can track every sale back to the media which initiated the activity which resulted in the sale, you could have good hard numbers on which to base your decisions.

The first problem is that most of your prospects have been subjected to any number of lead generation messages. I recently received a call from a prospect who said that he had received 17 mailings from me over the years. (He had saved them all in a folder.) He finally had decided to subscribe to my newsletter. It is easy to argue that all of these mailings, ads and card decks should receive some credit for his sale. I can't deal with that. My rule is that the contact which finally pushes the prospect over the edge and causes them to respond gets the credit. "Winner takes all." This seems to be the only practical approach.

The next problem is that when people call in, some percentage of them don't know where they saw information about your product. Perhaps they made a note on a slip of paper. They just don't know. (There is always the chance that your sales/order takers didn't ask.) My thought is to prorate the unknowns over all of the programs. Thus, if half of your orders don't have a lead source, I would assume that all of the programs really generated twice as many sales as the basic numbers indicated. This assumption probably introduces some systematic biases since some lead programs make it very easy for the prospect to respond so that we know what they responded to.

Chapter II. Lead Generation

For example, direct mail which includes a coded order sheet and a reply envelope should generate a lot of leads/sales which are clearly attributed to that mailing. Display ads with a phone number and mailing address may generate more calls where the customer wrote down the address, but they can't remember where they learned about your product. If you are concerned about this issue, you might establish several unknown categories: unknown mailing, unknown card deck, really unknown, and so forth. This will reduce the probability of distortion.

If you have a reasonably short sales cycle, there isn't much elapsed time between the lead response and the sale. The prospect can recall (and you can find out) what caused them to respond.

If you have a long sales cycle (six months to a year), the prospect probably doesn't recall what they responded to. If you have a computerized lead and sales tracking system, your system should contain this information. On the other hand, if you still have a manual system you may have to dig out the folders, ask the sales people, and even call your customers to see if they can remember. This can be quite a bit of work if you can't instill the discipline to collect the information when the prospect first responds.

I have worked with clients who pull this information together manually once a year. It is a great deal of effort, but the results often prove to be surprising. In one recent case, we discovered a number of surprising findings.

The first was that over 40 percent of their sales came from current customers or references from customers. The second was that display advertising was prohibitively expensive on a cost-per-sale basis. The third was that card decks were two to three times better than direct mail on a cost per sale basis. Directories were five times better than card decks.

This information resolved a number of ongoing debates within the company. It is really nice how data can turn emotional discussions into productive decisions. We decided to dramatically increase our customer oriented promotion, cut back on display ads, and increase the card deck utilization.

Finally, I would urge you to strive for a balanced mix. Don't push the numbers to extreme. Display ads help reinforce your other marketing programs and reach people who don't get or read your direct mail or card decks. Use the cost-per-sale information to fine-tune your marketing programs, but don't become a slave to the numbers. Good luck.

8. Beyond Computer Magazines

How can I get to that 70 percent of computer users who don't subscribe to computer magazines?

I am assuming that your product is a vertical application. If you are selling a horizontal (general purpose) PC product, you have to advertise in PC magazines (which is very expensive) and you have to build a dealer network which is even more expensive.

I continue to be surprised at how hard it is to build a dealer network. I have a client who has one product which has sold over 20,000 copies. It retails for $99. It is also a very nice looking package. In spite of all of these factors, this company has only 400 dealers and they are still struggling to get into the major chains like Egghead, MicroAge, Computerland, etc. If it is this tough for this company, please don't underestimate how hard it is going to be to get an unknown product into distribution.

Back to the vertical market product. If you have a vertical product, there probably are magazines which cater to that market. In fact, my definition of a vertical market is a population with one or more good mailing lists and one or more magazines which address this market. (In fact, there are a number of vertical sub-markets which are 20 or 30 percent of the readers of certain magazines. For example, there is no magazine for all software companies. Most of the magazines cover a technology area and are read by both the vendors and the customers.)

If you have a tough-to-find market, the first approach is to test the available magazines, card decks and lists. Design your mailing to draw in responses to build your house list. The lack of a great list can be a two-edged sword. At first, it is tough because you are spending money to build your list rather than marketing your product. The good news is that once you have built your list and are known to this list, your list becomes a major strategic asset.

Once you have developed such a list you can look for other products which you might market to them. This is when you will get the real payoff from all your hard work and investment.

9. Lead Tracking Software

Dear Dave:

In your June 1989 issue you wrote some interesting comments on how few companies even track their cost per lead. This is true across the board, and we've found in our work with advertising agencies that very few of them (or their clients) do any real measurement.

So, in March of last year we began development on a desktop system which would "manage" direct response campaigns. We took some elements from FASTRACK, our agency traffic management system (which sells for $2,500), and joined forces with one of the top direct response firms in Atlanta to develop this system.

We've named it FASTRACK II and are releasing it this month (January 1990) for $495.

We like this program so well that we've been using it ourselves to track our own businesses. We enter every valid lead and even enter small costs, such as the cost of demo disk and postage for all the cells.

Also, we use our system to track income and costs on consulting work as well as on other software we produce and sell. The system allows us to set up separate campaigns for each product.

I think you will find this program extremely useful for your own business. It does project management (everything from scheduling the production and printing a brochure to scheduling a seminar). It does all of the key ratios for direct response management and advertising. Finally, it sets up and manages a database of all my good prospects and customers for follow up, sales, etc.

This may be the kind of program you would like to recommend to your clients. Our manual will be finished in several weeks, and we already have back orders for the new program as a result of word-of-mouth.

Tom Boylan
Senior Consultant
TBX, Inc
(404) 234-4260

Dear Tom:

Thanks for the package. I have to track my direct mail campaigns to market my newsletter and semi-

nars. I will try FASTRACK II and report on it in a later issue.

Thanks,
Dave

10. Converting Leads into Sales

We have finally mastered the art of generating leads on a consistent basis at a cost that we can afford. What can you suggest as far as a fulfillment package that will help us follow up with leads and convert them into demos/trials and then into sales?

Going from a lead to a sale consistently makes the difference between having a marginal business and having a great business. The first thing that you have to analyze is your sales cycle. The sales cycle is the typical decision path that most of your customers go through on their way to buy your product. What questions did they answer, and what information did they need at each point?

You should be able to come up with a good idea of your sales cycle by working with your sales and support people who work with prospects during the sales cycle. A simple example for a vertical market accounting system might include the following steps:

1. We are interested in automating our business.

2. We are willing/able to spend over $50,000 to do this.

3. This product can meet our needs technically.

4. We can see ourselves working with this product and doing our jobs.

5. We have negotiated a good deal.

Your lead generation material must produce people who are at least stage one. I have seen cases where the companies generate so many leads that they try to screen out the small budget prospects with the initial lead generation materials. They did this because they were swamped by low-end prospects who were looking for a $1,000 solution when their minimum package cost $20,000.

I would prefer not to actively discourage prospects at the lead generation stage. Rather than saying, "Don't call or write unless you are prepared to spend $20,000", I would prefer to say "Are you losing out to your competitors who have better profitability? Would you like to have a sophisticated financial control system which will help you improve your bottom line?" I have signaled that we are selling an expensive/sophisticated solution, but we haven't rubbed their nose in it.

The initial response package is probably the most important piece (after the lead generation materials) since they don't know a lot about your company. This is where you explain that you have a powerful and expensive system and that if they are willing to spend over $50,000 that you would be happy to sell them a demo for a minimal cost.

I tend to like to charge a fair cost for the demo package (2 times costs) to insure that we are qualifying the prospects if there isn't much direct sales contact with the prospect. If you have sales people working with the prospect at this stage, the sales people can insure that the prospect is really well qualified.

You may have noticed that I haven't talked about a fulfillment package yet. The reason is that you can start off and work with any one of a number of good systems, or you can actually do everything that you need with a simple database which allows you to select prospects and print labels. I would urge you to get one of the contact management packages and use it to generate follow up letters, and to support your sales people.

One of my pet crusades is to get companies to follow up aggressively with the leads that they generate. I have seen any number of cases where companies generate leads and send them one package, and never contact them again. They continue to mail to cold lists, and pull in fresh leads, but they are not exploiting the leads they have already paid for.

Most sales people will want to call all the leads. They feel that if they can just get on the phone with the prospect that they can sell them the demo and move them to the next stage. This is probably true (There are some prospects who will react badly to the pressure of the sales person on the phone at this stage), but it is almost impossible for sales people to allocate the time consistently to this early stage lead qualification.

In most cases, there is a much better payoff for the sales person to focus on customers who have bought the demo and who are deciding if your product is technically capable and then are trying to envision whether it can really solve their problems.

My experience is that if you can implement an automatic follow up program with your leads that you can double or triple the number of demos you produce per hundred leads. The economics are very compelling. You might spend $50 per lead or more to get the initial response. For another $5 I could send this prospect another 10 letters. If this second $5 doubled my number of demos, I have cut my cost per demo from $500 per demo (assuming that 10 percent of the leads buy the demo) to $275. Once they have raised their hand and expressed interest, you can afford to spend a significant amount of money to help push them to take the demo.

This is the area where a contact manager can really pay off. I like to set up a follow up program where the lead might get two letters a week apart, after they receive the initial lead response package. Then I like to have a monthly letter to all the leads who have responded in the last year. Part of this process is to stay in front of the prospects. These letters don't have to be a hard sell. They can be very effective if they just mention something new that you are doing and keep your name in front of the prospect. This will increase the odds that when the prospect decides to do something that they call you first.

If you don't have a sophisticated contact manager, you can implement this type of follow up program by printing multiple sets of labels at the initial point when you produce the first labels. I have clients who started out with 10 sets of labels and put them into folders. Thus they were able to start implementing a lead follow up program before they had the contact manager installed.

Once they got the contact manager, they got more sophisticated and sent personalized letters and automatically avoided sending follow up packages to people who had already proceeded to buy the demo. It is nice to get this type of sophistication, but don't let the lack of sophistication of a manual system keep you from implementing a basic follow up program this summer.

11. Telemarketing Service Bureau

Dear Dave:

We have worked with a Telemarketing Service Bureau (TMSB) , and we had a very bad experience. We found that we had to make a high time investment. The TMSB made no performance guaran-

tees. This made sales projections almost impossible. The TMSB took no responsibility for sales. Finally, they have high turnover, but they won't cover the cost of training new hires. All in all, we believe that your readers had little interest in TMSBs because they aren't effective for software companies.

No name given

Dear Reader:

I agree with your assessment that setting up a TMSB requires a high time investment. I believe that this is because you are developing your sales and marketing programs. You would have to develop these programs no matter what program you chose so you shouldn't really view this cost as unique.

The problem of responsibility for sales is difficult. In truth, no one really knows how well a new product will sell via a TMSB. You have the same risk when you hire sales people. Some TMSBs will accept partial payment as commission.

The turnover problem also exists when you hire your own sales people. The only issue is did the TMSB mismanage their employees. This is an area where I have seen that you get what you pay for. If you pay too little, you can get people who aren't as skilled as you need, and you can't retain the people who are good. I was involved with one product which took a little longer to get the scripts right and get the sales going. We met with the TMSB and the phone reps, and I decided to pay two of the reps an additional dollar per hour for a couple weeks to get them to stay with the program.

My experience with TMSBs is 60/40 favorable. My best experience was with a simple 800# order taking situation. I am sorry that your experience was so negative. I would like to hear from other readers who have worked with TMSBs. Thanks.

Dave

Another Perspective

As I was writing this issue, I read the following article on how to decide to build your own internal telemarketing organization or to buy the service from a TMSB. The article started with several user quotes:

A large printing company

"We have to stay in house." This firm has over 5,000 products and one change to a paper stock could affect 100 products.

A direct marketing advertising agency executive

"As long as a vendor demands and maintains professionalism of its staff, there's no reason not to use a service bureau." This individual wouldn't trust customer service to a service bureau.

A manufacturer in Georgia

Expertise - heavy applications - are probably best handled in house, but "other than that, doesn't everyone use service bureaus?..."

A food processing manager

"We do a little of both." They handle small and complicated projects in-house. They use vendors for roll-outs which will generate lots of volume.

A nutrition company

"We could use outsiders to handle our calls, but we don't. Our services are personal and sensitive."

The vendor's perspective

Dale Broekemeier, President and Chief Marketing Officer for Idelman Telemarketing, Inc. (ITI), in Omaha, Nebraska suggests that prospects answer the following questions:

1. **The level of telemarketing experience within the company. If your company has little telemarketing experience, a service bureau may be best.**

2. **The predictability of call volume. Seasonal or short term volume can be handled less expensively by a service bureau.**

3. **How fast the project must begin. Service bureaus can come on-line much quicker.**

4. **The corporate culture and how well it can deal with telesales. It might be best to prove that telesales can work using a service bureau.**

5. **Equipment, capacity and location. Getting set up can require a significant investment.**

6. The quality of personnel on the phones. If the application requires very well trained people, it may be best to do it internally.

7.   Costs and financial stability. Short term costs are lower with a service bureau.

The article also pointed out that there are two types of service agencies: "production oriented" companies and "customized service bureaus." The production agencies have hundreds, even thousands of reps and handle large volume accounts. The custom firms usually have 50 to 100 reps and are geared more to business-to-business   campaigns.

This distinction reminds me that when buying any service you should make sure that they have worked with accounts like yours on similar projects. Do your   homework.

Reference : "The Showdown: In House vs. Service Agency", By Carol Scovotti, TeleProfessional, Winter 1989.

Carol is President of LC&S Direct, a consulting firm specializing in direct marketing and telemarketing conception, design and implementation. Her address is 100 Cedar Street, Dobbs Ferry, NY 10522, (914) 693-2834.

F. Directories (1990)

1. Directory of Top Computer Executives

I have received requests for good lists of top computer executives. Computer Intelligence and Focus are the most common list providers for the IBM mainframe sites. Most of my clients who market to the IBM mainframe sites buy their lists from either Focus or CI, but they are too expensive for many startup   companies.

ACR publishes a directory with 11,000 mainframe sites and 35,000 executives. They offer a single edition for $250 for both east and west ($150 for one half only). They also have magnetic tape, mailing labels, custom directories, and prospect sheets.

Reference: Applied Computer Research, PO Box 9280, Phoenix, AZ 85068-9984, 1-800-234-2227, FAX (602) 995-0905.

2. Prospecting Directories

If you sell directly to businesses instead of to MIS departments, you might find the following prospecting directories useful. They have state and regional directories for manufacturers, as well as services and distributors. The books are $59 to $200, and they also make their lists available on diskettes, mag tapes, etc. They have the name of the CEO.

Reference : Manufacturers' News, Inc., 4 East Huron Street, Chicago, IL 60611, (312) 337-1084.

Leadership   Names

Monitor Publishing sells a series of directories:

* **Corporate America**
* **US Financial Institutions**
* **International Companies**
* **Canadian Businesses**
* **Congress**
* **Federal Agencies**
* **State Governments**
* **News Media Organizations**

The directories are $100.

Reference: Monitor Publishing, 104 Fifth Ave. 2nd Fl, New York, NY 10011, (212) 627-4140, FAX (212) 645-0931.

3. Another Computer Installation Book

IDG has announced the Installed Technology worldwide database of 160,000 computer installations. According to their ad in Varbusiness they have information on hardware installed, software, decision makers, as well as purchase plans. They offer a free guide.

Reference: Installed Technology International, an IDG Database Company, Five Speen Street, Framingham, MA 01701, (800) 347-3484.

4. Macintosh Market Report

If you are in the Macintosh market, this report might be invaluable. It covers:

Market Stats
Apple Financials
Top 200 Advertisers
Advertising   Analysis
Ads in Non-Mac Pubs
Product Review Index

It is published ten times a year and costs $185/year.

Referenc: Macintosh Market Report, (714) 756-1319.

5. Microleads Vendor Directory

They have 11,000 companies in the current edition. Listings are free.

Michael J. Shipp
President
Chromatic Communications, Enterprises, Inc.
PO Box 30127
Walnut Creek, CA 94598
(415) 945-1602

6. Sourcebook

This is a 189 page book which includes publishers, development groups, programmers, game designers, graphic artists, publications, software tools, and other products and services. To list your company:

Infinite Automata, Inc.
3305 W. Spring Mountain Rd, Suite 60
Las Vegas, NV 89102

7. SCOUT Mid-Range Software Directory

Lists over 11,000 applications and 1,400 vendors. SCOUT focuses on software for IBM's mid-range systems: System/36, System/38, and AS/400.

Software Press
4391 Sunset Blvd, Suite 290
Los Angeles, CA 90029
(818) 785-3585

Dear Dave:

We have found that the best general business directory is from Trinet (Contacts Influential). More specialized directories depend upon the industry.

L. Taylor
Abacus Data Systems

Dear L. Taylor:

Thanks for the information. I use Trinet via Dialog, but I believe that it is available on Lexus or Nexus at your local library. Even though these on-line services aren't cheap, they make an awesome amount of information readily available.

Dave

8. List Quality

Dear Dave:

I enjoy reading Software Success, even though there is nothing for me to digest for Data Processing Digest. I share it with my business manager in Los Angeles, and we have found some very helpful ideas in it.

Marketing software is quite different in many ways from marketing a publication, as you no doubt know. But if software vendors use mailing lists as we do, they must be getting ripped off as we are if we aren't careful. I am wondering if you are aware of and have done any research on the state of mailing lists.

The only comparatively clean lists are those of careful publishers who value the accuracy of their subscriber addresses. Gisela Wermke, my above-mentioned business manager, has been examining mailing lists she has exchanged with or rented for the past several months. She was able to reject one foreign list she has purchased from a reliable broker because when she told him the state of the list he was mortified and asked her to send it to him so he could see it and chew out the owner. I don't believe either compilers, renters, sellers, our users look at the lists they are dealing with, or they would not allow such garbage to circulate in the market. We have been hard put to find lists that are clean enough that we would not be losing thousands of dollars in postage and printed materials if we sent them out. I am thinking of writing to the Direct Mail Association about it. It has become a scam and a scandal,

Margaret Milligan
Editor/Publisher
Data Processing Digest, Inc.

Dear Margaret:

Thanks for the letter. The quality of lists that you use are critical to the success of your mailings. I be-

Chapter II. Lead Generation

lieve that this is the fundamental reason that prospect pooling works so well. The best list that you will ever have is the people who have responded to your marketing.

I have looked at mailing lists that I have been using, and in several cases I have been appalled by the qualitative quality of some of the lists. I feel that you can use this flinch test to eliminate the really poor lists, but I would be reluctant to reject tests because I don't like the quality of the list. I have had several clients who have gotten good results from apparently poor lists. It appeared that this was due to the fact that these lists hadn't been worked as actively by marketing companies.

I find that many times aesthetic preferences don't work out in direct marketing. I often have clients who feel very strongly that they only want to send out personalized letters on very nice letterhead with first class postage. They believe that cutting corners will be disastrous to their results.

I have found that it is very important to test these assumptions. I read an article in Marketing Computers which discussed the two schools of marketing. John Adams described the direct marketing school analysts as followers of B.F. Skinner while the ad agency account executives as the disciples of Sigmund Freud.

The Freudian view is "that it takes a long time to develop positive feelings and brand name recognition. Just because we don't know what happened doesn't mean that the ad didn't work." "Skinner's marketing behaviorist would quantify the most effective ad strategy based on some immediately measurable criteria. For the Skinnerians, a postage stamp ad that delivered one sale for $20 would have measurably outperformed a four color ad that delivered ten sales at a cost of $2,000 (at $200 each). Forget image, Skinner, the direct mail marketer would say."

Refrence: "Skinner and Freud Return - As Marketers", By John Adams, Marketing Computers July 1990.

I am very much in the Skinner camp even though the image of torturing poor little rats makes me cringe. I believe that small companies need the immediate results and the immediate sales. I have watched too many companies wait for their ship to come in from image ads. I guess that one of the rea-

sons that I make the distinction between lead generation and promotion is that I feel that companies must start by generating hard leads that can turn into sales. At the same time, they should begin to set aside some of their budget for long term awareness. Press releases, articles, etc can have very good long term benefits, and they aren't real expensive in the short term.

One final thought that I have on the list quality issue is to ask the list provider about the non deliverable rate. This is a number they should know. The Skinner analyst in me really dislikes spending money mailing packages that end up in the garbage. Since most direct mail programs are sent third class mail, you usually don't have a clue about the non deliverable rate.

There are two things that you can do (other than mailing first class). The first is to put address correction requested on your envelope. This will get you some of the address corrections and the non deliverables, but you have to pay for the return postage. I do this with my mailings for lists that I have purchased for multiple usage.

Another approach is to send a double post card mailing to the lists that you are considering. You can send a double post card first class for only $0.15. First class address correction is better than third class with "address correction requested" because the post office views the third class address correction as somewhat optional. They try to do it, but it might take a year or more for them to process the correction. I did this with a number of lists that I was considering. The results were astounding. The non deliverable rate ranged from 20 percent to 0.2 percent (that is right, a factor of 100 difference). I turned out that the worst list was only slightly worse than the best list on a cost per lead, but the poor quality of the list did dramatically lower the return from my mailing.

I felt very good about taking these results an asking the list vendors for refunds, or credits for the non deliverables. I gave them my returned post cards so that they could update their files. I would be interested in other experiences with the quality of lists.

G. Getting the Mail Through (1990)

1. Corporate Mailrooms

The July 9, 1990 issue of Postal World [(301) 961-8777] had a very interesting article about a catalog mailer who did a survey of corporate mailrooms about their internal/incoming mail policies. They asked the following questions:

1. **Do you treat 1st class mail differently than 3rd class mail?**
   _ **We process incoming 1st class mail only.**
   _ **We process all incoming mail the same way.**
   _ **First class mail gets priority over 3rd class.**

2. **Do you use internal delivery codes or mail stops?**
   _ **Yes! We require them for delivery of mail.**
   _ **We prefer them on incoming mail, but they aren't required.**
   _ **We don't use them.**

3. **Would you help us update our list if we call you/send it to you?**
   _ **Sure! Give me a call!**
   _ **Sure! Mail me your list!**
   _ **I prefer not to.**

4. **What happens to third class mail that's title addressed (such as "purchasing agent") with no real name?**

5. **What happens to third class mail that's addressed to someone who is no longer with the company?**

6. **If several third class pieces, such as catalogs, all arrive in a single parcel, will you open the parcel, and distribute the contents at the sender's request?**

7. **Is your company a:**
   _ **Manufacturer**
   _ **Non-Manufacturer**

8. **Please attach your business card or fill in the information below.**

(I have found that your response improves if you can mail merge some or all of the information.)

The company which did this survey found that "No one has turned down a request for mailstop codes or internal updates."

The 20 percent of companies who don't even try to deliver title addressed mail could put a crimp in any mailing without titles.

Overall, I was impressed at how few companies are discriminating against third class mail at this point. There are a number of studies showing that the post office fails to deliver 15 percent or more of the third class mail even if it is correctly addressed. This is a much greater factor than the mail rooms at this point in time if you are marketing to smaller companies. In larger companies, their refusal to deliver third class mail is increasing significantly. I would suspect that there is even more non delivery of third class in companies where it isn't the formal policy, but it is okay to trash the third class "junk" mail.

It is very clear that mailstops are mandatory in large companies. If you are mailing lots of pieces to one organization, you might try contacting the mailroom supervisors. I have talked to companies who have mailed their lists to companies, and the companies looked up the mailstops for paid magazine subscribers.

If you only mail one or two pieces to large organizations, this could get expensive. You might consider mailing a double post card asking your prospect to correct the mailstop. If that fails, you could call and get the mailstop. I would be very interested in any results in this area.

2. Testing Response Rates

There was a recent article in What's Working that suggested that mailroom employees and secretaries were trying to screen out laser printed personalized letters by running a finger over the envelope. If it is smooth it was printed on a laser and thus wasn't really personalized.

Oster Communications, Inc., printed 70,000 letters with real typewriters as part of their launch of a controlled circulation magazine called "Corporate Risk Management." They got a 9.1 percent response rate which is very good.

The envelopes were printed by a bank of 22 computer-driven typewriters. "The printing program included address explosion, punctuation, and genderization so that the personal effect wasn't blown by telltale 'computer-ese.'"

They also tested live first class stamps and pre-canceled bulk mail stamps and found no difference in either delivery time or response. It appeared that both the USPS and the mailrooms treated the pre-canceled bulk mail stamps as first class.

The same agency used the same technique for a farm-oriented advisory newsletter and found the higher costs brought no improvement in results. Your basic corn and soybean grower doesn't have the same gatekeepers as CEOs, CFOs, and Corporate Treasurers.

Reference : "Back to the Future - with Typewriter Personalization", What's Working, November 1989.

3. How IBM Handled Misaddressed Mail

The following article discussed how IBM dealt with misaddressed mail at its Boulder campus where they have 5,000 employees. Every correction had to be looked up through an on-line system.

Given the volume of mail, they decided to approach the problem by the type of mail. Internal mail was a major source of misaddressed mail. They solved this by updating the internal directory every six weeks instead of every six months. They contacted the 51 magazines who were sending misaddressed mail and 31 sent their subscriber lists so that they could

be updated. This project saved over 300 manhours a month.

Reference : "101 Mailroom Tips, Tactics, and Techniques", Postal World, (301) 961-8700.

If you are mailing to corporations, this is the type of operation that you are dealing with. I found it interesting that the mailroom people didn't even discuss bulk mail. Given the fact that they are spending 300+ hours correcting addresses, I can easily see them trashing any bulk mail which isn't easy to deliver. They aren't being malicious, just busy.

The January 22, 1990 issue of Postal World had an article which said that SUN announced a policy that no more third class mail would be delivered without a mailstop after November 1989. They estimate that this will save SUN $11,300 in the first year.

The volume of third class mail was 271,220 in a recent year, most of it with no mailstop.

4. Getting Past the Federal Mailroom - Tips for Mailing to Governmental Agencies

The following list are tips from the **Association of Mailers to the Federal Government (AMFG)**:

* **Always go first class.**

	Small Co < 2,500 employees	Large Co > 2,500 empl
Deliver 1C mail only	3%	10%
Give 1C preference	10%	35%
No difference	87%	55%
Trash title addressed	20%	20%
Attempt to deliver title addressed mail	80%	80%
Require mailstops	7%	25%
Prefer mailstops	12%	45%

* Make sure you use the agency accepted acronyms. For example, the Bureau of Land Management is LLM, not BLM!

* Make sure you use the federal zip code (this is different than the non-federal address next door.)

* Use mailstops. Title slugs are useless.

* Forget the bells and whistles.

* Be careful with FREE BONUS offers. Offers greater than $5 are taken as a bribe and could get you on a federal blacklist for a couple years.

What's Working
September 24, 1990

AMFG
Mark Amtower
PO Box 339, Ashton, MD 20861
(301) 924-0058

5. Another Promo List

Nufax Demographics has lists of new software users, shareware users, computer buyers & sellers, computer magazine editors, and so forth. For more information:

Nufax
131 Kent Ave, Suite A
Kentfield, CA 94904
(415) 488-4760

6. Poor Quality Mailing Lists

Dear Dave:

I was surprised to see my letter about poor quality mailing lists in your August issue, but pleased, too, as it may cause others to consider the problem I raised.

I realized, however, that I had not been explicit enough in my complaints. It appeared that I was complaining about the customer value of the lists - that is, how many responses we would get. What I am complaining about is the totally erroneous information in so many of the labels, particularly those in foreign lists.

The persons hired to key the original information into computer systems seem to be both sloppy and ignorant, and obviously they are unchecked for ac-

curacy. It appears that many lists are typed from cards hastily filled out by conference attendees. They must be entered by untrained typists who are ignorant of geography, and the fact that the computer cuts off an address line arbitrarily when it reaches the end of the allotted number of spaces.

We have found that Quito is in Sweden and Budapest in Oman. We find street addresses such as: Boulevard de la.... chopped off by the digit restriction. We have also found foreign lists filled with irrelevant businesses such as shoemakers and hairdressers — apparently padded to fill out the required number of names with random selections from a telephone book.

These are the kinds of rip-offs which concern me. As many as two-thirds of foreign lists (even one from the U.S. Department of Commerce) have been filled with such garbage. It is obvious that those who are marketing the lists have not checked the quality of the product they are selling. Nor is the list compiler being responsible in checking the accuracy of his product.

This is the scam and scandal I deplore. Anyone using a marketing list should check it out thoroughly and demand his money back if it doesn't come up to a reasonable accuracy level.

Sincerely,

Margaret Milligan
Editor/Publisher
Data Processing Digest

Dear Margaret:

Thanks for the clarification. I agree that the type of practices you are describing are deplorable. Anyone using foreign lists should heed your warnings and check the lists before they mail.

Sincerely,
Dave

7. Two-Tiered Telemarketing

We are considering using a two-tiered telemarketing approach with a qualifier and closer. The closer would have more technical and sales skills. Our product costs $5,000. What do you think?

This approach can be managed a number of different ways. The basic idea is to use the qualifier to leverage the more senior sales person. I believe that this is basically sound. The challenge is to manage it effectively.

The simplest way is to have the qualifier be an administrative person who is paid by the hour. Part of their job is to make calls and ask qualifying questions. This can be done with no sales commission and you can get the basic questions asked. With this approach, the telemarketer isn't motivated to answer questions or to sell (even very low key). While this isn't fancy, it might be a good way to start.

The next stage is where you want the qualifier to help push the prospect to the next stage in the sales cycle. "Would you like to talk to our sales rep about scheduling a visit?" If there is an observable event that the rep is contributing to, it might be wise to pay them a small bonus. A reward of $25 per visit scheduled could be a significant motivator if they could get an additional couple of hundred dollars a month. I tend to believe that the qualifier should be paid this bonus even if the senior sales rep has to close on the visit. If the qualifier only gets paid if they schedule the visit, they will be motivated to push as hard as possible to close the sale, and they may waste some leads that the combined team might have sold.

This simple bonus works well if there is a well-defined handoff. The qualifier works the leads until they are scheduled for a visit, and after that the senior sales rep runs with the ball.

The more complicated situation is where the technical sales person works with the senior sales person all the way through the sale. The classical case is the IBM SE who was a technical person who supported the sales person. The IBM model was that the SE had a bonus based on the success of their sales person or their office. This bonus was small (five to ten percent) and was on top of a good salary. It was the icing on the cake. This can be very effective if the SE can off-load significant time from the sales person and allow them to increase their sales. I worry that the natural laziness of sales people tempts them to slack off after the SE starts to pick up their work. I would insist that the sales people sign up for a higher quota if you provide them with an SE.

8. Inquiry Handling Service (IHS)

IHS hired an independent market research firm to survey 20,000 leads from 23 business-to-business companies. The key finding, as disclosed in "Prospects Stay Interested Six Months," by Sue Kapp, published in Business Marketing, was that 56 percent of the respondents were still in the market for the product or service they inquired about six months earlier...33 percent of the respondents who requested literature still had money budgeted to buy the product. Where could you find a better list?

The study had a number of other interesting findings:

* **91% of the people remembered requesting the information.**

* **86% recalled receiving it.**

* **39% had been contacted by a sales rep.**

* **16% contacted the company themselves.**

Thus, there is good evidence that leads are still good prospects and that if you don't follow up, your competitors will.

9. Personalized Cartoons

We have had several articles in the last few months about getting your mail past the mailroom. "Results of this Promotion are No Laughing Matter" from What's Working, is about using personalized cartoons on the outside of the envelope. WX Wordtronics, a printer and mailshop, mailed 10,000 letters and generated 900 leads. The cartoon and mailing were created by Stu Heinecke & Partners.

This is an interesting twist. Much of the advice of getting past the mailroom is to look more like business correspondence. In this case, they looked like cute promotional mail and got a very good response.

They are cooking up a "Project X," which will offer marketers a bank of cartoons that can be used to reach a variety of audiences. Unit cost for a 20,000 mailing will be less than $1, plus postage.

Howard Stone
WX Wordtronics
(201) 956-5600

Stu Heinecke
Stu Heinecke & Partners
(213) 273-8985

10. Media Selection

Dear Dave,

In the August issue of Software Success, you addressed a question concerning media selection for

marketing and how to determine which media is bringing in the most (or the best) leads. One of the biggest problems with the analysis of media success which you discussed is that prospects don't remember where they read about or saw the product, and so there is a significant number of leads resulting from "unknown" sources. This requires, therefore, that an "unknown" category be included when marketing analysis statistics are generated.

I am the President of Hamilton Software Inc., a company which develops and sells investment and financial software. We have successfully used a common technique to trace leads back to specific ads which I thought would be worth mentioning. We incorporate a specific ad identifier into our company address; for example, if we run an ad in two publications, we would list our address as Hamilton Software Dept. A, and so forth, in one of the ads, and Hamilton Software, Dept. B in the other. Prospects will not write down where they saw the ad, but they almost always write down our address, so this information is obtainable even if they contact us by phone. If they write to us, of course, the information is on the front of the letter.

This technique isn't foolproof, but it's easy and works well with all kinds of media.

Sincerely,

Scott Hamilton
Hamilton Software

Dear Scott,

I like your approach. It is simple, and it sure looks like it would work well. Another idea that I recently had was to take the 800 number extension idea and just apply it to my regular phone number. As I am

sure you know, many 800 numbers have extensions, since more than one company shares the 800 number. People will write down the extension number

because they think they need it to make the connection. You could put extensions on your non-800 number. The concept is the same as your "Dept X" idea.

Thanks,
Dave

H. General (1989)

1. Definition

Lead Generation is the process of identifying serious prospects for your product who are worth a sales effort. In theory, if you had endless resources you could have a sales person ask everyone in the world if they would like to buy your product. While this sounds very far fetched, we have seen a number of companies who viewed their lead generation in this light. They had very expensive approaches to lead generation. Often their lead generation costs were greater than their gross margin from their sales. Rather than viewing their problem as inefficient lead generation, they viewed it as inadequate capital. In fact, additional capital wouldn't have solved their problem, it would just have postponed it.

Another important point: lead generation doesn't include company promotion. As you may recall from the January 1989 issue, promotion includes the corporate and product visibility efforts which aren't directly targeted to get prospects to respond. This isn't meant to imply that promotion isn't good, it just isn't lead generation.

2. Successful Lead Generation

As with any other business endeavor, you need a plan to successfully and cost-effectively generate enough leads to keep your company going and growing. We recommend the following steps:

First Step — Identify Your Market

The first step in lead generation is to identify the target market. Who is going to buy this product, and why? In our consulting practice, for example, we define our target market as those companies who have two attributes:
1. Looking For Help — We serve Software companies who are looking for outside marketing and business advice.
2. Can afford to Pay — The ability to pay is just as important as possessing the basic need.

Second Step— Find the Hot Button

The second step is to identify your customers reason for buying — the hot button. Why will they want to buy your product? What are the benefits from your customer's point of view? Note that we are talking about benefits here, not features. Many technically-oriented software people use product features instead of benefits at this stage and thereby miss finding the real hot button.

Third Step — Get the Message Out

The third step is to get your message to your target market in a way that will encourage them to respond. You will actually generate the lead with this step. A critical aspect of this step is to define the sales cycle. Do you want the prospect to request information, buy a demo disk, or buy the product? You must clearly understand your sales cycle and know exactly what you want your prospect to do.

3. Healing the Rift Between Marketing & Sales

The task of generating a lead, typically the domain of the Marketing Department, is complete once the prospect has been turned over to someone from Sales. This makes it easy for Marketing to wash their hands of the responsibility for converting leads into sales. This is a major problem in many firms. Sales isn't organized to systematically follow up on leads (they are too busy selling) and Marketing isn't motivated to stay involved (they are busy generating more new leads). This split motivates marketing to generate more less qualified leads and motivates sales to demand a few really good leads (like the Marines). The problem gets worse when the Sales Department won't (or more likely, can't) track the lead source for prospects that ultimately become sales.

There are several things that you can do to remedy this situation:
1. Technical Solution — The first is technical: implement a computerized lead tracking system.
2. Administrative Solution — Institute an administrative procedure whereby your people can't send a demo or trial package unless the source of the lead is correctly identified.
3. Cooperative Solution — Convince the sales people that identifying the best lead generation approach is critical to their personal success.

Lead Tracking Systems

There are a number of good systems which will automate your lead tracking and follow up. This will allow you to track the information once the lead source is entered. The challenge in this case is to motivate your sales force to identify the lead source.

Administrative Solution

An administrative solution is to institute a procedure that your administrative people can't send out a demo or trial system unless the lead source is entered. This can only be overridden with top management approval. This simple policy will insure that a lead source is entered for every demo or trial, but it doesn't guarantee that the sales people will make a serious effort to provide the correct lead source. As long as they view this as an administrative effort, they won't give it their full attention.

Creating cooperation

The best approach is to convince the sales people that identifying the best lead generation approach is critical to their personal success. When we consult for software companies with this type of problem, we approach this by telling the sales people that they have a budget of $X/month for lead generation. (If their quota is $50K/month, give them a 10% — or $5K — as a budget.) Next we typically talk about how they might spend their budget. For example, they might run one $5K ad and get 10 leads, or they might send 5K letters and get 50 responses, or have 5 card decks and get 100 responses, etc.

If you only know the cost per lead, you can't really create an optimal marketing mix. For example, advertising might produce the most business per marketing dollar because it produces the best qualified leads. We can only know this if the sales person tracks the lead source for the trials. We usually make the assumption that the conversion of trials into sales is independent of the lead source. That is that once a prospect has agreed to trial or demo your product, that they are serious. You might check this assumption to see if your win rate is dramatically different by lead source. As you can see, this involves a great deal of work, but the results are worth it.

The purpose of this whole exercise is to find out the best way to reduce the amount of selling that your sales force has to do. Producing more and better leads make it easier for the sales force to close a given amount of business. Once your sales people see this they will aggressively support your lead generation efforts.

Lead Sources

Q. We are trying to track our cost per lead, but we are having problems tracking our lead source for phone in or write in leads. Any suggestions?

A. This is a very common problem. Fundamentally, it is difficult because you are asking people to go out of their way and get the additional information for a very long-term reward. In many cases we have seen a significant improvement by reporting what the unknown rate is. If you provide a monthly report on lead tracking, and include the percent of unknown leads by sales person, the sales person won't like to have poor numbers.

There is another, more punative way to solve the problem: Generate a policy where information is not sent out without knowing the lead source. Before you implement this policy, make sure that you really mean it. There will be leads who don't know where they got the information from, but they may still be a good prospect. Our experience is that while this type of information is difficult to gather, you can dramatically improve the results over time. There is nothing like a graph by sales person over time to get their competitive juices flowing.

4. Processing the Leads

One common problem with companies who are trying to systematically generate leads for the first time is that they aren't prepared to process the leads. As the leads come in, singly and in groups, they are handled uniquely and are individually processed. Response letters are written and rewritten by each sales person, calls are exchanged and the needed responses simply stack up. While this may look like loving care for those few leads that get a response, for many others there is no response at all

All of this individual attention and effort results in very few sales and lots of negative feelings about all the effort that was expended. We believe that the poor results are due to the fact that the software company didn't take a consistent and holistic approach to closing the sale. If you are developing and redeveloping each piece, they can't work consistently together. The second problem with the ad hoc approach is that it isn't timely. It takes time and energy to redevelop the follow up pieces. Your prospects cool off and react negatively when they are contacted months later.

Developing a Marketing Production Line

Rather than a project-oriented, ad hoc approach, we believe that it is much more effective to develop a direct marketing production line. If you have the letters "in the computer", your administrative group can send them out on a predetermined schedule. Administration makes schedules, and marketing and management don't.

If you can develop a steady stream of prospects moving through the sales cycle, you will avoid overloading any group within your company. This will be much more effective. You are making the move from the specialty job shop to a production line with the resulting efficiencies. Another benefit of the production line is that you must standardize the steps which insure more consistent quality

There are some very real pressures to print all of your letters at one time because of the economies of scale in printing, but you might choose to stagger the time when you actually mail your batches to facilitate processing the leads. Depending upon your mailings you might be able to print one mailing every month or two, and then spread the mailings. If you also generate leads from advertising or card decks you should take this into account when you time your mailings.

Measuring Progress

One thing that we have found very effective to implement this type of thinking is to track the number of prospects every week or month for each stage in the sales cycle. For example, we usually measure the following items:

* How many mailings or advertising exposures?
* How many leads?
* How many demo disks sold?
* How many follow up letters sent?
* How many systems sold?

If you display these statistics in a visible location, everyone will begin to think in these terms and they will find ways to make the production line more efficient.

5. ARENS Lead Generation Example

Arens is a Software Success subscriber that publishes Presentation Graphics software. They also do a very good job of tracking their cost per lead. They created the graph shown on the next page to help them measure the effectiveness of their various lead generation options.

When graphed this way, it is very easy to look at the effectiveness within the groups: Shows, BRCs (Business Reply Cards) and Ads. It is also interesting to compare the effectiveness of the three groups. The median cost for the BRCs are the lowest, and the shows are second. There are a couple shows that appear out of line. Given the fact that you can only put so much money into any one channel, we could easily justify using both BRCs and trade shows.

Analysis

The cost per lead for advertising is five to ten times higher than the other methods. This is a lot more difficult to justify. *This is a case where tracking the lead to purchase ratios are critical.* If 10% of the advertising leads buy, for instance, the lead generation cost per sale would be $2K which is quite high for their product (which sells for $3K to $10K). If 1/3 of the advertising leads buy Arens software, however, the cost per sale drops to $450. That number is quite acceptable.

Our a priori objective is to hold lead generation costs to 10 to 15% of revenue. This isn't possible with a 10% conversion ratio for the advertising. BRCs with a $30 cost per lead would have a $300 cost per sale with a 10% conversion which would be quite acceptable.

REFERENCE : PRESENTATION GRAPHICS BY ARENS; (301)258-0970

6. Let Tactics Dictate Your Strategy

Al Reis and Jack Trout have written a very interesting book, Bottom-Up Marketing. We really liked it because it matched so many of our experiences.

Reis and Trout argue that instead of strategy dictating the tactics, that companies should use their tactical success to influence the strategy. They suggest that this approach will avoid committing "one of the two cardinal sins of business: (1) the refusal to accept failure and (2) the reluctance to exploit success." If you stick to top down thinking, you tend to overlook any factors that don't fit your preconceptions.

Their definition of tactics is also interesting: "A tactic is a competitive mental angle." It is differentiating

Reference: Presentation Graphics by Arens

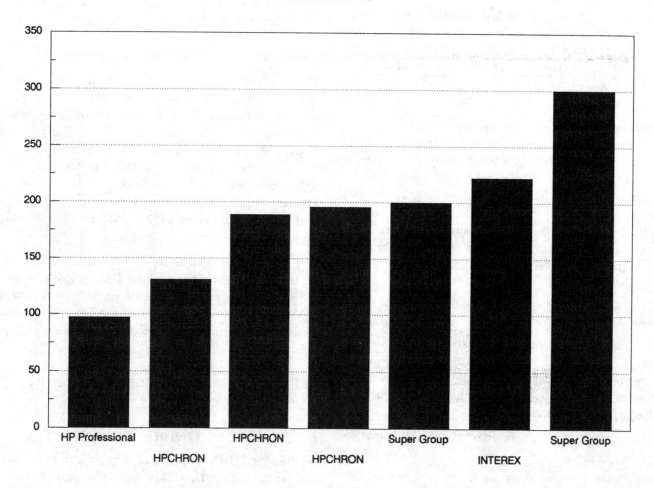

Lead Generation: Ads

Reference: Presentation Graphics by Arens

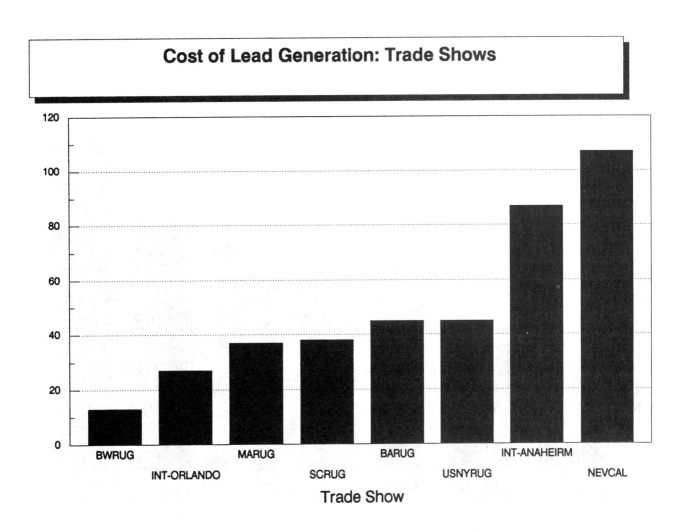

Reference: Presentation Graphics by Arens

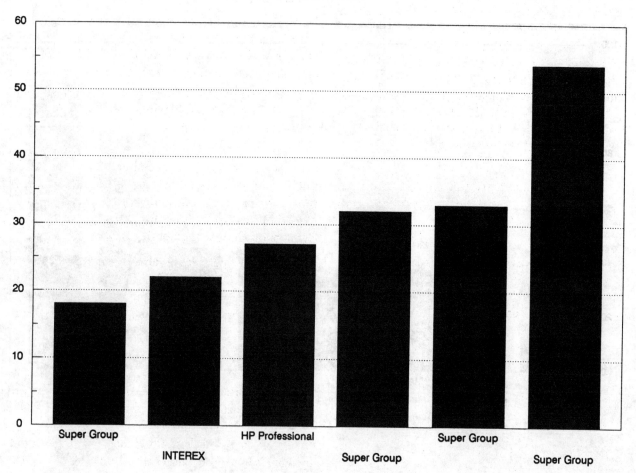

Chapter II. Lead Generation

your product by establishing a new product positioning.

Their definition of strategy is: "a coherent marketing direction". In their thinking, you use the strategy to focus your tactics in a particular direction so they reinforce each other. Their new twist is to find the tactics which work and then build it into a coherent strategy. If you find that different tactics work better, use this to adjust your strategic focus. This is an exploitative approach that can work very well for smaller companies.

In the course of our consulting, we deal with many companies which have good products and adequate sales but no strategic direction. Rather than philosophizing about the best strategy, we analyze where they have been getting their sales. We find out which tactics have been working. When we complete this analysis we know that we are working with proven winners. Then we proceed to build a strategy that reinforces these already-working tactics.

At the same time, once you generalize your experience into a strategy, you may learn some lessons and identify some new tactics you hadn't identified.

We have a client who sells a retail system that they were much more successful selling to companies with two locations. These firms were also much more likely to have had a pre-existing computer system. These insights resulted in two tactics:

1. Go after **two-location companies**
2. Focus on **prospects who have some computer history.**

This increased the effectiveness of their marketing programs and increased their awareness of their market position.

REFERENCE: Let Tactics dictate your strategy **Sales & Marketing Management**, December 1988, reprinted by permission of McGraw-Hill Book Company from **Bottom-up Marketing** by Al Reis and Jack Trout copyright 1988 by McGraw-Hill, Inc.

7. Strategic Marketing Issues

While you may not realize it, there are a number of questions about your business objectives which will influence your lead generation programs. In an article published by Direct Marketing, Jim Kobs identified seven questions which you should answer before you formulate your lead generation program:

1. **Is it more important to build sales or profits?**
2. **How heavily should a company invest in new customer acquisition?**
3. **Can present customers be profitably contacted more often with existing products or services?**
4. **Should a company try to grow the product category or penetrate it?**
5. **How to position and price a product or service?**
6. **Can the media or distribution channels being used be expanded?**
7. **Should a company try to add new products, launch new businesses, or develop new markets?**

If profits are more important you should stick to the tried and true lead generation programs. On the other hand, if your objective is to increase sales you may have to experiment with marginal lists and advertising media or increase your frequency with your primary lead generation programs which may reduce your effectiveness.

New customer acquisition is a longer term version of the sales versus profits question. In many business with recurring revenues it takes one or two years to recoup your initial marketing and sales investment. Typically this isn't true for software sales, but it might apply if you rent or lease your software.

We feel that you should always work your customer base as actively as possible. In most case this offers the highest return on investment. We feel that this should be independent of your other lead generation issues.

The decision on growing the product category versus penetrating the niche is very common for software companies. Often you can increase your effectiveness by focusing on the segments where you sell well. At the same time, you might be able to open up new niches with technical changes to the product and/or sales and marketing literature. These changes require an investment and they are risky since you don't know if you will really generate the sales if you make the investment.

Product positioning is critical to lead generation. How do your materials look compared to your competitors? Do your materials reflect your positioning? Are you targeting the appropriate people who will respond to your positioning?

Chapter II. Lead Generation

Your media channels include direct mail, telemarketing, seminars, dealers and distribution, etc. Developing alternate channels will require marketing investment, but this might dramatically increase your sales potential. Don't underestimate the effort required to become proficient in a new channel.

The new product or market question really depends upon whether you are happy with the growth that your current product can offer. If you can meet your revenue objectives with your current product, why do you need a second product? Make sure you take the long term view of this question. In many cases, we have seen companies where the current product would carry the growth for one or two years, but there were significant risks beyond that. In those cases, we advised the companies to initiate new product introduction plans.

It takes a number of years to develop, introduce, and then generate significant revenues from a new product. Commonly we see that companies take one year to develop a product. They introduce it in year two and generate modest revenues. In many cases, they lose money or break-even, at best, in year two. By year three the new product may be generating significant revenues. Your experience may be better than this, but we wouldn't count on it.

Reference: Marketing Strategies for Maximum Growth, by Jim Kobs, *Direct Marketing*, May 1987.

8. Sales Cycles

We often encounter several published works dealing with the same topic. Three articles dealing with sales cycles and their references are excerpted below:

Itch Cycles

Unless you really understand how your prospects decide to buy your category of product, you may be missing points in time when your prospects would be most receptive to your message. Biddulph gives two examples of "Itch-Cycles". The first is cash registers which are typically bought three months before the new business opens. The second is office art which has a small peak when companies open their first office, and has a much larger peak several months after they move into larger facilities.

You could identify tactics to exploit this information. Perhaps you could use new business license information to sell cash registers to companies who haven't opened yet. The office art example might allow you to sell a very nice lost leader art piece to new businesses. You are making this offer so that you can get these companies on your mailing list and hitting them hard when they move. If you refer to the second location retail situation, you could select companies who now have two locations rather than one. While this will require some effort, these prospects might warrant a call from a sales person.

REFERENCE: "Itch-Cycle Marketing", By David Biddulph, Direct Marketing, October 1988.

Fishing From Two Holes

Brucker identifies the steps in the sales cycle as follows:

1. **Unidentified problem**
2. **Suffering - Fishing Hole B**
3. **Investigate the problem**
4. **Identify the problem**
5. **Investigate solutions - Fishing Hole A**
6. **Select and buy**
7. **Solve the problem**

This is a very common profile for complex sales which require significant investigation. His point is that the marketing challenge is very different for Hole A than for Hole B. Most companies don't know how to exploit the fishing Hole B prospects. They categorize them as literature collectors and discount them.

It is possible to develop a two-step process that maximizes your sales potential. It starts by asking your prospect their buying time frame. If they say that they plan to do something immediately, you know that they are clearly at fishing Hole A, and you can unleash your sales-reps on them. If their plans are less immediate, you might consider sending them an educational article every month or two. Help them investigate and identify the problem. This might include application stories, and examples of the before and after for your customers. You might find that a very successful long term strategy is to establish yourself as the leading light in your segment. Speak at conferences, offer educational seminars, give away educational materials as premiums, etc. If you continue to work your Hole B prospects once you have identified them, you should garner lots of sole-source business when they get ready to buy.

Chapter II.   Lead Generation

REFERENCE: "The Two Fishing Hole' Telemarketing Model", by Roger W. Brucker, Business Marketing October 1988.

Resource Allocation In Closing a Sale

In a recent article, Ghingold (see the Reference, below) focuses on the later stages of the sales cycle once the customer has identified that they have a problem:

1. **Problem/need recognition**
2. **General description of product characteristics or quantities needed.**
3. **Definition of precise product specifications.**
4. **Search for and qualification of vendors.**
5. **Request for and analysis of proposals**
6. **Evaluation of proposals and supplier selection**
7. **Order transaction**
8. **Post-purchase performance feedback.**

As you can see, he is moving into the area of sales, but marketing and lead generation follow up continue to be involved in some of these phases.

Stakeholding

Research has shown that individual's influence in buying decisions depends upon their "stake" or self interest in the outcome of the decision. This is intuitively correct since people who feel that they have the most to win or gain will get involved. Defining stakeholding more precisely is tricky. The individuals with as stake may care because:

1. **Personal Use — They personally use the product or service in their own tasks.**
2. **Use by Others — Use of the product by others will impact their efforts**
3. **Providing Expertise — They have provided some expertise during the buying decision which, in part, makes them accountable for product performance.**
4. **Affects Responsibilities — Purchase and/or use of the product service may affect specific managerial responsibilities such as:**

   - **Supervisory responsibilities (department, plant, division) where the product or service is to be used.**
   - **Responsibilities for outcomes (e.g. sales, profits, costs)**
   - **Financial responsibility for the purchase (e.g. budget approval).**

This is certainly more pervasive than we would have thought on the surface, but when we think about how people act in these complex sales we can recall cases where people felt that they had a greater stake in the decision than we would have anticipated.

Recent industrial buying studies found that stakeholders were most likely to be involved early in the decision process. "Stakeholders seem to make an early effort to be heard and have their criteria and preferences included to guide the buying decision, but then tend to fade out once they have voiced their concerns and preferences, yielding to transactors and/ or legitimate authority."

We must admit that this pattern is opposite what we would have guessed. We commonly see authority figures entering the buying process late in the game. We all know of deals that were thrown off track at the last minute. Thinking about it, there are two very different processes at work. The stakeholders put their word in and stay aloof as long as they are comfortable with the progress. The transactors and/or legitimate authority will get involved as the deal progresses. Introducing a new authority figure late in the decision process is a proven negotiating technique which is unrelated to the stakeholder phenomenon.

The stakeholder involvement profile has significant implications for marketing and lead generation. You should identify as many of the stakeholders as early as possible and address their issues as quickly as possible. In many cases, you can't interact directly with the stakeholders. Your advocate/ contact must convince the other stakeholders that this is the best approach. You should consider developing marketing materials for the common stakeholders. Identify their key issues and address them in your marketing and sales materials. We have found that developing very simple mini-brochures is an effective way to address this type of issue. Even if you can talk with the stakeholder, it is quite effective to follow up with a letter and the mini-brochure. In many cases the mini-brochure is just a four page (11" by 17" folded over) one or two color document. If you have to deal through the advocate/contact, the mini-brochures are invaluable in arming your advocate to make your case. If you make him look good, you will benefit.

REFERENCE: "Bridging theory and practice in the allocation of Sales and Promotion resources within customer organizations", Morry Ghingold, The Journal of Business and Industrial Marketing, Volume 3 Number 2 Summer 1988.

9. Market Research and Surveys

The most basic objective for market research is to allow you to be more accurate in targeting your lead generation efforts. You need to know who are your best prospects and who are your non-respondents. *Profiles* are the common denominators. They give you a few attributes which describe most of the people on your file.

We would start with the selection criteria on the available mailing lists. What are the attributes that you can select on and what values are available? To the extent that you can limit your mailings to high probability prospects, you will have taken a big step toward increasing the effectiveness of your lead generation. While you are talking to your list broker, you should ask them about the list usage. How often is this list being used? Are your competitors using it? How often is the list updated?

Software Success has had the non-deliverable rate range from 0.7% to 22% on lists for software company CEOs. Ask the list owner what to expect so that you can be prepared. Ask questions like these:

* What return rate can we expect?

* What percent will be undeliverable?

* Is there a rebate or refund if there is an excessive undeliverable rate?

* What about special selections?

* Are there options which aren't available on the data card?

Good vs. Bad

One of the challenges is to identify an attribute that will predict both a good prospect and a very bad prospect. While this isn't obvious, there are some attributes which are necessary but not sufficient. A prospect with attribute #1 can still be a very poor prospect if they have attribute #2. If you can develop these screens with the list selection criteria, you will have a major tool.

In many cases, one of these attributes either isn't gathered by the list vendors or the quality of their data is too poor. For example, all the companies who have lists of IBM mainframe sites have data fields for software products installed. The data fields were fine, but very few of the respondents have provided the data.

Finding Key Secondary Attributes

As long as these secondary attributes are easy for your prospects to answer, you should be able to get the information. If you let your list provider know that this is important information to you, they will make an effort to improve the quality of their information. You can also conduct a survey of your house list and improve your own information. Finally, you can gather this information as part of your lead generation effort. Put the questions on the response card!

Adding a Qualifying Question

We have worked with several clients who identified a set of attributes which increased their sales-rate by a factor of five. An example was a vendor with a sophisticated vertical market package. They found that prospects *who had already installed a computer system were much more likely to buy their system.* The non-computer prospects were much more likely to do nothing. They put this question on the response card and asked for a phone number so the sales person could discuss their current system with them.

This process reduced the number of leads slightly, but the company capitalize on this additional information; they developed two lead follow up programs. They had an intense one for the computer prospects and an inexpensive one for the non-computer prospects. It is important to note that they did this without any support from their list providers. After a while, their in-house database was updated with this information and became the primary marketing mechanism.

So far these attributes have been company oriented. As long as you are selling to companies, you also must decide who to sell to in target company. There are a number of alternatives:

The manager/owner/president.

* **The purchasing agent.**

* **The operations manager.**

* **The selection committee.**

Chapter II. Lead Generation

Often you need to sell to each of these people during the course of the sale. One of the critical decisions in your targeting process is to decide who initiates the process to evaluate a new system. In many companies, the president controls the initiation decision. Proposals which have the president's blessing may still stall out with the other people in the chain, but at least you minimize the risk of selling the operations manager, the selection committee and the purchasing agent only to have the president say, "We don't need a new computer!!".

Using a Decision Model

In one instance we created a decision model that worked well. We postulated that the decision to acquire a new computer system was based upon the following:

1. **President — We said that the president decided that it was time to get a new computer system.**
2. **CFO — The CFO initiated the search for alternative systems.**
3. **Office Manager — The office manager conducted the evaluation.**

With this model we were able to tailor a very effective lead generation program:

* We sent the CEO a letter asking them if they were happy with their computer system.

* We sent the CFO a letter proposing that his company consider our system if they are investigating new systems.

* We sent the Office manager letter featuring the time savings and improved control.

Our company sent all three letters to these players one week apart. They were very successful sparking a decision to acquire a new system by getting the discussion going.

Improving Survey Response Rate

Once you have decided to conduct a survey, you need to improve your response rate. An article in Research Reporter found that "The two best ways to increase your response rate are through a mailed incentive or with a second mailing."

They found that A $1 bill will at least double your response, usually resulting in a rate of between 35% and 50%. They also experimented with taping coins in the mailing and found that the response rate boost was less than the additional effort to tape the coins

into the mailing. They also found that promised incentives don't work as well as mailed incentives. People respond to immediate gratification.

A second mailing adds about 10% to the response rate. The second mailing should go out two weeks after the first so that the recipients still remember getting the first survey. They found that 75% to 85% of the eventual return should be back within two weeks. This profile probably depends upon the target market.

We have found that we get 50% of our return within three weeks for people requesting a free issue of the newsletter, but once you develop a profile for your market you can use your mid point return to decide whether you want to follow up with a second mailing.

They also found the following things would help the response rates:

* Addresses typed directly on envelopes

* Personalized cover letters are expensive but may be justified if you are surveying executives.

* Post cards sent before the survey may increase the response.

* Include a postage paid return envelope.

* The questionnaire should look professional.

* One or two page questionnaires do 10% better than longer ones.

The results on all of these detailed variables depend upon the specific mailings. The old advice of test, test, test, ... continues to hold true.

Reference: "Mail Surveys: How to Get a Good Response Rate", Research Reporter, CMP Publications, (516) 365-4600.

10. How To Sell Software By Mail

Robert Bly has developed some guidelines on selling software by mail.

Price is more important than you think.

He feels that you should offer the mail prospects a discount and identify it as such. This will help provide the impetus for immediate action. We are concerned with the long term impact on your pricing integrity. If you decide to use a two-step sale where you develop an active list of prospects who have responded, you must be very careful not to offer a better deal to cold prospects than you are offering to people who have already responded. We are more comfortable offering a premium, (e.g. three months free maintenance, an extra utility, etc.), rather than a simple discount.

One step or two?

He feels that if the price is below $299 that one-step is best and over $1,000, a two-stage sales cycle will work better. He suggests that you test your response if your product is priced in the middle. While this is a good starting point, the complexity of the product is important. If the prospect knows exactly what you are selling, they are much more likely to buy it directly. If it is a new concept, you may have to go through a two-step sale even if you have a low price.

The free-trial approach.

Free trials are very common for high-ticket mainframe software. The risk with a free trial of the production version of the software depends upon the visibility and assets of the company trialing your software. Your risk with isolated individuals might be pretty high if they can use your software with little visibility. On the other hand, we had a client who sold investment software to very high net worth individuals. Their partners and brokers were aware of the software these investors were using so the company felt that there was very little exposure. Their experience supported this conclusion.

The other end of the spectrum is the Fortune 1000. As long as you get an authorized signature from a Fortune 1000 company your risk is quite low since they don't want to get sued. Our experience is that if you get a signature from an officer or owner in smaller companies that you can manage the exposure. This insures that your trial gets management approval and gives you someone to call if you have a problem. All in all, we have had very good luck with free trials, as long as the prospect was willing to invest the time and energy in trialing the software.

To demo or not to demo?

Robert advises companies not to send out demo disks unless they are great. We agree that a poor demo can kill the sale. He likes the limited-use demo which is crippled. It can be sold for a reduced

price of $10 to $50, and this price should be applicable to purchase. We have also seen this used effectively on the middle and lower tier of the market. We wonder if you wouldn't be better off to just trial the product. We have found some of these limited demos to be very frustrating. We invest the time and energy to learn the product, but we can't really use it.

We have also observed that selling a demo system isn't the last step in the sales cycle, but the first step in the next sales cycle. We continue to be surprised at the number of companies who work very hard to sell a demo system and then don't continue with the sales follow up.

Visuals.

If you are going to illustrate your software in your sales materials, show only the key screens. Make sure that you have captions so that they can really understand what is going on.

Please ensure that the visuals are easy to read. We occasionally come across an advertisement or brochure that shows a completely unreadable screen. Not only does it not persuade us to buy the software, but we are left with a little bit of distain for the company. "What kind of company would spend all the money to publish this advertisement/brochure and then not take the care to have it be legible?"

"Concept products"

Our experience is that "concept products" require more steps in the sales process and that each step (mailer) can only move the prospect one step. For example you might have the following steps:
1. We don't have financial control of our company.
2.. A new computer system might help.
3. There are a number of systems which can do the job.
4. This is the best system.
5. This is a fair price for this system.

Usually concept products are back at stage 1. You have to find companies who have the problem that you are trying to fix. The second stage is to convince them that there is a solution to their problem. You can offer them an article reprint or a mini-brochure describing the generic problem and the possible solutions. Only when you have gotten them to this stage is it appropriate to start to sell your product.

We have worked with a number of clients who started to sell the operations people that they had a technical solution before management had agreed that there was a real problem to be solved. This can lead to a great deal of wasted time and energy. Make sure that you map out the sales decision process and develop the materials to move prospects through the pipeline.

REFERENCE: "How to sell software by mail", By Robert Bly, Direct Marketing, September 1988.

11. Market Segmentation

Market segmentation is a concept which sounds very fancy, but in practice is quite simple. We recently read an article on this area in *Direct Marketing* Magazine. In this case history, the client got a 15% response rate from 5,000 prospects (75 new clients). They found that 64 of their new clients were out of a segment which was 40% of the population (2,000 prospects). When they analyzed the cost of just mailing to the 2,000 the investment per client was less $12.81 versus $19.33 even though the cost per letter was higher $0.41 versus $0.29.

It can be profitable to narrow your focus on the more productive segment as long as you can produce adequate leads out of the smaller segment to support the desired sales level. This is a secondary analysis which isn't simple to do exactly.

a. Segmentation Example

As an example, let's say that you are mailing to a list of 5,000 on a quarterly schedule. You could provide as many leads by mailing five times a year to the smaller list. This would result in 320 leads versus 300 at a cost of $4,100 versus $5,800. More leads for less money — sounds like a good deal to us.

Reaching Burnout

If you narrow your segment too small, you can improve your cost per lead or client very dramatically, but you can have such a small universe that you have to hit them too often. This can cause your list hit "burnout". We have seen cases where clients began to mail to their most productive segment monthly. This worked well initially, but the re-

sponse rates began to decline as the prospects got saturated.

You can do a number of things to avoid this burnout:

* **Change your creatives frequently.** Make your marketing materials fresh and new. You should remember that this also impacts your economics.

* **Change your organizational contact.** Mail to more people within the prospect organizations. You can use any number of people to generate the initial lead. This reduces the burnout versus always hitting the CEO.

* **Conduct a more intensive campaign.** Generate more leads per exposure. For example, a double post card may be quite effective if you are marketing to a large population. If you can narrow in on the 20% of your market which generates 80% of your business, you might be better off to send a letter and a brochure.

12. References

Over a period of time we have picked up really valuable information regarding lead generation. Here's a list of some of the more significant items:

* *Free Informational Brochure on the new SIC codes* - Information Access Company, 362 Lakeside Drive, Foster City, CA 94404, (415) 378-5000, (800) 227-8431.

* *The complete Direct Mail List Handbook* - By Ed Burnett, Prentice-Hall, 744 pages, $49.95.

* *Herschell Gordon Lewis on the Art of Writing Copy* - By Herschell Gordon Lewis, Prentice-Hall, 424 pages, $49.95.

* *Integrated Direct Marketing.* Techniques and Strategies for Success. - By Ernan Roman, McGraw-Hill, 239 Pages, $29.95.

* *Successful Direct Marketing Methods.* Fourth Edition. - By Bob Stone, Crain Books, 596 pages, $29.95.

* *Effective Inquiry Management Seminar* - Inquiry Management Institute, 25 Drydock Avenue Suite 500, Boston,MA 02210, 1-800-848-4400.

* *The Marketing Audit Workbook* - Institute for Business Planning, Inc. Englewood Cliffs, NJ 07632 446 Pages.

* *TSR.TST An Interpersonal skills/personality test to help employers recruit, hire, assign, train, and keep the best telemarketeers for the Job.* - Telemarketing Design Inc., 15427 Summerwood, Omaha, NE 68137, (402) 895-9399.

- *Direct Mail Seminar, Teaching the art of Direct Mail Communications* - Direct Mail Advisory Services, 7650 Charles Page Blvd., Tulsa, OK 74127.

- *Free Rules Tools & Checklists 888 Ideas for success in Direct Mail* - AMS Response, 16105 Gundry Ave., Paramount, CA 90723-4830, (213) 634-6484.

- *The Complete Direct Mail List Handbook* - By Ed Burnett, Prentice Hall Book Distribution Center, Route 59 at Brookhill Drive, West Nyack, New York 10995, $59.95.

- *Audiotex Directory - automated telemarketing buying guide* - ADBG Publishing, PO Box 25961, Los Angeles, CA 90025, $25.

- *How to compile and maintain a mailing list.* - Quill, 100 South Schelter Rd., Lincolnshire, IL 60069 (312) 634-4850, Free.

- *Free Quarterly Newsletter on direct response card decks* - Solar Directions, Solar Press, Larry Bauer, 1120 Frontenac Rd., Naperville, IL 60566, (800) 323-2751 or (312) 983-1400.

- *Fundamentals of Direct Mail One day seminar.* - Center for Direct Marketing, 10 Bay Street, Westport, CT 06880 (802) 757-2391.

- *Direct Marketing: How you can really do it Right!* - by "Rocket" Ray Jutkins, C/O TDS Direct Marketing 1122 Fourth Avenue, Suite #400, San Diego, CA 92101, 1-800-642-1144, $29.95.

- *Telephone Selling Report magazine* - 15427 Summerwood, Omaha, NE 68137 (402) 895-9399, $99/year.

- *Encyclopedia of Telemarketing* - Telephone Selling Report (above), $72.95.

- *Inquiry Handling service Newsletter* - 200 Parkside Drive, San Fernando, CA 91340, (818) 365-8131, Free.

13. Nice Little products

The initial idea

Q. What should we do about small, stand-alone products that aren't used with our main products, but are of interest to the same customers?

A. Deciding what to do with the "nice little products" (NLP) that someone inevitably develops can be tough. We have seen a number of situations where companies with NLPs spend a lot of time and money on products which are doomed to failure. NLPs can be very useful to your customers, but in most cases these products fail.

Why NLPs Fail?

Here's why they fail: NLPs require you to develop a totally unique marketing program that you don't have any experience with. They usually are much cheaper than the basic product so the primary sales approach doesn't work. It is also difficult for the company to justify investing in marketing and sales for the NLP. This scenario often results in the NLP developer leaving the company after the company has wasted too much money developing, documenting, and marketing the NLP.

Selling NLPs

The best approach that we have seen is to market it as a mail order product. Think of it as starting a new company within the context of your existing business. If you have a great NLP, you may actually start a new line of business. While this is possible, there are very few NLPs which are good enough to make this work.

Other Strategies

The real motivation for most of these NLPs is to allow your developers to gain some visibility for work they have done internally. The products aren't developed as economic exercise, they're done for ego. Since there is no real money invested, you can think creatively: What about shareware? If you made your NLP available, you should generate enough revenues to cover your expenses when the customers register their software. There are a number of benefits.

You can use your NLP as a low-cost premium to generate leads. If you put the documentation on the diskette (which is common with shareware), you have a very low cost premium to give away. This will help you generate leads for your primary product. Another benefit is getting your company name in front of your prospects. Even if they don't register their product, they will be using your software and will know your company name. Put a logo on the initial screen with your phone number. Finally, you should be able to get good publicity from this project. Magazines should be happy to publish a press release announcing that your NLP is available at no cost from you.

Chapter II. Lead Generation

Dear Dave,

Several of us at New Generation Software, Inc. (NGS) have become avid readers of Software Success in recent months. We particularly enjoyed the March 1989 issue discussing Lead Generation and the subsequent issue that talked about "Nice Little Products" or NLP's.

Two of our developers were in the midst of completing a NLP at the time and just as you said, the product did not fit into our existing product line, the sales staff had no interest in selling it because of the low price and marketing could not justify taking funds away from the primary products of the company to launch the NLP.

Based on your advice, we decided to turn the product into a publicity and lead generator for our other products. We sent out press releases announcing that the product was free to any IBM AS/400 user who contacted us by October 31, 1989. We received front page coverage in one of the primary publications in our market and additional press in three other magazines. We even wound up in a cover story in MIS WEEK.

As of this week we have received nearly 700 calls and shipped approximately 250 copies of the software. This is a market where even the most popular third party software prodcuts rarely exceed 1,000 installations in their lifetime. To get the maximum mileage from the marketing program, we ask each company that wants to receive the free software to complete a survey in which we ask them about their reading habits, ways of gathering product information, current software and planned purchases.

We have generated over 100 qualified leads for our other products from the completed surveys. To put this in perspective you need to understand that our company typically generates about 25 qualified leads per month under normal conditions. One last point; 62 percent of the survey respondents indicated that they had never previously heard of our company - now they use one of our products.

Best of luck for continuing success with your consulting and publishing business.

Thank you.
Bill Langston
Marketing Manager
New Generation Software

14. Vertical Marketing

Q: We have a vertical market product. How should we market it?

A: Since a vertical market is limited in scope, it's ideal for direct respnse marketing like direct mail, card decks, and telemarketing. Since most vertical markets have less than 10,000 prospects, you can mail them all a letter for just $10,000.

We suggest that you suggest that you start by analyzing what your competitors are doing, and how their marketing programs have changed over time. Test the various alternatives to identify the optimal mix. You should keep in mind that the optimal mix will change over time as your company matures and as the market changes. Keep testing and keep your eyes open. Plagiarism is the sincerest form of flattery. If your competitors come up with a great idea, use it.

15. Up-Scale Lead Generation

Q: How should I generate leads for a high-priced, strategic product?

A: This sounds like an upper management sale. See our earlier article on "Selling to Management.

There is one distinction that we want to make. Certain decisions are made by senior management and other decisions require senior management approval. In the previous article we were discussing decisions where senior management and middle management were involved in the selling process. The point there was to ensure that high-level executives were brought in early in the sales cycle. With some high-priced strategic products, middle management may not be involved in the decision process at all.

If this is your situation, you should study other companies who sell t senior executives. Think big. Look at how the "big Eight" accounting firms make executive-level inroads. See how management consulting companies get their business.

Selling the CFO

If the Chief Financial Officer (CFO), for example, is typically the decision maker for the product, you should look at the companies who sell expensive accounting systems. Include systems integrators in your survey. In most cases these companies have very polished senior sales people — people who are backed up with top-quality marketing materials and technical support. Once you understand what it takes to sell to CFO's, you can develop your own version of this sales program.

Generating Leads

Some of our clients have had good luck with direct mail to identify prospects with specific problems that their product solves. You can make points by being specific about the problem you solve and targeting the piece to a specific type or level of executive. Typically the interested CFO won't respond directly, but will ask one of his subordinates to contact you for information. In many cases, however, the CFO will sit in for part of your sales representation.

Other clients have had equally good luck using a telemarketing campaign to reach senior people. While it can be effective, this approach is invariably frustrating because it is so difficult to break through the wall protecting the senior managers.

In some cases a combination of direct mail and telemarketing can be very effective. This is especially true if you have a very small universe of prospects: The combination of direct mail and telemarketing has been shown to generate a greater response rate than either both mail or telemarketing used alone.

The executive sell-cycle

Usually, you must make a direct, in-person sales call on the senior executives to deliver your sales pitch. This expensive technique will be justified if your revenue per sale is sufficiently high and your close rate is OK.

Managing the sales cycle and the number of visits is critical to the success of this type of marketing program. You must analyze the sales cycle and very clearly classify various stages. This will guide you kin your meetings to focus on moving the prospect from stage one to stage two, on t stage three, etc. This is especially true with complex sales which have a long drawn-out sales process. It is very easy to get los tin the details and invest to much energy in poor prospects who will devour your time.

Another difficulty with this type of sale is that it is so involved that it is difficult for one person to see all of the facets of the deal. We urge you to have a management review of all the sales situations at least weekly. It is very easy for your sales person to get sucked into the details and lose track of the larger picture.

Inspite of all of these difficulties, selling a strategic product at a high price can be a very good business once you figure the pattern our. It isn't easy, but it can be done if your product is really good and if you focus on managing the sell cycle.

16. Generating More Leads

Q. We aren't generating enough leads to support the sales that we would like. What can we do?

A. Before we can launch into an answer, we need to set the stage by talking about sales cycles briefly.

Every software product has a sales cycle. How you approach lead generation is strongly affected by what your cycle is. If you sell direct to your customers on a one-shot basis, then you have a single stage sales cycle. If your customers try out your product by purchasing a demo disk, having a personal demo or installing the software on their system on a trial basis, then we call that a two-stage sales cycle. In this scenario you convert leads into demos or trials, and then transform these trials into sales. This two-stage cycle is typical of larger, more expensive, and more complicated sales environments. Our readership is mostly composed of firms with this type of product, and so we'll concentrate on the two-stage sales cycle.

In our experience, it's the marketing department that gets the leads in the door, the sales department that sells the customer on trying the product, and the product and/or the technical people who close the sale. For this reason, we will focus on getting more trials out of our lead generation budget.

There are a number of alternative approaches to solving your lead generation problem. You'll probably find the right answer in one or more of the following:
1. More of the SameSpend more money doing the things that you have already done.
2. Lower Lead CostsLower your cost per lead so you can get more leads for the same money.
3. Better Leads Generate better leads for the same money.
4. Better Conversion Ratio Increase your lead to sale conversion rate.

Chapter II. Lead Generation

Spend more money

This is the easiest thing to do but is the least practical in most situations. Advertising and direct mail typically can absorb more money. Incremental spending, in most cases, will yield results equal to or better than your present experience. There are a number of factors which will improve your lead efficiency including better recognition, and higher-quality materials.

In some cases, your efficiency may decline if you have already saturated your best channels. For example, if you already have a full-page, four-color ad in the only relevant magazine, additional advertising expenditures will be less effective.

Unless you have extra money to burn, we recommend that you start spending smarter, not more. Explore the alternatives discussed in this article.

Cheaper leads

There are a number of ways that you can generate cheaper leads.

Lower your costs The first and most obvious thing to do is to find cheaper ways to implement your marketing programs. There may be more to gain here than you might have guessed. In our experience, small mailings can cost $1.00 to $2.00 each. If you go to larger mailings (more than 3,000 pieces), you can slash your costs dramatically — a 75% to 80% cut is feasible. Your incremental printing cost may be only $0.25 to $0.35 per piece (these are the costs for printing and lettershop work to stuff the envelopes). You can also cut your postage cost from $0.25 to $0.167 by using third class mail.

Lowering your advertising costs isn't as easy, but some magazines will haggle. In particular, you can often negotiate a very good deal if you commit to a number of ads in the next year. This allows you to maintain a regular presence while getting a better deal.

Marketing tries harder Part of the marketing process is to develop better marketing materials. In our experience this is an evolutionary process. Much of marketing and most of lead generation is "test, test, test,....". You find what works through trial and error and you consistently improve the quality of your materials. We would like to recommend that you set aside some of your budget (10% say) for experiments. Unless you try some new things, you

will never get any better. While many of your tests won't work out, the payoff from the ones that do work can be really significant.

Once again, you must track your costs and your results if you ever hope to improve. We continue to be depressed at how few software companies even track their cost per lead. While it is a great deal of work, the cost of tracking your lead generation is negligible compared with the amount you are spending on lead generation.

It has occurred to us that many people may not track their lead generation because they don't want to be confronted with just how poorly they are doing (so they imagine). When our firm is called into a software company to help out, often times the marketing people are terrified that they will be fired when the (terrible) results come in (as we actually calculate their lead generation costs). This isn't the case at all!

Rather than viewing these lead generation costs as absolute, they should be seen as relative. The rate of improvement is a much better measure of the marketing staff than the absolute cost per lead. Your product may have an intrinsically high cost per lead, but if you can improve that by 20% you have really helped your company. You also shouldn't underestimate the long-term potential to lower your cost per lead if you work at it. A number of our clients have slowly and steadily hacked away at their costs with amazing results! In one case lead costs were lowered from $200 per lead to $20 per lead. In another, costs were cut from $1,500 per lead to $100 per lead. This is one area where persistence really pays.

Modify your marketing mix There are any number of ways that you can generate leads. While you should compare your programs within each approach (trade shows, seminars, PR, direct mail, etc), you should also compare the costs for the different approaches. We had one client who made heavy use of trade shows and generated most of their leads this way. They also had started advertising in one magazine and found that the cost per lead and the cost per sale for the advertising was dramatically lower than their trade show costs. They began to cut back on the shows they were planning on attending and invested the money in advertising. At that point they tried direct mail, and found that it was very competitive with the advertising. In fact, the better direct-mail lists proved to be better than the secondary magazines.

Over a couple years they continued to shift their budget and refine their approaches. Even though it appeared that the advertising was more effective than the trade shows, they didn't drop all trade shows. There were two (out of twelve they were attending) which were competitive with the other alternatives. As you can see, this is an evolutionary process, but it can dramatically lower your costs.

Focus on the right segments Another alternative is to focus your mailings and advertising on people who respond. You should survey your market and see if you can identify factors which make people more likely to buy your product. In the case of marketing *Software Success*, we have found that our response rates for smaller software companies were much better than larger software companies. We have seen situations where the response rate by SIC code is dramatically different.

As you can see, direct mail is a very easy way to test to see if your market is segmented in some way or other. While you are limited to the factors available from your list vendors, the amount of information available to make your selections on some lists is really impressive. We have also noticed a steady increase in the quantity and quality of information available from list vendors.

In addition to sending your basic mailings to selected lists, you might try tailoring your mailings for your hottest prospects. For example, if you found that three segments were very responsive, you could print up custom mailings for these segments which address their concerns directly. A letter starting out "Dear Small Software Company President:" has a lot more going for it than one addressed to "Dear Resident". Depending upon the size of these segments you might be faced with increasing your printing costs. If this is the case, you might print enough mailers for the next several mailings to get the cost back in line. This would allow you to have semi-custom mailings at close to a mass mailing price.

This concept can also be applied to advertising. If you find that your primary appeal is to one job title, you can analyze your cost per exposure to this title for various magazines. Magazine space reps like to talk about a cost per thousand (CPM), but it is an undifferentiated exposure rate. You might find that

the smaller magazine which targets your job title might be more cost effective than the larger circulation magazine which is read by a much broader market. You can use your CPM by job title to negotiate with the magazines.

It turns out that you can apply this concept to almost all the alternatives for lead generation. It may be more difficult to get the data you need for some of the alternatives, but the concept applies. Once you know who you are selling to, you can really do a better job of targeting your lead generation. At first the trade shows and smaller magazines may not have the information that you need, but if you ask around you will be surprised at how much information is available.

Better Leads

Sales people everywhere want better leads. One of the reasons that many sales people love advertising is that people who call in from an ad are much more likely to try the product quickly than someone who responds to a mailer. The problem is that there is a fundamental tradeoff between quantity and quality.

There are a number of ways that you can improve the quality of your leads. The first is to make it harder to respond. The higher you make the hurdle to respond, the more the prospect really was interested in your product. They are qualifying themselves by responding. You can ask tough qualifying questions on your response card or in your ad. Maybe you can force them to call you. As you can see, many of the ideas will improve the quality of leads by discouraging the softer leads from responding. As long as you have the resources to follow up with the softer leads, we believe that you are better off to pull in as many moderately interested prospects as possible.

Another thing that you can do is to improve your description of your product, its costs and benefits. Help your reader really decide if they can benefit from your product. On the surface this sounds great, but the drawback is that if you tell your prospects what your product really costs, they may disqualify themselves too early. If they had requested information and had talked to a sales person, they might decide that they really could afford or justify your product.

Chapter II. Lead Generation

Ideally you will bring in as many leads as you can effectively qualify. There is a trade-off between the optimal lead quality and your lead qualification resources. If your sales people have time on their hands, generate as many leads as possible (and don't worry about how well qualified they are since almost any lead is better qualified than a cold-call). On the other hand, if your sales people are swamped, you don't want to overload them with soft leads.

In most companies, lead qualification is a sales function, but you can augment your sales force by using marketing and administrative resources to qualify and process your leads. In this way you can effectively handle softer leads even if your sales people are busy.

Increase lead to sale conversion ratio

On the surface, increasing your conversion ratio sounds like you are simply beating on your sales people to do a better job. This is the classic sales and marketing clash where sales says that the leads are lousy and marketing says that sales is skimming. While sales management is important, it isn't anything that marketing can directly control. On the other hand, marketing can make sure that there is a systematic program to follow up with the soft leads. We have found that a monthly mailing to soft leads can dramatically increase sales. During the initial weeks after the prospect has requested information, you may find that an even faster pace may pay off.

We have seen far too many cases where sales is supposed to follow-up with the leads, but their follow-up isn't consistent. There are a lot of reasons: the sales person was just too busy, they didn't like calling prospects who wouldn't talk, they forgot, etc. You don't have to put up with the excuses: install a standard follow-up program which can be implemented much more efficiently. Design follow up letters and have them sent out on a pre-arranged schedule. You will be surprised how efficiently this can be done. You can print all the labels for the follow-ups on the initial data entry, etc.

Newsletters are a very effective way to continue contact with the soft leads. In many cases, newsletters are quarterly so you will need some interim mailings. You might just try a simple self-mailed press release. Yes, we're talking about sending a press release to your prospects, not the press. This is easy to

produce, and is inexpensive. At the same time it gets your name and your product name in front of those soft leads that haven't yet bought. You may find that these mailings have the greatest return of anything you are doing. That really makes sense. You have invested a great deal of money to get them to respond, the final incremental effort to get them to buy can be very effective

I. Survey (1989)

Earlier this year we enclosed a survey on lead generation. In this survey we asked a series of questions designed to tell us about the practices and success of our readership in the area of Lead generation. The results of that survey are reported below.

Please note that because multiple selections were allowed, the total of many questions adds up to more than 100%.

1. Computer Type

Q1. On what type of system does your software run?

While most of our respondents have products that are intended for microcomputers, we had a good representation of both minicomputer and mainframe software systems. This simply illustrates that our readership represents a diverse cross-section of the software industry. The figure showing this distribution is shown on the following page.

2. Software Type

Q2. What type of software do you sell?

Most of the firms characterized their software as vertical, but in reading the product descriptions, it became clear that vertical software is really a marketing decision in many cases. If your marketing & advertising budget is severely limited, you can get the best milage for your product by identifying your target market, and then zooming in on it.

Item	Value
No reply	13.3%
Vertical Software	66.7%
Horizontal	20.0%

3. Distribution

Q3. How do you sell your product?

Almost everyone sells their products direct. We were, however, surprised at the number of firms who sell indirect (through Distributors, Dealers, and VARs) and have OEM arrangements. The percentage of firms who sell through OEM arrangements in particular is encouraging. This number is a testimony to the increasing maturity of our business.

Item	Value
No Reply	13.3%
Direct	93.3%
Indirect	40.0%
OEM	26.7%

4. Sales Volume

Q4. What is your annual software sales volume? ($/year)

The average size of the respondents was larger than the average size for Software Success readers in general. This may be due in part to the fact that larger firms do more lead generation. Is it possible that they are larger because they have more formal lead generation programs?

Item	Value
No Reply	6.7%
$0-$250K	13.3%
$250K-$500K	13.2%
$500K-$1M	33.3%
$1M-$5M	26.7%
over $5M	6.7%

5. Market Size

Q5. How big is the size of your target market?

Most of the companies feel that their potential target market is quite large.

Item	Value
No Reply	26.7%
less than $5M	6.7%
less than $50M	6.7%
less than $500M	20.0%
less than $1B	13.3%
more than $1B	26.7%

6. Lead Generation Activity

Q6. How many leads do you generate per month?

On average, our survey respondents only generated about 45 leads per month. See the graph on the next page. This number is well below what we would have expected. When we compare this with a median company revenue of $1 Million a year, we arrive at one of the following conclusions: 1) many of the companies are selling expensive products, or 2) they are only supporting part of their sales via lead generation, or 3) they are selling a high percentage of the leads. The truth is probably a combination of these.

7. Lead Sources

Q7. What is your primary source of new leads?

As you can see from the graph on the next page, many companies selected several primary sources of leads.

Referral Leads

Q8. What percentage of your leads come from referrals?

We found this reply interesting. Many firms (33%) selected referrals as one of their primary sources of leads, but the median response to this question was less than 10%. Referrals are great leads to get but they are difficult to stimulate.

Item	Value
No Reply	20.0%
1%	6.7%
5%	33.3%
10%	13.2%
20%	20.0%
40%	6.7%

PR Leads

Q9. What percentage of your leads come from general PR?

These responses are bimodal: half of the companies do very little PR(and yield very few PR leads); some companies are active users of PR and yield more than respectable results. Getting 20% of your leads from PR is a real accomplishment.

Item	Value
No Reply	53.3%
less than 5%	13.3%
less than 10%	6.7%
less than 20%	20.0%
less than 30%	6.7%

Trade Show Leads

Q10. What percentage of your leads come from trade shows?

Once again we have a bimodal distribution. Half the companies don't generate leads from trade shows (presumably because they don't exhibit or attend shows); one-quarter generate a lot of leads from trade shows.

Item	Value
None	40.0%
1%	6.7%
less than 5%	13.3%
less than 10%	6.7%
less than 20%	6.7%
less than 40%	20.0%
greater than 60%	6.7%

Article Leads

Q11. What percentage of your leads are generated by published articles?

Having an article published on your company and/or product can be accomplished in one of two ways: 1) Someone in your firm can write a technical article and negotiate a placement in one of the technical trade magazines. 2) An article can be written by an outside reporter. Getting an article published on your company and/or product is quite a PR coup (assuming that the article is favorable, that is).

While articles aren't very common they can be a very cost effective way to generate leads and credibility.

Item	Value
None	66.7%
1%	6.7%
less than 5%	6.7%
less than 10%	6.7%
less than 20%	6.7%
less than 60%	6.7%

Existing Customer Leads

Q12. What percentage of your leads come from follow-up sales to existing customers?

We hope that the high "None/No reply" response was just a problem in interpreting the question. Once a customer is signed, you should do your best to sell them more products.

Item	Value
None/ No Reply	46.7%
0% - 1%	6.7%
1% - 5%	13.3%
5% - 10%	20.0%
10% - 30%	13.3%

Advertising Leads

Q13. What percentage of your leads come from advertising?

Advertising can come in many forms: you can run a one-inch notice in the back of a "classified section of PC Magazine for a few hundred dollars; you can take out a half-page ad in a limited-circulation, industry-specific magazine that might cost several thousand dollars; or you can run a multi-page, full-color spread in Business Week and expect to pay several hundred thousand. The range of advertising possibilities (and costs) is nearly limitless. Nonetheless, many of the smaller firms don't feel that they can afford to advertise and therefore don't. This is really a shame because advertising can be very effective. A number of firms, including most of the largest, generate a significant portion of their leads from media advertising.

Item	Value
None	53.3%
0% - 5%	6.7%
5% - 10%	6.7%
10% - 20%	6.7%
20% - 30%	6.7%
30% - 40%	6.7%
40% - 50%	6.7%
more than 50%	6.7%

Product Review Leads

Q14. What percentage of your leads come from product reviews?

How low can you go!!

Lead Generation Activity

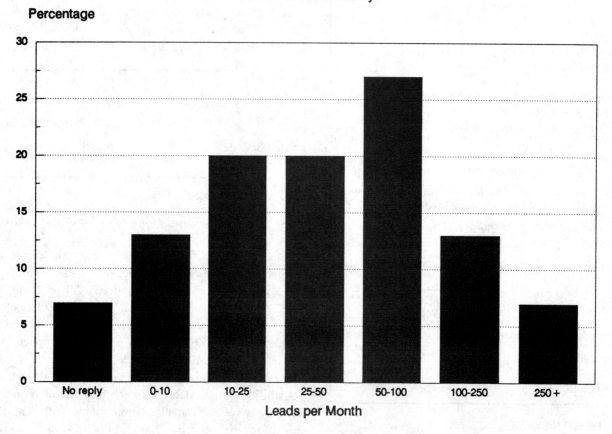

Percentage

Leads per Month

Primary Lead Sources

Source

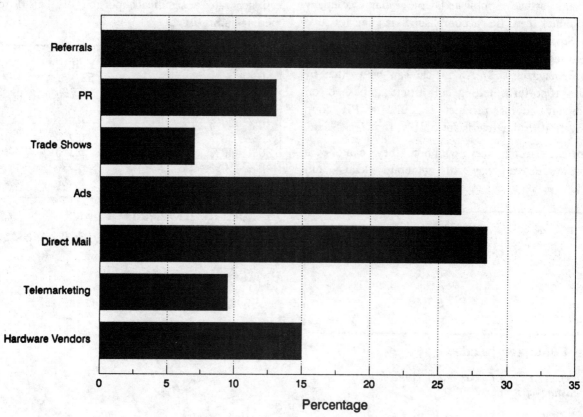

Percentage

Item	Value
None	86.7%
1%	13.3%

Direct Mail Leads

Q15. What percentage of your leads come from direct mail?

Direct mail is an important source of leads for many of our respondents.

Item	Value
None	33.3%
0% - 5%	6.7%
5% - 10%	26.7%
10% - 40%	13.3%
40% - 50%	13.3%
more than 50%	6.7%

Telemarketing Leads

16. What percentage of your leads come from telemarketing?

We expect that the high "No reply" rate means that most companies don't have a formal telemarketing program.

Item	Value
No Reply	73.3%
5%	6.7%
10%	6.7%
20%	6.7%
greater than 20%	6.7%

Seminar Leads

Q17. What percentage of your leads come from seminars?

Holding a seminar to educate your potential audience on your product or technology is a time-honored software lead generation technique for big-ticket software packages — mainly mainframe software. If your software doesn't cost at least $50,000 per unit, you probably can't afford the $/ lead. Not surprisingly, this method is unpopular with the majority of our respondents.

Item	Value
None	80.0%
0% - 1%	6.7%
1% - 5%	6.7%
more than 5%	6.7%

Cold-call Leads

Q18. What percentage of your leads come from cold calling?

Really???

Item	Value
None	73.3%
0% - 5%	13.3%
5% - 10%	6.7%
more than 10%	6.7%

Dealer Leads

Q19. What percentage of your leads come from dealers?

With rare exceptions, dealers are vastly over-rated as a source of leads for small software companies.

Item	Value
None	80.0%
0 - 5%	13.3%
more than 5%	6.7%

Vendor Leads

Q20. What percentage of your leads come from hardware vendors?

Hardware vendors rarely generate steady leads for software companies.

Item	Value
None	73.3%
0% - 1%	6.7%
1% - 5%	13.3%
More than 5%	6.7%

Software Directory Leads

Q21. What percentage of your leads come from Software Directories?

We have assumed from this response that most companies just can't track their directory leads. The return on directory listings is usually very good.

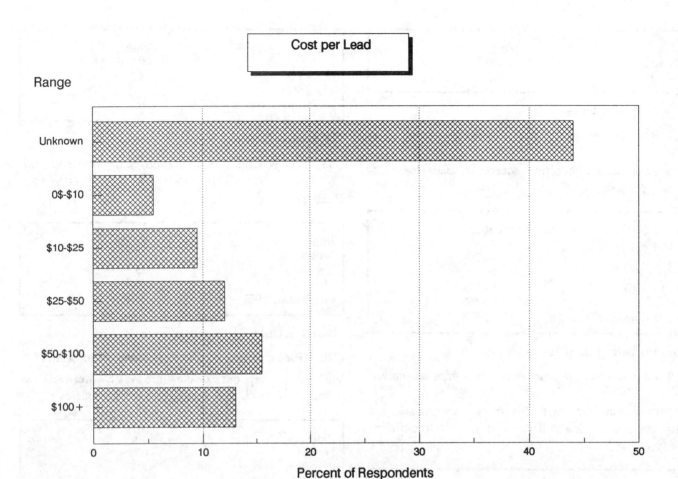

Cost per Lead

Range

- Unknown
- 0$-$10
- $10-$25
- $25-$50
- $50-$100
- $100+

Percent of Respondents

20 -- Cost per Lead

Item	Value
None	73.3%
0% - 1%	6.7%
5%	6.7%
10%	6.7%
20%	6.7%

Item	Value
No Reply	60.0%
$0 - $500	13.3%
$500 - $1K	26.7%
$1K - $2.5K	6.7%
more than $2.5K	13.3%

8. Lead Costs

Q22. What is your cost per lead?

Very few companies actually track their cost per lead. While it is a great deal of work, we feel that it is an absolutely essential step. You will never improve your lead generation efficiency unless you can track your cost per lead. You need to be able to verify the impact of changes.

Cost per Sale

Q23. What is your cost per sale?

The significance of this depends upon the product price. We should have asked lead generation costs as a percent of sales revenues.

Return on Investment

Q24. What is your return on the lead dollars that you invest?

All the companies who track their costs for lead generation show that they generate at least twice as much revenue as they spend on lead generation. In this case our respondents spend 50% of revenue for lead generation, which yields a Return On Investment (ROI) of 2.. A ROI of 10 is equivalent to spending 10% of revenue on Lead Generation, which is a common guideline.

Item	Value
No Reply	60.0%
0 - 2	6.7%
2 - 3	13.3%
3 - 5	6.7%
5 - 10	6.7%
greater than 10	20.0%

Item	Value
No one	6.7%
CEO	40.0%
Marketing	53.3%
Sales	26.7%
Outside	6.7%

9. Lead Generation Responsibility

Q25. Who is responsible for lead generation in your organization?

Unless Marketing is responsible for lead generation, we don't feel that the company is very serious about generating leads. The CEO is too busy, and Sales is too short term oriented.

10. Lead Generation Budgeting

Q26. How do you decide on your budget for lead generation?

The proactive firms spend the money to generate the future leads while the smaller, reactive firms are limited by their bank balance.

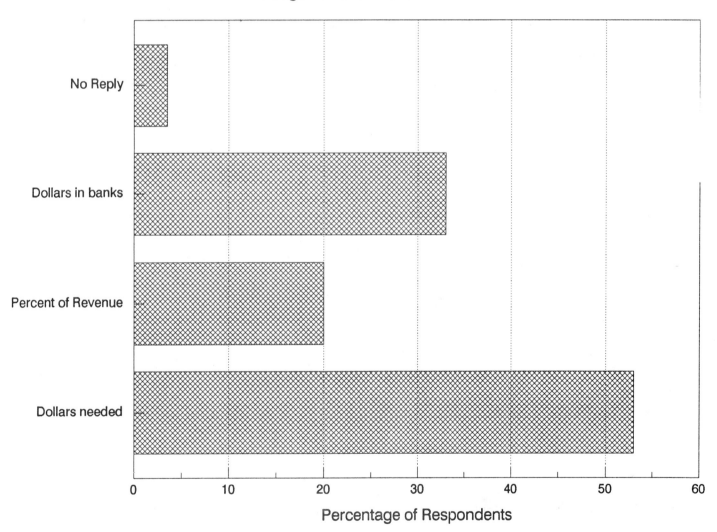

Budget Criterion Used

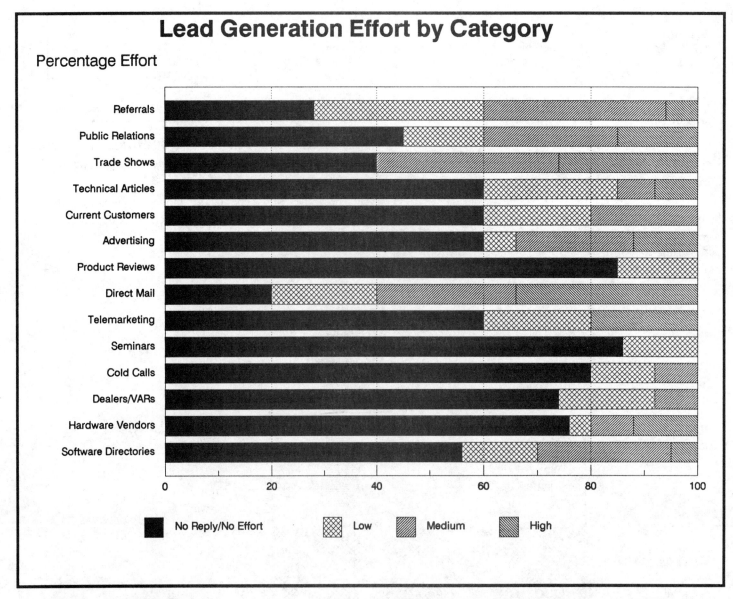

Lead Generation Effort by Category

Percentage Effort

Categories (top to bottom): Referrals, Public Relations, Trade Shows, Technical Articles, Current Customers, Advertising, Product Reviews, Direct Mail, Telemarketing, Seminars, Cold Calls, Dealers/VARs, Hardware Vendors, Software Directories

Legend: No Reply/No Effort, Low, Medium, High

11. Level of Effort

Questions 27 through 40 asked, "How much effort do you spend to encourage leads from xxxxx method." Rather than print a separate table or graph for each question, we graphed them together. We thought it would be more interesting to see how our survey respondents spent their efforts when viewed in aggregate.

Please, therefore refer to the larger figure — Q27-40 — when reading the following analyses.

Referrals

Very few firms have active programs to encourage referrals. An example of such a program is to offer a financial or non-financial incentive for leads. You could give free maintenance, free product upgrades, additional support, etc.

Public Relations

Some firms do nothing to encourage positive PR. Those that do put forth an effort tend to invest more in this endeavor.

Trade Shows

There is no such thing as a low level of effort with trade shows. You either go — and bust your buns — or you don't go at all. Seems reasonable to us.

Technical Articles

Very few of the firms write articles, and the effort varies considerably.

Chapter II. Lead Generation

Existing Customers

Half of the firms reported no effort, and no one had this as a "high" category. We wonder why. Following up with your existing customers doesn't take much effort and it can pay considerable rewards.

Advertising

As the promotion issue pointed out, if you are going to advertise you will need to make a serious commitment. This is probably why so many firms hesitate to start advertising when they don't have the money to follow through.

Product Reviews

You can't really invest a lot of energy in product reviews, but they can really pay off. (Oftentimes this effort is buried in the PR budget.) For the most part, product reviews take quite a long time to get published.

Direct mail

Almost everybody does some form of direct mail. And while direct mail can be started with a low level of effort, it can justify a significant effort.

Telemarketing

Telemarketing is flexible in that you can tailor how much you want to put into it.

Seminars

Product introduction seminars require the support of other marketing programs and are appropriate only for a certain class of high-priced software. Seminars can be very expensive and can consume an enormous number of non-financial resources. It is not surprising, therefore, that the vast majority of our respondents spent no effort and the others responded "low.

Cold-Calling

You can't really do a lot to encourage leads from cold calls other than buy a list for your sales people to call.

Dealers/VARs

This has decreased steadily over the last few years as software vendors have gotten disillusioned about selling through dealers.

Hardware Vendors

Several firms have based their entire marketing strategy around their alliances with hardware vendors. Most firms, however, don't bother.

Software Directories

Directories involved more effort than we ever would have guessed.

12. Tracking Results

Questions 41 & 42 asked our respondents how well they measured the results of their efforts. If there is a software marketing panacea, this is it — measure & track the results of your efforts. All too often, however, we find that objective measurement is lacking. (Everybody has an opinion, however — we don't even have to ask.)

13. Tracking Costs

Q41. How do you track the cost for lead generation programs?

The low level of commitment to tracking lead generation costs really limits how effectively most firms can monitor their programs.

Item	Value
None	40%
Low	33%
Medium	3%
High	14%

14. Tracking Results

Q42. How do you track sales related to lead generation programs?

Even fewer firms make an effort to relate sales to specific lead generation programs.

Item	Value
No Reply	40%
No Effort	20%
Low	26.7%
Medium	6.7%
High	6.7%

15. Lead Follow-up

Q43. How do you follow up on leads?

Most firms turn their leads over to the sales department for a sales-call follow-up. Some simply send out Marketing Literature and hope the customer buys.

Item	Value
None	13.3%
Marketing	33.3%
Sales	53.3%

16. Six-Months Purchase Cycle

Q44. What percentage of your leads buy within 6 months?

Most firms have a sales cycle greater than six months from lead to purchase or they convert less than 10% of their leads to sales.

Item	Value
No Reply	40.0%
0 - 10%	33.3%
10 - 20%	6.7%
20 - 30%	6.7%
30 - 50%	6.7%
more than 50%	6.7%

17. One Year Purchase Cycle

Q45. What percentage of your leads buy within 1 year?

Slightly more leads buy within one year, but the median industry lead to sale conversion rate is less than 20%.

Item	Value
None	33.3%
0 - 10%	26.7%
10 - 20%	6.7%
20 - 30%	13.3%
30 - 40%	6.7%
40 - 80%	6.7%
greater than 80%	6.7%

18. Literature mail-out

Q46. Who do you send literature to?

While a fair number of firms send out literature to all their leads, a significant number have marketing and sales follow up and qualify these leads before literature is sent.

Item	Value
One	13.3%
All leads	46.7%
Marketing qual	33.3%
Sales follow-up	26.7%

19. Good Leads

Q47. What percentage of your leads are "good leads" that your sales people pursue?

Unless you have formalized your lead qualification criteria, sales will pursue all leads with equal vigor which isn't necessarily good.

Item	Value
None	20.0%
100%	33.3%
75%	13.3%
50%	6.7%
25%	13.3%
10%	13.3%

Measuring Good Leads

Q48. How do you determine a good lead?

Most firms felt that they had a good lead if it was from their target market. Firms with a more immediate focus would disqualify a lead if it didn't have budget or weren't planning to buy soon.

Item	Value
None	13.3%
Target market	46.7%
Budget	33.3%
Timing	33.3%
Authority	6.7%
Application	13.3%
Source	13.3%

Literature Collectors

Q49. How do you categorize literature collectors?

While almost everyone sends information, some firms felt challenged to try to convert literature collectors into customers.

Item	Value
No Plan	20.0%
Send no info	6.7%
Cheap lit	20.0%
Good lit	33.3%
Sales effort	20.0%

20. Automatic Follow-up

Q50. Do you have an automatic procedure to follow up on cold leads?

Not following up on cold leads is a real shame. They are the best list you will ever find. Depending upon your lead to sale conversion rate and the length of your sales cycle, automatic follow up on cold leads can be key to your marketing program's success.

Item	Value
None	7.0%
No	40.0%
Low	20.0%
Medium	13.0%
High	20.0%

21. Dollar Allocation

Q51. How do you decide how to allocate your lead generation dollars?

Item	Value
None	40.0%
History	46.7%
Budget	0.0%
Competitors	6.7%
Whim	6.7%

Just as test, test, test is the basic rule for lead generation, history is often the best guide to what works. The budget usually reflects history.

22. Best LG Technique

Q52. What is your best lead generation technique?

Direct mail is the favorite and PR is second.

Item	Value
None	20.0%
Referrals	13.3%
Direct mail	26.7%
Advertising	13.3%
Telemarketing	6.7%
Trade shows	6.7%
PR	20.0%
Hw vendors	6.7%

23. Competitive Differences

Q53. How does your lead generation differ with your competitors'?

Most attributed the differences to marketing budget and company size. However, a significant number just felt more comfortable using a different approach, (i.e., preferring direct mail over trade shows).

Item	Value
None	26.7%
We're smart	6.7%
Budget	40.0%
Size	26.7%
Different Approach	20.0%

24. Budget Limitations

Q54. What aren't you doing in lead generation because of budget?

While advertising requires a significant budget, you can start direct mail on a limited budget.

Item	Value
None	26.7%
Adv	53.3%
Direct mail	26.7%
Telemarketing	6.7%
Trade shows	13.3%

25. Things not Done

Q55. What aren't you doing in lead generation because of time and energy?

Direct Mail and PR are both very labor intensive. PR has an especially high labor to dollar ratio so it is very good for smaller firms.

Chapter II. Lead Generation

Item	Value
None	33.3%
Direct mail	33.3%
Telemarketing	6.7%
Trade shows	6.7%
Cold calls	6.7%
PR	33.3%

26. Controlling Sales

Q56. Do you feel that you are controlling your sales via lead generation?

Most of the firms were dissatisfied with the control over sales that they were getting via lead generation. The lucky few were quite pleased.

Item	Value
None	13.3%
No	13.3%
Low	40.0%
Medium	6.7%
High	26.7%

27. Summary

Lead Generation is a critical marketing issue for many firms. It is the first step in the sales cycle, and you can't close the sale unless you open the dialog.

In our experience, the quality of Lead Generation is the difference between successful firms and unsuccessful firms. If you can develop a formula to generate leads on a consistent and cost effective basis you can then proceed to fine tune your sales cycle. Without an effective lead generation program your sales force is always going from one crisis to another.

We urge you to read the results of this survey carefully and see what other software companies do. You should also look at your own past efforts. Then you should identify a new program which you would like to try. As long as you are trying approaches which other software companies have found successful, we don't have strong preferences. We believe that a consistent lead generation program is much more important than any particular program.

If you haven't been aggressive in your historic lead generation, we often find that starting to send direct mail to the prospects who already responded can be very cost effective. These prospects already expressed an interest in your product so they are better than any list you could buy.

The second thing that we find is developing a program to automatically follow up with your leads will increase how much business you are getting out of your lead generation efforts.

Whatever you decide to do, view it as an experiment. You will make mistakes, but you will learn what works as you proceed. Good luck.

J. Program Alternatives (1989)

Many companies have difficulty deciding how much money to spend on lead generation and promotion. In particular they would like to know how to evaluate the effectiveness of their marketing programs. Our general guidelines are that software companies should spend 10 to 15 percent of revenues on promotion and lead generation. This excludes the salaries for marketing personnel, but it includes all outside costs.

The first step that you should take is to look at your budget and determine your current spending level. This will give you your first level indication of where your marketing program stands. There are a couple typical situations which might apply to your firm.

1. No Marketing is not good marketing.

We find that many small companies do no systematic marketing. They may go to one or two trade shows, but most of their leads are either through word of mouth or from cold calls by the sales people. The only real marketing expenses are for some basic marketing materials.

Typically the cost of marketing for these firms is less than 5% of revenues. Since these companies are small and growing, they are proud of the fact that they are holding down their costs — sometimes to their own detriment. Our view is that this type of firm is unlikely to grow out of their current sales level unless they begin to invest in marketing.

2. Low Cost, High Impact Campaigns

The challenge for these early stage firms is to find low cost and high impact programs to increase sales. There are typically a number of promotional items like press releases, articles, and product reviews that offer fantastic return on investment (ROI). They require time and energy, but very little cash.

Lead generation can also be approached on a step by step basis. We usually find that all firms have built up a house list of prospects who have requested information. Mailing to a house list can be a great way to generate lead activity and early sales. A newsletter can be another inexpensive marketing device that can have a number of uses. You can send it to your house list and to new prospects a month or two after you send them product literature.

3. Finding more money for Marketing

By implementing these small projects, you should be able to generate some additional revenue to fund further projects. At the same time, you might consider trimming your other costs to help fund the marketing. Often we find that technically oriented companies will continue to invest in additional new development, even when they have the most technically sophisticated product. The ROI from marketing is likely to be much higher than additional development.

4. Fast Growth, High Costs

Fast growing companies, those growing 50 to 100 percent per year, are another common occurrence in the software industry. Often their marketing costs are 15 to 20 percent of revenues — or even higher — because they are investing in marketing programs to support their growth objectives. The marketing dollars must be spent now to generate the sales later, and sales revenue lags most marketing programs.

Given the dynamics of this type of situation it is very easy to let your costs get out of control. Simple quarterly or annual calculations of marketing as a percentage of sales shed very little light on the fundamental quality of your marketing programs.

5. Measuring Results

It is critical to track the results of your individual programs so that you can evaluate the effectiveness of the various programs. If you are using direct mail, card decks, and advertising you must know the cost per lead and the percentage of leads which buy for each category.

We work with a number of mainframe software companies that track their costs per lead very closely. The following costs are based on a

hypothetical $20K software product being sold directly (via telephone) to customers:

- Advertising — Print media advertising might yield a $500 cost per lead. If 20% of the leads end up buying the product, the marketing cost per sale is $2,500 or 12.5% of revenues. Not bad.

- Direct Mail — A direct mail campaign might yield a $150 cost per lead. The quality of these leads will typically be less and result in a lower close rate — 10%. The cost per sale is therefore $1,500 or 7.5% of revenues. Good, very good.

- Card Decks — Card decks can be very effective for the right product at the right time (they can also be very bad). It the cost per lead was $50 while the close rate declined to 5%, then the cost per sale will be $1,000, just 5% of revenues. Great results if you can get them.

We would like to emphasize that the above is just a generalization about how a mixed-media lead generation campaign might work. Your results might be exactly opposite! Measuring the cost per lead and the close rate for each category of lead is the most important element.

6. Spending Smart, Not Spending More

Your first decision is how to spend your lead generation budget among the likely alternatives. You must look at the available vehicles and their costs. For example, there might be one card deck which all of your competitors use which costs $1K per month. A direct mailing might cost $3K and a quarterly schedule will help maintain a steady presence with your prospects. There may be one magazine which is the obvious place to advertise and the minimum serious ad costs $5K every other month.

We would start by assuming that we split our budget across these three categories evenly. Then we would start with the most effective vehicle and determine the minimum reasonable program. It might take 40% of your budget to be in every issue of a hot card deck. We urge you to make sure that you do each program well before you try something else. Running an occasional card in this or that deck is a sure way to waste your money. Next we would look at direct mail and determine what makes sense. Lets say that takes another 40% of your budget. That leaves you with 20% to test the advertising. While you can't have a big ad campaign, you should be able to find some inexpensive magazines with good readership, or classified ads in a more expensive magazine. You should revisit this macro budget on an annual basis as you learn more and your budget increases with greater sales.

7. Getting the maximum/Marketing Dollars

The next task is to insure that you are getting the best milage out of your marketing programs. By that we mean that you are using the best card decks, that your mailings are as effective as possible, and that you are running the best ads in the most appropriate magazines. In order to determine this, you must test alternatives within each category and compare your results.

Keeping a contingency reserve

You should keep at least 20% of each program's budget in reserve so that you can take advantage of unforseen situations. You'll run into one-time-good-deals, last-second cancellations that you can pick up for a song, etc. Having some money in reserve will mean that you can snap up these gems.

Creative haggling over price

You will get calls from the other magazines and card decks asking you to advertise. (It shouldn't be too surprising to realize that reading the competition is a good way for a space rep to generate his own leads.) If you have some money left in your budget you might be able to do a little horse-trading. Tell them about your limited budget. Tell them that you'd love to be in their deck/magazine. Tell them that cost per lead is your most important measure. Point out that they can help their cost per lead by lowering their cost. Let them make you an offer you can't refuse.

8. Milking the Cash Cow

A cash cow is an older, mature product that can yield cash benefits. You can milk a cash cow to fund your new products. There will be a lot of momentum from your prior advertising so you can cut back on your expenditures. We would expect that you could lower your marketing costs to the 10% level without significantly impacting sales. This is one case where the detailed analysis of the individual programs is really important. You can cut out the less effective programs because you are getting adequate leads from your better programs. At the same time, you might consider cutting back on some of your image advertising. The major problem with these cutbacks is that you might not see the results for six to twelve months. If you cut back too severely, you may damage the long term revenue that you will get out of this product, and it may be almost impossible to reverse the trend by the time it becomes apparent.

9. Sales Price Determines the Way You Market

You may have noticed that we haven't talked about the what kind of computers the products being considered run on. That is because we believe that the price of a software product is much more important to its marketing than what type of hardware it runs on. There are magazines, card decks, and direct mail lists for every hardware market. While they alternatives that you can select among may vary depending upon your hardware platform, the basic constraints are a function of the price level. We will give a couple examples to explain this.

$100,000 product

At this level you can spend $1K per lead, and still be OK as long as seven to ten percent of the leads buy. This allows you to use seminars, very fancy direct mail, and to make direct sales calls to establish interest. Prospects want a lot more personal attention before they decide to get interested at this price level.

$20,000 product

This could be a mainframe utility or a high end vertical market product on LANs

Often you find that the cost per lead is $150 and that 5% of the leads buy within six months to a year. This gives you a $3K cost of sales which is 15%. Direct mail can be quite effective for products at this price point.

$5,000 product

Unless you have a really hot product, it is difficult to market these products effectively through direct mail. If you could get the direct mail cost per lead down to $100 (a one percent response rate with $1/letter), it would take a 20% lead to sale rate to maintain a 10% cost of marketing. Card decks are typically more effective because of their lower cost per lead. At $50 per lead you will need a 10% lead to sale ratio to get a 10% cost of marketing.

$500 product

This is a very tough never-never land. Unless you get 100% lead to sale ratio and a $50 per lead, your marketing costs will be out of line. You almost have to go for the sale in the lead piece. You can't afford to send information out and have a secondary percentage of the responses eventually buy. Classified ads can work at this level if people will buy with limited information. You have to be very effective at generating leads very cheaply to make a go of this.

$100 product

Everybody wants to do another Borland, but this is a really tough act to follow Long term you can't afford to spend more than $10 to $15 per sale. We had one client who was able to generate leads for $30 per lead and convert 100% of these into sales for a $150 product. Thus they had 20% of revenues in marketing which was marginal. The really tough factor in their situation was that the leads declined slightly over time as the early adapters had tried the product and the company was talking to a more cautious group of buyers. Controlling marketing costs are critical for this type of product.

10. Distribution Evolution

In the above discussion, we have assumed that you would sell all of these products directly. It is obviously quite difficult to sell the less expensive products directly unless you can generate a large number of end user responses through advertising. After they have been brought through the distribution channel by expensive advertising, these products are typically sold on a continuing basis through distribution channels. Initially you, the publisher, will have to establish that there is end-user demand by selling direct. Once you have established that the product does draw, you can begin to talk to dealers and distributors, but you should expect this to be expensive.

11. Conclusion

We have given you a number of examples of situations commonly experienced by software companies. Your next step is to analyze your numbers to deter-

mine your situation. Then you can start to improve your effectiveness. This will be hard work, but the results will be long lasting.

12. Other Alternatives

Lead generation is a systematic program to contact cold prospects and to elicit warm prospects who are interested in learning more about your product. One of the difficulties that some people have in distinguishing between promotional programs and lead generation programs is that you can use the same vehicle for both. The intent is what distinguishes them. We will give some examples of simple lead generation programs and then lead generation programs that use promotional vehicles.

The simple lead generation programs are direct mail and cold calling. Direct mail pieces with a reply mechanism are classical lead generation. The same holds for sales people calling cold prospects to see if they would like to learn more about your product.

K. Image Advertising (1989)

Advertising can be used in both programs depending upon the structure of the ad IBM image advertisements about their contribution to science are clearly promotion, and hard product sell ads with a reader service number, a 800 number and a reply coupon clearly intended to generate leads. Our opinion is that it is almost impossible for an ad to meet both objectives. If promotion is your intent, you will go for the 'pretty' ad, while a lead generation ad will have lots of text to sell people on responding. We have seen a number of cases where companies tried to accomplish both objectives and wasted their money.

1. Cost-per-Lead Figures

Q. I would like some tips for interpreting and comparing cost-per-lead figures. In addition, I have a question on how best to allocate our advertising funds. My two questions are:

1. When comparing the cost-per-lead associated with trade journals, how great a difference do you need before you would consider it significant given that your advertising costs increase in uneven increments as you increase ad size or frequency?

2. If you have a smaller advertising budget than your competitors, and there are between five and seven relatively strong publications serving your niche market, are you better off putting most of your money in two of the publications and getting maximum exposure with those readers, or going for a more modest level of exposure in all of the publications where your competitors are advertising?

A. On your first question, I would study the variation in my cost per lead associated with one ad size in one journal. You might find a 20 percent variation for the very same ad. This might be partially due to seasonality, but it is probably due in large part to the small sample size you are dealing with.

Implicitly, it appears that you are concerned about testing a larger size, color, or greater frequency because of the structure of the magazine's price list. I suggest that you talk this over with your space rep from the magazine. Tell the rep that you hope to generate more leads with a bigger ad (or that you would like to test this concept). See if you can get him or her to work with you on this.

Let the rep know that you would like to run an experimental ad or two. If the results are good, you will modify your ad plans and they will get more money.

In one case that I was involved with, we wanted to go from a quarter-page ad to a full-page, four-color ad. We had run one full-page, four-color ad and had gotten very good results, but we were nervous going from $1,500 to $5,000 for a full page ad. We explained our dilemma and we proposed that we would pay $2,500 for a full page ad, plus additional payments if we received more leads up to a maximum of $6,000. Our historic cost per lead had been $50, so we agreed to pay them $50 per lead for any leads over 50 up to the $6,000 maximum. The magazine was willing to go along with us on this, and we both ended up winning.

Your second question is tough. My intuitive reaction is to pick the top magazine or two and make sure that you have strong coverage in them. If their ads are four- color, full-page in every issue, I would want to be in every issue. While I might not go for four- color, I would really want my ads to compare well with their ads. This strategy boils down to insuring that we cover our bases with the first magazine before we go on to the second.

The risk in this approach is that if some significant part of your market doesn't read the primary magazines, they will never see you. This is something you can determine by asking your customers and prospects. I have seen both cases with magazines. In some markets everyone reads one or two primary magazines, and they read one of the secondary magazines. In this case you only have to cover the primaries. The other case is where your market is segmented and prospects don't all read one magazine. In this situation, if you focus on the one or two largest magazines you risk losing significant parts of your market. If you are in this situation, you might consider running large ads in the one or two magazines that you can afford while to have classified ads in the others. I am not thrilled with having classified ads competing with display ads, but it is probably better to have some advertising in these secondary magazines than none at all.

I suspect that you already have an idea of the answer to this question based on your contact with the market. If you aren't sure, you could always ask your customers and prospects. Once you have this data, you can plan your stategy.

L. Trade Shows (1989)

1. Is it lead generation?

Trade shows are another switch hitter. You can go to a trade show to 'be seen'. You want to create a good impression, but you aren't intent on generating leads and business directly from the show. On the other hand, you can go to a show to sell product. This might be either at the show or shortly thereafter based on the leads that you generate at the show. Different shows are oriented differently. For example some shows forbid vendors from selling at the show while others encourage it. Our rule is that lead generation programs are graded based on leads and then sales that you generate. If you aren't tracking leads, then it isn't a lead generation program.

2. Trade Show Objectives

Q. We are trying to establish objectives for a trade show we plan to attend, but we aren't sure what our objectives are. Can you give us some examples of objectives?

Chapter II. Lead Generation

A. The objectives should be clear before you decide to attend a trade show. I have clients who attend trade shows simply to generate leads and sales. Their objectives are to generate a pre-specified number of leads from each show. Assuming they do not have historical information regarding the cost per lead from shows previously attended, they determine the target (desired) number of leads by dividing the estimated cost of attending the show by the objective or target cost per lead. They may also have secondary objectives on cost per sale for these leads. Comdex is one show for which you might have a number of objectives. I went to Comdex with a client for whom this was the case. First they wanted to generate enough sales to recoup their cost of going to the show. Their second objective was to generate twenty five large account leads for their sales person to follow up. In addition, the President wanted to meet with six distributors and sign up one of them. The dealer sales person wanted to sign up fifty dealers and get a minimum order from each. Toward this end the company put together a special show package to encourage dealers to sign up. Finally, the Marketing Communications Manager wanted to meet with ten editors and generate one article or review.

As you can see, each person who attended the show had specific objectives in addition to the overall objective of generating enough sales to cover the cost of the show. I worked with the company management to determine reasonable objectives for each possible attendee and then to evaluate whether these objectives justified sending that person. The result was that there were people who wanted to attend the show, but didn't have enough business objectives to justify the cost of their attendance.

One way to get people to clarify their objectives is to ask "Why should we go to this show?" "What won't happen if we save the money and don't go?" If you can't come up with good objectives ask yourself why you should go. If the only real answer is to show the flag, you might consider whether spending that same money on advertising might not do more to show the flag. Don't assume that you have to go to a trade show just because your competitors do. You won't be successful if you don't have clear objectives.

M. Telemarketing (1989)

1. Background

Telemarketing is a versatile tool that can have many uses. We would like to discuss some of the alternative applications of telemarketing to provide a framework for this discussion. Outbound Telemarketing involves calling cold prospects. This can be done to both sell and inform prospects. Cold Calling is a common name for sales people calling cold prospects and trying to get a sales dialog going. The other alternative is to have non-sales people call prospects and deliver an informational message. Usually, this is done in conjunction with a direct mail campaign. Let's call this Informational Calling.

While most sales people don't like the idea of non-sales people talking to their prospects, it can be very effective. In the article below, a company marketing a feed-grain additive called 700 broiler chicken breeders to let them know a mailing piece was on its way. The TSRs also told the prospects that the mailer offered a chance to win a prize. They got a 27% response which was much greater than their typical 12% to 17% control case.

REFERENCE: "Direct Mailers: Reach Out And Phone Someone", *Sales & Marketing Management*, September, 1988.

Another use for telemarketing is to qualify leads. This is usually done once the prospects have responded to an advertisement or a direct mail vehicle. Typically, the objective is to gather additional information so that sales can be more effective. Let's call this Lead Qualification. If you are offering a premium, lead qualification is useful to confirm that the prospect is a qualified lead.

Telemarketing can also be used as your sales channel. We call that TeleSelling. In this situation, your sales people conduct all their sales processes over the phone instead of making direct sales calls or selling through dealers and VARs. Teleselling can be either inbound or outbound. That is, you can use direct mail or advertising to motivate prospects to call in to request information or to place an order. While some of the topics in this article apply to Teleselling, the focus of this article is on generating leads by telemarketing, either cold calling or informational calling.

How many times must you call?

One of the most difficult aspects of telemarketing is the number of calls you must make to reach your prospect and close the sale. Sales and Marketing Magazine executives did a survey and found out that the following % of sales were closed:

- 2% on the first call
- 3% on the second call
- 4% on the third call
- 10% on the fourth call
- 81% on the fifth call

The likelihood of completing a business call also increases as you make more calls:

- 17% are completed on the first attempt
- 26% almost always connect by the second attempt
- 47% of the time the third call did the trick

2. Alternative Approaches

There are an increasing number of alternatives to trading phone calls all day. In the survey, *Sales and Marketing Management* looked a number of these options. The results of this survey are shown below:

Alternative	% using	Computer Executives
First Class Mail	55%	40%
FAX	52%	74%
Next Day Mail	50%	58%
Electronic Mail	28%	52%
Same Day Courier	23%	0%

As you can see computer executives are much more likely to use FAX and Electronic Mail, and less likely to use First Class mail.

REFERENCE: "Telephone "Tag" Is A Reality For Most Busy Executives", Sales and Marketing Executive Report, January 4, 1989.

We have found these alternatives to be especially effective if you are about to give up on someone who has been impossible to reach. Put your message on their desk and let them respond. Make sure you tell them that the ball is in their court. You aren't planning to call so they must call you if they wish to continue the dialog.

3. Synergistic Lead Generation

Telemarketing can be used to augment your direct mail programs and increase your close rates. "Close rates of 20 percent to 30 percent of targeted and qualified prospects are not uncommon," says Richard Bencin in the article referenced below Richard recommends the following steps.

1. Define a narrow target market (use SIC-code or some other well-defined qualifier).
2. Buy a list with phone numbers.
3. Call to verify the names and titles.
4. Mail an introductory letter.
5. Call to introduce the company and qualify the prospect.
6. Get their agreement to review your material.
7. Mail the material.
8. Call to verify they received the material.
9. Turn the prospect over to sales.

Very few small companies conduct this type of sophisticated marketing campaign. Usually, they try to implement it by having the sales people make the calls. This doesn't work in our experience because this type administrative call is too boring for sales people. The sales people also want to start selling too early in the process. If you can integrate administrative people into the process to make these non-sales calls, you can really enhance the effectiveness of your sales people.

REFERENCE: "Synergistic Business-to-Business Direct Marketing", Richard L. Bencin, Direct Marketing, December, 1988.

4. Examples of Telemarketing Lead Generation

The following article described three synergistic lead generation programs.

Calma Corp.

Calma sells a $50K CAD/CAM system and generates over 1,000 leads a month for 40 salespeople. They implemented a lead qualification program to verify that the prospect has an application and that they have budget. They categorized the prospects into four categories:

1. Passionate plan to buy within six months,
2. Hot plan to buy within 12 months,

Chapter II. Lead Generation

3. Lukewarm plan to buy but aren't sure when, and

4. Cold aren't interested in CAD/CAM.

Relieving the sales people of the responsibility for qualifying their prospects solved one very important problem: The sales people were so busy selling to passionate prospects, they didn't qualify their new leads. They just didn't have the time. The statistics show why:

In the first three months of the program, 4,800 calls were completed. These completions were the result of 16,000 dials. The completed calls resulted in 1,500 leads. Of more than 10% of these leads, 160 contacts were considered passionate. Closing 10% of these passionate leads generated in the first month of the program would result in approximately $1 Million in sales.

Calma has extended this telemarketing program to keep prospects informed of new developments and to keep their database current. They also call the customers to survey their needs and see if there are new sales opportunities. This also generates leads for the sales force.

Texas Instruments

Texas Instruments decided to use telemarketing to sell equipment service contracts as a response to third party maintenance vendors. The objectives were to maintain existing business, improve customer contact, and identify both problems and opportunities. While this program was active, "the rate of maintenance contract renewals was increased considerably".

Initially TI didn't provide their telemarketers with any technical training. Listening to the conversations, they realized that training would enable the telemarketers to communicate more easily with the prospects. At the same time they implemented a system to send contracts out within 48 hours and to follow up in two weeks if the contract wasn't signed and returned. They also scheduled a second follow-up for one to three months later.

Based on their early success, TI expanded the program to become more proactive. They included outbound calls to new computer users, large multilocation prospects, non-contract users, contract users in advance of their expiration date, and ongoing customer survey calls.

The Slide Factory

The Slide Factory produces and sells computer designed slides. They place space ads in regional magazines which encourage the readers to call. Depending on the prospect, they either qualify, sell, or schedule a personal visit with the prospect. They then send out an information package and schedule outbound calls to coincide with the package reaching the prospect.

They also classify their prospects: A) major purchaser, B) purchasers who do not justify personal follow up (they use direct mail and telemarketing to keep these prospects active), and C) prospects who can only justify direct mail. The Slide Factory was able to increase its sales 2.9% while the industry was dropping 49%.

In reviewing these cases there are several common points:

1. The ongoing customer contact programs are very effective in that they identify problem customers so that their problems can be addressed. "Up to 95 percent of the dissatisfied customers will continue to do business if the company does something about their problem in a timely manner."
2. Technical training isn't necessary to qualify prospects.

REFERENCE: "Telemarketing Spurs High-Tech Sales", by Richard Herzog, *Direct Marketing*, February, 1988.

5. More Information

Q. Where can I get more information about telemarketing?

A. Telemarketing magazine is $49/year. It is available from Technology Marketing Corporation, One Technology Plaza, Norwalk, CT 06854 (203) 852-6800. The topics it covers are:

Business-to-Consumer Telephone Sales

- Business-to-Business Sales
- Obtaining leads and qualifying prospects
- Integrating mail and phone selling
- Making appointments
- Overcoming objectives and closing the sale.
- Handling customer complaints and building goodwill

- Upselling and Cross-Selling
- Negotiating

You also get Telemarketing's 100 Do's and Don'ts with your subscription.

6. Telemarketing Seminar

There is also a March 28-30 conference in Long Beach, "The Telephone is the Marketing Tool of the '80s and '90s". The cost is $300 for three days including a wide variety of seminars. For more information call 203-852-6800.

7. Using a Telemarketing Service Bureau

Q. What about using an outside telemarketing service bureau?

A. Traditionally, telemarketing service bureaus have either accepted inbound client telephone calls or placed outbound client telephone calls. Inbound calls may include — but are not limited to — catalog orders, media advertisement orders, and dealer-locator or product information inquiries. Outbound calls may include market survey questions, calls to qualify prospects or telephone sales calls. Contemporary service bureaus are able to use their computer systems to offer even more services. According to the article below, you should evaluate three things to determine if a service bureau is optimal:
1. **Functional Capabilities** — These include number of phone lines, number and quality of telephone service reps (TSRs), and computer and phone support for TSRs.
2. **References** — When you check references make sure that you ask them about both the good and the bad situations. Ask the Service Bureau for references who aren't on their standard reference list. You should also ask for software companies and companies in your local area.
3. **Price Structure** — Make sure that you establish the service levels (busy rates) for the prices you are quoted. Some firms manage to provide lower prices by having fewer TSRs and poorer service levels. Decide the service levels that you are comfortable with and then compare alternative service bureaus who can provide that level of service.

The inbound call rate structure of service bureaus usually have a fixed rate per call and a variable rate per minute per call. If your script or calls appear to be difficult, you will be charged on a per minute rate which usually results in higher charges. You should consider starting with very standard scripts and data collection to hold your costs down. Then you can experiment with adding additional questions.

The outbound call rates are a mix of fixed hourly charges, hourly profit incentives, and back-end reimbursements for customers who later cancel. The appropriate structure will depend upon your objectives for the program. If you want the TSR to sell like mad, give them an hourly incentive. If you want them to be thorough, pay them hourly.

There are a number of other charges which you must clarify and understand. They include charges for inquiries and complaints (yes, you *do* have to pay for these). There are also front-end charges to get going. The article mentioned that these front end charges can range from $15,000 to $50,000 in a case which required programming in addition to script development and administration. The final charges are for the back-end transmission of information to you. In another case, a client found that order transmission increased projected project costs by 25%.

Make sure you understand and pin down exactly what they will do, what you must do and what all the costs will be. Get their promises and policies in writing to avoid later confusion and upset when the bill arrives. Given the up-front costs, and the investment in training a new service bureau, it becomes very expensive to change service bureaus. A telemarketing service bureau can be a very effective tool in your marketing arsenal, but it can easily be a failed experiment.

REFERENCE: "Selecting a Telemarketing Service Bureau", by Paul Mohr and Seldon Young, Direct Marketing, June 1989.

N. Hardware Vendor Relationships (1989)

1. Cultivating a strategic relationship

Q. How should I cultivate a strategic relationship with my hardware vendor?

A. A good strategic relationship with your hardware vendor can be very beneficial, but it takes a major investment in senior management time. Typically the hardware vendor is much larger than the software company, so it is quite difficult to determine who to approach in the hardware company Usually you can find out the person with the formal responsibility, but often there are other key players who must buy into the process. For example, the hardware vendor usually has a software vendor liaison, but often they have little clout in their organization. You may need to win over the industry marketing people, or the local sales manager.

The pattern is different for each hardware software pair so you have to check it out. The CEO or VP of Marketing of your company must make the commitment to meet with the vendor personnel and establish relationships. This includes the sales people who are giving you leads. See if you can make presentations to the sales force or the industry marketing groups. Put them on the distribution for your newsletter. As you see what works, you can refine your approach. In dealing with large hardware companies, it may take one to two years before you start seeing the results. This may seem like a high price to pay, but we have seen very few cases which produced significant and steady results much faster than this.

2. Strategic Alliances

Q. I hear a lot of myths about strategic alliances with computer hardware vendors. What is the reality?

A. The computer hardware vendors talk a good line, but they all want you to port your software to their system at your own expense. With very few exceptions, the hardware vendors are so infatuated with their hardware that they feel you should pay them for porting. In the absence of hardware vendor support, you should only invest in porting to a new hardware platform based on customer demand. Make sure that you are making a good business decision before preceding.

Difficulties arise when the computer hardware vendor wants to jointly market your software. The very best case can be quite good. For instance, I have a client whose software was selected by a hardware vendor as part of a strategic initiative. The vendor had previously evaluated the software and then purchased it for internal use. They subsequently developed glossy marketing materials that featured the software and their endorsement of it. They trained their technical people to demo the software and their technical support people to help sell it. This was great, but it doesn't happen very often.

The more likely case is that the hardware vendor liaison personnel will describe the aforesaid as possibilities, but then will be unable to commit resources to carry out these programs. Make sure you ascertain who in the vendor organization has the budget and the staff to help market your software before you make investments. Meet with the responsible management and ask them to put their commitments in writing.

Marketing programs can change quickly in large companies and I have seen too many cases in which software vendors made major investments in strategic alliances and didn't get corresponding returns. I would urge you to be very self-protective in your dealings with large hardware vendors. For them to write off a program in which they have invested $100K is inconvenient; for many small software companies it could be disastrous.

3. Multiple Hardware Vendors

Q: How can we handle multiple vendor lines and still receive leads from these vendors? They're afraid that if they give us a lead that we will bid somebody else's iron.

A: You can make this work, but it's hard. You must convince them, and your own people that you have an iron-clad rule: if the hardware company provides the lead, you will only bid their hardware. This means that you won't try to substitute another hardware platform if you are about to lose the bid. You have to go down with the ship.

You should think carefully about this before you implement such a policy. It may not be workable in your marketplace. Are you willing to risk losing a major new client? On a lead that you probably would have got eventually anyway? Ask yourself (and trusted subordinates) wheter this practice makes sense for your firm. This requires a great deal of internal discipline and apllied integrity. To make it work, the "no switch" policy must be an iron-clad rule.

The second thing that you can do is have different individuals in your firm be the primary contract/advocate for your different hardware lines. If you do this it is easy for the advocate to tell the hardware sales people, "I'm in your camp. Please help me win over the boss by developing good leads and helping me promote my product." Dealing with multiple hardware vendors is like having more than one girlfriend. It can be done, but you have to take car,e and you will have problems on occasion. As long as you help the hardware vendor's sales people class the sale, they really don't care what you do with the est of your time. Make sure that your people are responsive and you should keep all of your vendors happy.

O. Direct Response (1989)

1. Getting the mail through

Business-to-business direct mail is a very effective way to market software. You can rent the best list in the world and still have your mailing be ineffective if it never really gets to the intended recipient. We recently encountered several articles that addresses a key question: How do you avoid having your mail diverted before it reaches your prospect?

Mail-Room   Practices

If you market to executives in large corporations, your letters have to run the gauntlet. The first barrier is to get through the mail room. Diane Curran, a VP and group management supervisor for Smith-Hemmings-Gosden, reported on her survey of Fortune 500 mailroon directors. The key results were:

- 41% had a formal policy on the internal delivery of business advertising mail.
- 40% said that third class mail would not be delivered with a title (no name).
- 19% said that first class mail wouldn't be delivered without a name.

A lesson here is that non-specific or low-class letters stand a chance of being automatically screened out by the corporate mailroom. In planning your direct-mail budget, weigh the increased cost of postage and the list rental against the increased effectiveness of the mailing. If this is a crucial item for your firm, test it out both ways.

REFERENCE: *Friday Report,* April 7, 1989.

The Importance of a Secretary

The next roadblock is the executive secretary. A poll of 52 executive secretaries of industrial manufacturing companies revealed that they toss one-fourth of the promotional mail that their boss receives. Another 24% is rerouted, and only 51% of promotional mail ever reaches the executive. On average, the executives surveyed received 20 promotional pieces per day. If you want to be one of the lucky 10, you must get past the secretary.

REFERENCE: "Entice The Gatekeeper", *Business Marketing* , March 1989.

Getting past the Secretary

The Richmark Group conducted in-depth personal interviews to better understand the selection criteria the executive secretaries use. They concluded that executive mail should:

1. Acknowledge the secretary as your initial audience.
2. Differentiate yourself on quality and image.
3. Keep it short, simple and easy to understand.
4. Personalize your letters.
5. Develop accurate lists.

The research found that secretaries have three key questions that they ask as they screen their boss' direct-mail:

1. Is it credible?
2. Is it relevant?
3. Is it personal?

The credibility screen reflects on the judgement of the secretary so this is a serious screen. Surprisingly enough, the criteria were quite standard. Don't waste money on a very expensive envelope — secretaries throw the envelopes out. On the inside, secretaries want to see color, clarity, and a professional presentation. The secretaries surveyed disliked tacky mailings and inaccurate addresses. Informational mailings are valued by the executives since they estimated that 54% of the executives keep information "on file" for later retrieval. Finally, the secretaries liked new, original mailings and disliked repeat materials.

The relevance test depends upon the secretary being able to understand the product and the benefit. If it isn't readily apparent what you are selling, the secretary will assume that your piece isn't relevant — out you go. Since the typical secretary spends 65 minutes per day screening mail, your piece must state quickly and clearly what you are offering.

Mailings with a business card or personalization were more likely to be passed on.

Chapter II. Lead Generation

Getting Read by Your Prospect

The final hurdle is for the executive to read your mail. Even if your piece has made it past both the mailroom and the executive secretary, you still must entice the executive to read your mailing. Executives studied typically prioritize their reading using the following hierarchy:

1. Time sensitive materials.
2. Personnel or compensation matters or company superior correspondence.
3. Customer letters.
4. Internal memos.
5. External promotional material.
6. Magazines.

REFERENCE: "Getting past the secretary", Richard Kerndt, *Direct Marketing*, January 1989.

Reflecting on this obstacle-course, you can see ways that you can make your mailings more effective by focusing on getting past the gatekeepers. Even if you don't sell to Fortune 500 executives, your prospects have their own screening criteria. We urge you to talk to your customers and prospects to see what their rules are. Use these insights to make your marketing more effective.

Corporate Mailrooms

A recent article discussed the fact that some corporate mailrooms have stopped delivering third class mail. As an example, General Motors announced that it would no longer distribute third class mail or controlled circulation publications at any of its plants. This policy can be traced to corporate cost-cutting.

Even if companies don't prohibit third class mail, many of them require mail stops for all mail. The article referenced below listed a dozen ways to get past the mailroom.

REFERENCE: "The Mail Stops Here!" by David Enscoe, TARGET MARKETING, September 1989.

2. Direct Mail

Double Post Cards

The double post card — one half for your pitch, the other half for your prospect's reply — is the current lead generation bargain. First class postage is only 15 cents versus 16.7 for bulk. They are especially effective when the product or service doesn't demand lots of explanation. You might find that double post cards are very effective with your house list, but less effective with cold lists. The familiarity of cold lists might change over time so that you might be able to do more of your lead generation with double post cards. We have had several clients who mailed a brochure type mailer and sent a double post card as follow up. This proved to be very cost effective.

There was an example in DM and Fulfillment where a double post card got a 30% greater response and a 60% lower cost per lead. We also experimented with a double post card to promote Software Success. Our response rate was comparable with letter mailings which we had previously used, and the cost was 35% less. This included the fixed cost for buying labels which is significant in our mailings. In spite of these costs, our cost per lead improved by 35%. We believe that we were able to get the same response rate with the double post card as the letters because of all of the promotion we have done over the years. We also found it easy to describe the newsletter within the confines of the double post card.

There's a stringent specification on what is allowable in double post cards. The following is a quote from Post Office's Domestic Mail Manual, section 332.2

"... A double post card consists of two attached postcards, one of which may be detached by the receiver and returned by mail as a reply. Each card is subject to the First-Class rate. However, postage need not be paid on the reply portion until it is detached and mailed as a reply. The paper or card stock used for single and double postcards may be of any light color which not prevent legible addresses and postmarks from being placed thereon. Brilliant colors must not be used" The permitted sizes: no smaller than 3 1/2 X 5", no larger than 4 1/4 X 6". (For each card.)

REFERENCE: "Whats Working", *DM and Fulfillment*, January, 1989.

Newsletters

While you may not think of a newsletter as a lead generation mechanism, it can be very effective as one of your regular mailings to your prospect list. It also gives you something to send to leads a couple weeks after you have sent them your information pack.

Q: We've heard that company newsletters are a good way to stay in contact with our customers and prospects. Is this true? Should we start a quarterly newsletter? What experience have other software vendors have with newsletters?

A: Almost all the software companies feel that they are very effective marketing pieces. Youi can use them for direct mail to cold lists, and they make a very nice credibility piece to send tonew leads. They give you a very easy way to stay in contact with your customers and all of the prospects who have contacted you in the past.

Writing the newsletter

The hardest thing about a newsletter is getting it written and produced on a regular basis when youhave limited resources. Very few small companies can afford to dedicate an in-house person to write the newsletter. Using an outside agency can be very expensive. This means that the task of writing the newsletter falls on sales and marketing,and management. If you have lots of good writers in your company, this may not be a problem. For many companies it is very difficult to vet the quality and dquantity of articles that they want for the newsletter.

Budgetary   Competition

You shuld also weigh the fact that newsletters use marketing dollars which might be better used for hard marketing programs (direct mail letters or advertising for example). It often seems that a software company would get more immediate results from a harder marketing rogram than the softer results of a newsletter. You can try tomeasure the leads to quantify the benefits, but you are really comparing apples and oranges.

'Initial Issue' Syndrome

If you do decide to publish a newsletter, be realistic about what you can accomplish on a regular basis. We feel that many companiew set their standards too high (too glossy a look, or too long an issue) with their initial issue. This makes it very difficult for the next issue to hold up to the standard that had been established. We believe that it is fat better to under-achieve on your early newsletters, and continue to improve them over time.

Pick the right frequency

Picking the right newsletter frequency is important, too. Producing a monthly newsletter is almost always overkill. A quarterly newsletter is right for most situations. But you may find that coming out with two newsletters per year is just as effective as publishing itquartrly. Publishing a semi-annual newsletter is the minimum schedule that you should countenance; if you publish less than twice a year, you begin to lose much of the continuity benefits.

How do Americans want to receive info?

American Banker magazine found that the top preferences were:

* Direct mail 57%

* In person 33%

* Telemarketing 2%

We have seen very real differences depending upon the market you are segmenting and the person you are trying to contact. This is something you could ask your customers in your annual customer survey.

3. Card Decks

Card decks are perhaps the most commonly disliked lead generation media. Many marketing people apparently feel that this lead generation approach is "low class" or "junky". We don't share that feeling about card decks. We have found, however that card decks can be an effective component in the lead generation mix for many companies.

The following mini-articles cover different aspects of using card-decks for lead generation.

Card Decks Work

The most important thing to know about card decks is that they work in many situations to effectively generate leads. This means that the use of card decks is expanding.

According to the SRDS Card Decks Rates & Data, card deck listings increased by 7% in 1988. There are 601 business card decks and 38 consumer card decks available.

REFERENCE: "Sales and Marketing Executive Report", Dartnell, 4660 Ravenswood Avenue, Chicago,IL 60640 (312) 561-4000).

Chapter II. Lead Generation

Increasing Card Deck Response

There was an article in the *Card Pack Currents* by Francine Picco that had a number of concrete suggestions on how to increase the response rate to Card Decks:

Use a catch headline or hook statement, identifiable graphics and photos, and concise, readable copy.

- Place graphics and photos in the right-hand area of the card.

- Highlight free offers.

- Use "800" numbers.

- Move the phone number of the recipient fill-in section to just after the name and title, and leaving plenty of room to write.

Francine felt that card decks could be used for testing demand for a new product and to build a mailing list. We have seen card decks be very effective in generating a large volume of inquiries at a very low cost. The challenge seems to be to be able to condense your offer down to the limited format of the post card. Free offers are also very effective given that you have limited space to tell your story.

REFERENCE: "Three Perspectives on Card Packs" by Francine Picco; *Card Pack Council Newsletter*, 6 E. 43rd St., NYC, NY 10017.

We recently encountered an article which detailed a test marketing program to test selling audiocassette programs on success motivation, positive thinking and self-improvement. Ed Wertz, the author, wrote that the card deck that he wanted to test cost $3,000. (This is the upper end of the range in our experience. The prices for cards is often between $1,000 and $2,000.) The cost of creating his ad (copy, design, type and mechanical) was $500. By comparison, he said that the cost of a direct-mail campaign would be $400 per thousand (Note that this is on the inexpensive side. We see many homegrown mailings which cost $1,000 per thousand. Another article mentioned that card deck costs were typically $18 per thousand which is twenty times less than direct mail.) Holding the amount of money spent as a constant, Ed could only mail a piece to 9,000 names by direct mail (the card deck goes to 150,000 names). On the other extreme, if he matched the circulation of the card deck with a letter, he would spend $60,000 instead of $3,500.

Sadly, Ed doesn't tell us how well the experiment worked. We would guess that our clients have felt that card decks were effective 50% of the time. Oftentimes, the difficulty is that the client isn't prepared to build a data base, and then market to their in-house data base. In many cases, card deck inquiries are much more in the information gathering stage. They are less likely to be ready to buy. On the other hand, your cost per lead for card decks can be dramatically lower than other alternatives.

REFERENCE: "The Great Equalizer" by Ed Wertz, *Direct Marketing*, January 1989. Designing Card Decks.

Ed Wertz wrote another article in which he gives thirty pointers on effective use of card decks:

1) Use a strong, benefit-evident headline such as, "Mailing Labels at 1/2 price."
2) Show an easy-to recognize photo or illustration of the product.
3) Use action-word, benefit oriented copy.
4) Try to make copy points in as few words as possible.
5) Use the largest possible type size for headlines, subheads and body copy.
6) Make an irresistible offer; if that's not possible, make it seem irresistible.
7) Highlight the free trial, money-back offer or guarantee.
8) Do 95 percent of the selling on the front of the card. Leave the back for the information gathering or business reply card.
9) Do not overuse color. Overuse of color misdirects and confuses the eye. Use four-color to show the product at its best advantage; use two-color to emphasize the strongest selling points.
10) Use reverses only for short headlines - never for body type.
11) Use a horizontal format. Avoid vertically designed cards that must be turned to read.
12) If the reader is to turn the card over tell him so with a bold arrow, line copy or turned corner graphic.
13) Show payment methods with graphics - VISA and MasterCard dingbats for example - when possible.
14) Use angled type only for one-word or two-word headlines.
15) Qualify prospects with check-off questions.
16) Use business reply mail when looking for a high quantity of less qualified leads.
17) Have the prospect use his own stamp when looking for fewer more qualified leads.
18) Sell only one product, one service, one idea or one related group of products, services or ideas.

19) Make the fill-in area look as much like a coupon as possible.
20) Put the fill-in coupon on the front of the card whenever possible.
21) Be sure to ask for all the needed information: full name, company, title, address, telephone, etc.
22) If prospecting for inquiries from businesses only, say so. Tell the prospect what he must do: no post office boxes, card must be signed, you must answer the questions to receive, etc.
23) If no salesperson will call, say so.
24) Make price charts clear and readable. Eliminate some choices if necessary to present material clearly.
25) If seeking an order to be followed by a bill, say so. If payment is due up front, say that also.
26) Make the 800 number stand out. State calling hours.
27) When space allows, place the company name and logo on both the front and back of the postcard.
28) When showing old prices compared with new lower prices, cross out the old prices, making sure they can still be read.
29) Use original graphics, borders or attention getting photos to make the card stand out.
30) When using screened photos, check with the publisher/printer to avoid murky reproduction.

REFERENCE: "Designing Card Deck Cards" by Ed Wertz, Direct Marketing, April 1989.

Software Success & Card Decks

Our own experience using card decks to promote Software Success exemplifies both the strengths and weaknesses of card decks. Our first problem was to identify a card deck targeted to software companies. The best we were able to do was to test card decks which targeted both vendors and end users. Thirty five percent the decks that we tried were software or hardware vendor personnel. It wasn't clear what percent of these were software marketing or management personnel. In retrospect, all of the successful card deck experiences have depended upon finding the appropriate targeted deck. We would recommend that you not try a card deck unless you can get a high degree of coverage on your target market. While you start out with a twenty to one cost advantage over direct mail, direct mail should get significantly better exposure than card decks so you can't afford to give away too much to too many bad names on the distribution of the deck.

The best thing about using the card decks was that we found some companies who weren't on the direct mail lists. This is the positive side of the broad exposure. On the other hand we drew responses from a lot of flakes. In retrospect we should have made our qualification stronger and clearer. If you only want business responses, say so.

Finally, card decks are easy to respond to (in some cases it almost seems too easy) so you can generate a lot of leads. As long as you are prepared to follow up on the leads, it is probably worth a test to see if card decks can work for you.

4. Classified Ads

We view classified ads as postcards in a magazine. They have the same basic limitations that card decks have, and they have the same appeal. Their basic problem is that you have such a constrained format that you can say very little other than FREE!!. The appeal is that the cost is much lower than display advertising so the potential cost per exposure is much lower. You must be really creative to insure that you draw attention to your classified ad to compensate for the size.

There are two other factors which make classified ads even more challenging. The first is that they are expensive on a cost per inch basis. You are paying for the opportunity to only buy a couple inches. The second is that they are more competitive. Everyone who is reading the classified ads is considering answering someone so your ad is competing directly with the other adjacent ads.

Classified Ad format

Q: We have had a lot of response to classified ad listings when there were no display ads interjected. It's like the readers were really reading the listings. Once display ads crept into the text listings, our response diminished. Do your think that the format change for the classified ads could really account for the reduced response rate?

A: Classified ads are very different from display advertising. They are much mote like directory listings. It is very important for your prospects to be able of find information quickly. If it is hard to find the information, the impact of the classified ad is diminished.

In the PC marketplace, PC WEEK has a very good corporate and dealer readership but their classified ads are a jumble. While some companies have a good success running a small display ad week after week, many others come and go.

PC and PC WORLD magazines, on the other hand, are less on the corporate buyer, Their classified sections are better organized, and they are much more effective in generating leads. Many people know that PC MAGAZINE has an extensive classified section, and we know dealers who check there first when they get a request for a new product. They view it like a weekly software directory.

If your current "book" has a confused, disorganized classified section, we suggest that you look around to find another, better organized classified section for your ad. Test it before you switch, but see if you can't improve your results.

More Guidelines

Q. What guidelines can you offer for small classified ads?

A. Ken Eichenbaum has published a book that sets out to guide people who are creating smaller ads. "This isn't design institute stuff", he says, "just practical guidance to ad layouts that won't get lost on the page." Some examples are:

- **Headlines** — Sans Serif faces are more readable than Roman and words set in upper and lower case are easier to read than all caps.

- **Body Copy** — Set body copy no smaller than 9 or 10 point sizes, and the line length should never exceed in picas more than two-and-a-half times the point size.

- **Go Outside** — Pay extra to have your ads set outside.

- **"Statisticall** y a two column by five inch ad will be read by 12% of the readership. Half page ads are read by 30%. (These statistics are based on data gathered by the Newspaper Advertising Bureau.)

- **Use your Space Rep** — If your readership/ lead generation isn't what you'd like, try complaining to your ad rep. Get them to try to improve your placement in an effort to improve your readership.

- **Borders** — Use a heavy border to create an island of copy surrounded by white space.

- **Headlines** — Make your headlines shorter and heavier.

- **Graphics** — Use illustrations and avoid photographs.

- **Layouts** — Develop consistent layouts.

- **Borders** — Settle on a standard border.

- **Coupons** — Coupons can increase readership by 8 to 10%.

- **Color** — A second color can add 10% to 20% to readership if the color is well-done or unique.

Two thirds of the book is devoted to samples from ad agencies. This may give you something to copy. There are also sections on readership segmentation, copy and design, measuring response, and establishing a newspaper advertising budget.

REFERENCE: *How to create small-space Newspaper advertising that works.* Unicom, 4100 West River Lane, Milwaukee, Wisconsin 53209; (414)-354-5440; 159 pages; $24.50 plus $2.00 handling.

Data Literature Advertising

Dear Dave,

I ran across a fairly inexpensive method of magazine advertising that seems to work. As with most small software companies, our budget is very limited so we looked for alternatives to 4 color, full page layouts. Some of the major trade publications now offer "data literature advertising". This method works as follows: We send the magazine a copy of our latest literature. They photograph the literature and provide room for a 60 word description that we supply. This form of advertising occurs three to four times per year per magazine at an average rate of $600.00 including reader number, photography, typesetting, etc.

The most interesting factor is that, of the companies we investigated that ran full page ads, and utilized the data literature advertising, the response in all cases was greater on part of the "data literature advertising" by 2 to 1.

In one magazine, the full page spread costs over $6,500.00. For $600.00, in that magazine, more leads for less money was a real advantage. I've enclosed a copy for your review.

Sincerely,
Al Salerno
President
Salerno Manufacturing Software

Dear Al,

Looking at the copy that you enclosed we were surprised that the "data literature ad" was only 1/6 page in size. Given that size the literature is little more than a picture, you can't read any text in the photo.

The best that we can figure is that two factors are helping. The first is that customers keep these issues and use them as mini directories. This would give them longer shelf life. The second is that there may be some implicit endorsement by being in this section.

This is a great story to remind us all about the value of experimentation and research. We were impressed that you called the other advertisers and gathered your facts before you embarked on this project. Good work.

Direct Response Source

Q. Do you know of a source of information on direct response?

A. There is a direct response conference October 16-17, 1989 in Washington, DC presented by What's Working in DM & Fulfillment. The entire conference is focused on the creative aspects of direct response: strategy, letters, packaging, execution, testing, and format. Further information can be obtained by calling (800) 223-9335.

5. Direct FAX

FAX marketing is a hot new topic that seems to stirring up a great deal of controversy. There are a number of states which are considering outlawing unsolicited FAXs. The penalties appear to be large enough that running afoul of these laws could be a major problem. It also appears that there is a strong potential for a backlash. There was a special report in the May 8, 1989 issue of What's Working in DM and Fulfillment, "A fast look at fax marketing" which mentioned a "5% response to fax promotion to 31,291 names ... - 3% were complaints and 2% were inquiries about how the promotion worked."

It appears that the root problem is that people object to paying for the paper to be used to receive unwanted direct response solicitations on their fax machines. The fact that the paper only costs pennies per page seems to be irrelevant. There seems to be the principle of infringing on the prospect's space. Using their paper or tying up their fax machine is questionable unless people have expressed an interest. We like the analogy of sending direct mail letters postage due or sending someone a bill for an unordered good. In these other contexts you just wouldn't do it, and we predict that unsolicited direct fax will never become successful.

There are other uses for FAXs which we believe will become popular. Sending in orders or returning information to a vendor are popular uses. A number of mail order firms are doing up to 35% of their orders via fax and we expect this to grow. Day-Timers has also used confirm imprint proofs with their customers. The difference seems to be that the parties have a business relationship and there is an agreement to accept the fax. Given this restriction, we believe that direct fax will become much more important in business communication.

6. Demo Disk Marketing

Q: We would like to use demo disks in our marketing. What do you recommend? What about follow-up to prospects who purchase the demo disk.

A: The answer to that question depends upon the cost of your demo kit. At one extreme your kit may consist of only the disk. At the other extreme it might also include slick packaging, some documentation, a brochure, and other collateral materials. Since the cost of a demo can range from $0.50 to $25.00, your strategy can vary widely.

Basic Strategies

There are several basic approaches to effectively using demo programs:

* **Unsolicited, free distribution— You might consider this if your product demos well without instruction or guidance, and if you can ensure that the demo recipients are qualified.**

* **Free to requestors — You won't charge for the demo program, but someone must request it.**

* **Sell your demo — The real advantage of selling a demo disk is that it qualifies the buyer.**

Unsolicited Distribution

If a low-cost strategy seems appropriate, you might try just mailing the demo disk to your prospects. The advantage of this approach is that everyone gets to see your demo if they bother to open your mailer and run the demo. The problem is that they probably won't. An unsolicited demo may generate a dis-

Chapter II. Lead Generation

appointing response: there is little reason for your prospect to actually run the demo and then contact you with a positive response. And if they don't contact you, you'll never know if they're interested.

While individual demo disks may be cheap, the conversion rate, (sales per demo), is so low that this method may end up being quite expensive.

Summary: You need to have a compelling reason to use this method — a sure-fire list of prospects that are dying to see your product, for instance. Said another way: you should have a good reason to believe that the cost per sale will be comparable to other techniques.

Free to Requestors

Another strategy is to offer your prospects a free demo. This can be via a direct-mail solicitation, through magazine advertising, or even as part of a trade show. (Demo disks at trade shows have proliferated in recent years.)

There are two important points about giving away free demos:
1. Make them ask. Be sure that your prospect wants the demo by requiring a positive action on their part.
2. Be prepared to follow-up. Ensure that you get the prospect's name and phone number for the follow-up. We'll discuss this more later-on in the article.

Our firm is currently using a double post card to offer a sample issue of this newsletter to potential new subscribers. (A double post card is two 4" X 6" post card perforated and folded back to front. This card can be mailed first class for $0.15 and can be printed for about $0.05 each. This makes for a simple and cheap mailing. Another advantage to using a double post card is that you can print a picture of what you are offering. This makes it very easy for people to respond. We have gotten good response rates with this technique.

Summary: We have several clients who are routinely offering demo disks via direct mail with reasonable success. When done properly, this technique can yield a very attractive cost per lead.

Selling a Demo

Should you sell your demo or give it away? Our feeling is that unless your costs are close to $5.00 per demo, it is better to give it away for free.

How much to charge? Our rule of thumb is that it is fair to charge two times your direct costs for a demo disk. If you charge much above this you risk offending your prospects. Any less and you won't even cover your expenses. This allows you to recover your indirect costs, but you won't really make any money. Prospects accept this as a reasonable business proposition. This type of pricing is only a problem with a small minority of prospects.

Don't be afraid to charge more for your demo if the circumstances warrant, however. We have one client that charges $100 for a crippled "test drive" of their product. The fee is warranted by the fact that a serious prospect will likely spend several weeks using a demo, and by the price of the full system: $15-25k.

In some cases your sales people will need the flexibility to send ut a free demo disk to a large prospect, or other unique situations.

Summary: The principal benefit of charging for your demo disk is that it qualifies your prospects. When someone pays money for an item, even a nominal amount, you can be sure that you have a serious prospect.

The importance of follow-up

Once you have sent your prospect the demo disk, the battle has just begun. You haven't won the war just because they requested a demo disk. You have to make sure they actually review the demo, and proceed to buy your product. While there are some individuals who will look at the demo and immediately order. That is the exception and not the rule. Our experience is that the close ratio for demo disks without sales follow-up is quite low. To make effective use of a demo program, you need to have a thorough, methodical follow-up program. Here's a generic version of the follow-up program. Here's a generic version of the follow-up program that we help our clients implement:

Follow-up Letter

We recommend that you send a follow up letter one week to ten days after the demo disk was mailed. This letter should cover the following points:

1. We hope that your demo disk arrived in good shape. If it didn't please call for a replacement.
2. If you have any questions, please don't hesitate to call customer support.
3. We would be happy to work you through the demo if you would like the help.
4. A sales rep will be calling next week to answer any questions.
5. The price is $nnn, please order.

Salesrep Calls

The next step is to have a salesperson follow up. The salesrep should only try to call and leave a message two or three times. If they are unsuccessful in contacting the person directly, your sales plan should call for sending a final letter which offers to schedule a time to receives the demo.

Tracking the Results

While we realize that this sounds like a great deal of work, it should dramatically increase your sales once you have generated the interest in the demo. You must track the costs and the benefits to make sure that your are making money on this sales effort. This can be marginal with low priced products, less than $200, but the economics depend on your statistics. Test it and find out. While your are at it, have your sales people ask your prospects for feedback on the demo kit. Perhaps you can improve your effectiveness by modifying your demo kit. Unless you get the customer feedback, your efforts at modifying your approach will have little intellectual basis and most likely will be controlled by emotional opinions.

P.   Lead   follow-up   (1989)

1. Mail Versus Phone for Lead Follow-ups

Q. Should we follow up on our leads by mailing them information or by calling them first?

A. With unlimited resources or inadequate leads you should put the most energy into each and every lead and call them. Visit them if possible. (This is a joke.) In the short term, your sales people have to make do with the leads they have. If they don't have any or

enough leads to follow up, they have to generate their own leads by making cold calls. Given this alternative, calling up leads before you send them information is certainly more productive than making cold calls. At least the leads have indicated some level of interest.

In the short run, I believe you should allow your sales people to decide how to manage their leads as long as they respond in a timely manner to the interest of each prospect. I personally believe that you should respond to a lead within a week of receiving a request for information. If your sales person can call back within that time frame, great. If weeks or months will elapse before that call is made, you are certainly better off mailing the information and then following up afterwards.

I am biased toward instituting an administrative system which automatically sends the response package, and then following up on a periodic basis. A series of letters is often effective, with one letter going out every two weeks for the first couple of months. Thereafter, send letters monthly. By instituting this type of system you can insure that the prospect is getting a minimum level of sales information automatically.

If the sales person has the time to call the prospect and start a dialog, all the better. It is, however, important to avoid the all too common situation where the sales people follow-up inconsistently; their responsiveness typically depends upon how busy they are closing sales. Such a feast or famine cycle for sales people is all too common. Once the sales people get involved in closing sales, they stop prospecting. When they close the business, they realize that their pipeline is dry and it takes several months or more to develop the prospects and establish their sales momentum again. The automatic prospect mailings can help continue the sales process independent of the efforts of a sales person. When the prospect decides that they are really serious and call or send in an additional reply card, the sales person can then spend the time to close this prospect.

Thus far my arguments have been to use mail because it is consistent and dependable. You could achieve the same effect by hiring more sales people and/or managing them to ensure they make the necessary calls on a timely basis. I have clients who have done this by hiring outbound telemarketers to make the follow-up calls. With this type of system in place, you can insure that the calls are made promptly as required. If you are considering this alternative, you must look at the economic tradeoffs. If you send a letter series to prospects, you might spend an additional $5 to $10 (maximum) to get the most mileage out of a lead that you spent $25 to $200 to generate initially. Contrast this with $15 to $50 to follow up this $25 to $500 lead using telemarketing. Is this a good use of your money?

It doesn't take much of an increase in conversion rate of leads to sales to make a letter series pay off. This is the case due to the low cost of the letter series relative to the cost of originally generating the lead. You are investing additional marketing money to generate more sales. I have yet to see a case where this doesn't make sense, but you should try it and gather the information to validate the techniques and costs in your case. Once you have established this as your base case, you might try hiring a telemarketer to follow up on leads and see if they can be cost effective in converting leads into serious sales prospects upon whom your sales people can call. I have seen several cases where this type of outbound telemarketing can be cost effective, but the economics are tough. A telemarketer can cost $25 to $50 per hour including salary, phone costs, etc. If they have a five to ten minute conversation with each prospect, they may have three to five conversations per hour. This depends in large part on how easy your prospects are to reach. Thus it might cost you $10 per phone conversation. I have seen cases where the cost per conversation was much higher ($20 per conversation), and only 20% of the conversations resulted in further sales action. A best case might be $10 per conversation with a 50% conversion rate or $20 per serious prospect. The worst case might be $20 per conversation with a 20% conversion rate or $100 per serious prospect.

This telemarketing investment might make sense depending upon your cost structure, your conversion rate of serious prospects into customers, and the price of your product. You do, however, have to be sure that you are generating more serious prospects by going to the additional expense of calling them. If you find that 10% of your leads become serious prospects when you conduct follow up mailings, you have to compare the additional cost of telemarketing with the incremental number of serious leads this activity generates. This is a stringent

requirement, but there are situations where applying it can make real business sense.

In conclusion, I would advise you to implement an automatic letter follow up program and collect statistics on your conversion rates of leads to prospects to sales. Once you have this in place, see how much time your sales people have for telemarketing lead conversion. If they don't have time to do the conversion, consider running an experiment with outbound telemarketing in an attempt to convert leads into serious prospects. After running such an experiment (with either your sales people or telemarketers), you will have the data necessary to evaluate the effectiveness of this additional investment in converting your leads via telemarketing versus generating more leads and just using letters to convert them.

2. Automatic Leads Follow-up

Q. We have a mass market product priced at under $500, and we generate leads by the thousands. We literally generate several thousand leads a month. How should we follow up on these leads?

A. Automatically and cheaply! While I don't know your numbers, I will describe a case which is similar so that you can see the basic constraints in this situation. Let's assume that you can generate leads for $10 each, meaning that you spend tens of thousands of dollars each month in advertising. This is typical for this type of mass market advertising. Next let's assume that 10% of your leads result in sales meaning that your lead generation cost per sale is $100, or 20% of revenue.

While you can live with 20% of revenue spent on lead generation, you can and should work to cut it to 10%. At the same time the situation is worse than I have described. Your cost should include not only the advertising cost per lead, but also the cost of response materials. The cost of a package of materials which you mail to your prospects can be as high as $5, particularly if you include your labor costs. This materially impacts your lead generation cost as a percent of revenue.

The first step to reducing your lead generation cost involves developing an inexpensive information response package. If you need to send a lot of information, you might want to consider a self-mailer containing a brochure, an order form and a reply envelope. For instance a 24 page flyer might cost $0.50

to $0.75 each to print in the large quantities you would use. Such a flyer will lower your reproduction costs and your labor costs. It can also be sent at bulk postage rates due to the quantities you are dealing with. An unexpected benefit of this flyer is that you can send your full package to anyone who inquires, for instance bingo card respondents and other marginal groups.

Now that you have saved some money, I urge you to reinvest a little to fully exploit the leads you have generated. Put together a series of two to four mailings to spur prospects to buy. If you sent the flyer third class, send them a double postcard first class to confirm that they received the flyer. Make it easy for them to request a copy of the flyer or to suggest someone else who might be interested. Send this a week or two after the flyer was sent. Make sure that you print out the labels for all of these follow-up mailings at the same time you print the initial labels. Use a manual system with folders to control when the follow-up mailings are sent. If you make it very simple to do, it will happen automatically. If it is at all complex, it won't happen.

Any subsequent mailings should be informational and or sales oriented. You might send one sales letter followed by a press release or article. Given your quantities I would be tempted to make these self-mailers to hold the costs down.

The payoff from these follow-up mailings must be monitored. Before you start, establish your lead generation cost per sale. Then track it as you refine your lead follow up procedures. My experience is that as long as you hold down the cost of follow-up mailings, they can be very cost effective. Once you have spent the initial $10 to generate a lead, spending an additional $0.25 to send a follow-up flyer can result in a very high return on the incremental ($0.25) investment.

Q. Database   marketing   (1989)

1. Mining a Prospect Data Base

Q. We have thousands of prospects in our database. What are the best ways to mine them?

A. You must establish the quality and relevance of the prospects in your database I have seen a number of databases containing prospects from trade shows five years ago. These generally aren't worth mailing

to. First re-qualify the leads which are more than a year old. To do so send them a simple mailer with a reply card, which asks them if they are still interested. Would they like a current copy of your marketing materials? Do they want to stay on your mailing list? Would they like a call? Depending on your feelings about the quality of these leads, consider a "Please respond or be purged from our list..." mailing. As part of this re-qualification process, you might also consider mailing a survey to gather information about your prospects.

After cleaning up your database, put together a program for regular mailings. Many companies mail to their prospects base monthly while others mail bi-monthly or once per quarter. I feel you should strive to mail to them monthly. At first this seems overwhelming, but remember that a mailing needn't be fancy or expensive. A quarterly newsletter for your customers could take one slot each quarter. Other candidates include press releases, product fact sheets, application articles, and letters of an informational nature. The objective is to remind the prospect of your presence and of what you are selling. Make sure you always include a simple reply card so that it is easy for them to ask for more information or a sales call. Do this with a simple flyer attached to a reply card. I would also give them a "Drop me from your list" option on the reply card.

The final stage is automatic purging. Send them a "Respond or be purged..." mailing at the end of a year. If you don't do this, the size of your list will grow, its quality will decline, and your return from it will drop.

2. Trading Mailing Lists

Q. We have been approached by a non-competitive company who also sells to our prospects. They would like to trade mailing lists.

A. On the surface this is a great opportunity to gain access to potential prospects. This is especially attractive if there are no good lists available for your market.

The first consideration I would have is whether this a good company. Are the people ethical? Do I really trust them to live by our agreement? If you can't say "yes" to this, don't proceed. You are about to entrust one of your company's critical assets with an outsider. While you can put some controls in place, you are only asking for trouble if you don't trust the people.

Even if you trust the people, you must be very specific about the arrangement. A common approach is to send a set of labels to a letter shop and have the lettershop apply the labels to their mailing. You can make it very clear that they have one-time use only. By making it clear to the lettershop that this is the arrangement, you can use the lettershop to help enforce the one-time use of your labels. My experience is that lettershops take this type of restriction very seriously.

The next step is to seed your list with decoy names. Make sure that you include some out-of-state names. This will allow you to detect when your list is used without permission. In addition to the simple provision that they won't use your list more than once, I would consider a penalty schedule for each illegal use. For example, $10,000 for the first offense, $25,000 for the second, and $100,000 for the third. If you have this in place, they will have to pay you money if they use your list illegally.

I would check with my attorney to make sure that this schedule wouldn't undermine my right to prevent them from using it more than once. If you take these steps, I believe that you should be reasonably protected. If the company you are talking to is bothered by any of these precautions, I would seriously reconsider the trade. They are protected by these same provisions.

3. Managing Mailing Lists

Q: How should I manage my mailing lists?

A: We would like to distinguish between two types of lists:

Hot Lists

Hot or 'active' lists are prospects who have responded to your marketing efforts in the past. The hot lists also include your customers, friends, and other industry contacts that you want to stay in touch with.

Cold Lists

Cold lists are lists of 'suspects' that are rented or purchased from list brokers or other direct-mail professionals.

Maintaining a Hot List

You must keep your active list up-to-date yourself or you must pay someone to keep it current. We urge you to do this internally because you will have many uses for this list. It is an important company asset and should be cared for and protected as you would your source code. Keeping the addresses current can be a problem. We have fund that the following technique works well: send a first-class mail piece to everyone on this i● at least once every six months. Request address correction on the envelope. The Post Office will send you change of address notices and will return the undeliverable items. Use those items to keep the names on your list current.

Purchasing Cold Lists

Cold lists are the real dilemma. You can pay as much as $100 per thousand labels to $250 per thousand for a one-time use of a well-targeted list. Some list vendors also offer unlimited-use. This fee is typically twice or three times the one-time use rate. If you are planning a marketing campaign with multiple mailings in a short period of time, the unlimited use option seems attractive. (We should also mention that you can pay to have names entered into your own database from printed directories for the same two- to three-times multiplier the one time use costs.)

Advantages of buying Cold Lists

Before you decide to get an unlimited use data base, we would like to give you several reasons that the one-time use approach might be best:

1. FLEXIBILITY — You retain the flexibility to try new lists. You should test all of the reasonable lists before you commit to one. (Remember the first three rules of direct-mail marketing?L Test, Test, Test!) We suggest that you try the same mailing to all of your alternative lists so you can rank their effectiveness. In particular, we urge you to conduct at least one first class mailing to each list to measure the non=deliverable rate. We have found that this rate varies from 0.7% to 22% for the same target market. You might find that the bargain labels aren't the real bargain that you thought.

2. LIST MAINTENANCE — The cost of maintaining a list is much higher than you would guess. You must update the change of addresses as well as personnel changes. This can easily require a full-time clerical person to keep the list clean. If you let the quality of your in-house cold list decline

because you don't want to incur clerical expenses, you are being penny wise and pound foolish.

Our Recommendation

If you can find good-quality lists from outside vendors, and if they keep these list up-to-date, we recommend that you buy your cold lists. Once you select a list vendor you can usually negotiate a quantity discount if you are willing to commit to a specific purchase quantity.

4. Caring for In-House Mailing Lists
Maintaining a Prospect File

If your mailing list is on a computer, the postal service will clean up city names, addresses, and ZIP codes at no charge. (Call 1-800-842-9000 ext. 271, ask for name and number for your local postal rep.) Having a clean prospect list will save you the obvious costs of non-deliverables and change of addresses.

Fingerhut is a very large direct-mail marketeer that recently chopped their costs by cleaning up their lists. Even with all this effort, they still have a 3% inaccuracy rate. Two thirds of this are change of address and one-third are undeliverable. Fingerhut feels that they are much better off with a "clean" list as opposed to the national average of 9% bad names.

When you start a lead generation program you should capture the prospect information in a computer readable format.   In many cases, software companies have generated lots of leads which lie fallow in shoe boxes. You should examine these leads and see how good they are before you pay to enter them into your prospect file. Entering hand written names from a trade show five years ago may not be cost effective. In a number of cases, we have sent one mailing to the questionable names. We let them know that they would be dropped from the list if they didn't respond. This can generate some lead activity, but at the same time it also purges a lot of poor quality prospects.

At the same time, it is more important to capture all the new names you are generating. Make sure that you get these names and that you systematically exploit them. Make sure that you include a complete set of possible fields to track a lead through the sales cycle until they become a customer.   At the same

time make sure you allow track adequate information. It is much easier to track fewer fields instead of more over time.

Reference: "List Hygiene Saves Fingerhut $25 Million, 'Dirty' file brings lost income down to a manageable $12.8 million.", Catalog Business, March 1, 1989.

Maintaining List Security

Your prospect list is a business asset and as such you should protect it. Copyrighting your list is one step that you can take. You can apply for Copyright Registration for a nondramatic literary work (Form TX). Write to the Copyright Office, Library of Congress, Washington, D.C. 20559. The form is free; it costs $10 to register your copyright.

The next step is to seed your list with seed identifiers (errors in spelling, odd street codes, etc). Many companies have both internal and external seeds.

Using Trade Secret Protection

The next area of security is trade secret protection. To preserve the "trade secret" status of your list, you must proclaim that it is a trade secret to your employees, and you must monitor everyone who has access to the list. Furthermore you must limit access to those who have a "need to know." The precautions to protect a trade secret include:
1. Warning notice on every list.
2. Limited circulation.
3. Employee education.
4. Signed contracts including non-disclosure agreements.
5. Access control via signs and company procedures.
6. Restrictive licenses if you sell your list.
7. No overkill (e.g., don't mark everything trade secret).

If you think that these steps are too much work, think about how you would feel if one of your employees left to work for a competitor with a copy of your house list, and you had no recourse. We realize that this may seem remote, but it can happen, and you will be powerless unless you take the above steps.

REFERENCE: "List Security", Robert J. Posch Jr., Direct Marketing, November 1988.

Chapter II. Lead Generation

List Valuation and Renting your list

One of the benefits of developing a prospect list is that you can generate some revenues by renting it. The going rate for a list ranges from $40 to $250 per thousand for one-time use List rental income can add up and can help offset your maintenance expenses.

If you decide to rent your list, you should study the list security issues. There are companies who will help you monitor your list.   For as little as $60 per year they will monitor 5 cities and tell you if your mail is being delivered, how long it takes to be delivered, and if your list is being used without authorization. This is a small cost given your investment in your list and the replacement cost.

Even if you don't rent your prospect list, you might consider the list rentals you would have to pay if you didn't have your own prospect list. In our case, we have a prospect list of 2,000 names which we mail to monthly. If we paid $125 per thousand, we would pay $3,000 per year in list rentals. We have a client whose prospect/customer list is 150,000 names and they mail quarterly. At $100 per thousand their annual cost would be $60,000 which is getting significant.

One of the factors which must be considered before you rent your list is the revenue opportunity versus the security risk. If you implement the trade secret and copyright procedures, you should minimize your security risk. A formal rental contract is another prudent step. Finally, you might limit your rentals to firms who use reputable lettershops. The lettershops will be much more cognizant of the technicalities of protecting your list. With all of these steps you should be legally protected.

The other exposure is that you won't approve of the mailings. You can deal with this by reviewing the mailing. Insist on reviewing the actual mailer including the order sheet, etc. If you aren't comfortable with the mailing, you can always say no.

REFERENCE: US Monitor Service, (800) US Monitor.

5. Marketing Your Customer Database

What is all the to-do about marketing your in-house database of prospects/customers? Why is it suddenly important? The first reason is that with micro-computers the cost of managing a database is much lower. This is a technology driven reason and as such, it may or may not make business sense We believe that the real reason that database marketing is so important is because the world is becoming more and more competitive and companies are realizing that their relationship with customers is their most important asset.

In the good old days, sales people maintained extensive customer files. As long as employees stayed with the company, individual files were company assets. There are a number of risks in this approach. The first is that when the sales person leaves, the company loses that information. In fact, they might even compete directly with you using information they gathered while they were your employee. You can protect yourself with confidentiality and noncompete agreements, but it is still an exposure. While you can minimize the risk that your ex-employees will use this information to compete directly against you, you can not guarantee that your company will be able to exploit this information.

A second problem, is that different sales people will exploit this information inconsistently. One salesperson may be very good at keeping up their files, while another may not have the interest or aptitude. The third problem is that you aren't getting this information at the corporate level to aid in management and marketing decisions. Once you start to collect your own internal information you can augment it with externally available information. While this will require some programming, you will be surprised at the amount of information you can end up with. Your internal sources of information include but aren't limited to: warranty cards, rebate information, survey data, customer service, and your contracts and accounts payable departments. This is probably the most significant factor, as you are losing the opportunity to make your marketing smarter.

6. Examples of Database Marketing

Daytimers sells time management products and they have made extensive use of data base marketing to be more effective. Among other things they collect home addresses so they can follow individuals as they change companies. They have built a data base of two million buyers. They classify their buyers as user, influencer, decisionmaker or buyer and they target mailings to these individuals based on their buying patterns.

REFERENCE: "Business-to-Business Database Marketing", *What's Working*, March 1989, JPL Publications, (301) 961-8777.

The Conference Board markets a Marketing Conference to senior management. They felt that a centralized source of marketing data allowed them to:
1. Specialize by industry.
2. Increase cross selling.
3. Focus marketing programs.

They also found they were able to dramatically increase "word of mouth endorsements" by providing their sales people with information in the marketing data base.

REFERENCE: "Database Marketing Moves Into The Service Industries", *Sales and Marketing Executive Report*, February 15, 1989.

7. Building a Customer Database

This article stated that it takes 9 to 12 months to "transform separate files for invoicing, prospects, customers, products, promotions, and others into a single, up-to-date information source." Jennifer Barret, VP Business Development for Acxion Corp. provided the following checklist:
1. Establish your business objectives.
2. Get corporate commitment.
3. Identify funding for the project.
4. Establish a development team including the user groups.
5. Survey your marketers on their special objectives.
6. Deciding whether to do this inside or out.
7. Identify the sources of names.
8. Negotiate with data and name suppliers.
9. Collect the data. Netting duplicates.
10. Integrate the data.

One company spent $200,000 to establish a system with 2 million names, not counting management time. Another consultant, Jacob Schwartz of Statistical Research Systems, claims that you can have a system for $100,000 (including hardware but excluding consulting and personnel costs). John Klein has a one-page worksheet for calculating the cost of developing and maintaining a business to business data base. Send a stamped #10 envelope to:
What's Working Data Base
4550 Montgomery Ave.

Suite 700N
Bethesda, MD 20814

REFERENCE: "Taking A Giant Step Forward: From Customer File To Data Base", *What's Working*, February 27, 1989.

8. Using Technology to Cut Database Costs

Mary Ann Kleinfelter provided the following checklist to see if a firm could cut costs by using more technology in their database area. She conducted a survey which showed that less than one-fourth of mailers had incorporated an enhanced database as part of their strategy. Here is her checklist:
1. Is the information on your customer file adequate and accurate? This information won't be accurate unless you have a program to keep it up to date.
2. Is your order form working up to its potential? While there is a reluctance to ask too many questions, she has found that you might find one or two simple questions which could be very important.
3. What if the order form is not enough? SIC coding, census data, D & B financial information, etc. can't be gathered from the order form, but these types of information can be critical.
4. What can you do about rented prospect names? If you find that the above special information is critical, you might consider overlaying this information on your cold lists before you market to them.
5. How can you make postal processing part of your database marketing strategy? You can clean up your data base with ZIP correction and NCOA (National Change of Address) processing. The post office will process your list for you, or your lettershop may have software available to do this for you.

REFERENCE: "Building A Business-to-Business Database", by Mary Ann Kleinfelter, DM News, March 15, 1989.

9. Using a Customer Database

Rich Crocker wrote an article that had a list of possible uses for a prospect database:
1. Direct mailings targeted by territory.
2. Introduce a new sales manager to your prospects.
3. Identify prospects who haven't been called on.
4. Follow up mailings to inquiries.
5. Did you buy survey?
6. Announce new features to prospects.
7. Announce your presence at a local show.
8. Prepare a show report.

9. Give a salesman a disk with all his prospects.
10. Invite prospects to a local seminar.
11. Follow up on last year's show.
12. Generate lead forms for prospects who have been qualified.
13. Let your sales force know that they can use the data base.

REFERENCE: "Inquiry Data Base, Make It Work For You", Rich Crocker, *IHS Newsletter*, 1st Quarter 1989, (818) 365-8131.

The National Center for Database Marketing conducted a conference on "Database Marketing: The Revolution." They look like a possible source of more information. You can contact them at (916) 292-3000 or (212) 465-1801.

Summary

Database marketing is one of those buzz words that sounds great, but not a lot of people really do it. In part they don't because it is hard work, but we also believe that a lot of people talk themselves out of it. They decide that this is really a $100,000 to $200,000 project and that they can't afford that. These costs are very real and very easy to identify. The problem is that the costs of not upgrading your database are hard to identify, but are equally real.

We urge you to look over the lists of possible benefits and applications and see which ones you might like to try. Which ones might really pay off? Try to assign a value to these capabilities. Next see what you can do to test the value of this capability. For example, if you identified follow-up mailings to inquiries who haven't bought as being critical, you might consider printing multiple sets of labels when you print the label for the inquiry. A very simple manual system with labels in folders can be used to send out follow-up mailings. You can even establish procedures to pull labels when someone buys part way through the process. This manual approach isn't perfect, but it should give you a good idea of the possible benefit. Once you are convinced of the value of the capability, you should be prepared to implement a system. As a final note, please don't let your techies shame you into scrapping manual systems which really work. The objective is to solve your business and marketing problems, not to build a monument.

1992
Software   Success
Reference   Book

Chapter III
Pricing

A. Competition Survey (1991)

We had 191 responses to this survey, which is another record. I was pleased with the response since a number of companies which don't have direct competition might not complete the survey. We had a number of incomplete surveys which listed this comment.

1. Company Revenue
The respondents are very similar to the Reader Survey last fall. In both cases, over ten percent of the respondents have over $5 million in revenue.

Company Revenue	% Resp
No Reply	2.1%
<$250K	15.5%
$250K-$500K	8.3%
$500K-$1M	20.2%
$1M-$2M	21.8%
$2M-$5M	20.7%
>$5M	11.9%

2. Computer Type
We had slightly more LAN companies and somewhat fewer mainframe companies. I think that the increase in LAN companies reflects the increasing number of LAN companies and products. I suspect that some of our mainframe readers don't have much competition and so fewer of them responded.

Computer Type	% Respondents
PC	59.6%
LAN	20.2%
Mini	16.6%
Workstation	10.4%
Mainframe	6.7%

We had 219 responses to this question which is 1.2 times the number of respondents. This means that 20 percent of the companies operate on two platforms.

3. Product Price
This was quite similar to the reader profile. While it isn't cut and dried, you can see some consistent patterns in product pricing. The most popular price range is $1,000 to $10,000. I see many vertical market products in this range, as well as tools for corporate America.

The next most popular price range is over $25,000. If you are selling a significant product to large compa-

nies, raising the price to over $25,000 makes a lot of sense. These big companies want the full solution and they are willing to pay for it.

4. Number of Competitors in a Typical Sales Situation
If you look at the pie chart above, you will see that the most common response and the median response was to have three to five competitors in a typical sales situation. This is far more competition that I had expected. A number of my larger clients are dealing with this level of competition. Most of my smaller clients have much less competition. My experience is that heavy competition during the early growth period can be very damaging. It is hard to maintain prices and profits to fuel growth if you have competition in most situations.

5. Number of Competitors
When you look at the total number of competitors, it is even worse. The median answer is six to ten, but the most common answer is more than ten!

Furthermore, I was surprised that so few companies had either no competitors or only one competitor. It is possible to keep the level of competition under control if there are just two of you. Once you are in the two to five competitors environment, things tend to get out of control.

# of Competitors	% Resp
No Reply	1.6%
None	5.7%
One	3.1%
2-5	28.5%
6-10	27.5%
More than 10	33.2%

This level of competition is even more significant; if you refer to last year's issue on Pricing you can see that things really have gotten worse in the last few years. (See the table on the next page.)

Product Price	% Resp
No reply	8.3%
<$100	9.3%
$100-$500	14.5%
$500-$1K	9.3%
$1K-$10K	31.1%
$10K-$25K	14.5%
>$25K	16.1%

Number of Competitors in a Typical Sales Situation

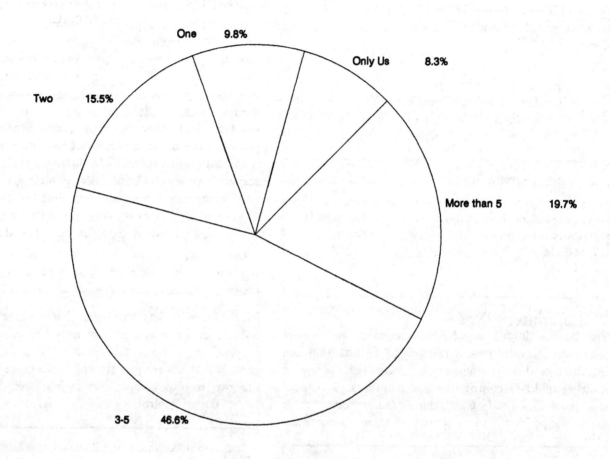

Number of Competitors	1989	1990	1991
None	14.5%	2.9%	5.7%
1	36.0%	13.0%	3.1%
2-3	30.0%	46.4%	28.5% (2-5)
4 or more	19.5%	33.3%	60.7% (> 6)

The number of people with one or no competitors has dropped dramatically in the last two years. It was 50.5 percent in 1989, 15.9 percent in 1990 and now it is 8.8 percent. There has been a corresponding increase in the number of markets with four or more competitors. Things really are getting tougher. It isn't just our imagination.

6. Number of New Competitors

There are more and more new competitors every year. In particular, I was interested in the number of people who had two or more new competitors each year. Anyone who has two new competitors is dealing with a competitive situation. The cumulative effect is even worse. Unless they have gone out of business, they see more competition every year.

Number of new competitors	1989	1990	1991 Expected
No Reply	10.9%	6.2%	10.9%
None	28.5%	21.8%	21.2%
One	23.3%	27.5%	22.3%
Two or more	37.3%	44.6%	45.6%

7. How Might the Numbers Stabilize?

I have heard that 20 percent of small software companies go out of business every year. If you have ten competitors in a market, two of them might go out of business. They might be replaced by two new competitors. I have seen several markets similar to this. The only difference in real life is that a number of the companies don't go out of business. They just become part of the "living dead." The principal continues to support his customers and make the occasional sale. In most cases they stop marketing, but they will receive calls because of their prior marketing. These "living dead" companies can hurt everyone in the market. They will lower their prices and discount at the drop of a hat. The don't make many sales but they do get some revenge against their competitors.

8. Percent of Time Someone Discounts

The median is that someone discounts 20 to 40 percent of the time. This is fairly tough. The markets that I hate are the ones where someone discounts more than 60 percent of the time. Sixteen percent of you have this unfortunate situation.

When you compare these results with last year's survey, there are some markets where no one discounts (it didn't occur last year) and there are more markets where discounting occurs over 40 percent of the time.

Discount amount	% Resp
No Reply	7.3%
None	13.0%
<5%	3.1%
5%-10%	15.5%
10%-20%	38.9%
20%-40%	20.2%
>40%	2.1%

I had expected more small discounts under 10 percent, but as you can see in the box above, this is uncommon. The 10 to 20 percent discount is most common. I have seen a number of situations where sales people can discount up to 20 percent without management approval. Corporate buyers also like to get a 10 to 20 percent discount.

% Time Discounting	1990	1991
Never	0%	14%
<10%	29%	17%
10%-33%	47%	31% (10%-40%)
>33%	24%	33% (>40%)

9. Amount Discounted on Average

I continue to be surprised at the small markets where no one discounts. That would be very nice. I have encountered very few situations in my consulting where there is no discounting.

The over 40 percent discounts are serious, and fortunately quite rare. The heavy action is the 20 to 40 percent range. This is similar to the group that had five or more competitors in a typical competitive situation. This certainly fits my experience that when the competitive situations are too busy, discounting accelerates.

If you compare these results with last year's survey you will find that there is less discounting than we found last year.

Percentage of the Time Companies Give Discounts

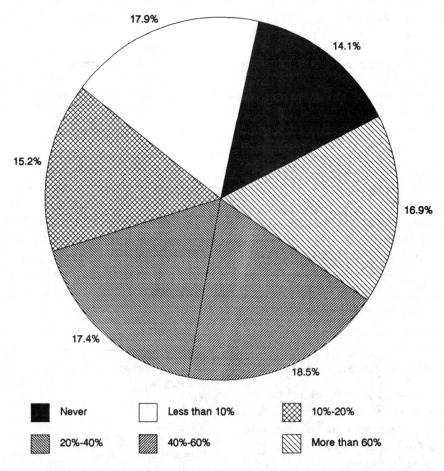

While my ranges are slightly different, it appears that there has been a real decline in people offering really large discounts. I believe that this is a good sign. Offering discounts over 35 or 40 percent rarely wins the business. Even if you do win, it tells the customer that you were really charging them too much. Finally, it is very hard to stay in business, let alone be profitable, with this level of discount. It appears that as an industry that we are learning that this type of behavior isn't good business. My only hesitation is that last year's survey had less than 60 responses, so I am concerned about the validity of the statistics.

10. Discount Amount versus the Number of Competitors

The table at the top of the next page shows the discount amount by the number of competitors. The first general observation is that the median discount amount increases as the number of competitors increases. This is as it should be. There are a couple of interesting observations that I wouldn't have guessed.

Why do 30 percent of the companies with no competitors discount 10 to 20 percent? Is this really the standard discount for all products in certain markets (like the DP MIS market)?

With no competitors or one competitor, people don't discount more than 20 percent (thank goodness). Once there are two or more competitors, 25 to 30 percent of the people encounter discounts of over 20 percent. Looking at the data, there are a reasonable number of samples in these three cells so the statistics seem okay. I would have thought that the situation for companies with ten or more competitors would be dramatically worse than those with two to five. I guess that once you are in the two to five range things get hot and it really doesn't get much worse after that.

Discount Amount	1990	1991
0%-5%	9%	16%
5%-15%	42%	39% (5%-20%)
15%-35%	32%	20% (20%-40%)
>35%	17%	2% (>40%)

#Competitors	No Discount	<5%	5% - 10%	10% - 20%	20% - 40%	<40%
None	50%	10%	10%	30%	0%	0%
One	40%	0%	40%	20%	0%	0%
2 - 5	19%	0%	19%	36%	25%	0%
6 - 10	8%	6%	13%	43%	30%	0%
>10	6%	3%	15%	50%	18%	6%

11. Length of the Sales Cycle

It takes three to six months to sell most software products. This is the most common answer and the median answer. Very little software (less than 20%), sells in less than three months. A significant number of products take up to a year to sell.

I think this is the real reason this is such a tough business. We are asking people to change their behavior and they take their time to decide to buy our software products. I suspect that the sales cycle for hardware products is significantly shorter. One minor bit of good news is that very few companies have a sales cycle over a year long (5%). I suspect that companies with this length sales cycle go out of business fairly often which would keep this population down. I have encountered several products with sales cycles well over a year. They were all sold by very large companies and the average sale was $500,000 to $1.5 million. With this sized sale, you can afford to fund the extremely long sales cycle.

Length of Sales Cycle	% Resp
No Reply	2.6%
Immediate	3.1%
<1 week	1.6%
<1 month	4.7%
1-3 months	23.7%
3-6 months	33.2%
6-9 months	14.0%
9-12 months	13.0%
12-18 months	3.6%
>18 months	0.5%

12. Change in Sales Cycle

I should admit that I asked this question expecting to find that people had seen an increase in the sales cycle. There were several reasons for this hypothesis. The first was that I have a number of clients who have had very poor sales since August. In particular, companies selling to the Fortune 500 have seen a number of acquisition decisions postponed. The prospects didn't decide not to buy, they just put it off. In some cases they instituted additional approval levels, while in other cases they just pushed the decisions out two to four months.

My other reason for expecting an increase in the length of the sales cycle was that I thought additional competition would drag out the acquisition. I have seen this any number of times. In a very competitive situation, it can take more time because everyone is throwing curves at the prospect.

Anyway, the data says that the sales cycle hasn't changed.

Change in Sales Cycle	% Resp
No reply	3.6%
Reduced 3 months	3.1%
Reduced 1-2 months	11.4%
No change	58.0%
Increase 1-2 months	16.1%
Increase 3-4 months	2.6%
Increase more than 4 mos	5.2%

In thinking about why we didn't see a change in the length of the sales cycle, I have a couple of thoughts. First, most of you aren't selling to the Fortune 500,

Length of the Sales Cycle

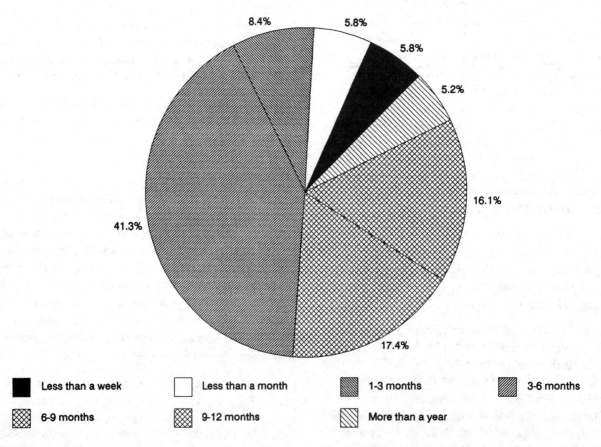

■ Less than a week	□ Less than a month	▨ 1-3 months	▨ 3-6 months
▨ 6-9 months	▨ 9-12 months	▨ More than a year	

and those of you who are selling to the Fortune 500 are also selling to other market segments. Most software companies can adapt to economic conditions by marketing to the sub-markets who are doing well (or who aren't in really bad trouble). One of my clients who has had some problems with the Fortune 500 postponing decisions has increased its marketing niche to include some non-profit segments like health care and county government. These segments are still buying and you can motivate them with a sale.

The other reason that people may not see this as a trend is that they are dealing with some very specific sales situations. It takes time for this to become a trend. I went back and asked my clients who had suffered poor sales because of the postponed sales if they believed that the length of their sales cycle had increased. They all said that they felt that these were isolated situations and that they didn't see it as a fundamental change. This implies that it might

take a year or two for a change in the length of the sales cycle to become apparent. What will the next survey show?

The final thought is that the sales cycle might be more under the prospect's control than I thought. Perhaps they have a time table in which to make this decision. They are in control and increases in the level of competition or the economy don't change their behavior. If this is the case, we may see a decrease in the average sales cycle as products become more of a commodity. The first person to buy a computer really took their time. Buying a PC today is no big deal. Almost fifteen percent of the companies had a reduction in the length of their sales cycle. Reductions in price can also have the same effect. In fact, my computer example has a lot to do with the decline in price as well as the degree of perceived risk.

13. A Final Thought

The software market is maturing. This means more competitors. We are much more likely to discount, but we are learning that huge discounts aren't good business. If you look at other competitive markets, some of them seem to control the competition before everyone goes broke. Others, like the retail computer stores, heat up to the point where no one makes any money. You think that the pressure will finally drive out the weak ones and that prices will stabilize. Airlines are an example of this. The securities analysts keep saying that the airlines are all killing each other. They have to stop this rampant discounting and let everyone get some reasonable profits. They begin to raise prices and then someone announces bargain airfares. Within the week, they are at it again.

The economists would tell us that eventually the situation will stabilize and that the players will learn to not destroy their collective business environment. The endless supply of new players seems to postpone this stability. Software has quite a low barrier to entry for most products. By that I mean that it is fairly easy to develop most software products with a combination of self funding and customer funding. Few products require investors to develop the product. This suggests that we will have lots of new competitors (see the earlier section on new competitors) and that we may see declining prices or higher discounts.

B. Miscellaneous (1991)

1. License Transfer (Apr)

Q. We sell a $4,000 product in a small vertical market. How should we deal with transferring our software license when one of our client companies is sold? What about when they sell the computer that runs our software? (Sometimes the companies go out of business and sell off their computers.) One of the data base companies that is active in our market charges a $350 re-buy fee. We have been charging a $250 re-license fee. We also require the new user to prepay $400 for ne year of maintenance. What do you see other companies doing about this?

A. The most common answer is to ignore the issue. Many license agreements prohibit the transfer of software, but this is an antagonistic position. I recall reading where Computer Associates was requiring customer to relicense their software when they turned their data center over to a facilities management firm. The software was going to be running on the same hardware and supporting the same users. CA just wanted to get paid again. As you might predict, the customers took CA to court. I don't know who will win the suit, but small companies can't afford to go to court with their customers.

If the company is purchased, I feel like you should offer a reasonable transfer fee. I think that your arrangement is reasonable. As we talked about it, this really wasn't an issue.

The difficult issue is when your customer sells the computer and software to another company. The really strict position is that you should try to force the buyer to pay full price for the software. Neither you nor I thought that this would work. They thought they were getting the software along with the computer, so they don't want to pay again. They have no investment in your software, so it is easy for them to go out and buy equivalent software from one of your competitors. They would tell everyone how you were bad guys.

In a small vertical market, you can't afford this bad press. This seems like a pretty bad situation all the way around. On the other hand, if you collect the $250 plus the $400, you have a little money, and you may have a new customer who will pay maintenance over the years. While this isn't a great outcome, it is a good one. Thus, I would apply the same policy to all license transfers.

I would be interested in hearing from others who have dealt with this situation to learn what works and what doesn't.

Sales Success Profile

I received a card from a reader advertising a sales skills test. It is the $ales $uccess Profile and the points were:

* **50 question multiple choice sales skills test, measuring 12 sales skill areas.**

* **PC compatible scoring software provided for instantaneous results.**

* **Originally developed for a Fortune 500 Company**

* Validated against over 11,000 salespeople, accurate and legal to use.

Only $199.

Lousig-Nont & Associates, Inc.
3740 S Royal Crest Street
Las Vegas, NV 89119-7010
(702) 732-8000

I don't have any experience or know of anyone using this test. I have had a couple of clients who used this type of sales tests and a number of times the sales managers swore by the test that they liked. All of the managers who really used these tests had made a real investment in understanding the test and then calibrating their sales people. It takes time to really get the results from this type of effort.

The people I know who have used this type of product have used services offered by consultants. They received tests from the consultant, and mailed the tests back to the consultant. It often took a week or two to get the results back. All other things being equal, getting the results instantaneously would be a real advantage. Louise-Nont offers a 30-day money back guarantee, so it might be Worth a try if you are looking for a test to help you hire better sales people.

2. Network Licensing and Pricing (May)

Dear Dave,

Whenever I read Software Success, I get the sense one of the benefits of being a subscriber is becoming part of a software networking group. In this group everyone (or many) seem pretty open about sharing their ideas or concerns.

The last time I wrote to you, I offered your subscribers a complimentary copy of the "White Paper" I prepared on software pricing using network license servers. I've heard from several of your subscribers and I'd be happy to send it along to others who may have missed the first offer.

In addition to the Pricing White Paper, we also authored a three-volume report on how customers would use license server-based products (once these products were available from vendors). The report was based on a $150,000 research project we did as part of a 1988 multi-client project. The 30 or so companies that have bought the report since 1989 have been able to use the information to repackage their products, develop new pricing structures and new marketing programs.

I'd like to offer other Software Success readers a special $200 discount off the $795 price of the first two volumes of our report "Network License Servers: Challenges for Vendors and End-Users". These volumes cover vendor recommendations and profiles of 20 companies that were offering software that could be flexibly licensed.

Anyone interested in ordering the report, or finding out more about it, should let me know.

Best Regards,
Jim Geisman
Marketshare, Inc
(508) 358-2154

Dear Jim,

Anyone selling Network License Server priced software can probably benefit from your reports. Thanks for offering Software Success readers a discount.

Dave

3. Source Code Pricing (Jun)

Dear David,

We offer a mid-range/mini based software product for a vertical market that runs on AS/400 and HP3000 computers. The run-only license fee is $10K to $15K. We are considering the sale of source code as an option. I do not find any articles you have published on source code pricing. We are looking for a recommended ratio to selling price of object code only or do you suggest some other method of establishing a price?

I would appreciate your comments as soon as possible.

Keep up the good work. Your newsletter has had great info in it!

Richard Cartier
Logistic Concepts
(616) 772-0028

Chapter III.   Pricing

Dear Richard,

Many developers don't want to sell their source code because they fear that someone will steal their secrets. (i.e. give/sell it to someone else or use it to develop a product that will compete with the originator.) This isn't a problem, in my mind, as long as your customers have real assets that would more than repay you for any transgression on their part. I would deal with this issue, by having a good attorney write a very tight contract for the source code purchase. This is a simple non-negotiable issue. If anyone wants to buy the source code, they have to live with your contract.

The next part, setting a price, is relatively easy. My experience is that you arbitrarily pick a number. Often it is equal to the object code fee, but it can be larger. In almost all cases, it is a nice round number like $100K. In your case, you mentioned that the customer, who was considering the source code license, had five object code licenses, so the number that came to mind was $100K. This is another non-negotiable item. If he wants the source code, he has to pay the price. If you decide that the right number is $100K, he can pay the price or not. You really don't care. It's your product, so he can "take it or leave it".

The difficult area is ongoing support and maintenance. Once you ship the source code to a customer, you lose your ability to provide him with support. If he is making modifications and wants you to support him, he has made a real mistake. My basic philosophy is, when a customer buys the source code, then he is on his own. You may provide consulting at an hourly rate, but this has to cover the time to look at his modifications, install them on a test system (he has to pay for the computer resources to install his modifications on your machines), and then he has to pay for your time to debug his system. This is very expensive and he MUST pay the bill.

The next problem issue is updates. Say, for instance, one year after he has bought the source code, and has gone on his merry way, you come out with "Version Two" of the source code. He will probably want you to marry your changes to his modifications. This can be very messy and very expensive. Again, I'd be happy to do this, but he would have to pay for all of the time. It isn't wise to bid this on a fixed price. This has to be time and materials. In some cases, when you are limited on key resources,

you can't afford to put your best developers on this project. You need them to be developing the next version of your product. I have seen a case where a software company hired a contract programmer to do the update modifications for the customer and added 10% to cover the management cost. This was a lose/lose situation. The customer complained that the deal was way too expensive and the software company felt that it lost money on the project.

My preference is to sell the updated source code to the customer for a fixed fee. In one case, a client charged 15% of the object code fee plus the source code fee, or 30% of the object code fee. The customer was then free to program to his heart's content.

I believe it is really important to impress upon your customer the fact that he is buying the source code, and is going into the development business, and won't be able to keep his system current with the state of the art. I have seen very few cases where this really makes sense for the person buying the source code.

In most cases which I have seen, there is a programmer who wants to play with the system.

The programmer hopes he can get the source code for very little money and play with it. This is the reason for setting a high price and not negotiating.

As an aside, the one real security risk is that a programmer who works with the system leaves the customer and develops a competitive product. To deal with this risk, your customer must have all programmers with access to the source code sign non-disclosure and non-compete agreements.

The second reason people want the source code, is so they can make the little changes to the system. You can be responsive to this by offering contract programming and making their changes part of the system. If you fold their changes into the base system, the ongoing maintenance is a moot point.

The final reason that people want a source code option, is in case you aren't responsive and they have to make modifications to meet their own business requirements. This is a valid reason in my mind. If they exercise their option to get the source code because you aren't being responsive, they should expect to do all of their own enhancements. In my experience, if you discuss these issues with your prospects and customers, then very few of them will

Chapter III. Pricing

actually buy the source code. A number of them do want to have the option, but that is fine. I hope that this discussion helps you steer your customers and prospects in the right direction.

Thanks,
Dave

4. Price Ranges $1K–$5K (Jul)

Dear Dave,

I have a theory and a comment about your surveys. I think that the range $1K–$5K is too wide for your surveys. My theory is that customers have a significant psychological barrier at $1,000. Sometimes this is related to how much the end user can sign for, without getting his boss involved. Sometimes it just seems that $1,000 is too much to pay. If other vendors have found this to be the case, I would expect fewer products to be priced in the range $1K–$2K than above or below that range. If a customer is willing to pay $1,000, he is probably willing to pay somewhat more. A similar effect may occur somewhere around $3,000 (this is less visible to me because our products are priced well below that). It seems that $5,000 products are more like $10K or $20K products than $1K products. In order to test such a theory, you would have to adjust the product pricing ranges in your surveys to include perhaps $1K–$2K and $2K–$4K ranges (or something like that).

Our basic products are priced in the $500–$1K range, but with options sometimes prices can go into the $1,100–$1,300 range. If my theory is right, I have a dilemma on raising prices with future releases. Since it seems that I would not want a product in the neighborhood of say, $1,500, I will have to greatly increase the functionality of the products and options so I can double my prices. How do other companies in this price range increase prices as the functionality of their products improve?

Sincerely,
Michael S. Mort, Ph.D.
President
Signal Analytics Corp USA
(703) 281-3277

Dear Michael,

I have observed both the $1K barrier and a $2K barrier, with the next common barrier level at $5K. You are right in suggesting that these barriers occur partially because of budget authorization levels and partially because of customer perception. In many cases, customers convince themselves that they want a product under $1K, and they won't even consider a product over $1K.

I agree that, in many cases, a $5K product is quite different than a $1K product, but the $10K and $20K products are in yet another league. I will try providing more ranges in my surveys to see if we can uncover some of these differences.

During our phone discussion, you mentioned that you have 3 competitors at $1K, $2K, and $3K. (I will call them competitor #1, #2, and #3.) Right now you are competing well with #1, and you have been adding functionality so that you have more features than #1 but you still have less features than #2. It sounds as though your product is really worth $1.5K.

I think the worse thing you can do is raise your price to $1.5K and bundle all your options. At this price point, competitor #2 would beat you on features and competitor #1 would try to eliminate you on price. I have worked with several clients who were caught in this type of crossfire. They ended up lowering their base price to $1K with more functionality than competitor #1, and provided the options as separately priced add-ons. This is your current position and I think it makes sense to stay here until you have the functionality to compete with competitor #2.

Once you are ready to reposition your product to $2K, you might announce the product with a new release or a variation in the name. At that point, you have two choices. On one hand, you can offer to sell the options to your customers, while the other choice is to give everyone all the functionality of version 2 as long as they pay for maintenance.

Most companies try to sell their options to their customers to recoup some of their R & D costs. I have seen a couple of cases in which the vendors aggressively market these add-ons to their customer base. Even these aggressive vendors get less than 30% of their customers to buy the options. I suspect that in this industry, companies, on the average, get less than 10% of their customers to buy their options. The bottom line is, as an industry, we don't get much of this add-on revenue.

The advantage of giving your customers the add-ons for free is that you will increase your maintenance revenues and you will have all of your customers using the best software that you have available. What you want to avoid is a bad reference by a customer who still has the old version of your product, and who would have had no complaint with the newer version. ALso, having all of your customers on the same version will also reduce your support expenses.

The extra maintenance revenue can be quite significant. In fact, this concept is much like the situtation in which a vendor gave away free software in order to obtain future maintenance revenue. If you double your price from $1K to $2K and your maintenance is 15% of the current price, your maintenance fee will go from $150 to $300. If most of your customers (80% or more) pay the higher maintenance fee, you will probably make more money over the next few years by giving version 2 to your customers for free.

The only loose end in this strategy is taking care of the customers who paid you for the options when your base price was $1K. I would probably give them a credit toward future maintenance based on the amount they paid for the options.

Good Luck!
Dave

5. International Pricing (Aug)

Dear Mr. Bowen:

I am a recent subscriber to your publication and have noticed that you are generous enough to reflect upon your expertise and dispense advice to those who ask. Well, I am in a position where your advice on setting up international distribution would be of great use to me right now, so here goes.

My company, Computer Mail Services (CMS) has been marketing an electronic mail gateway product called M-Bridge to connect Novell local area networks to the public services of MCI Mail. Recently, as MCI has been actively establishing foreign partners to act as local representatives of their services, CMS has been made a beneficiary of all this activity — we have been getting requests from all over the world about local distribution of our product. Since our company has been fulfilling past foreign requests directly to the customer, these requests have been a source of some anxiety as I have to decide how I will structure these distributor relationships.

My questions to you are numerous, but let me start with the most pressing ones. Obviously, they all deal with setting up international distribution for our product.

* Do you have any suggestions on how differently we should structure our agreements with foreign resellers compared to domestic resellers? Perhaps you may have some examples of how other software companies have structured their foreign reseller or distributor agreements.
* On the topic of product discounts, should foreign resellers get a different discount schedule compared with the domestic one? Should we have different discount schedules for different countries or regions of the world?
* Should we price the product differently? Presently the domestic retail price for M-Bridge is $995. Should CMS dictate what the local "retail price" should be in each specific country? Or should we permit the reseller to determine this price?
* Who pays for import duties for our product? What about freight?

As you can tell from these questions, I am very ignorant about this subject. As this is our company's first time to do this, I really would like to get a pattern that is optimal for our future partners and ourselves since I intend to use this pattern for our other LAN connectivity products.

Any ideas, comments, suggestions you might have on this subject would be greatly appreciated. In fact, please feel free to jot down your handwritten responses and FAX them to me. I anxiously await your reply.

Sincerely,
Lih-Tah Wong
President
Computer Mail Services
TEL (313) 352-6700
FAX (313) 352-8387

Dear Mr. Wong,

On your first question of the format for the legal agreement, I suggest that you gather as many of these agreements as possible. Several of the industry associations (Software Publishers and Adapso) have standard agreements. You also should contact attorneys who specialize in software companies and who have already negotiated these types of agreements. Finally, the distributors will all be eager to send you copies of their agreement that you would like to sign. While there are a number of issues in international agreements, I am sure that the trade offs facing you will quickly become very clear to you. I do advise you to get an attorney with experience with these types of agreements. You don't want to be paying for his education or having him develop his first copy of an international distribution agreement on your nickel.

Typically, foreign distributors get a higher discount than domestic distributors or resellers because the foreign distributors are doing more. They have almost all the responsibility for marketing in their country. Domestic resellers and distributors, on the other hand, almost always depend upon the software publisher for marketing. Typically, I see foreign distributors paying 50% of the US list price. They then sell for more than US list price in their market. I have seen some cases where the international distributors have sold for double the US price. Thus, they ended up with a 75% discount in their market.

While this may be a little high, I feel it is important to give your international distributors adequate margin to develop the markets in their countries. I believe that software companies should spend between 10% and 20% of their revenue on marketing. Thus, the international distributors should receive 10% to 20% more than domestic distributors who provide equivalent services.

Pricing products in foreign markets is a difficult issue. In many cases that I have seen, the US vendor says that he wants 50% of either the US list price or the actual sales price whichever is greater. Then, he depends upon the international distributor to determine the local price. This is fine as long as there is no other way for the international distributor to receive payment from his customers. I heard of one case in which the distributor always sold the software at US list price, but also provided high priced consulting services. It appeared that the distributor was receiving excess consulting fees rather than selling the software for a higher price. The customers didn't care what was on the invoice, and the distributor didn't have to share these excess dollars

with the US company. The same situation occurs when your distributor is selling other software products to the same customers, but unless you have a reference point, this may be as good as you can do.

Your situation provides you with a nice solution. Your international distributors are also selling Novell networks so you can link your price to Novell's. If you are 1.5X a small Novell LAN in the US, you should be 1.5X a small Novell LAN in Hong Kong, etc.

My experience is that the buyer pays for import duties and freight, but this is always negotiable. Again, I would see if I could get a copy of the agreement between Novell and the international distributors. Following the precedent that has been set by Novell will make everything much easier for both you and the international distributors.

Good Luck!
Dave

C. Case Studies (1991)

1. Managing a Product Transition (Sept)

The company in this case study sells a specialized product to a very large vertical market. Historically, they have sold their product at the $595 price to the high end of the vertical market. This product has been named editor's choice every time it has been reviewed. It is seen as the technically best product in its category. It requires at least a 286 processor with a large hard disk, which limited the market several years ago.

Historically, the company investigated ways to tap into some much larger segments. These were groups with less money who could use the product. A couple of years ago, the company looked at this segment and decided not to pursue it because a mass market product would require a significant development effort to run on less expensive computers. There would also be a significant effort necessary to lower the product's cost of goods sold. At the $595 sales price, the $30 product cost was only 5% of revenue which was acceptable. If the price dropped to $100 - $200, the $30 product cost would become a real problem. For all of these reasons, this pursuit was discontinued.

Chapter III.   Pricing

Earlier this year, as the development of the next generation product was proceeding, the company began to look at how to manage the transition from the old product to the new product. The new product has been designed once again for the high end people who purchased the old product in the early days. It is going to set a new standard for technical excellence in this market.

In the meantime, the company implemented some changes to lower the product costs. They went from using three ring binders to perfect bound manuals when they introduced a new version of the product. They had enough upgrades to justify printing 1K manuals perfect bound. They also switched to high density disks with compression to reduce the disk costs. This lowered their product costs to $15 which made a price of $100 to $200 now seem possible.

As with any new product introduction, there was a great deal of uncertainty about when the new product was going to be available. This is a small company and the support people were involved in testing the new product. The developers talked to customers, so the customers knew that the new product was on the way. The company felt obliged to tell the customers that they would be getting an upgrade to the new product rather than an upgrade to the current product.

This is a really difficult issue. It is easy to say that you don't want any information to leak to the customers and prospects, but that just isn't reasonable in the real world. Information does spread, and good companies also feel obliged to tell their customers what they are doing. It just doesn't feel right to stonewall your customers.

Given these realities, the information does spread and the sales to the primary market tend to slow down as the word gets out. You can combat this by offering a full credit for money paid for version one of the product toward version two. However, most customers won't want to invest the time to learn version one and then have to learn version two. They'll say, "I'll wait until version two is available and then I will buy."

The company in this case study began to experience a significant drop off in sales of the old product (the current product at that point in time) at the same time the schedule for the new product continued to slip.

This is a common situation for companies that have one product and are coming out with a major new version of that product. At the point when the company is making a major investment in the new product, the revenues from the old product decline.

2. Price testing and new markets (Sept)

One of the manifestations of the slow down in sales had been a decline in lead to sales conversions. The company was still generating a good number of leads, they just weren't buying. This was caused by some indirect competition from some general purpose products with added features which made them an alternative for casual users. The old product was still better than these general purpose products, but the general purpose products were much cheaper ($200 to $250). The sales people felt that they had to reduce the price on the old product if they wanted to maintain sales.

The company decided to do some test mailings offering lower prices to see if they could pull some sales out of the leads they had already paid for. They sent test mailings out at $195 and $295. At the same time, the product cost had been lowered from $30 to $15 down to $10. At this point we decided to test the $99 price to a broader market.

The broader market mailing went out at $99 and $199. There was no demo disk offer. It was a "Buy It! You'll like it!" offer and the $99 offer generated three times more revenue for the same number of post cards. The company was using up some old product inventory, but with the new lower product cost, the revenues would be 1.6 times the cost. This calculation was very simple because the only offer available was a straight product purchase. This was great news because it opened up a new broader market.

Historically, the company had generated leads via direct mail (post cards) and card decks, and had mailed a number of follow up pieces to these leads. The close rate on these leads had declined to 2% in the last year because of the new product rumors and the increased indirect competition.

Originally, direct mail had generated leads for $6 each. Then, the company spent another $5 per lead to follow up for a total of $11 for each lead generated. Thus for each 100 leads generated, $1,100 was spent. If out of these 100 leads, the company got a

2% sales rate, they would get 2 sales at $595 each or $1,190 in revenue. If you add in the cost to produce 2 products at $30 each, the total costs come to $1,160 netting the company only $30 for all their efforts. The product costs were $30 for printing, three ring binders and the disks. If 2% of the leads buy, the financials for one batch of 100 leads are:

Revenue		
2% buy	2 * $595	$1,190
Costs		
Lead generation	100 * $6	$600
Follow up	100 * $5	$500
Product Cost	2 * $30	$60
		$1,160
Profit/(Loss)		$30

In previous years the lead to sale conversion rate had been between 5% and 10% and the lead generation had been much more profitable.

When the company began offering the new lower price of $195, they began generating more revenue, but their economic picture didn't improve (In fact, they LOST money.) The lead to sale conversion rate increased to 6%. At the same time the product cost was reduced to $15. The financial picture with 100 leads was:

Revenue		
6% buy	6 * $195	$1,170
Costs		
Lead generation	100 * $6	$600
Follow up	100 * $5	$500
Product cost	6 * $15	$90
		$1,190
Profit/(Loss)		($20)

At this point the company put all but the most profitable marketing programs on hold. The new product continued to slip and the company couldn't afford to invest in new marketing programs. The marketing department reduced the cost of the lead follow up from $5 to $2 and further reduced the product cost from $15 to $10. With these reduced costs, the financials became:

Revenue		
6% buy	6 * $195	$1,170
Costs		
Lead generation	100 * $6	$600
Follow up	100 * $2	$200
Product cost	6 * $10	$60
		$860
Profit/(Loss)		($310)

This reduced cost marketing program was implemented using the very best mailing lists and card decks available and helped generate some cash to help carry the company. I must point out that these programs probably weren't profitable when you allocated the overhead costs. Thus, these programs were just providing contribution margin. On the other hand, the overhead costs were fixed costs that couldn't be reduced because they were for facilities and the core team. In this type of situation, if you can't cut your overhead costs, you should generate as much contribution margin as possible to minimize your losses.

The company learned a couple of lessons from this exercise:

1. New products always take longer than planned.

2. Managing the product transition is a difficult issue because information always leaks.

3. You should re-examine the implications of changes in your lead to sale conversion rate on your economic formula. (The company profiled here should have cut costs for its lead follow up much earlier.)

4. As you drop the price of your product, the nature of your business changes and cost savings become even more critical.

D. Pricing Survey (1990)

This survey received quite a good response. We received 69 completed questionnaires which is close to 10 percent of the subscribers at the time the survey was distributed. I really appreciate the fact that so many of you take the time to complete the surveys.

1. Background
Company Revenue

The responses were fairly evenly distributed among companies under $5 million in sales. The distribution is similar to last year's pricing survey, but there are almost twice as many responses this year so the spread is more even.

Annual Revenues	% Resp
<$500K	26%
$500K-$1M	17%
$1M-$2M	26%
$2M-$5M	22%
>$5M	8%

2. Computer Type

The respondents are pretty heavily PC oriented.

Computer Type	% Resp
PC	80%
LAN	10%
Mini	13%
Mainframe	18%

These numbers total 121 percent which says that 20 percent of the companies are on more than one platform. If we assume that all of the LAN companies are also available on PC's, we have an additional 10 percent which are either mini or mainframe companies. Thus 11 percent out of the 31 percent of the mini or mainframe companies are offering their products on another platform. (There are 31 percent of the companies on mini and mainframe.) This is higher than I have seen in the past, and I expect it to increase in the future. I believe that this reflects the strategic direction of companies like IBM, DEC and HP to provide solutions on multiple platforms. Vendors who are on these mainframe or mini platforms are beginning to offer their products on other platforms.

An interesting distinction is whether these vendors are selling the PC versions of their products directly into the PC market, or if they are planning on selling PC copies to through the same people who are selling their mini or mainframe product.

My experience is that it is very difficult for a company to effectively learn how to sell a different version of their product to a different audience. On the other hand, selling a different product (the PC version) to the same person is reasonably easy. In particular, the PC market for a pure PC program is much more demanding than the market for a PC version of a mainframe product.

3. Type of Product

I asked the readers to classify the type of product they are selling. The categories were:

Leader: the top product;

First tier: one of the top products in the category;

Second tier: you have five or more competitors who are better established than you; and

Young Turk: is a new product which is establishing a name for itself.

New product.

We asked this question last year in the pricing survey. The number of First Tier Products have decreased significantly while the number of Leaders and New Products have both increased. I believe that part of this is that new subscribers may have more new products, but I believe that there is more to it.

It is difficult to achieve success as a First Tier product on a limited budget. The leader always has the alternative of coming down on top of you. You can't really control your pricing and, in general, profitability for leaders is much better than for followers.

Type of Product Table

Type of Product	1990 Survey	1989 Survey
Leader	39.1%	31.1%
First Tier	26.1%	45.9%
Second Tier	8.7%	9.8%
Young Turk	2.9%	6.6%
New Product	20.3%	4.9%

I have seen a number of cases where companies have repositioned their product from one of many generic products (First Tier) to the best product for

XXX (Leader or New Product). There is usually some concern that the company is losing something by focusing on the smaller niche market. My feeling is that if you can achieve all the growth you need for the next five years in the smaller niche that you aren't giving up anything.

I strongly feel that it is more important for small, self-funded software companies to find a niche where they can grow and be profitable. Once you have the growth and profitability, you can focus on expanding your market. I should note that funding is important to this trade off. If you have professional investors, the correct strategy may be to go after the much larger market rather than fooling around with the small niche market.

My conclusion is that part of the shift in the last year has been readers repositioning their products into niches where they can be the leader. I would be interested to hear from any of you who have made this type of change.

4. Market Size

We are beginning to get a much better response to the market size question. This year, 95 percent of the respondents answered this question.

I am looking for the annual sales of products in your category. The easiest way to determine this is to look at the competitive products and estimate their annual sales. While it is very difficult to estimate is accurately, you should be able to get this within a factor of 2X. If nothing else, call up your competitors and ask them how many copies of their product they have sold in the last year. If you use list price, that is clearly an upper limit on market size. If you cut their sales in half and assume a typical market discount (what is your average discount?), you should have a reasonable estimate. The responses were:

Market Size	% Resp
<$1M	13%
$1M - $10M	33%
$10M - $100M	28%
>$100M	22%

There are some important ramifications of the market size which you should consider. You should make sure that your market size implications are consistent with your company goals and objectives.

<$1M

Markets less than a million a year in sales are great for very small "family" businesses. It is reasonable to grow between $250,000 and $500,000 and have a very nice business in this type of market. If you get established in this type of market, you are fairly sure that a big player won't enter your market and mess things up unless they really miscalculate. If they do make the mistake, you should be able to hold on, and resume your roll once the big player realizes their mistake and pulls out. They might not pull out, but they will certainly cut their marketing investment.

$1M - $10M

If you want to have a $1 million, ten-person company, this is the right market to be in. If you can be the leader in this type of market, you can have good profits which you can take out as very nice salaries. One limitation with this strategy is that it is difficult to sell a $1 million software company. You are really selling the product at this level. On the other hand, you can make a good living and have a lot of fun.

$10M - $100M

This is where things start to get interesting. It is reasonable in this type of market to get to $25 million and go public if you are the leader and a number of first tier players can get to $5 million in sales and sell their company. The bad news is that type of market is very attractive to a broad range of investors so there is usually much more competition. The good news is that the potential payoff is much better with this market size.

> $100M

This is the type of market that professional investors really like. You can go public at $25 million with a prospectus that shows how you can grow to $100 million in the next five years. The catch is that the venture capitalists want you to find this market before everyone else. That is when the market has the potential for more than $100 million in sales, but before the sales have reached that level. They want the potential to be the leader in a more than $100 million market.

If your market has already gotten to this level, you no longer have the risk that the customers won't buy this category of product. This is a significant risk if you think back on all the hot markets that never materialized. The bad news is that if the market has gotten this big, that there probably are several very strong competitors. Starting a software company by going up against a strong competitor is a very risky proposition. I would advise you to see if you can find a niche where you can dominate and get to $1 million in sales before you go after the $25 million leader.

5. Type of Companies by Market Size

The bar graph on the next page shows the distribution of the type of company by the size of market. In the small market ($1 M) most of the companies are either young turks or new products. I feel that this is the only way to start a new product company.

The $1 million to $10 million market has more young turks than I would have guessed, but there are fewer second-tier firms. If you are going to be a second-tier firm, do it in a large market. (There are a lot of second-tier firms in greater than $100 million markets.)

I was also pleased to see a good number of first-tier firms in the under $10 million market. It is reasonable to grow to $1 million as a first tier firm. The leader might have a 25 percent market share, or $2.5 million in sales. Thus, the leader would be 2.5 times as big as the larger firm, they can swamp the smaller firms with their R & D power.

Market Share

The biggest news is that almost 90 percent of the respondents were able to estimate their market share. Last year less than half of the respondents answered this question.

The pie chart on the next page shows the distribution of the responses for market share. As you can see, a significant number of companies have less than one percent of the market (17.5 percent this year versus 7.1 percent last year). I believe that this is due in part to the increase in new product companies. On the high end, we also showed an decrease in the top two categories, which were over 25 percent. Last year, 42 percent of the companies

were over 25 percent, while this year 23 percent were.

I believe that last year a number of companies took a very narrow view of their market. It is easy to justify a high market share if you define your market narrowly enough. Getting 25 percent market share in a serious market is a real accomplishment. Thus I view last year's responses as too high.

6. Competition

The level of competition has increased in the last year. See the table on the page 5. As you can see, the number of companies who feel they have a low level of competition has de-Market Sharecreased and the number with a high level has increased by almost the same amount.

Level of competition is subjective in that it is hard to come up with a measurable criteria which corresponds to the level of competition. For example, I looked at the number of competitors as a function of level of competition, and there was no clear pattern. Level of Competition

Level of Competition	This Year	Last Year
None	5.8%	6.6%
Low	21.7%	29.5%
Medium	49.3%	49.2%
High	20.3%	14.8%

I think the real issue is how much your actions and decisions are affected by your competitors. You might have so much business that you don't really care if you lose a particular deal. You won't discount just to get one deal. I would suspect that discounting is the best predictor of competitive level. I would appreciate any other thoughts on questions that I might ad to next year's survey.

7. Number of Competitors

There has been a dramatic increase in the average number of competitors.

These numbers tell much more about the competitive environment in 1990 than the general level of competition. My experience is that anyone who has four or more competitors in a typical sales situation is faced with serious competition. With that many competitors at the table, there is almost always someone who is desperate and is willing to cut their price to try to buy the business. Even if they don't

Type of Company by Market Size

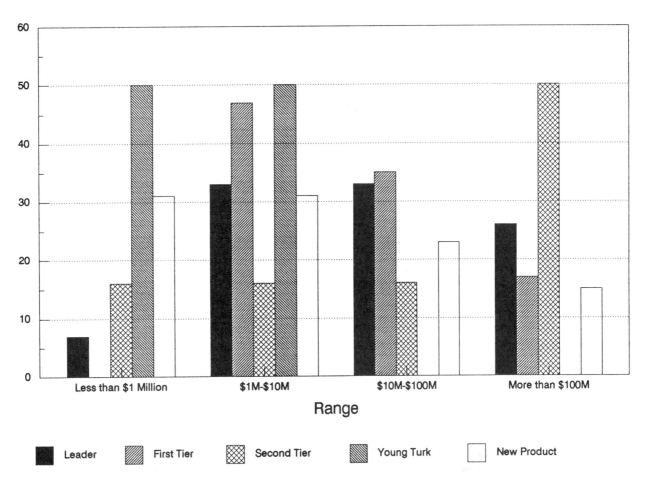

win the bid, the desperate bidder can force the winner to make major concessions to win the business.

Typical Number of Competitors

Number of Competitors	This Year	Last Year
None	2.9%	14.5%
1	13.0%	36.0%
2-3	46.4%	30.0%
4 or more	33.3%	19.5%

Depending upon the relative size of the market, and the profitability of selling to the market, you can have a tense situation when you have two or three competitors. Often the tone in the market is set by the leader.

8. Number of Competitors by Type of Company

The graph above shows how many competitors companies typically deal with depending upon the type of company.

Only new product companies have the freedom of no competitors in a typical situation, but the most common situation for a new product company is to have two or three competitors.

Leaders are also most likely to encounter two or three competitors. I suspect that in many of these situations, the leader initiated the evaluation. The customer felt obliged to look at the alternatives, but as long as the leader is in control they should do well.

First-tier companies are slightly more likely to have four or more competitors than leaders, but their profiles are quite close. I have found that many first-tier companies can position themselves as the leader based on some issue or another. Thus, they get some

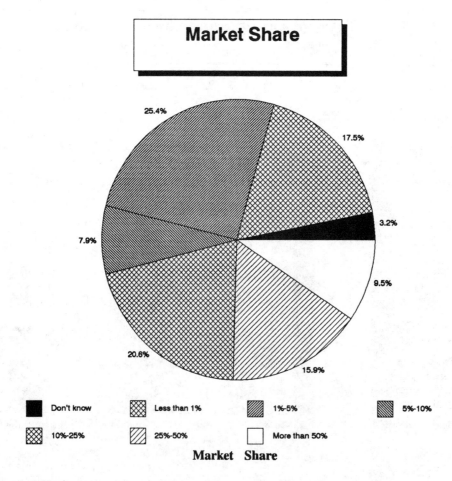

Market Share

■ Don't know	⊠ Less than 1%	⊠ 1%-5%	⊠ 5%-10%
⊠ 10%-25%	⊠ 25%-50%	□ More than 50%	

Market Share

of the benefits of being a leader. This is especially true if the first-tier company can cultivate a relationship with the prospect and control the evaluation. If you have a unique attribute and you can sell the prospect on the need for this attribute early in the sales cycle, you can develop sole source business. This is true even if the prospect goes through the motions of evaluating the alternatives. We have all be involved in bids where it was clear that someone had already wired the deal. While it isn't much fun to be on the receiving end of this situation, it is great to dish it out.

Second-Tier companies are most likely to be one of four or more competitors. It is almost impossible for them to be a subleader. The only case where I have seen a second tier firm achieve a sub leader status was by focusing regionally.

Young Turks are always battling two or more competitors.

While new products can get no competitors or one competitor, they often face two or more competitors.

My experience is that new products need a honeymoon period where the have no competition. This allows them to quickly get an installed base which will help increase future sales.

9. Pricing Structures

The graph on the next page confirms that the single CPU license is the most common pricing structure offered. There are three answers on the graph. The first is what is the primary pricing structure. The second is what alternatives does your firm offer. The final question is what is offered by the competition.

The average company identified alternatives as the primary pricing structure. I have seen cases where companies stressed different pricing for different markets. For example, you might stress the single-copy price for your low end market, and sell your multi-copy or site license price to your larger prospects.

Pricing Structures Offered

Percentage of Respondents

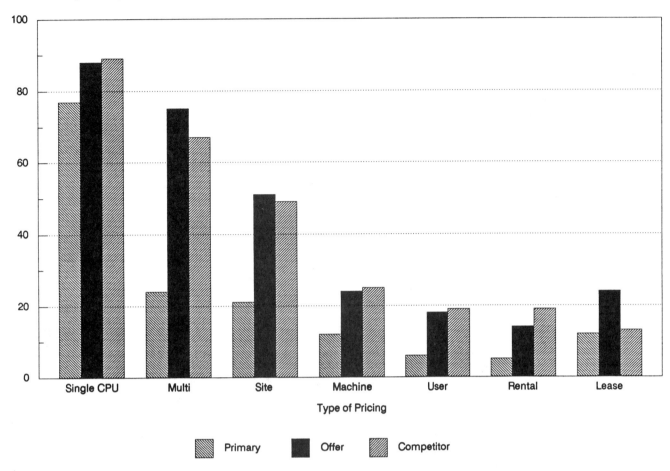

Type of Pricing

Primary ▨   Offer ■   Competitor ▨

I was interested to note that the relative ranking of the alternatives was the same for the primary offering and what people offer. The rankings from most popular to least popular are:

* **Single CPU**

* **Multiple copy**

* **Site licensing**

* **Machine Base**

* **Leasing**

* **User based**

* **Rental**

I was pleased to see that leasing wasn't at the bottom. There was an article in the March 1990 issue of Datamation about Candle's new leasing program. In six months they had 30 leasing deals, and they be-

lieve that they wouldn't have gotten the deals otherwise. Their primary product is $100,000 to $140,000 a copy, but most of the leasing deals have "come from cash-strapped organizations needing the $5,000 performance-measuring component to squeeze more power out of exhausted CPUs." Thus, it appears that Candle got 30 new customers because of its leasing program.

For the most part, the competitive offerings matched the respondents. There were two exceptions. The first was that the competitors were more likely to offer rental. The second was that the respondents were more likely to offer leases. I am concerned that these findings aren't real solid statistically.

10. Price Structure by Computer Type

The graph on the next page shows the differences in the pricing structure offered based on the computer type (platform).

Price Structure by Computer Type

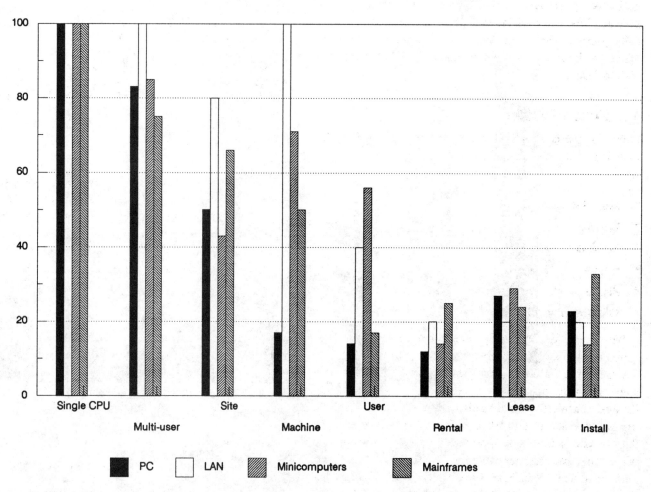

Everyone offers single CPU licenses. Multiple copy pricing is more common for LAN software, but it is pretty popular with the others. Site licenses are most popular with LAN and Mainframe companics, and is moderately popular with micro and mini companies.

Machine-based pricing is very popular with LAN and mini companies. I was surprised withthe LAN companies, since I expected them to be focusing on user-based pricing. I was told by several LAN companies that they had found user-based pricing too difficult to sell, and they had gone to machine-based pricing. They know the maximum number of users that a network file server could support. They used this to set their machine-based price. There has been a long tradition of machine-based pricing in the mini world because of the broad range on power for mini vendors. I suspect that many of the LAN vendors are also mini vendors so I would believe that they extended their mini-oriented machine-based pricing to their LAN offerings. I was somewhat surprised

that only half of the mainframe vendors offer machine-based pricing. This matches my experience, but every time that I say that machine-based pricing has been slow to take off in the mainframe world, I get calls from subscribers who say that IBM endorsed machine-based pricing in 1984 and that everyone who is anyone is doing it by now.

User-based pricing was most popular for the mini vendors. I have added a workstation category for future surveys, but I have included the workstation companies in the mini category for this survey. I have found that user-based pricing is very popular for networked workstation software.

Rental wasn't very popular with anyone, but it was most popular with the mainframe vendors. I suspect that this is related to the average product price. If your product sells for under $1,000, rental just doesn't make sense, but at $20,000, the vendor can afford the administrative effort to invoice for rental.

Chapter III. Pricing

Leasing is equally popular for all types of computers. It is offered by 20 percent of the companies. Installment purchases were similar in popularity to leases. The only difference is that the vendor typically carries the loan with an installment purchase where a financial institution takes the financing risk with a lease.

11. Plan to Offer

Only 25 percent of the respondents answered this question, but the most popular alternative to offer was:

* **Site License**
* **Leasing**
* **Multiple copies**
* **Rental**
* **Single CPU**
* **Installment Purchase**

I have received a steady stream of calls from subscribers who have a prospect who is asking for a site license price. I think that you should sit down and come up with prices for a site license, multiple copies and rental. If you do this and you are asked for a quote, at least you have a price. My experience is that if you admit that you don't have a site license price that you are encouraging the prospect to bargain on price. You may have to bargain even if you have a starting point on paper, but I think you will end up with a better final price.

12. Other Pricing
Multiple Copy Discounts

As you can see from the table at right, companies offer higher discounts on the third copy than they do on the second copy. My standard multiple copy discount schedule is 20 percent off on the second unit, 30 percent on the third, and so forth. If I am eager to get more multiple copy sales, I am willing to increase the discounts by 10 percent, (e.g. 30 percent on the second unit, 40 percent on the third, etc.). I usually recommend a maximum discount of 50 percent.

Multiple Copy Discounts

Discount	Second Copy	Third Copy
No change	21.7%	13.0%
10%	20.3%	14.5%
10%-20%	13.0%	15.9%
20%-30%	8.7%	13.0%
30%-40%	10.1%	15.9%
>40%	13.0%	3.0%

My discount schedule is deeper than the respondents are offering. There are several reasons that I am more eager to discount the multiple copy deals. The first is that I want to encourage customers to buy as much as possible at one time. This is the easiest time to get more money out of them. The second concern is that most companies do a poor job of going back to their customers and selling them the add-on sales. It isn't a lot easier than making a new sale, but you get less money. My final reason is that I would prefer to set the discount too low. I would love to sell too many additional copies. If the price is too low (or could be higher), you can always raise it. I would much rather sell more copies at a lower price and get the maintenance, than set the price too high and not sell any additional copies

Site Licenses

Almost half of the companies answered this question, and their answers were:

Site License (X CPU)	% Resp
1X	19.3%
1-2X	9.5%
2-3X	6.4%
3-5X	25.8%
>5X	38.7%

I was perplexed with the people who price a site license the same as a CPU license. It seems they don't have a real one CPU price.

The price for a site license is a tradeoff between getting more money from your customer (up front) rather than waiting and selling them single CPU copies over time. I assume that in most cases that the maximum revenue potential is to sell CPU copies to half the machines in a site. I assume that the customer can cut his cost in half just by having his people move from machine to machine.

The next factors seem to balance out. The vendor wants to get the money now, and the customer doesn't want to have to manage who is licensed to run the software and who isn't. My experience is that if you get a reasonable estimate of how many CPU licenses the customer might really buy (in your dreams), that they might pay half this for a site license.

Using this rule of thumb, you might find that mainframe customers will pay between two and three times the CPU fee maximum because very few mainframe sites have more than six CPUs. Minicomputer site licenses can go as high as five to ten because customers may have a larger number of minis in one site. This is especially true if you extend the definition of site to a corporate license.

My final thought on a site license is to set the price low. Sell a few, and then consider raising the price. I have seen far too many cases where people have set the site license fee so high that they never sold any. The principals were too worried about leaving money on the table. My feeling is that I would much rather get the large customer who might serve as a reference for you than hold out for the last dollar. I have found that if you ask the customer to write an article, this can be a useful concession and can help take some of the sting out of "giving away a site license."

Rental

Only 22 percent of the companies answered the question about rental prices since rental is so unpopular. Nevertheless the responses were:

Monthly Rental %	% Resp
<5%	40%
5% - 7%	27%
7% - 15%	20%
15% - 20%	13%

Thus, the median rental price is probably 6 percent. I believe that this is too low. If maintenance is 15 percent per year, 1.25 percent per month is for maintenance. Thus we are netting 4.75 percent per month which will recover our 85 percent purchase price (I took out the maintenance since we are collecting it monthly), in 18 months. This is ignoring interest. If you put in a reasonable small company cost of capital, the payback period is probably closer to 24 months. If you start offering purchase credits,

renting is even more attractive. It is apparent that most of you feel that you can't charge more than 7 percent for rental and you know that you can't afford to rent at this low a price.

I would suggest that you set the rental price at 10 percent of the purchase price with no purchase credits. If installation and training are required, the customer has to pay for these services. At this rate, 8.75 percent applies toward purchase and you recover the full purchase price in 10 months. This is a price at which you can afford to rent.

When your prospects complain that your rental price is too high, you should just respond that you aren't a bank, but you have decided to offer a rental as a convenience for your customers. If cash flow is a problem, they can lower their monthly payments with a lease. On the other hand, if they need the convenience of a rental you are happy to do it at your price. I have seen this work, and generate net additional business. Try it. The worst that will happen is that no one will take it which is where you stand now.

E. Questions and Answers (1990)

1. Geography based pricing

We sell software which includes maps. We are selling to a very large company which has many offices and we are hoping to sell them one copy for each office. How can we keep them from using our software in multiple offices?

The first step is to have a license agreement which limits them to using each copy of your package on a single machine. This will keep them from using it at different locations at the same time, but it doesn't keep them from shipping the licensed machine from city to city.

If you really want to limit each license to its city, then just include the maps for that city with the package. Thus, if I licensed your product, I would get the product and the San Jose map. You might consider pricing the maps separately. For example, I might want the maps for San Jose and San Francisco. Splitting your price between the product and the map will be an interesting exercise. You also need to think through the packaging. I assume that you will package the maps separately and facilitate loading the map into your program.

Dave

2. Pricing
Establishing Quantity Discounts

Dear Dave:

Here's a question that some of your Software Success readers might find interesting. I could use some advice from you on this question ASAP, since I'm entering a negotiation right now, so if there's any way you could respond before this question appears in the newsletter, I'd appreciate it.

We are marketing end-user software for the UNIX environment, and we are pricing the software on a "per-user" basis (using a floating license manager.) Coming from a mainframe background, we have little experience in large quantity discounts and distributor discounts. We have seen software price lists which offer from 50 percent discount at quantity 200 (SUN) to 90 percent at quantity 200 (SAS), as compared to the quantity one price.

We're not sure what the large corporate customer will expect for large quantity discounts, or server and site license fees, nor what a distributor will expect as his discount. Could you share with me some of your pricing experience in the Unix or PC marketplace?

Sincerely,

Ed T. Spire
President
Dynasoft

Dear Ed:

When I called, we focused on the site license option since that was the specific deal with which you were faced. Your single copy price is $2,000, and you thought that a site might use 100 copies maximum of your software.

I feel that you shouldn't discount software below 50 percent to end users. I have seen cases where customers buy a site license and they want additional physical copies of the packages. It is reasonable to me to sell these at two times the cost. If your product cost is ten percent of revenue, your materials cost would be twenty percent, but it is usually described as two times the cost or $50. The ten percent figure is common for PC software, but should be lower for mini and mainframe packages.

Now that we have established that we will sell the customer incremental copies for $1,000 each (50 percent), we need to decide how many copies we will equate to the site license fee. My thought is to price this at 50 percent of the reasonable maximum or 50 units. Thus, my suggestion was that you price your site license fee at $50,000.

I have a number of clients right now who are looking at site licensing pricing. The real dilemma is that the sales person always thinks they can sell 300 copies at $2,000 per copy to this one special customer for $600,000. They look at my $50,000 suggested site license fee and scream that I am giving it away. They suggest that they think we should cut the guy a deal and offer him a site license for $400,000 which is still eight times my number.

My very strong feeling is that you should set the price low enough to make some sales. Over and over I see people chasing the very high dollar site licenses, and they almost never close a site license contract. They put in a great deal of energy and come up empty, or perhaps they sell a handful of copies.

My approach is to deliberately set the price low and make some sales. I would ask these early site licenses to agree to articles. Once you have made some sales, you can always raise the price. I realize that this approach may end up leaving some money on the table, but at least it gets the ball rolling.

U.S. distributors want between 50 percent and 65 percent off list price for PC software. This discount can go as high as 75 percent to 85 percent depending upon what services the distributor provides. Marketing companies who sell and support mainframe products typically pay the developers only 15 percent to 25 percent of the revenue. This is reasonable to me if the marketing company is providing first level support, distributing the physical product, producing the manuals and tapes, and so forth.

As you can see, it is very important to delineate who does what before you settle on a price with a distributor. Once you have that understanding, you can agree on a fair price. I would suggest that if there are responsibilities that you are concerned that the distributor might not fulfill that you should agree in advance how the revenue split would change if you had to take over these responsibilities.

You should also define what it means for the distributor to fail to provide the service. I have seen a number of cases where the marketing company failed to make the investment to provide first level support. The development company ended up picking up this work without the ability to get paid for it.

3. Bundling OEMs

I was impressed with the following article:

Microsoft has bundled Microsoft Works with the IBM PS/2 25, 30, 50Z, 55SX, the Commodore PC 20-III, the Mitsubishi 286L, the Packard Bell (286s), and the Hyundai (all 8086 machines).

Software Toolworks has bundled five of their products on five Headstart machines Grollier's is also bundling their New Grollier Encyclopedia on the Headstart LX-CD and III-CD.

MECA bundled Managing Your Money and Tax Cut, and Sierra On Line bundled Hoyle's book of Games and King's Quest IV on the above IBM machines Tandy has bundled Quicken from Intuit, Instant Pages from Electronic Arts, and RightWriter from RightSoft on their Tandy 1000 SL/2.

Some key points from the article include:

$2 - $7/unit.

As low as $0.50/unit for entertainment titles.

10,000 to 150,000 minimum guarantees.

$100 suggested retail price is typical.

Ease of use is important.

Publishers rarely get more than ten percent of their sales via OEM deals.

The vendors don't view bundling deals as profit centers. They are low risk and low return.

Bundling can allow you to reach first-time buyers.

The major benefit may be the high promotional value without direct cost.

Reference: Call the Shots", Software Industry Bulletin, Digital Information Group, (203) 348-2751

I think that it is interesting to note that almost all of the vendors are quite successful and they are bundling at least moderately successful titles. I have watched a number of small firms pursue OEM deals with very little success. I don't mean that it can't succeed. Just make sure that you control how much

time you invest and that you structure your deal to minimize your risk.

4. Site Licensing

We have a PC product which connects to mainframe computers and we have been approached by a number of our customers about corporate and site licenses. There seem to be a wide variety of alternatives. How should we define the various product offerings and what basic guidelines would you suggest?

The simplest step is a site license. That is one mailing address. Sometimes you even try to limit this to one building, but that depends on how your customer is organized.

Setting the price for a site license is quite qualitative. Conceptually, you estimate how much the total revenue potential might be if you sold single copies Then you negotiate a discount with the customer for the unlimited use at that site. Often the site license discount is as high as 30 to 50 percent. It is critical to get the prospect to buy into this process. In most cases, the site license fee is the basis for all the future negotiations.

The next step is a corporate license. In this age of mergers, the definition of a corporation is critical. I suggest that you limit it to companies doing business under a common name. Given that definition, you need to know how many sites they have in the corporation.

Determining a corporate price is really a function of discounting the site license fees. Rather than a typical 10 percent off for each additional copy:

Typical Multi Copy Discounts:

# Copies	Discount
1	0%
2	10%
3	20%

I have seen that most companies expect and most vendors offer higher discounts to get a corporate license. In many cases I have seen an incremental discount of 20 percent:

Corporate License Discount:

# Sites	Discount
1	0%
2	20%
3	40%
4	60%

This is just a starting point. For most companies, a corporate license is a windfall. For the customer, the acquisition is typically driven by one site. While the other sites, might be interested, they are reluctant to spend their money on something driven by another organization. For both of these reasons, the calculated corporate license fee is just a starting point. The first step is to round it down to a nice even number. Then you start to haggle.

My advice in most cases is to accept as little as 1.5 times the site fee for a corporate license, but insist on maintenance fees based on the calculated prices. Give ground on the initial purchase, but don't mortgage your future. The other concession that you can ask for is for the customer to agree to an article on their corporate license and how they are using your product.

If they want to use your product in companies which go by a different name, I would look at that as a second corporate license. It might be 30 to 50 percent less than the first corporate license.

Worldwide rights are another alternative. Most software companies get 30 to 40 percent of their revenues internationally. I would think that pricing the world wide license at 1.4 times the corporate license would be reasonable. You might look at how much usage they would make of your product internationally, but I believe that it will be difficult for you to get a lot of money for the international rights.

One area that I haven't discussed is product delivery. This is a mundane detail which can be very important if you are selling PC products with hundreds of copies. Most companies conclude that they really want to have shrink wrapped product to give their people. The really don't want to duplicate disks and copy documentation. You can do it cheaper, and better. Make sure that you specify how many copies of the product they get for each license, and what the incremental cost per copy is. I would price the incremental copies at 2X direct cost which should break even.

As I think about it, there is lots of room to discount the initial license fee on these licenses, but you must be very careful to protect your maintenance revenue. While your incremental costs to sell an additional site are usually minimal, the support costs are very real. I would price the maintenance for a site at 15 percent of the site price per year. Additional sites can get discounts if they go through the primary site for support. If they want to call you directly, they should pay the site maintenance fee.

The final issue that you should address is the cost of updates. How many copies of the updated product will they get as part of their maintenance fee? How much will additional copies cost?

5. Software Leasing

Dear Dave,

Thank you for your suggestion regarding software only leasing. I contacted ManDahl Leasing Corp. in San Francisco and it seems like they might be able to help us out. Our problem is: I have been trying, quite unsuccessfully, to find a company that will finance a software only lease. (Our software licenses range from $8,000 to $60,000+.) Because there is little or no hardware involved, companies view the transaction as an unsecured loan. ManDahl will do a credit check on the prospect and requires the lessee be a Fortune 1000 company. Unfortunately, most prospects looking for a leasing arrangement are not in the Fortune 1000! I am curious as to whether you or your readership has had any similar experiences or are aware of organizations offering software only leases based solely on credit history.

Michael G. George
Marketing Manager
Cascade Technologies
(212) 768-7380

Chapter III. Pricing

Dear Michael,

Studebaker Worthington is the company that promotes software only leases. In our initial phone call you mentioned that they weren't really interested in software only leases except to the Fortune 1000 and for more than $20,000. It also wasn't clear that they really wanted to write any software only leases.

I gave you the introduction to ManDahl:

Melvin Lemberger
ManDahl Leasing
50 First St. #500
San Francisco, CA 94105
(415) 777-3775

I don't know of any other companies writing software only leases. I would appreciate hearing from any readers who have tried to get software only leasing.

Dave

Dear Dave:

I thought your readers would be interested in the following information on software leasing.

Does leasing have a place in selling software? The simple answer is "yes," but there are still many questions regarding the issue of leasing, such as:

* **What are the ground rules? Who are the candidates for leasing?**

* **When should leasing be introduced as an option?**

* **What's in it for me, the vendor?**

* **How do I go about coordinating the lease activity?**

Here are some of the ground rules:

1. **The financial stability of your prospect is vital. The lease, in effect, becomes an unsecured debt. Upon signing the lease, the lessee (your customer) is guaranteeing to make payments for the length of the lease.**

2. **Leasing should be offered as an option at the beginning of the selling cycle. When you know and understand your prospect's requirements, you can indicate that the software may be leased at a modest cost per month or purchased for the full amount of the software.**

3. **If your customer decides to lease because of the low monthly payments, you (the vendor) get paid in full when the customer signs all the lease documents.**

4. **Call your leasing company and they will handle all the paper work and also provide lease quotes for your proposals. The usual range is from $5,000 to $5,000,000.**

5. **One caveat: By signing a non-cancelable lease, your customer (the lessee) is financially responsible for all lease payments. It does not matter if they are not happy with the product, ore even if your company is no longer in business. The lessor does not want to get involved with new software. Therefore, your software product should be seasoned by having been sold to several end users. This helps demonstrate reliability.**

Finally, I would be happy to provide any more leasing information that your readers might require. Of course, there is no obligation.

Mel Lemberger
ManDahl
(415) 777-3775

Dear Mel:

Thanks for the information. I know that a number of my readers who market to smaller businesses have problems because of the lack of creditworthiness of their customers. If they want to pursue this, I suggest they call you.

Dave

F. Pricing (1989)

Pricing is one of the most hotly debated topics in software companies. Everybody is an expert at pricing. Development types typically want to charge high prices for the software (relatively speaking) because they know how many hours of work went into the product; they want a high price to pay for the product's "goodness". Salespeople tend to want low prices so that the software will sell easily. The CEO wants the "right" price.

But what is the "right price"? Ask any MBA. He'll tell you that "The Right Price" (otherwise known as TRP) for almost any product is the price that yields the maximum possible profit for the company. If you don't shut him up in time, your MBA may launch into a discussion of Cost of Goods Sold, Gross Margin, and other irrelevancies. We believe that with regard to software, the traditional pricing models are wrong, or at least miss the point: software company profits closely follow revenues – in maximizing revenue you also maximize profits.

Your pricing strategy is the fundamental linchpin of your software marketing plan. Once you have set the price, you have limited your degrees of freedom on many aspects of your marketing program. The price of your software determines a number of marketing issues:

- *Distribution channels available* – Are you going to sell direct, through distribution, or through VARs?

- *Sales Cycle* – Selling expensive software takes longer – a *lot* longer.

- *Type of salesperson hired* – Telephone order-takers are *much* different than Executive "Account Representatives." Not surprisingly the compensation is different, too.

- *Advertising Plans* – The type of magazine and the size & frequency of your "spread" are determined by price (and cheaper software doesn't mean cheaper advertising – just ask Phillipe Kahn of Borland.)

- *Installation & Support* – Your installation & support plans will be strongly affected by the price of your product. A two-week on-site training and installation visit is much different than a dial-in BBS system and each of these is appropriate for differently priced software.

There's an interesting corollary the software pricing issue: while it is difficult to set the prices initially, it is *even more difficult* to change them after the price has been established. We believe that this is due in part to the fact that so many factors are based on the product's price that everyone in the company is effected if the price changes and if the corresponding factors don't change.

Your level of support is an example of one such factor. If you start with a low price on your software product, you won't have the money to pay for extensive support. Both you and your customers must become comfortable with "bare bones" support. If you raise your price, your customers expectations will change accordingly. If your support people don't adapt, your customers will be very critical of support which they previously considered adequate. You can make similar cases for a long list of other factors.

Even the simplest software product faces complex pricing issues in the modern corporate environment. Must each user purchase a separate license? What about site licenses? How about pricing when used on a LAN? Do we have Mainframe pricing? The list of questions goes on and on.

This article will focus on a number of complex pricing issues which occur again and again.

- In the minicomputer and LAN-world the pricing strategy is moving from CPU-based to network-based.

- In the IBM mainframe arena, software prices are often set according to a multi-level or "tiered" pricing strategy.

- PC-based software vendors typically use operating system based pricing.

We'll address each of these pricing schemes in this article.

1. Value-based Pricing

The objective of all of these plans is to price the software based upon the **value** delivered by the software. If a customer really uses your software, and assigns many users and resources to it, you'd like to receive more money from that customer. If there is another customer that wants to purchase your package, but will likely subject it to only limited use, you'd like to have a pricing strategy that offers a lower (and more justifiable) cost. While the objective of value-based pricing is laudable, implementing it is tricky.

Chapter III. Pricing

Dear Dave:

One point that was missing from the pricing issue is the justification of price in value received to the customer. This is typically broken down into two parts — identifiable costs (such as connect time savings and lower training costs) and 'new math' costs (such as the value of more effective communications to a sales group).

Harry E. Brawley, Jr
Sigea Systems, Inc.

Dear Harry,

Value based pricing is difficult to establish, and even more difficult to maintain. In my experience, value often influences the decision to implement a new system, but the fair price is usually based on more mundane factors like competitive alternatives. If you look at some of the basic utilities in your life, like running water, they have incredible value, but you would be outraged to pay for running water based on its value to you. As long as you have a monopoly, you can use value based pricing to justify the price you have already settled on. In most cases the prospects have alternative (even indirect ones) which put some limits on what you can charge.

G. Network & User-based Pricing (1989)

Networks circumvent the traditional CPU based pricing which was common in the VAX world. In CPU based pricing vendors traditionally had three or four price levels which corresponded to hardware categories. (See the following discussion on tiered pricing for a discourse on how this works.)

The difficulty with networks is that once you install your software on the network, you lose control. You have no control, for instance, over what CPUs are connected to the network and which users downloaded your software onto their machine.

1. What doesn't work

We had some clients who tried to extend their CPU-based pricing metaphor to networks. This didn't work at all.

This client tried to add up all the processor power for all of the CPUs on the network (calculated in Millions of Instructions Per Second [MIPS]), and

used this aggregated CPU power as the basis for their price. There were a number of things wrong with this approach:
1. Their network prospects were faced with very high prices because of all the CPU power on the network.
2. Existing customers complained that under this approach they would have to contact the software vendor every time they added or dropped a CPU from their network.
3. There was infinite disagreement about the real MIPS generated by the networked CPUs.
4. The final issue was that the customer might have a network with hundreds of nodes but only one or two people actually using the software.

If this vendor insists on pricing their system based on the total CPU power, they will price it beyond the customer's value threshold. Our conclusion was that the CPU metaphor falls-apart when you attempt to equate value to CPU-power on a modern networks.

This lack has made many software companies look towards user-based pricing.

As the corporate-wide networks become more complex, people began to look for a convenient way to provide flexible access for customers which provided adequate vendor safeguards. A new technology called 'network license servers' (NLS) is emerging from the engineering workstation environment.

NLSs allow MIS departments to offer access to authorized users. It also allows occasional users to access the software within the copies that were purchased. The vendor embeds 'locks' in their software and the customers purchase 'keys'. The number of 'keys' determine the number of copies of the application which can be in use at one time (maximum concurrent users). Some vendors charge a premium for keys which are issued over the phone, and in some cases you can even rent a key for a crash project. MIS departments like this controlled access approach because it facilitates "charge-backs" and thus lessens the impact on the MIS budget.

REFERENCE: PC Week, "License Servers Offer Network Users Reliable Software Distribution System", March 15, 1989.

2. Conversion to User-based Pricing

There are a number of practical issues which come up in real life. If you implement user-based pricing on a product which was previously priced on CPU-basis, how do you convert the CPU-licenses over to user licenses? You may think that you can ignore this "minor" issue. Forget that thought! Your customers will force you to deal with it when they convert to networks.

The most equitable approach that we have seen is to give the customer a credit for what they paid for the CPU license. This credit is applied toward acquiring a "new" user-based license. As long as the prices are similar, this won't cause a great deal of difficulty.

We have seen a number of cases where older CPU licensees were faced with paying three or four times their original price to upgrade to a user-based license for their usage. Almost all customers view this price increase as unacceptable. Most software vendors end up having to negotiate these conversion deals individually with their older customers. In the end, most software firms end up giving in and accepting what the customer is willing to pay. There's a reason why this pragmatic attitude makes good sense: While you may not be realizing any conversion revenue, you can gain increased revenue by charging more for software maintenance on your products.

3. Maintenance & Support Fees

Maintenance and support fees are often an issue with user-based pricing. We think that this is true because customers don't think of the user license as a purchase agreement. Since they typically add users every year, they usually must add to their license by sending in additional license fees as they add users. They think, 'Why should I send in money for maintenance fees this year? I am about to pay X dollars for additional users.' Don't be surprised if your customers want to work a deal where they pay a discounted amount for both items.

4. New Pricing Algorithm Teething Pains

While part of this negotiation is your classical "lets get as good a deal as possible out of our vendor", it also reflects the fact that you are introducing a new pricing algorithm. Your customer is afraid that he is being taken advantage of so he wants to test your limits. Everyone involved in the purchase will want to test your flexibility. At the same time, new pricing often ignores very real customer issues. You will have to work these issues out with your customers.

Over time new pricing will become established and there will be less negotiation, but for now accept the questioning as part of the evolution of a new pricing structure.

5. Adding Users

The pricing strategy for additional users is critical to the success of user-based pricing. If you don't impose a penalty for adding users later, all your customers will sign-up for their minimum number of users. When they need to add to their user-base, they simply purchase more at minimal cost.

We have a client who is selling their software product based on user-based pricing. They came up with the idea of 'zero based pricing' for additional users. See the graph on the next page.

Their pricing per user declines significantly as the number of users increase (in this case the price per user declines on a log or a quadratic scale). The tenth user, for instance, may only cost one-third of what the first user cost; and the fiftieth user may only cost 20%. This type of pricing is used to encourage customers to buy as many keys as possible because each purchase cycle starts at zero users: there is no credit for prior purchases (hence "zero-based"). This policy insures that the customers won't deliberately under-buy. Here's an example showing how it works. If the initial purchase is for an eight-user license, the customer's cost will be $9,000. The customer must think carefully about future additions before making up their mind. Doubling the number of maximum users to 16, at the time of initial purchase, only costs an additional $6,000. If, on the other hand, the customer buys an eight-user license and then later needs to add more users, an additional eight-user license is another $9,000.

If you elect to use this approach, it might be reasonable to give the customer a limited time where they can reconsider and add additional users onto the original purchase (60 to 90 days perhaps).

The major benefit of this approach is that is offers a powerful incentive to customers to purchase the maximum reasonable number of user-licenses at the time of initial acquisition. It certainly ensures that you haven't made it too easy for your customers to put off buying additional users.

Number of Seats vs. the Price of Software

(Courtesy of Businesswise, Inc.)

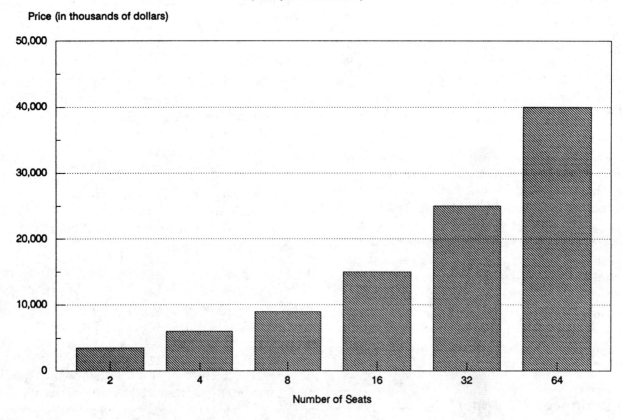

Figure 1 -- Zero-Based Pricing

6. User Access Control

If you control the maximum number of concurrent users, you are encouraging your customers to buy fewer keys than they might actually need. If a customer has 50 people who might use the system, they may buy only 25 keys on the assumption only half of the potential users will actually need to access the software at any given time. This situation creates a "scarce resource" mentality that can encourage hording behavior. Some users come in early and sign-in thereby using one user count. They remain logged on even when they don't really need access to the system — just to ensure availability at a later point in time.

"Hard" vs. "Soft" Keys

Another problem which occurs in time of shortage is that not all users are really equal. Most customers/applications have soft occasional users who won't be impacted if they can't sign on the system today. There are also "hard core" users who must have continuous, on-line access all of the working day. If these users can't get a key, they will raise hell with everyone within reach. This puts the MIS department and the vendor through a fire drill to get them a phone key ASAP. (For some reason most customers rarely think about asking non-required users to sign off.) This raises the issue of whether you make the limit on the number of keys hard or soft. (A hard limit prohibits additional sign ons while a soft limit merely sends a warning message.) If you make it hard, you run the risk of upsetting the users (note that this especially bad if your pricing encourages them to buy as few keys as possible). The soft approach is to give them access to additional keys. Rather than denying additional users access, the system sends a message to the administrator, "You have exceeded your allotment of keys, call XYZ software to buy more". This approach depends upon significant trust in your customers and guarantees that you will sell fewer marginal seats.

Reserved Seating

Another approach is to sell assigned seating and open seating. We have a client, BusinessWise, who is selling a package that provides on-line tech support and problem tracking. As with most applications there is a group of "hard core" users (the support technicians) and another group that is more "soft core" (development, marketing, and sales). BusinessWise came up with the idea of selling "seats" rather than "keys" and of having assigned seats for the support reps, and having an open pool of seats for the soft group. The idea is that the system cannot deny a support tech access to the system since they can't do their job if they don't have access to the system. While it might be inconvenient for someone in the soft group to be denied access, it won't be a crisis. If it becomes a real problem, that individual should really be in the assigned seat group.

Reference: BusinessWise, Inc.; Steve Hartman; (408)866-5960

7. Minimum Prices

Another real issue is how low you can actually afford to go in selling your system. As an example, if your system sells for $10K for a typical 10 user configuration, what is the minimum acceptable price that you can afford to sell it for? Can you make money at $5K for 2 users? Rather than offering linear pricing you might offer modest discounts for limited usage. Digital Equipment thinks that it has the answer. DEC implemented pricing based on a maximum of 4 concurrent users. They offered customers 5 - 20% discounts if they limited the maximum concurrent users to 4 for their Datatree data retrieval package, the VAXnotes conferencing package, and their Teamdata programming package. They might extend this to other software packages. You also need to consider your lower limit when you think about maintenance pricing. You might need to have a higher percentage for maintenance on the smaller configurations.

REFERENCE: ComputerWorld ,"DEC:New Limited-Usage Pricing for Software", 4/25/88.

8. Network License Managers

Dear Dave,

I thought the readership of Software Success might be interested in some work Marketshare has done with respect to licensed software. As you may know, Apollo, Sun, and Dec have all announced products that can control the number of simultaneous users of an application package. Using these tools, software vendors can offer their customers flexibile licensing alternatives that mean more access to software on a local area network.

In a survey we did of technical software vendors, we are looking at a 50% increase in the use of these network license managers from 1988 through 1989. Allowing for a one year lead time, we will probably see the number of products offered in this particular technical software segment to double sometime in mid 1990.

Some of the highlights from this major research effort might be of interest to your readership:
1. Network license servers are a new way to create value added by improving access to applications.
2. License servers offer new ways to charge for software and make software rentals a real possibility.
3. Premium pricing is possible for many applications but this depends on factors such as price of application and frequency/intensity of use.

You might let the readership know that we have prepared a white paper on software pricing and the impact of network licensing. This white paper is available at no charge if people will give us a call (508) 358-2154 or send us a FAX on their letterhead (508) 358-6350.

Sincerely,
Jim Geisman
President
Marketshare

H.   Tiered   Pricing   (1989)
IBM introduced its four-tier pricing in October 1986, and many software companies have been evaluating tier-based pricing ever since. Conceptually it is very appealing.

1. How it works
The enormous spread in CPU power from the bottom of the IBM line to the top has made it necessary

to assign an individual machine to one of four groups:

- Small
- Medium
- Large
- Very Large (humongous)

Software is priced according to which "tier" the target CPU is assigned to.

2. Pricing Variations

It has been very common to have different charges for the different operating systems (DOS and MVS). Vendors and customers felt that this was fair because the more sophisticated operating system (MVS) provided a lot more functionality. (It also helped that the MVS customers were used to paying more for software.)

The major attraction of tiered pricing is that it enables vendors to open up a new market in smaller sites would never have been a prospect at the higher price.

One drawback is that if you are currently selling your product at full-list to some firms with small CPUs, you will automatically reduce your price to these customers. This will reduce both your sales and maintenance fees. This can be especially expensive if your product has an extensive customer base of smaller machines. You will have to deal with customers who want to reduce their maintenance because they are using a smaller CPU. While we haven't seen this level of detail in how people implement tiered pricing, we think that you may have to allow customers downgrade their license and pay the lower maintenance fee. Hopefully, you could discourage most of your eligible customers from downgrading and reducing your maintenance fees.

There's a bit of silver in that dark cloud, however: if your customers do migrate at a later time to a CPU in a larger group that they will be required to pay an upgrade fee.

3. CPU Licenses

Many software firms sell their products based upon a "CPU License". This means that the customer is licensed to use the software on one particular machine, oftentimes specified in the license by CPU Serial Number.

The CPU licensing can be a real sticky issue. This is especially true in very large sites which move machines around like toys. Customers the "Fortune 500" category often have datacenters containing dozens of CPUs. This type of site might need to change the target CPU once per quarter. Tracking CPU serial number (and providing serial-dependent upgrades) is totally unmanageable. Software sales-reps with this type of customer would be wise to encourage the purchase of an unlimited or 'site' license if you require the customer to specify specific serial numbers. More commonly, modern license agreements restrict the software to one production machine and one backup machine without specifying serial numbers.

We have clients who have faced resistance from their smaller customers when they upgraded their CPU. These small customers resist paying more for software which won't be providing any more value just because it is running on a faster CPU. There are two objections that these customers bring up:

1. "Why should I pay more when I am not receiving any more value?"
2. "You are holding me hostage, and I refuse to pay your unreasonable charge."

Some of our clients have been surprised and dismayed at the vehemence and obstinacy of the customer.

4. Upgrade Dilemma

A historical example might help you see why some customers feel this way, and how easily a really big dollar-amount can be required. Let's say that your software product originally sold for $5,000 five years ago when your customer was running on a machine group 10 CPU. Group 20 CPU fees were then $10,000. Over the five years your customer has had some awareness that prices were going up (because their maintenance fees have been increasing), but this doesn't get a lot of attention. If your prices have increased an average of 20% per year over the five-year time-frame (a not-unreasonable price growth, see the next article, *How to Raise Prices*), your present prices will require a $10,000 fee for group 10 machines and $20,000 fee for group 20.

Our example customer would be asked to pay $15,000 to upgrade to a group 20 CPU (the new group 20 price minus 100% of what they paid). From the vendor's point of view, we are being very fair by giving the customer 100% credit for his software (wouldn't it be great if hardware vendors were that nice). The ungrateful customer, rather than appreciating our concern, is outraged that we want him to pay three times as much for the upgrade as the initial purchase price. This difference can become even more extreme if they got a great discount in your distant past (of course you don't discount now, do you?) or if your prices have gone up even more in the meantime.

You will undoubtedly have a very emotional confrontation with your customer. The real problem is that your customer (typically the MIS manager) was surprised by the magnitude of the upgrade fee and will look bad to his management. Chances are that this isn't a budgeted expense, and we all know how management hates surprises. Given this real-life situation, you'll most often be wise to bend or soften your policies.

5. Making Peace

In the example above, we would probably recommend offering the customer the full credit for the *current* price of the model that they own. While this is hard to justify intellectually, it will probably result in $10,000 in revenue and a reasonably happy customer since we have given our advocate something to show his management that he got for his company. (If you make this current-price trade-in a formal company policy, that can become a selling point for your software.)

You may also be required to make some concessions on the maintenance. 15% of $20,000 is $3K per year which is 60% of the original price.

There's a real lesson to be learned here: don't let your customer be surprised by the impact of your upgrade fees. Call them frequently, mention your policy in your newsletter, offer periodic "upgrade sales" to encourage voluntary and relatively painless upgrades. (This last item can also provide a beneficial revenue boost during the slow summer months.)

6. Version Upgrades

Another variation on tiered pricing is to call the new release a new version which must be paid for. The amount of credit for version 1 toward version 2 can range from 0% to 100%. New version pricing entails many of the same issues that we just discussed under CPU upgrade price increases. The upgrade fee is a surprise and the customer doesn't really feel that they should have to pay for the new version. They have been paying you maintenance all these years under the impression that they were going to get all the features in the new version at no additional cost. While IBM can get away with this type of heavy handed action, a small software company can't.

7. Mainframe Pricing Trends

Users have become much more price sensitive in the last few years, and some vendors attribute this to IBM's tiered pricing. Another reason is rising software prices, and the general retrenching of American business. Finally, the software industry is maturing and there are many more product categories which now have commodity status where price is the only factor.

There are also some vendors who will discount very aggressively at the drop of a hat. David Tory of Computer Associates said, "We're no more aggressive than anyone else, but we've always taken the view that we will not walk away from a deal because of price."

REFERENCE: Software Magazine, "Price is more sensitive, IBM's tiered pricing scheme is having an impact", March 1988.

I. Hardware/OS-based pricing (1989)

In the IBM mainframe world software vendors have been pricing their software differently on different operating systems which run on the same hardware. Part of the justification is that the lower operating system users (DOS) are getting less value than the larger operating system users (MVS). While this may be true, there is an underlying economic reality that can't be avoided. The MVS sites are accustomed to paying for software while the DOS sites are much more cost conscious. The customers who are cost conscious will tend to buy DOS because it has much less overhead. The MVS customers are larger and have more of a need for the extra functionality that MVS offers and they are willing to pay the price.

Chapter III. Pricing

The same situation exists in the personal computer world. A TRS-80 customer is quite different than an Apple II customer who is totally different than an IBM PC user. When you look at mass-market PC software in the entertainment and the individual productivity markets, you will notice that there are real price differences on the different machines. A lot of this reflects the underlying preconceptions that users have.

When Visicalc a best-seller on the Apple II, it was priced at $195. Lotus then introduced 1-2-3 at $495 and went on to reap hundreds of millions of dollars in sales. We would not be surprised to see an OS/2 version at a higher price level. While some of these differences are really arbitrary, we would like to discuss some of the factors which should be considered.

1. Competitive Pricing

The first thing to look at is the competitive pricing on the target machine. What have other vendors done? If everyone else charges $10 less for a product on the Commodore 64 (C64) than the Apple II and $10 more on the Commodore Amiga, you should have a very good reason to buck convention. There is a fair amount of group-think that is fairly compelling. If your pricing is perceived as being out of line, you will have a real problem.

Make sure that you don't limit your price-comparison search to direct competitors. If your product costs $150 on the IBM PC, see what other vendors with similar priced products on the PC have done when they ported their product to the target machine. Your prospects will be looking at alternatives. If they feel that you are priced too high or too low, you will put them off.

2. Technical Differences

The technical evaluation of the quality of the product and/or the customer benefits is another factor which must be considered. If the C64 version of your product isn't as good because of the limitations of the C64, it is probably wise to lower your price. At the same time, the Amiga version of your product might be really great and might justify a higher price. We believe that this is the real underlying reality and that it explains much of the conventional wisdom for the hardware price variations. The vendor is often the worst person to really evaluate any product quality variation from machine to machine.

There is another aspect of the technical evaluation: You must insure that your converted product meets the common standards on the target machine. Look at the other software available for your target machine and set your standards accordingly. There is nothing worse than converted software which looks 'ugly'. This can kill an otherwise good product.

Technical programming difficulty is another reason that vendors want to charge more for software on one machine. This is a very tough factor to include in your pricing decision because you don't know if the programming difficulty is specific to your programmers or really dependent upon the target computer. If the problem is with the target computer, there should be little software available and you might have an opportunity to charge more. We recommend focusing on the competitive external situation rather than the internal factors. If you have programmers who have trouble programming a new machine, view that as their personal problem. If you try to pass the buck to your customers by raising your price above market, you will guarantee that your product does not sell.

3. OS/2 Pricing

The next pricing frontier will be the OS/2 pricing for PC software. Everyone is expecting that the software prices for OS/2 products will be higher. Initial OS/2 product introductions have borne this suspicion out. Justifications for a higher price include the following:

- OS/2 users have lots of money. (Just look at how much more the hardware costs.)
- OS/2 sure is more sophisticated.
- OS/2 software will do more for more people.

We expect that we will see higher prices for OS/2 versions of MS-DOS products, but unless they are really better we don't expect them to sell well. Great products which really exploit OS/2 will command a higher price because they offer more value. In the end, the software marketplace pays for value.

J. CPU vs. Site Licenses (1989)

Q. We have traditionally sold most of our software on site (per location) licenses. My sales staff is telling me that we are loosing revenue — everyone else is charging on a per CPU basis. What's the real truth? What is the state of the art on CPU versus site licenses?

A. Almost everyone that we know of is offering CPU licenses. In cases where two vendors are competing and one is offering a CPU license and the other is offering a site license, only rarely will a customer pay more than 10 percent additional for a site license. This means that you are potentially leaving money on the table with a site license.

The only situation where we would recommend that you consider staying with a site license as your primary price would be if you have strong competition which is pushing site licensing.

K. Setting a Price (1989)

The price of software has been going up dramatically over the past few years (see the following article for more statistics.) We have felt that much of these increases were due to the fact that the customers were getting more for their money.

1. Price per Pound

We recall reading an article in a PC magazine which suggested that micro software prices were strongly correlated with the weight of the package. The author had analyzed the price and weight of a number of PC packages and had come up with a reasonably good correlation. The writer had determined that software cost $79 per pound. While the writer made fun of his findings, we believe that the amount of documentation is often tied to amount of perceived benefit. A bigger program requires a bigger box of documentation.

2. Price per Byte

Jim Knowles, President of the Futures Group, has studied PC pricing and has come up with a similar, but much more useful analysis: The amount of compiled code and the price of the package are strongly related. Jim pointed out that "With Visicalc you got maybe 50K of compiled code. Today you get a megabyte of code, the software does more and it has a better user interface." To quantify his point he compared the prices of software and the amount of compiled code.

He found that the price per byte of compiled code has declined 17% to 19% annually. As he pointed out this is comparable with the decline in the hardware cost per MIPs (Million of instructions per second).

REFERENCE: VarBusiness , "Will Rising Software Prices Lift VAR Profits?", March 1988.

3. Continued Improvement

This analysis sheds some light on another feeling that we have had. We feel that software vendors must continue to enhance and extend a product to keep it viable. If a software vendor wants to maintain the price of a product they must increase the amount of code by 17 to 19% per year. If you don't enhance your product, your cost per byte won't remain competitive and you will either have to drop your price or suffer a decline in sales.

4. Death of Old Software

This helps explain the problems that some old products have whose sales decline steadily over time. We have seen a number of good, and functional products which suffer this slow death. The frustrating aspect of this situation is that they are great products which can do the job. The vendors are very reluctant to drop the price because that will diminish the maintenance revenues which have become the major source of revenue. It may be that this price per byte is one of the driving factors in long term pricing. This also would help explain the hardware/operating system pricing variations. We really would like to hear your thoughts on this. In particular, we would be very interested if anyone can plot the cost per byte for an older product which continues to sell well. Has it kept on the 18% per year curve?

5. Mainframe Prices for Micro Software

There are also examples of PC software companies who charge mainframe prices. IMRS markets Micro Control which is 'advanced accounting software' which they have found to be very price insensitive. The price of Micro Control was raised from $30K to $70K in four steps in two years. In fiscal year 1988, they expect to double their income to $7 Million. This clearly is a case where the customers feel that they are receiving good value even at the higher price.

6. Initial Release Pricing

There are a number of common mistakes made in setting software prices. The major reason is that far too many people assume that price is *the* major issue for their customers. New companies, in particular, tend to badly underprice their products. There are a number of reasons that cause this:

- They try to use low price to compensate for other shortcomings.
- They lack confidence in the value of their product.
- They fear that they will starve if they don't make the sale, and half a loaf is better than no loaf.
- They give away secondary products and services to close the sale.

7. Demand Curves

Ideally, you should set your initial price correctly so that you don't have to increase it dramatically later on. Larger companies use focus groups to test consumers reactions to new products and use this as a major input to the pricing decision.

We have worked with a number of smaller companies who have conducted market surveys to determine if their was a market for their new product and to get some idea of what the demand curve is like. A demand curve is the percent of qualified prospects who would be interested in the product at a given price. Once you get your survey results you have to plot the cumulative percentage of customers who would buy at a given price. The curve starts at 100% at $0 for qualified prospects and goes to 0% at $1M or some other outrageous price. Once you have the demand curve you can analyze your economics at different price points.

Believing the Customer

When we discuss the problem of performing customer surveys with many technical people, they often express the concern that customers really won't tell the truth. They think that all customers will tell you the lowest possible price.

Our experience is that this isn't true. Customers will most often give you good, honest-for-them answers. You may decide that they are understating their threshold price by 10 to 15%, but this is just noise in most pricing discussions. After all, we are trying to decide orders of magnitude in pricing: Should we sell this product for $100 or $1,000?

8. First-year Pricing

Our feeling is that you want to start off with your sales objectives and set your price based on the percentage of the market that you must get in the first year.

For example if you are in a vertical market with 10,000 potential customers, and you need to sell 100 customers, you might need 1,000 serious prospects to get the 100 sales. If this is the case, we would set prices high so that only 10 to 20% of the prospects would seriously consider the product at that price-level. If you priced your product at the one-half of this optimal level you might be leaving a great deal of money on the table.

A higher price level may provide the revenue to pay for all the marketing materials, and development to make your product what you want it to be. This reminds us of the quote, "Be careful what you pretend because it will become true." If you start off with a low price, you run the risk of being perceived as having a cheap and shoddy product. This can be a very difficult impression to change.

We worked with a PC product company where we did a survey and created the demand curve. In that case we assumed that the unit cost of marketing was fixed, and we set the price to optimize the gross margin. The product cost was 25 to 30% of the lower prices so gross margin was a real issue with this product. In higher priced products where sales costs become more important, you might include sales as part of your fixed cost. If you optimize the contribution margin, revenue - product cost - cost of sales and support, you might be on a better path to determine your optimal price level from your survey.

In reality, the demand curves that we have seen often have very simple and powerful messages. We was involved with a vertical market package which might have been sold for $100 to $1,000. At the same time, there was a wide variety of possible functionality in the product. When we got the surveys back, we found out that $500 was a real price barrier. We also had the input on the priority for the possible features and functionality. With these two sets of information, the developer was able to focus his development on building the best $500 product.

Price Demand Curve: Percentage of Customers Buying

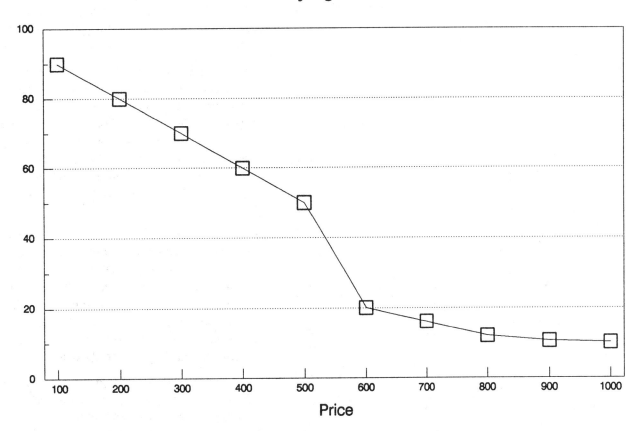

Figure 2 - Price Demand Curve

If we had known then what we know now, we could have analyzed the cost per byte for their competitors and told them how many bytes they would need to support the $500 price on the year of planned introduction.

L. The wrong way to Raise Prices (1989)

1. Apple's RAM price increases

Apple's price increase last year are a good example of the wrong way to raise prices. We are sure that Apple felt that their loyal customers would gladly pay more for Macs. At the same time they had the excuse that RAM was more expensive. They didn't anticipate the reaction from their customers: the customers felt that they were being taken advantage of. The customers postponed acquisitions and bought smaller machines with lower margins. This resulted in sharply lower second quarter net income and a drop in stock price. We believe that the Mac advocates felt betrayed by Apple and that the IBM advocates used this excess to argue that their company shouldn't buy proprietary machines which would make them hostage to the rapacious vendor. The long term impact might be a sharp reduction in new accounts. You should never underestimate the ethical outrage that price a increase may generate.

2. Lotus, too

Lotus Development Corp may be going down the same path. "Pricing in our industry needs to evolve," said Robert V. Schecter, senior VP for finance and operations. "We need to get paid more for our product." He then went on to explain that support for multiple environments was increasing Lotus' costs, and he felt that these costs should be passed along to the customers. We were really offended by this. Lotus is porting their software to other environments because they had a business case: that they will make money selling it in those other environments. It sounds to us like Lotus wants the MS-DOS customers to subsidize their move to OS/2 and mainframe platforms. Given the fact that Lotus charges top dollar for its products, and that they are faced with a great deal of quality competition with lower prices, I wonder if they aren't following Apple down the road to a customer revolt.

REFERENCE: Software Magazine, "Lotus wants higher prices", January 1989.

M. How to Raise Prices (1989)

Raising software prices is a very common phenomenon. The software market has been growing 22% a year, and the price of common packages has been growing 12% a year. According to a survey by Culpepper & Associates, the price of the average software product jumped 38% from 1984 to 1987. The increase by software type was:

- Cross-Industry   25.6%
- Vertical Market   27.1%
- System/Utility   44.5%
- Microcomputer   49.7%
- System Control   63.5%

1. Unbundling Prices

The above price increases are probably limited to the list price on the software package. In many cases you can effectively increase your software's prices by unbundling. By this we mean that instead of including training, support, extra documentation, etc in the basic package, these products and services are available on an extra price basis. This is an easy way to increase your prices because these secondary items are rarely subject to the pricing scrutiny that the basic product price is. This is analogous to car dealers focusing on the basic car price and making their margin on the add on options.

2. How and Why

If you decide that you must raise your price, you must consider a number of issues. The first issue is why you really believe that you can get more for your product. In many cases this is a function of the competition. How often do you lose a deal based on price? How often does the prospect complain about price? Our feeling is that unless 10% of your prospects are complaining about price, your price is too low. While we dislike discounting, we feel that unless you are being forced to do some discounting it is safe to assume that your price is too low. The only major exception to this is if your product is positioned as the bargain basement product. If you raise its price out of the bargain basement, you may lose your market. Otherwise, if they aren't complaining, your price is too low.

3. Maintenance Impact

The next issue to examine is your maintenance impact of a higher price. If you dramatically increase your price (double it perhaps), your customers would probably complain if their maintenance prices doubled. In some cases they may have escalator clauses in their contract which limits your annual maintenance price increases to 10 to 15% per year. If this is the case, their maintenance prices will lag the maintenance prices for new customers, but they will catch up. If your customers don't have this type of escalator clause, you might consider a half way step. Under this approach you increase their maintenance half way between the old price and the new price in year one. In year two they will pay the full current maintenance price. Our experience is that this is seen as fair by most customers. Your people can say, "We value you as a good customer and while we are increasing your maintenance fees, we are splitting the difference with you to show our appreciation. Instead of focusing on this price increase you should be looking at all the great things we will be coming out in future releases of the product, and don't forget that your maintenance dollars are helping to make it happen."

4. Announcing the Increase

We recommend that you announce your price increase for 30 to 90 days out. This gives the current prospects in the pipeline a chance to buy at the old price.

Now you have to turn to your sales pipeline. The moment you announce a new, higher price, you will pull a significant amount of business forward in the pipeline: some prospects who were planning on buying later in the year will buy now before the price goes up. Our experience is that if you announce the higher price effective now, that you end up with a number of unhappy prospects. Software companies often end up giving those who buy the old price. Rather than going through this battle, we find that it is much better to give them a reasonable amount of time to act.

Make sure that you allow enough time for yourself: if they don't make the deadline that you need to feel 'OK' about refusing to honor the "old" price — because they blew it. (No matter how firm you want to be, reserve some room for practicality: you will need to give time-extensions to get final approval, obtain proper signatures, etc.)

5. New Marketing Programs

The next challenge is to set the marketing programs in place to rebuild your pipeline. The price increase will create a bubble in your sales pipeline. If you don't do something to generate leads to fill in this bubble, you will suffer from the classical feast & famine syndrome.

You should analyze your sales cycle. How long does it take to generate leads, turn them into prospects and then turn them into sales? With many complex products it takes six to nine months to turn leads into sales. If you are planning on announcing your new prices effective in three months, you could face a three month drought.

We recommend that you coordinate your follow-on lead generation program with the timing on your price increase announcement and cutover to the new prices. If we were faced with the above parameters, we would probably hold off the price announcement for a month or two to give the follow on lead generation program time to start leads into the pipeline.

6. Increase Timing

The timing in your market is another factor when you are considering announcing new pricing. We have found it most effective to use a price increase to accentuate your best selling season rather than trying to improve your off-season.

In much of the mainframe and large-system software world, the fourth quarter of the year is the best selling season and the first quarter is the worst. Many companies announce new prices effective January 1. This helps to pull as much business as possible into December. It also depletes January sales, but you were faced with rebuilding your pipeline in January anyway. It also helps that the January pipeline is a new set of people.

You can make it difficult for yourself if your prospects knew a great deal about the old price. In many cases, they find it difficult to accept the new price and the leftover accounts (the ones who failed to buy before the price increase) are very poor prospects because of the residual effect of their failing to buy.

7. Avoiding Price Comparisons

Given the fact that you don't want to pollute your next wave of prospects, you should de-emphasize or eliminate price in your marketing materials in the months before you announce a price increase.

Your prospects will be able to find out your old price by checking the directories, but you shouldn't rub their nose in it. At the same time you should start pushing the features and benefits of your product. It really helps if you have a new release tied in with the price increase.

The objective is to make it easy for your prospects to understand and explain your price increase. While we all know that the real reason that you are raising your price is the fact that you product is currently underpriced, customers really don't like to hear this. If you were dramatically underpriced, this explanation may be OK, but otherwise you should come up with a better story.

8. Price Increase Justification

One rationale that we have seen used for products with more features than the competition at the same price was: "We looked at these three extra features that we provide and we realized that the competition didn't have these features and they were worth $X." This helps your advocate explain to others internally why your product is worth the new, higher-price.

9. Internal Education

The final preparation for the price increase is to educate your entire staff on what you are doing. And we do mean your entire staff. It is important that they all know exactly what you are going to do, and how it is going to be implemented. While your sales people must understand your pricing program in detail, Your customer support and administration people can undermine a carefully crafted price increase with a simple off-hand comment.

10. Summary

While this may seem like a lot of work to just raise your price, you must follow these steps to optimize your results. We have seen several cases where companies raised their prices and then had to lower them. This kind of confusion can put you out of business so make sure that you think your price increase through carefully. It isn't wise to increase your prices more than once a year so don't rush the process. On the other hand, if you can increase your prices by 20% you could go from a nagging loss to a nice profit. Higher prices can also give you the cash for more marketing, or to develop the additional features your customers have been calling for.

11. Dear Dave,

Your recent article on Software Pricing arrived 90 days too late for us. North Edge Software recently raised the price of *Timeslips III* [a time & billing package - ED.] from $199.95 to $299.95 on April 1st. So, instead of looking to your article for advice, we used it as a score card. Here's what we did:

- We pulled all advertising for 120 days prior to raising the price to remove the possibility of user confusion with the old price. (interestingly enough, sales increased during that period)
- We sent letters to all prospects offering them Timeslips III at the old price, plus an additional 25% discount for ordering before the end of March.
- We sent our (known) dealers a special promotion postcard and included information on the price increase.

- We sent all registered users a letter informing them of the price increase and gave them a chance to upgrade at the old price before the end of March.
- We launched a new ad campaign with a whole new look, more professional, more polished more "benefit oriented" starting on April 1st. The May issue of PC Computing carries our new advertisement.
- We also (by chance) happen to have won Macuser's Editor's Choice Award for best new business financial package. See May issue.
- We've redone all our collateral to reflect a new, more vital business image.
- We flushed all sales out of the pipeline and, as expected, April is pretty dead. I prepared for this by placing as many new catalog ads as possible which should drop during April and May. This will give us additional visibility with end users.
- We will soon launch an end-user based direct mail promo to sell existing customers our line of Timeslips accessories, such as Remote, Timeslips III Accounting Link (TAL) and Speller.

We expect the drought to last about 90 days, which appears to be the normal sales cycle. That leads us into July and August which are supposed to be slow. September through December roar back and usually are responsible for "making the year" excellent. Additionally, we will have a major new release in December (which will be an upgrade) making December through March unbelievable revenue months. Six months later, a new MAC product will be released. Again, excellent revenue months ahead.

So that's our plan. I don't know if we violated the basic rule by not coupling the upgrade with a new release or unbundling the features and selling them separately. I do know that Timeslips III was severely underpriced and that many, many customers expressed great hesitation about using an "under $200.00" program to run their business. At $299.95 list, that problem should be solved. Additionally, when Timeslips III was initially released, we sold over 70% direct. Now we sell less than 20% direct, and it's heavily discounted. Even with the new pricing, PC Connection is selling it for $169.00. Those who call and have sensitivity to the higher price are referred to Egghead or PCC.

Mitchell A. Russo, President
North Edge Software Corporation

Dear Mitch,

It sounds like you did just fine to me. You obviously put a lot of thought into your price increase and prepared your market properly. Good going! One thought, however. $299.95 is <u>still</u> a low price-point for run-the-business software. I think your market could afford to pay a street price of $200 - $250 for your package. This means that full-list might go to $395 or even higher. Your firm would have good company in making this type of move. Symantec has very succesfully re-positioned and re-priced <u>Q&A</u> up to this level after its initial introduction with a $149-level price-point.

N. Price Discounting (1989)

There are many different perspectives on discounting. In some industries, companies sell off the price list and discounting is unheard of. In other industries, everyone discounts and you feel stupid if you don't get a discount. Discounting is rampant in the software industry. There are very few vendors who generally don't discount, and in almost all cases even these leading vendors discount occasionally. Our rule of thumb is that if at least 10% of your prospects don't complain about price, your price is too low. In those rare cases where the product is so undervalued that the software vendor never is asked for a discount, we urge the vendor to raise their prices.

1. Is your price correct?

Before we address discounting, we would like to discuss the pressures to lower your price and how they manifest themselves in the sales cycle. If your price is 'totally out of line', prospects will simply not respond. If someone does call, it will be to verify that you are really charging outrageous prices. This will be followed by an abruptly terminated conversation.

2. Niche Pricing

It is important to point out that 'totally out of line' often depends upon the user. We have seen a number of cases where a product grew up in a specialized niche with a very specific need. Because the need was very specific, and the other alternatives were even more expensive, the product was perceived as being fairly priced. As time goes on, this niche will tend to become saturated: it's time to look for a larger market.

The software vendor will often identify a larger secondary market which could utilize their product, but it's often troubling to sell the full-featured niche product at the (lower) price level dictated by larger markets.

If this is your case, you must decide two things:

- Do you really want to participate in this larger market.
- How you can rationalize the two different price points.

3. A "New" Product

In this situation you can simply create a "new" product: one that has been "feature-reduced" or "downsized" for the target marketplace. It is important that the simplified product be adequate for the larger market and inadequate for the niche market. Assuming that you can define this feature mix, you can minimize the number of your niche customers who buy the cheaper mass market product.

4. Price Pressure

If we assume that your product is fairly priced for the served market, you will still get price pressure. The first source of pressure is from savvy prospects who have learned that many sales people will give them a discount if they just ask. Typically these customers will acknowledge that they are just asking for a deal, and will rationalize it by saying, "No harm in asking, is there?" Some markets like to bargain and aren't happy if they don't get a deal. In many cases, you can package your pricing so that everyone gets a deal. For example, you might un-bundle the cost of documentation in a complex system. Then when the salesman gets down to closing the deal, they can offer to throw in $100 of documentation to close a $10K deal. If your customers are accustomed to getting deals, structure your price list so that it is easy to give them something that isn't too expensive. Make sure that your sales people know what they should give away first and how far they can go. We view this type of discounting as "give me something to close today". As such it is fairly innocuous as long as it is managed.

5. 'Wrong Customer' Discounts

A second type of discounting occurs when the prospect doesn't see as much value in your product as a typical customer. In some ways this is a result of poor qualification. You should have weeded this prospect out earlier in the process, but often they want your product — it just isn't worth list price to them.

In these cases you have to decide if you are willing to meet their price or walk away from the business. This becomes an especially difficult decision if your company is cash short and/or the sales person has invested a great deal of effort in this prospect. On one hand half a loaf is better than none, but you can really damage your price integrity if you drop your price to one-half or below.

We find that the salespeople are the most affected by this type of discounting. Many salespeople find it very difficult to distinguish between prospects who are complaining about price just for fun, and prospects who would not buy at your regular price. In many cases the sales person doesn't know if the prospect is really bluffing. The best approach is to give the salesperson a limited discount range (e.g. they can't discount more than 15%) and have them play it out until the prospect says no. The sales person can truly tell the prospect, "I have given you my best possible deal. I can't do any more for you." Once the salesperson has lost the deal, the sales manager calls up the prospect and tries to find the compromise price position which is acceptable to both parties. Having the sales person out of the process reduces some of the emotional impact of the deep discounts that these situations often require.

The one risk in this situation is that once the prospect has said no, that you won't be able to open the door again. Our experience is that since this prospect is looking for a low price, they will be happy to talk. The only exception is if this is a competitive situation and one of your competitors might meet their price while you are out of the picture.

6. Competitive Pricing

We have finally gotten to the dominant reason that most companies discount: **competition** . Once you are down to the close in a sales situation your marketing, sales, and development costs are all sunk costs. At that point in time, anything you get from the sale is almost pure margin. (We realize that there are some costs for documentation, disks or tapes, and perhaps some training, but for the pure software your gross margin is very high.)

The other factor is that most of the vendors in the software market are small companies which have the flexibility to make the decision to discount. Typically larger companies are reluctant to discount because of the problems in control. The CEO of a small software company can look at a sales situation and analyze the trade-offs in dropping his price. In many cases he is only an office or two away from the salesperson.

7. Dramatic Price Cut?

Q. We are having trouble selling our product, which is priced at $5,000. We are considering dropping our price to $500. How can we predict if our sales will increase by at least a factor of ten to generate the same or greater revenues?

A. What you need is a demand curve. This is the percent of prospects who would buy your product at various different prices. I would start by drawing what you believe to be the demand curve. Have several knowledgeable people in your company draw the same curve, and then compare them. My experience is that while it is difficult to know the exact shape for such a curve, most companies have an intuitive feeling for its appearance. For example, your sales people may know that 90 percent of sales prospects won't consider paying more than $1,000 for a product of this type. Often this depends upon the size of the company you are considering. Companies with revenues over $100 Million will act differently than $1 Million dollar companies.

Take your hypothetical curves and combine them to show possible variations in the demand curve. Use them to estimate your potential revenue at different prices. They will give you a forecast of possible unit sales and total revenues at different prices. Next you must work through the cost implications of selling different quantities at different prices. In many cases this academic analysis of cost implications will help you eliminate certain alternatives. It will also give you a feel for the probabilities that one of these alternative scenarios might work out.

Next survey your prospects about the probability of buying your type of product at various prices. I have found that asking them the highest price they would pay for this type of product is a question that many people will answer. This is exactly the type of information you need for your demand curve. Just for fun, compare the survey demand curve with the ones that you drew initially. How are they different? Why? The final analytical step is to calculate the profit as a function of price. Do this by computing gross revenue (price times volume) and subtracting fixed and variable costs at each price point of interest. You can then determine the optimal price, at which the highest profit is generated.

Once you have determined that you could possibly make more money at a different price point, you must transition from your current price to the new price. There are a number of issues which you must consider before changing your price. I urge you to refer to the March, 1989 issue of Software Success for the factors you must consider before changing your price.

O.   Discounting   Styles   (1989)

1. Discounts 'IBM Style'

In most markets the roles of the players tends to be very clear. At the top there are the 'IBM style' companies who almost never discount. These companies have published prices and are on the GSA schedule: you can easily determine how low they can go. (Remember, GSA pricing is guaranteed "most favored nation" pricing — they cannot go lower.) In most situations, these firms are selling their benefits rather than discounting.

Our experience is that these companies only start to discount after they have lost a number of competitive situations. They require a policy decision to allow discounts and they must have proof that without discounting they will lose a significant part of their business.

It is interesting to note that these companies typically view discounting as a temporary expediency. usually they will concurrently start a development effort to differentiate their product and to allow them to return to their 'take the high road' style of business. They need high prices to support their overhead and they will have to dramatically change their style of doing business if they begin to discount with any consistency.

2. Middle Of The Road

The middle firms will discount a limited amount, but they have their limits. They realize that they may have to discount against the 'IBM style' competitor to win, but 15% to 25% should be adequate to win most of the situations. At the same time these companies are under pressure from the underdogs, who will cut their price to any level just to win the business. While middle-ground companies may win against the upper firm by discounting, they can't afford to fight it out on price with the lower tier firms.

They have to play Mr. Upper Crust when they get into heavy competition with a lower-tier firm. When the lower-tier firm offers to sell their product at 10% of your price, they must say, "They sure don't think much of their product to offer it at that price. Don't you agree? Can you see how they are going to stay in business and continue to develop the product and offer support at that level. Do you really want to buy an unsupported product?"

In many cases, the firm which is overaggressive in dropping their price is really undermining their own credibility. As long as the middle firm isn't losing consistently to the lower firm, it is safe to limit discounting. (This is much like the situation with the upper firm resisting price competition.)

3. Pricing Counterattacks

The tricky point is when the little guy begins to take away business. Most firms ignore the situation until the little guy is an established player. If you wait too long to counterattack, you may not be able to dislodge the little guy and the prices in your market may come down. The other alternative is to attack them and to try to avoid losing *any* business to them. This is Computer Associates' strategy. (See their quote earlier in this issue.) Their motto is (in effect), "We will lose no business based on price."

While it is best to control the ability to offer extraordinary discounts (much like the secondary prospect situation), this strategy can be effective in hurting a small undercapitalized company. We have often suspected that it is also an indirect way to teach the new kid on the block the rules of the pricing game: do not to rock the boat. If the new kid is willing to discount to 10% of your price, you may have to respond with equally outrageous discounts to keep him from winning the business, but if he only discounts 50% and your limit is 25% you may not be compelled to invoke extraordinary discounting. This is a risky strategy which depends upon several factors to be effective:

- The little guy has to have minimal resources so that you can hurt him without destroying the market.

- You must have tight enough controls that this level of discounting doesn't get out of control in your sales organization.

- You must have a better product than the little guy so that long-term you can support your price level. If the little guy really has a better product, he may win the business even after you meet his price.

P.   Miscellaneous   (1989)

1. Discount Schedules

Q. *It is standard to use discount schedules that give distributors greater discounts than dealers. Is this practice legal?*

A. Until recently we would have answered that these industry standard discounts reflected economies of scale for the vendors and thus were legal. We have advised our clients to base their price list solely on the quantity ordered rather than the type of company placing the order. This eliminates the problem of determining who is a distributor, etc.

We ran across two items recently which make us wonder if this isn't going to change. The first was an article in the *San Jose Mercury News* on December 23, 1988. "The FTC issued complaints against six of the nation's largest book publishers Thursday for allegedly discriminating illegally against independent bookstores by selling books at a discount to major bookstore chains.... The complaints said the publishers charge a lower price per book on large orders and treat orders placed by bookstore chains as a single order, even if the books are shipped separately to individual chain outlets." If the FTC rules that books publishers can't sell to chains cheaper than independent bookstores, we would look to them to apply the same logic to software sales. Before you non-PC publishers tune out, saying that this doesn't apply to you, we would like you to consider your quantity discount pricing. Almost every mini and mainframe vendor that we know offers multi copy discounts to large companies. We would anticipate that the FTC would rule that these discounts are no more legal than the chain discounts so you may have to change your pricing structure.

The second item was in the November 15, 1988 issue of *Soft*Letter*. "In a move that caught software distributors and dealers by surprise, Lotus this month unveiled a new discount structure for resellers that effectively eliminates all *volume discounts*. Under the new plan, virtually all dealers and distributors will pay the same list price for Lotus products, regardless of order size — 45% off list for old titles ... and 40% off for new titles... The new pricing structure — which becomes effective in mid-January — replaces a multi-level price list that has given distributors a 43%-47% discount and large house accounts a 47%-48.5% discount." It is interesting to note that Lotus will get $20 more per copy which will help profits.

This may be part of a growing trend, but we will have to watch both the FTC and the leading vendors. We would be very interested to learn of any cases of changes in discount pricing structures.

2. Multi-Site Discounts

Q: What is the industry-standard pricing practice for multiple sites? Is there a difference between the initial sale and ongoing maintenance?

A: First of all, review the March issue of SOFTWARE SUCCESS (vol.3, #3). THat entire issue was devoted to all types of software pricing issues.

The next thing you can do is to get copies of the GSA schedules for any large competitors in your market.

Our general advice it to provide an increasing discount for each additional copy purchased on the same PO. Typically we suggest 10% off on copy number two, 20% on the third, 30% on the fourth, 40% on the fifth, and 50% off on any sites beyond number 5. We don't recommend that you ever offer more than 50% off.

You might, however, adjust the 50% point based on the price of your product and the number of sites your prospect has. For example, if you had a prospect with 5 sites who was seriously considering two copies and was talking about all five, we would probably offer 10% discount for site number two, 25% for the third site, and 50% off for site number four and beyond. This would make copies 3-5 very attractive.

How you charge for maintenance depends upon sho is authorized to call for support. If your customer has one point of contact for maintenance, then we suggest offering maintenance for 15% of the then current price of the number of copies that they bought. On the other hand, ifall the sites call without coordination or concentration, they all should pay the single copy maintenance fees.

3. Maintenance Fees for Site Licenses

Q. How should we price maintenance when we sell a site license or a multi-copy deal?

A. You must ask your customer if they are going to have a single point-of-contact for maintenance or if every CPU will have someone who will call in. If they are willing to designate one person to be your point-of-contact, you should base your maintenance on the site or multi-copy price. At the same time you should establish the provision to increase your maintenance fees over time. As long as this price (site or multi copy) is on your price list, you can increase your maintenance when your customer's corresponding list price increases.

If your Customer received a special price, you could index it off your single copy price. For example, if you sold a site license for 2.3 times the single copy price, you could base your future maintenance price on 2.3 times the future single copy price. If your customer feels that each site/CPU needs direct access for support, they should pay the single copy support price. One issue that you should clarify is what maintenance is included in the sales price. Is the first year of maintenance free? For all sites in a site-license deal? Even though each site will have unfettered, direct access? Lack of clarity on these issues can cost you big.

We know of one situation where the vendor felt that the site license price assumed one point-of-contact for support. When it became clear that direct support was going to be required, the software vendor wanted to increase the initial price. The software purchaser was quite upset because they had made the assumption that they were getting direct support for the site license fee. To make matters worse, the individual buying the package had presented it this way to their management: they didn't want to go back to management and request a higher price. The vendor ended up giving in and providing direct support for the initial fee. The real cost was that the deal was at risk for a period of time and that the decision was delayed for over a month.

This points up a general piece of advice when you encounter this type of situation. Don't throw out a number too early in sales cycle. Make sure that both you and the customer really understand exactly what is involved. Tell them that until you both understand what is really required and what they want, you are only guessing about the price. Often large companies will throw out the bait that they might buy 20 copies of your product. If you volunteer to sell them 20 copies at half-price, you've damaged your sales-effort in several important ways:

1. Your price is softWhile your price may in fact be somewhat negotiable, you've just thrown the price list out the window.
2. You can't negotiateThey haven't made any commitment, but you already slashed your price in half!
3. You don't know what they wantPrice adjustment is a poor substitute for really knowing what your customer wants and needs.

We have seen software companies who have ended up selling two or three copies of their software at half-price because they threw the price out too early and allowed the customer to selectively remember what they wanted. While this is common in all sales situations, it is especially common in complex and expensive deals.

4. Getting a GSA Schedule

Dear Dave,

In the April issue of your newsletter, in answer to a question about pricing, you say, "The next thing you can do is to get copies of the GSA schedules for any large competitors in the market." We inferred from this statement that GSA schedules show vendor pricing. Is this correct? If so, how does one go about getting GSA schedules?

Diane M. Butler
Vice President
Third Eye Software, Inc.

Dear Diane,

You are correct, the GSA schedule does show vendor pricing. The GSA schedule is the government price list. Companies on the GSA price list guarantee that the GSA schedule pricing is their most favorable pricing (this is done in a separate GSA contract). They can sell to any government agency by referencing the GSA schedule. There's one important fact about being ont the GSA schedule: while you list your lowest prices on the GSA list, they often end up being the highest prices that you'll receive, as well. You can use the GSA schedule to know how low your competitor can go without getting into difficulty with GSA.

You can request price-list information under the Freedom of Information Act. The group in GSA that distributes the information is the Information Resource Management Service. The person that we have gotten information from is:

Ms. Charlotte Thompson
General Services Administration
IRMS-KES
18th & F Street NW
Washington, DC 20405

You should write her with the list of companies you are interested in getting the GSA schedule Group 70 for. Once you find out which companies are listed, you will need to find out the fee for getting the information. In our experience this is a nominal fee.

Q. Survey (1989)

1. Survey Background

Eighty-two percent of the respondents were software companies. The remainder were equally split between software and hardware companies and dealer/VARs. Annual software revenues were under $5 million for most of the firms. The companies were fairly evenly distributed between two categories: less than $250,000 and $2 million to $5 million. Total company revenues were slightly higher due to hardware and other non-software revenues. Interestingly enough, there was a dramatic increase in the number of firms in the $2 million to $5 Million range compared to the reader survey in July. This increase ranged from 11% in software revenues to 26% in total revenues.

2. Years in Business

Most of the companies had been in business six to ten years. The detail was:

# Years	%Resp
1	1.6
2	3.3
3	9.8
4	4.9
5	6.6
6-10	50.8
> =11	11.5

3. Number of Employees by functional area

The number of employees by functional area is shown in the table on the next page. As you can see, the median was one person for marketing, two people for sales, three people for development, two people for support, and one person for administration. This is your classical nine-person software company.

Most companies had only one salaried marketing employee. The results were:

# Sal Mktg	% Resp
No reply	34
1	39
2	9
3	7
4	8
5	2

This is consistent with the low level of marketing budgets.

Seventy-two percent of the companies sold vertical software, 23% horizontal and 6% system utilities.

4. Average price per unit

Price	% Resp
under $250	14.5
$250-$1K	14.8
$1K-$2.5K	16.4
$2.5K-$10K	23.0
$10K-$25K	13.1
$25K-$100K	16.4
over $100K	3.3

	Mktg	Sales	Devel	Support	Admin
No Reply	34.3	39.3	11.5	18.0	13.1
1	39.3	13.1	16.4	18.0	24.6
2	9.8	23.0	21.3	21.3	13.1
3	6.6	11.5	14.8	13.1	9.8
4	8.2	1.6	11.5	8.2	11.5

Number of Employees by Functional Area

5. Sales channels

The sales channels used were:

Channel	% Resp
Direct	93.4
Telemarketing	39.3
VAR/ Dealer	47.5
OEM	9.8

Direct selling is the primary channel and accounts for over 76% of the respondents' sales 52.5% of the time. Telemarketing is a secondary channel and accounts for over 76% of sales in only 9.8% of the companies. VAR/dealer sales are of varying importance to the respondents.

6. Percentage of sales through VARs

% of sales	% Resp
no reply	50.8
< =10%	18.0
< =25%	9.8
< =50%	9.8
< =75%	3.3
> =76%	8.2

OEM sales were made by only 9.8% of the respondents and they made less than 25% of their sales through this channel.

I was surprised at how small most of the respondents viewed their market size. Sixty percent of the companies didn't reply and half of those who did respond viewed their market as having a potential under $10 million in sales.

The graph on the next page shows that there is a correlation between market size and type of product position. Most of the leaders and first tier products were in smaller markets. While second tier and young turk Products were in larger markets. New product can either be in small or large markets.

7. Marketshare

At the same time, I was surprised at the number of firms who felt that their market share was quite high:

Marketshare	% Resp
No reply	54.1
< =1%	3.3
< =5%	13.1
< =10%	3.3
< = 25%	6.6
< = 50%	9.8
< = 75%	3.3
> =76%	6.6

8. Responsibility for Pricing

The table at the bottm of the next page shows who is repsonsible for setting list prices, establishing discount guidelines, approving discounts and handling complex deals. In most cases, the president is involved in making these decisions. Sales executives were more involved with approving discounts, but complex deals were likely to come back to the president.

Type of Product by Market Size

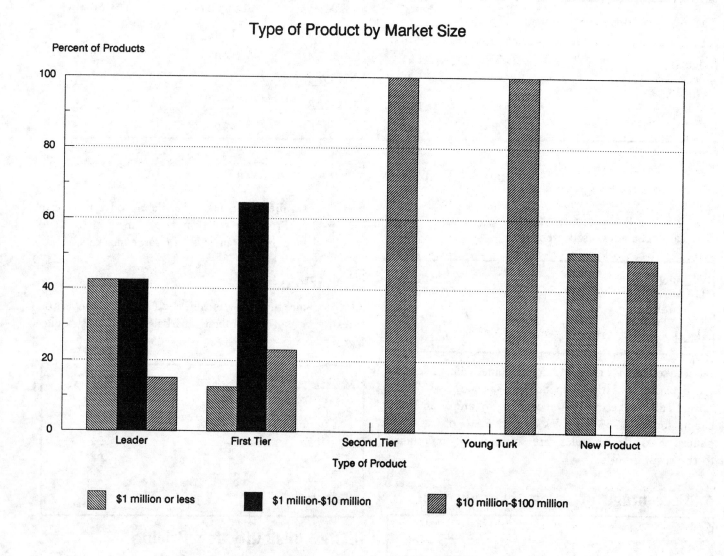

Figure 3 -- Type of Product by Market Size

	List Prices	Discount Guidelines	Approving Discounts	Complex Deals
President	68.9	62.3	52.5	75.4
Marketing	32.8	32.8	29.5	18.0
Sales Exec	11.5	19.7	26.2	9.8
Sales Rep	1.6	1.6	0	1.6
Finance	6.6	4.9	6.6	8.2

9. Product Benefits

The key product benefits were:

Benefit	% Resp
Productivity	77.0
Hard costs	34.4
Soft costs	47.5
New analysis	31.1
Control	32.8

I was surprised that productivity was the clear winner among product benefits. I was also disappointed that soft costs were significantly more common than hard costs, but I guess I shouldn't be surprised since everyone who has hard costs has additional soft costs. Thus, we have 13% of the respondents who had soft costs and no hard costs. Looking at it that way, it isn't too high.

10. Competitive Environment

How would you characterize the competitive environment?

Level of Comp	% Resp
None	6.6
Low	29.5
Medium	49.2
High	14.8

I believe this relatively low level of competition is related to the fact that many of the respondents are smaller companies who are focusing on markets with low levels of competition. This is an important factor in running a small business. If you get into a large market with a high level of competition, it will be very difficult to grow and be profitable.

11. How many competitors typically encounter

# Competitors	% Resp
None	21.3
1	52.5
2-3	44.3
4-5	19.7
6-10	4.9
>10	1.6

Among the companies with low competition, 15% usually don't encounter a competitor. The 14.8% who feel that they have a high level of competition encounter four or more competitors.

12. Flagship product market position

Market Position	% Resp
Leader	31.1
First Tier	45.9
Second Tier	9.8
Young Turk	6.6
New Product	4.9

The graph on the prior page shows that there is a relationship between the number of competitors typically encountered and product position. Leaders encounter four or more competitors less than 10% of the time. Second tier and young turks are faced with a much more competitive environments. This is consistent with the strategy of picking a niche and focusing on it. The young turks and the new products are trying to break into mature markets. This is a much tougher challenge.

13. Attention paid to competitive products

Attention	% Resp
None	4.9
Some	13.1
Medium	62.3
High	18.0

"No attention to competitive products" corresponds to "no competitors," which makes sense.

14. In-house competitive evaluations

Evaluations	% Resp
No	19.7
Sometimes	32.8
Occasionally	26.2
Continually	18.0

I believe that this low level of competitive evaluations reflects the technical background of many people in this industry. Many technical people don't want to look at their competitors because they don't want to see that the other guy may have a better product. Many of them don't feel that it is ethical to evaluate other products. While I understand these feelings, I feel very strongly that companies must understand their competition if they are to succeed in the long term.

15. How do you get competitive information

Information	% Resp
Trade press	59.0
Customers	86.9
Direct	47.5
Trade shows	54.1

It is pretty easy to get information on your competitors and everyone is doing it. If you aren't doing this consistently, you are missing the boat.

16. Marketing Budget

I continue to be surprised at the spread for software companies. While 10 to 30 percent is a common range, there are a significant number of companies who spend less than 10 percent on marketing.

I am more comfortable with the small companies who spend more than 30 percent. I see them as trying to launch new products. They are spending on marketing in anticipation of sales.

17. Pricing Structures

What type of end-user pricing structures do you offer for your primary flagship product?

Structure	% Resp
One price only	52.5
User based	34.4
Site license	37.7
Machine size	31.1
Monthly rental	11.5
Leasing	18.0

I was surprised at the number of firms who are offering complex pricing: user, site, or machine-based. This reflected the continuing innovation in our industry, particularly among smaller companies. At the same time, I was disappointed at the low number of firms who offer rental and lease programs. My philosophy is to determine the price at which you are happy to rent and to put it on the price list.

Rental might be at ten percent of the purchase price per month with no credit toward purchase, but make it available. If you need money to cover installation and training which you bundle with a full purchase, you can unbundle these items with the rental. If you make this option available, you just might get another sale which otherwise might have been lost. Make sure that you don't underprice these alternatives and convert sales into rentals.

18. How are your prices published?

Price List	% Resp
Public	63.9
Private	29.5
Guidelines	11.5
Semi-custom	6.6
GSA	8.2

While I wasn't surprised, the low level of participation in the GSA price list, it is noteworthy. I would be interested to hear from anyone who has listed their product on the GSA price list. What did it cost? Has it brought you more business? Was it worth it?

19. Discount Policies

How often do you grant price discounts beyond those offered on your price list?

Discounts	% Resp
Never	9.8
Seldom 0-10	52.5
Occasionally 10-33	26.2
Often 33%	6.6

I don't really believe these answers. I do believe the 9 percent who say they never discount. I have trouble believing that the majority of software companies discount less than 10 percent of the time. I wonder if we aren't just kidding ourselves.

If you do grant price discounts, how much are they?

Discount	% Resp
Small 0-5%	27.9
Medium 5-15%	57.4
Steep 15-35%	34.4

I believe that people answered based on the word and not the percentages. I agree that most companies offer medium discounts, I just think that they are more than five to fifteen percent.

20. Secondary price concessions

Secondary	% Resp
Never	13.1
Seldom 0-10	50.8
Occassionally 10-33	19.7
Often 33%	8.2

Apparently, our respondents aren't very likely to grant secondary price concessions.

If you do grant secondary concessions what are they?

Concessions	% Resp
Extend terms	27.9
Free maintenance	24.6
Free training	29.5
Installation Support	29.5
Free Programming	26.2
Extra modules	19.7

As you can see, no one item is much more likely to be given away.

21. Competitor's end-user pricing

Type	Comp	Resp
One price	42.6	52.5
User based	21.3	34.4
Site lic	21.4	37.7
Machine	26.2	31.1
Rental	4.9	11.5
Leasing	8.2	18.0

Our respondents consistently offer more pricing options than their competitors. This is consistent with the fact that they are smaller, more responsive companies.

22. Competitor's prices published

Published	Comp	Resp
No reply	24.6	3.3
Public	34.4	63.9
Private	36.1	29.5
Guidelines	8.2	11.5
Semi-custom	11.5	6.6
GSA	1.6	8.2

The most significant difference is that the respondents are much more likely to publish their price list.

23. Compeptitors price discounts

Freq	Comp	Resp
No reply	44.3	4.9
Never	0	9.8
Seldom 0-10	16.4	52.2
Occas 10-33	26.2	26.2
Often 33%	13.1	6.6

I find the estimates on how often the competition offers discounts to be much more believable.

24. How much are they?

Discount	Comp	Resp
No reply	52.5	16.4
Small (0-5%)	4.9	27.9
Moderate (5-15%)	23.0	57.4
Steep (15-35%)	18.0	34.4
Fire sale (>35%)	9.8	1.6

Some of this difference is due to the fact that our respondents are market leaders or in the top tier. As such they should discount less.

25. How often do they grant other concessions?

Concessions	Comp	Resp
No Reply	52.5	8.2
Never	1.6	13.1
Seldom (0-10%)	13.1	50.8
Occas (10-33%)	26.2	19.7
Often (>33%)	6.6	8.2

I wonder if the perception that competitors are making more concessions is partly influenced by negotiating tactics on the part of prospects. A prospect might tell a sales person that they got a great deal from the competition to get rid of the sales person or to see if they can get an even better deal from the losing vendor. The competitors are about as likely to grant the same secondary concessions as our respondents. I find this graph very interesting. 1986 was a very mixed year. Some prices were going up while others were going down. 1987 was a year for the industry to catch its breath. Most of the respondents made no change or increased their prices less than 10 percent. In 1988, more companies were increasing their prices, and some were making large cuts. In 1989, companies were raising their prices.

This is as good as it gets. We all must remember that 1989 was an abnormally good year. 1990 is likely to be less upbeat. The economists are anticipating some sort of a recession. I expect that we will see pricing actions more like 1986 with some cuts and few increases, but primarily with holding actions on the pricing front. If demand is soft, it is very difficult to raise your prices. This is especially true in competitive markets.

26. Unbundling over the last few years

Year	% Unbundling
1986	5.7%
1987	9.6%
1988	0
1989	4.2%

These percentages of unbundling are even more significant when you realize that not every company can unbundle.

27. Price Changes

Why the most recent price change?

Factor	% Resp
No reply	62.3
Competition	9.8
Opportunity	23.0
Maintenance	6.6
Costs/ profits	4.9
Distributors	1.6
Other	1.6

1989 was the year for opportunistic price increases. I anticipate that the answers for 1990 will be much different.

Stress of the last price change?

Stress	% Resp
No reply	63.9
No problem	27.9
Modest blip	6.6
Moderate impact	0
Disasterous	1.6

The disasterous situation was a price change tied to a new product introduction. It appeared that a major part of the problem was due to the delays in the product availability.

Who was most sensitive to price change

Who	% Resp
No Reply	63.9
Prospects	8.2
Customers	6.6
Sales reps	13.1
Tech support	0
Management	8.2
Development	0
Dist/ dealer	6.6

It makes sense that the sales people are most sensitive to changing the prices. They have to represent the product and the company. Sales people also have fairly narrow price ranges that they are comfortable selling it. My own consulting experience indicates that, in many cases, the sales people are pushing to raise the price. They aren't having to discount to close the business, and they aren't getting beat up on price.

My feeling is that if you aren't getting beat up on price by tenpercent of your customers, you are leaving money on the table. The optimal complaint level may even be higher depending on the product and the market. I found it interesting that support and development weren't sensitive to price changes. They are happy to put in their opinions, but once the changes are made they don't care. In many companies, the developers are very resistant to raising the price. It is much more important to them that the company sell many copies than that the company make a profit. They want the prestige and exposure. They are also afraid that at the higher price level that the prospects will have higher expectations and this will put more pressure on them.

28. Conclusions

1989 has been a very good year for most software companies. Software companies have been able to raise their prices with little resistance. The more sophisticated companies are offering more pricing alternatives so that they can be responsive to different customer situations. The president is key to pricing decisions in most smaller companies. Marketing executives take over this responsibility in larger companies.

Price Changes

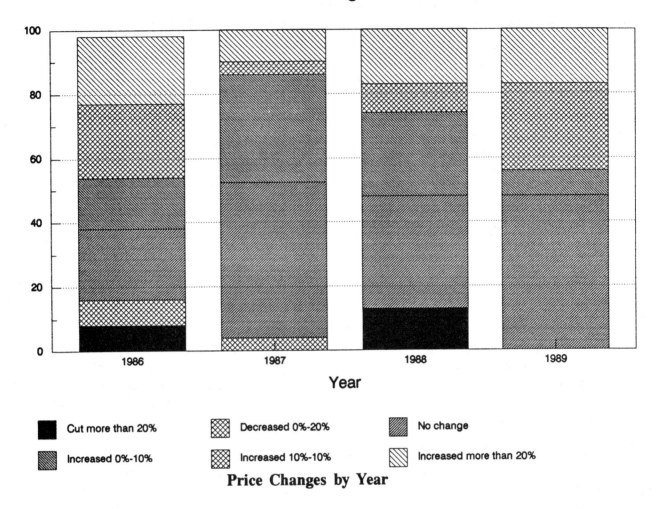

Price Changes by Year

1992
Software   Success
Reference   Book

Chapter   IV
Distribution

Chapter IV. Distribution

A. Distribution Survey (1991)

We received 139 responses to this survey. Once again, it is a good response, but it is a little lower than our prior record since 45% of our readers get 0% of their sales through distribution.

1. Company Revenue

The distribution of company revenue was very similar to our past surveys. We had slightly more companies in the $250K to $1 Million range than in prior surveys (41% vs. 21% last year). This seems to be a revenue range where companies often try to establish distribution. I have seen a number of cases in which companies have generated some sales in their local markets and have had problems selling outside of their local markets. Many of these products require training and support, so a local presence is important. These companies then decide that they need local VARs or dealers to sell their product in other markets. At the same time, these small companies are looking to the VARs to invest in establishing their product in new markets. In my experience, this is much like the "blind leading the blind". The VARs want the Software Vendors to invest in them, and the Software Vendors want the VARs to invest in marketing their products. A significant investment is required from both parties.

The question later in the survey about the cost of acquiring and training a dealer got some interesting answers. 45.3% of the respondents said they don't spend money on dealers. 63.3% of the respondents' companies had revenues under $1M. My experience has shown that it is very difficult for small companies to launch a successful dealer program without outside investment.

Small companies have another problem attracting dealers. Dealers want to sell a successful product that is also easy to sell. The best proof of an easy-to-sell product is the large number of copies sold. This makes it easier for larger companies to recruit dealers, since they have a larger installed base to make the dealers more comfortable.

A final problem faced by small companies is that their products are "young". They aren't complete, and in most cases, the documentation, packaging, etc, isn't as mature as more established products. The lack of product maturity makes selling these young products more difficult. Dealers have learned they can do much better by selling more mature products which carry more of the burdens of making the sales.

2. Product Price

The products in this survey had lower prices than previously indicated (Fall 1990 Subscriber Survey). Only 28.8% of the products in this survey had prices over $10K while 36% of the Fall 1990 respondents had prices over $10K.

It appears that products priced over $10K are more difficult to sell through distribution, due to the training and support requirements. The most popular range of products sold through distribution is $1K to $5K.

Product Price	% of Respondents
Not indicated	0.7%
< $100	2.2%
$100-$200	8.6%
$200-$300	2.2%
$300-$500	9.4%
$500-$1K	12.9%
$1K-$5K	27.3%
$5k_$10K	13.7%
$10K-$25K	14.4%
> $25K	14.4%

3. Number of Prospects

The number of prospects this year was slightly higher than we found in last year's survey, especially in the 10K to 100K market range. This is an encouraging trend since larger markets make it easier to get distribution.

Number of Prospects	This Year	Last Year
Not indicated	5.0%	7.1%
< 1K	13.7%	9.5%
1K-10K	26.6%	42.9%
10K-25K	19.4%	11.9%
25K-100K	22.3%	9.5%
> 100K	13.7%	19.0%

There was a decline in the number of companies whose market had over 100K prospects. This may be due to companies in these larger markets focusing on more manageable "niche" markets. One of the keys to success in building a software company through self funding is to set your sights realistically. Rather than going after 100K+ prospects with 50+ competitors you might be better to focus on a 10K niche with only one or two competitors. As you grow, and you begin to be limited by the size of the market on which you are focusing, you can begin to target other niches of 10K prospects. In this way, you can have an adequate market potential at any point in time, without taking on competitors who might put you out of business in the early stages.

More respondents this year than last indicate that having a large market helps in getting distribution. I believe that this year there are more small companies in large markets, but they aren't investing in getting dealers. The appeal of the large market doesn't compensate for these other shortcomings.

4. Computer Type

This survey had fewer PC products, more LAN products and very few mainframe products.

Computer Type	% of Respondents
Not indicated	5.8%
PC	55.4%
Mac	8.6%
LAN	17.3%
Mini	14.4%
Workstation	8.6%
Mainframe	3.6%

I think there are fewer PC products than in previous surveys, because dealers and VARs are inundated with PC products. It is very difficult to come up with something unique that is going to get the attention of dealers in the PC market.

I expected to see more LAN products because this is an area where software companies are introducing a lot of hot new products. It is easier to be unique and interesting when you are exploiting some new hardware like LANs. We saw the same thing in last year's distribution survey.

There are very few mainframe dealers, so you wouldn't expect to see many mainframe companies in this survey. Most mainframe companies want to set up distribution for PC products which they have developed. They are accustomed to selling high priced mainframe products, and they know their sales people won't be as effective selling lower priced products. While I agree that sales people who sell a $50K product can't and shouldn't be selling a $500 product, it is very difficult for a mainframe company to make this transition. Using direct mail and telemarketing to initially sell the $500 product is often a necessary step to getting a dealer channel established.

This survey only had 1.08 responses per company. Past surveys had 1.2 to 1.3 responses which indicated that twenty to thirty percent of the companies supported more than one platform. Thus, it would appear that only offering your product on one platform and making it the best it can be, for that platform, helps get distribution. Dealers and VARs don't want a watered down version of the product for a secondary platform. It is very difficult for software publishers to make money with versions of their product that have been ported to another platform. It is nice to say you support "this platform" and "that platform", but it requires a major investment to turn a technical conversion into a profitable product.

Your choice of computer type still seems to affect your chances of success in establishing distribution (primary or successful).

Computer Type	% Successful This Year	% Successful This Year
PC	12%	34%
Mac	8%	NA
LAN	20%	25%
Mini	10%	31%
Workstation	40%	NA
Mainframe	0%	14%

I believe that this year's lower percentage of PC companies ranking themselves as successful is partially caused by the overabundance of PC products currently being offered to dealers. I also suspect these numbers reflect the probability that many of this year's respondents are new readers with small PC companies which don't have the money to train and/or acquire new dealers.

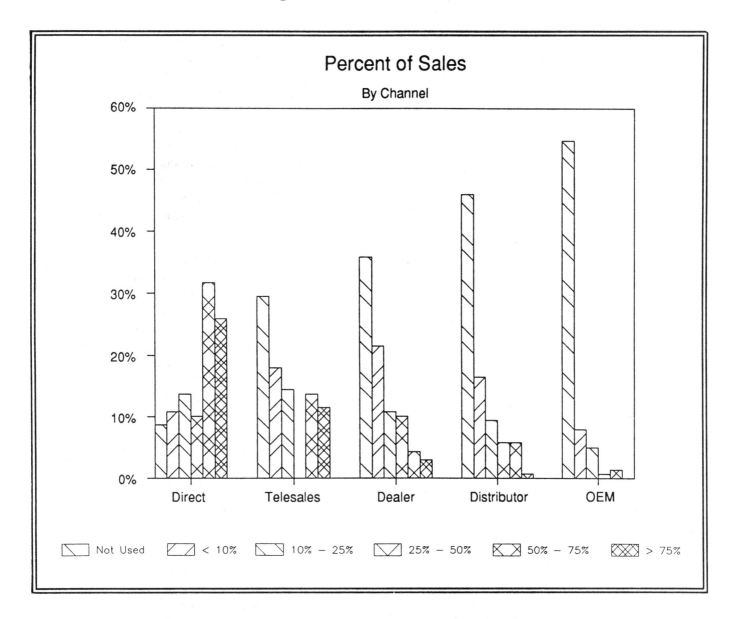

This year, for the first time, I've included the MAC as a computer type in the distribution survey. I am not surprised at the MAC companies' difficulty to succeed in distribution, given the fact that there are fewer dealers who carry much MAC software.

It appears that many of the workstation companies responded as Minicomputer companies last year, since I didn't offer a workstation choice. This is based on a small sample, but it appears that there is good demand for workstation software with dealers. I also suspect that these dealers are more likely to be VARs.

5. Percent of Sales by Channel

Direct

If you look at the graph (Percent of Sales) above, you will see that, even for this survey, software companies depend primarily on direct sales. Only 8.7% of the companies make no use of direct sales, and 57.6% get over half of their sales directly. Last year's results were similar.

Telesales

In Telesales, the sales person never meets a prospect face to face. The entire sale is made via the phone. 29.5% of the companies did not use this sales channel, but 25.2% get over half their sales via Telesales. The usage of Telesales has increased dramatically since last year when we found that 64.3% hadn't used Telesales. This is consistent with my observations. Companies are making more use of Telesales, and prospects are becoming less apprehensive about buying products over the phone.

Dealer/VAR

35.9% of the companies make no use of dealers / VARs and only 7.2% get more than half their sales through dealers and VARs. Last year 47.6% of the companies made no use of dealers/VARs, but 16.6% got more than half their sales through this channel. We also had significantly more companies getting less than 10% of their sales via dealers/VARs. My experience shows that many dealers have been hurt by the current recession and companies selling through dealers have also suffered. When companies are also selling directly or by Telesales, they can compensate for declines in dealer sales by increasing their direct or Telesales efforts.

Distributors

46% of the respondents don't use distributors and only 6.5% make more than half their sales through distributors. Thus, only 10% of the companies who sell through dealers don't sell through distributors. If you are serious about selling to dealers, it really helps to sell through distributors. Distributors provide a number of services to dealers which make it easier for dealers to buy your products. As you can see, most of the companies who get over half their sales through dealers also sell through distributors (6.5% via distributors vs. 7.2% via dealers). It is difficult to get more than half your sales through dealers without using distributors.

OEM

54.7% of the respondents have no OEM sales and only 1.4% get over half their sales via OEMs. This shows more OEM activity than we last year, when 83.3% of the companies didn't have OEM sales and none of them had over half of their sales via OEMs. I am pleased with this increase. I have talked to several readers who get 5% to 10% of their revenue via OEMs. A few of them said that their OEM revenues provide most of their profit and require very little incremental effort.

6. Experience with dealers

Experience	% of Respondents
Not indicated	8.6%
Never tried	30.2%
Tried & Failed	7.9%
Some sales, no investment	18.0%
Still trying to build	23.7%
Primary Distribution	5.0%
Succeeding	9.4%

There are a few more companies who have never tried to establish a dealer channel than there were last year (30.2% this year vs. 23.8% last year). Perhaps these people are considering selling through dealers, but haven't decided to yet.

Only 7.9% of the respondents tried but failed to establish sales through dealers. 18.0% reported "some" sales. I suspect most of the failures have made some sales, but have stopped making an investment. Very few cases are such failures that they didn't make some sales. If you combine both of these responses together, a total of 25.9% this year failed. This is higher than last year's 19.0% who tried and failed. This is consistent with the fact that this last year has been very tough for dealers.

23.7% of the companies are still trying. This is about the same as last year which was 26.2%. My experience has shown that it takes a year or two to get a successful dealer program launched.

5.0% of the respondents depend upon dealers as their primary channel of distribution. This corresponds to the 7.2% who report more than half their sales via dealers. Another 9.4% feel that they have succeeded with their dealer program even if it isn't their primary program. These combine to 14.4% who have been somewhat successful. If you add the 18% who are making some sales, but not making any more investments, 32.4% were somewhat successful. Last year 28.6% of the respondents felt they had succeeded. The questions are different this year, so it is difficult to compare the results exactly. However, it appears that companies might be getting more successful with their dealer programs. Next year, it will be interesting to see how the numbers play out.

Discounts

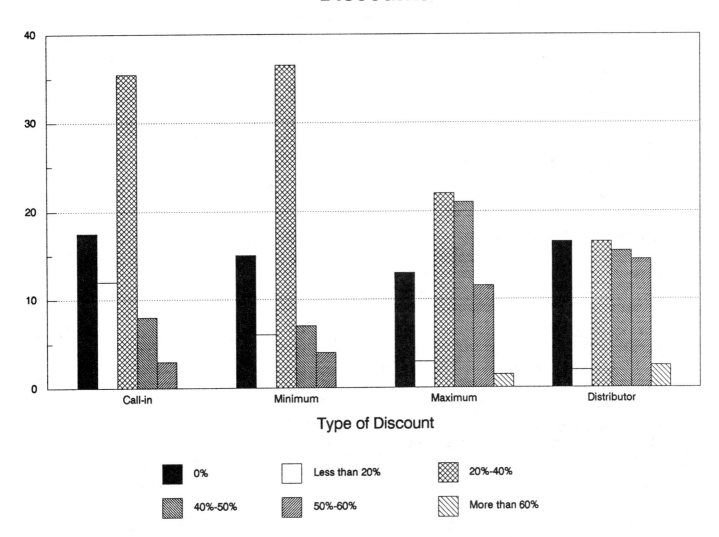

Type of Discount

Legend:
- ■ 0%
- □ Less than 20%
- ⊠ 20%-40%
- ▨ 40%-50%
- ▧ 50%-60%
- ◩ More than 60%

7. Training Required

Significantly more companies are selling products which require no training (28.1% this year vs 11.9% last year). Also, there has been a decline in products requiring more than one week of training (17.3% this year vs 40.5% last year).

These changes are in the right direction. Last year 40% of the products requiring no training were successful, and only 18% of the products requiring more than a week of training had successfully established a dealer program.

Difficulty getting dealers/distributors

27.3% of the people who "don't know how hard it is to get dealers" corresponds to the 34.5% who haven't

used dealers and VARs. We also had more people this year who've experienced little difficulty in getting dealers (12.9% this year vs. 4.8% last year). I wonder if the increase in products with no training has turned into a corresponding increase of companies who found it easy to get dealers.

Difficulty	% Respondents
Not indicated	11.5%
Don't know	27.3%
High	31.7%
Medium	18.0%
Low	12.9%

8. Cost of Acquiring and Training a Dealer

The largest group of respondents don't spend money to acquire or train dealers. With this attitude, I am surprised that these companies have had any success with their dealer programs. The most common investment was $1K to $10K. This is enough money to send some materials and to pay for a couple of trips. In my experience, it often takes two or three trips with one or two people to get a dealer trained. Once again, I am impressed at how careful the respondents are with their money. (We saw the same type of results in last year's trade show survey where over half of the companies attended national trade shows for less than $10K.)

Another 13.7% of the respondents spent $100 to $1K. I wonder just how much these companies can accomplish for less than $1K. If they are visiting the dealers, either they are within driving distance or the companies are really controlling their costs.

6.4% of the respondents were spending over $10K on new dealers. This is similar to the percentage of respondents where dealers are their primary distribution channel.

Cost of Acquiring and Training Dealers	% Respondents
Not indicated	15.8%
Don't spend	45.3%
< $100	4.3%
$100-$1K	13.7%
$1K-$10K	15.8%
$10K-$25K	3.6%
$25K-$50K	1.4%
> $50K	1.4%

There is a strong correlation between company revenue and the likelyhood of spending over $1K on acquiring and training a dealer. Overall, 22.2% of the respondents spent over $1K on acquiring and training dealers.

Company Revenue	% of Companies Spending over $1K
< $250K	6%
$250K-$500K	19%
$500K-$1M	16%
$1M-$2M	35%
> $2M	40%

The amount you spend acquiring and training dealers makes a dramatic difference in a company's success with dealers. **You have to pay if you want to play**. Only 9% of the companies who don't spend money getting dealers are successful (Successful or Primary), and 75% of the companies who spend over $10K are successful. The mid range companies who spend less than $10K are successful 16% to 23% of the time.

9. Discounts

The graph on the previous page summarizes the discounts offered by the respondents under various conditions.

Call in

A "call-in order" occurs when a vendor hears from a dealer for the first time, after that dealer has received a request from a customer who wants to buy the vendor's product. The vendor's reputation or marketing has created the "pull" to bring the buyer into the dealer's showroom. The bothersome point here is, the dealer has done nothing to deserve the discount. 17.3% of the respondents stick to their guns and won't give the "call-in" dealer any discount. (You may recall that this was Deneb's policy in a recent feature article.) This is an admirable policy, because these vendors would rather lose a sale than risk a customer buying from an unqualified dealer who will offer no support. However, this can be risky, as far as sales go, because if there is a comparable product which will give the dealer a discount, then the dealer will undoubtedly try to sell the customer that product.

12.2% of the respondents offer the "call-in" dealer a token discount of less than 20%. This isn't what the dealer wants (40%), but it is better than nothing. If your product requires support, then you should not sell through unqualified dealers, no matter what your discount is. However, if your product is a commodity product requiring no support, then it's OK to offer your standard discount to "call-in" dealers.

The most common discount for call-in orders is 20% to 40%. This was offered by 35.3% of the respondents. Only 12.2% of the respondents offer discounts of over 40% for call in orders. Unless you can get the dealer to buy and stock some additional product, I can't see why you would give them more than a 40% discount. I would appreciate hearing from anyone who does this, to better understand your motivation.

Minimum Dealer Discount with signed agreement

This is very much like the call-in discounts. It doesn't appear that we give dealers much benefit for signing our agreements. In theory, it seems that we should offer them some additional discount since they have given us some information and shown some level of interest and commitment. It may be that most of the call-in orders are willing to sign a non-binding, non-committal dealer agreement to get the minimum discount. This would explain why these two discount schedules are the same.

Maximum Dealer Discount

The maximum dealer discounts are somewhat higher than the minimum, but not as much as I would have expected. 38.1% of the respondents keep the maximum dealer discount 40% or less. This occurred 57.6% of time for the minimum discount so 19.5% of the respondents offered larger discounts to their best dealers. The other way to say this is, 66% of the companies who limit dealers to less than 40% with their minimum discount, also limit them to less than 40% for their maximum discount. (e.g. 2/3 of them don't give dealers any opportunity for higher discounts.)

The companies who offered higher maximum discounts tend to limit their discounts: 20.9% are 40% to 50%, 11.5% are 50% to 60%, and only 1.4% are over 60%. My tendency is to offer greater discounts to dealers who can sell the product in volume. If you are generating sales of $1 Million a year, and a dealer comes along who can can sell an equivalent amount, doesn't he deserve a great discount?

Distributor Discounts

Distributor discounts are slightly better than the maximum dealer discounts. In particular, 17.3% of

the respondents offered distributors discounts over 50% while only 12.9% offered dealers a maximum discount over 50%.

One of the problems I have with this type of distinction is deciding who is a dealer and who is a distributor. There are any number of companies who are hybrid organizations. They may be dealers in their own market, and they may sell to other dealers or reps in other markets. If someone can get a larger discount by claiming to be something else, you can depend upon them to claim to be the correct type of organization. It is questionable to have this type of semantic difference in discounts.

My first concern is, this isn't fair. You might have a dealer who is actively marketing your product and selling a great deal of your product. I really think that this dealer deserves a greater discount than someone who calls himself a distributor and yet offers very few services.

I have been involved with several efforts to define stages of support for dealers and Super Dealers. The concept is that Super Dealers do a specified list of tasks (support and volume commitments) which entitles them to greater discounts. The concept is great, but, in practice, my clients have ended up in endless debates with their resellers.

My current approach is to base the discounts on the number of sales actually achieved. This is very simple to monitor and everyone understands what it means. It also seems to eliminate the debates that take everyone's energy away from selling software.

The only exception which I find necessary is offering distributors greater discounts for initial orders. It appears that because of their services and costs, you may have to give distributors slightly higher discounts than dealers. Unless you allow for the 7% distributor markup, you will end up competing with your distributors by offering your dealers a better price than they can get from the distributor.

10. Dealer Agreements

The 33.1% Not Indicated corresponds to the 34.5% of the respondents who aren't using Dealers and VARs.

I was surprised that 18.7% of the respondents do not require a signed dealer agreement. I wonder how many of these companies are making sales to dealers. I really think you should have a signed agreement with any dealer who is selling your product. At the very least, the dealer should agree to pay the bills and not steal your trade secrets.

The most common requirement indicated was a simple agreement (which I think is appropriate). Very few companies require a credit application. This reflects the fact that few software companies extend credit to dealers.

Indicating that industry experience and references are important is very appropriate, especially with the more expensive applications and vertical market applications. A reseller who doesn't understand the market can seriously damage the reputation of any product which he tries to sell.

Dealer Agreement	% Respondents
Not indicated	33.1%
None required	18.7%
Simple agreement	38.8%
Credit application	7.9%
Industry Experience/References	10.1%

11. Credit

34.5% of the respondents indiciated they will extend credit to dealers if a credit application has been completed. This is far more than the 7.9% who indicated, in the prior question, that they require credit applications. 36% of the companies who indicated they do not require a credit application still extend credit. I hope these companies aren't really extending credit without first requiring and checking a credit application. I know of one case in which a vendor extended credit for small initial orders to hundreds of dealers without requiring credit applications. Over time, the amount of credit became significant and the vendor still didn't have any information on the dealers. At this point, the company had significant exposure. To make a long story short, the vendor was never paid by at least 20% of the dealers to which he'd given credit. His mistake was shipping more product to these dealers before insisting that they pay for their previous orders. It is a great deal easier to require a credit application and check the information before extending any credit, than it is to monitor the amount of credit and insist on a credit application from someone you are already doing business with.

Credit	% Respondents
Not indicated	38.8%
COD	29.5%
Terms if credit application	34.5%
Credit card	15.1%

I thought more companies would be selling to dealers via credit card. This is an easy way to help a dealer buy without taking the credit risk. I realize that getting credit card merchant status is difficult for startup software companies, but this can be a good option for dealer sales.

12. Dealer Prices

If you don't believe that your dealers add any value to your product, then it makes sense to have one price for all of your dealers. 20.9% of the respondents do this.

Volume based pricing appeals to me. It rewards the dealer for selling more of your product on the assumption that he is making an investment in marketing. Therefore, he deserves a higher discount.

Dealer Prices	% Respondents
Not indicated	34.5%
One price for all	20.9%
Volume based	25.9%
Pre-buy product for discount	6.5%
Vary by dealer category	13.7%

Pre-buying product, in order to get the discount, used to be very common in the mini computer market. You also see this practice with some larger data based and 4th Generation Language Development tools. Only the very powerful companies who have their resellers "locked in" can insist that their dealers pre-buy product. 6.5% of the respondents are offering this now, and it is growing less common.

I was bothered by the fact that 13.7% of the respondents vary their dealer prices by category. I understand that people do this, but it seems to invite problems. I have seen more problems trying to define and enforce differences by category. This becomes especially difficult when you realize that the same people may be doing business under a number of different names. They might have a storefront dealership, a custom programming VAR business, and a consulting Rep company. Each of these companies might be nothing more than a checking account "doing business as". If you give VARs a better discount, then today I'll be a VAR. If you decide to do this, I hope you will think long and hard about the best ways to describe and enforce the differences in categories.

13. Dealer Training

25.2% of the respondents indicated they don't provide training. This corresponds to 28.1% whose products don't require training.

25.2% of the products required less than one day of training. This seems to correspond to the 17.3% who make training available (not required).

Looking at this from the other end, 17.3% of the products required more than one week of training. If you add up the two "required" answers (free and they pay), you get 18.7% which seems to correspond to products requiring more than a week of training.

It isn't clear whether dealer training is required for those who indicate they go to the dealer's location (free or paid). If we add them in as "required" you get another 7.9%, which raises the total to 26.6% requiring more than one week of training. My experience shows that even with products requiring less than one week of training, it is important to train the dealers, and it seems as though some of the companies with less than one week of training, do require their dealers to get trained.

Dealer Training	%	Respondents
Not indicated		36.0%
Not available		25.2%
Available, but not required		17.3%
Required, but free at our location		12.9%
Required, but pay at our location		5.8%
At dealer's location		3.6%
Ar dealer's location, paid		4.3%

Of the vendors who require training, at their location, there are twice as many who provide it free as there are who charge a fee. It is difficult to get dealers to pay for training. They will pay travel expenses to come to your location, but once they get there, they will balk at writing a check for the training.

When vendors go to the dealer's location to train them, they are only slightly more likely to get the dealer to pay for training (4.3% pay vs. 3.6% free). I suspect that the vendors aren't getting the dealers to pay for much more than out of pocket expenses. In my experience, the dealers will pay the vendor's airfare and motel expenses, but will resist paying an hourly or daily rate for training.

14. Initial Stocking Order

Most respondents indicated they do "nothing special" on the initial stocking order with dealers. It appears that, even if you offer a really great deal, very few dealers will take you up on it. Initially, you must "prove yourself" first, by giving them a product that sells well.

In the past, some vendors were able to force dealers to pre-buy product when they signed up initially. As I indicated in the dealer pricing section, this practice isn't very common. Very few vendors have the power to force dealers into paying up front.

Initial Stocking Order	% Respondents
Not indicated	38.8%
Nothing special	55.4%
Super discount on initial order	3.6%
Extremely good deal (3 for 1)	2.2%

15. Co-op Programs

Co-op programs are rebates from the vendor to the dealer to pay for dealer marketing programs. The amount of rebate is a percentage of the dealer's sales of the vendor's product.

Most respondents indicated that they don't make co-op programs available to their dealers. My advice is, don't contractually commit to co-op programs if you can avoid it. In my experience, the large companies will take credit for all the co-op programs they are entitled to and do as little as possible, while the small dealers won't take advantage of the co-op programs. Another problem with contractually committing to co-op programs, is that you, the vendors, have to accrue the expense, even if the dealers don't make use of the co-op programs.

I am not saying you shouldn't provide a co-op program for your dealers. Just be sure you carefully manage it, to insure getting the benefits you deserve.

Most large chains and sophisticated dealers will negotiate very hard for co-op programs. You will have to work with these sophisticated dealers to get as much exposure as possible for your money. Assuming that they are going to get your money, focus on getting as much as possible out of them.

With the smaller dealers, the money you were planning to spend on co-op programs will be better spent in providing them with everything they need to run ads or do mailings. For example, in one case, we took the dealer's logo and had our graphic artist incorporate it into our ad. We then mailed the ad to each dealer, with a check to pay for running the ad in the local paper. We even charged them for our administrative time to put everything together (as well as the bill from the graphic artist). These dealers really appreciated the fact that we were providing them with a turnkey service. Once we had run the first ad, we just accrued their co-op money until they had enough money to pay for the next ad. This program was very well received, and the dealers appreciated the fact that they actually got the advertising run. I have seen this same type of program done using direct mail with similar results.

Co-op Programs	% of Respondents
Not indicated	38.1%
Not available	46.0%
<1%	4.3%
1%-2%	5.8%
2%-3%	5.0%
3%-4%	0.7%
4%-5%	1.4%
>5%	2.2%

16. Exclusivity

Exclusivity means that only one dealer can sell in a territory. The territory is typically defined geographically. You are guaranteeing that you won't authorize other dealers to sell in your dealer's territory.

33.1% of the respondents don't make exclusivity available. 35.3% of the products had prices under $1K. Therefore, it is logical that very few of these low price products would offer exclusivity.

The most popular approach is to give exclusivity on an informal basis such as verbal agreements and no signed contract. The success of this depends upon the dealer committing to making the investment necessary to establish the product. In the initial phase of these informal arrangements, the focus is on the dealer's effort rather than sales. During the early stages, sales are hard to predict. If sales are slow to build up, the dealer shouldn't be judged unfairly.

Only 5.8% of the respondents grant exclusivity to get a dealer to sign. I have seen this done to sign up top-notch dealers. In some markets, there are dealers who are clearly market makers. Everyone knows and respects them, and it is valuable, to a software company, to have these power dealers carry your product. If you do this, I think that you should give them an exclusive for some period of time, but after that, they should have to deliver sales in order to keep the exclusive.

Very few (2.2%) of the survey respondents sell exclusivity. In my experience, the amount of money the dealers are willing to pay for exclusivity, is significantly less than the territory is worth. At most, a dealer might be willing to pay $5K to $10K for a territory which might generate $20K per month in sales. Getting the up-front money and then, not getting the sales doesn't seem like a good deal.

Guaranteed sales is a good way for a dealer to maintain an exclusivity for a product with a track record. If dealers have been selling your product for several years, and you know that your good dealers can sell a certain percentage of the prospects in their territory each year, it becomes reasonable to set quotas. With young products, without this type of track record, it is very difficult to set quotas. In many cases, the dealers set unrealistic quotas for themselves (After all, they *are* sales people). When a dealer fails to make his quota, the software vendor has a real dilemma. Technically, the vendor can cancel the dealer's exclusivity, but there is the problem of finding someone who can produce more sales from that territory. The dealer is also discouraged that he failed to make the quotas and wants a second chance. In most cases, the company ends up rescinding the quota and extending the exclusivity. Thus, the arrangement goes from quota based to informal, since the vendor wasn't really serious about the quota. I advise you not to implement a quota unless you are really willing to drop the exclusivity if the dealer fails to make the quota. *Don't bluff*. Once you have the data to establish realistic quotas, then you can go ahead and do so.

Exclusivity	% Respondents
Not indicated	35.3%
Not available	33.1%
Informal	16.5%
Grant it to sign them up	5.8%
They pay	2.2%
Guaranteed sales required	12.9%

Lower priced products are less likely to offer exclusivity. (i.e., more high priced products do offer some form of exclusivity.) 45% percent of products under $500 don't offer exclusivity and 26% of those over $500 don't offer exclusivity.

17. International Sales

Software Success readers don't make a lot of international sales. Large software companies often get 30% to 50% of their revenues internationally, but it is very difficult for small companies to make the investment required for establishing international sales.

% of Annual Revenues from International Sales	% Respondents
Not indicated	30.2%
None	20.1%
<10%	28.8%
10%-20%	11.5%
20%-30%	2.9%
30%-40%	5.0%
>40%	2.9%

7.9% of the respondents get more than 30% of their sales internationally. Only 10.1% of the respondents had annual revenues over $5 Million. This corresponds with my experience, showing that, unless a software company has over $5 Million in annual revenue, then it is unlikely to be successful selling internationally. You may pick up a few random international orders, but it is difficult to get a return on your investment. The only exception is if you have a really hot product, or you have a product that is especially well suited to the international market. For example, in the game business, Amiga is much more popular in Europe than here in the U.S. Thus, a game company with Amiga products might do better by marketing in Europe, than a non-Amiga company of the same size.

18. Conclusion

The possibility of mass distribution is one of the appeals of software. If you can find the right formula to sell your product, you'll have the opportunity for others to market your product and make you rich. It is tough to establish distribution for a software product, but I hope these discussions and survey results will help guide you in setting up a successful distribution program.

19. Distribution Outlook (Jul)

The May '91 issue of VARBUSINESS focused on Distribution, and presented the best discussion of the distribution industry I have ever read.

In his article "Distribution: 1991 Outlook", Richard March talks about the current battle royal between industrial distributors and the computer distributors. Industrial distributors originally sold chip level components and have grown into selling custom mini and micro computer systems requiring high levels of support. On the other hand, the computer distributors sell off-the-shelf shrink wrapped PC products requiring lower levels of support.

With today's trend toward LANs, both of these industry segments are butting heads, each with its own set of problems in adapting to serving LAN users. The industrial distributors will need to de-customize and lower prices to compete, while the computer distributors will need to offer more support and raise prices.

I found the following quotes from March's article especially interesting:

"... from 1986 to 1990, sales of computer products through distributors nearly tripled from $2.1 billion to about $5.8 billion. Atlanta brokerage Robinson-Humphrey Co. Inc. forecasts no cooling off in 1991, with sales expected to hit at least $6.5 billion."

"When Microamerica Inc. and Softsel Computer Products merged their operations last year and formed $1.2 billion Merisel Inc., the company conducted a $100,000 study to determine what resellers wanted. The study found the top three demands were brand name products, availability, and attractive prices."

"The biggest question mark for the future success of the industrials will be falling profit margins. The industrials are used to operating with gross profit margins of 23 percent to 25 percent, while the computer distributors are comfortable with 10 percent to 13 percent gross margins. As a result, the computer distributors can accept lower profit margins and still make money, while the industrials cannot."

If you are serious about selling to resellers through distributors, you should read the trade magazines such as VARBUSINESS, which cover the distribution industry.

For more information call:
CMP Publications
(516) 562-5000

B. Miscellaneous (1991)

1. Staffing Dealer Sales (Feb)

Dear Dave:

I just received my first copy of Software Success, and found it not only interesting and informative, but thoroughly enjoyable as well. I look forward to the next issue. As the Director of Channel Sales for Micrografx, you touched on several subjects under my domain: Customer Support, lead generation, sales force compensations, and marketing issues. I'm going to route my copy to several others in the department.

One subject that I am very curious about is the industry-wide setup and staffing of field sales forces to meet the needs of corporate accounts and reseller accounts. Our company is very split on how this should be handled; our Corporate Sales Director feels that all field sales personnel should focus on the corporate "pull" side. I feel we do need that functionality, but there also needs for a "dealer only" sales force, to "push" the product line as well. This is done as reps perform the daily spreading of the gospel to the dealers, via store calls, training seminars, and joint sales calls. My experience is that most of my competitors successfully operate in this fashion. Perhaps this is a subject you've already covered, and if so, please send me any back in-

formation you might have. If this is an untapped subject, I'm sure you will find a great deal of interest in the following areas:
- **How and when to staff the field**
- **Concentration of a force in a few select territories versus a more shallow, but broader coverage**
- **Percent of field force focusing on retailer/resellers versus end-users/corporate accounts**
- **Best source for locating new reps**
- **Responsibilities of reseller reps and corporate reps**

I think that Micrografx is a fairly representative "mid-sized and growing" company. There are even more like us who face these same questions. I look forward to your insight.

Sincerely,
Keith F Magee
Director of Channel Sales
Micrografx, Inc.

Dear Keith:

I appreciate your letter. I don't have personal experience with a company with your sales mix: outbound corporate sales and dealer sales, but I will describe the generic approaches that I have seen.

Companies who have all distributor or reseller sales have sales people who call on the distributors and chains. Even the small companies end up making personal sales calls on the large distributors. My experience is that these companies act as a distributor for the unaffiliated dealers.

As the pseudo dealer for these unaffiliated dealers, they seem to have a telesales department. The phone reps take the calls and fill the orders. In some occasions they also make outbound calls to generate sales. My guess is that this proactive effort is less than ten percent of their time and maybe less than twenty percent of the sales.

Another common situation is vertical market companies which have to recruit, train and support VARs. Most commonly these are more expensive packages (over $5,000 in most cases). These companies usually have a sales person who visits the dealers, selects the dealers, trains the dealer and helps them sell. These companies almost always end up with an inside dealer support rep who takes their calls and fills their orders.

Chapter IV. Distribution

Thinking about these experiences and applying them to your situation a couple things jump out:

1. Your large distributor chain accounts probably warrant concentrated sales focus and sales calls.

2. The mass of dealer or resellers need inbound phone support, but probably can't justify direct sales calls.

To answer your questions specifically:

I would probably start with locating the distributor sales people at corporate. They probably can't visit the distributors or chains much more frequently than every two or three months. Thus, if someone focuses on the top ten accounts they might make one trip a month. This would allow them to visit the current accounts and do some prospecting.

I would focus on the large dollar volume accounts initially rather than trying to cover everyone. If you prove that you can increase sales with these accounts, by investing in sales coverage you can consider expanding your coverage. At the same time, I am sure that it doesn't make economic sense to visit all your dealers.

The split of resources between the resellers and the corporate accounts is more difficult. In theory, I would like my cost of sales to be similar by channel. The difficulty is that I am giving the dealers and distributors a very significant discount to pay them for selling my product (in theory). Thus I sometimes feel that the dealers and distributors should run their own ads and sell the products that they are reselling (this is a joke, for those of you who are agreeing strongly.) Seriously, when we are offering a distributor a discount of 60 percent or more it seems like we should get a lot for our money.

Direct sales to corporate accounts is much simpler. My experience is that most companies pay approximately ten percent in sales costs for direct sales. This is a combination of expenses and may vary by a couple points, but it is pretty common.

Sales expenses for distributor and reseller sales should be much lower. Reps who work with very large reseller accounts often receive less than two or three points on the sales to the reseller. I have worked with a client who had a sales person who received a one half of one percent bonus on distributor sales over a base amount. While this doesn't

sound like a great deal of money, it was very significant in the context we were dealing with.

I would probably start addressing this issue by listing the objectives that I wanted to achieve. (In one case the company paid a five percent sales commission on sales to a list of desired accounts.) Then look at how much you are willing to spend to achieve these objectives.

If you are focusing on the major accounts, finding someone who has worked with these accounts is a major plus. There is a great deal of networking in this business and people with contacts usually are more effective. Depending upon the state of the economy you may have to use references, ads or recruiters to find this sort of sales person. I would think that this would be a good time to find such people.

The responsibilities for the reseller reps have to be tied very carefully to their objectives. The corporate reps are more classic sales people with a quota and a territory. Go get those sales.

One final thought is on your long-term ability to manage the channel conflict with selling to both end users and resellers. I predict that as you become more successful that there will be more pressure from the resellers to turn the corporate accounts over to them. If you resist this, you are creating a weak point for a competitor to exploit.

Good luck
Dave

2. Kenfil Distribution (Jul)

This month's feature article is not about a software company, but rather, a "software only" distributor. I thought it would be interesting to see things from a distributor's point of view. The following information on Kenfil Distribution is from the company's literature:

"Kenfil Distribution is the largest software-only distributor in the U.S. and the ninth largest computer products distributor overall. The company is the market leader in the rapidly growing business productivity and utilities segment, where it is heavily targeting the emerging opportunities in mass merchandising. Kenfil commands about 15 percent of the U.S. wholesale software market. The company carries more than 2,000 personal computer software ti-

Chapter IV. Distribution

tles, and stocks inventory in warehouses located on both coasts. The company forged a pattern of continuous sales growth since its founding in 1983. In 1989, it generated in excess of $140 million in revenues."

"Unlike other distributors which carry educational, entertainment and other consumer oriented software, Kenfil carries only three types of software – business, productivity and utilities."

"While Kenfil pursues a focused product strategy, the company serves a diverse customer base. Its customers include independent and franchised software specialty retailers; computer chain stores; mass merchandisers; mail order firms; value-added resellers; and computer consultancies. Kenfil also provides the only source of product marketing support for a growing variety of non-traditional outlets such as discount warehouses, bookstores, record and tape stores, and office supply houses."

I spoke with Irwin Branksy (818) 785-1181, Kenfil's President, and asked him the $64,000 question,... "How do you get a software product into distribution?" Irwin said that Kenfil carries 2,000 SKUs (SKUs are stocking units. Each version of a product (IBM, Apple, etc.), is a SKU.) Every month, Kenfil gets 15 to 20 new products submitted for evaluation, but only accepts *6 new products every year* from those products submitted. That is 6 out of 180–240 or 3% to 4%. (This seems almost as hard as raising venture capital!) I figured Irwin must take on more than 6 new products per year when he carries 2,000 SKUs. When asked where the others come from, he answered "from my customers." The dealers and chains who buy from Irwin, often hear of another product and ask him to carry it. This virtually guarantees success for him, because the need has already been determined. It also helps that he has pre-sold some copies of the product.

At this point, the most important factor is the product's uniqueness and the least important is price. Irwin strongly believes that offering a distributor a deal on price would have very little positive impact.

As an aside, Irwin almost always advises vendors to raise their prices when they sell to him. He uses an actual formula, to determine prices, based on what the vendor wants the "street price" (price the end user pays) to be. Irwin believes it is more important for consumers to perceive the price they pay reflects

a good discount from list price rather than paying a low absolute price. His experience has shown that distributors mark products up by 7% and the dealers then mark them up again by another 15 to 20%.

The terms list price and suggested retail price mean the same thing. To simplify things, I'll use "list price" throughout the rest of this article.

Distributors usually receive a 40% to 60% discount from list price. For a product which has a list price of $100, the distributor pays $40 (60% discount), and marks it up 7% to $43. The dealer pays $43 for the product, and then marks it up 15 to 20%. The dealer sells it for $49 to $52, which is 50% off list price. In another situation, a distributor gets a 40% discount (e.g. they pay $60), and the distributor marks it up 7% to $65. The dealer then adds his 20% markup and the street price becomes $78 which is only 22% off list price.

Other distributors may have significantly higher markups. An article in VARBUSINESS (May '91) suggested the most common distributor markup is 10% to 15%. If we assume a 15% distributor markup and a 20% dealer markup the street prices would be $55 (60% discount to the distributor), and $83 (40% distributor discount) for a product with a $100 list price.

The VARBUSINESS article went on to say that industrial distributors mark up their products even more, and this causes competitive pressure from the computer product distributors.

I agree very strongly with Irwin on two points:

* Keep your eye on street prices.

* Set your list price so that you can give everyone the discounts they are accustomed to.

I have a client whose product was listed at $99. The company president had decided he just wouldn't sell it to the distributor for less than $58 (42% discount). The distributor then marked it up 15% and sold it to the dealer who then marked it up another 20%. Thus, the street price was $80 which had a "ho-hum" discount of only 20% off list price.

This lack of margin was an on-going problem with the distributors and dealers. We finally raised the list price to $129. At the same time, we changed the discount to 50%, and sold the product to the distributor for $64.50 which was 11% more than we

Chapter IV. Distribution

had been getting before. The distributor and dealer still marked it up 38% between them (15% distributor and 20% dealer) to $89 which is 31% off the list price of $129. Obviously, the fundamental assumption was that consumers would be willing to pay the additional $9. The interesting thing is, it appears the product is more attractive (it's selling better) with the higher discount from list price and the slightly higher absolute price. Given this improvement, the fact that the vendor, the distributor, and the dealer are all making more money per unit is just icing on the cake.

If you are trying to decide on a street price for your product, I suggest that you start by collecting some information. Visit some retail stores which could carry your product. Look at the list prices and street prices of products similar to yours. You want to make sure your discount from list price is at least as good as the discounts of the other products on the shelf. This is particularly true when you look at comparable products at the same price point. If the comparable products are selling at 30% off list price and your product will only be 10% off list price, you won't look so good.

To recap Irwin's pricing formula:

1. Set your street price (the price which end users will pay). Determine this by researching retail stores with products comparable to yours.

2. Check the discounts being given. If all of the boxes on the shelf boast "50% off list price" then you'll have to do the same or better.

3. Decide on your list price based on competitive discounts and street prices. For instance, if products comparable to yours have street prices of about $50 and boast 50% discounts off list prices of about $100, your list price should be $100 or over. Being a bit over is OK (up to say, $130), but going too high will make you no longer comparable and will cause you to have a higher street price and more of a discount. The danger here is having the end user see your product as overpriced and lower quality. If your discount ends up being 60% off list price, this may "red flag" your product as one which the store is trying to get rid of due to some defects (e.g. it's old, low quality, etc.) This is where conformity will work in your favor.

4. Once you have set your list price, then you can set your discounts for your distributor(s), commonly 40–60%.

5. The distributor will usually mark up anywhere from 7% (Irwin's markup) to 15–20% (according to VARBUSINESS) and sell to the dealers.

6. The dealers then markup another 20% or so and label the boxes with their street price, the list price, and the amount of discount to the end users.

Once you have a unique product with a good price, then the next most important consideration is packaging, according to Irwin. A vendor he has worked with recently, has a product box with loose front and back covers like a book. This gives the vendor two more panels on which to put information. Irwin believes that successful products will sell themselves visually. (I strongly agree with this.) Assuming this is true, the additional two panels of information on the box will translate into more sales.

Irwin also stressed that you need to put very specific information on the outside of your product box. What system does your product run on? Also, bar coding is now required on all packages and Irwin's company can do this for a fee.

Also, make sure the name of your product is on both vertical spines of the box, along with the system requirements. Boxes get placed on the shelf every which way and you want consumers to get the information as quickly as possible without having to pick up and turn over every box on the shelf.

Irwin strongly believes in the demand/pull strategy. (In my own experience, I've also found this seems to work best.) With a demand/pull strategy, the vendor does everything possible through heavy promotion and advertising to create "demand" and get consumers into the stores to "pull" the product off the shelf. This is the most effective way to get a product into distribution. If people are coming into the retail stores and asking for a product, the dealers will then call their distributors ask them to carry this product, because they know it will sell.

This strategy is appropriate even for companies with well known products. Symantec is introducing a new version of Norton Utilities at a special introductory price. Given the success of the first version of this product, you wouldn't think this strategy is really necessary. But, Symantec wanted to get the product into distribution as quickly as possible. In this case, the strategy served to renew and increase reseller enthusiasm for a product that could have been perceived as "ho-hum".

Chapter IV. Distribution

Seasonality is another factor Irwin feels must be considered. He believes distributors tend to pick up new products in May and June. Dealers continue to pick up new products through August. All new products must be into distribution by September for the Fall selling season.

In my experience, software companies usually make 40% to 50% of their annual sales in the fourth quarter. This is even more pronounced in consumer sales, where Christmas sales totally dominate the year.

Another reason vendors have difficulty getting distributors and dealers to take on a product is the fact that this is a zero sum game. For every product added, one must be dropped. One thing a vendor can do to make his product more attractive is to spend money with the dealers in other ways. The super stores give vendors even more ways to spend their money, such as paying money to be in their catalogs or giving their sales people "spiffs" (special performance incentives for selling vendors' products.) This might be $10 for every package sold or a chance to win a drawing for a big screen TV or vacation. These things will create pull, and if the vendors spend money to create pull, they will generate stock turns, which then provide ROI, which is what this business is all about. These added incentives make your product more attractive for the dealers and improve the odds of getting your product added to their product line.

As an aside, it should be obvious that the vendors whose products are already into distribution are aware of this zero sum game. They are dealing with the distributors, dealers and super stores, on a regular basis, trying to figure out how to keep you *out*. Therefore, all's fair ...

When asked about other requirements for distribution, Irwin replied that for the last 2 years, all contracts he has signed have basically been contingency deals in which Kenfil has the option to return a product, at any time, for 100% credit with no questions asked. In return, his dealers have the same option to return a product to him. Therefore, he can't afford the risk of getting stuck with any returns. Along with this, Irwin uses a formula to test the financial viability of vendors to guarantee their ability to re-pay, if necessary.

When a new vendor signs up with Kenfil, Irwin asks for 60 day payment terms on the initial order. Once

a product has been successful for three to six months, he likes to set up 30 and 10 day pre-payment discounts to improve his margins. If a product is returned to Kenfil and then to the vendor, that vendor must re-pay Kenfil within 10 days.

At this point, I realized there is a real risk period in which the distributor is exposed. This may partially explain why the distributors are so cautious about taking on new software products. Let's assume that, at the end of 60 days, the distributor pays for the first order. He has a 3 month risk window before he really knows how well the product is doing. The following schedule shows this window:

Jan 1 - Vendor ships product to Kenfil.
Feb 1 - Kenfil's catalog goes to the dealers.
March 1 - Kenfil pays vendor for January 1 shipment.

- Dealers place orders with Kenfil.

April/May - Products are on dealer shelves.
June 1 - Dealers either re-order or return the products.

I must admit, I didn't quite realize just how much exposure the distributor has in this situation. It sure makes it much easier to understand why distributors are so risk adverse.

Last month I spoke with a consultant who works with software companies which sell through distribution. He works with venture capitalists to help their investments establish distribution. As we talked, it became clear that his clients had been much more successful than most of my clients in getting distribution. At the time, I figured his clients' had better distribution because they were venture backed and could afford bigger ad campaigns, thus creating more pull. I believe there is another reason, which may be even more important. If a company has raised several million dollars in venture capital, a distributor can be assured of repayment if a product must be returned. With small self-funded companies, the re-payment risk is much higher.

Conclusion

As I've said before, it's tough to establish distribution for software products. With a better understanding of the distributor's end of the business, you should be able to evaluate more objectively whether you should approach distributors and dealers. If you

Chapter IV. Distribution

think you should, this information should help you. Good luck!

Also, I would like to hear from any of you who have had great success in getting distribution. Tell us the magic answer!

3. Distribution Book (Oct)

I recently talked to Frederick L. Cooper III, an attorney who has published a book on software distribution titled "*Software Distribution: How to Develop a Successful Marketing Plan.*" He sells the book for $49.95, plus $2.00 for shipping. For more information, call the following numbers:

TEL (404) 729-1336
FAX (404) 729-1338

This book looks at the link between indirect-channel marketing and intellectual property law. If you are trying to establish multiple channels, this book provides a unique perspective.

C. International Distribution (1991)

1. International Distributors (Apr)

Q. We have been contacted by a distributor "go between" who wants to act as an agent between our software company and international distributors. Do you have any experience with this type of situation?

A. I have a couple of clients who have worked with this type of agent or broker. My first advice is to check their references. Have they worked with similar products? I find that most people don't check people out. You can significantly improve your odds if you do your homework first. A "go between" or agent should have a track record. In fact, they should have a track record with similar products to yours.

The next real issue is to clarify for whom the agent is working. On occasion, I have been uncomfortable because I have felt that the agent was really working for the foreign distributors (who were local to them). I don't feel the agent should be working for the international distributor. Part of the appeal of working with an agent is that you feel this person is watching out for your best interest.

I have had two clients who have hired brokers on a consulting basis. The broker came up with a list of distributors, did some background research on the distributors, visited the distributors and reported on their interest and their capabilities. One client paid the agent $5,000 for this initial study and the other client got a study for free.

The agent's report should list the prospective distributors, provide background on the distributors, and summarize the results of the visits. Your agent can get you the U.S. companies which these distributors are representing so you can approach them. I believe that you are better off paying for this report because it clearly establishes that the agent is working for you.

I am not sure if there are any legal implications regarding this, but it makes me feel better. You are also in a much better position to get exactly what you want if you are paying the bills. For example, if you are paying the agent, it is quite acceptable to ask the agent to run credit checks on the distributors. I might be reluctant to do this if I wasn't paying for the consulting.

The real reason the agent wants to do this is that they want part of the ongoing revenue. It seems like their share ranges between five percent and ten percent. It also seems like they take their share out of the distributors discount. For example, in one case, my client was planning on giving the distributor a 50 percent discount. The agent wanted five percent so the agent was responsible for convincing the distributor that 45 percent was fair. The agent had to commit to provide some services for the distributor to justify this split. I think that this arrangement makes a great deal of sense if the agent sets up relationships with multiple distributors.

One point that I haven't made is that getting European distribution will probably cost you between $100,000 and $250,000. This will cover the legal costs plus travel to meet and train the distributors. If you want to make your distributor effective, you will have to make this investment. I have never seen a case where setting up European distribution generated a short-term positive cash flow. It seems to take a couple of years before the cash flow is positive.

The situation with Japanese distributors can be more positive in the short term. I have been involved in a number of deals with Japanese distributors that generated a short-term positive cash flow. The common scenario was, "We were found by a Japanese distributor who is interested in our product. They agreed to pre-paid royalties, and guaranteed quarterly payments. We went ahead because we needed the cash, and we weren't going to do anything in Japan in the meantime."

In the short term, these were good deals. In the medium term, we wonder if we wouldn't have been better off to wait on doing business with Japan. It turns out that the distributors who approached us were second-tier distributors. There are other distributors who might have been much more effective at selling our product in Japan. I realize that this sounds like sour grapes, but there are a number of questions that can't be answered:

1. Would the bigger and better distributor have been interested at that initial point?
2. How much would we have had to invest in selling the bigger distributor?
3. How much less cash would we have gotten from the bigger distributor?
4. Would they really have sold more?

My final thought is that you are making multi-year decisions when you begin to set up international distribution. Take your time and think it through. I have seen far too many deals which were hurried and didn't pay off. Take your time, do your research, and then back your decision with the necessary investment. If you do it right, you should get a good return on investment.

2. Doing Business Internationally (Apr)

I recently received this FAX from a subscriber in Hong Kong:

Dear David:

Now I need your help. I am a the software distributor in Asia. My company size is small, but we are carrying over 100 titles. Recently, we are astonished by a few publishers who are more than willing to renounce their business credibility.

1. Very often publishers charge our credit card without notifying us when and the total. Then they ship out the order after our repetitious fax and phone calls. It's often 30 to 60 days later. Is this typical behavior for publishers within this special category?

2. For better reliability, we request our publishers mail all materials to my box address. Some refuse, and the products are lost. For example, we specially instructed a company to ship 10 copies of a particular publication to my box address.

As of today, we have not yet received the shipment. Even worse, our customers phone us every day complaining about our delay. They first agreed on the phone to FedExp (at my cost) the 10 missing copies. Then I received the enclosed fax message this morning. Again, he broke his promise. Now he insists either we have to wait till 3/8/91 (this letter was dated 3/1/91) or we have to accept a new order of 10 copies. Being a small company, it is financially difficult to accept either offer. I have already paid dearly to follow up the shipment problem by fax and long distance.

While Americans face a trade deficit and are increasingly losing marketshare to the Japanese, I'm the one working very hard in Asia to improve the situation by selling more American software products. Fortunately, a few American publishers explain clearly and loudly that it's Americans conduct which is unfair business.

David, given the long distance, how can I effectively manage such an unfortunate violation of business integrity we so cherish in a civilized business world?

Look forward to hearing from you soon.

Thank you.

Best Regards,
Armstrong Wong
Armstrong Systems
Hong Kong
FAX (852) 363-8560

Dear Armstrong:

I am afraid that there are a few people who take advantage of a situation like selling internationally to cheat others. At least by paying for your orders via credit card, you can get your money back through the credit card company.

The more difficult problem is dealing with companies who really aren't set up to do business internationally. There are a number of details that companies have to figure out. What are the best ways to ship internationally? What charges do you add on for international shipment? You need to be explicit about these shipping charges and the method of shipment.

We started getting a number of international orders for our books and newsletter earlier this year. We didn't have an international price list. We finally developed one and it is very explicit about how we ship things. As you know, even airmail can take quite a long time to ship internationally. Once we developed this price sheet, we have faxed it to all international orders and inquiries. People are able to look at this and request Federal Express shipment and charge it to their credit card.

My advice to U.S. companies is to be very explicit on your policies for international sales. Do you accept credit card purchases only? Do you accept checks in U.S. dollars? Are invoices allowed? I think that a lot of the confusion and misunderstandings come from this type of lack of clear policy. These types of policy decisions take some time, but once you sit down and work it out you will be able to consummate the international business that comes your way.

I hope that my readers will look at how they are set up to do business internationally and will make the necessary improvements.

Thanks for the letter and the subscription.

Dave

3. Source Code — International Distributor (Jun)

Dear Dave,

I have been approached by a US based company which specializes in exporting technology to Korea. They have won the contract to supply a hardware board on a large government procurement. Now the government wants them to integrate software with their hardware board. There are a number of companies which have software which could meet this requirement. The export company has approached all of them, and they have selected us. (Most of the companies are larger companies and weren't able to meet the timeframes that this project involves.)

The time frames are very tight. The government wants to see a working system within 3 months.

The distributor wants to know my price for my source code so they can make these modifications and submit the system to the government. They are also asking about rights to distribute my software in Korea, as well as the rest of Asia. At this time, we don't have plans to market the product in Asia, but have received other inquiries about Japan.

Thanks for the help.
Anonymous

Dear Anonymous,

During our phone discussion, I concluded that giving your source code to the distributor during the demonstration phase seemed very risky. It doesn't sound like he has the funds to pay significant money up-front for the source code until he wins the contract. It also sounds as if illegal copying is a major problem in Korea. (The distributor wants to augment your software copy protection with a hardware key. He also wants to serialize the software so each copy only works with one hardware board.)

When we talked about the work to prepare for the demo, there were three distinct parts:

1. **Translate the documentation into Korean.**

2. **Translate the screens and messages into Korean. Thankfully, all of the text is isolated in one part of the program, the external section.**

3. **Make the necessary changes to work with the Korean BIOS. (The system calls may be slightly different.)**

The first two don't involve any risks for your company and the distributor should be able to proceed on them ASAP. A programmer will need access to your source code to make the BIOS modifications. I think you should control this part. You mentioned that you know a Korean programmer who can work with you on this phase of the project. If you need help from the distributor's U.S. based programmers, you shouldn't have any significant risk (as long as they don't walk away with the source code).

If you give the distributor the source code, he is going to have to pay people to make the BIOS change, and you are going to have equivalent expenses. Hopefully, your expenses will be less because you know the product. At the same time, you don't know about the tools that run on the Korean BIOS, so your costs might be higher. The most efficient solution should be a joint project where you know the required modifications and the distributor's programmers help you with the tools for the Korean BIOS.

We concluded that you could prepare for the demo without releasing the source code, and still meet the timeframes for the demonstration to the government.

The idea is that you will distribute a copy protected disk to the distributor. The distributor will print the documentation, but you will control the number of copies which he can install. As we discussed, the easiest approach is to continue shipping copy protected disks to him until he purchases the source code.

Now, we have to give the distributor a price for the software with and without source code. Your product sells for $495 and you have already agreed to sell him the software for $200 (60% discount), if he buys a significant quantity. This is probably OK as long as you are shipping disks and know that you are getting paid for all of the copies he sells. It also sounds like this price is going to enable the distributor to reduce his price to the government and help him win the bid.

Selling the source code to the distributor makes it much more difficult to verify how many copies of the software the distributor sells. Once he has the source code, he can make his own copies. Even if he contracts to only sell in Korea, there is also a risk that it would be very difficult for you to keep a third party from taking your product and selling it elsewhere in Asia.

Here are three pricing proposals:

1. **Sell them disks at $100 each.**

2. **They pay $200K for the source code. They also pay $100 per copy. The $200K may or may not be a prepaid royalty. (If the $200K is a prepaid royalty, the distributor will get the first 2K copies of the product with no further payments.)**

3. **The distributor pays $1 Million for the source code and all rights to sell the product in Korea.**

As I think about it, I like options 1 and 3. However, I have mixed emotions about option 2 because of your risk of losing control. Perhaps you should make the $200K a source code fee, with no credit toward royalties. This will give you some money to hire a Korean law firm to audit the contract and insure that you get paid for everything they sell.

This is an unusually complex deal, but as we discussed, we both agree it is important to work with the distributor so that you win the business together. This is a potentially very lucrative contract for both of you.

Good luck!
Dave

4. Japanese Market Consulting Firm Jun)

Dear Mr. Bowen,

Unimont Research is a computer consulting firm specializing in the Japanese market. We see a rapidly growing demand for U.S. computer systems, software and peripherals in both our clients' and our own operations.

Many Japanese companies are looking for software, peripherals, and hardware to distribute or represent in Japan. Others are searching for promising high tech companies to invest in. Demand, in this case, far outstrips supply.

You would be the best person in the closest contact with the vibrant US high technology sector.

Unimont's offices in Tokyo and Osaka distribute software, systems and peripherals throughout Japan. These offices also consult to many of Japan's largest companies looking to expand their product lines or make strategic investments. Our offices in Princeton and Los Angeles consult to US software companies planning on entering the Japanese market. Our Los Angeles office also directs Japanization efforts (the translation of foreign software to run on Japanese systems and display Japanese text).

We believe we are well placed to hook up promising US companies with capable and interested Japanese distributors and/or investors. And we hope you will consider the potential of the Japanese market, the world's second largest for computer technology after the US.

Chapter IV.   Distribution

The Japanese computer market is growing at rates in excess of 10% per year. URI estimates that by 1995, Japan's total annual expenditures on computer technology will be $80 Billion. US companies possess often superior technologies that can succeed in Japan, if only they knew how to enter the Japanese market. We believe we can help.

If you would like more information please feel free to contact me.

Sincerely,

Masa Matsuo
Unimont Research, Inc.
(213) 544-1103
FAX (213) 544-1399

Dear Mr. Matsuo,

Thank you for your letter. If U.S. companies are interested in exploring the Japanese market they should send you their product literature. You also have offered to help educate people about the Japanese market.

You said that in the last two years you have concluded distribution arrangements for 10 U.S. software products. This is quite an accomplishment given the effort to negotiate one of these distribution agreements.

You also stressed that you can arrange to Japanize products for U.S. companies.

Anyone who thinks their product(s) might do well in Japan should contact you and benefit from your experience in transferring U.S. products to Japan.

Thanks for the information.
David H. Bowen

> Dear Readers,
>
> I talked with Mr. Matsuo and he seemed very knowledgeable about distributing U.S. products in Japan. I am very interested in hearing from any of you who contact him to learn the realities of exploring distribution of U.S. products in Japan.
>
> Dave

5. Japanese Distribution (Jul)

I recently met with Mr. Takahashi, Editor in Chief of Package Software Magazine in Japan to discuss his publication and its purpose. Package Software Magazine is dedicated to promoting the concept of "package software" in Japan as opposed to "custom software", which is much more common there.

Package Software also publishes a directory of software products. Their last directory, published in January, 1991, listed 7,465 products. The July 1991 directory will list over 10,000 products, indicating rapid growth in the Japanese package software market.

In talking with Mr. Takahashi, it became very apparent that the current Japanese distribution system is much like the U.S. software distribution business in the early 1980s. The few distributors in Japan sell high priced products with high margins. Typical distributor margins in Japan are over 20%, compared to 7-15% in the U.S. (See the Kenfil feature article earlier in this issue.) PC software in Japan retails for over twice the price of comparable products in the U.S.

In Japan, the distributors are responsible for marketing the software and the software publishers have a more passive role than their U.S. counterparts. Mr. Takahashi was very surprised to learn that the U.S. distributors did no marketing. However, when he learned about the comparatively low U.S. distributor margins, he understood why this is so.

Recently, in Japan, a PC magazine company introduced a word processing product and used the magazine to promote the product directly to end users. (This was one of the first Japanese companies to use this type of demand/pull marketing where the software publishers markets directly to the end users creating a demand to then pull the product through distribution.) This product has been very successful.

In this situation, the distributor demanded higher margins (greater discounts) from the software publisher, and threatened to carry a competitive product if the publisher didn't agree to increase the discount. The publisher won this battle, because his product was well established and he could easily find other distributors. The publisher called the distributor's bluff and won.

I expect that the Japanese distributors will become much more like the U.S. distributors, as the software publishers realize they must promote their products themselves.

I feel that it is appropriate for the publishers to take the marketing and promotion risk, because ultimately they will reap the benefits if a product becomes successful. If a distributor invests in marketing and promotion, and gets a product launched, he runs a risk that the software publisher will then go to a discount distributor and undermine the first distributor. Unless the distributor gets an exclusive deal on a product, he has no control or power. If he gets an exclusive deal for a product, he is then really functioning as a publisher (there are a number of publishers who sell other people's products, so this is a viable business.)

Reference: Mr. Takahashi, Editor in Chief, Package Software Magazine, FAX 03-5472-1875.

6. Export Management Company (Jul)

Dear Mr. Bowen,

We are an Export Management Company that concentrates solely on exporting American software to Europe. I came across the April 1991 issue of Software Success while visiting one of my clients.

In the "Questions & Answers" column of this issue, a developer said that he had been approached by a distributor 'go-between', and asked your opinion on this matter. I'd like to describe to you how we work, not to take issue with your response, but to make you aware of some other options available for your clients and readers.

We are, in effect, our clients' international marketing department. Working for developers, we:

Create a country specific or pan-European marketing plan

* Arrange for distribution in Europe:

  – Find and screen distributors (or VARs, resellers, integrators, etc.)

  – Negotiate pro forma contracts between developer and distributor

  – Develop goals and quotas

* Manage the physical ordering, payment, licensing, and export process.

* Monitor distributors' performance versus quotas and goals.

* Provide periodic sales and opportunity reports to the client.

* Arrange, on a sub-contracting basis, for product localization:

  – Translation (interface, on-line help, manuals).

  – Packaging

  – Marketing/promotion

Depending on the marketing channel chosen, some of the above tasks are not necessary, or fall within the purview of the distributor; nevertheless we manage the entire process, freeing our clients to concentrate on domestic marketing and software development.

At all times, our primary fiduciary and moral (if you will) responsibility is to our client, the developer. We do not take title to products. We encourage our clients to enter into non-exclusive arrangements with many distributors, which in fact enhances our value since we manage them all for the client. We stay on top of the sales process, and constantly evaluate the distributors' success.

We are paid by our clients, the developers, in two ways. Primarily, we earn a commission based on royalties paid to the developer, not on end-user price. In this way, we are highly motivated to maximize their revenues. Secondarily, we earn a management fee for any localization work that is done, a fee which essentially covers our time and costs in arranging and supervising this work.

Unless called upon to act in a consulting capacity, we require no initial fees, nor do we sell distributor lists, feasibility studies, or our own research. While your point about getting what you pay for is well-taken, we have found that our customers are often unable to justify high initial outlays, even with the significant carrot of the European software market dangling in front of them. We want them to get into Europe with minimum cost and risk, and thus are interested in the views you expressed on this matter. Finally, while we do often counsel a client to fully localize their products (which could be the subject of

Chapter IV.   Distribution

another letter!), that decision remains theirs to make when they feel ready.

In sum, I think we offer a real alternative for certain kinds of developers, those without enormous marketing budgets, those with a long term commitment to the promise of Europe, and those with legitimately interesting and useful products. For us, it's fun and challenging work.

Please call either me or my partner, Joe Brunoli. We would welcome a chance to chat on this and other issues.

Sincerely,
Samuel E. Taylor
Renaissance Business Group
TEL (415) 454-3577
FAX (415) 454-9886

Dear Samuel,

I received a call from one of my clients who is considering working with your firm to market her product in Europe. I like your business concept. I think you should be able to lower the cost for small companies to introduce their products into Europe. You can visit several distributors on behalf of a few U.S. companies on one trip, allowing the U.S. companies to effectively share your expenses. I also expect your expertise might benefit the small companies who otherwise couldn't afford someone with your experience.

Even with your help, I am still skeptical that some of these low budget developers can achieve success. Companies who try to establish international distribution without being thoroughly prepared to make the investment rarely succeed. The low level of international sales reported in the survey earlier in this issue supports this. I hope that you are able to lower the threshold for companies to get into the European market.

You mentioned that you are just starting this venture, even though both of you have years of experience marketing U.S. products in Europe. You also mentioned that you have talked to a number of developers and have just signed your first agreement. I wish you well and advise any of my readers who are interested to contact you. Please keep me informed on your progress.

Good luck!
Dave

Addendum:

As a result of working with my client who is negotiating with Renaissance, I became aware of a sticky issue that must be resolved in all distribution agreements. The issue is what happens if the agreement doesn't work out and one party fails to renew the agreement. If you are only dealing with a distributor, you usually end up with a certain number of deals that are in limbo. In practice, it usually turns out that the distributor has a period of time to close some named accounts. (This is much like the rights a sales person often retains when management changes his territory.) Even with these types of provisions, I have observed a number of unpleasant situations in which the distributor agreements fail.

With an agent, you may have a situation in which one of his distributors is really successful, but the developer wants to cancel the agreement because the agent isn't meeting the developer's needs. The agent wants to protect himself against being cut out of the business with the successful distributor. I feel that the agent established this business and deserves the commissions.

A common attitude from an agent is the "fire me, fire my distributors" approach. He asserts that if you cancel the agreement, then you can't work with any of the distributors he introduced you to. This sure helps protect him, but it can really cripple the developer. This is especially true if one of the distributors is making sales.

It seems to me, one alternative is to allow the developer to continue working with the distributors referred by the agent, but to continue paying the agent a declining commission. I have seen agreements where these severance commissions were paid over a few years on a declining scale. This seemed to reward/appease the agent, but allowed the developer to continue to work with the successful distributors.

When I was studying Physics, one of my professors said, "All of the hard problems in the world are at the transition points. Everything is easy at a steady state." The issue of agent/developer agreements is one of these transition point problems. I suggest that you carefully think about the transition points in all relationships and contracts which you are negotiating. These are the times when assumptions change and the situations need to be specifically addressed. You will lower your risk of ending up in a difficult situation, if you do a thorough job of anticipating these issues.

Good luck,
Dave

7. More Japanese Marketing (Sept)

Dear Dave,

In the last two issues, you have featured letters about the Japanese market. This definitely is following an industry-wide trend. As the rate of expansion of the software market in America slows, people are increasingly turning their attention to even historically difficult markets like Japan, Korea, Taiwan and Brazil. I believe that this heightened interest in Japan couldn't come at a better time.

Recent developments in PC technology are resulting in 25% growth rate in PC sales and, additionally making the localization of software, orders of magnitude easier. Laptops, Windows consistent (relatively) API, DOS/V, Low-cost Macs and scalable font boards are all innovations that are reaping major changes in the demographics of the Japanese PC market, bringing PC's out of the corner, where they ran custom developed software almost exclusively, and putting them on individuals' desks. I am including the first few copies of a newsletter that we are producing that discusses specific issues we believe will have a great impact on the Japanese PC industry.

As you pointed out in your July issue, the Japanese distribution system resembles the American system in the early 1980's. While any generalizations about Japan are dangerous, many aspects of the Japanese computer installed base such as end-user sophistication, degree of LAN integration and amount of migration from Mini's and Mainframes that has taken place, can best be described as similar to America in the early 1980s. This is, however, changing rapidly and should near parity with America in the next 5 to 7 years.

While I don't agree with Mr. Matsuo's comment that demand for US computer products outstrips supply, I do believe that Japanese companies rarely fall victim to the NIH (Not Invented Here) trap and that there are real opportunities for long term growth in

Japan. However, the reputation Japan has gained for being a difficult market is well deserved, and companies such as Mr. Matsuo's and Mr. Takahashi's can provide invaluable guidance. For example, in your Japanese distribution article in the July issue, you present a hypothetical example of a software publisher who takes advantage of the demand for his product, created by a distributor who has invested heavily in marketing and promotion, and switches to a discount distributor. This, in Japan, is an almost certain recipe for failure. It would be considered a major breach of faith and would completely wreck the publisher's credibility, making future deals with any major players extremely difficult.

I encourage anybody who is considering making a move into Japan or just has questions to call or Fax me. I will do my best to answer any questions and am always interested in hearing about others' experiences.

Sincerely,
David Zook
M.P. Technology
Shinjuku-ku, Sanei-cho 8, #501
Rokuyu 25 Bldg
Tokyo, Japan 160
TEL 81-3-3358-9800
FAX 81-3-3358-9802

Dear David,

Thanks for the information and the offer of help. I sense that the Japanese market will be a major opportunity for the companies who can find a niche and fill it.

I have two clients who have Japanese distributors and they both have found a major distributor who made quite significant guaranteed payments to my clients. These were multi year deals so the amount of money was $200K to $600K which was significant.

In both of the cases, with extremely different products, the distributor's sales in Japan have been extremely disappointing. Both of these distributors have lost money several years into the deal. Unlike US companies, they view this as part of their investment in opening the market. When there is a high barrier to entry in a market, you can justify making an investment to open the market since you will have a much greater opportunity to exploit the market.

I would also be interested in hearing from readers about their experiences with selling in Japan.

Thanks again for your comments.
Dave

D. Distribution Survey (1990)

1. Results of Distribution Survey are Analyzed

We got quite a good response to the distribution survey. The respondents were consistent with the Software Success Readership except that we had fewer companies who sold both hardware and software. I would guess that companies who sold hardware were somewhat competitive with dealers who want to add software value to their hardware.

Company Type	% Resp
Software Publisher	38.1%
Software and Hardware	9.5%
Software Developer	54.8%

The median revenue was the same as the reader survey, but there were more companies with over $5M in Revenue.

Annual Software Revenue	% Resp
<$250K	9.5%
$250K-$500K	11.9%
$500K-$1M	31.0%
$1M-$2M	14.3%
$2M-$5M	7.1%
>$5M	11.9%

This survey included more system utility companies than the reader survey which surprised me.

Type Of Software	% Resp
Vertical	52.4%
Horizontal	16.7%
System Utilities	26.2%
Horizontal Micro	9.5%

There were significantly more companies with products less than $1,000. It was also interesting to note that the firms in this survey had products in more categories. I believe that some of them had introduced lower priced products to get distribution.

Price Per Unit %	Resp
$1K	35.7%
$1K-$10K	38.1%
$10K-$25K	23.8%
$25K-$100K	23.8%
$100K	7.1%

As expected, these companies make more use of distribution, but they also make much more use of telemarketing and significantly more use of OEM sales. All in all the respondents to this survey were trying more alternative channels. They were more sophisticated in their approach.

Sales Channel	% Resp	% Rdr
Direct	92.9%	83%
Telemarketing	42.9	32%
VAR/ Dlr/ Dist	54.8%	46%
OEM	19.0	12%

As you can see in the table below, most of the companies get most of their sales directly.

Telemarketing is not used by 64 percent of the respondents. Only 4.8 percent of the respondents get over 75 percent of their sales via telemarketing.

Only half of the respondents use VARs, Dealers, or Distributors. Again it is difficult to get over 75 percent of your sales through distribution.

Seventeen percent of the companies have OEM arrangements which is higher than typical. Only 4.8 percent of the companies get over 10 percent of their sales from OEM deals and no one gets over 50 percent of their sales by OEM.

CPUs Supported	% Resp%	RDR
Micro/ PC7	6.2%	74%
Lan/ Multi-user	57.1%	38%
Mini	38.1%	35%
Mainframe	16.7%	21%

We had more LAN product offerings which may be due in part to the changes in the last six months. I also believe that this reflects the fact that LANs are hot with dealers. They may not sell a lot of LAN products, but they sure love to talk about it. This motivates vendors who want to sell through dealers to provide a LAN version.

Percent of Sales by CPU

Percent of Sales	Micro	LAN	Mini	Mainframe
No reply	28.6%	50.0%	69.0%	88.1%
< 10%	2.4%	19.0%	2.4%	2.4%
10%-25%	9.5%	14.3%	7.1%	0.0%
25%-50%	7.1%	7.1%	2.4%	2.4%
50%-75%	7.1%	2.4%	4.8%	2.4%

We had fewer mainframe companies which reflects the fact that there is less distribution for mainframe products.

As you can see from the table below, most of the companies which sell micros make most of their sales on micros, while very few companies make significant sales on LANs. Companies which sell minis and mainframes tend to sell mainly on this primary platform, but they are more mixed. I suspect that some of them have introduced PC versions to open up larger markets for their base technology.

The most common number of prospects is 1,000 to 10,000 which is a common number for a good vertical market. For example, there are 8,000 software companies. The second most common population is over 100,000 which is your classical mass market.

Number Of Prospects	% Resp
No Reply	7.1%
<1K	9.5%
1K-10K	42.9%
10K-25K	11.9%
25K-100K	9.5%
>100K	19.0%

Regarding Distribution	% Resp
No Reply	2.4%
Never Tried	23.8%
Tried and Failed	19.0%
Still Trying	26.2%
Succeeded	28.6%

Realizing that this is a biased sample because companies who had never tried to build a distribution program would be less likely to complete this survey, fifty percent more people succeeded than failed. On the other hand, there are an equally large number of companies who are still trying. In my experience, many of these are failures who haven't admitted that they have failed yet.

Most of the companies were either average in the documentation or excellent. I expect that if you feel that your packaging is rudimentary that you aren't even thinking about distribution.

I wonder about the people who feel that they have average documentation. It would be okay to be average if you were comparing yourself with others who are selling at retail. If you are average with companies who are selling direct, you may have a real problem.

Packaging/ Documentation	% Resp
Rudimentary	4.8%
Average	45.2%
Excellent	54.8%

Percent of Sales by Channel

Percent of Sales	Direct	TM	VAR	OEM
No reply	11.9%	64.3%	47.6%	83.3%
< 10%	11.9%	9.5%	11.9%	9.5%
10%-25%	7.0%	9.5%	11.9%	2.4%
25%-50%	16.7%	7.1%	11.9%	2.4%
50%-75%	11.9%	7.1%	9.5%	0.0%
> 75%	40.5%	4.8%	7.1%	0.0%

I was really surprised that so many of the products required more than a week of training. I am very surprised that people consider trying to get distribution with a product which requires over a week of training. There are a couple problems for a reseller with this type of product:

Complex products require a complex sell which make the sales job more difficult. The reseller must train their technical people well enough to make sales calls. The reseller is faced with a tough decision to either train their people or lose the support and training revenue.

I would have thought that products which required less than one week of training would be marginal for distribution, but companies must be finding creative solutions to these technical support and training issues. I would like to hear from readers who have dealt with these issues.

Training Required	% Resp
None	11.9%
<1 day	21.4%
<1 week	6.2%
>1 week	40.5%

There was a fairly even spread in the level of competition.

Level Of Competition	% Resp
High	28.6%
Medium	47.6%
Low	23.8%

Most people felt that it was difficult to get dealers or distributors to carry their products.

Difficulty Dealer/Dist	% Resp
No Reply	2.4%
High	54.8%
Medium	21.4%
Low	4.8%
Don't know	16.7%

2. Experience with Dealer Programs by Type of Software

All of the Horizontal product companies have tried to get dealers, and they have been fairly successful. Unless you are very well capitalized, you must have distribution to sell a vertical product to its fullest potential. You can start off selling direct through the mail and advertising, but you aren't getting all the prospects.

Vertical market companies and system utility product companies have been less willing to try and less successful. The vertical companies have failed almost as often as they have succeeded. The system utility firms don't fail they just keep trying. Their success rate is the same as the vertical market companies.

With a horizontal product, almost any dealer can carry your product. Almost by definition, their are no special training or support requirements for a vertical product. I am not sure that this is 100 percent true, but it applies to most of the horizontal products that I can think of. If you think about word processing, spread sheets, and data base products, they can all be sold without specialized knowledge. There is an implicit assumption that the horizontal vendor can provide phone support.

Vertical market companies must find dealers who either know their vertical market or are willing to make the investment to learn about their vertical market. This is a significant difference. I have worked with a number of vertical market companies trying to recruit dealers and time and time again I have seen prospective dealers who either knew the market or knew how to sell software, but didn't know both. Dealers who only have half of the requirements have a hard time succeeding. I have almost concluded that you shouldn't sign up a dealer unless they meet all the requirements. You are going to make a major investment in their training, and you can't afford to sign up dealers who fail.

	No Reply	Never Tried	Tried & Failed	Still Trying	Succeeded
Vertical	5%	27%	23%	18%	27%
Horizontal	0%	0%	14%	43%	43%
System Utility	0%	27%	0%	45%	27%

3. Experience with Dealer Programs by Price per unit.

For the most part, lower priced products are more likely to achieve successful distribution. You are also more likely to try to get distribution the lower your price is. The only exception are the products valued over $100,000. There were only a few products in that category, so I would discount those results. I suspect that lower price corresponds to easy to use which is what the dealers really want.

	No Reply	Never Tried	Tried & Failed	Still Trying	Succeeded
< $1K	0%	13%	13%	20%	53%
$1K-$10K	0%	25%	13%	25%	38%
$10K-$25K	10%	40%	0%	30%	20%
$25K-$100K	0%	30%	30%	30%	10%
> $100K	0%	0%	67%	0%	33%

4. Experience with Dealer Programs by CPUs supported.

Micro products have been most successful, which isn't surprising since most of the VARs and dealers are micro-oriented. One-third of the micro companies had successfully built a dealer program, which is pretty good.

Mini products have been reasonably successful getting dealers, but minis have more failures. I was also surprised that so many mini vendors had tried to get distribution. I guess this is from the network of mini-oriented VARs who where technically sophisticated and sold sophisticated software with minis as turnkey solutions.

LANs have also gotten more failures, but they have a reasonably good success rate. I expect that the LAN failure rate is higher than the micro because so many micro dealers try to sell LAN solutions, but don't know what they are doing. Their failures become your failures.

The mainframe companies never fail, they just keep on trying. Few of the mainframe companies feel that they have been successful.

	No Reply	Never Tried	Tried & Failed	Still Trying	Succeeded
Micro/PC	0%	25%	13%	28%	34%
LAN/Multi User	0%	17%	25%	33%	25%
Mini	6%1	3%	25%	25%	31%

5. Experience with Dealer Programs by Number of Prospects

In general, the more prospects you have, the more likely your dealer program was. The only exception was the less than 1,000 market. I suspect that that isn't statistically valid.

I am really impressed that all of the companies with more than 100,000 prospects have either succeeded or are continuing. None of them failed or never tried. Perhaps all the companies with more than 100,000 prospects who failed to get distribution went out of business.

The other interesting fact is that as your market gets larger you are much more likely to try to establish a dealer program (e.g. the percent never tried drops). The failure percentage is 20 percent to 25 percent except for the markets over 100,000. I suspect this is just an indication that somewhere between 1/2 and 1/3 of products just aren't good enough to succeed in distribution. The failure rate drops as the market size increases because there is more pressure to make your product acceptable to distribution if you are selling to a larger market.

	No Reply	Never Tried	Tried & Failed	Still Trying	Succeeded
<1K	0%	50%	25%	0%	25%
1K-10K	6%	28%	22%	33%	11%
10K-25K	0%	20%	20%	20%	40%
25K-100K	0%	25%	25%	0%	50%

6. Experience with Dealer Programs by Training Required

If your product has less than one day of training, you can't fail to get dealers. Seriously, products with less than one day of training have a 50 percent chance of success. Depending upon the outcome with the "still trying" accounts, the final success rate could be pretty good.

When the training required goes above a day, the failure rate goes up and the success rate drops dramatically. I believe that this is the limit of what dealers can handle. If your product requires more than a day of training, the dealer has to make a major investment in training his own people to be able to provide training. If the dealer doesn't make that investment, he is only selling hardware, which is a low-margin business.

	No Reply	Never Tried	Tried & Failed	Still Trying	Succeeded
None	0%	20%	0%	40%	40%
< 1 day	0%	11%	0%	44%	44%
< 1 week	0%	27%	27%	18%	27%
> 1 week	6%	29%	29%	18%	18%

7. Experience with Dealer Programs and difficulty getting dealers.

As you would expect, companies who succeeded feel that it is less difficult to get dealers than either those who failed or those who are still trying, but the difference isn't as dramatic as you might think. In my experience, it is initially difficult for almost everyone to get dealers and making them successful. As a company begins to build a dealer network, it gets easier because they get smarter and because new dealers are willing to follow the dealer network. Dealers often act based on advice from their peers. This would explain why companies with successful dealer programs thought it was easier to get dealers. Now that they are successful, it is easier. Surprisingly enough, 42 percent of the successful companies still feel that it is difficult to get dealers. They have just learned how to do it.

	No Reply	High	Medium	Low	Don't Know
Never Tried	0%	30%	10%	0%	60%
Tried & Failed	0%	75%	13%	0%1	3%
Still Trying	9%	73%	18%	0%	0%
Succeeded	0%	42%	42%	17%	0%

8. Experience with Dealer Programs and Percent Dealer Sales

I was surprised that some firms who never had tried to get dealers got 10 percent of their sales through dealers. It was also interesting that some firms whose dealer program had failed were still getting 25 percent to 50 percent of their revenue through the dealers. The companies who were still trying were getting mixed results. In fact, they were getting fewer dealer sales than those who had failed. Success can mean quite different things to different people, but most of the companies who were successful got over 25 percent of their sales though dealers and many of them were over 50 percent. My experience is that if you begin to get some momentum in the dealer channel, you have to commit all of your sales through dealers. I have never seen a really successful dealer program where the vendor also sold significant product direct.

	No Reply	< 10%	10%-25%	25%-50%	50%-75%	> 75%
Never Tried	80%	20%	0%	0%	0%	0%
Tried & Failed	25%	38%	25%	13%	0%	0%
Trying	55%	18%	9%	0%	9%	9%
Succeeded	8%	0%	8%	25%	25%	33%

This survey was analyzed using Quik Poll from TBX. I have been using Quik Poll to analyze my surveys. It is very easy to use and allows you to tabulate and do cross tabs. The price is $495. TBX, 106 Woodcrest Dr., Rome, GA 30161, (404) 234-4260

E. Directories and Other Information on Dealers and Distributors (1990)

The following factors give you the best chance of building a successful dealer program. That isn't to say that you can't do it if you don't have one of these characteristics, but they all help.

Horizontal product
Price $1K
Micro or Mini
>100K Prospects
< 1 day training

1. National Association of Computer Dealers (NACD)

The NACD publishes a number of books which cover manufacturers, Distributors, Service Companies, and Secondary Dealers. These books are in the Profile series which start at $99.95. (It is a twelve volume set.) They also publish the National Directory, which is "the industry's Yellow Pages" - $49.95.

NACD
13103 FM 1960 West #206
Houston, TX 77065
(800) 223-5264
(713) 894-1983

2. Distributor Phone Numbers

Dear Dave:

I just received the 1989 Reference Book that I ordered. It looks like it will have a great deal of useful information. However, one thing that I was hoping it would have is the phone numbers for Micro D and Softsell. If you have this information, could you fax it to me?

Thank you,
Scott Warner
Athena

Chapter IV. Distribution

Dear Scott:

The phone numbers are
Ingram Micro D
(800) 456-8000 or
Softsell
(213) 412-1700
Dave

3. Microcomputer Dealer Channel

Chromatic offers their database list on disk and on paper for unlimited usage. Their address is:

Chromatic Communications Enterprises, Inc.
P.O. Box 30127
Walnut Creek, CA 94598
(415) 945-1602

The costs and counts are:

	US	Canada
Paper	$345	$325
Disk	$595	$495
No. of Stores	5,135	1,126
No. of Contacts	7,367	1,543

4. International Legal Issues

Dear Dave,

In this global marketplace of the 1990's, it will be critical for software companies doing business outside the Untied States to understand the international laws and regulations governing their businesses.

If your readers would like some information on this topic, I have some publications that might be of interest to them.

Very truly yours,
Susan H. Nycum
Baker & McKenzie
960 Hansen Way
Palo Alto, CA 94304
(415)856-2400

Dear Susan,

I enjoyed reading the articles that you sent me, and I think that anyone who is involved or contemplating getting involved with international sales could benefit by reading them.

For my readers, your firm is the world's largest law firm with offices around the world, and you are a partner specializing in representation of software companies.

Having international representation is critical if you are going to do business internationally. I have a client who was owed $50,000 by a distributor who used every excuse in the book. Within three months of getting a local attorney, my client got their money.

Dave

5. Foreign Distribution Channels

Dear Dave:

In recent months I've been involved with developing foreign distribution channels for high technology hardware and other products. In each case, foreign distributors of these products have urged me to supply them with software products as well as hardware. In particular, it seems there is a crying need for PC-based software products in Japan.

In response to this need, I've put together a team of experts who specialize in exporting U.S. products to foreign markets. One person, Alex Mavronicles, is a long-time resident of Japan and has extensive contacts there. He reports that English is much more suited for Japanese business than is the native language. Therefore, most large Japanese businesses require the use of English in internal communications. Thus, many U.S. software products are readily exportable to the Japanese market because little or no product modification is required.

On the other hand, the European expert on the team, Barbara Le'ger, reports that Continental Europeans prefer to interface with the software in their native tongue. This often means modification of output screens and reports is necessary before the product can be sold. Barbara has helped numerous companies enter the European market and is excited about joining Alex and me in this endeavor.

If any of your readers are interested in the Asian, European, or other foreign markets, please have them contact me at (408) 973-0297 or FAX: (408) 973-9063.

Sincerely,
Jim Shaw
Shaw Resources

6. Experience Porting to the NEC Personal Computer

Tapping into the Japanese Market

We are thinking about going into the Japanese market, and we are investigating porting our product to the NEC Personal Computer, which has 70 percent of the Japanese market. We found a company in Seattle which specializes in ports to the NEC, but their prices appear high. Do you know of any other alternatives?

I don't know of anyone else porting their own products to the NEC on their own. My experience is that the first step is to find a distributor or agent in Japan who thinks that there is a market for your product in Japan.

One of the judgements that your distributor should make is to what machines your product should be ported. In most cases, the distributor arranges for and pays for the port. It may be an advance against royalties, but they provide the cash. I would be very reluctant to invest money in a technical port without a strong indication that there really is a Japanese market for your product.

7. Another OEM Deal

Dear Dave:

We have a software product which adds value to a class of hardware boards. We sell our software directly, but our sales have been disappointing. We have been approached by one of the hardware vendors. They would like to OEM our product. One of their competitors has already bundled software with their board. It appears that the hardware company that contacted us is concerned. It also appears that they don't have the technical capability to produce this software with their current staff. If they hired someone with the right background it might take a man year to develop the equivalent functionality.

We sell single copies of our product to end users at $150. We sell single copies to resellers for $100. We push a five pack for $250 to resellers or $50 per copy. Most of our sales are at the $50 per copy price.

What should we expect from this arrangement, and how should we try to structure the deal?

Signed,
Anonymous

Dear Anonymous:

You also mentioned that the hardware company had approached the third (and only other software company) and they had rejected them because of product quality. Thus, your direct competition for this contract is some unknown developer who is probably working on his bid to develop the software for the hardware company.

You felt that this bid might be $100,000, based on the skill level required to do the work. I think that you might get a maximum of $125,000. If you ask much more than that, the hardware company will be very tempted to develop it themselves.

The hardware company is selling slightly more than 1,000 units a year, and their sales appear to be increasing. You expected them to sell this product, or a follow-on for the next five to ten years. They are financially sound and you aren't in any great hurry to get the cash up front.

I felt that you might get $75,000 if you wanted the cash up front, and you might get $25 per unit with a 1,000 per year guarantee for five years with a cap of $125,000. The $25 per unit is half the dealer price, which seems high to me. The board was an $800 board, so $25 per unit is three percent of retail which probably seems very high to the hardware vendor. Given the cost of developing this software, they may not be able to avoid this high cost. If you price it like this, you are protecting your interests, and you shouldn't be undercut by the programmer who submitted the bid to them.

Good luck,
Dave

8. A Bundling Deal

I am often approached by companies who would like other more prestigious companies to bundle their product. In most cases, the host company doesn't feel any pressure to do this and the small company usually invests a great deal of time and energy with nothing to show for it.

I received a press release from Interactive Development Environments (IDE) on their reselling Saber, FrameMaker, and Interleaf. They hailed this as their "new expansion strategy - IDE becomes a CASE Environment Integrator."

I would like to point out that IDE is reselling these other products. This is a practical approach to this problem. If you would like to integrate other products, I suggest that you follow IDE's approach and resell the other products.

I would expect that making modifications to the other products to allow them to tightly integrate is much more difficult to accomplish. I have been involved in a number of these discussions which haven't worked out. It just seems that it is too complicated and too many people want it to fail. In particular, the development people for the other products don't want to have to deal with you modifying their code.

The one approach that I have seen work is for one of the companies to modify their product by providing an exit that anyone can use. The other company can achieve the tighter integration without interacting with the development team once the exit is done.

9. Japanese Market - Results of a Survey by Market Share and Babson College

Dear Dave:

We have recently conducted a survey of U.S. computer companies currently selling their products in Japan in conjunction with the MBA program at Babson College. We mailed 700 surveys and more than ten percent responded to the ten-page survey. Forty-four percent said that they currently export to Japan. The exporter's average revenue was $62.5 million while the average of all of the respondees was $47 million.

Eighty percent of the companies selling in Japan used distributors, but we felt that very few of them have used the distributor relationship to its fullest.

Most found the Japanese distributor a way to lower risk, speed up product sales, and learn Japanese business practices quickly. Very few companies use their distributor as a source of venture capital. None of the companies use their distributor to gain access to new technology or monitor competitors, as Japanese companies often do.

The survey also showed that more than half the companies selling products in Japan had been approached by a Japanese distributor, rather than having pro-actively sought one. Most companies entered distributor agreements with little or no knowledge about the distributor, its customer base, or its corporate affiliations.

Marketshare has successfully matched dozens of U.S. companies with appropriate Japanese distribution partners.

The company has developed a checklist of what to look for in a Japanese distribution partner, and a set of questions that help predict whether a company can successfully sell products in Japan. Both are available at no charge if your readers call or write me.

Sincerely,

James H. Geisman
President
Marketshare, Inc.
21 Cochituate Rd
Wayland, MA 01778
(508) 358-2154
(508) 358-6350 FAX

F. Traditional Distribution (1989)

Retail distribution is new to the computer industry because only very recently have computer products been offered at retail prices. A $100,000 minicomputer system is a direct sale; such is not the case for $5,000 microcomputers and $100 software products. Thus I believe that our industry's problems with retail distribution largely reflect our inexperience in this area. Below, I will present some sample articles that discuss distribution for more mature industries. Don't let the fact that these articles aren't specific to the software industry keep you from learning the lessons they offer.

1. Retail Chain Buyer's Decision Factors

Two university professors asked thirty-six buyers (i.e., purchasing agents) at five grocery store chains how they decide to support one manufacturer's product promotion over another. Responses were as follows, listed in descending order of importance.

Manufacturer Reputation A solid reputation depends upon both the quality of the promotion as well as the service provided to the dealer.

Item Profitability This is based on the gross margin of the product before the specific promotional deal being offered.

Promotion Elasticity This is how responsive the item is to promotion; i.e., how much will sales increase as a result.

Item Importance This refers to the buyer's receptiveness to this type of promotion at this time.

Promotion Wearout This results from overexposure of the buyer to the promotion; it will hurt the prospects of a promotion.

Sales Velocity This factor represents dollars per unit time; it can motivate buyers to push secondary brands.

Incentive Amount This dealer discount, when combined with item profitability and promotion elasticity, determines the profitability of the product being promoted.

Manufacturer Brand Support This factor was rated last because buyers assumed it would be good, and thus it wasn't a differentiating factor.

I was fascinated by the complexity of the buyer decision process. It wasn't a simple economic analysis. The fact that manufacturer reputation was first is very interesting. I suspect this has to do with a desire on the part of buyers to minimize risk. Manufacturers with a reputation for good promotions are more likely to insure that a particular promotion succeeds. By contrast, a terrific deal from a poor manufacturer may not, in the buyer's mind, be worth its risk. This may be in part due to the risk/reward system for the individual buyer. For example, if they back a "good" promotion, no one will fire them for not getting a better deal. However, if they take a chance on a risky promotion with very high profit potential, they could be in trouble personally if it fails dramatically. This situation is analogous to software evaluators in large corporations.

REFERENCE: "What's Key to Retail Support? Survey Quotes Buyers, Who Say it's Reputation, Reliability.", by Amy E. Gross, Promote, October 10, 1988.

2. Real Life in Consumer Distribution

Most of us in the software industry are impressed with consumer product distribution techniques, such as coupons and point of sale displays. We wonder why the computer industry can't have the same level of sophistication with regard to distribution. A recent ADWEEK article discusses conflict in the distribution channels for consumer products. I was surprised at the percentage of their budgets manufacturers spend on promoting products to the trade (retail store purchasing agents) and the resulting reduction in promotional dollars directed toward consumers. The numbers presented in ADWEEK are as follows:

	1984	1988
Trade	35%	44%
Consumers	30%	25%

This situation has gotten so bad that Procter & Gamble has stated publicly that it intends to reduce trade promotion spending so it can spend more on consumer advertising. At the same time, retailers are competing with manufacturers by selling private label brands. To shed more light on this tug of war, let's consider some of the ways in which retailers are extracting money from manufacturers.

Super Valu Stores demand that manufacturers pay a flat fee of $2,000 for every new product that doesn't meet its sales quota. These "failure fees" are catching on among food distributors. Lucky Stores sets per-product sales figure quotas that must be met within 120 days. If a quota is not met, it requires the manufacturer to pay the retail cost of any unsold inventory. Adding fuel to the fire is the breathtaking pace of new food product introductions. The number of new food products introduced per unit time reminds one of the software industry. For instance, there were 7,000 new food items in 1984, and there will be as many as 12,000 in 1989. The failure rate on new food items is 50% to 90%, depending on the type of item. Because of this, retailers have begun to pass costs along to manufacturers in addition to failure fees. Examples of costs now being passed to manufacturers include:

Presentation fees of $50 to $500 for making a sales presentation to a retailer's employee.

Survey fees for a retail chain to survey its own stores.

Slotting allowances may be cash or free product in return for a retailer stocking a new item.

Trade allowances are discounts for buying product in volume, as well as fees for in-store demonstrations, store displays and ads in store circulars.

Annual renewal fees are paid to keep a good product on the shelf for another year, even if it is meeting its sales quota.

REFERENCE: "Conflict in the Aisles: Getting Them Coming and Going.", by Christine Donahue, ADWEEK's Marketing Week, September 4, 1989

G. Dealers and VARs (1989)

This section begins by defining and providing background information on dealers, VARs, VADs and other types of resellers. Statistics are presented regarding who they are and how they are doing financially. Next, features of several successful VAR programs are tabulated. Completing this section is a review of recently announced dealer programs.

1. Definitions

Value-Added Resellers (VARs) resell hardware and provide a total or turnkey solution. The average VAR has been in business 5.5 years and had gross revenues of $1.4 million in 1988. Many VARs were formerly OEMs who took minicomputer hardware and provided software to form a complete solution. Their margins were very good so long as they were selling systems with prices in the hundreds of thousands of dollars. The sharp drop in hardware prices that began with the introduction of microcomputers has forced these companies to rethink their strategies.

Independent Software Vendors (ISVs) sell their own and other vendors' software packages. Often they modify packages on a custom basis. They don't sell hardware.

Value-Added Dealers (VADs) are high-class storefront retail operations. They sell off-the-shelf hardware and software and add value in terms of installation and support. These firms are under extreme margin pressure and appear to be reducing the level of service they provide since they have difficulty getting paid for it.

System Integrators purchase and interconnect hardware and software from numerous vendors. They are independent of any particular hardware vendor. Many of them are very large and service federal and state governments.

Storefront Resellers push iron, i.e., off-the-shelf hardware. They have an outbound sales force because often only 20% of their business comes from walk-ins. They may offer classes to attract prospects, but they don't see themselves as being in the service business.

2. Background Information

The number of microcomputer VARs grew 28% annually from 1983 to 1987. In absolute terms it grew from 1,800 software and hardware VARs in 1983 to 4,750 in 1987. "Analysts are predicting minimal growth for the next five years to slightly more than 5,000 through '92."

REFERENCE: "VARs: Growth Stabilizing", Computer Retail News, February 29, 1988.

If you look more closely you see hundreds of small computer stores losing money and closing their doors. To date, 1,500 such stores have closed their doors forever. There have also been a number of mergers. Intelligent Electronics acquired Entre and

Chapter IV.   Distribution

Converging Point, and Businessland is acquiring Dardick, Inc.

Reference: "Computer Retailers Crash, Burn, Bleed", by Michael S. Malone, San Jose Mercury News, October 2, 1989.

The margins for computer dealers have dropped from over 34 percent in 1979 to below 20 percent today. These are figures assembled by Sherman Uchill, a consultant who sold his dealership in 1988. Sherman believes that this margin pressure has killed dealer support and service.

Reference: "PC Industry Slowdown Reveals Flaws in Dealer Channel", By John Gantz, Infoworld, July 17, 1989.

Examining the statistics further, consultants and independent software vendors have margins of 24 to 25 percent, VARs, VADs, and System Integrators have margins of 22 percent, and storefront resellers have the lowest margins, only 17 percent. This data was collected in a survey of 2,500 VarBusiness subscribers conducted in August 1988 (see the reference below.)

Reference "The Widening Channel", VarBusiness, 1988 State of the Market by Michael McTwigan.

As the margin pressure on storefront resellers increases, (driven by the mass market discount retailers) these resellers begin to act as VARs. The VARs in turn begin to publish their own software. This migration toward specialization and higher end products is being encouraged by hardware and software vendors, who are looking for more efficient ways to sell their products and to train users. For example, Businessland recently announced that they will be carrying the Next Computer and are forming an Advanced Business Systems Division to focus on networking services.

3. Sample VAR Programs

Table 1 summarizes some basic information regarding several of the leading software companies that have successful VAR programs. As you can see there are certainrequirements that all dealers should meet. For example, every reseller needs a valid resale license. In addition, you need to have each one fill out a credit application. You must establish financial guidelines that must be met before you extend credit. Toll-free telephone support must be available to all dealers. Large manufacturers typically do not charge for marketing materials.

4. Seven Dealer Programs Reported in the Press

I recently collected a random sample of seven press releases announcing dealer programs. The results are summarized below. Many of these exemplify vendors trying to attract dealers.

Sanyo announced that within the last year they had doubled their reseller base to 600. They felt their success resulted from a "virtual exclusivity since all orders are channeled directly through territorial manufacturer's reps". They also have a one price policy for all dealers (i.e., price does not vary with volume) that inhibits the development of a grey market. They also don't sell to "distributors, warehouse clubs, mail order companies, or organizations that cannot offer service and support".

Practical Computer Technologies, Inc. sells add-on disk drives. Their press release announced a no-nonsense dealer assistance program for small and medium-sized dealers. They offer co-op advertising money and provide technical and marketing support during and after the sale. There are no quotas or cumbersome qualifications.

American Business Systems, Inc. released the following: "ABS offers new dealers a free, in-house accounting system, plus instant discounts during its summer recruitment program." The free sign-up incentive package is valued at up to $1,500 (at dealer list price), and allows the dealer to use the software they sell. Dealers also get automatic entry into the "Super Dealer" program at the 10% discount level with an initial order of $1,200 instead of the normal $3,000 requirement.

Borland introduced its "champion program" to identify resellers and send them additional materials. The materials include a "three ring binder reseller guide with product spec sheets."

Unify 's "VAR Sales Accelerator" program offers resellers support in sales, marketing, and business planning. They also offered their development system at an 80% discount off list. The program offers consulting, promotional and demo materials.

Program Requirements

	Marc	Micropro	R Systems	WordPerfect
Number of Resellers	200	2,500	415	2,500
License Requirements	State Requirements	Purchase Commitments Reseller Tax ID	Resale tax ID Dealer training	Resale tax ID Distributor arrang.
Market support	Demo copies Training Joint sales calls	Point of purchase materials Joint sales Calls no charge	Literature Leads No charge	Literature No charge
Technical Support	800# no$ Users pay	800# no$ Users pay	800# no$	800# no$
Reseller Selection	Credit appl Two weeks	Minimum purchase requirement Four days	Hw and OS knowledge Ability to respond to customer needs 5-10 days	Consultants work out of home/VARs at home or business 10 days

Systems Plus Inc. announced four reseller training seminars. These two day conferences prepare their dealers to market, sell, install and train users on all of their accounting modules. There is a $250 fee which entitles a dealer to attend the seminar and receive all course materials.

Microrim 's program, called the Sales Promotion Allowance (SPA), offers incentives for aggressive R:Base resellers. Under this program, resellers receive allowances to offset promotional investments. The funds are provided for mutually agreed upon sales promotion programs. This is in addition to their Merchandising Performance Allowance (MPA) and Market Development Funds (MDF). The latter is similar to other co-op programs.

H. Key Business Issues and Trends (1989)

This section discusses a number of issues that are becoming of increasing importance for software sellers.

1. Allocating Your Marketing Mix

A key decision when implementing product distribution plans involves allocating your marketing resources between push and pull through programs. Push marketing focuses on attempts to close a sale. One example is a sales person calling on a dealer or end user. Pull through marketing techniques create company awareness, leave a positive impression and generate sales leads.

Manufacturer reputation is built by pull through marketing. A public relations effort that places articles about your technology is an example of pull through marketing. I believe that, in general, most software companies allocate too much of their marketing budgets and efforts to push marketing and not enough to pull through marketing. This in turn makes it much more difficult for push marketing to work. Once you understand how your dealers decide what products to carry and which ones to push, you can decide how to allocate your marketing budget. As a rule of thumb, spend more at the outset on pull through than push. When more than 10 dealers who don't stock your product have called saying they have a customer for your product, start a larger push program.

2. Maturing of Software Distribution

While I haven't seen among software retailers the types of extreme demands found among consumer product retailers (see "Real Life in Consumer Distribution" above), I would expect movement in this direction as the software industry matures. During this maturing process, experienced people from the retail business will move into computer retailing and the distribution channels will begin to be consolidated. By consolidation, I mean a reduction in the number of companies owning and operating sales outlets. Rather than being disgusted by the prospect of paying these fees, we must understand that retailers and manufacturers have found this to be the best way for this business to work. I suspect that the same fundamental realities will come into play in the software industry over time.

With regard to computer industry consolidation, an article Business Marketing indicates that this process is already occurring. For instance, according to StoreBoard Inc., the market share of microcomputer sales by type of dealer is:

	1985	1988
Independents	45%	40%
Chains	37%	34%
Franchises	18%	26%

REFERENCE: "The channel challenge", By Kate Bertrand, Business Marketing, May 1989.

I would expect that retail software revenues are even more consolidated since many of the independent retail stores are pushing cheap hardware, while the large chains like Egghead sell a broad line of software. In the coming years, I expect major chains and

franchises to charge software manufacturers stocking and other fees to carry their products. As these retailers gain market dominance, their ability to extract additional concessions will increase. I would be very interested to hear about your individual experiences with such distribution concessions.

The break between Compaq and Businessland may be an example of the type of battle to be fought as computer industry retail outlets are consolidated. Businessland negotiated steep discounts with both IBM and Apple, but Compaq refused to match those discounts. Compaq elected to spend its money on promotions for its resellers in an effort to insure that the resellers are profitable. Compaq feels that giving the resellers discounts will result in the retailers cutting their prices rather than spending the additional margin on product promotion.

3. Channel Conflict

Every retailer is worried about channel conflict, especially when channels of distribution are in flux as they are now. Historically, VARs have focused on vertical markets and the retail chains have gone after Fortune 1000 accounts with outbound sales teams. I expect that these boundaries will blur as the level of competition increases.

Software-only Retailers

The software-only retailers have experienced dramatic growth in the last three to four years. Their size and growth rates are astounding. According to an article in Business Marketing, the leading chains and their current numbers of stores are:

Chain Name	# of Stores
Software, Etc.	240
Egghead	180
Babbages, Inc.	121
Software City Inc	90

At the outset, these chains exploited the fact that hardware retailers didn't promote software because their salespeople were busy selling hardware. The hardware stores were reluctant to commit shelf space to software because they were getting better margins from hardware at the time. Finally, as the market for software grew, software-only chains

Chapter IV. Distribution

could economically exploit this niche, resulting in their heady growth.

One surprising statistic in this article was how successful these chains have been with corporate buyers. It cites a 1988 survey by Sentry Market Research reporting that software distributors (including the chains mentioned above) were the most preferred source with 42% of the corporate buyers, software publishers were second with 24%, and retail stores were third with 15%. The software-only chains offer a great combination of good prices and very good service, including returns and technical support.

If you have a PC product that is sold to the corporate market, you should try to get software-only chains to carry it. Even if they won't stock it in their stores, get them to stock it at their warehouse(s) and put it on their price lists. By doing so, the store can take the order and have it delivered by overnight mail. As the competition between these chains heats up, software vendors may gain leverage with software retailers that will help them move their products into new distribution channels.

REFERENCE: "Software's Hard Charging Channel", by Robert F.McCarthy, Business Marketing, October 1989.

4. Restocking Rights

The shelf life of most software packages is only four to six months, so stale inventory is an important issue. If resellers order a software product from a distributor, they can typically return it for a credit that can be applied to future orders. Distributors normally have sufficient clout with software vendors to insist on restocking rights. This is an important issue for a vendor with only one product. On the other hand, a vendor with multiple products can offset returns of one product with shipments of another product to the same distributor. Even if you have only one product, it is better to offer restocking rights to a distributor than to a reseller since the distributor can take returns from one reseller and offset them with orders from another reseller.

5. Emphasis for 1989

ABCD/Computer Dealers conducted a survey in 1988 asking reseller executives (of VADs, VARs, etc.) the question "In which of the following areas do you plan to increase your emphasis in 1989?" The responses were:

Area of Emphasis	% Responding
Sales of service, support, and training	75
Value added sales, less discounting	72
Sales of networking products	65
Sales to vertical markets	61
Consulting Services	44
Outbound sales to business, government and schools	42
Sales of software	33
Telemarketing	27
Rentals and Leasing	24
Home market sales	15
Low margin, large account sales	15
Mail order catalogue sales	10

As you can see, the vast majority of resellers want to move up market and add more value to each sale. They are fleeing mass market retailing, which thrives on high volumes and low margins.

6. Importance of Software or the Lack Thereof

I was a bit disappointed that software was of so little importance to the resellers surveyed by ABCD/Computer Dealers (see above). I think this reflects both the fact that reseller margins on software are no better than those on hardware (20%), and that unless they make a substantial investment, their software sales will follow the Softsell Hot List. Selling commodity software is really no different than hawking office supplies.

7. Selecting Products

Product selection is a difficult issue for resellers. To see how they go about this process, let's consider an article written by Michael Major, VP of Merchandising for Connecting Point Computer Centers. His approach breaks the analysis into the following sections: technical, support, merchandising and marketing, and profitability, giving each category equal weight. Each reseller is encouraged to alter the relative priorities to better match their own needs. His categories and the criteria for each are:

Technical Analysis

* **Quality assurance - Does it work?**

* **Specification performance - This would focus on software features.**

b. Support Analysis

* **Level of Support - What will be required of the dealer? Less is better.**

* **Training the end user - What will this cost the dealer?**

* **Training the infrastructure - What is required to train dealer employees?**

* **Technical compatibility issues - How will they be resolved? By the vendor.**

* **Serviceability - How easy is the product to service. This applies only to hardware.**

* **Vendor support - Vendor technical support, stock balancing, etc.**

c. Merchandising and Marketing Analysis

* **Position in the marketplace - Is the product a market leader? Will the dealer have to advertise to generate interest?**

* **Method of distribution - Is the dealer buying from a distributor? Will the distributor sell to other dealers? Will the vendor sales people sell direct in the dealer's territory? Will the dealer receive an exclusive in its territory? If so, for how long?**

* **Strategic or step - A strategic product is one that will enhance the credibility of the store. Step products are a step up from the standard offering and have higher margins, lower volumes, and lower quotas.**

* **Feature/function/value - Can the customers be convinced that this value is worth buying?**

* **Marketing programs - Are there co-op or market development funds available? Co-op funds are rebates which the dealer can use to market the product. Market development funds are typically cost-sharing co-op programs. What about contests and spiff programs for end users, sales people, dealership owners, etc?**

* **Point of sale materials - What brochures, banners, displays, etc., are available from the vendor?**

Profitability Analysis

* **What is the gross profit percentage?**

* **How will this affect cash flow? Cash flow is typically affected by vendor payment terms and frequency of shipments (which impacts inventory levels).**

* **What will be the support and marketing costs?**

The above approach is exhaustive. You may find dealers who aren't this organized, but they aren't likely to do well marketing your product. At the other end of the spectrum, the really successful firms probably have an even more extensive evaluation process. I urge you not to ignore these questions. You must address them if you hope to ever sell effectively through distributors. At the same time, consider these same issues with regard to your own direct sales. I find it useful to look at software companies as being comprised of both product and marketing companies. The marketing companies are similar to a captive dealership with an exclusive territory. Your captive dealership must face the same issues as the external dealer you are trying to recruit, except that they aren't as free to complain.

REFERENCE: "Evaluating Products: "Keeping the Emotions Out", by Michael Major, Reseller Management, July 1989.

8. Co-op Programs

Co-op programs are a common way for manufacturers to help their dealers sell products. Co-op funds, which are normally used to advertise or otherwise promote a product, typically range from 2% to 5% of gross purchases. This sounds like a great concept, but there are some difficulties with its application. The first reality is that most of the money set aside by vendors for co-op programs goes unused. This is especially true for smaller dealers. At the other end, very large resellers are known to take co-op money without running the corresponding promotions for a specific product. They will run a general ad or create a flyer in which the product is mentioned, and then take the entire co-op budget as a credit.

If you want to try a co-op program, start one on an experimental basis. Don't formally reserve 2% to 5% of your revenue, as your accountant may require you to accrue this as an expense even if it is not being spent.

Next, do everything you can to facilitate your dealer's promotions. I would suggest that you take your most effective marketing program and offer to tailor it for your dealers. You might allow them to use their co-op budget to modify your ad. Using your ad agency will reduce learning curve costs. I have also seen vendors offer advertising artwork to their dealers at cost as part of a dealer program. This type of service can significantly increase the number

Chapter IV. Distribution

of dealers who make use of your co-op program. Remember, if dealers make use of an effective marketing program, both the dealer and the vendor win.

Next, lay out and determine the cost of a full dealer marketing program. Then estimate the resulting sales and determine how you should establish a more complete dealer co-op program. Software companies often start by offering very high discounts to solicit new dealers at the time they establish their dealer channel. Dealers typically use these discounts to lower end user prices. While this might help sales in some cases, it doesn't fund the marketing program. I would consider giving dealers a very high co-op program rate (10% to 15%) for the initial six months to a year. Then I would cut the rate to 7.5% for the next year and 5% for the following year. I would talk to my dealers about these guidelines, but wouldn't commit myself beyond the first year. Such a program addresses the market recognition issues that dealers have with a new product and should help insure that your product gets the necessary exposure.

Q. How should I deal with co-op advertising with my reps and dealers?

A. Very carefully. Make sure that you provide them with ad copy and artwork which feature both your company and product name. (Don't forget to include trademarks and copyright notices.) You also need control over where they run the ads and how much you pay. While co-op advertising can be very effective, make sure you are getting your money's worth. You also need to set a time limit on how long the money is available. Make sure that you get *both* a copy of the advertisement in question *and a* copy of the invoice to them. It is very easy for a rep or dealer to think of the co-op money as theirs, and for them to bill you for ads that give you very little value.

Direct mail is more targeted so you don't have the issue on what percentage of the ad applies to you. The most generous direct mail co-op program is where the vendor to provides the brochures and sales literature and the dealer pays for the postage and stuffing the envelopes. If the vendor has mailing labels they may provide them or the dealer may get them out of the phone book. It is also very common for vendors to sell the sales literature at cost to their dealers.

The key with both of these types of programs is to ensure that you get what you are paying for. It is very easy for co-op programs to be a great waste of money, but if they are managed they can be very effective.

9. Exclusivity

Exclusivity is something that every reseller wants. They all fear making the investment necessary to develop the market for a product and then being unable to reap the benefits. On the other hand, the vendor is afraid of giving the reseller an exclusive territory that the reseller won't work properly; the result is fewer sales than expected. A common vendor reaction is: "Make the sales and I will give you the territory." The dealer's reaction is: "It takes time to develop a territory for a new product and it is very difficult for me to tell you how fast this will take place. The last thing I want is for this development to take slightly longer than expected, and then to have you authorize cut rate dealers in my territory who will reap the benefits of my investment."

Exclusivity is a difficult issue for most vendors. I have found that there are two widely used approaches to this problem. The first is to achieve the broadest distribution possible. The second is to attempt to develop a limited number of very good resellers. Which approach you choose depends upon the nature of the product. If a product can be sold as a black box without technical or sales support, broad distribution is the best approach. While you won't get support or any investment on the part of your dealers, this type of product doesn't require it.

On the other hand, if your product requires the reseller to invest both sales and technical time to learn the product, you really should give the reseller a reasonable exclusive. There are a number of cases in which prestigious vendors have given distributors an exclusive to secure their assistance in developing the market. For example, Aldus gave MicroAmerica an exclusive for PageMaker. This exclusive translated into a higher price to the dealer, but it motivated them to provide the higher level of support. Another benefit to the vendor is the ability to insist that the distributor or reseller pay immediately when the product is sold.

With an exclusive, the distributor typically commits to a minimum level of sales. If this level is not met,

Chapter IV. Distribution

the distributor either pays a penalty or loses the exclusive. This means of using an exclusive is an example of channel push. Properly managed, exclusives can be an important carrot to get and keep top quality resellers focused on your product.

I. Launching a Massive Dealer Program (1989)

1. Program Materials

If you have a great product which you believe will be of interest to and can be effectively sold by resellers, start by creating the documents describing your dealer program. These include a brochure about your dealer program and the various dealer agreements you will want them to sign. Refine these documents through several revisions before you actively market your program. As part of this process, take your package to the VARs and dealers you already know and ask them to review it. Also try to contact some local VARs and meet with them to see what they think about your materials. This package is extremely important. If it is amateurish, it will scare away any of the good VARs you might otherwise attract.

2. Attracting Dealers

Once you have the program materials, you must start marketing with them. Purchase appropriate dealer and VAR lists and develop a direct mail program to recruit dealers. Because VAR turnover is extremely great, I don't know of any list that is truly up-to-date. These lists also contain consultants and other types of businesses, especially when VARs have changed to consultants and then to dealers as they try different business formulas. In spite of this, it is important to have a sales piece (brochure). You will be generating VAR leads and you need to send them something other than your full dealer package.

The alternatives to direct mail for generating VAR leads include press releases and ads in dealer magazines. Given the volume of dealer program press releases, make sure you have something snappy to say and that it is well written. Otherwise you won't get the editor's or the VAR's attention. Also, editors get huge numbers of press releases, so be persistent.

Advertising in dealer magazines can be quite expensive. You might consider running classified ads with a headline such as "Looking For Quality Dealers".In my experience, getting an initial set of dealers is fairly easy. Establishing a profitable relationship for both the dealers and yourself is very difficult. Initially, you will have to expend the same energy with your dealers as you would with direct sales and will get only half the revenue. Experiment with a variety of techniques, including:

- **Local advertising**
- **Seminars with and without vendor participation**
- **Joint sales calls (vendor and VAR).**
- **Technical and sales training**
- **Special sales literature**
- **Demo systems**

This initial stage requires a major investment. Don't underestimate how big this might be. It is easy to spend $100,000 launching this type of program. You will have to dedicate a sales/marketing person to the dealer program. This person must travel to qualify dealers, run seminars, and go on joint sales calls. This is in addition to the advertising and direct mail costs, and the initial cost of developing the dealer package and recruiting materials.

3. Captive Dealership

Establishing a dealer program quickly is very expensive and very risky. As you know, it is hard to sell a new software package. It is even more difficult to sell a new software package developed by another company. Consider setting up a captive dealership. If you can't operate a dealership profitably as an adjunct to your software publishing business, why should anyone else be able to do so? Taking such an approach is educational and allows you to work out the kinks in your own marketing and sales equation. Once you have the equation, put it in writing and make it part of your dealer package. The practical experience of running a dealership will be invaluable in recruiting and qualifying dealers. Now you are ready to start to recruit additional dealers.

4. Additional Dealers

The approach I prefer is based on identifying key cities where you want to establish a dealer. These are often cities generating a steady stream of good leads. When visiting these cities, meet with dealers to begin the mutual qualification process. If you identify a good candidate, give them an exclusive based on the requirement that they generate a specified minimum sales volume. Give them six to nine months to achieve this level of sales.

Intensively support this new dealer. Have your dealer sales rep spend several days a month on site. You can't support a large number of new dealers during this stage. This is also the stage where it is easy for the relationship with a new dealer to go sour. If the dealer fails to reach sales goals and loses enthusiasm, you will have a hard time rekindling it in the future. For this reason, I have found it best to limit the number of dealers you sign up. One or two a month might be the maximum level you can support during this phase.

While in this phase, have your dealer sales person document the materials which will allow future new dealers to become effective with much less personal support. Develop the slides and script for a seminar for prospective users so that it can be done by a dealer. Develop a script for demos. Generate lists of questions and corresponding answers for a dealer's technical and sales personnel. As you develop these materials, send them out to new dealers. Track the time required to support new dealers and plot their sales success. Determine whether you are getting better at bringing new dealers up to speed. Improvements will generally result in part from better selection and in part from better training.

5. Dealer telephone support

As you reduce the time required to support new dealers, your dealer sales person can handle more new dealers. You will probably also need a person who handles the day to day dealer telephone support. Don't expect the dealer sales person to handle this role for very long. Their job is to continually recruit new dealers and get them up to critical mass and nothing should detract from their ability to accomplish this. Once a dealer is rolling, a maintenance person is required.

6. Reference

Q. Where can I get some information on building a distributor network for my software?

A. This is one of the most common questions we get from PC software companies (mainframe and mini companies ask about sales compensation). The American Management Association (AMA) has a three-day seminar on "Managing the Distributor Sales Network".

- **The AMA advises that the seminar will help attendees:**
- **Choose the right distributor for each market segment**
- **Make the market tell you who your distributors should be**
- **Increase your share of distributors' selling time**
- **Negotiate distributors' investments in your inventory**
- **Control the distributors' market areas - legally**
- **Get your sales force, manufacturers' agents and distributors to work together**
- **Structure distributor pricing and discounts**
- **Reduce your cost of sales dramatically**
- **Determine how many channels/tiers of distribution you really need**
- **Enforce service requirements**
- **Protect your patents, trademarks and logo**
- **Prevent legal problems**
- **Introduce new products through distributors**
- **Negotiate realistic sales forecasts with your distributors**
- **Measure distributors' markets**
- **Make joint sales calls more effective**

Even if you decide not to attend this seminar, we believe that this is a very good list of issues: everyone who is selling through distribution will face these problems. While this course isn't focused on software companies selling through dealers, we believe that it could be very good education for anyone trying to build a distributor network.

REFERENCE: To register or meeting information call (518) 891-0065 Ext. 410. It is a three day seminar which is available in Los Angeles, Boston, Dallas, Chicago and New York. The fee is $795 for AMA members and $915 for non-members.

7. Managing and encouraging Dealers & VARs

Q. How can I support, manage and encourage dealers and VARs?

A. In trying to identify the success factors in clients who have been successful in developing dealer networks in the last few years, we found a couple common points.

- **The companies were technically oriented and were committed to distribution.**
- **They had technically advanced products developed with 4GLs.**
- **The CEO was personally committed to this program and spent time with prospective and active VARs.**
- **They made the 12 to 18 month investment to get their initial VARs.**

While we don't know if these are truly requirements for building a new dealer network, we haven't seen many other cases of success in the last year or two. Once again, we would love to hear about your successes and your failures. (And for the mainframe and mini readers, we'd also like to hear about your efforts to get agents and reps.)

8. Sales Rep Compensation - Dealer Sales

Q. We sell primarily through distributors and dealers, and we would also like to have telemarketing sales reps call dealers and sell. It is difficult to directly attribute sales to this telemarketing effort because most of the dealers will place their orders through their distributor. In fact, we don't want to aggressively encourage direct sales and antagonize our distributors. How should we compensate these sales reps?

A. You are correct in assuming that the compensation package for these sales reps should be different than that for sales reps who are selling directly to customers. In general terms you must increase the fixed component of the compensation package for sales reps who call dealers. At the same time you want to motivate them as sales people. To do so requires some variable compensation which gives them the immediate feedback and thus motivation that sales people need. Consider the following approaches:

The first involves working with your distributors to sort sales information by region and then have your sales reps focus on a specific region. If one rep can call all your west coast dealers once a month, you could have a commission plan based on west coast sales.

Another approach combines a survey with the sales call. Often vendors have very little information about their dealers. If you make filling out a short questionnaire a part of the sales call, you can pay your reps an additional fee for each completed questionnaire. This approach only works well once; creating a second round of feedback is difficult. This approach is useful if you are starting a dealer program and you want to develop a data base of your dealers.

Another, although more difficult approach involves having the rep inform the dealer of a special promotion which they can redeem through their distributor. Redemption involves a trackable piece of paper which indicates to you which rep made the sale. This approach requires the distributor's support and can be unwieldy. There are a number of implementation issues for the distributor which will probably keep the distributor from considering it seriously.

Another involves having your company handle the rebate. Your sales rep tells the dealer to place their order with the distributor and then send proof of purchase to you so that you can send them the rebate. This provides you with the specific information that the sales rep's call did result in an order, permitting you to justify paying a commission to the rep. I have a couple of concerns about this approach. First, you may giving a selective discount depending upon the geographic completeness of your telemarketing coverage. It might be much more effective to make this special offer available through the distributor. My other concern is that the dealer may order the software to get the rebate and then return the software to the distributor.

After enumerating all of these alternatives, I really wonder if it is that important to compensate each sales rep individually. I have a client who sells through distribution and has a sales staff which receives bonuses based on overall revenue targets. These sales reps sell to distributors and large chains, permitting sales to be tracked, but management felt that the sales reps really had limited control over the eventual sales to end users.

In the final analysis, a product only sells and stays sold if customers go into stores to buy. This is a pull through sale. By contrast, all that indirect sales people can do is push the dealers and distributors to stock product. Thus I don't feel that it is really fair to make their compensation highly leveraged. You can still use normal management techniques to make sure that they are doing a professional job. It just isn't a high commission position.

9. Reseller Discount Schedules
Q. What are general guidelines for reseller discount schedules?

A. In the PC world, dealers get 40% to 50% off list price and distributors get 60% to 70% off. These ranges are for established companies and products. As with most things, the actual prices depend upon negotiations which extend over years.

The situation for new products with new companies are entirely different. Software publishers have typically offered their product discounts as a direct function of the volume that the reseller buys. Thus the reseller is making very little money on the first sales, which are the most difficult. Once they get the system worked out, their selling costs decline and the product costs go down. This is very difficult for the reseller to understand. They are making a serious investment in selling your product and they feel that you should make it easy for them to get started.

Getting Started in Distribution

Special Introductory Pricing
We have seen several cases where companies offered special introductory pricing for new dealers for a limited time. Usually these deals go as high as 66% off for an initial order of 5 or 10 units. By offering the dealer unusually high margins you can get them started carrying your product. This also allows you to brag about how many dealers are carrying your product. You should realize that some of these early dealers won't stick with you when you raise your prices. They are bargain shoppers, and they will be looking for the next deal.

WordPerfect in 1984
We recall that WordPerfect Corp (then Satellite Software Inc.) sold their product on 90-day contingency

back in 1984 in order to get dealers. Their offer was a simple, straightforward good-deal for retailers: "Stock our product. At the end of 90 days pay us or return it." This is a no-risk deal for the reseller, and it may have been one of the factors that got distribution for Wordperfect.

Complex Products
The other side of the issue is that complex products require dealer commitment. Unless the dealer is committed to your product, chances are the dealer won't really be successful. You must make sure that you qualify your dealer's interest, but at the same time don't make the dealer feel that you are penalizing him for the fact that he is just starting.

J. Low Priced Products (1989)
The dealer program described above assumes that you need to train your dealers and work with them so they can sell and support your product. If your product doesn't require technical training, it can probably be categorized as a lower priced utility. Products costing less than $500 have their own set of problems, the worst of which is that they typically don't have enough gross margin to attract most resellers. Storefront resellers who are primarily selling hardware can't get interested in a $200 software product. The software-only resellers might be interested if they think they can generate sufficient volume.

1. Generating Pull
Generating volume through distribution with a low price product requires a great deal of pull. You have to advertise, generate regular press releases and get magazine reviews. Advertising in mass market magazines is expensive. Getting reviews can take six to nine months from the time your product is provided to a magazine, assuming you can get the attention of the reviewers. This delay is due to the normal production schedule of a magazine. The editor must identify which products to review, assign a reviewer, review the review when it is complete, and then schedule it for publication. In my experience it is very difficult to get top drawer distribution without excellent magazine reviews.

2. Direct Selling
As a result, selling new low priced products through distribution requires two stages. The first is direct

selling. Direct mail, classified ads and targeted telemarketing are the common techniques at this stage. As sales increase, you will get a few dealers based on your sales and marketing efforts. These will typically be adventurous dealers calling to inquire about carrying your product. You will also make sales to corporations that have policies requiring them to buy all their software through certain approved dealers. Once you have made the sale to such a company, they place the order through their approved dealer. Surprise, surprise, you just lost 40% to 50% of your margin. The positive side is that you have gained another dealer.

3. Initial Dealers

Even though the volume sold through dealers is low at this stage, it is very important that you have dealers and that you iron out the details of your dealer program before dealer sales become critical to your revenues. It is easier to attract new dealers if you can say that you have had a dealer program since 19XX and that you now have XX dealers.

Selling price is another area to be carefully considered. If you plan to sell through distribution, make sure you take this into account when you price your product. Discounts of 40% to 60% are common for dealers, chains and distributors. Make sure you have set your price high enough so that you can comfortably give these discounts. Vendors often don't want to give dealers the margins they need to make a reasonable profit. The vendors feel pressed because their original price was based on the assumption that they would sell direct and that they would sell at a low price to attract interest. I urge you to set your price at the distribution list price, and then possibly offer introductory discounts, especially for direct sales. Doubling your price when you begin to sell into distribution can really confuse the marketplace.

4. Attracting New Dealers

Once your product has been reviewed and your dealer program is starting to work, consider special programs to attract new dealers. "Comdex Specials" can be an excellent mechanism for signing up new dealers. You can also design special programs which you promote through mailings and press releases. Telemarketing to dealers can also work to attract new dealers if your sales people have a program to offer. You must simultaneously continue to market

to your customers and generate demand. By and large, demand for products sold through distribution depends upon creating customer demand and "pulling" product through. It is very, very difficult to push dealers to sell your product. Many people feel that dealers do very little for their 50% of the revenue other than take orders, but this is what you should realistically expect. Feel very lucky if a dealer does more for you, but don't feel upset if this doesn't happen.

Building a dealer channel for a low priced product is slow and requires a significant marketing investment. The good news is that if you can get established in distribution, your product will continue to be sold. Most dealers are reluctant to drop a product that has been selling just because there is a new and better alternative.

K. VAR Development Center (1989)

Applied Business Computers (ABC) is a dealer for Shaker Computer and Management Services, Inc., which has developed a software package for construction companies called COINS. ABC also sells two other specialized software packages, one for manufacturers and the other for distribution companies. ABC is a "Super Dealer" for COINS; as such, it provides training, software and hardware support, customized programming, maintenance and other assistance to its customers. ABC has ten employees, only two of whom actually sell products. One of these salesmen is company President Dan Pultz.

Dan has developed his own somewhat unique "Selling System", which is based on a lot of client "hand holding," detailed specification of services provided, and a true "service orientation." With this approach, ABC sold seventeen copies of COINS in twenty four months, more than all other COINS dealers combined. His success sparked an interest in what ABC was doing that other dealers weren't.

Dan invented the idea of a VAR Development Center, which he subsequently discussed with Shaker. The plan proposed to help other VARs structure themselves in such a way that they would be able to support high end systems in a vertical market. The training at the center would deal with such topics as departmental staffing, cost accounting, and successful selling and marketing techniques. Also, hardware, software and language manufacturers would provide special programs allowing the VARs to do in-house testing of the equipment and software they are considering selling.

Using Dan's concepts, a VAR staffed similar to ABC and selling one $50,000 system per month would generate $1 million in annual sales and a 10% net income. The advantage to hardware, software and language manufacturers would be a network of VARs who could successfully and with little support install and maintain high end systems. The advantage for the VAR would be an exclusive territory for a vertical market package and an effective "delivery system" for getting that package to the market.

The VDC seemed like a good idea, but Dan was unable to get funding for it from software manufacturers. I believe we will see companies implement this idea in the future as our industry matures, and people are able to develop successful road maps and use them to train others. I have heard of other companies who are offering this as a service to their customers, and I would be very interested to learn more about it. Any comments on this topic are most welcome.

L. Distribution (1989)

In the last ten to twenty years, companies have gotten much more sophisticated about distribution, which has become a fundamental part of a company's marketing strategy. This is being driven by the increasing sophistication of the marketplace and the increasing level of competition. Rather than living in a "one size fits all" world, the 70's ushered in an era of market and product segmentation. In the 80's, many large companies gave up on the low end of the market as competition in this segment became intense and margins eroded. They simply couldn't compete on price at the lowest tiers of the market. As an alternative, they increased their focus on the middle and upper tiers. Over time these companies realized they were ignoring a significant segment of the market. As a result, there has been a great deal of experimentation and innovation in the area of distribution. It just isn't retail distribution as it was formerly known. Let's look at some specific examples.

1. Minicomputer Distribution

"Hewlett-Packard has turned to industrial distributors for the first time to sell its workstations..." "Hewlett-Packard is not alone in approaching distributors. Motorolla recently signed an agreement with Ingram Micro D for the distributor to carry its line of workstations."

REFERENCE: "Dealers Move Up", VarBusiness, June 1989.

These vendors expect many of their small resellers to buy directly from distributors rather than from them. This arrangement allows vendors to focus on the larger accounts rather than servicing the smaller VARs. It is interesting to see that HP is offering its resellers a choice between a higher discount or greater sales and marketing support from either HP or an OEM. More specifically, the resellers can pocket 3% and forego the support. HP has 1,500 OEMs and 1,000 VARs worldwide (half are in the US). Small resellers will now actually receive a better discount from the distributors than from the manufacturer. I believe this is motivated in part by the fact that distributors can support resellers more cheaply than can HP.

The trend toward industrial distributors is also taking place in the VAX business. Many Digital distributors have sold other hardware, including terminals. As a result, they felt that selling systems would stabilize their business. The distributors have increased revenues by servicing the small VARs, but they "have found that servicing these VARs has been more of a headache than they first thought."

REFERENCE: "The Channel Stretches - Value that Resellers Add Varies", by John Gantz, Digital News, September 18, 1989.

At the same time that HP and Digital are increasing their reliance on distributors, there is a great deal of turmoil with some of the other minicomputer vendors. "Data General Corp. stopped using distributors about two years ago, for the simple reason that 'they really didn't add any value'." It appears that part of the problem is a lack of agreement about what a value added distributor is and how much they should be compensated for filling this role. Is it just an example of classical distribution? What role does technical expertise play? What about business planning and sales training? It seems that the industry is encouraging distributors to pretend to offer full service, but no one is willing to pay for the additional value. As long as this is the case, there will be an irresistible trend toward less and less service.

REFERENCE: "VARs Get Little More Than Sweet Talk From Distributors", by Susan Greco, Var-Busines,   April,1989.

2. Microcomputer Distribution

Microcomputer distribution is also in a state of flux. There are two major national distributors: Softsel and Ingram Micro D. The other source of national distribution is the major chains: Computerland and Businessland. Distribution has become a big business; a $5 Billion business according to Ingram Micro D. It is, in fact, growing larger; the growth rate for distributors is expected to be 24 to 38 percent for 1989. The national distributors hold 50% of the market, multi-regional distributors 13%, regionals 13%, software only 5%, and specialized other 19%. The national distributors increased their market share from 45% in 1988 to 50% in 1989. Ingram's acquisition of Micro D during this time made it the largest distributor in the country. It appears that consolidation in this industry will continue.

REFERENCE: "Distribution Channel Changes to Keep Pace With PC Market", by John Gantz, Infoworld, June 26, 1989.

Many companies believe that signing up either a distributor or a dealer is the same as adding a sales and marketing organization. In both the dealer and distributor cases, it is one thing to sign up a reseller; it is quite another to make them effective. Distributors offer a number of positive characteristics: they stock software, they can create product awareness, they can distribute product, and they offer credit to dealers. If the small vendor wants to increase the distributor's focus on their product, they might consider an exclusive arrangement with one distributor. This provides additional visibility within the distributor's organization. The distributor is also more likely to invest in developing the market for an exclusive product.

Credit is a very important service that distributors offer to dealers. Some distributors offer easy credit in order to increase market share. At the same time,

distributors are asking dealers to provide more and more background information. Many distributors are coming to fear the very real credit risks dealers can pose. Floorplanning describes the process of a third party "flooring" company like ITT, TransAmerica, or Chrysler First Corp. assuming this credit risk. In this scenario, the reseller has a fixed period of time to pay the flooring company; they are required to pay even if they haven't sold the product.

REFERENCE: "Distributors and Credit: The Big Chill", Reseller Management, April 1989

Distributors are critical to the efficiency of the software business. They allow customers to buy products much more cheaply than they could if purchases were made directly from the manufacturers. The importance of distributors will increase as the software industry matures. At the same time, I expect that distributors will use their increased clout to bargain for more favorable terms with both manufacturers and resellers. This is already becoming true with microcomputer distributors. I expect to see the same trend in the next year or two with the minicomputer distributors. Finally, I expect that we will see experiments with mainframe distributors as mainframe vendors feel the heat from the mini and micro systems.

3. Manufacturer Reps

Reps are a very common method of distribution for manufacturers in other industries. In these , reps are independent sales agents who represent a number of lines. They call on their customer list, hand out sales materials and take orders. Consultants who take commissions in our industry are quite similar to reps. Let's look at how vendors select and motivate reps in traditional (non-computer) industries.

The first step in selecting a rep is to develop a profile of the ideal rep firm. The factors to be considered are: market focus, compatible product lines, and technical background. The first test involves whether the rep is actually calling on your target customers, and, if so, whether he is calling on the right person in the organization. Next, make sure you are comfortable with the product lines they carry. On the one hand you don't want them to carry a competitive line. On the other hand, they should be selling similar and complementary products, which require a sales process similar to the requirements of your product. For example, if you have a complex product, you don't want a rep who sells fasteners. And finally, the rep firm must have the technical credentials to represent your product properly. Look at your own sales people to see what is really required with regard to technical background.

REFERENCE: "Yes, There is a Perfect Rep", by Harold J. Novick, Business Marketing, February, 1989.

If you want reps to work effectively, you have to work at motivating them. Scrutinize the relationship and determine what you can do to make things work smoothly. Ask your reps for feedback and then act on it.

Lavin Associates surveyed 25 reps who represent 272 manufacturers and found that only 9.2% of the manufacturers gave any commendations to their reps. Reps are people; they need positive feedback just like the rest of us.

REFERENCE: "Few Manufacturers Motivate Their Independent Reps", Dartnell, May 10, 1989.

4. System Integrators

Traditionally Big Eight accounting firms concentrated on strategic alliances with major hardware vendors. Consulting divisions at the Big Eight accounting firms focused on the leading cross industry financial software. Recently these large accounting or professional service firms have decided that they can gain a competitive advantage by striking an alliance with emerging technology companies. They are looking for small firms who can help them get into a new market. Such vertical market alliances work well because the small, emerging technology company can have a significant presence is a vertical market.

These alliances can take one of many forms. The professional services firm can act as a value added reseller, a distributor, a co-marketer of the products and services, or as a provider of services after the product has been sold (installation, demonstration, training).

REFERENCE: "Smaller, Specialized Firms Key Targets in Recent Alliance activity", System Integration Age, February, 1989.

Alliances with professional service firms are difficult to consummate. Such service firms are not accustomed to investing in marketing in the same way that product firms are. Unless they are being driven by customers and contracts, it is difficult for them to invest in these types of alliances. This is especially true when large professional service firms are talking to smaller software vendors.

Most alliances are with the very large software companies: Pansophic, Computer Associates, MSA, McCormack & Dodge, ADR, etc. There are a few with smaller software companies who have products which dominate their niche. One example is Index Technology. If you are approached by a professional services company, be self protective. Ask yourself if you would make the investment if you were working for the service firm. Don't risk or invest more time and money than you can afford to lose. Take into account the fact that these alliances are very risky.

5. Shareware

The final distribution alternative is shareware. The concept is that software is distributed free of charge, and users are obliged to pay a fee to register if they find the software useful and they would like both a written manual and product updates. There are over 18,000 public domain, freeware/shareware programs on file at Ferris State University (FSU). The PC-SIG (PC-Software Interest Group) at Ferris offers a laser disk with 817 floppy diskettes of applications, utilities, and games.

REFERENCE: "Teaching Computer Literacy With Freeware and Shareware", THE Journal, May, 1988.

Shareware is distributed in several ways. The most popular is on-line through BBS' or commercial on-line sources such as Compu Serve. A cheaper alternative is U.S. mail. The author of the below-referenced article calculated that one would pay $17.56 to download PC-Write from CompuServe; ordering it through the mail would cost $9.00. The mail order sources are user groups and commercial enterprises. The PC-SIG and the PSL (Public Software Library) offer many of the amenities of ordinary resellers: standard packaging, advertising, 30-day return policy, technical hot line, quantity discounts and credit cards. There are a number of smaller, secondary sources of shareware.

Chapter IV. Distribution

REFERENCE: "Through the Mail: On the Right Road to Shareware", by Alfred Glossbrenner, Personal Computing, May, 1988.

Just when I thought it was safe to categorize shareware as hobbyist software, I read that shareware had spread to corporate America. Initially it was underground, but Marshall Magee estimates that over 90 percent of his shareware firm's customer base is corporate. "The guys that are doing well in shareware — all their products are business oriented." The PC-SIG even launched a Shareware Magazine for the corporate market.

REFERENCE: "Shareware Finds a Niche in Large Corporations: Once Scorned Public Domain Software is Rapidly Gaining Corporate Credibility.", by Marilyn Stoll, PC Week, February 9, 1988.

The recent publicity about viruses has put a damper on shareware. It is commonly suggested the use of public domain and shareware software can raise your exposure to viruses. This general advice fails to account for the differences between public domain software which is distributed on BBSs and shareware which is distributed by companies. Note that even shareware from one of the recognized companies could be modified by someone who works with it in the production process.

"Despite concerns associated with the possibility of virus attacks, shareware has found a niche in the computers of corporate America." "Corporate buyers use shareware because of its low cost, free evaluation and typically strong support of individual users." Shareware vendors have started to act more like classical software companies in order to gain more corporate attention. They have offered site licenses and in many cases they deliver the software directly to the customer doing the evaluation. This helps address the virus scare. "At Pratt & Whitney in East Hartford, Conn., John O'Boyle, a manager of office-systems technology, explained that the virus scare has 'prompted a mandate at the corporate level that we will not use software that comes off bulletin boards.' However, 'Once we send an order out through purchasing channels, we don't consider the product as shareware, he said."

REFERENCE: "Shareware Gets a Foot in the Door of Corporate USA.", by Dale Lewallen, PCWeek, February 20, 1989.

Shareware is a valid distribution alternative that might work for some software companies. If you have some nice utilities which aren't really worth packaging and marketing, consider putting them out as shareware. Send the shareware disks to your target market with a letter asking them to register it if they find it useful. These registered users could be a major asset in your marketing. They know your company and have used some of your software products and thus are good prospects for your full commercial package. I would be very interested in hearing about anyone's experience with shareware as a PR and lead generation tool.

M. International (1989)

1. New European Common Market

Q. We are concerned about planning for the changes in Europe which will occur in 1992. [The Common Market will abolish all internal tariffs in 1992. Goods and services are projected to move very freely, creating a huge, "open" market — Ed.] How will marketing in Europe change? For the better, or for the worse?

A. From what we have read, many of the changes won't have as much impact on software companies as on hardware companies.

Hardware companies who are shipping boxes across national boundaries have to deal with significant paperwork. Software companies have less paperwork because in many cases they have a distributor in each country who has a master copy of the software product and who distributes it within their country. The need to have a master copy for each country is cultural and language-based, not legal. (The French won't buy German or English software, and vice versa.) The trade law changes won't affect this type of bias.

We believe that the most significant change for US companies will be that more European Distributors are organizing themselves to cover all of Europe. This will result in much better distribution for a small US company. Having one master distributor to deal with will be much more efficient than dealing with four or five independent distributors.

2. International Distributors
Q. What issues should we consider in developing international relationships?

Chapter IV. Distribution

A. Developing international relationships requires a serious investment and a long view. You must be prepared to visit your distributors once or twice a year to keep them going. These visits will help you establish a solid relationship with your distributor. It is also important to have one person whose top priority is to keep your distributors happy. Ideally this is the person who visits with them. You will be surprised at the ongoing stream of issues which need attention. The final issue is how well your product fits other markets. Don't assume that what sells in the USA will sell in the UK. You may have to modify your product to meet the needs of these other markets. This will test your commitment to the international market. We wouldn't go international if we weren't prepared to make these investments. If you do you might be generating 30 to 50 percent of your revenue internationally in three to five years, but the up-front costs are high.

1992
Software Success
Reference Book

Chapter V
Management Issues

Chapter V. Management Issues

A. Fund Raising Survey (Jun 1991)

We had 152 responses to this survey. Once again this is quite a good response. However, it is somewhat less than the Support and the Demo Surveys, since not everyone is interested in Fund Raising. Less than half of the companies who completed this survey even attempted to raise capital from Private Investors. I believe that a number of people didn't respond because they have never tried to raise capital. This may indicate that many Software Success readers are still in the "bootstrap" stage, or are still determined not to use outside money.

1. Venture Capital Really is Harder to Raise (Oct)

Based on what my clients have told me, 1991 has been a difficult year to raise venture capital. Still, since I had only a relatively small sample, I wasn't sure if it was a general trend.

...1991 investments will be at about $740 million, compared to 1990's full-year total of about $1.9 billion. Not since 1980 have disbursements slipped under $1 billion.

Then, a client who is trying to raise second-round venture capital sent me an article titled "Disbursements' Decline Deepens: First Quarter Results Point to Weakest Year in a Decade," published in the July 1991 issue of *Venture Capital Journal*.

The article was written by David Schutt, the journal's editor-in-chief, who uses the results from the first quarter to estimate that 1991 investments will be at about $740 million, compared to 1990's full-year total of about $1.9 billion! Not since 1980 have disbursements slipped under $1 billion.

The news for companies looking for seed investments was even worse. "In contrast to later-stage funding, seed disbursements fell more rapidly than the market as a whole. Seed investments came to $4.2 million in the first quarter, down from $16.9 million a year ago–a 75% descent."

The positive news is that three of the ten largest deals were software companies. (These ten largest deals represent almost half the entire amount dis-

bursed in the first quarter of 1991.) The largest outlay went to Central Point Software, which received $17.2 million in first-round financing.

When venture capitalists have investment opportunities in established companies like Central Point Software, it is easy to see why they have so little enthusiasm for the small software company with one hot product and limited sales.

I've said it before and I'll say it again. Be careful and smart with your money. Fund your company yourself if you can. Live below your means and run a tight ship. But remember to have a sense of humor, and don't give up on your dreams.

Good luck to all of you who are looking for investment money.
Dave

In contrast to later-stage funding, seed disbursements fell more rapidly than the market as a whole. Seed investments came to $4.2 million in the first quarter, down from $16.9 million a year ago–a 75% descent.

---

2. Company Revenue

The companies who responded to this survey were slightly larger than typical. I believe that this reflects two factors. The first is, companies who raise money probably have greater revenues than companies who don't raise money (i.e. revenues increase with outside capital.) The second reason is, companies with greater revenue and greater revenue potential are more interesting to investors. Private investors typically want to see a potential for $5 Million in sales so that the company can be sold to a larger company later. Venture capitalists want to see an absolute minimum annual revenue potential of $25 Million and many have lower limits of $100 Million.

Company Revenue	This Survey
< $250K	21.7%
$250-$500k	15.1%
$500K-$1M	21.7%
$1M-$2M	17.8%
$2M-$5M	12.5%
> $5M	12.5%

Paid-in Capital

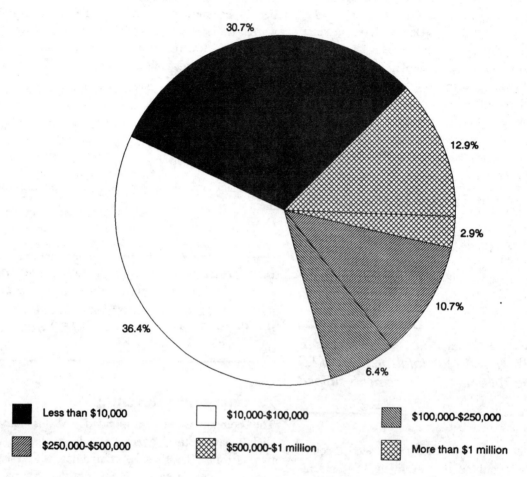

■ Less than $10,000	□ $10,000-$100,000	▨ $100,000-$250,000
▨ $250,000-$500,000	▨ $500,000-$1 million	▨ More than $1 million

3. Title

Most of the respondents are Presidents. This is appropriate, since the President/CEO is responsible for fund raising, which is very difficult to delegate. A number of Vice Presidents noted that they are one of the founders or owners, which involves them in fund raising.

Title	% Respondents
President	61.8%
Vice President	21.1%
Director	9.2%
Manager	9.2%

4. Area of Responsibility

The respondents were most likely to be in Management and least likely to be in Finance. The typical respondent indicated being involved in two areas of responsibility. For example, some were in both Management and Marketing, etc.

Area of Responsibility	% Respondents
Management	68.4%
Marketing	44.1%
Sales	30.9%
Support	21.7%
Development	23.7%
Finance	13.8%

5. Paid-in Capital

Paid-in capital is money invested in a company for equity and the most common amount for this survey is $10K to $100K. This is a common range that founders can fund from their own personal savings.

There were a surprising number of companies which had less than $10K in paid-in capital. My experience has shown that many of these companies understate their capital and have invested more than they realize or give themselves credit for. I often see companies whose founders only invested $5K in hard cash, but then didn't draw a salary for a year. In true economic terms, they also contributed a free year that might have been worth $50K. This would make their paid-in capital total $55K. As long as you never intend to look for investors, this is probably the simplest and best approach. On the other hand, if you are showing your financials to potential investors, paid-in capital is one of the things they look at when trying to determine a pre-investment valuation. The pre-investment valuation is the amount the business is worth before the investment is made. One of the factors investors consider is how much money has been invested in the company so far. If you underrepresent the paid-in capital by not drawing a salary for a year or more, you are reducing the amount that the investor will see you have invested, and therefore are effectively lowering his perception of your company's value.

I have been told by several venture capitalists that the entrepreneurs are better off to pay themselves a salary and then turn around and reinvest the money in the business. This makes the paid-in capital accurately reflect how much money you actually put into the company. One disadvantage of this approach is, you can end up owing taxes on income for which you don't have cash. In particular, you don't have cash to pay your taxes. You can reduce your taxes if you incorporate as a Subchapter S. With a Subchapter S corporation, the losses revert to the stockholders and your losses should come very close to canceling out your salary so that you end up with very little net income. When I started my own software company, this approach ended up being 90% effective. I still ended up paying some taxes since some incorporation and startup expenses must be capitalized and thus, can't be completely deducted in the year you have the corresponding income. Check with your accountant to see what the current tax rules are, and if this approach might be worth considering.

6. Ownership

Most software companies are very tightly held (i.e. there are very few owners and a dominant share of the stock is held by owner/operators). "Several partners" is the most common form of ownership for this survey's respondents. This can be a very good way to start a business, if you can get several partners with different skills. The risk here is the inherent risk in all partnerships — divorce.

The second most common form of ownership indicated is "one owner". In my experience, many sole owners had a partner at some point in the past and have vowed never to have another. This style of ownership imposes some limitations on the company's ability to attract high level employees with stock options. It is also more risky for an employee in a small company with one owner. In particular, it is quite risky if the owner is technically oriented and the employee is sales and marketing oriented, or vice versa. In many cases the technical founders will place all blame on the sales and marketing employees rather than seeing things objectively.

Less than 20% of the companies who responded have outside investors. This assumes that we didn't get multiple responses from people who have one form of outside investment.

Ownership	% Respondents
Not Indicated	5.9%
One Owner	29.6%
Several Partners	42.1%
Employees	11.8%
Private Investors	10.5%
Venture	8.6%
Public	2.6%

7. Growth rates

The graph below shows that, as an industry, software companies are growing very fast (increasing revenue). The median growth is 20% to 30% per year. Most respondents say they know their expected growth rate for this year. Over 10% didn't recall last year's growth rate. While this isn't a major part of the sample, I believe that everyone should keep good records and use history to guide their current decisions. There were a number of humorous comments on "Expected Five Year Annualized Growth Rate". These readers felt that five year projections were totally incomprehensible. While I don't believe it is worthwhile for small companies to

Expected Growth Rates

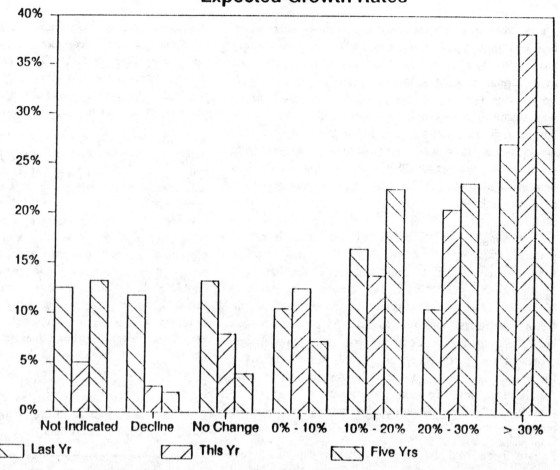

spend months and months on detailed five year plans, I do believe that it is useful to have a basic understanding of where the company is going. If your market is growing 20% per year, and your company has been growing 20% to 30% per year, then it is reasonable to expect this trend to continue.

Even with this minimal level of detail, you can do some basic strategic planning. Ask yourself how many people will be in the company in five years if your headcount grows 20% to 30%? This will give you an estimate of how much office space you might need. In most small companies, growth in revenues are generated by adding sales people. If this is your case, you can use the revenue growth rate to drive your sales force hiring plans. (Make sure that you factor in the training time required for new sales people to become effective. It might take three to six months for a new sales person to become effective, so, if you want to calculate the impact of adding a new sales person, you will have to take this ramp-up time into account.)

Slightly over 10% of the respondents had a decline in revenue last year. This is a tough business and last year's economic turmoil hit some companies hard. In my experience, certain sectors showed real declines in purchases last year: manufacturing, retail, and the Fortune 500. This was especially true after the start of the Gulf War. My guess is, 10% of the respondents will show a decline for this year (1991) when we do this survey again next year (1992). Entrepreneurs are overly optimistic as a group. (Why else would we venture off and start our own companies? If we were realistic, we would all still be working for someone else!)

Very few respondents expect a five year decline in revenues, but be forewarned. Such a decline could actually occur. When our companies are young, we all believe that we can sustain these incredibly high growth rates forever. I have clients in the home entertainment market where industry sales have actually declined several times over the last 10 years. These declines were due to hardware life cycles, macro economic trends, and consumer burn out, but they did occur.

I think we will see more examples of declines in industry sales, within saturated market segments, as our business matures. I have several clients who sell vertical applications to saturated market segments. The overall levels of sales to these markets are declining since a good percentage of the potential market has already purchased software, and they don't need significantly more capabilities. If this is the situation, the vendors who decide to stay in the market must lower their prices to attract the marginal buyers who didn't decide to buy in the past. This will become more common as our industry matures.

While the median growth rate was 20% to 30%, the most common response was "over 30%". This was true for last year, this year, and the next five years. The "over 30% expected" was especially pronounced for this year's expectations.

8. Company Objective

When you compare the results of this year's survey with the results from last year, there is surprising consistency on the number of people who want to sell their company or take it public.

Response	This year	Last Year
Income principals	51.3%	71.0%
Good place to work	32.9%	50.7%
Sell company	28.3%	29.0%
Go public	13.8%	14.5%

There are fewer people who indicated that income for the principals or creating a good place to work were the primary company objective. I noticed that we received slightly fewer multiple selections this year than last. (This year the responses add up to 126% and last year they were 165%.) It appears that this reduction in multiple responses resulted in fewer people indicating income or a good place to work as an objective, rather than any fundamental change in people's objectives.

Past Funding — Amount Tried to Raise

The responses to this question point out the problems software companies encounter in raising capital. I suspect that many of the "not indicated" companies never tried to raise outside money. They didn't think it was worth the time and energy, and, chances are, they were right.

The most popular amount companies tried to raise was under $10K and that probably came from the

principals. This is the classic bootstrap. You put in the minimum amount to open the doors, and then sweat until the business starts to make enough money to pay yourself a minimal salary. Eventually, you can pay yourself an above average salary which begins to repay you for your sweat equity.

Amount Tried to raise	% of Respondents Trying	Actual Paid-in Capital
Not indicated	30.3%	9.2%
< $10K	22.4%	28.3%
$10K-$100K	8.6%	33.6%
$100K-$250K	10.5%	5.9%
$250K-$500K	8.6%	9.9%
$500K-$1M	5.3%	2.6%
> $1M	15.1%	11.8%

If you look at the $10K–$100K range, it is clear that most of the companies who have under $100K in paid-in capital didn't raise the money from outsiders. The funding came from the principals and their family and friends. I believe that this is how it should be. As an investor, I get very nervous when I see companies in which the principals haven't put up any money. Even if they don't have any money, in almost all cases, their family and friends do.

This is a concept that professional investors understand. I met an entrepreneur who was trying to raise $750K from a seed capital firm. The venture capitalists wanted 60% of the company for their $750K. The entrepreneurs decided that this was such a great deal that they wanted to raise $250K from their own resources and their family and friends. They wanted to invest along with the venture capitalists (as part of the $750K). The venture capitalists were thrilled, and they said that if the entrepreneurs were willing to come up with the $250K, then they'd be willing to increase the valuation for the company, before the investment, from 40% (of the final valuation) to 60%.

Let's walk through the numbers. In the first case, the venture capitalists said that the pre-investment valuation was $500K. If you add $750K from the investment, the post-investment valuation is $1.25M and the founder's stock is worth 40% ($500K/$1.25M). When the founders decided to come up with the $250K, the venture capitalists increased the pre-investment valuation to $1M. Thus, the post-investment valuation was $1.75M and the founder's stock was 57% ($1M/$1.75M). Thus, the founders'$250K investment increased their share another 14% to a total of 71%.

The bottom line of this example is that the venture capitalists doubled the pre-investment valuation because the founders were willing to put their own money at risk. They knew that because the money was from friends and family, the founders would be much more likely to go the extra mile to make the company work. If a company fails, it is much easier to walk away from it and let the venture capitalists and outside investors take the loss than explain to Aunt Matilda how you lost her life savings. (NEVER ask people to invest in your company if they can't afford to take the loss.)

At the other end of the spectrum, 15.1% of the responding companies tried to raise over $1 Million, but only 11.8% have over $1 Million in paid-in capital. This is pretty close to the 11.2% who had either venture or public ownership. My experience indicates that, unless you can justify over $1 Million in investment, then the venture capitalists won't be interested. Their management costs are too high for smaller investments. There are some smaller and specialized firms which make smaller investments, but these firms are difficult to find.

The toughest range of funding for a software company is in the $100K to $1 Million range. In many cases this is too much for the founders (unless they go to their RICH family and RICH friends), and it is too little for venture capitalists. This is the range where private investors can make sense. 10.5% of the companies had private investors as owners. 18.4% of the companies have $100K to $1 Million in paid-in capital. I would guess that 57% of these situations involved private investors (10.5%/18.4%).

9. Fund Raising Attempts — Private Investors

43.4% of the companies who responded to the survey have tried to raise money from private investors, and 52% of the companies who tried to raise money from private investors were successful. This is pretty good. Last year we found that 34.2% of the companies were planning on getting private investments and another 24% were considering going on to raise venture capital and/or go public. This is very consistent with this year's results.

Private Investors	% Respondents
Not indicated	48.0%
Attempted	43.4%
Successful	23.0%
Raised Less $ than desired	6.6%
More Stock given up	1.3%
Unsuccessful	5.3%

The most common problem with private investors, in my experience, is that they start off with a fixed amount of money which they want to invest, and they won't put more money in even if the situation requires it. Venture capitalists usually reserve two or three times their initial investment for subsequent rounds of investment. While the venture capitalists will negotiate very hard and will evaluate the wisdom of investing good money after bad, they do have the money to make the subsequent investments. Private investors, on the other hand, often decide that they want to invest a fixed amount in one investment and then they go on to other investments. They don't want to take too much portfolio risk by putting too much money into one deal. I have been involved in several deals with private investors providing first round financing. We then brought in venture investors for a second round of financing. These companies had some problems and we were trying to raise additional money from the venture capitalists under difficult conditions. The venture capitalists were willing to put additional money into a third round, but at a lower price than they paid in round number two (their initial involvement). The venture capitalists almost always structure their investments so that if a later round of funding comes in at a lower price, they will, in effect, pay that lower price for their first round of financing. What happens in practice, is that they get more stock retroactively for their initial investment.

The net effect of this process is dilution of the common shareholders, who are typically the founders and the private investors. In the cases mentioned earlier, the private investors were furious. They didn't want the venture capitalists to get more stock for the first round, but the private investors weren't willing to put in any more money themselves. The founders looked at the numbers and realized that if they participated in the new penalty round (what a great name!), then they could actually improve their ownership position. The penalty round was such a

Chapter V. Management Issues

great deal that everyone who owned stock should participate in it. It was structured to penalize anyone who didn't participate. The private investors didn't want to participate and were unhappy with being penalized.

Very few of the private investors forced the founders to "give up more stock/control than desired". My experience shows that most private investors are almost passive about the company valuation. In many cases, they are investing based on personal confidence rather than on strictly financial criteria. It is almost too easy to price the stock too high (set too high a valuation on the company) for the private investors.

I can hear you asking, "How can I set the stock price too high?" The first issue is to make the private investors feel they made a good investment and did well. These are friends and acquaintances, so there is a non-financial side to the transaction. If you look at the final outcome, and you sell the company for $10 Million in ten years and you end up with 12% of the company and screw the private investors or you get 10% of the company and the private investors do very well, I would personally choose to take less money to maximize the odds that my private investors do well. You may start another company and look for private investors once again in the future, so this isn't a totally philosophical issue.

The next and much more practical reason for setting a fair price for the private investors is the importance of the stock price going up from round to round. If the founders buy stock for $0.10 per share and issue 1 million shares, the initial valuation is $100K. Six months later, the founders have earned some sweat equity and have a product which has made some initial sales. This might raise the valuation to $500K or $0.50 per share. You might sell 200K shares to private investors at that point for $100K. Now the post investment valuation is $600K and the company has 1.2 million shares outstanding. If the company takes this $100K and the product built with sweat equity and gets the sales to $1.2 Million per year, the valuation might be $1.2 Million, or $1.00 per share. (I picked reasonable numbers, but have made them convenient.) At this point you might bring in $1 Million at $1.00 per share from venture capitalists.

At this point, the company would have 2.2 million shares of stock and the founders and venture capital-

ists would have 45.5% of the stock and the private investors would have 9%. Let's see what would have happened if we had sold the stock to the private investors at $1.00 per share. They would have only received 100K shares and there would only be 2.1 million shares outstanding after the venture round. The founders and venture capitalists would have 47.6% of the stock each, and the private investors would only have 4.8%. As you can see, the founders only gained a couple percent of the company and they ran the risk that the private investors would block the venture round.

In theory, if the founders realize that they priced the stock too high for the private investors, they can go back and sell the private investors more stock at a very good deal to retroactively adjust their stock position. This is possible, but it is difficult to implement in practice. Once you have placed a valuation on the company, it is emotionally very difficult to reduce the valuation. This is similar, on a personal level, to the difficulty of taking a job for a lower salary.

The other problem is that each subsequent round of investors wants to squeeze the previous investors. While the investors want to squeeze the founders, they need the founders to make the company succeed, so they can't take too much out of the founders. Private investors from an earlier round are much more exposed. If they aren't participating in the current round, they are of no use to the new investors. If the new investors can dilute the earlier investors without hurting the founders, the new investors have improved their investment. (This is very much a zero sum game.) For these reasons, once you tell the new investors how much stock the private investors have, the new investors will strongly resist giving the prior investors more stock. They would rather receive the stock for themselves.

The bottom line is, it is important that you establish a realistic valuation for the private investors, and I would urge you to try to slant the valuation toward the low end of the realistic range.

Only 23.0% of the respondents were successful in raising private money. 4.3 times more companies were successful raising private money as were unsuccessful (23.0% vs. 5.3%) Another 7.3% appear to have given up if you compare the number of people who attempted to raise private money and the ones who were successful, raised less money than desired, gave up more stock than desired, and were unsuccessful. Overall, this suggests that it is reasonable to raise private money for software companies.

10. Fund Raising Attempts — Venture Capital

29.6% of the companies have tried to raise venture capital. Last year 15% of the companies wanted to raise venture capital and 8% wanted to go public. If you combine these (raising venture capital is conventionally a step toward going public), 23% of the companies should be considering venture capital. Thus, these two surveys are reasonably consistent.

This year 37.8% of the companies who attempted to raise venture capital were successful (11.2% vs. 29.6%). Last year we found that 28.8% of the companies who tried to raise venture capital were successful. I am pleased that the success rate has improved. Last year 50.2% of the respondents had tried to raise venture capital and 14.5% had succeeded so 28.8% of the companies were successful in raising venture capital last year.

This year we have a smaller group who tried to raise venture capital, but a higher percentage of them were successful. In absolute terms, fewer of the respondents were successful this year than last year (11.2% this year vs. 14.5% last year). I suspect with all of the economic uncertainty in the last year, fewer companies have tried to raise venture capital. I have talked to a number of software companies who have postponed looking for venture capital because they feared they would be wasting their time looking in this economic climate.

Venture Capital	% Respondents
Not indicated	62.5%
Attempted	29.6%
Successful	11.2%
Less $ than desired	3.9%
More stock than desired	6.6%
Unsuccessful	7.9%

Venture capitalists negotiate very hard on price. 58% of the successful situations involved giving up more stock and control than desired (6.6% more stock vs. 11.1% successful). Only 5% of the successful private investor situations involved giving up more stock and control.

I was surprised that 34.8% of the successful venture investments raised less money than desired. (3.9% vs. 11.2%). This is even higher than the experience with private investors where 28.6% of the companies raised less money than desired. I know that the venture capitalists have the money, and when they decide to back a company, they want to put in as much money as is reasonable. One problem that software companies have as a class of investment is, most software companies don't require the big multi-million dollar investments that venture capitalists like to make. There are a number of large firms which won't invest less than $1-2 million and they won't allow other venture firms to participate in the investment since they want to keep their minimum investment at a reasonable level.

One explanation is, some of the respondents started off with totally unrealistic expectations. I talk to people who say, "I think I would like to raise ten or twenty million dollars for my company." While this might explain some of the responses, I don't think that it should be a major factor since I think that, early on, most people get a realistic idea of how much money is appropriate to raise.

One common scenario is the founders hoping to raise several million dollars to complete the development, test market the product, and then launch the product. The venture capitalists look at all these risks with great concern. In many cases, they will fund the company in stages. They will give the company $250K to finish the product and get the first ten customers. There might be another $500K for an initial test marketing phase. Once the company passes these levels, the venture capitalists would fund the full marketing roll out. As I think about it, this probably explains why so many companies raised less money than desired from the venture capitalists.

7.9% of the respondents were unsuccessful in raising venture capital. This is 26.6% of those who attempted to raise money. This is lower than the 12.2% of the companies who were unsuccessful in raising private money. I believe there are two factors at work here. The first is that it is very easy to begin looking for private money. Many times, people begin looking for money without first having a business plan. They just talk to the people they know. Looking for venture capital requires much more of an investment and most people think about it a little more seriously than looking for private money. The second reason is, venture capitalists are experts at saying "maybe". They almost never say no, they give you suggestions, or tell you to come back once you have jumped the next hurdle. From their point of view, as long as they don't spend much time with you, they should keep you on the string. Who knows, next year you might turn into a great investment opportunity. One real problem I see with small companies trying to raise venture capital is, it is easy to put good time after bad trying to raise venture capital when your odds are really poor. There is a very high opportunity cost for companies looking for venture capital because the people involved with writing the business plan and meeting with the venture capitalists could be raising money by selling the product to customers.

11. Fund raising attempts — Public Offering

As we all know, it is difficult to take a software company public. Only 4.6% of our respondents even tried. This is 36.8% of the respondents with over $5 Million in revenue, which is fairly high (4.6% vs. 12.5%). Only 1.3% were successful, which is 28.2% of those companies that tried to go public. This is only slightly lower than the 37% success rate in raising venture capital.

I don't understand why so many people raised less money than desired with a public offering. I really would appreciate a call from anyone who had this experience.

Public Offering	% Respondents
Not indicated	89.5%
Attempted	4.6%
Successful	1.3%
Less $ than desired	2.6%
More stock than desired	0.7%
Unsuccessful	2.6%

12. Effort spent looking for capital

If you look at the table on the next page "*****" represents the estimated amount of time the successful firms spent looking for money. I made the assumption that people who spent the most time were most likely to be successful and that many of the people who spent very little time decided early on to not

pursue this source of funding. As an example, two of our respondents were successful in going public. 18 people answered this question about how much time was spent trying to go public. One person spent over a year, and two people spent between six months and one year. I marked the six months to one year as the estimated minimum amount of time spent looking for this form of funding (when the companies were successful).

As you can see, this isn't exact, and the statistics for the public offering question are weak (they also happen to be reasonable). If I had to guess, I think that it might take more than one man year to prepare for a public offering, but most companies which are planning to go public start the process several years ahead of time. They get one of the BIG 6 accounting firms, and hire the CEO and CFO for the road show. They start meeting with the investment banking firms a couple of years ahead of time. Often, they do a mezzanine round of financing, where they bring in the investment banking firm which is going to take them public, as an investor. This allows the investment banker to do much of his due diligence as an investor and board member. As you can see there are a lot of hidden costs to going public.

I think that these estimates are quite good for raising private investor money and venture capital. It is quite reasonable to raise private money with one to three months of work. This usually only requires a short business plan and a lot of personal relationships.

My experience is that it usually requires one person working full time for six months to one year to raise venture capital. I think that our estimate is a little low because other people also have to be involved to develop the business plan and field the questions from the venture capitalists and the experts they hire to do the due diligence.

13. Time looking for venture capital

When you compare the time that companies spent looking for venture capital (depending upon whether they had raised venture capital or not), there is a clear indication that dedication pays off. Part of this may also be that some companies learn early in the process that their company isn't likely to be funded and they cut their losses.

Effort spent looking for	Private Investors	Venture Capital	Public Offering
< 1 MM	44.4%	17.8%	66.6%
1-3 MM	30.6%****	30.3%	0%
3-6 MM	13.3%	14.2%	16.6%
6 MM-1 Year	12.5%	17.8%****	11.1%****
> 1 Year	1.3%	17.8%	5.5%

While the sample isn't huge, it appears that companies spent more time this year, than last, looking for venture capital. This is consistent with my impression that this past year was a tough time to raise capital.

	Not Successful		Successful	
Time Spent	Last Yr	This Yr	Last Yr	This Yr
< 3 MM*	65%	77%	30%	27%
3-6 MM	30%	0%	30%	13%
6-12 MM	4%	23%	20%	27%
> 12 MM	0%	0%	20%	33%

*MM = Man months

14. If unsuccessful, why?

My first observation is that a good number of people who were unsuccessful at raising venture capital didn't answer this question. One reason for this is, it isn't very comfortable to dwell on past failures. Another is, it is difficult for most sales people to really face why they lost the sale. Raising money is a very difficult sales job and it takes all of the sales management skills you possess (and then some!).

Reason Unsuccessful	% Repsondents
Not indicated	73.0%
Too much work	3.3%
Didn't want to give up control	10.5%
Revenue potential not enough	9.9%
Didn't need enough money	10.5%
Management team	5.3%

My experience shows there are a number of fundable deals which don't receive funding because the principals aren't willing to make the time and energy investment to convince the investors. Thus, I would expect that "Too much work" is more of a factor than these results show.

Not wanting to give up control shows up as the top reason, and this fits my experience. One of the primary motivations for entrepreneurs is the independence, and you give up much of this independence when you take someone else's money. I am surprised at the number of entrepreneurs who believe that the investors won't have control as long as the entrepreneurs retain more than 51% of the stock and control of the board of directors. This may be true if you have private investors and they have the same class of stock that the founders have. If the investors have preferred stock, I would assume that they, at least, have veto power. Most capitalization decisions require a majority of all classes of stock, so the preferred stock holders can block many major decisions. (Please consult your attorney if you have preferred shareholders. If you are considering selling stock, please find the best attorney you can. Venture capitalists use stock agreements which have been refined over the years to control entrepreneurs. Therefore, it is very important that you understand the real implications of any and all agreements which you are considering signing.)

There is another way investors have practical control over the companies they invest in. It is the old golden rule, "He who has the gold rules." In almost every situation where companies take money in, the concept is that the company will take this round of money and grow the company to the next stage. When management can show that they have made good use of the first round money, they tell the investors how they will use the next round of money. If you need money and you go back to your investors, they have all the control they need. It is very difficult to go find another investor group to buy out the first group unless there is an incredibly good reason that the first group should be bought out.

I have met a number of entrepreneurs who start out saying, "I want someone to give me a couple million dollars." I explain that no one "gives" you a couple million dollars. They may invest their money in your company, but they are going to do everything they can to guarantee that they can control the business, if necessary, to protect their money. We are talking about a great deal of money and it is very reasonable for the investors to require these safeguards. I think it is important for me to state that I believe it is appropriate for the investors to have this level of control. One of my rules for investing in small software companies is, I will only invest if I think the company is venture fundable. Thus, I like to get in at the private investor round with the anticipation that the company will raise venture capital. If this happens, I can then count on the venture capitalists to do their best to make the stock worth something. Of course, there is always the risk that the venture capitalist will make his stock worth more than mine, but I believe that this risk can be managed when you negotiate the initial deal with the venture capitalists.

A perceived low revenue potential is a real reason why many software companies aren't funded. In my experience, a software company has to have annual revenues of at least $5 Million to be an attractive acquisition candidate, $25 Million or more to take the company public. Most venture capitalists will only consider investing in a software company if its revenue potential is $25 Million to $100 Million (the particular number depends upon the venture firm). There are a lot of really good software companies which might get to the $5 Million level and be a great place to work. The venture capitalists don't view these as good investment opportunities. Private investors, on the other hand, might be more interested. The risk for the private investors is that the founders may change their minds and decide not to sell the business. The founders can keep the business and pay themselves very well and be happy. Private investors often don't share in this economic success. This is especially true if the private investors have a minority ownership position. For this reason, I am reluctant to become a minority investor in a company where the founders have the option not to cash the company out.

Requiring too little money is also a very legitimate reason for not getting funding. There are very real management costs for venture capitalists which make small investments non-economic. Most venture firms have strict minimum investment amounts which are fairly easy to find out. The same situation applies to going public. The legal and accounting costs are fixed so these fees become prohibitive when you look at raising smaller amounts of money with a public offering. In most cases, private investors don't have similar minimum investment problems since they don't spend time managing their investments. Private investors who are mini-venture capitalists and work with their investments on an active basis end up with their own minimum investment levels.

It wasn't a surprise that the "management team not being good enough" wasn't perceived as a reason for being unsuccessful. Asking a management team if they are lacking is difficult to acknowledge. I also believe that there are real differences in opinion between entrepreneurs and venture capitalists about what it takes to manage a company. Part of this difference is ego on the part of the entrepreneurs. They have brought their company this far and they truly believe that they can get it to wherever they set out to go.

Another reason for the difference in opinion is that the demands on the management team, in a bootstrap operation, are much different than in a high finance "warp-speed" company. In several of Software Success' feature articles, the founders commented that they felt their companies had benefitted by NOT having money. They didn't have the money to make big mistakes and they had the time to learn. If you have a couple million dollars of other people's money and your objective is to grow the company to ten million dollars in revenue in five years, you don't have time for trial and error. It is really important to have someone with prior experience in this situation. In my experience, the most common reason for investors not investing is lack of confidence in the management team.

15. Company Revenue — Cross Tabs

Company Revenue vs. Objective

Income for the principals is a very common objective for the companies under $1 Million in sales (45%), and it becomes less important as the revenues grow (it is only important for 18% of the companies over $5 Million in sales.)

Creating a good place to work and selling the company is independent of the company revenue.

Only 5% to 10% of the companies under $2 Million in sales are considering going public. This jumps to 23% when the revenues go over $2 Million. You may recall a survey from last year where the compensation for the CEO jumped significantly when the revenues went over $2 Million. I suspect that this is caused by the same underlying reality. I predict we will find that companies with over $2 Million in sales are much more profitable than those under $2 Million.

Company Revenue vs. Approaching Private Investors

Lack of revenue didn't discourage people from trying to raise money from private investors. The companies that were over $5 Million in revenue were significantly more successful than the smaller companies in raising money from private investors. I wonder if the private investment really makes a difference in helping the company grow. The other explanation is, private investors push the companies to grow, since the investors aren't likely to be well rewarded unless the company gets over $5 Million in revenues.

Company Revenue vs. Approaching Venture Capitalists

Once again, lack of revenue doesn't discourage people from approaching venture capitalists, but the success rate below $5 Million is under 20% of the companies who tried. For companies over $5 Million, 45% of them succeeded in raising venture capital.

Company Revenue vs. Public Offering

No one with revenues under $5 Million even tried to go public, and both of the companies over $5 Million who tried to go public succeeded.

16. Ownership — Cross tabs
The company objective is linked to the ownership. With one or several partners, income for the principals is the dominant objective (over 40% of the time). These companies with one or more partners are moderately interested in selling the company (20%). At the same time, the companies with only one owner aren't that interested in going public.

I was very interested to see that companies with employee ownership were very similar to those with private investors. I guess the employees think of their stock in much the same way private investors would. The employees were even more interested in going public than the private investors. This is the classical way in which stock options really become worth something. 39% of the companies with venture capital were interested in going public and another 39% were interested in selling the company. Very few of the companies with venture capital rated "income for principals" or a "good place to work" as an objective.

17. Expected Five Year Annualized Growth Rate — Cross Tabs
The company objectives don't seem to have any correlation with the five year annualized growth rate. I almost believe that people start with their own agendas for the business, then they develop a product, and the product has it's own growth rate potential.

Having a high growth rate (30% annually) helps somewhat to raise private money. 56% of the companies with over 30% growth rate expectations were successful in raising private money. Only 33% of the companies with 1% to 10% growth rate expectations were successful.

It appears that an expectation of a low growth rate kills your chances of raising venture capital. No one with expectations under 10% was successful in raising venture capital, even though they tried. I was a little surprised at the firms with 10% to 20% expected growth rates who had been successful in raising venture capital. I wonder if they pumped up the numbers to raise the venture capital, and now they are trying to downplay them to avoid getting fired by the venture capitalists.

18. Conclusions
Fund raising is the one task I believe the CEO MUST do himself. You can hire a marketing and sales executive, or you can get someone to handle development. But, investors want to talk to the person at the helm. In my experience, finders are rarely successful in getting companies funded. The CEO has to get in-

volved in developing the plan and has to be able to convey that he/she will make it happen.

One of the real risks for small companies is wasting too much time chasing unrealistic funding alternatives. I hope that you can use the information provided here to help you determine the realistic odds of getting your company funded. If the odds are poor, you are probably better off putting the energy into making sales and getting the capital you need from your customers.

On the other hand, software companies CAN get funded and appropriate funding can really help the company grow. Hopefully, this information will help you develop the most appropriate plan for your company.

Good Luck!
Dave

B. Operating Expenses (Sept)

We received 50 responses to this survey. While this seems low, I am pleased with the response. Historically, it has been difficult for the Software Success readers to provide operating expense information. In last month's survey we found that CEOs were least likely to have a financial background. At the same time, this is an area of high interest. There are very few financial benchmarks for small software companies and this information is critical to the successful management of your business. I appreciate the time that the respondents took to complete this survey.

1. Company Revenue

The respondents to this survey were slightly more likely to be in the $1M to $2M range and less likely to be either smaller or larger. I suspect that in the larger companies, the marketing managers may not have easy access to financial information. They are functional managers responsible for their own specific area. Upper management is responsible for managing the budget between the functional groups.

With the smaller companies (under $250K), the financial results become much less clear. The primary expenses are personnel expenses and each person has different responsibilities. There were a number of people who noted that they are individually

responsible for development, support and general administration. Some of them provided an estimate of the expense allocation by functional area, based on how they divided their time. However, a number of them could only guess.

Company Revenue	This Survey	1990 Reader Survey
< $250K	14.0%	22.4%
$250K-$1M	34.0%	21.2%
$1M-$2M	30.0%	23.5%
$2M-$5M	18.0%	22.4%
> $5M	4.0%	10.6%

2. Product Price

Compared to last year, there are slightly more products with prices under $1K, but the difference is not significant.

3. Computer Type

We had 1.59 responses per respondent which implies that 60% of the respondents are marketing their products on two computer types. This is higher that the 1.3 responses per respondent we have found in earlier surveys, and it is dramatically higher than the 1.1 responses per respondent we found on the distribution survey.

Why were the distribution respondents on fewer platforms?

I suspect that companies who are selling through distribution, or trying to sell through distribution, are putting all of their energy into making their product the best it can be. When you go into distribution, you are putting your product on center stage with all of your competitors. Thus, your product is under greater pressure to excel.

On the other hand, if you sell direct, the prospect has less chance to compare you with the competition. It may be more important to provide your product on the plaltforms which your prospects might consider, than to make those last incremental improvements to your product.

We have a new category for this survey, "multi user PC". Even though these products run on PCs, I agree with the readers who suggested this new category that they are different. I was impressed at the number of firms who provided this response. The number of workstation vendors was less, so I wonder if some of the multi user companies previously indicated they were workstation companies.

LANs showed the largest increase for this survey, but I am not sure if this change is statistically significant because of the small sample size. If it is, the migration to LANs is turning into a stampede.

Computer Type	% Respondents
PC	54.0%
LAN	30.0%
Mac	14.0%
Multi User	12.0%
Workstation	6.0%
Mini	22.0%
Mainframe	20.0%

I was surprised to see the significant increase in Mac products. This has been close to 8% in previous surveys. A dramatic increase in Mac companies isn't consistent with my experience. I am seeing less emphasis on new Mac products in my consulting which conflicts with the increase in Mac usage indicated in this survey. Many of the previously indicated "Mac only" companies are now focusing on Windows development. In the last year, very few companies have been starting up as "Mac only" software developers.

I haven't seen an increase in Mac software products to match the increased shipment levels of low cost Macs. It may be that this is just a delay as software companies develop software for the Mac, or it may be that many software companies have written off the Mac as a viable market for their software. It will be interesting to see if we continue to get this high level of Mac usage in future surveys.

We also ended up with higher levels of mainframe and mini respondents which I don't believe is significant.

4. Funding

The companies in this survey were much more likely to have outside funding (34%) compared to the recent survey on funding where we found 21.7% of the companies had received outside funding (private, venture or public). I believe that companies with outside investors are more likely to keep better financial records than self funded companies.

It appears that venture funding contributes to higher growth rates in revenues and profits than self funded companies or companies with private investors. I realize that venture capitalists hope that their funds help their portfolio companies grow, but it is nice to see some data to support this belief. (I should note that these cross tabs are based on quite a small sample size so you shouldn't put too much confidence in the results.)

% of Companies with...		
Funding	> 50% Revenue Growth Rate	> 50% Profit Growth Rate
Self	14.0%	20.9%
Private	10.0%	20.0%
Venture	33.3%	50.0%

While these results wouldn't make a statistician happy, they do seem reasonable. It is interesting to note that private investors don't seem to improve the growth rates. I suspect that the private investors are too "nice" (less demanding). I believe that the tough positions taken by the venture capitalists are fundamentally positive. As an entrepreneur, I may not like their "high pressure to achieve" mentality, but it is probably the right way to run a business to produce the best results.

5. Growth Rates in Revenue and Profits

The median increase in revenues and profits was 10 to 20%, but a significant number of companies are doing much better. 14% of the companies are increasing their revenues by more than 50% and 22% are increasing their profits by more than 50%.

Growth Rate	Revenue	Profits
> 20% decrease	0.0%	6.0%
0%-20% decrease	2.0%	8.0%
No change	24.0%	24.0%
> 10% increase	6.0%	2.0%
10%-20% increase	26.0%	28.0%
20%-30% increase	4.0%	6.0%
30%-50% increase	24.0%	4.0%
> 50% increase	14.0%	22.0%

The other surprising news is that only 2% of the companies reported a decrease in revenues and 14% reported a decrease in profits. That isn't bad performance for a year with a recession and a war.

6. Number of Employees

There were fewer one person companies than I had expected, but in thinking about it, most really small companies have at least two or three employees. There are very few individuals with all of the skills (or time) to run a company.

Number of Employees	% Respondents
1	8.0%
2-5	18.0%
6-10	24.0%
11-20	22.0%
21-50	28.0%

7. Primary Distribution

Direct sales continue to be the most popular distribution channel, but the telesales and dealer channels are also popular alternatives. Building a company with OEM sales as your primary distribution channel isn't very common. Developers who want to focus on developing their technology can use the OEM approach if they keep their costs low. It also takes time for OEM sales to build up.

Primary Distribution	% Respondents
Direct	68.0%
Telesales	18.0%
Dealer	14.0%
OEM	4.0%

8. Impact of the Economy

The answers were:

12.0%   Said "Our sales dropped last August, and show no sign of improving."
32.0%   Said "Some decline, but improved since the end of the war."
22.0%   Said "No impact that we can see."
34.0%   Said "We're doing great."

As you can see, less than half of the companies felt any impact of the recession. This is consistent with the earlier finding that the median growth rate in revenues and profits was 10% to 20%. Anyone who is growing 10 to 20% per year doesn't have much basis to complain about the economy.

A number of people felt that they were somewhere between "no impact" and "doing great". There were comments like, "Tougher year, but we intend to make the numbers." I think that this is what makes the software business such a great business. If you have a really great product and you are offering excellent service, you can continue to grow when the large traditional companies are laying off tens of thousands of people. No wonder so many people are starting software companies.

9. Reducing Costs

The most common answer here is that people aren't reducing costs. If you are growing 10 to 20% per year, you have to increase costs, not reduce them.

Method for Reducing Costs	% Respondents
Aren't	64.0%
Layoff marketing	8.0%
Layoff sales	8.0%
Layoff administration	10.0%
Layoff R&D	16.0%
Cut marketing budget (non-salary)	20.0%

As you can see, cutting the non-salary marketing budget was the most common approach. While I am sure that every marketing budget has some room for more careful trimming, I am concerned about the long term impact of these cuts. I hope that those of you who did cut your marketing budget didn't trim it back too severely.

I was really surprised that R & D was the department most likely to have layoffs. I had expected that the technical founders would have protected their technical people and let the sales and marketing people go. This is easy to justify since the layoff is caused by the lack of sales. Sales and marketing personnel were least likely to be laid off. I think that management understood that the problems were macro economic and that they needed to protect their sales and marketing people to continue to make sales.

This is also a short term versus long term decision. The extra programmer is likely to provide more features in your product release next year. He won't generate revenue this year unless he does consulting or training. The sales and marketing people will produce sales this year.

10. Revenue Per Employee

The average revenue per employee is $105K per year.

It appears that companies with product prices between $1K and $10K are much more likely to have a revenue per employee of over $150K.

Product Price	% Resp with Rev/empl > $150K per year
< $1K	7.6%
$1K-$10K	22.2%
> $10K	5.5%

With low priced products you have to generate an incredible volume to sell over $150K per employee. You would think that high priced products would make it easier to generate the high revenue per employee, but there are a number of factors that work against this:

*The longer sales cycle with higher priced products.

*Greater consulting/support content in the sale of a high priced product.

*Greater specialization makes it more difficult to recruit sales and technical people for high priced products.

*Customer expectations are higher and they want more for their money.

Dealer sales and telesales are also more likely to generate more than $150K in revenue per employee. With direct sales, the business is pretty labor intensive which makes it difficult to get high levels of revenue per employee.

Primary Distribution	% Respondents with > $150 Revenue/Employee
Direct	9.1%
Telesales	22.2%
Dealer	28.6%

I think that this is one of the basic appeals of building a distribution channel. If you can get other people to sell for you, you can leverage your people and your resources. The only problem is the investment necessary to get your dealers to a profitable level in selling your product.

11. Comparison with Vertex Management Report

The Vertex Management Group published a report, titled "Information Technology Industry, Human Resource Productivity, Performance and Trends. 1991 Survey Results." Tel (404) 396-6600, FAX (404) 391-0132. They surveyed 48 software companies, 11 of which were under $5 Million per year in revenue.

"The average revenue/employee for software products firms declined about $30K this year, most likely due to the recession and increased price pressure on products."

The median for all software companies in the Vertex report was $99K which is consistent with this issue's survey results. They found that, for companies under $5 Million it was $113K, and it was only $77K for companies over $100 Million.

The Vertex report went on to say, "Furthermore, larger firms experienced the greatest decline, this perhaps due to some inflexibility to cut back as required, more competitive products in some markets, and saturation in others."

These results make the results of the Software Success readers seem even more positive. As a group, the Software Success readers didn't suffer the revenue per employee drop that Vertex found in the larger companies. Small companies can be much more responsive to changing conditions, and it appears that this has helped the Software Success respondents get through this recession with minimal impact.

Operating Expenses

Category	This year	Last year
Revenue		
Product Revenue	76.8%	84%
Support Revenue	15.4%	8%
Professional Services	7.8%	8%
Cost of Sales		
Hardware	5.9%	3%
Royalties	4.4%	4%
Other COGS	5.5%	7%
Total COGS	**15.8%**	**14%**
Gross Margin	**84.2%**	**86%**
Marketing Expenses		
Salaries	3.0%	6%
Promotion/Lead Gen	11.1%	11%
	14.1%	17%
Sales Expenses		
Salaries	5.6%	8%
Commissions	4.5%	2%
Other	0.6%	0%
	10.7%	10%
Support Expenses		
Salaries	8.6%	8%
Other	1.0%	1%
	9.6%	9%
Development Expenses		
Salaries	15.0%	13%
Computer	3.0%	3%
Other	1.7%	1%
	19.8%	17%
Admin Expenses		
Salaries	6.8%	9%
Facilities	5.3%	4%
Other	7.0%	8%
	19.1%	21%
Total Expenses	**89.0%**	**87%**
Profit Before Tax	**11.0%**	**13%**

12. Product Revenue

The product revenue went down as a percentage of total revenues because of the increase in support revenues.

13. Support Revenue

The most significant change is the increase in Support Revenue. It is almost twice the percent of revenue as last year, and the support expenses are no higher. Maybe the Software Success readers are beginning to charge for support.

When you look at the profitability of the support department, this year it is making money and last year it didn't.

Support P&L	This year	Last year
Support Revenue	15.4%	8%
Support Expenses	9.6%	9%
Profit/(Loss)	5.8%	(1%)

I should point out that I haven't allocated part of Development to the support expenses. I usually think that the development expenses (including fixing bugs) are incurred to keep the product competitive in the market. Thus, the development expense would not be allocated to support.

14. Professional Services

The average percent of revenue from professional services is almost unchanged from last year. This year I calculated the percent of revenue for professional services for those companies who have any revenue from professional services. These companies average 14.6% of their revenue from professional services. This is pretty significant and represents a major profit opportunity for the companies that develop this revenue area.

15. Cost of Goods Sold (COGS)

The total cost of goods sold (COGS) increased slightly over last year. I wonder if this reflects the increased discounting pressure many companies felt in the last year or if it is solely due to the higher hardware cost of goods sold.

16. Hardware COGS

The average hardware COGS doubled from 3% last year to 5.9% this year. When I calculated the hardware COGS for the companies who sell hardware it was 18.5%. With many of my clients who sell hardware to mature markets, half of their sales include hardware and half don't. This would imply that these companies' hardware COGS might be as high as 37% on the sales with hardware.

My experience is that in many cases hardware loses money for software companies when you look at all the costs involved. Companies who sell hardware along with their software almost always think that they are making very good profits on the hardware when they compare the direct costs and the revenue. Many of them believe that providing the full service expedites making the sale. The difficulty is that many of the costs are indirect: the extra sales time to close a more expensive sale, working with the hardware vendors, spare parts inventory, and unreimbursed support because you are now responsible for supporting the hardware. I would appreciate hearing from readers who have analyzed their situation in detail and are willing to share this data (I will be very happy to provide anonymity.)

17. Royalties

Average royalties remained 4%, but companies who pay royalties average 11.1%. My experience is that royalties average 10% to 20%. Most companies who pay royalties have both internal and external products. Thus, their average royalty will be reduced based on the weighted average sales.

The royalty percentage varies based on who does what, but very few software companies can make money if they pay more than 25% royalty. This corresponds to the average development expense of 19.8% and part of the 9.6% support expense. If you pay a 25% royalty, you can only afford 5% of revenue for your development and support expenses. This assumes that the external developer is carrying almost all of the development and support responsibilities. If the publisher has to start staffing development and support, he will have to either reduce his profits and/or reduce his marketing and sales expenses.

I think that it is very important for royalty agreements to be tied to responsibilities. If the publisher has to assume certain responsibilities that the external developer was responsible for, the royalty payments have to be reduced.

18. Other COGS

The other COGS are usually the manuals, disks, tapes and packaging to deliver the product. It is lower this year than last, but it was 7.1% for the companies who provided this information.

19. Marketing Expenses

The marketing expenses this year are a little lower than last year, and all of the change is in the salaries. This is an area that was difficult for many people filling out the survey. In a small company, the president may be the chief marketing officer and may allocate 20% of his time to marketing, but all of his salary is listed under administration.

The marketing salaries were 5.2% of revenue for the companies who answered this question which is close to the 6% we found last year. The promotion and lead generation budget of 11.1% is very close to last year. Almost everyone spends some money on promotion and lead generation so the average of those who responded was 12.0% which is very close to the overall average.

There were a number of companies who were spending 20–30% of revenue on marketing. I found it interesting that, although all of these "heavy marketing investment companies" had lower profit before taxes, none of them were losing money.

The companies who were spending over 25% of revenue on marketing were increasing their revenues 30% on average and their profits 20% on average. This is quite good. Normally, when you make a heavy investment in marketing, revenues grow, but profit increases lag initially. The increased investment does pay off however. It takes about a year for profits to catch up and become higher than they would have been without the marketing investment.

Only PC and Mac companies spent over 25% of their revenue on marketing. None of the mainframe or multi user PC companies spent over 15%, and the others spent, at most, 15–25%. This probably corresponds to the fact that only companies with product prices under $5K spent over 25% of revenue on marketing.

20. Sales Expenses

Sales expenses remained steady at 10%. Salaries for companies who pay sales salaries were 7.1% which is identical with what we found last year. In many companies, management personnel are the only sales people, so there are no sales salaries or commissions.

The commissions were 6.4% for the companies who paid commissions.

If you combine these for the companies who pay commissions and sales salaries, the total expense is 13.5% and 53% of that is salary. Last year we found that salaries made up 80% of the sales expense. I wonder if this really reflects a change to more emphasis on commission compensation.

Other sales expenses were travel expenses. These weren't significant to many companies, but they were 8.0% of revenue for the companies who included this rcsponse.

21. Support Expenses

Support expenses have only increased slightly even though revenues are almost twice as high. The other support expense is phone expenses for most companies, and this was 2.4% for the companies who answered this. Many companies include the phone expense under the other administrative expenses.

22. Development Expenses

Total development expenses increased slightly over last year. I suspect that many companies hired the development staff based on the sales plan and that their revenues were less than they had anticipated.

23. Administrative Expenses

Administrative expenses declined 2%. I think that this was part of a very widespread cost control effort in our industry. A very significant number of readers noted that they were controlling their costs and trimming expenses. I see this as a sign of the increased maturity in our industry.

24. Profit Before Taxes (PBT)

PBT declined 2% over last year. This is the bottom line. It has been a tough year, but not a terrible year for software companies. The bad news is that 14.6% of the respondents lost money. With undercapitalized companies, you can't afford to lose very much money or your business gets into real problems.

Companies with direct sales are more likely to have profitability over 15% (33%). 22% of the companies who sell via telesales have profitability over 15% and only 14% of the companies who sell via dealers have profitability over 15%. I had expected that companies who sold via dealers would have lower profitability because they were sharing the margin with the dealers, but I would have thought that the telesales companies would have had the best profitability. This may just be a problem with the small sample size.

A number of the smaller companies, with revenues under $1 Million, reported profits over 25%. This is misleading since the owner operators aren't drawing a salary. Rather they take all the "profits" or lack of profits as personal compensation. A number of these respondents pointed out the problem when they were filling out the questionnaire, but they didn't know what a "fair market salary" would be for them so that they could more accurately understand what was the "real profit". This is an issue that buyers face when they are evaluating buying small companies. In many cases, when the new owners determine the cost of paying an employee to run the business, the profits are dramatically reduced. There are a number of businesses that are great owner/operator business which would be mediocre owner/employee business.

All of the companies that had over 25% profit before tax were self funded. I believe that these are also the owner/operator companies that I discussed in the prior paragraph.

There was no correlation between revenue growth or profit growth and profit before tax. Some of the companies with very high profitability are also growing very fast. I think that these are the small owner/operator business we have been discussing. In general, I find that most companies are faced with trade-offs between profitability and growth, but we don't have the data to clarify that relationship.

Another factor that can distort the statistical relationship is the "hot new product" syndrome. I have seen a number of situations in which a company comes out with a "hot new product". Revenues are growing very quickly since everyone wants the product and short term there is no competition. The company is also able to set a high product price due to high demand. Thus, a company in this position can experience a honeymoon period of high revenue growth *and* high profitability.

The bad news is that nature abhors a vacuum and competition will be attracted to this great opportunity. I have one client who found a niche and developed a product that had this great combination. They were able to grow to $10 Million in revenue with profit before tax over 30% before the bad guys introduced competitive products. This year four major competitive products were introduced. This company is now faced with some difficult strategic issues on how they are going to deal with their competitors. Which is more important? Revenue growth or profitability?

This is really a short term versus long term question. There are any number of studies that show that companies with dominant market share receive higher levels of profitability. If you can sustain high levels of revenue growth, you are maximizing your long term market share and your long term profitability. On the other hand, if you focus on short term profitability at the expense of revenue growth you risk ending up at a competitive disadvantage in the future which could jeopardize your long term profitability potential.

25. Comparison with Vertex PBT

Vertex found a 7.5% median profit before tax for all software companies. For companies under $5 Million they found only 3.8% median profit before tax which is significantly lower than the 11% we found. The only group that they found had high profitability was the $5M to $20M with 14% PBT.

I would like to believe that Software Success readers are significantly more profitable than other software companies. I am interested to hear about any other surveys of software company profitability that we can compare with our survey.

26. Vertex Payroll by Functional Group

Vertex analyzed the payroll by functional group as a percent of total payroll expenses. Software Success readers spent less on marketing and sales salaries than the Vertex respondents. Part of this is due to the fact that in small companies the president is the chief marketing officer, but typically we don't allocate part of his salary to marketing or sales.

The Software Success readers spent more on support than the Vertex respondents. I believe that this is related to the emphasis which Software Success respondents put on increasing their support revenue.

The development and administration expenses were pretty close for the two groups.

Functional Group	Vertex	Software Success
Marketing/sales	28.5%	22.0%
Support	18.1%	22.0%
Development	35.2%	38.4%
Administration	18.0%	17.4%

27. Conclusion

I hope that you find these results as interesting as I did and that you take the time to compare your results with those in this survey. I also hope that you start using this information to help run your business. Perhaps next year we can get a much larger sample and have statistically more reliable cross tabs.

C.   MISCELLANEOUS   (1991)

1. Information Services Company Valuations (May)

Readers have often asked me how to determine the reasonable ranges of valuations for software companies. My usual range is from 0.5 to 2 X Annual Revenues. This is based on anecdotal experience (deals I am involved in and people I talk to). I recently received some information from Broadview Associates on "Price to Revenue Ratios". It seems like the range is actually a little tighter than I have been thinking. Very few of the deals are under 0.4 or over 1.6.

Price to Revenue	% of Valuations
0-0.4	8%
0.4-0.8	27%
0.8-1.2	25%
1.2-1.6	22%
1.6-2.0	8%
> 2.0	10%

Information provided by:

Chris Schember
Broadview Associates
(415) 391-7300

2. Midnight Engineering (May)

Dear Dave,

Being a new subscriber, I'm not sure where most of the other subscribers fall in company size, annual revenues, etc., but by your editorial comment, I suspect they tend to be small. An excellent source of information (hands on) available for small software companies is the magazine *Midnight Engineering*. Although it deals with hardware products too, it is a great source of information on running a business on a tight budget. Their number is (303) 225-1410 (Do you advertise there?).

Speaking of tight budgets, the person who wrote to you on low volume printing (February 1991) would be interested in material provided by Don Lancaster at Synergetics, PO Box 809, Thatcher, AZ 85552. He wrote the book (no pun intended) on low cost publishing.

Anonymous

Dear   Anonymous,

Thanks for the note. I do advertise in *Midnight Engineering*, and I enjoy reading it. I appreciate your sharing resources and information with all of the Software Success readers.

Thanks,
Dave

3. Surveys — "Other" (Jun)

Dear   Dave,

Some of your questions should include an "other" box and an opportunity for the writer to fill in a response. While this means a little additional work for you, some of us round pegs don't always fit into your square holes. The numbers always work but the categories seldom do. For the fund raising survey, there are more ways of raising money than those indicated.

In the past I have begun to answer a questionnaire only to find that none of the answers fit. Once per questionnaire is OK, but after two or three, the questionnaire goes in to the circular file and never sees the light of day.

Thanks,
Anonymous

Dear Anonymous,

Thanks for the feedback. I read all of the survey forms and all written comments, so please add your comments to the questionnaire. I will also take your suggestion and add more "other" boxes so all of the round pegs get their day in the sun.

As always, I welcome comments, such as yours, to help me understand what I really should have asked. It is this type of feedback and collective thought that helps make Software Success more useful to its readers.

Thanks!
Dave

4. Hardware Marketing (May)

Q. We sell a vertical market package written under Unix that runs under several platforms. We try to avoid sales under $20K and have sold it for as much as $300K. As margins on hardware are getting smaller, we are finding it harder and harder to get hardware vendors to help us market our software. What do you see as the trends in hardware marketing and what should we be doing to prepare for the future?

A. Given your questions, I assume that you have been making significant dollars in the past off the hardware margin. Chances are, you also got significant support from the hardware vendors. The trend I am seeing is that the margins available to software companies on hardware are dropping rapidly. In most cases, it appears that selling hardware is break-even or a "loss leader" (a necessary product sold below cost to draw in business). This is non intuitive to most companies who are selling hardware along with their software. They will say, "I sold that last system for $30K and I only paid $20K so I made a quick $10K." When we dig into it and begin to allocate the sales and support time to make and complete the sale, our margin begins to drop. You also need to look at the cash flow. Are you paying for the hardware before you get paid? Do you have to buy some spare parts, cables, etc? What about the free hardware support after the sale? Take a hard look at it and see if you are really making money. My experience is that you probably aren't.

5. Credit Card Merchant Account Status (Jun)

An interesting article appeared in the May-June 1991 issue of Midnight Engineering. Written by Greg Kirkendall, this article recounted Greg's attempts to get credit card merchant status. Greg had developed a software product and was planning on selling it to college students via mail order using Mastercard or Visa.

Greg was turned down by his bank and they suggested that he contact a third party credit card service. The third party credit card service company said that unless 60% of his business was wholesale or retail NO ONE would offer him credit card services.

He was also told by the third party services that, in addition to submitting a business plan, and personal financial statements, you have to buy (not rent) your credit card reader from them. The cheapest price he found was $1,095!!!

The article also listed the following alternatives:
Golden Retriever Systems (Dick Mulhern, Sr.) 602-496-8430
BanCard Systems (Ronald Warren) 818-965-8700
Star-Byte (Wall Fredrich) 800-243-1515

Another alternative was DemoSource, a distribution and sales company that also provides credit card services.
DemoSource (Brian Berman) 800-283-4759

I know that getting credit card status can be difficult if you don't have a track record, and I was surprised at the extremely high fee from the third party companies. I've had a few calls from readers asking for advice on how to get credit card status, so I would be interested to hear from anyone who has worked with one of these third party service companies (either successfully or unsuccessfully). Also, if any of you has an interesting story about your own quest for credit card merchant account status, please call or write.

Thanks,
Dave

Greg Kirkendall may be reached at 47 Hiawatha Avenue, Westerville, OH 43081, 614-794-1365

6. Offshore coding–Philippines (Jul)

Dear Mr. Bowen,

I have recently become a subscriber to Software Success and have been quite impressed with the format and content of your publication. I am writing you specifically because of my interest in offshore coding and software conversion.

My company has been involved in offshore data encoding for several years. This process involves converting a company's raw data into computer readable format. Our processing facilities are located in the Philippines which gives us several unique advantages. Among the benefits are the large pool of low cost, English speaking, computer literate workers.

As a logical extension to this business, we are looking at offshore coding and software conversion. We are not primarily interested in designing the software. Rather we would like to concentrate on the "grunt" work such as converting existing software so that it runs on different hardware platforms. We believe that we can do this work at half what it would cost to do in the United States.

We believe that there is a market for this service in both large and small software companies. We believe that American companies can benefit greatly from this service. Lowering the cost of the labor intensive component brings down the breakeven cost for software makers. For smaller companies, being able to tap a large pool of programmers means being able to get a product to market that much faster.

I would be very interested to hear what you or your readers think of this market.

I look forward to speaking with you soon.

Sincerely,
George Martels
Vice President
Systems and Encoding Corp. (SENCOR)
205 E 95th St., #22G
New York, NY 10128

TEL (212) 735-6190
FAX (212) 735-6191

Dear Mr. Martels,

I am pleased that you want to do conversion programming in the Philippines. The economic advantage is mostly lost when offshore programmers are brought to the U.S. This is not very cost effective due to travel expenses and the high cost of living here.

Although you have many good references for offshore data encoding, you are just starting the software conversion business. At this point, you're concerned because you don't have references in the software conversion area. Hopefully, your good reputation in the encoding business will help get your conversion business off to a good start.

Good luck and thanks for the letter!
Dave

7. Selling A Company (Aug)

Dear Dave:

We talked a few days ago, and I asked you about evaluating and selling a software company. You suggested I write you a letter, so here's my story:

My company has been developing a "multimedia" presentation authoring language and interpreter for this language for the past three years. Originally developed for in-house production of touchscreen training and information systems, it was released as a presentation product called XYZ one year ago.

Our three years of developing and using the product have made it strong (we know the recipe's good because we've had to eat our own cooking for three years!) Because we've had to make money using these tools, we have been able to position our product quite well for the first customers of this new "multimedia" market. Unfortunately, those first customers are the pioneers, and there are not many.

We ran two months of small color ads in InfoWorld from November to January, and we were disappointed — we only received 300 phone-in leads during that time. Next we placed a small 1/4 page black and white ad in Byte in January and that ad did a little better, netting 300 more leads, but most were "bingo card" leads. Finally, we changed the name of the product to ABC, emphasizing the synchronization capabilities of the system, and placed full-page, full color ads in Byte and Videography magazine. We've also received a little free press from the four or five press releases we've distributed to various editors in the media. This press is responsible for more than 500 bingo-card leads, and the list is continuing to grow.

The leads are coming in, but only about 5% are buying. Our product averages $500 per system, and we make about $200 on each product sold. The customers we do have are quite happy with the product, and have already seen a return on their investment.

The market for our product is quite immediate and will explode as "multimedia" becomes less of a novelty and more of a tool in the next couple of years.

The problem is that we've accumulated a fair amount of advertising debt, and it's going to take even more consistent advertising, consistent PR and consistent development to make us succeed as the standard for PC-based audio/visual post production .

I now have a few questions:

1. How do we determine what the company is worth? How about the product itself?
2. Where do we find a "strong partner" with the resources, the experience and the vision to carry our product to its full potential?
3. What are all the mistakes we are about to make at this point?

Thanks for your time. I've enclosed our latest ad and some of the press releases we've had success with.

Sincerely,
Anonymous

Dear Anonymous,

My first reaction is that it is going to take time to find a buyer. Also, you have to keep this business going and growing if you hope to get anyone to take it off your hands. Most software companies' valuations are based on annual revenues, so a company with zero revenues is worth zero. From our discussion, it sounds as if your revenues are pretty low.

My arithmetic indicates you may have generated a maximum of 3,000 leads and that if 5% of these leads buy, you may have sold 150 units at $500 each. Thus, your maximum annual revenue at this point may be $75K. Depending on your advertising debt, I can imagine a buyer offering to take the product off your hands in exchange for taking responsibility for the advertising debt. The buyer would then negotiate that debt down and buy you out for $10K to $25K depending on how much debt you have and how determined the magazines are to collect payment.

The one exception to this is if the product contains proprietary technology that someone really wants. I have a friend who sold a product which generated less than $500K in annual revenues to a very large company for $8 Million. His product had special features and the large company wanted these features at any cost. This type of situation is the exception that proves the rule. So, unless your product has this type of rare potential, don't get your hopes up.

Next, I will focus on your specific questions. Then, I'll evaluate what you have done and what I think you should do in the immediate future.

Because of the formulas commonly used to valuate software companies, your company is presently worth zero and the product is probably worth very little. In a potential buyer's eyes, you haven't proved that there is a market for your product, thus creating significant risk for anyone who proposes to take on your product. People who take over the marketing of other people's products like it if there is a large number of good customers. These companies are able to tell potential buyers, "We market our product by doing (whatever) but, our growth is limited by our financial resources. If you add in X amount of money, then you can expect to get the following sales.". Buying a product like this is very low risk, and can be quite lucrative. Your situation is much, much riskier because you don't have an established track record and that depresses your perceived value.

The one exception would be to find someone who already believes your "vision" (e.g. he thinks that "multimedia" is the wave of the future and he wants to get in quickly and "ride the wave".) This is your "strong partner". My guess is, there are people out there who share your vision, and they might get interested if they believe that you and your product will get them to the promised land more quickly.

Chapter V. Management Issues

You must make sure that you don't get too discouraged. (This is the reason I want you to re-establish some type of positive marketing program.) If you convey that you have lost faith in the vision, you will scare off any "strong partners" and, they will have no interest in buying your product or working with you. In my experience, visionaries who want to enter an emerging market tend to screen out negative input. This affects their ability to see things realistically because they want so desperately to "make it happen". If you convey any negative attitudes, they will shut you out, and rationalize that you just don't have the "right stuff". Anyway, it will definitely kill any chance of making the sale to them.

Finding a strong partner who shares your vision takes time and receptivity. You need to cast your net far and wide. While you can put energy into this type of search, you can't force it to happen. You might approach a business broker, but I would be surprised if one would be very interested in working with you, unless he has a client specifically looking for products in multimedia.

I fear the greatest mistake you will make is giving up on running your business. If you decide that you are going out of business and you want to find someone to buy the product, your company and product will lose all their appeal. You have to keep your energy up and keep the dream alive. A good friend of mine told me a story about the gazelles in Africa. While they graze, they each periodically jump straight up, as high as they can. They do this for the benefit of their predators, the lions. By jumping, the gazelles are telling the lions, "Don't come after me, I will make you work too hard for your dinner. Eat my lazy or sick buddy." As a small company, you have to do the same thing to keep your business alive. At this stage of the game, staying in business is an emotional act of will. It is up to you.

I'm impressed that you generated 300 leads from one small ad. I know that the classified ads in Byte cost $525, so even for a 1/4 page ad, your cost per lead is pretty good. Rather than going for the full page four color ad, I would have spent my money on classified ads. Your challenge right now is to generate leads and make some money. Lets' assume you could generate leads for $2 each from classified ads. (I am assuming that the classified ads pull better over time and that you test various magazines. Also, you might haggle with the magazines, and get the

ad costs down a bit.) If 5% of these leads buy, your cost per sale is $40. You net $200 on each product sold so your revenue/cost is $200/$40 = 5 to 1. That is pretty good.

There would be some time delay (two or three months?) for the ads to turn a profit, but if you can work your way through that problem, you should start to generate some revenues to help cover your costs. This is also the type of information that potential buyers really want to see.

You need to deal with your advertising debt. Tell the magazine that the fancy ads were a mistake and you are now going to focus on classified ads. Also, tell them that you did generate leads from the bigger ads and tell them when you expect to make sales from those leads. With that information, you should be able to set up a payment schedule. While the magazines aren't thrilled with this type of situation, they will appreciate your efforts to pay them.

Send your press release to everyone in the world. Get one of the lists of 700 computer magazine editors and maybe even the lists of newspaper computer editors. Given your success with the four or five press releases you've already distributed, this press release mailing might help provide a supply of leads in the next few months while you are trying to reduce your advertising debt.

My last concern is your net of only $200 on a $500 sale. It sure sounds as if you aren't charging enough to cover the cost of the hardware which you bundle with your software. You should have at least a 20% margin on the $300 hardware sale plus your $200 software sale. I think a 40% margin on the hardware would be even better. Please look hard at this.

Hopefully, all of these ideas will help you figure out a solution.

Good luck!
Dave

Note to Readers

If you would like to contact this company, please give me a call.

Chapter V.   Management Issues

8. GSA (Aug)

Dear Dave:

One topic I haven't seen you discuss in Software Success or your Reference Books is GSA. In our efforts to sell to Uncle Sam, we've been asked to get our company and products listed on a GSA Schedule. Apparently, this is not easy to do (at least for the neophyte), but once a company is listed, it makes selling to Uncle Sam a whole lot easier.

We're about to embark on the GSA trail. I'd appreciate some information on GSA: What is it? How to get on it? Finding, qualifying, using, "GSA agents" (aka "beltway bandits")? Maybe this is an idea for a future article?

Regards,
Dorian Hausman
TBS Software, Inc.
(416) 940-9373

Dear Dorian,

First, I'll answer your questions.

Q. What is the GSA? How do I get on it?

A. Basically, the GSA or General Services Administration is the purchasing department for the Federal Government. In order to purchase products and service for the government, the GSA must carefully screen all potential vendors.

If a vendor has completed the GSA application and has qualified for listing on the GSA schedule, he has a better chance of being chosen for sales to the government. If the government is looking at 2 competing products, and one is GSA listed and the other one is not, the GSA listed vendor stands a better chance of getting the sale. However, being GSA listed is not essential to securing a government contract. It just cuts through the red tape and speeds up the process. To get a GSA application, call (202) 708-5082.

In my follow up call, your marketing manager told me that if TBS had been listed on GSA, you would have signed a contract with one of the government agencies. Since TBS isn't GSA listed, the government must go to outside bidders. This involves a delay, but TBS should get the contract anyway, as an outside bidder, since there is no direct competition.

Q. How do I find, qualify, and use a GSA agent (aka "beltway bandits").

A. GSA agents basically try to convince companies of the importance of being GSA listed. These agents then charge high fees to complete the GSA application for you.

I have two clients who paid GSA agents high fees (up to $25K) to complete the GSA applications. In both of these cases, the companies weren't sure the consultants really earned their fees. The clients had to supply all of the information for the application and the agents just filled in the blanks. (At least this is how it felt to my clients.) If you have to spend time finding the information, why not fill in the blanks yourself and save the money?

Also, being on the GSA schedule didn't bring these companies any increase in revenue. At least you had one situation where being on the GSA schedule would have helped. You've tentatively concluded that hiring an outside consultant to complete the forms would be unwise because you would end up spending too much time teaching him about your product and your business.

Thanks for bringing up the subject of GSA. I'd like to hear from other readers who have taken both approaches (hiring someone vs. completing the GSA forms yourself.) Also, does being GSA listed really help a small software company?

Thanks,
Dave

9. Advertising for Sales and Marketing People in Northern California (Aug)

Dear Dave,

We have a friend who owns a very successful software company in Australia. He wants to start up an American branch, and wants to know the best places to advertise for technically oriented people with some sales ability. He does not want to use employment agencies.

Apparently in Australia there is some section in the daily newspapers dedicated to computer related positions. Is there an equivalent publication in Northern California?

Anonymous

Dear Anonymous,

The San Jose Mercury News has a very large classified advertising section and is well read by the high tech industry here in Silicon Valley. The also have a special computer section in the Sunday paper that contains classified ads. Their phone number is (408) 920-5111 or (800) 287-7878.

Dave

10. Credit Card Processing (Aug)

Dear Dave,

This is in response to your request for information about credit card processing companies. We originally tried BANCARD Systems (in 1990) and found them very difficult to do business with. They submitted one lease agreement for the equipment, which we signed. Then, some time later, they returned a blank form and said that they needed to make some changes from the original, and to please sign a new form. Of course, we refused to sign a blank document. They called us and came by our office a few times and tried to pressure us into signing. Eventually they stopped. We never heard from them again, but they had opened an account for processing transactions for us with a bank in Southern California, who began charging us a monthly service fee (automatically deducted from our bank account), even though we had no equipment or merchant number. I wrote to the bank and they stopped charging us, but never gave us a refund or replied to my letter.

Then we were contacted by PeachTree Bancard and, have been using their service for about nine months. They are O.K. but the fees and charges are high. We pay about $100.00 a month on the equipment lease and a minimum service charge of $35.00 a month. The "discount" rate is 3.35%. This means that we pay 3.35% on all transactions. If these transaction fees are low, we still pay the minimum. Since we still receive most of our payments by company check, this sometimes happens.

Other minor problems: the amount of time before money is deposited into our account has been as much as seven days. PeachTree blames this on our bank, which may be true. Also, the deposit amount is our sale minus the 3.35%, so we have to calculate that number and it doesn't match up with our invoices. This means more bookkeeping headaches. We must keep very careful records. For the first few months we didn't even get statements from them. Now they do issue statements monthly, but they aren't very clear. They list the totals from each batch of transactions processed, then in another part of the statement list the monthly fees and service charges. It's time consuming to go back and calculate the fees and reconcile everything.

I hope this information is helpful to others who are thinking of setting up a credit card account.

PeachTree Bancard Corporation
2001 Butterfield Rd, 13th FL
Downers Grove, IL 60515
TEL (708) 719-1188

Very truly yours,

Pamela Fanstill
Austin Software Products
TEL (415) 589-9244
FAX (415) 589-9245

Dear Pamela,

I am pleased that you did manage to get a credit card account. Your story does indicate, however, the hassle this may involve. On the other hand, offering to accept credit cards may significantly increase your sales.

With our own account here, we don't calculate the discount rate on each transaction. The bank sends us a statement each month letting us know the amount automatically charged for that month. We then deduct that amount from our account and enter it in our accounting systems as a "credit card — bank service charge". Maybe it's easier for us because we're dealing with our bank and not a credit card service bureau.

Now that you've got a track record for credit card transactions, perhaps you can go back to your bank and try again to set up your credit card merchant account with them. I suspect you'll have better luck this time and you'll find your accounting hassles will greatly decrease.

Thanks again for the information.
Dave

11. Another Credit Card Story (Aug)

Dear Dave,

We are in the retail mail order business (magazine subscriptions and other spin-off information products). Our average sale is $75. A credit card merchant account is important to us; it offers an immediate buying opportunity, enables us to take the telephone sales, and (especially) offers a hassle-free way of dealing with non-US buyers.

At one time we had a business checking account with Manufacturers Hanover Trust, a giant New York bank. They refused to open a credit card merchant account for us.

We transferred our business to a tiny county-wide bank — Gateway — who negotiated a merchant account for us, with clearing through Citibank, another New York giant.

When we moved our back office (fulfillment, accounting, etc.) to California, we heard reluctant noises from our proposed bank, Wells Fargo, a California giant. However, we filled out the application form, showed our track record (never a disputed sale), pulled personal ties (our Vice President had a long time personal account) ... and said we would have to go elsewhere if turned down for a merchant account. We got the account.

Clearly this is an experience similar to the "How to get your first credit card" story, and for the same reasons.

I am afraid I have a low opinion of banks, feeling that (a) whatever you want to do is what they don't want to do, and (b) they would rather deal with insane losers like Texas real estate or Polish pineapple groves than with someone substantive.

Sincerely,
Nicholas Zvegintzov
Software Maintenance News
TEL (718) 816-5522
FAX (718) 816-9038

Dear Nicholas,

Thanks for the letter. What I am hearing is that you CAN get a merchant account, but it isn't easy. I suspect that the banks can't differentiate between software companies and mail order porno companies.

We both sell soft goods and don't have a store front. I am sure that software companies are very good merchant accounts for the banks, and sooner or later one of them will figure this out.

Thanks,
Dave

12. San Jose's Center for Software Innovation (Sept)

I met with Sarah Daniels, a summer intern working for the City of San Jose Office of Economic Development to discuss San Jose's plans to develop a Center for Software Innovation. Although, the Center is still in the planning stages, its promotional brochure states:

The City of San Jose, through its Office of Economic Development, has established a goal of promoting local software development. The Center for Software Innovation will be a nonprofit corporation, sponsored by a coalition of government, university, software and computer businesses. Its main goals include:

*facilitating new software development by providing small business assistance activities and *access to equipment for porting and testing*

*supporting Silicon Valley's competitiveness by encouraging software application development for area computer businesses.

*creating an identifiable, physical focus of software activity in San Jose

*promoting downtown economic development, and both retaining and creating new area jobs

The key to this proposed Center seems to be providing a porting and testing facility which would include: multivendor equipment, software library, PCs, workstations, networks, and printers. The focus would be on assisting configuration testing, customer support, and enhancements and ports.

The initial response from small software companies has been very positive. Porting and testing with today's complex environments is becoming a real issue with many problems.

Many of my clients make use of a combination of vendor facilities and customer locations (this is called beta testing). The vendor facilities can work if you are lucky enough to be dealing with a single vendor solution and if your vendor supports you. The customer location testing can be very time consuming if you can only test there in the off hours.

Dishonest software developers, who lead their customers to believe the software has been tested when in fact it has not, will not only destroy their own reputation, but will tarnish the reputation of the whole software industry.

So, a testing center, such as the one proposed by San Jose, would greatly enhance software development. It appears that the city can get much of the hardware and software for free, but a number of issues still must be resolved:

*How much will it cost to staff the center?

*How much test time will companies need?

*What is a reasonable configuration for the center? What scope should it try to provide?

*How much will companies pay for this type of test facility?

I have suggested that they conduct a survey (what else would you expect), but I invite you to share your thoughts with them. The governments in many other countries are taking a very active roll in helping their software industries. If we want our government to help our software industry, we need to let them know we want help and provide them with our feedback.

For more information contact:

Sarah Daniels
City of San Jose Office of Economic Development
TEL (408) 277-5880
FAX (408) 277-3615

13. Merchant Credit Cards–More Information (Sept)

We received the following note from one of our subscribers: "We are a small 2 person software company with all sales via mail order. We live in a small town (60K) and our local bank had no problem giving us Master Card/Visa after we were in business only 3 months."

The following is from National Home Business Report, Summer 1991.

Obtaining Merchant Credit Cards. After battling with his bank to get merchant status, John Calli published a special report to help others solve this problem: "Strategies For Getting Charge Card Merchant Status at Your Bank – Even If You're Running a Home-Based or Mail Order Business."

"The secret," says Calli, "is to find out what your bank's policies are before you tell them about your business. Ask for your bank's merchant account information package, and then fill out the forms and tell them what they want to hear."

This 64-page booklet is packed with insider tips and strategies that have worked for others, plus special tips and samples of various merchant account application forms. $21.95 ppd. from Western Pub. Co., Dept NHBR, PO Box 365, Cody, WY 82414-0365.

14. National Association of Credit Card Merchants (Sept)

This company specializes in helping "companies that have had difficulty securing Visa and MasterCard status securing such accounts", as well as helping credit card merchants "control chargebacks, credits and frauds so as to prevent penalties by Visa, MasterCard and American Express", etc.

For $349.95 you get your application and immediate help in getting your merchant status,a guidebook on how keep your merchant status, a year's subscription to their "Credit Card Merchant Newsletter", and Problem Solving Hotline.

If you are having problems getting merchant status, these people might be able to help. I would call and ask if they have a money back guarantee before I paid the $349, but if all else fails they might be able to help. I talked to one of their sales people, but I haven't talked to one of their customers.

National Association of Credit Card Merchants
TEL (407) 737-7500; FAX (407) 737-5800

15. Bundling Software With Computers (Sept)

Dear Dave,

I enjoy your publication Software Success.

I would like to find out if you have any comments on the bundling of a software package with a computer at the manufacturing stage?

(Here's) Some background information on T.K.M. Software Limited:

TKM markets a library automation package. The package (MicroCAT) was developed under SCO Xenix using C and ported to DOS. MicroCAT is available in a single user configuration and a multi-user configuration. The package consists of a series of modules:

- cataloguing
- searching
- circulation
- authorization module
- serials
- acquisitions
- audio visual booking

The package conforms to international standards and uses variable length fields for the individual records. MicroCAT has been targeted to the school library market, although I think there are other markets which can use the product. I believe it has some generic appeal because of the variable length records and powerful searching system. MicroCAT uses a proprietary database. I am attaching current pricing information.

I am currently investigating the potential of having a computer manufacturer bundle the software with the computer which they distribute. My plan is to have some of the basic modules included (cataloging and searching), and the customer would be able to upgrade with more modules, or to a multi-user environment. Do you have any comments and/or suggestions on this approach?

Thanks!
Yours Truly,
Ross Eastley, C.A.
TKM Software
TEL (204) 727-3873
FAX (204) 727-5219

Dear Ross,

When we talked, you mentioned that the computer manufacturers you had talked to weren't willing to pay more than a couple of dollars per copy for your documentation to include with their system.

My experience is very similar. Hardware companies look at everything as cost of goods sold plus markup. I once negotiated a contract where our software added significant value to the hardware. The hardware sold for three to four hundred dollars and our software retailed for $150. We ended up getting $10 per copy and the hardware company thought that we were taking advantage of them since the cost of our manual and disk was only $2. I was called into a meeting with their controller who said, "You guys are taking us to the cleaners. You are selling at 5X cost which is highway robbery." He thought we shouldn't be getting more than $3 or $4 for our product.

As we discussed it, if you can't get more than $10 per copy, you are almost better to put out a basic teaser product as shareware. At least this would get it into broader distribution.

Given the fact that the lowest price on your price list is $299 for the single user cataloguing plus online public access, I can't imagine that you can find a hardware company that will pay you the $100 or more that you were hoping for.

Let me know if you find such a deal.

Thanks,
Dave

Note: I would appreciate hearing from any readers who have had experience with bundling deals with hardware.

D. MARKET RESEARCH (8/91)

Only 85 people responded to this survey, about half the number who usually respond. Although it shouldn't be, Market Research is a low interest topic for software companies and the response rate reinforces this. I am afraid that most small companies are so focused on short term survival , it makes long term strategy seem like a luxury.

The company revenues of the respondents were very close to prior surveys, with slightly more companies in the under $1M range. Looking at the cross tabs, a higher company revenue increases the likelihood of having a users group:

Comany Revenue	% With Users Group
< $1M	16%
$1M-$5M	29%
> $5M	77%

1. Years in Business

We're in it for the long haul!

The median years in business is 5 to 10, and only 2.4% of the respondents have been in business less than a year. Comparing the results with last year's reader survey, we find:

Years in Business	This Year	Last Year
<1	2.4%	9.3%
1-2	9.4%	
3-5	20.0%	27.9% (1-5)
5-10	48.2%	38.4%
10-15	12.9%	24.4%
>15	4.7%	

Each time I look at the responses on number of years in business, I am surprised at how long most of you have been in business. The median company has been in business 5 to 10 years and has a median revenue of $1M to $2M. This shows just how difficult it is to grow a software company. Older companies are more likely to hold users groups, but it isn't nearly as strong a correlation as company revenue.

2. President/CEO Background

Lots of Techies, Few Bean Counters

Most company presidents have a technical background, and business is a distant second choice. I expect that many of the CEOs with business backgrounds came from the industries to which they sell. For example, someone who runs a trucking company might become CEO of a software company which sells trucking software.

President/CEO Background	% Respondents
Technical	65.9%
Business	27.1%
Marketing	7.1%
Sales	5.9%
Other	3.5%
Finance	1.2%

I wasn't surprised that Finance was very low on the list. This has been very evident when I tried to get subscribers to provide operating expense information. For the most part, as an industry, we have very little financial information about our own operations. This will be evident in the September issue when I tally the number of responses to the Operating Expense Survey.

The CEO's background has very little impact on the type of customer surveys used in market research. The only possible exception is that 16.7% of the marketing CEOs do focus groups. This is greater than the 5.9% of all CEOs who do focus groups. This may be due to the fact that companies where focus groups are appropriate are more likely to have marketing CEOs. On the other hand, it may just be statistical variations with small numbers.

3. Computer Type

PC's rule, but minis and mainframes edge up

The response to this part of the survey was very close to prior responses. The mainframe responses were higher than we found for the distribution survey, but they are no higher than normal. The mini-computer responses are slightly higher than last month, but again they are well within the normal range.

Computer Type	% Respondents
PC	54.1%
Mac	8.2%
LAN	14.1%
Mini	16.5%
Workstation	8.2%
Mainframe	7.1%

10% of our respondents offer their product on two computer platforms. This is lower than the 30% we saw last year. It seems as though companies are learning to "stick to their knitting" rather than trying to be all things to all people.

The mainframe and minicomputer respondents were slightly more likely to have users groups. I suspect that these companies have more expensive products and their customers are more involved with these software companies.

4. Number of Prospects

The number of prospects indicated in this survey continues the trend toward larger markets. A few more companies even indicated markets with over 100K prospects. There are a number of explanations for this trend. The first is that Software Success readers may be doing a better job of finding more prospects who have been there all along. Another explanation is that you are shifting your focus to larger markets. A final explanation is that the number of prospects is increasing within your markets.

Number of Prospects	% Respondents
< 1K	7.1%
1K-10K	29.4%
10K-25K	18.8%
25K-50K	17.6%
50K-100K	8.2%
> 100K	22.4%

Part of this trend is that many of you know that identifying more prospects for your product is one of the lowest risk ways to expand your market. Rather than worrying about adapting your product to new markets, you can replicate your marketing and sales programs by searching out more expanded mailing lists and magazines which focus on your type of market.

5. Product Price

If you raise prices, you'll have to ask more questions.

There were more high priced products than we have seen in previous surveys. Perhaps market research is more appealing to companies with expensive products. Or maybe, with high priced products, more market research is essential. If you're going to charge this much, then you'd better know exactly what people want!

Product Price	% Respondents
Not indicated	4.7%
$100	1.2%
$100-$200	10.6%
$200-$1K	17.6%
$1K-$5k	28.2%
$5K-$10K	21.2%
$10K-$25K	23.5%
$25K-$50K$	9.4%
$50K-$100K	8.2%
$100K	7.1%

There were 1.27 responses per respondent. Therefore, these numbers add up to 127%, indicating multiple products.

Installed Base or Number of Products Sold

These results are consistent with the number of customers indicated in the January Support Survey, but this survey has more information on companies with more than 5K customers.

Installed Base	% Respondents
0	1.2%
< 100	24.7%
100-500	34.1%
500-1K	15.3%
1K-5K	14.1%
5K-10K	4.6%
10K-50K	2.4%
> 50K	3.5%

I expected companies with larger installed bases would be more likely to use focus groups, but this wasn't evident in the replies.

7. Level of Competition — Medium

Most companies felt that the level of competition was medium. The results are quite similar to what we found in the 1990 pricing survey.

Level of Competition	% Repsondents
Not indicated	1.2%
Low	21.2%
Medium	48.2%
High	28.2%

Companies with a high level of competition are more likely to conduct more formal mail surveys and ones with a low level of competition are more likely to conduct informal phone surveys.

8. Rate of Product Innovation — Moderate

Again it was a moderate "2 or 3 announcements per year".

Rate of Product innovation	% Respondents
Not indicated	2.4%
Very high	10.6%
Moderate	77.6%
Low	10.6%

9. Types of Customer Surveys

Formal Mail vs. Informal Phone

Mail surveys are most popular, but a significant number of people conduct phone surveys. A number of people noted that they follow up by phone with the people who don't return the mail survey. I expected a strong response to the informal type of customer survey and almost half the respondents indicated that they do this. This can be a very good way to gather information and contribute to good cusrelations.

Type of Customer Survey	% Respondents
Not indicated	2.4%
Mail	62.4%
Informal	49.4%
Phone	43.5%
Users group	27.1%
Focus group	5.9%

I was pleased to see that this many companies were conducting users groups. A company can begin conducting users groups with minimal investment by asking customers to pay for the cost of the meeting. The costs are usually minimal and customers should be willing to cover these costs if they are really involved with your product. You might query your customers and see how many of them would be willing to pay a couple hundred dollars to attend a users group. (Make sure that you explain the fee is to cover the cost of the meeting rooms, coffee, etc.) If you get a positive response, then you can proceed with the expectation that your users group will "break even". (I am assuming that people from your company will organize the users group for free.)

In this survey, very few companies conducted focus groups. I have only seen focus groups done with consumer products having very large markets and equally large installed bases. There was no apparent pattern to who was most likely to conduct focus groups.

10. Usage of Customer Surveys — 87.1% use

Only 15.3% have never tried a customer survey.

Most companies, 61.2%, make occasional use of customer surveys, and 25.9% make regular use of customer surveys. This is moderately high, but the people who completed the survey are much more likely to be conducting customer surveys.

11. Customer Survey Topics

Topic	% of Respondents
Product satisfaction	78.8%
Possible product features	77.6%
Support satisfaction	65.9%
Referrals	29.4%
Testimonials	28.2%
Sales informatioin	11.8%
Pricing	10.6%

Product satisfaction, possible product features, and support satisfaction are all primary reasons for conducting a customer survey. Any one of these can justify conducting a customer survey.

Everyone should ask for referrals and testimonials when they conduct a customer survey. You should also ask if the customer wants a call from an executive in the company. I have also seen companies generate a number of sales leads via the customer survey. This is especially true if your customers can buy multiple copies of your product.

Very few companies ask their customers pricing questions. Many people are uncomfortable discussing future prices with their customers. This can be a tense conversation if your customers feel that your product is overpriced or if you feel nervous about your price. People are much more likely to ask about pricing in their fundamental market research since they don't run the risk of offending their customers.

12. Fundamental Market Research Topics

Fundamental Market Research Topics	% Respondents
Product planning	42.4%
Competitive awareness	40.0%
Pricing	31.8%
Buying decision factors	24.7%
Company awareness	23.5%
Product acquisition plans	14.1%
Hardware configuraition	14.1%
Reaction of competitors announcement	9.4%

Product planning and competitive awareness are both primary reasons for conducting fundamental market research. I also expect that company awareness is a subset of the competitive awareness.

Pricing is a common subject for fundamental market research since many companies are uncomfortable asking their customers pricing questions. This is also one of the best sources of information for pricing on new products.

Buying decision factors are often part of product planning. I have had some luck researching decision buying factors in mail surveys, but I have had better luck with personal interviews.

Product acquisition plans can identify companies who will be buying a product in your category at a specified point in time. These are the world's greatest sales leads, and these leads have more than paid for a number of fundamental market research surveys I have been involved with. From the prospect's point of view, he would like to know of all of the products he should consider.

If you sell to prospects who may or may not have computer hardware already, it is important to know what hardware, if any, they have. The incremental cost of your system will vary depending on how much of their current hardware they can use. You might have two marketing programs. One for large prospects who are much more likely to have current hardware and who are just buying software. The other program would be for your smaller prospects who will be buying hardware and will require more training and support. This type of differentiation can improve the effectiveness of your marketing.

13. Rating Customer Survey and Fundamental Market Research

Very few people felt that market research was a waste of time, but relatively few felt that it was great. For the most part, it was good or OK. My own experience has been more positive, but I suspect that I am more interested in market research than the typical Software Success reader.

Satisfaction	Customer Survey	Fundamental Market Research
Not indicated	15.3%	42.4%
Waste of time	1.2%	2.4%
OK, but...	16.5%	20.0%
Good	48.2%	30.6%
Great	17.6%	4.7%

14. Conclusion — Enhance your Business Direction

Customer Surveys and Fundamental Market Research don't require a lot of time or money, and they can help direct your business. You also can avoid issues and make decisions that have long term benefits. If you are going to do one of these surveys, I urge you to cover all the bases while you are at it. Ask your customers for testimonials, referrals, and additional sales opportunities. Good luck.

E. Management Survey (1990)

This survey received the best response of any survey in the history of Software Success. In part this reflects the increase in readership, but the percentage response rate was also better than earlier surveys. I hope that this has been improved by our efforts to make the surveys easier to complete. On the other hand, it probably reflects the fact that there is very high interest in management and funding issues.

1. Company Revenue

The companies responding to this survey were larger than typical for Software Success. I believe that this is due to the fact that many of the issues in this survey are more important to somewhat larger companies.

REPLY	PERCENT
<$250K	18.8%
$250K-$500K	8.7%
$500K-$1M	14.5%
$1M-$2M	29.0%
$2M-$5M	18.8%
>$5M	10.1%

2. Title

More of the respondents were presidents or CEOs. Again, I believe that this is because these issues are of most interest to the top executive.

REPLY	PERCENT
President/ CEO	71.0%
VP	14.5%
Director/ Mgr	8.7%

3. Number of Employees

The number of employees follow the company revenues and are larger than average. I noticed two anomalies. The first was that 24 percent of the companies had revenues under $500,000 and only 20 percent of the companies had less than five employees. My rule of thumb is that software companies should average $100,000 per employee. Some of these smaller firms are averaging less than this. On the high end, ten percent of the companies had more than $5 million in sales and only four percent had more than 50 employees. Thus, some of the larger companies are getting more than $100,000 per employee.

These two situations support the theory that very small software companies are less efficient because they don't have the expertise to deal with the issues at hand. It is also nice to see that the economies of scale might become available at the "under 50 employees" level.

REPLY	PERCENT
<5	20.3%
5-10	20.3%
10-20	24.6%
20-50	29.0%
>50	4.3%

4. Funding

I was surprised at the number of software firms with one owner. I would have thought that there would have been more firms with two or more partners. I guess the technical partner who brings in a sales and marketing partner doesn't give the sales partner a piece of the rock very often. The next most common funding situation is private investors. I find this a reasonable approach if the principals can identify possible investors who either know them as individuals or who understand the market. It seems to be too difficult to sell both the people and the market to private investors.

Both of these investor groups have other reasons for investing. Investors who know the principals may invest because they want to see their acquaintance succeed. Investors who know the market may benefit from their association with the software company. They may want some marketing or product rights or other associated arrangements. This raises the issue of how the private investors get their money back. This is a very easy question for owner investors. They can get paid well and to the extent that they are paid more than fair market for their services (my apologies to the IRS), they are receiving a return on their investment. Venture investors will only consider companies which can go public so they have their exit strategy well planned.

Private investors, on the other hand, are stuck with the middle ground. In many cases, the companies they invest in don't have the potential to go public, but they might become a very nice $5 million a year business which could be sold as a division to another software company. I have seen a few cases where the investors wanted to sell the company, but the employee stockholders enjoyed their jobs and

Chapter V. Management Issues

didn't want to sell the company. If you get serious with private investors, I urge you to discuss the exit strategies in detail so that everyone has a clear understanding of the game plan.

The low level of venture and public investment in software companies is consistent with the size of companies in this survey. It also reflects the fact that there are many software businesses which can grow to very nice $5 million businesses, but will never be big enough to go public or interest venture capital.

5. Expected Revenues in Five Years

Software is clearly a go-go industry. Even doubling your revenues in five years would be considered very good in most industries. A compounded growth rate of fifteen percent per year would result in a doubling of revenues in five years; 38 percent per year would result in an increase to five times current revenues. Given these very high expectations, I anticipate we will have many software companies who are failing to meet their revenue targets. One of the most common problems for software companies is to put together a very aggressive sales plan, then spend in anticipation of revenues. While you must make some investments before you have revenues, spending money that you don't have is an easy way to put your company into hot water.

I have seen a number of good companies with excellent products push too fast and contract for advertising that they couldn't afford. The theory was that the sales would come in time to pay for the advertising. In many cases, even though the products were well received, the sales lagged the expectations and the companies hit the wall. They were unable to pay their advertising bills and were cut off from future advertising. Their customers and prospects saw the sudden stop in ads and began to get worried. In some extreme cases, the companies mismanaged their cash to the point where they were unable to cover payroll and they had to close the doors.

Even though I am optimistic and tend to believe that new marketing programs can generate significant new sales, I urge you to avoid risking more than you can stand to lose. Please consider small ads. If they work, you can always increase the size of your ads. There are also any number of promotional possibilities which require little cash, but can generate a significant number of leads and sales.

Future Financing

REPLY	PERCENT
1-2X	10.1%
2-5X	43.5%
5-10X	26.1%
>10X	18.8%

6. Company Objectives

If you look at these objectives, the funding patterns for software companies become very clear. Employees can benefit from the first two objectives (income for the principals and a good place to work). Selling the company is interesting to private investors.

The one discrepancy is that 29 percent of the companies want to sell their company and only 13 percent are either venture backed or already public. This means that another 16 percent of software companies are hoping to raise venture capital. It is pleasant that this is consistent with the 17 percent of companies who say that they desire to raise venture capital in the future. (Note that I am assuming that the companies who said they wanted to go public also wanted to raise venture capital. While this isn't always true, it is nice that the numbers are reasonably consistent.)

REPLY	PERCENT
Income Principles	71.0%
Good Place to Work	50.7%
Sell Company	29.0%
Go Public	14.5%

Past Funding - Tried

The most common attempt at funding was to raise less than $250,000. Only a modest number of firms tried to raise more than that. I noticed that some of the companies didn't answer this question if they didn't succeed in raising money.

REPLY	PERCENT
<$250K	55.1%
$250K-$1M	13.0%
>$1M	13.0%

Past Funding Succeeded

If you compare these raw statistics with the previous ones about what past funding people had tried, it appears that most of the companies who tried to raise less than $250,000 succeeded and around half

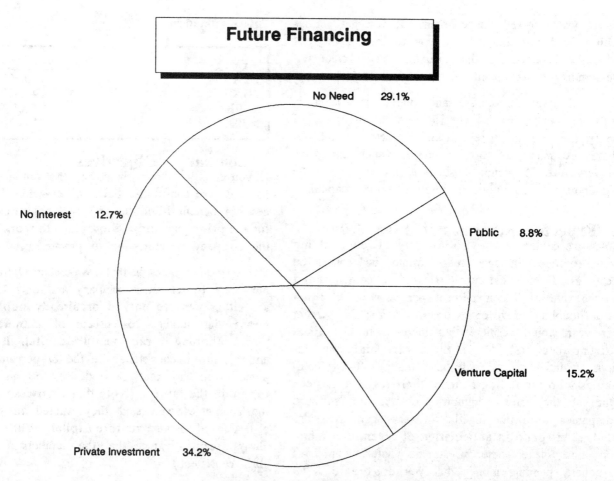

Future Financing

No Need   29.1%

Public   8.8%

No Interest   12.7%

Venture Capital   15.2%

Private Investment   34.2%

of the companies who tried to raise more than that succeeded. This is a little higher than I would have guessed. I believe that this is due in part to the people who didn't mention their failed attempts at raising venture capital.

REPLY	PERCENT
<$250K	53.6%
$250K-$1M	7.2%
>$1M	7.2%

Future Funding

The graph on future financing (at top of page) is quite interesting in that a large number of software companies aren't interested in outside funding. Either they have no need or they have no interest. My experience is that if you can get a software company established that you can grow very nicely from retained earnings.

Some of the categories have overlapping responses. For example, a number of companies said that they planned to raise venture capital and then go public.

7. If You Sought Venture Capital, Were You Successful?

Less than thirty percent of the companies who tried to raise venture capital were successful. This is closer to what I have observed. The reality is probably even lower because many of the people who said that they had spent time raising venture capital didn't answer this question. Nonetheless, raising venture capital is difficult for a software company.

REPLY	PERCENT
No	36.2%
Yes	14.5%

8. Effort Spent Looking for Capital

I was surprised at how short the time was spent looking for capital. This includes efforts to raise private money, which usually are less than three man months. My experience is that most companies who raise venture capital invest more than a man year when you include all of the people involved.

REPLY	PERCENT
<3MM	33.3%
3-6MM	14.5%
6-12MM	4.3%
>12MM	2.9%

When we broke out the time according to whether the company had raised venture capital or not, the differences became clear.

SUCCESSFUL REPLY	NO	YES
3MM	65%	30%
3-6MM	30%	30%
6-12MM	4%	20%
12MM	0%	20%

It is clear that most of the people who failed to raise venture capital quit after spending less than six man months. A good forty percent of the companies who succeeded spent more than six man months. While I still believe these estimates are low, I think that they make the magnitude of raising venture capital clear.

9. Acquisition of Products

I was really surprised at how much product acquisition activity has taken place. Given the abundance of good products which are created by individuals, this can be a real mutual opportunity. In particular, I was impressed that twenty nine percent had acquired a product.

REPLY	PERCENT
Have Done	29.0%
Evaluated	13.0%
Considered	1.9%
Never Considerd	24.6%

If "Yes," Why?

The most common reason to acquire a product was to exploit existing sales and marketing resources. This can be true even if the product is unproven. With established products, buying an installed base and eliminating a competitor can be significant reasons for an acquisition. I have seen a number of situations where eliminating a competitor was a primary motivator behind the acquisition, even though no one likes to admit it.

REPLY	PERCENT
Exploit Sales	46.4%
Installed Base	14.5%
Eliminate Competito	r4.3%

If "No," Why?

I have talked to many companies who weren't fundamentally interested in acquiring products because they saw themselves as development companies. They have a great deal of confidence in their ability to build excellent products, and they are less sure of their ability to market and sell products. Thus, they don't really feel that they have a sales and marketing capability to exploit.

The "no money" response may or may not be a valid reason not to consider an acquisition. I have seen a number of software acquisitions done with little or no money down. Many authors are happy if the marketing company will invest in marketing their product. In these situations, the most difficult issue in the negotiation is the minimum sales quotas that the marketing company must achieve to maintain the exclusive status. This negotiation is made more difficult by the fact that the marketing company isn't in a position to guarantee payments. (They didn't have any money.) The "build better" answer is really just a subset of the development company.

REPLY	PERCENT
Development	27.5%
No	$11.6%
Build Better	8.7%

10. R & D Capitalization

Capitalizing R & D is still an uncommon policy even though it is becoming more common. It was quite common for companies over $5 million (57 percent).

REPLY	PERCENT
Yes	31.9%
No	56.5%

11. Revenue Recognition

I was impressed with the quality of the revenue recognition. Only 8.7 percent of the respondents recognized revenue based on a verbal commitment. This can lead to difficulties since the customer isn't legally bound and it invites the sales person to be creative. It also allows the customer to renege on the deal.

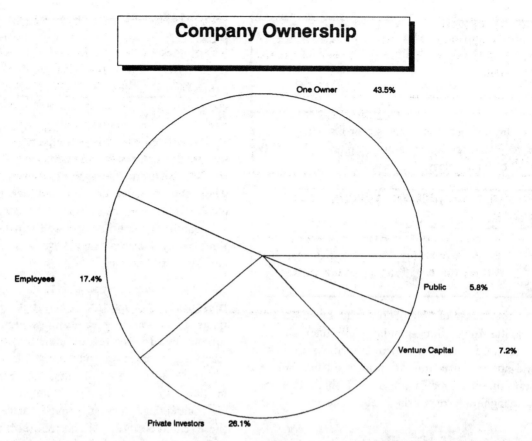

Company Ownership

One Owner 43.5%

Public 5.8%

Venture Capital 7.2%

Employees 17.4%

Private Investors 26.1%

Cash was the most common basis for recognizing revenue and it clearly is the best. A purchase order or a signed contract are pretty dependable if you sell to reputable businesses.

Delivery is okay as long as you have either a signed contract or cash. I sure wouldn't deliver my software without a binding commitment on the part of the buyer.

REPLY	PERCENT
Signed Contract	24.6%
Cash	39.1%
PO	33.3%
Verbal	8.7%
Delivery	5.8%

12. Maintenance Recognition

Most of the companies still recognize maintenance revenue based on cash receipt rather than prorating it as the maintenance is performed. The American Institute of Certified Public Accountants have proposed a rule that for software with post delivery obligations requiring maintenance revenue to be reported incrementally over the life of the maintenance contract.

Reference: "New Accounting Rules Would Affect Revenue Reporting", Software Magazine, December 1989

I feel that you should do this anyway for two reasons. The first is that it corresponds to the reality of the work and the costs that you have to incur to provide the support. The second is that it lowers your revenue and net income and thus your taxes. This saves you cash. It doesn't make sense to me for a privately held company to pay more in taxes just so that they can say that they made more income. I would rather have the cash and explain the difference. Companies under $2 million recognized maintenance on a cash basis (73 percent cash/27 percent prorate) while the larger companies (over $2 million) tended to prorate it (29 percent cash/71 percent prorate).

REPLY	PERCENT
Cash	53.6%
Prorate	30.4%

13. Line of credit

Most of the companies who tried to get a line of credit (LOC) did, but a significant number of companies never tried.

REPLY	PERCENT
Yes	56.5%
No, But Tried	8.7%
Never Tried	30.4%

14. Company Objective versus Funding

As you might expect, one owner companies were most interested in income for the principal and least interested in selling the company or going public.

Employee owned companies wanted to sell the company or go public. I was surprised that companies with private investors ranked income for the principals so high. This doesn't benefit the outside investors. As you might also expect, venture capital based companies are the most interested in selling the company or going public, but they aren't much more motivated than employee owned companies. Public companies can't sell the company or go public again so they focus on income or a nice place to work. I guess this reflects the fact that management in most public companies has little ownership.

	Income	Good Place	Sell Company	Go Public
One Owner	51	29	16	4
Employees	21	32	26	21
Private Investors	43	31	20	6
Venture	27	18	27	27
Public	50	50	—	—

15. Future Funding versus Revenues

There are a couple of strong trends. The number of companies who don't feel that they need funding increases steadily as the company revenues increase. Software companies should be self funding once they achieve a critical mass. At the same time, very few companies have no interest in funding once they get over $500,000. The interest in private investors is strongest in the $500,000 to $1 million size. I was surprised at the number of companies over $5 million who were interested in private investors. Perhaps they are looking at an ESOP. Venture capital and interest in going public grows as the company size increases. There was a drop in interest in venture capital over $5 million. This is probably because the leverage for the venture investors is less at this size, and there is less need.

	No Need	No Interest	Private	Venture	Public
< $250K	17	33	42	8	0
$250K-$500K	25	25	38	13	0
$500K-$1M	0	9	64	18	9
$1M-$2M	38	8	29	17	8
$2M-$5M	35	6	24	24	12
> $5M	57	0	14	0	29

16. Acquisition of Products versus Revenue

Most companies over $1 million in Revenues have considered acquiring a product and all of the companies over $5 million have at least considered it. Surprisingly, the percentage of firms completing an acquisition is fairly constant over $1 million. I am sure that if you sample much larger companies that the percent done approaches 100 percent.

	Done	Evaluated	Considered	Never Considered
$250K	8	0	50	42
$250K-$500K	17	0	33	50
$500K-$1M	20	10	30	40
$1M-$2M	42	16	26	16
$2M-$5M	36	21	29	14
$5M	43	29	29	0

F. Software Industry Business Practices Survey (1990)

Last year the Massachusetts Computer Software Council and Price Waterhouse produced this survey. This year the survey is being conducted on a nation-wide basis in conjunction with Adapso.

The survey seeks information on products, development languages and tools, support and maintenance, marketing, distribution, strategic alliances, growth, financing, and revenue and expense breakdowns. The survey will take about 20 minutes to complete. Replies will be held in strictest confidence by Price Waterhouse and only aggregated data will be released publicly.

Respondents may obtain a copy of the final report from Adapso for $50.00. Non Respondents may obtain a copy of the survey results by calling Adapso after. The fee is $200 for members, $500 for non-members.

I don't know what the non-Adapso member respondent fee is.

Luanne James
Executive Director,
Adapso
(703) 522-5055

G. The Operating Expenses Survey (1990)

We finally got enough responses to analyze. I really appreciate all of you who took the time to complete this survey.

1. Revenue

Support revenue was bi-modal. It was either very low (one or two percent) or it was ten to twenty percent.

Professional services were also split. Most firms get very little consulting revenue, but we had a few firms who got more than twenty percent.

2. Cost of Sales

Hardware costs can be twenty percent of revenue. I would guess that they are closer to 40 percent in sales which include hardware, but only half the sales include hardware for most firms which sell hardware with their software.

See the table on the next page for a breakdown of operating expenses.

Operating Expenses

REVENUE		
Product		84%
Support		8%
Professional Services		8%
	Total	**100%**
COST OF SALES		
Hardware		3%
Royalties		4%
Other		7%
	Total	**14%**
GROSS MARGIN		**86%**
EXPENSES		
Marketing	Salaries	6%
	Promotion/	
	Lead Generation	11%
	Total	**17%**
Sales	Salaries	7%
	Commissions	2%
	Total	**9%**
Support	Salaries	8%
	Other	1%
	Total	**9%**
Development	Salaries	13%
	Computers	3%
	Other	1%
	Total	**17%**
Admin.	Salaries	9%
	Facilities	4%
	Other	8%
TOTAL EXPENSES		**73%**
PROFIT BEFORE TAXES		**13%**

Royalties range from five to fifteen percent for the companies who pay royalties. I was surprised at the number of companies who pay royalties (almost half). The average royalty for those who pay royalties was eight to ten percent.

The other expenses were for packaging. In the recent issue on packaging, Darrel Monda suggested that packaging should cost less than ten percent, and our readers are consistent with that.

3. Marketing Expenses

A number of companies didn't break out marketing salaries because the CEO does the marketing. Most of the companies spend between ten and twenty percent on promotion and lead generation. There were a few who spend less than five percent. Most of these companies were quite small and I suspect they are spending time on marketing, but they can't really account for these soft costs.

4. Sales

I was surprised at several things on the sales costs. First, I was surprised that salaries were so much higher than the commissions. Second, I was surprised that the commissions were so low. The total of nine percent is about right, but the distribution surprised me.

5. Support

On average, support costs are almost equal to the support revenue. There seem to be two situations. When companies have low levels of support revenue (less than ten percent), they lose money on support. It almost seems that there is a minimum level of investment in support which is difficult to get below. On the other hand, when the support revenue gets above ten percent, the margins are very good.

6. Development

The level of investment in development seems to be related to the state of the product. Companies who are introducing a new product and have low support revenues have to keep their development expenses under ten percent since they are investing in sales and marketing to launch their product.

As companies mature they reinvest part of their margin from the maintenance fees in new development. If you combine the support and development costs, companies with less than ten percent of revenue from support invest 18 percent in support and development (these costs are 18 percent more than the support revenue).

Companies with more than ten percent support revenue invest seven percent of their revenues in support and development. They aren't investing as much as the young companies, but they are investing.

7. Administration

In most cases, administration is fifteen to twenty percent of revenues. There were a few cases where it was higher because of salaries or other expenses. I expect that these higher expenses were really for other functional areas, but they just didn't split them out. For example, you might put the President into administration, even though he is devoted to sales and marketing. There were also a few firms who had very high "other expenses" which affected the averages. Facilities were five to ten percent for the companies who broke them out. Some respondents included facilities in the other category.

8. Profit Before Tax

I was pleased with the twelve percent average PBT. There was a reasonable distribution on PBT. The upper limit seems to be 30 percent to 40 percent for PBT, and the companies with these high levels of profitability aren't investing in support and development personnel. I believe that you can't sustain these ultra high levels of profitability. Either competition comes in and forces you to cut your prices or to invest in your product. Ten to fifteen percent seems to be a sustainable profit level for many companies. Many of the companies in this range are investing ten to twenty percent in support and development while they are getting reasonable profits.

H. Company Benefits (1990)

I have gotten several calls about company benefits and I found the following survey results by NIBM on company benefits. They surveyed 1,500 companies and found that the percent of payroll spent on benefits had dropped from 29 percent to 25 percent over the past three years.

They felt that this is due in part to the trend to shift more of the health care cost burden onto employees.

"The average health care deductible for white collar workers is now $220."

1. Adapso Employee Benefits Plan

If your company is a member of Adapso, you can take advantage of their plan. It includes:

*   **Major Medical**

*   **Life and Accidental Death and Dismemberment**

*   **Dental**

*   **Prescription Drug**

*   **Short term disability**

*   **Long term disability**

Reference: Adapso Plan Manager,PO Box 907,Minneapolis, MN 55440-9863, (612) 588-2731

NIBM Benefits Survey

	Benefit	1986 Rank
1.Paid Vacation	92%	3
2.Hospital/ medical/ surgical	87%	1
3. Paid Holidays	84%	2
4. Group Life	82%	6
5. Paid funeral leave	70%	4
6. Paid sick days	69%	7
7. Paid jury leave	67%	5
8. Company paid health premium	57%	not ranked
9. Long term disability	52%	8
10. Dental Insurance	52%	13
11. Tuition Reimbursement	48%	10

I. Salary Survey (1990)

We had sixty responses to this survey. This was quite a good response, but it was a little lower than I had expected. It turned out that a number of people weren't able to complete the survey for a number of reasons:

*   They work for very small companies where the job categories don't apply

*   They worked for larger companies, but they only know the salaries in their department. The good news is that most of the people who filled out the survey took the time to fill out

most of it. We ended up with a great deal of information, and I appreciate the time people took to complete the survey.

1. Profile of Respondents

We had more respondents from larger companies in this survey. 39.4 percent of the companies in this survey had revenues over $2 million whereas only 18.3 percent of the companies in the July Lead Generation survey were over $2 million.

I think this is related to the fact that compensation in smaller companies is viewed as personal. I still remember the survey from a small company which said "Only our CPA knows the answers to these questions!" In larger companies, salary levels are more public and far less personal.

The distribution of computer type was much closer to the previous surveys. We had slightly fewer LAN companies and slightly more mini companies, but the variations were pretty small.

President

The salary of the president was provided by 75 percent of the respondents. The median salary is $80,000. There was a very broad range of salaries for presidents:

SALARY	% RESP
No Reply	25.0%
<$40K	8.3%
$40K - $60K	15.0%
$60K - $80K	15.0%
$80K - $100K	15.0%
$100K - $150K1	5.0%
>$150K	6.7%

I was generally surprised at how few presidents received significant bonuses or commissions. My experience as a board of directors member is that I like to see a software company president with a good salary in the $80,000 to $125,000 range, and a potential for a significant bonus. If the company has had a great year, it might be appropriate to pay a bonus as large as the base salary.

On the other hand, if the company has a disappointing year, the President might receive no bonus. I am very uncomfortable locking the company into a very high presidential salary given all the uncertainties in the software business.

Two-thirds of the respondents received little or no bonus (more than $5,000). The remaining third were spread from $10,000 to $120,000. Fifteen percent of the respondents received large bonuses (more than $30,000), and many of these were over $100,000. This supports my experience that the best way to reward the President when things are going very well is to pay them a very nice bonus. Lets hope that the small companies which aren't paying bonuses yet, will succeed so that they can reward the CEO.

The outlook for raises is pretty poor. A total of 82 percent of the respondents didn't answer or expected a raise of less than five percent. In most cases, they were expecting to raise other salaries in the five percent to ten percent, but they weren't expecting to raise their own salary. I guess they don't see 1990 as a great year. Only one person was expecting more than a 25 percent raise, and that was because they hadn't made very much last year.

2. Development

We had more spread on the highest development title reported.

TITLE	% RESP
No Reply	36.7%
VP2	6.7%
Director/ Mgr	13.3%
Senior Pgm	21.7%

I was surprised at the number of firms which had marketing vice-presidents, but the highest ranking technical person was the senior programmer. This may be due to the fact that marketing and sales people want and need impressive titles, while developers could care less in many cases.

In many of the cases, the companies had vice-presidents of marketing and a senior programmer. I suspect that these were marketing companies which acquired products from other companies. The development responsibility in these marketing companies is limited to the care and feeding of the current products. You may not need a vice-president of development in this type of situation.

The median compensation was under $60,000 and only five percent of the respondents earn more than $100,000.

SALARY	% RESP
No reply	36.7%
$20K - $40K	16.7%
$40K - $60K	25.0%
$60K - $80K	11.7%
$80K - $100K	5.0%
>$100K	5.0%

The bonuses for developers are even lower than for presidents, but they are expecting slightly better raises.

3. Marketing

We had a reasonable spread of marketing titles.

TITLE	% RESP
No reply	36.7%
VP	23.3%
Director	16.7%
Manager	16.7%
Coordinator	6.7%

I think this spread reflects the fact that most software companies start and grow without a marketing person in the company. Many smaller companies can't afford or attract a vice-president of marketing, so they hire a manager or coordinator. Over time, this person may grow and get promoted, or the company will be able to attract a more senior marketing person.

The median marketing salary is $40,000 to $60,000 and only 3.4 percent of the marketing people make more than $100,000.

SALARY	% RESP
No reply	36.7%
<$20K	6.7%
$20K - $40K	20.0%
$40K - $60K	20.0%
$60K - $80K	10.0%
<$80K	.7%

One misleading conclusion you could draw from these numbers is that senior marketing people don't make much money. My experience is that very good marketing executives typically make over $100,000. The problem is that there aren't a lot of experienced marketing people in the software industry. I expect that these numbers will change over time as our industry matures.

Given the relatively low salaries for the marketing executives, it isn't surprising that they receive very little in bonuses. They also are expecting slightly better raises than the developers.

4. Sales

We didn't receive a lot of information about the sales compensation. I expect that few of the marketing people know what their sales counterpart is earning. The sales titles were:

TITLE	% RESP
No reply	61.7%
VP	18.3%
Director	3.3%
Manager	16.7%

The median sales compensation was $60,000 and five percent of the sales executives earn over $100,000.

SALARY	% RESP
No reply	63.3%
<$20K	1.7%
$20K - $40K	11.7%
$40K - $60K	6.7%
$60K - $80K	6.7%
>$80K	10.0%

I was surprised that of the 35 percent of the companies who answered the bonus question for sales, that ten percent of them receive less than $5,000 in bonus. Only 8.4 percent receive over $20,000 in bonus.

While I don't believe that the sales executive should be on straight commission like their sales people, I like to provide the performance motivations that bonuses and commissions can provide.

5. Support

We had quite a broad spread of support titles.

TITLE%	RESP
No reply	36.7%
VP	11.7%
Director	11.7%
Manager	23.3%
Support Rep	16.7%

I was pleased at that the number of support managers was greater than the number of support reps. I have seen too many cases where companies had several support reps, but no manager. Everyone was reporting to the president or vice-president of development. I think that making someone manager of support is an important first step in elevating the importance of customer support.

The median support compensation was $20,000 to $40,000, which is a clear indication of the low level of priority that customer support actually receives. I want to remind you that this is the highest compensation for an employee in the support department. Thus it includes many of the managers.

SALARY	% RESP
No Reply	38.3%
<$20K	5.0%
$20K - $40K	35.0%
$40K - $60K	18.3%
$60K - $80K	3.3%

It appears that you have to be a director or vice-president of support to make over $40,000.

As you might expect, support people don't get bonuses but they do expect at least five percent to ten percent raises since they are paid so poorly.

6. Sales Compensation

The median sales person earns $30,000 to $40,000 in our survey. Only 3.3 percent of the companies reported that their average sales person earned over $90,000.

SALARY	% RESP
No Reply	45.0%
<$20K	1.7%
20K - $30K	10.0%
$30K - $40K	16.7%
$40K - $50K	11.7%
$50K - $60K	6.7%
>$60K	8.4%

This is quite different than the hype we all hear about software sales people pulling in the big bucks. On average, they aren't making a lot of money.

I asked about the maximum salary for sales people, and I expected to either hear no limit or a very high number. Almost everyone who answered this question gave a specific and a relatively low number. Usually the maximum that they stated was less than twice the minimum salary. In some other cases it

was even lower depending upon the compensation for the top sales executive.

In a large number of cases, people stated that a sales person couldn't earn more than the sales manager. I feel that there should be no limit to what a sales person can earn. As a sales manager, I will earn more because of my override, so I shouldn't want to cap the sales person's compensation.

The minimum compensation for sales people was somewhat higher than I would have guessed. The median was probably close to $35,000.

MINIMUM	% RESP
No Reply	48.3%
$20K	8.3%
$25K	11.7%
$30K	6.7%
$35K	15.0%
$40K	3.3%
$50K	6.7%

If you compare the average compensation of $30,000 to $40,000 and the minimum of $35,000, it appears that as an industry our sales people are much more salaried than I would have thought. The amount of leverage that the average sales person has is limited. I also asked people what the guarantee was for sales people. The median was $25,000 and 6.7 percent guaranteed $50,000.

GUARANTEE	% RESP
No Reply	43.3%
$10K	1.7%
$15K	6.7%
$20K	6.7%
$25K	25.0%
$30K	1.7%
$35K	6.7%
>$40K	8.4%

There is a $10,000 difference between the minimum and the guarantee. I think that this reflects the minimum sales level that companies will suffer. If they are using a ten percent commission rate, and the sales person sells $100,000 the sales person would get $10,000 in commission plus their $25,000 guarantee.

At this level, the company is paying 35 percent of revenue in sales compensation. If you double this to cover benefits, office space, phones, and management overhead, a sales person at this level is only marginally covered.

The most common commission rate is eight to ten percent, but a number of firms pay four to six percent in commissions. A very few firms pay the very high commissions which were much more common a few years ago.

COMMISSION	% RESP
No Reply	46.7%
>1%	3.1%
1% - 2%	3.1%
2% - 4%	12.5%
4% - 6%	25.0%
6% - 8%	9.4%
8% - 10%	34.4%
10% - 15%	3.1%
15% - 20%	6.3%
>20%	3.1%

We didn't get a very good answer to the "total compensation at quota" in that 63 percent of the companies didn't respond. There was a very broad range, and the median response was $40,000 to $60,000.

COMP QUOTA	% RESP
No Reply	63.3%
<$20K	3.3%
$20K - $40K	8.3%
$40K - $60K	8.3%
$60K - $80K	5.0%
$80K - $100K	8.3%
>$100K	3.4%

7. Salaries as a Function of Company Revenue

Presidents of software companies under $1 million in sales don't earn much more than their key developers. At $1 million the situation improves, and once the companies get over $2 million most of the presidents earn over $100,000, and sixteen percent earn over $150.000.

Developers also benefit when the sales go over $2 million. When companies are less than $2 million in sales, the lead developer makes less than $80,000. For companies over $2 million, 31 percent of the developers earn over $80,000 and ten percent earn over $125,000.

The pattern for marketeers follows the developers. They make less than $80,000 if the company is less than $2 million in revenue. If the company is over

$2 million in revenue 21 percent of them make over $80,000 and eleven percent earn over $100,000.

For sales people, 26 percent of them make over $80,000 in companies over $2 million, and eleven percent earn over $100,000.

8. Sales Rep Compensation

Compensation for sales reps is much less dependent on the company revenue. I believe this is due to a number of factors. First of all, most managers in small software companies have an equity share. They are investing in their company by foregoing salary since they believe that they will benefit from this investment. Very few sales people have an equity investment. For many of them, they want the immediate gratification of the cash.

I have been told by a number of very good sales people "I sell products, I don't build companies."

Given this philosophy, small companies are competing with larger companies for sales people and they have to pay cash (not stock). The percentage of sales people (average compensation) who earn over $50,000 doesn't change much for companies over $500,000.

REVENUE	% RESP
<$500K	0%
$500K - $1M	25%
$1M - $2M	13%
$2M - $5M	26%

The one area where larger companies are better to sales people is the minimum salary. Twenty-one percent of companies in the $2 million to $5 million range pay a minimum of $50,000 to their sales people. Almost none of the smaller companies pay over $35,000 as a minimum.

I had expected to find that the larger companies paid smaller commissions because they offered higher bases and more security. It turns out to be much more complicated.

Companies under $500,000 pay no or very low commissions. In many cases the founders are doing the selling so they don't get a commission.

Companies in the $500,000 to $1 million range offer the highest commissions of any group. Thirty-seven percent of them pay commissions over ten percent.

President Salary vs Company Revenue

Revenue	No Reply	>$20K	$20K-$40K	$40K-$60K	$60K-$80K	$80K-$100K	>$100K
<$250K	40%	20%	20%	20%			
$250K-$500K	0%	0%	0%	33%	33%	33%	
$500K-$1M	12%	0%	0%	37%	25%	25%	
$1M-$2M	25%	0%	6%	19%	19%	19%	13%
$2M-$5M	10%	0%	0%	0%	16%	16%	58%

It appears that these companies have decided that they need to attract professional sales people and they have to bribe the sales people with extra high commissions. Given the problems selling an unknown product which may not be as complete as products from larger companies, this seems fair to me.

Once the companies are over $1 million in sales, it is very rare for them to pay commissions over ten percent. The commissions in companies over $2 million are slightly lower than the companies in the $1 million to $2 million range. Twenty-six percent of the over $2 million companies pay commissions of four percent to six percent versus only six percent of the $1 million to $2 million companies.

9. Compensation at Quota

As you can see in the table below, there is no clear pattern in the compensation at quota by the size of company. I am afraid that part of this is the small sample size for this question when you segment it by revenue range.

We had three companies in the $250,000 to $500,000 and one of them paid $80,000 to $100,000 at quota. If you ignore this statistical aberration, the larger companies pay more at quota. The companies in the $2 million to $5 million range paid up to $150,000 at quota, and a majority of the ones who answered paid over $60,000.

The medians by company size were:

REVENUE	MEDIAN COMP
<$250K	No Reply
<$500K	$80-$100K
<$1M	$40-$60K
<$2M	$20-$40K
<$5M	$60-$80K

10. Development Title Compensation

The median compensation for the different development titles was:

TITLE	MEDIAN COMP
VP	$60K - $80K
Director	$40K - $60K
Manager	$20K - $40K
Sr Pgm	$20K - $40K

The spread is even more dramatic because nineteen percent of the vice-presidents make over $100,000.

11. Marketing Titles

The marketing spread is similar:

TITLE	MEDIAN COMP
VP	$40K - $60K
Director	$40K - $60K
Manager	$20K - $40K
Coordinator	$20K

Fourteen percent of the vice presidents make over $100,000.

Comp at Quota

Revenue	No Reply	< $40K	$40K-$60K	> $60K
< $250K	100%	0%	0%	0%
< $500K	67%	0%	0%	33%
< $1M	62%	0%	25%	12%
< $2M	56%	31%	6%	6%

12. Sales Comp by Title

Titles really translate into more dollars for sales people.

TITLE	MEDIAN COMP
VP	$80-100K
Director	$40-$60K
Manager	$20-$40K

J. Reader Survey (1990)

Record High Survey Response, Again

We received 86 responses to this survey. Once again, this is a record. (Even if it is only one more than the last survey.) Given the fact that this survey isn't on a specific marketing topic, I was very pleased with the response. Thanks for your time in filling out the surveys.

1. Company Revenue

The company revenue is fairly evenly spread. As you can see from the graph on page 21, our readers are pretty evenly spread among the under $5 million in revenue range. Only 10 percent of our readers have revenues over $5 million.

2. Computer Type

The table on the next page shows the distribution of sales by computer type. As you can see, PCs are the most common computer type, but we have good representation for mini, workstation and mainframe vendors. I am currently doing test mailings to lists which emphasize these other markets.

The average company had 1.21 computer types. Thus, one out of five companies offer their product on two platforms. This is a little higher than we have seen in the past. I believe much of the growth has been due to PC companies offering LAN versions of their products. We are also seeing more mainframe companies offering their products on the PCs and LANs as part of the IBM enterprise-wide computing.

If you look at the table on the next page, you will see that only 17 percent of the companies get no sales on the PC. Thus, there are many companies which offer other platforms and generate some sales on these other platforms, but they don't consider themselves a PC company.

Fifty-four percent of the companies are primarily PC companies in that they get over 50 percent of their sales on PCs. This is 77 percent of the companies who said that they offered PC products.

Only 8 percent of the companies are primarily LAN companies in that they get over 50 percent of their sales on LANs. This is 53 percent of the companies who said that they offered LAN products.

This is an improvement over earlier results. I expect this to increase in the next few years as LANs become a new standard platform.

Minicomputers are more isolated in that most mini companies are focused on the minis. 67 percent of the mini companies get over 50 percent of their sales on minis. Workstations are even higher, with 80 percent of the workstation companies getting over 50 percent of their sales on workstations.

I have gotten several calls and questions from people asking if I knew of workstation products which had successfully ported to PCs and vice versa. I don't know of any examples. I would be interested in hearing of any cases, successful or not.

I wonder if the companies with less than ten percent of their sales on workstations aren't more likely to be mini companies than PC companies. It turns out that there were eleven companies with one percent to ten percent of their sales on workstations. Seven of these were PC companies which is eleven percent of the PC companies. One was a LAN company which is seven percent of the LAN companies. Three were mini companies which is twenty percent of the mini companies. Thus it turns out that the

that mainframe companies get at least 25 percent of their sales on mainframes, but other companies get some mainframe sales.

I have one client whose primary product runs on the PC, but they have a mainframe product. This has been a real problem for them. The mainframe product has been supported by a programmer who is no longer a full time company employee. This makes it difficult for the company to provide technical sales support. Customer support is a little difficult, but the programmer manages to provide it while he is doing his primary contract programming business.

Since the mainframe is a secondary line of business, the company has to buy time on a computer service bureau. The disk storage and processor charges are considerable. It appears to me that these costs and the awkwardness will keep this secondary business

Table I - Percent Sales by Computer Type

Computer Type	0%	1-10%	10-25%	25-50%	> 50%
PC	17.4%	12.8%	4.7%	9.3%	54.7%
LAN	52.3%	16.3%	7.0%	16.3%	8.1%
Mini	73.3%	8.1%	2.3%	4.7%	11.6%
Workstation	79.1%	2.8%	2.3%	1.2%	4.7%
Mainframe	81.4%	3.5%	2.3%	3.5%	8.1%

mini companies are more likely to offer a product on the workstations, but there are more PC products because there are so many more PC companies in this survey.

I expected that the mainframe companies would be most focused on the mainframe. 70 percent of them get more than 50 percent of their sales on mainframes. This is pretty high, but it isn't the highest. A total of fifteen companies had some mainframe sales comparedwith ten companies who considered themselves to be mainframe companies. It appears

from ever being really profitable. I would be interested to hear from others who are supporting a secondary mainframe or mini product.

3. Market Size

I was pleased to see that 82 percent of the companies knew their market size. This is a significant increase over earlier questionnaires. I was also pleased that companies were focusing on larger markets.

Small markets are very difficult to base a company on unless they are really rich. I have also seen a number of cases with very small markets where one company will start in the market and be doing well. This will attract several competitors. Soon, there isn't enough business to support all the competitors and everyone is unprofitable. This is much less likely to happen with a larger market, and it takes longer to occur even if it does occur.

MARKET SIZE	% RESP
No Response	18.6%
<1K	5.8%
1-10K	25.6%
>10K	50.0%

The respondents to this survey view their markets as slightly larger than those who responded to the July lead generation survey. In particular, 14.3 percent of the July respondents felt that their market had less than 1,000 prospects. This is down significantly with this survey.

I hope that more companies are taking a hard look at their potential market and finding ways to expand it. While one approach is to modify your product or marketing to appeal to another market, you can make significant changes if you just begin to aggressively look for new magazines, lists, and so forth. I have seen a number of cases where a proactive program to identify more and better prospects has made a major change in the business.

First, develop a formula for direct mail or advertising which makes money. The next step is to "roll it out," to approach more people and make more money.

4. Product Price
The product prices are pretty evenly spread.

PRODUCT PRICE	% RESP
No Reply	10.5%
<$1K	23.3%
$1K - $10K	33.7%
>$10K	36.0%

I used these ranges because I find product marketing characteristics to be quite different at each of these levels.

Products under $1,000 are best sold through distribution or directly with a one-step sales cycle.

At this price level, you don't have enough money to work with prospects during the evaluation process. Our last distribution survey indicated that products under $1,000 are much more likely to succeed in distribution.

At the $10,000 level, we begin to be able to afford sophisticated sales and pre-sales support. My experience is that once the price gets over $20,000, a company can afford to travel to the customer to demo the product. Most products over $10,000 involve demos, and trial evalua-tions.

The $1,000 to $10,000 middle ground is tough. If you are selling a mainframe or mini product to large corporations, this range is equivalent to selling the under $1,000 product to individuals. Corporations will buy products in this price range with less evaluation and concern than the over $10,000 products. I believe this is related to the purchase decision level within large corporations.

Selling products in the $1,000 to $10,000 range to small businesses is really selling to individuals. In most industries, these businesses take decisions this size very seriously. I have seen a number of vertical market companies selling products in the $5,000 to $10,000 range wrestle with how to speed up the sale.

At this price level, you don't have the margin to support direct sales calls. If you can sell the hardware, that may help. One common approach is to try to do a remote PC demo to show the prospect the product. The success of this depends upon the level of PC literacy of the prospects and the confidence of the vendor's sales and support people. I have seen a couple of cases where this has worked.

Another interesting approach is to sell the product for half down for the trial period. The customers put down a deposit of 50 percent and then receive a trial period with extensive phone support. If the customer decides that the product isn't for them, they return it and their money is refunded. The company that does this is a leader in their market, and has done this for a long time. They have conditioned their market to accept this as reasonable. It also helps that they are the market leader.

The other approach is to try to hold down the travel costs by a combination of not traveling and sending a video, asking the customer to pay for the travel, calling on a number of prospects in the target city to prorate the travel over a larger number of sales, and/or working with local reps or dealers.

5. Company Type

The pie chart on the next page shows that Software Success readers are primarily software companies. The hardware and software companies typically bundle hardware with their software in an effort to improve their margins.

We have more consultants and programmers this year than last. Many of them have been doing custom programming and have developed a product that they would like to market. My experience is that the transition from a consulting and custom programming business to a product business is a difficult one.

Once you get a custom programming business rolling, the cash flow is pretty steady if you are doing a good job and are getting additional work with your old clients and new referral clients.

The development cycle for software is reasonably easy for programmers to estimate. The time and effort to develop a product is the first big surprise for this type of fledgling software company. The next big surprise is the sales cycle. It is really hard for people to believe that it really takes six to nine months to work a customer through the sales cycle.

6. Marketing Budget as a Percentage of Revenue

The graph on page the next page shows the wide range in marketing budget as a percentage of revenues. I explicitly asked people to include salaries, so I assume most respondents did this. The median was 10-15 percent, which is a little lower than I would have expected. I looked at the relationship between revenue and marketing budgets and there was a significant difference for companies above and below $2 million in revenue.

You may recall that we found that compensation for CEOs jumped significantly when company revenue went over $2 million. This was why I tried analyzing the marketing as a percent of revenue for companies above and below $2 million in revenue.

%REV	<$2 M	>$2M
<10%	35%	51%
10-15%	20%	21%
>15%	45%	28%

As you can see, a significant percentage of companies under $2 million spend over 15 percent of revenue on marketing. This drops significantly with companies over $2 million. There is also a corresponding shift in companies spending under 10 percent of revenue.

In retrospect, I should have asked about the anticipated revenue growth since I really believe that there is a strong relationship between marketing investment and future revenue growth.

Given the fact that I didn't ask the question, I will try to describe a model that I have and see how reasonable it appears. Lets assume that 15 percent of revenue is a reasonable marketing budget, but it is 15 percent of next year's revenue. As we all know, marketing is generating leads for next year's sales.

GROWTH RATE	% OF THIS YEAR
-20%	12.0%
-10%	13.5%
0%	15.0%
+10%	16.5%
+20%	18.0%
+30%	19.5%

While I am not real comfortable with the exact numbers, the concept seems right.

7. Sales Channels Used

If you look at the chart on page 347, you will see that 86 percent of the respondents use direct sales channels.

On the average, a company uses two channels. In fact, many of them report sales in more secondary channels that they don't report in this first question.

There have been some modest shifts in sales channel usage in the last year. Direct is unchanged at 86 percent. Telemarketing or telesales has increased from 32 percent to 45 percent. Dealer sales have decreased slightly from 48 percent to 43 percent. (Remember that these are the percent of firms using this channel.) Finally OEM usage may have increased slightly from 13 percent to 16 percent. While I

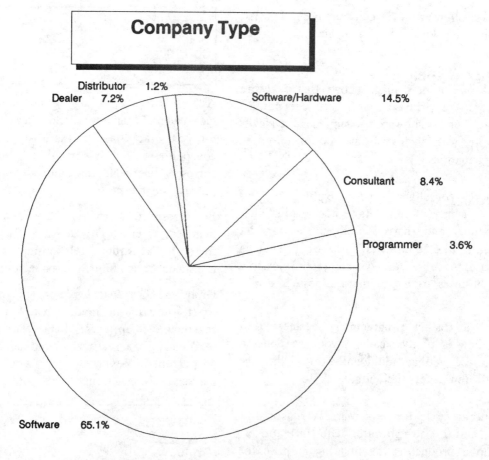

Company Type

Distributor 1.2%
Dealer 7.2%
Software/Hardware 14.5%
Consultant 8.4%
Programmer 3.6%
Software 65.1%

Marketing Budgets as a Percentage of Revenue

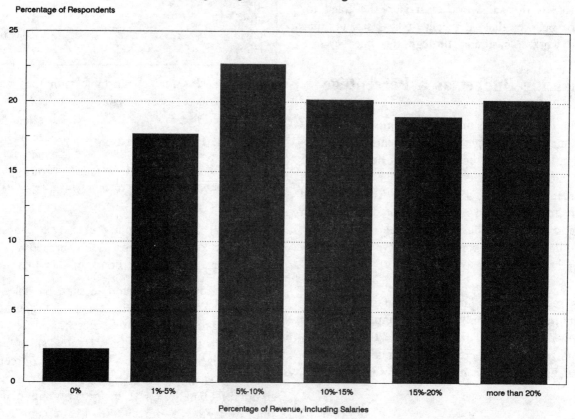

Percentage of Respondents

Percentage of Revenue, Including Salaries

Sales Channels Used

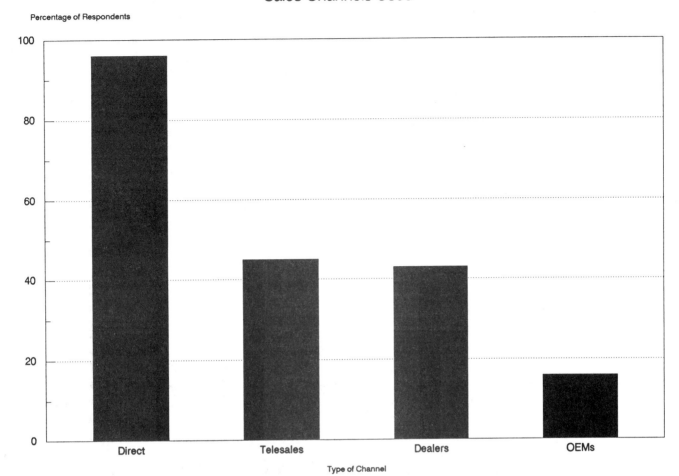

wouldn't bet on these specific numbers, the trends do seem right.

8. Sales by Channel

The graph at the top of the next page shows the sales by channel. The first and most obvious observation is that for most companies, direct sales deliver the bacon. Direct sales are the only category that delivers over 50 percent of the sales for most of the companies that use it. The table below shows the percent of companies using a channel that get more than 50 percent of their sales from that channel:

CHANNEL	% >50%
Direct	75%
Telesales	23%
Dealer	8%
OEM	7%

I was pleased to see that a reasonably high percentage of firms that use telesales get over 50 percent of

their sales via telesales. My experience is that telesales makes extreme demands on the marketing and sales sophistication of a software company. With direct sales, the skills of the sales person can help to overcome many flaws in the sales and marketing. If your marketing materials are second rate, the visual impression of the sales person will help to compensate. If the presentation of your product in your materials confuses your prospect, the sales person can pick this up and can address the confusing points. With telesales, the sales rep has less information about how the prospect is reacting and they have less opportunity to impress the prospect.

I wasn't surprised that only 8 percent of the companies who use dealers get over 50 percent of their sales through dealers. It has been difficult to build a major dealer network in the last few years due to a number of factors:

* **Software isn't important to most dealers.**

Percentage of Sales by Channel

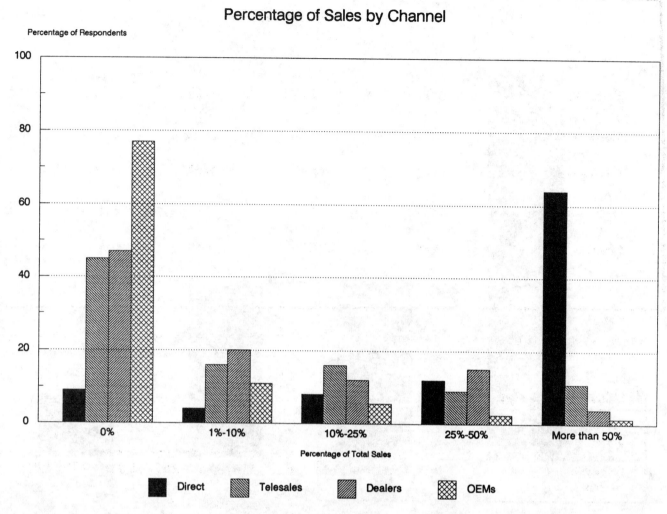

* **The number of dealers has been flat or declining the last few years.**

* **Everyone in the distribution channel is under severe profit pressure.**

* **It takes a major marketing budget to launch and support a product sold through dealers.**

* **Most dealer sales are at discounts of 40 to 60 percent, so the percentage of retail sales through dealers must be twice the percent of revenue.**

Thus, if a company generates 25 percent of its revenue via dealers and 75 percent direct, they must sell 50 units through dealers and 75 units direct.

The OEM percentage of sales is quite low, but the margins should be good. Twenty percent of the respondents used OEMs, and only 6 percent of these (or 1.2 percent overall) got over 50 percent of their sales via OEM. An OEM strategy can be a good way

to start, but it is difficult to build a big business with an OEM-only strategy.

9. Title

Our readership is split between general managers and marketing and sales management. My experience is that a good percentage of the general manager readers are also directly responsible for sales and marketing in smaller organizations.

TITLE	% RESP
No Reply	8.1%
General Mgr	41.9%
Prod Devel	8.1%
Mktg/ Sales	38.4%
Finance	7.0%

10. Time by Function

A high percentage of respondents spend a significant amount of time in management. Almost everyone is involved with sales and marketing. I assume the

Table II - Time by Function

Function	0%	1-10%	10-20%	20-30%	> 30%
Managment	5.8%	9.3%	20.9%	25.6%	31.4%
Development	19.8%	17.4%	14.0% 1	7.4%	24.4%
Mktg/Sales	4.7%	8.1%	11.6%	26.7%	41.9%
Finance	18.6%	33.7%	19.8%	14.0%	7.0%

people who spend no time in development and finance are the sales and marketing specialists.

11. Company Age

COMPANY AGE	% RESP
<1 Year	9.3%
2-5 Years	27.9%
5-10 Years	38.4%
>10 Years	24.4%

While we had a slight increase in the number of companies who had been in business less than one year (from two percent to nine percent), we have had a very significant increase in companies who have been in business five or more years (from 32 percent to 62 percent).

12. Interest by Type of Article

The most interesting articles were surveys (36 percent high) and questions and answers (36 percent high). Dear Dave (20 percent high) and essays (20 percent high) were less popular. The only other point was that a higher number of people (11 percent) rated Dear Dave articles as low interest.

One comment in the notes was that people were interested in learning more about other companies. I included a discussion of this in the cover letter for the November issue. If you would like to talk to me about being interviewed, please complete the response form.

The other recent change is that I have been getting more detailed questions mailed or faxed to me. This gets you a little free consulting and gets me more real-world discussion for Software Success. The articles in the remainder of this issue were all letters that I have received. Thanks.

K.   Management Essay (1990)

1. Funding

This article deals with issues related to obtaining funding. It includes a comparison of funding sources, tips for determining the market value of a business, and comments about the tax consequences of a sale.

The top priority of management is to ensure that the business has sufficient capital to operate. If you don't have the cash to make payroll and other expenses, you aren't a business. Undercapitalization is the leading cause of business failure and it can strike at any point in a company's evolution.

The starting point in dealing with capitalization is to understand your capital requirements. You need to have accurate cash projections. When I have run small companies which were very tight, I had weekly cash flows for the next two months and monthly cash flows for the next six months. Finally, we had quarterly cash flow requirements for the next two years. While this isn't perfect, it gives you

Chapter V. Management Issues

a very good idea of what you need to manage your business.

There are a number of alternatives to fund your company. You can use debt and borrow money or you can use stock and sell equity. The best choice will depend upon both the characteristics of the business and the personalities and motivations of the founders.

When you borrow money, the people who are providing you with the capital aren't actively involved with your business. They can get their money back without getting involved with the internals of your business. As long as they receive their loan payments, they are happy. In many cases, they ask the principals to guarantee the loan. This gives them alternatives, external to the business, to repay the loan.

Equity holders, on the other hand, must be much more intimate with the business. Their equity isn't worth much unless the business is fundamentally sound. The business could manage to make loan payments and still not be a good equity investment.

Most founders that I talk to assume they want to sell stock. They don't want to burden their company with making loan payments, so equity seems like a great deal. The costs of raising equity are subtle, but they are very real. You are giving up control because you now have outsiders who have a stake in your business.

Another issue that comes with equity is professional management. The investors will often require that the company hire professional managers to help grow the company and to watch out for their capital.

In many cases, the conflict between the founders and the professional management is seen as a personality conflict, where it is really the basic change in direction forced by the requirements of the capital. Growing a company very fast requires a number of changes, and some of these will be uncomfortable to the founders. Don't trivialize these issues by classifying them as personality conflicts.

The assumption that the investors control the business is one that I find many entrepreneurs find hard to believe. They assume that if they still hold 51 percent of the stock that they control their company. The classical funding scenario is that the investors receive forty to sixty percent of the stock for their first round investment. The next round of funding will receive twenty-five percent. After three or four rounds of funding, the founding group is usually down to under twenty percent and the CEO usually has only five to ten percent. At that point, it is very clear that the investors have control.

On another level, the investors have control as long as the company needs additional money now or will need money in the future. It is very easy for the investors to use their control of the money to control the company as they see fit.

Going Public = The Objective

The criteria for raising venture capital vary by fund, but they are looking for companies which can go public and make them an excellent return on their investment. In the late sixties and early seventies, you could take a technology company public based on a sexy name. As a result, there were too many public offerings of companies which were too weak. These stocks dropped after the initial public offering (IPO) and it became more difficult to take a software company public.

"Less than 25 percent of the [technology] stocks that went public through 1987 are trading at prices equal to their IPO price," said Edward Metz, a partner at investment banking firm Broadview Associates. In 1983 there were 74 technology issue IPOs and this dropped to 13 in 1988.

The first step in a public offering is to find an investment banking firm willing to underwrite the initial public offering. There are a number of subjective factors which investment bankers look at:

* **High quality company**

* **Good record and balance sheet**

* **Attractively priced**

* **Niche company**

At the same time, it appears that there is a minimum revenue level required for a good public offering. Several years ago this was $10 million in annual revenues. Now it appears that it is closer to $25 million.

Reference: "IPO Market to Grow Only Slightly in 1989", Deidre Depke, Computer System News, February 13, 1989.

That isn't to say that you can't go public on the Vancouver exchange as a start-up, or find some other creative approach. In fact, going public to raise your initial funding can be a possibility. You can raise money based on a business plan if you are willing to invest the $200,000 in legal and accounting fees and you don't care where you raise the money.

My experience is that if you raise money on one of the penny exchanges, your stock price will fall because your underwriter won't support your stock. This means that you are cut off from future funding, which may or may not be a problem.

You must also prepare to have a senior executive dedicated to dealing with your investors. The Financial Analysts Federation conducted a survey of 100 software companies. "The committee found that the average software company met with investors 25 times per year, issued almost 30 press releases and attended seven industry conferences. Despite this effort, the group concluded that most software companies are poorly understood."

These statistics support the full time job for someone to work with the investors.

Reference: "Street Talk - Poor Grades", Deidre Depke, Computer Systems News, November 11, 1988.

2. When to Fold

One of the issues that you must consider is that the objectives for investors and founders differ. Investors will want to shut down a company which isn't meeting their expectations. The reasons they may decide to withdraw support for a company include:

* **Another round of financing is needed**

* **Performance is below expectation**

* **Problems are tied to adverse funda-mentals**

* **No alternative funding options**

* **No revival strategy**

Reference: "VCs Must Know When to Fold", William Terdoslavich, Computer Systems News, April 3, 1989.

I am continually surprised by the number of people who believe that their business would succeed if they could just add money. Even if they raise millions of dollars, they hold onto this belief even if the facts are to the contrary. The article below is about Xanaro Technologies which was founded in 1985 with an integrated package called Ability. The company had spent $5.5 million to develop the product, and they spent another $10 million to promote their product.

Within a year they had only sold $3.3 million and they owed an additional $5 million to their creditors. The high point to their promotion was a 100,000 insert in PC World which cost them over $4 million.

This is a great example of how the investors pulling the plug was the best thing that could happen to the principals. I find that it is extremely hard for the principals to be at all objective about their prospects. I find it sad to hear about individuals who have poured very significant amounts of their own money into a hopeless cause. I really believe that one of the advantages of raising outside money is that the principals have an outside "reality check."

The Xanaro story has an interesting ending. Migent Software bought the rights for Ability for $540,000 in 1986. They recouped their money immediately by selling a cut-down version of the product to a text book publisher. They also sold another 100,000 copies at $259, spending less than $500,000 to promote it. (The first pass sold 5,000 copies at $650 each using $15 million.)

Reference: "Money Doesn't Change Everything", Bruce McDougall, Small Business, April 1988.

I have dealt with a number of founders who have been very frustrated with their investors because the investors had given up on their companies. The founders talked about their great products and how they were advancing the state of the art. I guess they really believed that the next product was their revival strategy. This rings hollow to the investor who was told that the last product was going to be so great that customers would knock down the doors.

3. Selling Your Company

Another alternative is to sell your company. This is reasonable at the level of $5 million in revenues. At that size, an acquiring company can make your company a division with its own general manager. You also have two levels of management which allow operations to continue if one or more managers leave in the wake of the acquisition.

If your company is smaller, closer to $1 million in sales, you are really selling a product and not a company. My experience is that with these product acquisitions, it is important that the buyer be selling into the same market as the new product. This allows the buyer to gain some synergy with their existing marketing efforts.

If you decide that you want to sell your business, retaining a business broker is a good first step. Selecting the right broker is important if you want to maximize your results. The following article suggested the following questions to ask when picking a broker:

What method will be used to value the business?

What specific services are provided as part of the fee?

What type of listing contract will be required (Open Listing, Agency Listing, or Exclusive Listing)?

Will the broker provide a sales brochure?

What will be the format for the buy-sell agreement? (Ask to see a typical sales contract.)

How will the potential buyers be handled? Will the broker accompany each prospect to the business?

What information will the broker need?

Reference : "How to Start, Expand & Sell A Business", James C. Comiskey, Venture Perspectives Press, San Jose, CA.

While I think that it is important to hire a broker, you must take responsibility for managing the broker. The broker is representing your company to potential buyers, but you have the most to gain and lose.

4. Valuing Your Business

The following article points out that valuing a business depends upon the question, "Who's asking?" Fair market value (FMV) is:

"The price at which the property would change hands between a willing buyer and a willing seller when the former is not under any compulsion to buy and the latter is not under any compulsion to sell,

both parties having reasonable knowledge of relevant facts" (IRS definition)

Valuations for the IRS (tax purposes) follow well defined procedures which involve the minimum possible interpretation. They use a number of different methods:

Net Asset Value

Excess Earnings Method

Capitalization of Earnings Method

Discounted Future Earnings Method

Reference : "A Guide to Valuing the Closely Held Business", Renno L. Peterson, The Practical Accountant, April 1989.

If you want to understand these approaches and other ones that are commonly used, refer to the references later in this article.

5. Tax Implications

There are a number of tax implications of how you structure your deal which can have a major impact on how much money you are left with. The following articles discuss some of these issues, but make sure that you talk to your accountant and your attorney before you get into serious negotiations with a possible buyer. This is also a good topic to discuss with possible brokers.

Reference: "Sell Your Business, Keep the Profits" Ronald M. Harwith, Gary A. David and James R. Farrand, VarBusiness, February 1989.

Reference: "To Sell Your Entire Business, Plan Carefully to Save Countless Headaches Down the Road," Steven A. Meyerowitz, Business Marketing, March 1989.

6. Additional Resources

The Valuation Report, $195 (516) 681-2111.
This actual report shows how all the theories, considerations and options explained in the manual come into play to produce a final answer to the question: How much is a business really worth?

A Checklist Guide to Successful Acquisitions

By Victor Harold, Pilot Industries, 103 Cooper Street, Babylon, NY 11702

Chapter V.   Management Issues

This 45-page booklet is written from the buyer's point of view. It has extensive lists of things that a sophisticated buyer will ask. If you really want to be prepared, you should go through these lists and have your answers ready.

How to Get More Value from What You Already Own

By Charles R. Ryan, ($37.50), (800) 634-3966 ext 8931This book focuses on developing your exit strategy.

This company also produces another book that might be of interest:

Valuing Small Businesses and Professional Practices

By Shannon Pratt ($62.50)

Merger, Buyout & Acquisition Catalog

Business Publications, Inc.
(619) 549-7200

This catalog has 51 practical publications and 7 easy to use software programs on mergers and acquisitions, business valuations and corporate finance.

ValuSource

Is a software company which has five easy to use software tools that will help you to: (1) value any business, large or small; (2) identify acquisition prospects; (3) sharpen your dealmaking skills; (4) structure and finance LBO's; and (5) analyze mergers and acquisitions.

(619) 483-1172

Valuation Reference Manual, ($59; full refund if not satisfied)

The Business Owner,
Tricia Walsh, TBO,
383 S. Broadway,
Hicksville, NY 11801
(800) 634-0605

"We have a comprehensive manual on how to value a business."

National Venture Capital Association

1655 North Fort Myer Drive, Suite 700,
Arlington, VA 22209.

Send a stamped, self addressed 9" X 12" envelope ($1.65 postage) for a directory of members.

Small Business Innovation Research, and Technology

1441 L Street N.W.,
Room 500, Washington, DC
20416.

International Venture Capital Institute, Inc.

PO Box 1333, Stamford, CT
06904 (203) 232-3143.

Ask for the directory of Venture Capital Clubs. It lists 115 clubs internationally, with 100 in the US. $9.95.

Venture Capital Network, Inc.

PO Box 882,
Durham, NH 03824-0882.

Offers a computerized matching service for entrepreneurs seeking equity.

Seed Capital Network, Inc.

Operations Center,
8905 Kingston Pike, Suite
12, Knoxville, TN 37923.

This network extends through the United States.

Nebraska Business Development Center

1313 Farnam, Suite 132, Omaha, NE
68182-2048.

Send a self-addressed business size envelope ($0.45 postage) for a list of approximately 60 venture capital clubs.

National Business Incubation Association

One President Street, Athens, OH 45701. (614) 593-4331.

For general information and the names of localincubators.

International Venture Capital Institute Inc.

PO Box 1333, Stamford, CT
06904 (203) 323-3143.

IVCI offers a directory of business incubators, listing over 640 business incubators in the US and Canada, for $19.95.

Small business investment companies specialize in lending to small businesses. Some invest solely in minority or women-owned businesses.

National Association of Small Business Investment Companies

1156 15th Street N.W., Suite 1101,
Washington, DC 20005
(202) 833-8230.

Send a check for $5.00 for "Venture Capital - Where to Find It," a directory of about 400 SBICs throughout the U.S.

National Association of Investment Companies

1111 14th Street N.W.,
Suite 700, Washington, DC
20005 (202) 289-4336.

NAIC has a directory of investment companies located throughout the US that finance minority-owned businesses. Ask for a publication called "For Entrepreneurs Only," $7.50.

National Association of Female Executives.

Women who own small businesses may qualify for venture capital funding. Contact NAFE at: 127 West 24th Street, New York, NY 10011. (212) 645-0770.

Small Business Administration

(800) 368-5855. (202) 653-7561 in the Washington DC metro area.

The "answer desk" provides recorded information on various SBA programs, as well as referrals to your local SBA office.

The SBA also publishes "The States and Small Businesses: A Directory of Programs and Activities, 1989," a 411 page directory. $12. To order, call (202) 783-3238.

7. Polished Plans

The ideal business plan should be seven to ten double spaced typewritten pages, according to The Coopers & Lybrand Guide to Growing your Business.

The plan should answer all the following questions:
Your objective
The strategy to reach the objective
How much money is required
When and how it will be spent
How you will repay it

You should also discuss the risks in your plan as realistically as possible.

I am surprised at how complicated most business plans that I read are. The writers feel that they have to answer all questions so they go into great detail. When I review business plans, I typically spend 15 minutes reading the executive summary and the cash flows to see if it has any merit. While I know that this seems unfair to the people who labored to create the plan, I suspect that it is fairly typical of people who review business plans for venture firms. If I like the plan after the first 15 minutes, I will then spend another hour reading it, but my total first look at a plan is 1-1/2 hours maximum.

If you think about it, the objective of the plan is to get investors interested. You can't answer all possible questions in a document, but your can confuse the reader so that they never take another look. I agree with Coopers that the initial plan should be short and to the point. You also need the 100-page version, but I would only send this out after I had talked to someone (preferably in person) and I knew that they were serious. Another issue is that the 100-page plans may contain confidential information. I would prefer to control distribution.

Reference : Items 7-18 on the previous page and the article on polished plans were from: "39 Sources of Cash to Help Your Business Take Off" By Mark Mehle, Success; December 1989.

8. Working with Banks

Banks end up being a major source of financing for many intermediate software companies. A significant number of our readers have obtained lines of credit to help finance their growth. Most companies open their company bank account with the same

Chapter V. Management Issues

bank that they have their personal account with. This is convenient, but it may restrict your business. The reasons that you might want to change banks include:

Growth - your needs exceed your bank's limits

Poor service - this can occur with larger banks if your account is relegated to junior officer

Personality conflict - this can be a valid reason for changing

If you are looking for a new bank you should consider your needs for the following:

Line of credit
Loans
Seasonal requirements
Capital acquisition
Credit card processing

This is a point where you need to look at your situation very carefully. You might need long-term loans to buy computers and other capital equipment. You might find non-banking lenders who are very willing to provide this type of asset-based financing. Their rates may be higher than your bank, but it is often reasonable to obtain equipment this way.

Another requirement is to finance your accounts receivable. If your business is seasonal, you can end up in your peak season with as much business as you can handle and no cash. In 60 to 90 days your customers will pay your invoices, and you will be in a very good position to repay a line of credit. If you are trying to fund long-term growth with a line of credit, make sure that your cash flow is such that you can occasionally pay off the line of credit.

Before you go out and approach the banks, make sure that you have your financials in order. Banks will want to see past financial statements, income statements, balance sheets, and personal statements for the principals, as well as projections for the next few years. As a starting point, you should look at your assets and have your accountant guess what a bank might loan you. They might give you 20 to 70 percent on accounts receivable depending upon your customers and your history, 70 to 80 percent of the appraised market value of your assets, and 95 percent for cash equivalents. You should know this number before you start your discussions with the bankers.

Reference: "Breaking the Bank Barrier", Karen Wilson, Varbusiness, April 1989.

Once you know what you are looking for, you should start your process by interviewing candidate banks. Ask them what they can do for you and what the costs are. Get their loan commitments in writing before you act.

Reference: "Finding a New Bank", A. Barry Cappello Small Business Reports, June 1989.

My experience with banks is that this is an area which can repay an investment of effort on your part. You may find a banker who is willing to give a small LOC with a personal guarantee. They will verbally tell you that if this works well that next year they will remove your house as collateral and the year after that they may remove your personal guarantee. My advice is to start with the best deal that you can get and get to know your banker. Fight the urge to feel hurt that this company you have built isn't viewed as creditworthy by your bank.

Software companies are hard for banks to deal with. We don't have a lot of collateral in the traditional balance sheet sense. For this reason, it is important to find a sympathetic banker and develop a relationship with them. If you get a trial line of credit, draw down on your line and then pay it back.

Using your line of credit all the time or not using it makes a poor track record. Ask your loan officer how the head office measures lines of credit. Tell them that you want to be a good customer so that you can qualify for more credit in the future and grow your business.

Some banks require that the loan balance be cleared up once annually for about thirty days. Doing this several times a year makes the bankers even more comfortable.

If you are concerned about the personal guarantee, you could draw the money out and put it into a money market fund. Leave it there for thirty days, and then pay down your LOC. This won't cost you much, but this exercise will allow you to get the LOC that you want in a year or two. If you don't walk with your bank, you will never be able to run.

9. Managing Your Accounts Receivable

So far, we have been focusing on borrowing money from others. Managing your accounts receivable is trying to minimize having your customers borrowing money from you.

The first advice is to stay on top of your accounts receivable. Someone in your company should be responsible for monitoring your accounts receivable. I have seen far too many crises which were initiated because a large customer was slow to pay. I had to get my first LOC when I had four large accounts receivable with four Fortune 500 companies. I didn't realize that you had to get on a first name basis with the accounts payable clerk and manage the process. I averaged over 120 days with these four accounts. It can happen to you.

The first reality is that AR doesn't age well. The percent collectable drops dramatically after 60 to 90 days. According to I.C. Systems, a national collections service, only 90 percent of past due receivables are collectable after 60 days, 67 percent after six months, and 45 percent after one year. More conservative sources claim that past-due receivables only retain 87 percent of their value after three months, 33 percent after six months, and 22 percent after one year.

Reference : "Managing Receivables Can Pay off", Doug Dayton, PC Accounting, Winter/Spring 1989

While I am not this negative, it is something to worry about. The first step is to have an aged monthly receivables report. You don't need a fancy accounting system to generate this type of report. I just have a Symphony database which I sort by invoiced date. This shouldn't be a real issue unless you are dealing with hundreds of invoices. If that is the case, you need accounting software and a collection clerk.

In a survey conducted by ABCD, 69 percent of VARs reported a collection period of over 30 days. Fifty percent reported 31 to 40 days and nineteen percent were over 40 days.

Reference : "Managing AR", Michael J. Major, Computer Dealer, August 1988.

You should review this every month with your finance person and your sales person. I believe that every business which sells on credit must have a credit manager who is responsible for managing the AR. This can be one of the principals, or your finance and administration person. In many smaller companies the office manager fills this role.

This person should call all outstanding accounts once a month. I tend to time my calls at the end of the month on the chance that I can get my invoice into the next month's batch. Make sure that you record who you talked to and what they said. It is especially important to note if the customer mentioned any problems with the product which my be holding up payment. Many larger companies will just not pay if they aren't happy. They won't complain; they Just don't pay.

The other thing that you need is a simple measure that you can look at monthly to see how you are doing. I like the average days' sales outstanding. You divide the receivables by your average daily sales (annual sales divided by 365).

My AR averages 45 days which is typical for a good 30 days payable. (You have to expect some days on both ends for transit and processing, so 40 days might be a practical lower limit if everyone paid 30 days after they received your invoice.) Monitor this number. It might vary plus or minus ten percent. Plot yours over time to see the reasonable range. Once it goes above the reasonable range, make it a top priority. Get it under control before you slide into a cash crunch.

An escalating AR period is just a warning signal. It may be caused by poor follow-up, an economic downturn, sales selling to marginal accounts, or your product not working. Think of it as a fire alarm, and act accordingly.

If you find that your bad debt is more than one or two percent, you should step back and look at what you should be doing. Should you not recognize the revenue until you have a signed contract or a purchase order? What is conventional in your marketplace? Should you require credit applications and run credit checks before you extend credit? Are your sales people promising too much?

Chapter V. Management Issues

10. Management References

1) **Personnel Policy Expert: "Software that Creates a Complete Employee Handbook,"** KnowlegePoint (707) 762-0333.

2) **Directors and Officers Liability Insurance: St. Paul's, Electric Underwriting Department,** (800) 328-2189 X7968.

3) **Personnel Law Update 1989,** $78 Book, Council on Education in Management, 325 Lennon Lane, Walnut Creek, CA 94598, (415) 934-8333.

4) **A User's Guide to Computer Contracting, Forms, Techniques, and Strategies,** $75, Prentice Hall, (800) 223-0231.

5) **ESOP Workshop National Center for, Employee Ownership, Inc.,** 426 17th Street, Suite, 650, Oakland, CA 94612., (415) 272-9461.

6) **Adapso 1990 Compensation Survey,** $700 nonmembers and $500 members, William M. Mercer, Meidinger Hansen, Inc., The National Survey Group, 1417 Lake Cook Road, Deerfield, IL 60015.

7) **The Complete Guide to Marketing and the Law**, Robert J. Posch, Jr., $69.95, Prentice Hall, Book Distribution Center, Route 59 at Brookhill, Dr, West Nyack, NY 10995-9901.

8) **The 1988-89 Hiring and Firing Policies Survey** can be purchased for $15, and the 1988 Office Turnover Survey Report for $30, from AMS Foundation, 4622 Street Road, Trevose, PA 19047.

L. Questions and Answers (1990)

1. Competing with The Big Guys

How can we compete on salary and benefits against big guys?

The first thing to accept is that the small company can't get "big company employees" unless you bribe them. By that, I mean that if someone really likes the security and comfort of the big company, they are better off staying with the big company.

On the other hand, there are people who are working for a big company who would love to work for a small company. While it might be difficult for them to take a pay cut, I have seen many of them come to a small company at the same salary. When you account for the benefits, retirement plans, and so forth, they really took a cut in pay. The reason that they did this is that they wanted to work for a small company. Perhaps you have a stock option plan, or are working in their area of technical interest.

The other alternative for small companies is to hire people who can't get hired by the big guys. Perhaps they don't have the degrees from big name schools, or perhaps they don't have a degree. Small companies are in a better position to evaluate the individual and modify the position to suit the individual. This type of flexibility can help you get some really special people.

My final advice is to avoid competing with the big guys. If you have a prospective employee you asks why your benefit plan doesn't hold up to the one offered by Amalgamated Food, I find that the best answer is that "we have an excellent benefit program for a small company." Small companies have their strong points, but if you are looking for the security of the big company I would advise you to go to work there. You will lose some prospective employees, but both of you will be better off with them working for the big company. The people who were just pushing you will admit that better benefits weren't very important to them after all.

2. Industry Consolidation

Do you think that there will ever be an industry consolidation in software like the auto industry where it all boils down to the "Big Three?"

My simple answer is "no." Software is an industry with very low barriers to entry. It is very easy for a good programmer and a designer to come up with a product concept and get a product developed with a combination of their own money and customer funding. The low price of PC hardware has made this dramatically easier and the proliferation of software companies is testimony of this trend.

Marketing products, on the other hand, does favor large established companies. There are economies of scale in marketing. I expect to see the large marketing companies get larger. The major companies have been growing faster than the industry averages though aggressive sales and marketing and acquisition.

The only counterbalancing force is that at some point the supermarket software companies begin to lose their effectiveness. It appears that Computer Associates may have passed the optimal point and that its sales growth may slow down. I suspect that the counter forces include:

1. **The super-large companies find it difficult to retain and attract top technical people.**

2. **Managing large sales organizations is difficult.**

3. **They become less responsive to the market.**

4. **They acquire substandard companies because they are so pressured to maintain their sales growth. They will acquire anything with good sales numbers even if the quality isn't there.**

I don't know where this will balance out, but I can't imagine a software industry without young startup companies with hot new products.

3. Virtual Companies
What do you think the advantages and disadvantages of small companies working together to form a "virtual company?"

I am against it. I have seen a number of "virtual companies" which got into trouble when things either went well or went badly. Most of these "virtual companies" had no formal contractual arrangements among the principals. Initially, they banded together as a confederation and cooperated with each other. I like that in principal, but I find that everyone forgets why they came together, what the deal was, and who owns what. The potential for ugliness is impressive.

In many of these cases we are dealing with a verbal partnership agreement. Law firms are often partnerships, and their partner agreements are lengthy documents for very good reasons.

If you find that working with other small businesses makes sense, I urge you to document each relationship in writing. It can be a simple letter agreement, but please put it in writing. It also helps if you don't assume that others will do unspecified things like "help out during peak periods."

4. Keeping Customer Expectations in Line

How can we keep our customers happy? (e.g., how can we keep their expectations in line with our corporate goals?) We want to be sure that we can offer good service at a good price. What can we do to help this?

The first step is to write this down for your own internal use. I'll bet you will be surprised at what your sales people think, your support people expect, and so forth. Have your support manager write a description of support services. Specify what the customers responsibilities are, how much they must pay, and what you will provide. Review this internally. I am very sure that your sales people have been misleading your customers. They have been doing it explicitly ("I thought we had 24-hour support") or implicitly ("I didn't want to tell them our support people don't start work until 9 A.M. California time"). If you aren't explicit, your customers will make the most favorable assumptions for themselves and you will have to live with their assumptions.

A common adage in training and support is to under-promise and over-deliver. If you start off by specifying the minimum that you will deliver, make sure you deliver it. Failing to deliver what you have promised will create major customer problems. This is the risk of documenting your support policy. The advantage is that you are starting to manage your customer's expectations.

5. Packaging for a Mainframe NLP
We have an NLP (Nice Little Product) which we would like to make available as a promotional item. It is a mainframe product. What are your thoughts on packaging, documentation and installation?

Make it simple, but nice. Your customers know that they shouldn't expect you to spend lots of money on an NLP, but it should look nice. There are a number of things which should be done that don't cost much, but are important to the customer impression.

I would start with the installation procedures and documentation. Please make sure that it is easy to install and that the documentation is very clear on this topic. The user might be reluctant to call your support people if they can't get your free software to work. They would worry that they aren't entitled to support because they didn't pay. In this case, they would throw the software in the trash and think bad things about you. If this happens, you have gone to a lot of time and effort to create a bad impression.

The next point is to make sure that the user can get going quickly and get some nice results. Send your tape and materials to some of your customers who are less advanced technically and ask them to critique it. Do the same with your less technical support people.

Once you are sure that you really have a nice little product (and not a nice piece of code), you can expend a little effort on packaging. Offset printed laser output is fine for the documentation. If personalized binders are too expensive, you could use standard three ring binders with clear pockets which you can insert your letterhead with the product name. You can buy these binders for $2.50 each in quantities of 24, so the cost isn't very high. Mini-reel tapes will also help you hold down the cost of the product.

My final test would be to show the package to some friends of the family and ask them to rate it. If they say "nice," but not fancy you have hit it just right. Good luck. I would appreciate your letting me know your success with your NLP.

6. Computer Industry Forecasts

We are trying to decide what platform and which operating system to develop a new product for. Do you know of any source of forecasts?

Computer Industry Forecasts is published quarterly. Each issue is over 100 pages. The forecasts are extracted from over 600 sources. The topics include:

* Computers (by type)

* Storage Products

* Software

* PC Software

If you don't find what you want from the data extracted in the report, all of the articles are fully abstracted so that you can get the full article. You can also find which market research firms are working in your area of interest.

The price is $295 for four issues, and they have a no risk guarantee.

Reference: Data Analysis Group, 3201 Hanson H Road, Box 4210, Georgetown, CA 95634, (916) 333-4001, FAX (916) 333-1247.

7. Career Paths

What are the career paths in software marketing? What about hiring college grads? Are there any key schools?

Software is a very young industry and as such, we don't have established career paths like our more established hardware friends. Another problem is that most good, experienced software marketing people either work for large companies with very nice compensation packages or are a principal in a smaller firm. In many cases it is difficult to attract a senior person without either a large compensation package or a significant equity position.

I have been involved with many companies where one of the founders is the marketing strategist. When they really think about it, they don't want to hire a senior person to take responsibility for marketing. For a wide range or reasons, I have found that over 50 percent of the people hired into senior marketing positions in small companies abort within six months. The reasons are numerous, but after six months they are gone.

You can easily spend $100,000 on such a six month experiment. This is salary, benefits, and some budget to allow them to try to implement some of their ideas. This level of mistake can really hurt a small company.

Another approach is to hire a marketing assistant. My profile is someone in their mid-twenties with a marketing degree who hasn't gotten a good job in marketing. Their salary is probably in the $20,000 to $30,000 range and they are willing to do the administrative work that is key to marketing. If you are doing direct mail, you need them to work with the printers, manage the creative process so that deadlines are met, and so forth.

At this salary range you are hiring someone out of your local market, so there aren't key schools to look for. Many schools offer projects for seniors and MBAs, and this can be a way to get some fundamental marketing done, and to meet some possible candidates.

One key aspect of the job is the opportunity for the person to grow with the job. If they do a good job and the company grows, there is every possibility that they could eventually become the Vice-President of Marketing. This can be very attractive to the right candidate.

8. What Do You Want To Be When You Grow Up?

In a recent planning session, a client was looking at a number of possible strategies. They ranged from very safe (consulting with value added) to very risky (raise venture capital and build the ultimate product).

While I was listening to the discussion, I realized that any of these choices were reasonable. The company actually had three alternatives which were viable. In fact, the risk and reward in each case was reasonably well balanced. I suggested that the decision depended upon what the principals wanted their company to be when they grew up.

The three alternatives that I proposed were:

The Family Business

In this scenario, you keep it small and focus on profitability and high salaries for the principals. You don't take risks since you want to ride this one for the long haul. You don't want any outside investment because you don't want the interference and you don't want to share the long-term wealth.

A Nice Private Company

The objective here is to get the company to the $5 million range so you can sell it. You may have to bring in some patient private money, but they can look to get a very nice return on their money within five to ten years. The employees get a combination of a nice place to work in the meantime and a very nice payoff if you manage to sell the company.

Go for the Gold

In this scenario, you want to build a $25 million company which can grow to $100 million. You will need venture capital to do this, and you will have to give up control when you bring in the money. In effect you are turning your company over to the god of money. This money god will dictate many harsh actions in its drive to force the company to grow as fast as possible. The founders are likely to be forced out, and have to feel that their stock makes this experience worthwhile. I started a company and left after I brought in venture capital, and I am pleased

that my company is going to do $10 million this year and that my stock may finally pay off.

I look at the decision in terms of a balance between current satisfaction (having fun and making a good salary) and long-term capital gains (stock). Any point on the spectrum is valid, but the point that your management team is at has a major impact on how you should direct your company. I have met with a number of family businesses who come up with ideas which might attract venture capital. They assume that they can bring in the venture capital without affecting the balance of the rewards they get out of their work. In many cases, they decide not to pursue the high road, because they don't want to lose control or to give up the security they currently enjoy.

This balance can change over time. After I left my company, I went into consulting, which is the ultimate family business. I am still running a family business, but I am making more investments in small software companies. I urge you to have an open discussion with your key players about these issues before you make any major changes in your product or your capita-lization plans.

9. Hiring Killer Sales People

We've avoided hiring high pressure sales people with that killer instinct. Are we kidding ourselves? We think our credibility is very important and don't want to hurt it for shortterm gain. Is this wise?

No. Even good products need to be sold, and good sales people will sell more of your products than non-professional sales people. I think you are mistaking good sales skills with ruthless behavior. It is important to hire sales people whose ethics and style of business match your company. For example, I can't imagine Joe Isuzu selling a Mercedes-Benz.

Don't assume that good sales people will trash your credibility. The best sales person I knew at Amdahl consistently sold two to three times quota even though they kept cutting his territory. He was a real gentleman. All his customers liked him, and he did everything right. In fact, he did all of the things that many of the other sales people claimed that they just didn't have time to do. He spent so much time on soft sales activities, like maintaining old customer accounts, that I was always amazed at his success.

If you have a good product which requires and deserves a professional sale, I am sure you can find sales people who will sell your product and enhance your reputation. Your challenge will be to convince them that you have a product that won't embarrass them. Good luck.

10. Setting Sales Quotas

We are a young company and we are hiring our first professional sales person. How should we set our sales quotas?

I assume you have been making sales with non-professional sales people. In most small companies, the president or founder is the sales person. This person is trying to make sales while they are also filling the presidential role. I suggest you count the president as one sales person. This assumes that this person's extra charisma and energy compensate for the other demands on their time. I would then use the past year's sales by month as the quota for the new sales person. If the sales are quite uneven, you might consider using quarterly quotas.

also assume that the president will continue selling independent of the sales rep. When the sales rep gets the president involved, I believe the rep should give up half the sale (for quota purposes) and half their commission. This makes sure that the sales rep doesn't exploit the president's time.

t this point, I can just hear the cries..."you are making it too easy for the sales rep, they are going to come in and make a fortune off our poor little company." First of all, I truly hope that you have to pay your rep large commission checks. Secondly, I am trying to set the quota low to maximize the odds that the rep will succeed. As a technically-driven industry, we tend to be far too hard on our sales people. Stepping in as the first sales rep after the founder is a tough act to follow. This is a low-probability-of-success job. It is also one in which the company really needs the sales rep to succeed.

As long as the only person who can sell your product is the president, your company can't grow. At some point, the president gets tired of working 70 hours a week and backs off and sales begin to fall. That is no way to live. You have to find out how to identify, hire, train and make new sales people effective. If you can solve this puzzle, you can grow your company. Thus, if I give the new sales rep an extra five percent to help ensure that they are motivated, I think that I am making a good investment. You can always increase your quotas in the future as you build more of a track record. Don't forget to have a contract with your sales person which limits the length of your agreement with them.

11. Financial Review

I have received several calls asking for more detail on the operating expense survey we reported on in the March issue. I didn't feel that we had sufficient data to support the type of detailed analysis that several of the callers were trying to make.

Sentry Market Research has published their "Software Industry Financial Review '90". It analyzes 140 leading (public) software companies and analyzes 18 financial ratios including: Net Income Percentage, International Revenue, Growth, Return on Assets, Current Ratio, Times Interest Earned, R & D and Marketing Expenditures.

The report costs $795 and data diskettes are $50 each. There is a 10-day money back guarantee.

Donna Belanger
Sentry Market Research
1900 West Park Drive
Westborough, MA 01581
(508) 366-2031

12. Overtime   Regulations

A recent law (H.R. 5382) has been introduced in the House of Representatives which would:

a. **Extend the professional exemption from overtime to salaried programmers. "This would alter the Department of Labor's long standing policy that programmers and analysts are not professionals."**

b. **Exempt highly compensated programmers paid on an <u>hourly</u> basis. "Under current law, all individuals paid on an hourly basis must be paid time-and-one-half for hours in excess of forty. Highly compensated is defined as 6-1/2 times the minimum wage, approximately $55,000 in 1992. The Adapso supported proposal would be the first exemption for individuals paid on an hourly basis."**

Chapter V. Management Issues

If you would like to help support this legislation, you can contact:

Mitchell Gorsen
Information Director
Adapso
(703) 284-5353

If you have any programmers who are paid hourly, you should be sure that they are currently being paid for overtime, even if they are highly paid.

13. Software Development Estimation Software

Dear Dave,

I am writing to tell you about CB CoCoMo™ - a new product recently introduced by Market Engineering Corporation.

CB CoCoMo is a computer product aimed at helping software developers reliably estimate the time and cost of a software development project. The product, developed especially for the Macintosh computer, is unique in that it integrates two established technologies - the Constructive Cost Model (CoCoMo) developed at TRW, and "Monte Carlo Simulation", a mathematical technique popularized by Market Engineering's Crystal Ball product. Thus, with Monte Carlo Simulation, the user can assign a range of probabilities to each input variable, such as program size or programmer ability, rather than one firm number. Instead of a single result, the output from the program is a range of possible estimates showing the best case, the worst case, and the most likely schedules and budgets.

We are particularly anxious that this product should be featured in your magazine. I do hope that this is possible and that the enclosed media pack provides you with all the information you require. If you have any further questions regarding CB CoCoMo or Market Engineering, please do not hesitate to call me or Mr. Eric Weismann, the company president.

Sincerely,

Catherine Le Roi
Marketing Manager
Market Engineering Corp.
1738 Wynkoop St #200
Denver, CO 80202
(303) 298-0020

Dear Catherine,

Thanks for the letter. Estimation software is an area that I have been interested in since my days at Amdahl in the early 80s when we used estimation techniques with some of our large projects.

I like your approach of bundling CoCoMo with the Monte Carlo front end, since my experience is that most developers are paralyzed by the requirement to provide hard estimates. I was also impressed that the price for your product including Crystal Ball is only $499. This is very cheap if people can achieve the benefits that you list:

a. .Obtain useful scheduling, staffing and financial information at the beginning, in the middle and end of any software development project.

b. Estimate how long a project will take to complete, what the optimal staffing should be, and how long one should expect to spend at every stage of the project design, development and testing.

c. Find out whether costs are in line with industry norms.

d. Assess the likelihood of achieving a certain schedule though the use of confidence intervals.

e. Revise estimates quickly and easily.

I was impressed to see that your estimates are based on only 19 input parameters.

1. Delivered source code instructions
2. Required software reliability
3. Database size
4. Software product complexity
5. Execution time constraints
6. Main storage constraint
7. Virtual machine volatility
8. Computer turnaround time
9. Analyst capability
10. Applications experience
11. Programmer capability
12. Virtual machine experience
13. Programming language experience
14. Modern programming practices
15. Use of software tools
16. Required development schedule
17. Development mode (organic, semi-detached, and embedded)
18. Annual change traffic (%)
19 .Cost per man month

The cost drivers (items 2 through 16) are rated from very low to extra high.

I would be very interested to learn of others' experience with your product and other products like this. It sure seems like this type of technology should have real benefits for our industry given the magnitude of our investment in software development.

14. Test Drive

Dear Dave:

After reading a letter to you regarding Disk Duplication Services in your August 1990 newsletter, I thought that you and your readers may be interested in knowing about our product - TEST DRIVE.

Although many software companies have their disks duplicated by an outside firm, there are usually occasions in which this is not practical, and update disks or special patches must be sent directly from technical support. In these cases, there must be some assurance that the drive used to write the diskette is in proper working order. Problems frequently occur when one drive is slightly misaligned in one direction, and another is misaligned in the other direction. Both drives may function just fine until they try to read a disk written by the other drive! The result can be very embarrassing when a customer receives a disk that he or she cannot read. They, of course, do not suspect their own computer.

TEST DRIVE is a floppy drive diagnostic tool. It can accurately measure and display a floppy drive's spindle speed, alignment, azimuth, eccentricity, hysteresis and more, all without system disassembly. Regular use of TEST DRIVE will ensure that a diskette is written with the highest degree of reliability.

I'd be happy to pass any information along to your readers, or answer questions they may have on the subject.

Sincerely,

Larry Polyak
MSD
4100 Moorpark Ave #104
San Jose, CA 95117
(408) 296-4000

TEST DRIVE is available for three formats: 360 KB 5 1/4, 1.2 MB 5 1/4, and 720KB & 1.44MB 3 1/2. It costs $115 for one format, $171 for two, and $215 for all three.

Dear Larry,

Thanks for the information
Dave

15. Commissions

We are trying to decide whether we should pay commissions on training, documentation and/or maintenance sold at the time of sale?

My initial answer is "no." I don't believe that you should pay commissions on these secondary items which all have associated costs. While you would like the sales people to include them in the sale, you can't afford to pay full commission. On the other hand, your sales people will sell more of these items if they are compen-sated.

Conceptually, you want to pay commission on gross margin for all your products. Thus, if your costs for training are 80 percent, you would pay only two percent commission, equivalent to a ten percent commission on your software. I have seen companies try to deal with this in two ways. The first is to offer a lower commission rate on all other items. You end up with one large debate, but once that is over, it is easy for everyone to know what commission is due. The other alternative is to calculate standard costs and gross margin for each item. When you apply the standard commission against this gross margin, you end up with a commission rate for each and every item. This is very tough to manage. It also invites the sales people to lobby for raising the commission on documentation when the price of paper goes down. As you can tell, I am not real thrilled about either of these approaches.

I would step back and ask how much influence the sales person really has on the sale of these items. Most initial training is prescribed by the vendor, and the sales person rarely sells additional training. My experience is that the training manager or the trainers are the only people who really sell training. Thus, I would reserve training commissions for them.

Documentation is even less elastic. I have trouble understanding how a sales person could really sell a customer on more documentation. I have seen one case where hundreds or thousands of people used a mainframe product where the manager of administration was able to sell additional copies of documentation, but this seems like the exception that proves the rule.

Prepaid maintenance is the one item where it might be worthwhile to pay commission. I believe that the sales person could influence this item. It is nice to get paid early for maintenance. I probably would agree to pay a commission on maintenance if I were eager to pull the maintenance forward. At the same time, I wouldn't allow the sales person to discount this prepaid maintenance at all. In fact, I might take every dollar of discount off the sales commission to ensure that the sales person wasn't tempted.

16. New Accounting Rules

New accounting rules have been proposed by AICPA, FASB, and SEC. There are two changes:

1. **For custom software which has a customer acceptance clause in the contract, no revenue should be taken until it is tested, complete and accepted.**

2. **Maintenance revenue should be accounted in equal increments over the term of the contract. When first-year maintenance is bundled with the purchase price, you will have to account for this separately.**

If companies institute these changes, their revenues will decline and their accounting bills will go up. The intent of these changes is to match revenue and expenses. One article that I read argued that while software companies should reserve the amount they expect to spend to provide the service, they should be able to book the profit initially. This is an interesting argument, but it just seems to me that it makes the accounting complexity much greater.

"The AICPA Proposal,
Good Intentions Gone Astray"
By Constance F. Galley
TSI International
The Software Industry Executive
May/June 1990

Adapso is fighting this change since many of the public software companies are looking at significant restatement of revenue and thus, net income. If you are interested in fighting this, call:

Douglas C. Jerger
Director
Adapso
(703) 284-5329

Business Potential

Your book and newsletter arrived on Friday and I ended up reading half the night. Your publication is the first one that I've found with practical information on marketing software. It answered quite a few questions that we had.

I am writing for some marketing advice. Do my products have potential with the correct marketing strategy or am I wasting a lot of time? Is the information we send out too factual? Any assistance would be appreciated.

History:

I have a full time job in the DP department of a major corporation and am attempting to start a business on the side. We have a separate business phone which my wife monitors in my absence. We have been selling one product for the last two years and recently announced a new product.

The problems we have faced:

1. **Reaching our unique audience (with our older product).**

2. **Closing the sale after the information has been sent.**

Staff Master:

Market: Utility companies, police, security, multi-shift organizations. During the last two years we have:

1. **Sent out numerous small mailings (100-250) with limited results.**

2. **Advertised once (1/4 page) in a state trade journal with no results.**

3. **Sent out press releases every six months (200-400). Four press releases were published (a couple of lines at most) with responses of 50 - 120 from each).**

4. **One newspaper article was published with a response of ten which lead to three immediate sales.**

5. **We are listed in a number of software directories, which have produced two to eight leads per month and a few sales.**

The responses from the press releases would seem to indicate a viable product. The number of sales to leads wasn't very high, so we changed our demo program (which was terrible) and lowered the price. This has increased the sales ratio considerably. But we can't live on press releases, and display ads are not cheap. Any ideas?

How would you proceed with a limited budget?

Sincerely,

Bob Eisman
Comsec

Dear Bob,

I would look at your return on investment for your marketing programs. It appears that directories and press releases clearly make money. What about the local newspaper articles? If you could spread the article elsewhere, it might help you generate some more quick sales.

Your real problem in my mind is establishing a primary marketing program that will generate the leads to generate the sales to build the business. Your choices appear to be direct mail and advertising. You mentioned that you had gotten a one percent response rate on your direct mail, which you felt was terrible.

Depending upon the average sales price, the cost of your mailing and your lead to sale conversion rate, direct mail may be profitable.

I personally like direct mail for small companies since you can test it with a limited budget and then expand your mailings as you reinvest your profits. Advertising, on the other hand, requires a significant investment to establish your presence.

There are two basic issues on the viability of your business. The first is: "Can you make money marketing your products?" That is, can you bring in more money from an ad or direct mail than you spend? If your ROI is less than one, this is a hobby and not a business.

The second issue is: "Can you generate enough contribution margin from your mailings to cover your fixed expenses and support this as a full-time business?" Let's assume that you can generate $2 in revenue for every $1 you spend on direct mail, and that your fixed expenses (including a salary) are $10,000 a month. Thus, you need to be able to spend $10,000 a month on marketing programs that will provide the margin to cover your fixed expenses. If your

mailings cost $0.50 per letter, this means that you need to be able to mail 20,000 pieces per month.

One of the most common problems that I see with small companies is that they never make the investment in marketing to start generating the level of activity to get the business going. Small mailings of 100 to 200 pieces will only generate a few responses and the cost-per-letter may approach $1.00. When you increase the volume, your unit costs decline and the absolute level of activity increases.

I realize that I haven't answered your question, but I hope that I have given you some guidelines on the questions that you need to answer.

Good luck,
Dave

17. Printing and Press Releases

Dear Mr. Bowen:

I have just this past week receive my first subscription to Software Success. Where have you been all my life? This is great stuff. It is nice to know that our problems are not unique, and that there is a vehicle for sharing problems and solutions.

I have two questions for you. The first question is this: In your book, as well as in your October newsletter, you mentioned that the printed interior of a manual should cost between $0.50 and $1.00 per copy. Obviously the cost is relative to the number of pages and the size of the print run. Please tell me the names of some printers that will do quality work for this price. Printing costs are eating me alive. One of our manuals, for example, is 90 pages, and the best prices we can get at a local printers is $4.35 (based on 100 quantity) or $3.96 (based on 500 quantity). We use standard IBM format. Note: These prices are for one color. In fact, at the 100 quantity, the printer uses a Xerox instead of offset, so the quality is not what it should be.

Sincerely,

William O. Limkemann
President
Software   Research

Dear William:

My first advice is to talk to your printers about what you can do to reduce your costs. They are experts and I have found that they have offered me suggestions that have dramatically reduced my costs with no discernable reduction in quality. You might find that going to a standard 5-1/2" by 8-1/2" format might save you some money.

You also should consider increasing your print run. Right now you are spending $435 to $1,980 to print from 100 to 500 of your manuals. I have a price schedule for one book printer and they will print 1,000 96-page books with perfect binding for only $1,222.

Printers you might call are:

G & H Printing
(415) 824-9750

Northwest Printing
(208) 345-4545

Printit
(317) 478-4885

Whitehall Printing
(708) 541-5890

The second question: For the past 6 years we have built a reputation developing and selling a great database management system to the CTOS (Unisys B20 distributed processing systems) market. This is a large, yet definitely niche, market. We have had good success and are well recognized in this market. We have also ported our package to UNIX and have begun gaining some success in parts of this market. As we have many dealers who also sell PC compatibles, we recently ported to MS-DOS, rewriting to make it have the look and feel of a generic MS-DOS product.

On September 1, we sent press releases to all the important industry journals. To my absolute amazement, we have not received a single mention in any PC journal (that I am aware of). Now I understand the enormity of the PC market, the number of database products that exist in the market, and the fact that editors must get swamped with press releases.

What is the secret of getting a new product in the PC marketplace mentioned in the popular PC magazines? How do I get the attention of editors? Also, once beyond this step, what ideas do you have for getting a product reviewed by a PC publication?

Thanks in advance for your help.
William

Dear William:

Getting press releases published in the major PC magazines is a very difficult task. I think that you set your sights way too high. I am sure that in your market you are one of the big players and that you can get your press releases published almost on demand. With the major PC magazines, it might take six months to get a press release published unless you are an Ashton-Tate or a Lotus. I would suggest that you get one of the lists of 600 editors and send out your press release again. You should also contact the magazines about submitting your product for review. Different magazines have quite different rules. This is going to take some serious work and time to break into the big leagues. One idea that you might consider is getting a PR agent who has worked with the major PC magazines. This is one of the cases where an agency might pay off. You might be able to find someone who has the contacts to break through the clutter and get someone to look at your press release and your product.

When I started my first company, my ex-boss told me "you think that it is a sprint, but it is really a marathon." I think that the same insight applies to breaking into the PC press. I would set my objectives to get some exposure within a year. If you can do better than that, you should be very proud. Don't be upset if you can't do it in sixty days.

Good luck,
Dave

18. Small System Design

Dear Dave:

We've been reading Software Success with great interest. It's hard to find information about small vertical market software companies that are self-funded. Your publication is the first that we have found that seems to be talking to us a sufficient amount of the time.

There are a few areas where we seem to deviate from most of your subscribers, in thinking over articles from the past year. For example:

- We write, support, market and sell construction accounting, job cost, estimating and payroll programs. Most sales are 7,000-12,000. We have about 20 employees, with total gross annual revenues of $1,000,000.

- We've been successfully selling service (maintenance) contracts to users since 1986. Support income is at least one-third of our revenues.

- We actively support 500 to 1,000 users. We bill users without service contracts for telephone calls. We handle about 1,000 calls per month. Service contract holders receive periodic updates throughout the year, and a discount on upgrades.

- Our sales account receivables average just over 10 days.

- We sell through dealers that we recruit or that find us, and directly to users in areas where we have no dealers. Of our product sales revenues, two-thirds is from dealer sales and one-third is directly to users. We have about 65 dealers that are actively selling our products.

- We have users who have become some of our most successful dealers.

The most significant thing that we've learned is that no one has absolutely correct answers. Sometimes we may re-invent the wheel, but more often we're blazing a trail that works for us. Thus, we never called for our consultation with you.

Please put us down to renew our subscription for the next year.

Sincerely yours,

Ann C. Weber
Vice President
Small System Design

Dear Ann:

Thanks for the letter. This is the type of real information that we all need to share. I encourage others to write in with similar profiles of their business. Learning about what has worked for others can really help your creative process and allow you to come up with better solutions. Good luck with your business.

Sincerely,
Dave

19. VISA/Master Card

Our bank doesn't offer VISA/Master Card. How can we become a VISA/MC merchant?

The first answer is to ask other merchants in your local area with whom they work.

There was a reference item in the newsletter below which identified another source of information. "A Special Report," by Larry Schwartz and Pearl Sax, directors of the Credit Card Bureau, provides information and a sample questionnaire for companies planning on applying. Also included is a list of sources for additional capital and a listing of banks that grant merchant status. The book is $49.95 plus $3.50 postage and handling. To order, contact The Credit Card Bureau, 217 N. Seacrest Blvd., Box 400, Boynton Beach, FL 33425 - (407) 737-7500.

Reference: "How to Get VISA and Mastercard Merchant Status", What's Working, January 1990.

20. Tracker Management

Dear Dave:

As you know, Tracker Management sells software to tow truck companies. I thought your readers might be interested in how we got into this business.

After owning my own body shop business and failing, I became an insurance adjuster for several years, which gave me the opportunity to talk with hundreds of shop owners.

I found out that it does not matter what size company you have. The size of the company only determines how much money you turn or collect. How much money you keep comes from your ability to control the money. In other words, how good your office expertise is.

I decided to focus on this fact, research it and find a way to apply it and share it. First, I took over a loser of a body shop at a Cad/Olds dealership. We turned it around and made it quite profitable.

I had a college professor friend of mine from Kent State write an estimate writing program and sold it as a complete package called Digi-tree. Now it's called Mitchell. Over about a three-year period, I sold their systems and slowly learned a lot about computers and business.

Thinking back to the good old days, I keep remembering all the paperwork with towing.

A towing company which generates $10,000 worth of work a week could be sending as many as 400 to 500 invoices to dealerships and police departments all over the city. I would have to keep track of cars for a night, or 30, 60, or 90 days or more—not knowing the owner's name at the time and getting stuck with the car, then needing a system to keep track of the car, file legal papers, etc.

There were a number of steps that I had to make to go into the tow truck software business.

First I needed to talk my wife into doing the programming. Then we spent another six months part-time, evenings and weekends, writing the very basic package. At that time, my wife quit her job and we went after the market full time. We talked with about 50 shop owners showing them what we had and asking for input on what they thought we needed. We added the important items, then we gave the program to a couple of shops. We had three beta sites use Tracker and give us input.

Was it easy after that? No way. We went to eight to ten shows and never sold one until the last show. In November of 1988 we sold our first system to Joe Linhard in Baltimore. After that it started to just snowball. We sold almost 40 systems in 1989.

I believe that part of our success is due to the fact that we are a family business. I think the towing industry as a whole is family businesses and they like dealing with a family business. Another thing that sets Tracker off from the others is we are one of a very few that are dedicated 100 percent to towing.

Lastly, I'd say we did a survey and we asked two questions: Why did you buy Tracker, and now that you have had it awhile, what do you like most? Answer to question number one was "It looked simple and easy." Answer to question number two was "It is simple and easy and support is great." I think that is the key.

Would you classify Tracker as a success? Yes, but remember success is a journey, not a destination. Another comment we make around the office a lot is it only took about seven years to become an "overnight success."

We tend to lean with the high-profit, low-volume philosophy. I know we cost a little more then the other systems, but we are darn well worth it. We make a decent profit on the systems we sell and then we feel obligated to service our customer. Plus, by selling a higher class system, we end up with higher class customers. They want solutions to problems and are willing to pay for service. They know the service will help them run their company better and generate more money than the service cost them in the first place.

Another thought that comes to mind was when one of my prospective customers asked me why we charged for service support after 90 days when most other companies did not. I asked him how good support would be if it was free. We charge a modest fee and then feel very responsible to give support and we feel good about it.

So, the bottom line is, we feel if we spend 80 percent of our time with our customers and 20 percent selling, we sell more. Doesn't seem right, but it works.

Well, there you have it — the inside view of a VAR (Value Added Reseller). A software company that helps tow companies computerize for the 1990's.

James (Jim) Weaver is founder and C.E.O. of Automotive Computer Enterprise, Inc., the parent company of Tracker Management Systems. You can ask Jim questions or get info about computer seminars at 1-800-445-2438.

21. Expanding Product Lines

We have a very successful and mature product. We would like to expand our product line. What are your thoughts on this?

The best product line extension is to sell more products to the same people. Many vendors have been able to ask their customers about additional products, features, modules, and so forth. These additional products can be sold to your installed base and to new customers. This allows you to increase the size of your average sale. Survey your customers and see if there are any good add-on opportunities.

The next step is to sell new products to the same company, but to different people. For example, you might sell an accounting system to the CFO and introduce a time and billing package for the office manager. This is a more difficult sale. You don't know the new person, and your sales people may not be effective selling this new product to a new person. In spite of these problems, I would examine this possibility second because their company knows your company. It also exploits much of your current marketing investment.

Selling your product into a new, but similar market is one of the toughest marketing challenges. Let's say that you have been selling to drug stores and you want to sell to hardware stores.

Your technical people have looked at the programming changes and they look minor. You have also looked at the effort to modify the documentation.

Your first problem is that you probably need to modify your marketing materials and documentation more than you really want to accept. You have fine-tuned your materials over the years for drug stores, and now you must do the same thing for hardware stores. Most of the horizontal product line extension failures that I see are a direct result of failing to make the necessary investment for the new market. Prospects can tell if you have just done a slip-shod job of tailoring your product for their market, and they don't like it.

The final cost of entering a new market is the marketing and promotion costs and delays. It is easy to spend $100,000 to $250,000 to introduce your product and company to a new market. If you think back on the pain and suffering of starting your company and introducing a new product, entering a new market is much like this. You don't know what works in this market and they don't know you. It is very easy to forget how much smarter you have become over the years by selling in your current market. This isn't to say you can't enter a new market. Just don't underestimate how hard it will be.

22. Local Developers Association

How should we go about starting a local developers association? What about membership and bylaws?

I don't know, but hopefully one of our readers do. If any of you have experience with a local developers association please drop me a line with the specifics. Thanks.

23. Trademark Information

The U.S. Trademark Association offers "The Official Media Guide and Trademark Checklist." The checklist includes over 1,000 word marks. The media guide contains rules on how trademarks should and should not be used:

Trademarks are proper adjectives and should be followed by generic terms.

Trademarks should not be pluralized.

Trademarks should not be used in the possessive form.

Trademarks are never verbs.

Tradenames and trademarks are not the same.

If you would like more information on these points call or write:

U.S. Trademark Association
6 East 45th Street
New York, NY 10017
(212) 986-5880

24. Market Research

We are introducing a new PC product and we are trying to research the market for our product. We have a twenty-question survey that we would like people to fill out after they have gone through our demo disk.

We are offering people a discount on the product if they complete the survey. We have sent out fifteen, but we have only gotten a couple of surveys back.

We got a new product mention in PC magazine and have 200 responses that we sent copies of our brochure. We have someone who can make outbound calls. Many of the PC Magazine leads have phone numbers. What do you suggest?

Getting two responses from fifteen surveys is great. You just need to get more of them out there. I would write a letter explaining that you would like them to go through your survey and demo disk to help you refine your marketing. I would offer them a free copy of the software for the first 50 to complete the survey. You might get away with offering a significant discount, but I would want the information.

I would mail this letter with the survey and demo disk to all of the leads who haven't gotten the survey. Depending upon the two- week response rate, you might follow up with calls to the people who provided phone numbers and haven't responded.

Another strategy that we discussed was to call the leads and ask them if they were willing to do this. If you got their commitment to review the demo and fill out the survey, you could send it out. This might get a higher response rate because they are making a commitment before you send the materials.

In practice, you might send the letters to the names without phone numbers, and call those with phone numbers.

Good luck,
Dave

25. Big Company to Small Company

We recently hired a marketing manager from a large company. He was very impressive, but from the day he started at our small company he was totally ineffective. Have you seen other companies experience this problem? What is the solution?

Making the transition from a big company to a small company is very difficult. In a big company, a middle manager has very narrow responsibilities and authority. They are also used to working with a mature infrastructure behind them. I think that many of them don't have a clue about what it takes to get the job done in a small company.

When I left Amdahl, my friends took me out for lunch a couple weeks later and asked me what I had done. I said that I had gotten a business license, office, office furniture, phones, and started on my business plan. One of them said, "Why didn't you have facilities do all that?" The moment he said it, he realized that I was "it," but ex-big company employees have many of these surprises.

Another source of problems is that most middle managers in big companies have limited and narrow experience. They may have been in marketing, but their experience may be with one phase of marketing. They also may be hampered by the fact that the things that work well for big companies may not work at all for small companies. I have seen cases where these experiences have given these managers intuitions that weren't appropriate.

The most extreme case of this was a CEO who was brought into a venture backed startup. He had worked for a number of the biggest and best firms in the industry. The company was struggling, and trying to raise a second round of financing. The company had gone through some really hard times and the employees were getting ready to pull in the belt and get the job done.

The new CEO decided that he needed a $5,000 desk since this is what he had had in his last job. This was his image of a CEO. The employees were outraged, but he stuck to his guns. While this wasn't the only problem, it was a very symbolic event that contributed to the company's woes.

The range of decision making authority in smaller companies is quite different from that in large companies. In a large company, a manager has a budget limit and feels free to spend up to that limit. In small companies, founders and owners take a much more personal interest in how money is spent, as exemplified by the desk example above.

It is often difficult for new managers to know what requires approval and what doesn't. My advice is that the manager should ask during the break in period, and establish a working relationship with the owner or founders. Over time, the manager should get a pretty good feeling for this.

The narrow experience situation is something that you really should discuss in detail. In most cases, the big company manager won't have all the breadth that a small company person would have. Make sure you discuss this in detail with them, and that you discuss how they are going to fill in the areas in which they don't have the direct experience. Perhaps they should have a reading program. Using consultants to fill in these areas is a reasonable approach.

The infrastructure problem requires a two-step approach. First, you must discuss these issues in great detail before the person starts. Can they use a PC to write their own memos? Do they mind sending their own FAXes? Do your best to make it real for them.

The next phase is to remind them of the modus operandi in your company. Don't let them "forget" and ask others to do things for them that they should do for themselves. If you did a good job in phase one, they should be receptive to your reminder. If they insist on flaunting the culture, point out to them that they will just create ill will and that they won't succeed.

People can make the transition from big companies to small companies. In fact, most of the people in the industry started off working for big companies. As the boss of a new employee, you should do everything you can to help them succeed.

My experience is that less than 50 percent of new marketing managers succeed and are with the company three or four years later. In many cases, it is the cultural and personality issues that are the real problem. Sometimes the difference are irreconcilable, but many times they are just minor differences that lead to major misunderstandings. If you realize this ahead of time, you should be able to improve your odds of success significantly.

M. Management Survey (1989)

We got a good response for the management survey. It was slightly lower than some of the more popular topics like customer support, promotion, etc, but we were very impressed with the amount of effort people expended in filling out this questionnaire. Thank you for your support.

Our respondents had a product mix that was typical for small software companies: 60% were vertical-market packages, 40% were horizontal. The distribution mix was strongly oriented towards direct sales: only 11% of the respondents used indirect (through distribution channels), while 59% were direct only, and another 30% used both direct and indirect methods

1. Capitalization

Most firms were primarily owned by their founders. 71% of the firms had no outside investors. 23% of the firms had private investors, 11% had venture capitalists and 11% were public. This fits my experience that most software companies can't offer serious private investors and venture capitalists the Return On Investment (ROI) that they require. Software companies are a great place to work and can be very lucrative for the founders, but often they are poor investments.

The founder's investments seemed to fall into two categories: either they invested less than $10,000, or they put in $100k to $200k. Our experience is that the companies which were founded on very little money were in niches with little or no competition. If you are facing any competition, you need at least $200k to get a company launched. Bank loans were a more significant source of financing than we had anticipated. 75% of the situations where the founders had invested $100,000 to $200,000 had also extended their leverage through bank loans. 17% of the companies were planning on additional debt financing (Line of credit or personal borrowing), while 23% were planning on raising money from private investors or venture capitalists. 60% of the companies were happy to finance the company out of retained earnings rather than via investors.

Company Objectives

The objectives of the respondents, relative to rewarding the shareholders, were as follows:

- Income for principals   64%
- Good place to work   58%
- Sell the company   35%
- Go public   23%

There is little apparent disagreement among the shareholders. Only 17% of the respondents perceived that there was any dispute over company objectives. Our experience is that there is in fact more disagreement and dissention than was reported. The CEO often doesn't see it or chooses to ignore the other shareholders. This is especially true if they are friends of the family or employees.

There is another hidden problem lurking in the bushes, waiting to leap out and consume the unwary: many shareholders don't (or won't) express an opinion until there is money on the table. We have seen major differences erupt once the company is worth something, or the company can afford to pay significant bonuses or dividends. This is an area where talking to the shareholders beforehand, can help to minimize the stress once the company has some excess money to deal with.

Raising Outside Funding

The companies who had raised money from private investors or venture capitalists were quite open about the amount of work involved. Typically it took one elapsed year and one and one half man years to close the financing. This represents a full-time effort on the part of the CEO and half-time for the sales and marketing VP. Managing the company on a day-to-day basis must be sandwiched in between investor visits, meetings with venture capitalists, phone calls to/from potential investors, and scouting trips. Several firms mentioned that they had wasted significant time trying to raise venture capital.

We have seen many cases where there was little hope of raising money from either private investors or venture capitalists, and the companies would have been much better off investing these one to two man-years in running the company. Even getting a line of credit takes time. This was less than raising capital, but you should anticipate three to six man-months.

Personal Objectives

When asked what they wanted out of the business, the answers that our respondents provided seemed to be dependent upon the company's method of capitalization. The companies that had raised professional money (from sophisticated private investors, venture capital, or public offering) said that they wanted high earnings per share. As long as these earnings are good, the company is perceived as doing well (such is the tale of American business.)

Companies without significant cash investment were oriented toward providing their employees (especially the founders) with a good, secure, and fun job. Lastly there were those companies that wanted to be sold or go public. These "wanna bees" need to grow their company so that they can progress down the path of raising money. With this as an objective, sales revenues are much more important than profits, since these companies are reinvesting all their available capital and retained earnings to achieve maximum growth.

When asked about the strength of the management team over half of the companies mentioned planning as their major strength. Only 11 percent of the companies mentioned sales or marketing as a management team strength. Technical know how was mentioned by 33 percent of the companies. The remainder of the responses were general management and people skills.

2. Competitive Rankings

We asked the respondents to rank their company and their competitor on the same items. We then compared how they ranked themselves compared to how they ranked their competitors. We determined what percent of the respondents ranked their company better than their competitors on each category. We are going to call this Bowen's "better than" ratio (BBTR). Here's the BBTR for the questionnaire categories, along with our comments.

On the average, the readers of Software Success run smaller companies (we will publish the survey results in the April Issue so we will know how much smaller than average they are), so some of these answers reflect their relative size.

Support — 100%

Everybody is better than their competitors, right? We see this unanimous response as technical ego. Everyone we talk to thinks that they have the world's best technical support. At the same time, they don't query their customers about their support, so this is just an opinion, not fact. This is a blind side in our industry. See the December 1988 issue of *Software Success* for more discussion on customer support.

Reputation — 95%

This is management ego. All software companies can't have a better reputation than all of their competitors. We find that many small companies define reputation in terms of being technically better. At the same time they offer price discounts on their products and don't understand why their larger competitor continues to win sales. The small technical companies who compete with IBM are a good example. They will tell you that they have a much better reputation than IBM since IBM products are no good. Since IBM is rated one of the top companies year after year, these actual surveys of potential customers usually tell a different story.

We urge you to conduct a market survey of how your customers and your prospects view you and your competitors. Do this anonymously. Once you have some data, you can realistically discuss your reputation. You can also discuss the steps you need to take to improve your perceived reputation.

Technical strength — 89%

This is probably true for many smaller companies. Part of this is that small software companies have less overhead to distract their technical people. The other reason is that with a small, young company, the technical people can focus on building new products. In a more mature company, much more of the technical resources are tied up in maintaining and enhancing older products. Larger/Older companies have too much money at risk in maintenance (and add-on product sales) to let the older products drop. At the same time, development on these older products is technically less interesting, because of the inherent technical difficulties in extending old code.

Chapter V. Management Issues

Market Knowledge — 83%

This sounds about right. Smaller companies *should* be closer to the market and their customers. Everyone in the company should have contact with the prospects and customers. Especially, the CEO. Any small company where the CEO doesn't really understand his target market is in deep trouble. Even if the CEO was a prospect, they must stay in touch with the market to keep their market knowledge current. Markets change, and if your company can't go with the flow you will find yourself out of business.

Management — 83%

This seems somewhat optimistic. While larger companies do lots of stupid things, most of them (especially in our industry) have lots of very good people. One of the major constraints for small software companies is management bandwidth. The managers in small companies are often very talented. But in many cases their talents are being misused or they are being asked to perform in areas where they don't really have the expertise. How many times have we seen a technical CEO stuck with managing sales people? How often does senior techie get stuck doing the books?

Small companies also usually lack depth in the management team. If one person gets overloaded, the other managers will have to drop some of their own tasks if they are to pick up the load. This results in a lack of continuity and consistency which is a major problem in small software companies.

The management strength for small software companies is that decisions can be made quickly. Most of the management difficulties in large companies can be traced back to two realities:

1. They have so many people to involve in the decision, that it takes a long time to make decisions.
2. Their environment is much more complex. They have large customer bases to deal with. It is also more difficult to deal with problems on a larger scale. If you have 100 customers, you can deal with changing your maintenance policy. With 100,000 customers this is much more complex. The recent discussion of IBM's new maintenance plans indicates how difficult things become when you are large. Small companies are like speedboats on the software lake, while large companies are like oil tankers. If you want to succeed, you better remember which you are.

Average Overall rating — 77%

We were impressed that 23% of the companies felt that their competition was stronger than they were across all the categories. This was more realistic than we would have anticipated. If you assume the this is really true 50% of the time we could calibrate all of the other ratings. *Of course, we assume that the readers of Software Success are much brighter and better than average. Don't you agree?*

Marketing — 77%

This is where the bigger companies begin to have the advantage. Their infrastructure and support staff make a difference in the marketing area. There are a lot of fixed costs in the marketing area. This gives the larger company a real advantage. Once the larger company has covered these fixed costs they can spend their money on the extras like seminars. Smaller companies have to be much smarter about how they spend their marketing money if they are to hold their own with the big guys.

Sales — 71%

We are surprised that this wasn't lower. We find that sales is a weak spot in small, technically oriented companies. If the management doesn't have a sales and marketing background, it is usually very difficult for them to build a strong sales organization. In many cases it is also difficult to recruit good sales people into a small company unless they are technical enough to evaluate a strong technical product. The really good salespeople are making so money with their existing company that they can't even think of leaving. Small companies also lack much of the infrastructure which is so critical to top quality sales.

Installed base — 69%

A significant number of the firms are competing against competitors who have larger installed bases. Part of the difficulty in assessing installed base is how you define the relevant market. We have seen a number of situations where small companies convince themselves that they have excellent market share by defining the market so narrowly that they are the dominant player. An example of this is the minicomputer software vendors who discounts customers who buy PC software as not really being in their market.   Make sure that you don't mislead yourself.

Financial resources — 59%

Everyone feels poor, no matter how much money they have raised.

3. Where are you going?

We asked our subscribers to list what one change they would like to make in their company. The replies are illuminating:

Better marketing — 41% This is classically the weak spot for software companies. Typically software companies are founded by technical people who understand their market. They can hire sales people to sell the product, and if it is a good product they will generate sales. Bringing marketing talent into a small undercapitalized software company is no easy challenge. First there are very few marketing people with industry experience so most likely you will have to find someone with some marketing experience who is interested in learning the software business. Training these people can be both expensive and time consuming, but unless you can attract an experienced player it is probably a good alternative. The *best* alternative, of course, is to hire Dave Bowen to help train your staff.

Better management — 37% This is another area where it is difficult to add people. Because of the small size and difficult financial straits of most emerging software companies, their managers must wear many hats. People who have worked in large companies often find this diversity distracting. They are used to having a very narrow focus, and in most cases they don't really have the exposure to manage other areas. In most cases the CEO acts as the marketing manager. (In some cases he is the Marketing Department!) At the same time he (or she) is also the sales manager because the sales people directly report to the CEO. A good administration manager/office manager and a programming & support manager will make life easier for the harassed CEO.

If you have these key functions filled (CEO, Chief Programmer, Marketeer, & Admin), you have the basis upon which to build a full-blown management team. If not, you need to stop and fill the gaps. While one person may fill two jobs (CEO and Chief Programmer, for instance), they cannot be expected to do a good job wearing three hats.

In developing a strategy to build your management team, we find that it is best to add one new manager at a time. This minimizes the organizational stress and makes it easier for the new manager to succeed. In our consulting assignments, we start by assessing the strengths of the current management team and building a priority list of which managers should be added, and in what order. The positions that most startup companies need to fill over the first few years are:

- Sales
- Marketing
- Support
- Training
- Finance
- Personnel

More capital — 17% - We were surprised that this perceived need was so low. It probably reflects the fact that 60% of the software companies we sampled didn't want outside capital. Almost half of the companies that *did* want to raise outside capital perceived that their competitors were in better financial shape.

More products — 5% - This doesn't surprise us. This is a technical industry. By and large we have much more product than we can effectively market. There are very few cases where the better mousetrap will carry the day without skillful marketing.

4. Objectives for '88 & '89

In last year's survey, when we asked our subscribers about their objectives for 1988, 76 percent of the companies wanted to increase sales and 29 percent wanted to introduce new products. We were surprised at the number of companies who wanted to double their sales in 1988 and felt that they had failed because they only achieved 70 percent of the plan. In any other industry 70 percent growth would be phenomenal. Too many software companies plan on 100 percent growth and get into trouble when they only achieve 70 percent. When you are making your plans for 1989, make sure that your revenue goals are reasonable. You might base your financial plan on 70 percent of the sales plan if you are shooting for ultra-high growth.

It was interesting that a number of the new products for 1988 were on new hardware platforms. This allows for horizontal growth. If you choose your new platform right you can open up significant new marketing territory with a new platform. (See the question in Q & A's on this issue.)

Everyone had sales as their 1989 objective, and 35% also mentioned additional product as an objective. Some of the product objectives were to introduce new products while others were to clean up existing products.

5. Acquisitions

36 percent of the respondents had acquired a company or product, and 47 percent were considering acquiring a product. The reasons for acquiring a product were:

- **100% Exploit sales and marketing** — Once you have made the investment in your sales and marketing engine, you can exploit additional products. This is especially true if your development staff is tied up supporting your existing products.

- **50% Buy an installed base** — When you buy an established product, you can cross-sell it to your installed base and sell your existing products to these new customers as well. This depends upon the match of your installed base and the installed base that you are purchasing. If there is a good match this could be very profitable.

- **12% Eliminate a competitor** — While this is the lowest reason given, in our experience this reason is more common than our respondents indicated. This is especially true with marketing agreements which lock the developers into subsequent product development for the marketing company. While the developers might not have been direct competition, the marketing company has insured that they won't become direct competitors in the future.

Reasons for no acquisitions:

The reasons that 53% of the companies gave for not acquiring product were:

- **55% We are a development company** — This is a good reason for many companies. If you know that you are a development company and not a marketing company, you shouldn't acquire products because you don't have the sales and marketing channel to exploit.

- **44% We don't have any money** — While this is a common answer, it shouldn't stop you if you

think that you can effectively *use* an acquisition. We have seen a number of cases where the marketing company had adequate capital to launch the new product, but they didn't have to pay the developers big bucks. The developers would receive 15 to 25 percent of the sales revenues and 50 percent of the maintenance revenues. These arrangements work where the marketing company is already selling into to the new product's target market.

- **22% We can build it better** — Maybe you can, maybe you can't. Don't let NIH (Not Invented Here) get in you way when you want to acquire an attractive product.

6. R&D Capitalization

Capitalization policies with regard to your Research & Development expenses can make a significant difference to both your P&L and Balance Sheet. The Federal Accounting Standards Board (FASB to all you accounting fans) has ruled that "at risk" R&D expenditures *must* be capitalized and amortized over the life of the product. In spite of this, a surprising 52% of the companies do not capitalize R&D. A full one-third of our respondents felt that capitalizing R&D was financially misleading

Of the companies who do capitalize their R & D, 25% felt that it was significant while 62% felt that only their accountant or their banker really cared.

Dear Dave;

This letter is in response to your February, 1989 issue of Software Success. I enjoyed the overall article very much; Hover, there were some misleading points concerning R & D Capitalization that I would like to comment on.

The first point is somewhat picky in nature. FASB stands for Financial Accounting Standards Board rather than Federal Accounting Standards Board. The FASB is very particular about any federal association. They have been adamant about being completely separated from the "Feds" and any related influence in the structuring and promulgation of financial accounting standards.

The second point concerns the proper accounting for R & D expenditures from a financial accounting standpoint. Please bear in mind the following may differ materially from a tax basis or related form of accounting. Statement of Financial Accounting Standards No. 86 issued by FASB during August, 1985 specifically deals with the proper treatment of R & D Expenditures as they relate to computer software to be sold, leased, or otherwise marketed as a separate product or as part of a product or process. The Statement defines both Research and Development Costs of Computer Software and Production Costs of Computer Software for clarification purposes. Moreover and more significantly, Paragraph 3 of the statement states "All costs incurred to establish the technological feasibility of a computer software product to be sold, leased, or otherwise marketed are research and development costs. These costs shall be charged to expense when incurred as required by FASB Statement No. 2, Accounting for Research and Development Cost."

Please do not regard this letter as undue criticism. I felt that most of the information contained within the article was very timely and informative. I did feel, however, that the R & D reference required additional clarification. Keep up the excellent work.

John L. Vininv, CPA
Executive Vice President
Mortgage Computer
Ogden, Utah

I appreciate the feedback,but I am even more confused than ever. I suspect that part of the problem may be the difference between financial accounting and tax accounting, Most of the information that I have seen has related to the tax accounting side of this problem. I urge everyone to review this with their own accountant.

7. Revenue Recognition

When you recognize sales revenue is a significant financial issue for software companies. You will remember that sales/revenue growth was the the top objective for both 1988 and 1989. Recognize the revenue too soon and you'll be kidding yourselves when you look at your P&L, wait too long, and you are being needlessly conservative. For our respondents, revenue recognition occurred at the following times:

- **47% Upon receipt of a signed contract — This is a reasonably conservative approach. Some of the firms also require a Purchase Order Number. When you have both of these documents in hand, you will have little risk of voided contracts. The risk depends upon how strong your contract is an under what conditions the customer can break the contract.**

- **29% When the cash is received — This is the safest, but most conservative, approach.**

- **29% When a Purchase Order is received — Half of these cases also require a signed contract.**

- **17% when they received a verbal OK —**

Recognizing verbal orders can be very risky. To minimize the risk in accepting a verbal order, have someone else follow up with the customer to verify the verbal order. You might have a contracts person call the customer the next day. Otherwise you run the risk that the salesperson will be mislead by the customer or will deliberately mislead management.

Accounts Receivable

The Accounts Receivable period ranged from 30 to 90 days. 45 days is probably the lowest that you can expect if you are selling to large companies.

Void Rate

The void rate is the ratio of those contracts that are ultimately rejected for whatever reason. The void rate was bimodal: 47% of the companies had 0% voids; 53% of the companies hold their void rate to 5%. We wonder how accurate these void rates really are. Would we get the same answer if we asked the accountants instead of the CEOs and Marketing Executives?

8. Line of Credit

29% of our respondent companies have lines of credit (LOC). 40% of the LOCs were personally guaranteed, and the other 60% were secured by the Accounts Receivable. Our experience is that banks will start a LOC with personal guarantees, but they will take them off as they get to know the company. Our advice is to start with a modest AR line with personal guarantees. Use it well and in time the bank will expand your credit, and it can become a real part of your cash management system.

Typically you can borrow up to 75% of your A/R (A/R over 90 days old will typically be excluded). One firm mentioned that development contracts were excluded from the borrowing base. The most the bank might want is a monthly review of your A/R borrowing base.

9. Maintenance Revenue Recognition

An amazing 64 percent of companies recognize all of their support revenue at once. We strongly recommend against this. The proper accounting is to prorate it over the life of the contract. While this may not seem significant when your maintenance revenues are low, it will be critical when your maintenance revenues approach 30 to 50 percent of your total revenues. There are two reasons to prorate it:

1. It will lower your taxes by postponing revenue.

2. It will avoid a major revenue drop when you eventually prorate it.

10. Sales Compensation

The average base salary was $25,000 per year and 35 percent of the companies pay 5% commissions, 23 percent of the companies pay 10% commissions, 11 percent of the companies pay independent reps 30% commissions, and 30 percent of the companies don't pay commissions.

Only 29 percent of the companies pay their sales people draws, 17 percent pay new sales people an extra base initially, but 64 percent pay bonuses.

Another crucial issue is determining when salespeople will be paid. The responses were as follows:

- **64% Upon cash receipt — This is the safest approach if you give your sales people any flexibility in specifying payment plans.**

- **23% Upon revenue recognition — This is OK if you have tight controls on recognizing the revenue. All of these companies giving this response required both a signed contract and a Purchase Order before they recognized the revenue — they're fairly safe.**

- **5% Upon contract execution — If you have experienced *any* voids at all, this is a risky proposition.**

11. Bonuses

Software companies don't pay a lot of bonuses. The frequency by title was:

- **47%   Management**

- **35%   Development**

- **35%   Company wide bonus.**

- **11%   A support specific bonus.**

We believe that more companies could make use of bonuses.

12. Compensation on Recruiting

77 percent of the companies said that they start with salary guidelines and find the best person that they can afford while 18 percent said that they go for the best possible person. One company said that they go for the best person when filling development positions; they start with salary guidelines when filling management positions; the find the cheapest person possible when filling the administrative positions, and they look for people who can be trained when filling support positions. This seems like a real pattern that many companies follow. We would appreciate comments on this.

N.   Miscellaneous   (1989)

1. Software Company Compensation

Q. What information is available on compensation for software companies?

A. The Association for Data Processing Service Organizations (ADAPSO) is conducting a compensation survey; the results will be available in May 1989. This survey will probably be the best source of nationwide salary levels for our industry. The cost is $500 for ADAPSO members and $700 for nonmembers. They are available from William M. Mercer, Meidinger-Hansen, Incorporated, The Survey Group, 1417 Lake Cook Road, Deerfield, IL 60015 (no phone number).

There are local salary surveys which might be more useful for your non-management or technical positions. Call your local Better Business Bureau to see if they know of a local salary survey.

Q: In a past issue you discussed how to get a local salary survey. Isn't there some place that has a nationwide computer salary survey?

A: One of our readers mentioned that you can get a free, nationwide salary survey from Source EDP. The survey reviews the latest salaries and career paths for over sixty computer job functions and experience levels. While this survey is oriented towards the job-seeker, you will get valuable information for employers, as well. Specifically you'll learn about:

Chapter V.   Management Issues

* Job growth trends.
* Which computer careers offer the most salary and career potential.
* How to assess your current position/
* What you can do to avoid career dead-ending.
* The 1989 "going rates" for professionals at different experience and skill levels.
* The six steps to computer management.

2. Competitive Co-operation?

Q. How can I foster co-operation with my competitors?

A. It is almost impossible to foster co-operation with direct competitors because of the competitive pressures. It just doesn't make sense to give a direct competitor any edge.

Indirect competitors, on the other hand, might both benefit from some industry interface standardization. WordPerfect Corporation and Aldus Corp recently announced, for instance, that they were co-operating on ways to have WordPerfect text imported directly into Pagemaker.

If there are several types of products which your customers might buy which could interface with each other, both vendors can benefit from having common interfaces. For example, the word processor to desk top publishing software interface helps both vendors sell their products. When you see this type of opportunity you can approach the other vendor and suggest a technical exchange to facilitate these interfaces. In theory you could form an industry committee to develop common interfaces. The new PC bus and OSF are both examples of this type of co-operation. We think that it is significant that both of these examples are being driven by larger companies which can afford to contribute both people and money to get these projects going. We don't believe that smaller companies can afford this type of complexity. If you know of any examples, I would be pleased to hear about them.

3. Saving the Company:Cutting Expenses

Q. We overestimated our sales and staffed up in anticipation of sales that didn't materialize. The company is now in trouble. How should I cut ex-penses? Is there any systematic way to approach saving my company?

A. There *is* a way. (And you'd be suprised at the number of software firms that find themselves in this boat.) The best way to deal with trouble is to anticipate it and deal with it early. The sooner you recognize that you are in trouble, the less painful it will be to make the necessary changes.

Getting in over your head

Sometimes these troubles are only brought on by a short term down-turn in sales, but in many cases they reflect the fact that your business has made the transition from the survival start-up stage to the competitive growth stage. In the survival stage you hold your expenses to the bare minimum, because of your cash constraints. Once your sales begin to increase it is very easy to add staff and buy additional equipment. There is often a strong sense of debt, "We owe it to ourselves since we have worked so hard and gone so long without the proper resources." There is also the feeling that creeps in: "If we have done this well with limited resources, just imagine what we can do with the right resources." For all these reasons, many young companies raise their fixed expenses above the level that they can realistically support.

A Relief Plan

Once you realize this, you have to develop a plan to lower your burn rate (how much money you spend every month) to a sustainable level. Look at your historic sales and make very conservative growth assumptions (how about no growth?). The next thing is to examine your expenses very carefully. The CEO should understand every line item. You should start with the non-people expenses first to find fat that you can cut without a layoff. We find in most cases that it is reasonably easy to cut the non-payroll expenses by 10 to 20 percent with minor inconvenience. While this isn't a large part of the monthly expenses, it is a very good signal to everyone in the company that you are cutting back. Make everyone aware that you are in a 'crunch' and that you are starting with the non-people expenses to see if you can weather the storm without letting people go. You will be surprised at the creativity of the suggestions to cut expenses. While some of them will be absurd, it gets the entire company involved.

Chapter V. Management Issues

Considering Layoffs

Laying off personnel is much tougher. We recommend that you have each manager rank his people based on their criticality to the business. Also ask them to identify the deadwood that is truly marginal. One of the benefits of type of crisis is that it is an opportunity to cut the deadwood. Under more normal circumstances, it is very difficult to let marginal people go, especially if they are trying to do the job. Letting them go as part of a company layoff makes it easier for you and saves them face.

At the same time you should have your accounting department studying your accounts receivables and accounts payables. You will be surprised at the impact of modest changes in improving your collections and delaying some of your payables. Within a couple weeks you should have a cash flow forecast for the next few months. This will determine how deep you need to make your cuts.

An Option:Temporary Salary Cuts

If your tough times are truely a temporary situation, you might want to consider a temporary salary cut. If you give the majority of your staff every other Friday off, for instance, you can effect a 10% across-the-board cut in salaries. (In these situations, management typically gets to work *more*, not less — you'll still need to come in every day.) We have seen several situations like this where a temporary salary cut obviated the need for layoffs.

Your company's culture will ultimately determine whether you can implement this type of salary cut. If you have developed a strong loyalty to the company, this approach will probably work fine. If you are in a very competitive market or have a brand-new situation, you might think twice.

Facing the inevitable: Layoffs

Finally we come back to determining who must be laid off. We come at this two ways:

1. Who is generating cash?
2. Who is expendable?

The key cash generators are individuals or groups who can't be replaced. If you lose them, most likely you will lose the cash. They must be kept.

There is a second category of employees which is helping to generate cash, but are not indespensible: others can take over for them. Individuals in this group might be candidates for layoffs — depending upon the availability of other resources.

Individuals and groups in the final category aren't generating cash in the near term. Often programmers working on R&D are in this final group. The challenge with this final group is to find ways to redirect their efforts to generate cash. This means that they may need to stop working on fun future projects and start contract programming or training which will help carry the company. Usually you can come up with creative ways to protect your key people.

At this point you have all the information to make your decisions. You know how much you have to cut and you have your priority list of who to cut. We know that this process isn't easy, but unless you make these tough decisions at some point you will go out of business and everyone will be out of work.

One simple but often overlooked principle works wonders with morale: keep your people informed. While it's a natural human tendency to keep all the bad news to yourself, don't do it. Have an all-hands staff meeting and lay it out for them. Tell them what you are doing and what you'll expect from them. Hold these meetings on a regular basis until the crisis is over.

4. Software Company Operating Costs
Operating Expenses 1988

Sentry Market Research (508/ 366-2031) recently published a report, *Software Industry Financial Review 1988*. They studied 81 leading software companies financial reports. Some of the relevant numbers from this study are shown in the graph below. In folding these ratios into your own business and/or sales plans, we sugest that you focus most on the *average* numbers for your market segment. The high-est numbers can be distorted by individual companies with unusual years or unusual situation. Another difficulty is that these are numbers for larger successful companies so it is unclear how well they apply to small software companies, but we don't have a lot of data.

Operating Expenses by Software Type

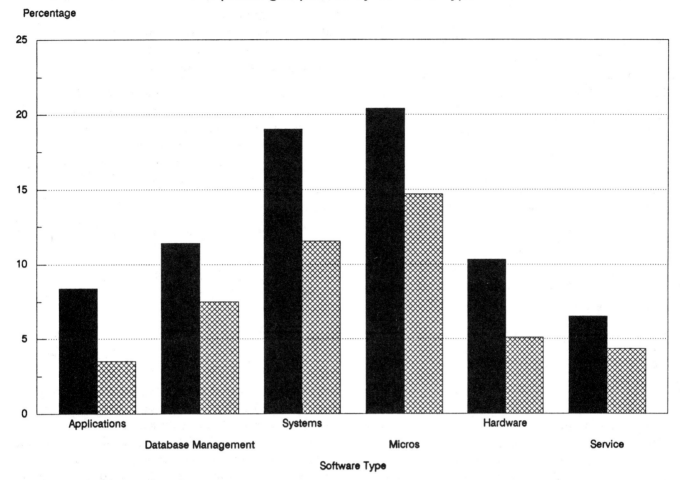

Percentage

Software Type

Operating Expenses 1989

Q. Where can I get information on software company operating expenses?

A. Sentry Publishing released their, "Software Industry Financial Review '89" in July. It is a 150 page report which provides in-depth financial investigation of more than 100 leading software vendors. Later this year we will conduct a similar survey of our readers which will provide you with the numbers for small software companies.

REFERENCE: "Sentry Market Research", Software Industry Financial Review '89, (508) 366-2031.

5. 1989 Software Forecast

Q. *What is the outlook for 1989 for software? Do you have any numbers that I can give to my investors?*

A. The Commerce Department just released their prognostications for 1989. Computer software sales are expected to rise by 24 percent, giving it second place in the services category. The only higher category was space commercialization which begins its first year of operation. While there will be variations by market segment, it looks like 1989 will be a good year. The current forecasts for 1990, however, show a recession coming on. Keep this in mind as you add staff in 1989.

6. Dealing with Consultants

Q. Our product requires significant consulting to tailor the application to the specific customer. Thankfully our customers are willing to pay for this. We would like to avoid building a large consulting organization. We have had some conversations with consulting companies who would like to work with

Chapter V. Management Issues

us. How should we deal with these consulting companies?

A. There is one fundamental question that you must answer first: "Can consulting companies really expect to make money installing and customizing this product?"

In spite of your belief that customers will be willing to pay for this service, they may not. In certain situations customers expect (demand) that the software vendor provide installation/customization as part of the purchase price. If this is true for your product, a consulting firm cannot make any money.

If you have experience with actual customers who are willing to pay extra for installation and customization, then the answer to our question above is "Yes". The next step is to find some consulting companies.

Finding Consultants

Exactly how to find consultants will depend upon the specific type of work that you are doing.

You should ask your customers for introductions to the consulting companies that they work with. Next you should meet with the consulting companies and review your consulting with them. See if they are, interested. If they are you should propose that the consulting company send their people to a training class on your product. While you shouldn't charge the consulting company for the class, you shouldn't pay for their time. If they aren't willing to make this investment, we would be very reluctant to make much of an investment in them.

Establishing a Relationship

Once the consultants are trained, you will have to work out the ground rules of your relationship. You must keep in mind that except in very rare cases, they will not be exclusive to you and you are under no obligation to them. They will be happy to perform similar consulting for your competitors and you will be happy to work with their competitors. As long as you keep this in mind you should be OK.

Finally, you should understand that in most cases consulting firms will be very reluctant to risk their reputation by endorsing your company or your product. While they may identify leads for your sales people, they will not sell for you. If they actually sell against you, you should drop your association with them.

Managing the Engagement

Once you have made the sale, they will want to move in and take over control of the project. This risks your connection with the customer because the consulting company has very limited loyalty.

In our experience, the best way to get good results is to insist that you maintain control of the project and use the consultants as contractors. As long as your person is the primary technical contact, you should minimize the risk that the consultant will damage your business relationship.

Payment Terms

In this type of relationship the consulting firm is simply working for you and you are responsible for paying them for their work. If you really maintain control of the project, you can understand why they don't want to bear the collection risk. You are their client and since they are working under your direction, it is only fair that you are eventually responsible for paying them. If they don't do good work, you can always refuse to pay them. If you are unhappy with the quality of their people, let their management know quickly. Don't keep someone on the job who isn't carrying his weight. If the consultants do their job, and you fail to collect it is your problem and not theirs.

Successful Relationships

We have seen several cases where software companies have managed to work well with consulting companies. But, to be honest we have seen many more cases where the software companies invested a great deal of time and effort with little result. If you are trying to build this type of relationship make sure that you manage it carefully. Monitor your investment and the commitment of the consulting companies. Clearly identify the next steps and be willing to drop them if they don't follow up.

7. Bonus and Profit Sharing Plans
Q. What is your experience with small company bonus and profit sharing plans?

A. The initial reaction to a bonus program is almost always positive. Everyone likes to be paid for doing a good job. This is especially nice when there are very specific parameters regarding what constitutes a good job. The difficulties with such a program occur later. To avoid them, make sure your initial program isn't so lucrative that you can't meet the expectations you have established.

One of my clients paid the staff 50% of their compensation in very high bonuses since they paid below market salaries. Once the company got going they started hiring regular employees at standard salaries, and they had to adjust the bonus program. At the same time, the old employees demanded that their salaries be increased to fair market value. When the company re-established bonuses at a fair level by reducing them significantly there was a great deal of resentment. Most of the initial employees left because they felt they had been treated unfairly. Perhaps the company should have made it clearer at the outset that part of the bonus was intended as a substitute for full salary and that the remainder was a real bonus, including combat pay.

Another client has a quarterly profit sharing plan. Their profits do, however, vary dramatically from quarter to quarter, causing bonuses to vary. Another problem is that the employees see very little direct correlation between their efforts and their bonuses. I believe that this company is getting little benefit from their bonus plan. At the same time, though, they have a bonus plan for managers that is quite effective in focusing them on company profitability. The managers will take actions to increase profits because they know this will increase their bonuses.

The final bonus plan example from my experience is the most successful. This company is in a very seasonal business in which most of the sales are made at the end of the company's fiscal year. The company has for some time had an employee and a managers' bonus plan, both of which are based on company profits. By the end of year, everyone in that company knows the expected profitability and the impact additional sales will have on profitability and on their personal bonuses. In addition, the board of directors has established special targets tied to company-wide profits. By the final quarter everyone in the company is aware of the end-of-year sales push, and they all look for ways to help.

In summary, bonuses work best when the recipients can have a direct impact on their bonus. It is also important to anticipate the long term impact of your bonus program. You can always authorize additional bonus payments, but it can be very demoralizing to your staff to reduce these payments.

8. Networking with Other Entrepreneurs

Q. What do you think about networking with other entrepreneurs?

A. I find talking to other small business people very useful. Many of the issues in small companies are independent of the type of business. Start getting to know other software company executives in your geographical area. Ask your accountant, banker or attorney for the names of other executives who might be useful to meet. Set objectives for yourself and go out and network.

9. Stock Versus Money in Recruiting

Q. We are trying to fill an important growth position in our company. Some of the candidates are more interested in money while others focus on stock and long term growth. How should we evaluate these differences?

A. Candidates' utility functions (how they regard value tradeoffs, in this case stock versus salary) differ and are unlikely to change. In most cases, the people who focus on immediate money are more interested in short term results, while long term players want stock. I believe that a person's focus of attention is directly related to their desired compensation plan. Thus if you are trying to fill a strategic growth position, make sure that the candidate is focused on stock or other long term payoffs.

10. Pre-Employment Testing

Dear Dave,

I just received the April issue of Software Success, where you asked for help from anyone who had experience with Pre-Employment Tests. I have experience, both as an employee, and later as an employer.

A few months before I graduated from University in 1974, I was interviewed several times by Canada's second largest bank for a job I dearly wanted: Assembler programmer getting in on the beginning of their on-line banking software development (first it was terminals for tellers in branches, then automated teller machines (ATMs)). The last step in the process was an aptitude test. It was scheduled for 5 hours. I finished it in just over 2 hours. Unfortunately, they did not tell me up front that the passing mark, as far as they were concerned, was 85%; I got 83%!

In 1977, I got the opportunity to prove myself. My employer at the time, Worker's Compensation Board of Alberta, was testing aptitude tests as a recruiting tool for the future. I was given the Wolfe Systems Programmer Aptitude Test and managed to score 100% on it.

As Data Processing Manager, I used the same test myself when screening Systems Programmers from fresh graduates in 1983 for an IBM mainframe Systems Programming position. Wolfe provides a full page letter outlining the pros and cons of hiring the individual, as well as what to watch for once the individual is on staff.

Meanwhile, in 1981, when hiring a Clerk responsible for interpreting (from bad handwriting) and entering data used to test the corrosion level on pipes in natural gas plants, I used an old aptitude test produced by IBM in the late 1960s to test logic among people off the street that IBM planned to train as potential entry level programmers. The results were surprising, but very accurate. The very outgoing individual who was lead contender for the position did quite poorly. The shy girl who had to be prodded to even apply scored far and away the best mark. She went on to produce practically error-free work. Two years later, I used the same test to hire a secretary who was also to be a part-time IBM mainframe computer operator, with similar positive results.

These are aptitude tests. As their name implies, they do not tell you how much a person knows, but what capacity the person has to learn skills in the area being tested. How do you determine how much the person knows?

Back in 1974, I was introduced to the Structured Interview. In fact, my success on it landed me my first job after graduation. It was a technique that I used whenever I did interviews in later years. Basically, you ask the person good technical questions in the area of expertise you need for the position you are interviewing for. The trick is to be sure you are asking a question that body language or luck (yes/no, true/false) will not reveal, yet can be answered in less than 60 seconds in a stressful environment (interviews are stressful for 90% of people). I have also successfully used very short paper exercises as part of a Structured Interview.

Recently, Wolfe has also come out with tests that determine expertise level. Although I have not used them, I did have the opportunity to look at one (for TSO, as I recall) and I was favorably impressed.

Wolfe's head office: Wolfe Personnel Testing & Training Systems Inc. - 99 Boulevard - New Milford, NJ 07646. I do not have their phone number as I have always dealt with the Canadian office in Montreal.

I hope that you will find this information useful. I probably should write a magazine article on the subject of interviewing and testing, because I rarely see it done in a manner that effectively tests anything but whether or not the person can hold a coherent conversation. After all, I have more experience than most: I probably have been through more than 25 interviews in the last 15 years.

> Jon E. Pearkins, CDP, CSP
> President
> Certified Software Specialists, Ltd.

Dear Jon,

Thanks for the letter. This is the kind of real world experience that is so useful. I would like to hear from anyone who has had similar experience hiring sales and marketing people.

11. Free Trials and Processing Paperwork

Q. We offer a free trial period when selling our product. We are always dealing with lengthy trials, and customers are slow to process their paperwork. What can you suggest?

A. It is important to stay in contact with the customer/prospect during the entire process. In many companies, contracts are sent to a legal department for review. If this is the case, find out who is reviewing the contract and when their comments are due.

Often your sales people can't call the legal department directly, but they can work with your contact or the prospect's contracts group. It often helps if you have a contracts administrator who interfaces with the contracts group in the customer organization. Having a second person involved with the customer can provide valuable insights into the progress of the sale. Active management of the contract and accounts payable process will reduce the time to close the sale and collect your money.

12. Managing Accounts Receivable

Q. How can we improve our cash flow by reducing our accounts receivable cycle?

A. Improving collections is an objective in every small company. There are a number of reasons that companies may be slow to pay:

1. They intentionally pay all of their bills slowly.
2. They are unhappy with your company and they are passively protesting.
3. They didn't really commit to buy at the point in time you thought they did.

Slow to pay

The first problem is simply that many companies are slow to pay. They often utilize complex procedures and bureaucracies to slow down payment. You can address this by having a contracts person who works with your customers, talking to the customer's contracts administrator and to accounts payable personnel. A good contracts person can be worth their weight in gold. They know how to work the system so that you get paid as quickly as possible.

Bugs in the software

The second problem occurs more often than we would like to admit in our industry A customer "buys" a software package, but it doesn't quite work as advertised. The vendor may have to make some changes, and the customer has to do additional work to get the desired results. Often in these cases, the person who signed the contract tells accounts payable not to pay the invoice until the vendor resolves these problems. I have seen this happen and when it does, vendor management often isn't aware that there is a real problem. Having your contracts person call the customer gives you a good check and

balance system. The customer's accounts payable clerk will pass along this information (that there is a problem) to your contracts person without pulling any punches. Your sales and support people often won't ask the hard questions and thus won't get the straight story. By contrast, this would all be in a days work for a contracts person.

Verbal PO

The final problem results when companies book sales when the sales person gets a verbal PO. Customers often view a verbal PO as something which helps the sales person, but isn't binding on them. They only feel committed when they have signed the contract. Your payment won't start to be processed until the contract is signed. Make sure that you keep this in mind when you look at your accounts receivables.

Realistic Expectations

Finally, most software firms find that large companies take from 45 to 90 days to pay, and some companies find the time slipping to 120 days. As long as your payment period is from 45 to 90 days there probably isn't a lot you can do to dramatically improve it. These techniques should help keep it from getting much worse.

13. Vacation Policy

Q. We are a small company, but we hire people from large companies. What do you feel is an appropriate vacation policy?

A. My initial answer is that I believe that employees should accrue vacation once they are off probation (three months). I personally think that you should start people at two weeks a year. While I realize that you can save a little money by only giving people one week initially, I think that this is penny wise.

In my mind, the real question is when to to give employees three weeks. As you mentioned, this occurs after five to ten years with most local companies. I would seriously consider offering this increase at three years. Part of my motivation is that many entry-level programmers and other professional employees begin to look around at other opportunities after two or three years. Having three weeks of vacation might keep a few employees.

Underlying my feelings on this topic is the reality that small software companies are very intense places to work. Employees who leave large companies to work at smaller companies are often surprised at how hard they have to work and how much they have to do. There is a high risk of burnout in this environment. Getting people to take vacation is a very good way to help minimize the risk of burnout.

14. Software vs. Hardware

Q. Will customers pay more for the software than the hardware?

A. A couple of years ago, we would have answered "No." There were very few software vendors who were selling software systems on PCs where the cost of the software was greater than the cost of the hardware. In the meantime the cost of the comparable hardware has dropped significantly, and software costs have increased for many software categories. You can now buy a well configured brand name 386 for $5K to $7K. At the same time, there are a large number of vertical market packages which cost $15K to $25K which will run on a 386. We believe that this isn't nearly the issue that it was in the past.

15. Moving into the Service Bureau Business

Q. Unlike many companies who have made the move from a service bureau business to the software product business, we are moving from selling turnkey systems into selling computer services — we're a service bureau. Do you know of others who are making the same move?

A. No, we don't. We have a number of clients who started out as service bureaus and have made the transition to the software package business. Most of them were able to finance this transition by selling their software package to their service bureau customers.

This process was made easier than normal by two factors:

1. The existing service bureau customers were experienced in using the software and had little sales resistance.

2. The amount of documentation needed for the service bureau customers was lower that it would be for regular customers — it gave the software

vendor some time to produce quality documentation.

In talking with this reader, it appeared that they were doing a number of things differently which might account for their success:

1. They were using modern hardware (DEC) which was very cost effective for the service bureau. The VAX architecture is designed for networking and allows them to be very cost effective.

2. The offer a 20% credit of all service bureau fees toward the eventual purchase of the turnkey system.

3. Their pricing is very simple. There is a fixed fee per report so the customer knows exactly what to expect. They actually bill the customers in advance.

4. They can offer significant cost savings for new and small customers.

Does anyone else have a similar experience to this?

16. Developing Managers

Q: How should I recruit and decelop managers in a software vendor environment?

A: Recruiting managers into a vendor environment is difficult because there are so few experienced managers in our industry.

Hire Professional Managers

In many cases you will have to take a good manager with less direct industry experience but strong management experience. (You might recall that Steve Jobs of Apple did exactly that when he hired John Scully away from Pepsi-Cola.) Often you can find strong managers within your prospects of customers who can understand your product. With these people you must train them about our industryand how things work ina small company. Often the small companyconstraints require a compete reeducation if they have worked in large companies fot their entire career. Promote from within

The other alternative is to promote from within. The idea is to train new managerswho already know yur business. We appaud this approach and have found that it is very good for company morale, but is has its own hazards. Please don't assume that a good programmer or salesperson will automatically become a good development manager of sales manager. Spend time with them coaching them on how to do their job. Send them to classes and seminars to help provide the background that they need. Encourage them to read management books and discuss these books with them.

You should expect that it will probably take at least a year before they become effective. If this isn't acceptable, don't put your good people into a position where they will fail. If you can't promote your prospecive managers right now because the immediate demands will be too intense, you might urge them to start on their education process. Then when a less intense position becomes available they will be better prepared to hande it.

Provide a fall-back position

Finally, you should address the fact that your fledgling managers might not succeed; they might want to return to their old position. Assure them that you are leaving the "back door" open for them. They might find that they reallydon't like being a manager, and that they really want to go back to their old job. If this is the case, you are much better off if they can stay in the company rather than being forced to leave.

17. Pre-Employment Tests

Q: Do you know of any employment tests which we could use to evaluate prospects?

A: Wonderlic publishes a battery of personnel evaluation tests. They include intelligence tests, a test for clerical skills, IBM compatible word processing skill assessment, etc. If you have difficulty evaluating word processing and clerical employees, these tests might be useful. Has anyone used these types of tests?

18. Using part-time experts

Q: We have been approached by a university professor who would like to trade for a copy of our product for services. He is moderately well known in our niche market (he published a book which is read by the trade). How can we get the most out of this situation?

A: If you don't manage the situation, you probably won't receive any benefit. The most likely outcome is that you will discuss some general ideas with your professor, and that you will give him a copy of your product. Time will pass, and while you may hear

from your professor occasionally, you will realize that you haven't received anything in return for your product.

Managing his Effort

To gain any benefit from this project, you must manage the professor. Pin the professor down. Find out what he is really willing to do. If he had written a book, he might be pleased to write an article. This could be very useful to your PR program and to your professor.

Before you give him your software, develop a schedule with milestones. Include drop-dead dates which will cause the professor to return your software if he fails to deliver agreed items by these dates. While this isn't a free (or even easy) way to get some work done in exchange for your software, it can be cost-effective.

O. Legal (1989)

1. Trademark Registration

Q. Is trademark registration of our company's software really necessary? It's expensive and time-consuming. Do I really have to bother?

A. If you don't care about your trademarks, then don't bother. If you've spent *any* time and money on developing name recognition (and who hasn't?) then you better register your product with the trademark folks. We read a recent article, quoted in part below, in the January 30, 1989 issue of *ComputerWorld* which makes the point quite well.

"Who has the most lawyers? Lotus apparently did things by the book when it named its new hard disk utility Magellan. It searched for previous trademarks, found none, and proceeded. But two companies using the name have already reared their heads. First a software reseller called Magellan Software Corp. popped up. The software developer Emerald Intelligence, Inc. surfaced with an artificial intelligence package called Magellan. It is likely, however, that Lotus will keep Magellan because both Emerald and Magellan Software failed to register their monikers."

Chapter V. Management Issues

Trademark Services

Dear Dave,

I noticed in the "Questions & Answers" section of the September issue of Software Success, a question about trademark checking. Your readers may be interested to know that information brokers, such as F1 Services, can provide this service quickly and economically.

We check databases which list both Federal and State registered trademarks; several online software directors, including the Computer Directory on CompuServe which corresponds to the print version of Data Sources; databases of articles from computer industry publications; and databases which list over eight million company names.

By using online databases, rather than printed lists, we can locate trademarks and company names which may be close to a company name under consideration to cause problems, even if they are not an exact match. Most trademark searches cost less than $100.

Although our trademark searches do not substitute for the services of a trademark attorney, they do enable our clients to save legal fees by prescreening possible names and eliminating those which have obvious conflicts.

I am enclosing a brochure which describes our services more fully. If you have any questions about our trademark searches or other services, please call me at (214) 746-3646.

> Sincerely,
> Chris Dobson
> Partner
> F1 Services

User Feedback/Trademark Registration

Dear Dave;

Please correct the mis-information on cost/time to obtain a registered trademark. I did it simply by getting the free form, filing it out, and sending it in — no lawyer, no fee except for a standard charge.

> No name given.

I guess that this is really a personal preference. When I started this newsletter it was called Software Strategies. I had to change that name because a consulting firm had trademarked it. I then registered it as Software Success with the help of an attorney. THe registration was protested by a firm which publishes "time dated materials" (calendars, appointment books, etc.) When that happened, I was pleased that I had an attorney to help reach an agreement. (I agreed not to publish calendars, and they agreed not to write a software newsletter.)

The initial expense for the attorney was primarily for the trademark search and an opinion on how close the other names are and how likely I was to have a problem. Given all of the companies named Software XXX, I appreciated this help, but you can do this yourself. The important point is to register your trademark.

Trademarks Costs

Q. We are spending lots of money with our attorney checking out trademarks. This is expensive and time-consuming. What can we do to improve this?

A. The first step is to check any proposed name against existing software companies in a directory like Data Sources. Check both the product and the company listings. While this isn't perfect, it will eliminate obvious problems. You can also purchase the Trademark Register listed below. While the cost may seem high, if you avoid legal searches the cost of the Register will pay off. In the end, you should register your trademark and go through the process of responding to the objections. These steps are intended to help you eliminate unnecessary searches.

REFERENCE: "The Trademark Register of the United States (1881-1989)". $288.00; (800) 888-8062

2. Program Ownership

Q. We use free-lance programmers. Do we have an exposure on who retains the copyright for our programs?

A. Yes you do. The High Court decided that independent contractors (e.g., free lance programmers) may retain the copyright on their works unless they are assigned to the employer in a contract. If you use contractors, make sure that you have a contract which specifically assigns their rights to your company.

3. Escrow Agreements Revisited

Q. Do you know of any real-life cases where a escrow agreement has made a difference?

A. The following story was published in the January 1989 issue of *VARBusiness* (only the names have been changed). The first company, let's call them Turnkey Systems Corporation (TS) had contracted with Programming Services Corp (PSC) for generic account software which PSC customized for TSC's mortuary niche. One day PSC dissolved and vanished leaving TSC unable to support their customers since they didn't have the source code. TSC didn't have an escrow agreement with PSC. Their only recourse was to sue PSC's remmnants to recover the source code. Because of the time it will take to go through the courts, TSC will soon be out of business. Because they didn't have an escrow agreement with their software vendor at a critical juncture, this company will loose everything.

This is a case that we hadn't really focused on, but many software companies have embedded code from outside companies. Make sure that you have the source or ready access to the source.

P. Sales (1989)

1. Sales Rep Management

Q. We're new to this business of having a full-time sales staff. While we understand how to manage and control programmers, it's not so clear how to handle sales-types. What is the proper way to manage sales reps?

A. Write up a contract which addresses the basic issues instead of working off verbal agreements. We continue to be surprised at the number of companies which have only verbal agreements with their sales people. Is it any wonder that disagreement between sales people and management are so common? Make sure that you address the following points:

- **Base salary**
- **Draw or loans and the terms for repaying these.**
- **Commission percentage and when it is paid.** Be sure to specify *upon what condition* (i.e. receipt of funds, delivery of goods) as well as **time-frame**.
- **Territory adjustments and hold-out or "House" accounts.**

- **What happens if you sell the company or the product?**
- **Terms and conditions if the sales person quits.**
- **What happens if they are fired?** Make sure that you specify what happens in both the "for cause" and "without cause" terminations. Delineate the conditions under which each event may take place.
- **Quotas and termination.**
- **Probation and a trial period for new sales people**
- **Trade secret protection and product information.**
- **A non-compete clause that bars them from employment with direct competitors for a limited time.**
- **Cross-sales agreements (headquarters in one territory and divisions in another territory). Commission splits.**
- **Cross product sales. (The salesman for product A manages to sell product B to one of his customers.)**
- **Duties of the sales rep.**
- **Pricing discretion allowed the sales rep.**
- **Term or duration of the agreement.**
- **As you can see, the relationship with a sales rep is complicated. We are sure that you will have your own specific issues in addition to the above general issues. Committing these issues to paper will reduce the problems that you encounter with your sales reps. While the legal costs for this are real, we believe that you will benefit by having a more rational relationship with your sales reps. We are interested in your experience with contracts with sales people.**

2. Qualifying Prospects for On-site demos

Q. We have asked our sales prospects to pay our travel expenses for on-site demos. We are getting a great deal of resistance from prospects regarding this. What is the experience of other software companies?

A. Very few software companies are able to get their prospects to pay for on-site demos. Customers view this as a sales call and feel that the vendor should bear the cost. I am impressed that you get prospective customers to pay. This is a great sales lead qualification step.   As we discussed, what you are really interested in is getting management to participate in the demo.   I feel that you should agree to visit a prospect as long as management agrees to spend time with you during the visit.   This will help ensure that you get the exposure and the chance to close your sale.

3.   Monitoring the Competition

Q. What should we do to monitor our competition?

A. This is an important issue, and I continue to be surprised at how few software companies understand their competition.   I suspect that many people are afraid the competition will look so good that they will be depressed.   Other people have expressed the feeling that it is immoral to analyze competitive products.   I feel it is critical to find out as much as possible about your competition by studying the information they have put in the public domain.   As long as you aren't asked to sign some form of non-disclosure agreement, any information you are given is in the public domain.

First identify your competitors.   You can do this through product directories, watching the trade press and talking to your customers, prospects, and to industry observers.   There is a great deal of available information if you just look for it.   It often helps to designate one person within your organization to compile all competitive information.   Have them keep copies of everything in a Competitors file.   This includes product literature, ads, directory listings, articles from the trade and financial press, etc.   You might consider conducting an occasional literature search on one of the public data base systems like Dialog.   This service is available through many libraries for a nominal fee.

Next compile competitive sales information.   You can start with competitive situations in which your firm is participating and associated information that you get from your sales prospects.   Often your customers will give you information after you close the sale.   If you are comfortable with some deception, you might call your competitor(s) and ask specific questions under the guise of being a potential customer or a consultant representing one.   As long as they are willing to give you the information, you aren't doing anything illegal.

4. Reacting to Competitors

Q. Our software product has several direct competitors. How should we react to their tactics and strategies?

A. The answer to that question depends upon your relative position within your market.   Are you the leader (Hertz), the number two and trying harder (Avis), or one of the young turks (Budget)?

The lower on this competitive pecking order, the more you stand to gain by aggressively responding to the competitors.   If you are a young turk, we believe that you should take advantage of every flaw or crack in your competitors products or strategies.

Being a "young turk"

If your competitors don't offer site licenses and your customers want a site license, give it to them. If their product doesn't match up to yours, create an A vs. B product comparison showing just how superior your product is. Flexibility and boldness are a fundamental advantage of being small.   Take advantage of your smallness.

The advantages of being #1

At the other end of the scale, the market leaders can't afford to acknowledge and or respond to the riff-raf.   IBM is the classic market leader.   They almost never respond directly to competitors.   When they do respond, they do it in their own time and in their own way.   This almost always takes the form of a product introduction or a strategy change.

The recent announcement of the 486-based PS/2 M70 upgrade is a case in point.   Nothing was said (directly) about Compaq, but the machine is designed expressly to slow down the Compaq sales juggernaut.   (You can bet, however that IBM sales reps are saying lots about the speed and upgradeability vs. Compaq when they hold private conversations with their customers.) This type of indirect, "we'll show 'em who's boss" response is very powerful.

The middle position is difficult.   It is OK to play against the #1, but you can't really afford to respond to your own young turks.   You risk undermining your relative leadership position.

Don't respond to "dirty tactics"

Finally, we believe that there are certain tactics (playing dirty) which should never be responded to. Our experience is that slander, etc., end up hurting the company that uses it. If one of your competitor's sales people is playing dirty, you might call your competitor's President and let him know what is going on. Don't trade slander for slander; don't get down to their level.

While there may be rare instances where companies have reaped short term benefits by playing dirty, most customers are really offended. We would be interested in hearing from others who have dealt with this issue.

5. Sales Manager Compensation

Q. Could you discuss sales manager's compensation plans in conjunction with sales rep commissions? What about commission splits?

A. Most companies want the sales manager to earn twenty to thirty percent more than the best sales rep. This can be thrown off if one sales person really hits it big, but in general the sales manager should earn more. In many cases you may be promoting one of your sales people into being a working sales manager.

During the first stage of their new tenure, your new Sales Manger will spend part of their time training and managing new sales people while they are selling the rest of the time. This is an incredibly tough position.

We have seen plans where the new sales manager's base salary is increased when they are promoted. They still retain their commissions on their sales, but the now have only half the territory and half the time. Their sales and commissions will go down. At the same time, they should be rewarded for getting new sales people productive.

We have seen cases where the sales manager gets a bonus equal to one tenth of the sales rep's commission. You can make this compensation plan work to your benefit: as you ad sales people, cut down the direct selling by the sales manager by increasing their salary.

6. Limiting Information to Prospects

Q. How much information should we give suspects and prospects?

A. Just enough to get them to take the next step in the sales cycle! It is very easy to inundate your suspect/prospect and confuse them so badly that they decide to do nothing. Moving forward through the sales cycle as a prospective customer is frightening. If you have a clear idea of what the next step is and you have the information to make the immediate decision, you can move forward with confidence. Some of your suspects/prospects may require additional information to make the decision. If this is the case, you must provide them with the required information. Providing excess information is analogous to the sales person who continues to talk after they have made the sale. The excess information may actually hurt the sale by raising issues which wouldn't otherwise arise.

7. System Sale

Q. We have a complex product which involves a system sale. Do you have any general advice on how to market a complex product?

A. We assume that you mean that your product involves a number of people in the buying organization. In cases like this, you have a number of different people involved in the sale. There is the person who initiates the sale. There will be one person who manages the evaluation. There will be technical evaluators, and other people who must buy-off on your system.

The best advice we can give you is to map out everyone who is involved. Ask your prospects who is responsible for what during the sales process. Ask them again after they buy. When the sale seems to hang up, see if you can't identify the hidden snags. Determine what issues are important to them and develop the materials to sell them. Provide these materials to your evaluator. Work together to make the sale and you both win.

8. Marketing Horizontal Software

Q. What general advice can you give me on marketing horizontal software products and productivity tools?

A. By definition, a horizontal product sells to a wide market — you must find a way to advertise and/or promote your product so that you can generate leads. In our experience, direct-mail works best for focused vertical-market packages; horizontal packages need to be advertised.

You must find a magazine where you can advertise effectively to sell your product. The other way to sell is through distribution (e.g. computer stores). Using distribution successfully also depends upon finding a magazine which creates interest in your product so you can pull people into stores. In our experience, you can't push product through the distribution channels. You must be able to create demand (e.g. pull people into the stores). Even if you are creating demand, it will take quite a while for the stores to shift from calling you to place orders to stocking your product. In the meantime, you must generate direct sales via your advertising. Another alternative is to use PR, but this is tough for a horizontal product. The horizontal magazines are hard to get coverage in, but this is worth a shot.

9. Choosing a Sales Method

Q. We are considering different styles of sales. In particular, we are trying to decide between high-powered direct sales people and telemarketing sales people. In particular we are considering moving to a telemarketing approach and away from our face-to-face visit approach. How would you advise us to make this decision?

A. The step you are considering is not just a matter of style, it is a fundamental part of your approach to your customer. Our experience is that it is quite difficult to make the transition from direct sales to telemarketing without a major commitment and investment.

Companies who have high-powered sales people calling on prospects can use some of their sales people's credibility and image to overcome their sales materials. When you are telemarketing, your written sales materials take on much more importance.

We would begin with the sales cycle and see if you can use telemarketing and direct mail or advertising to generate the leads and qualify the prospects. See how far your telemarketeers can carry the sale. As you work your way through the process, you will identify the bottlenecks and address them. Develop the materials for each successive stage.

As you progress you may find that you can cut the number of sales calls from four or five down to one or two. Eventually, you may be able to conduct the entire sale without visiting the prospect. In many cases, we have seen direct sales people make the transition to telemarketing. The key to having this happen successfully is to show them that they can close more business by selling over the phone. If you take this approach, you can make it win/win.

10. Operational Sales Statistics

Q. How should we track our sales people other than sales dollars?

A. While it is important to track sales revenues in dollars, you should track a number of operational variables which are key milestones in the sales cycle. One important rule is that you should only track points which are measurable. One client had a fairly complex sales cycle which involved a number of steps (the number of remaining prospects is shown in parentheses):

1. Initial inquiry (100)
2. Purchase demo disk (25)
3. Run demo system (20)
4. Technical evaluation complete (15)
5. Recommend purchase (10)
6. Purchase (5)

The numbers reflect this client's actual statistics.

The key point for this client was to establish how to categorize prospects, establish guidelines/targets, and then to measure them. This client needed each salesperson to sell five copies of their software a month. Using the ratios they then calculated the other numbers. One real benefit for the sales person is that having guidelines/targets at this level really help them manage their efforts. We have also found that having weekly and monthly reviews are a very good way to monitor the sales effort. Invite outsiders into these meetings and compare the targets and actual results. Often the sales manager conducts the weekly meetings and the President is involved in the monthly meetings. Make sure that the sales people prepare and present their statistics. This makes them accountable for their work and insures that they really understand when they are dropping the ball in one particular area.

Another client picked three key indicators:

- **Number of initial inquiries,**
- **Number of demo disks purchased, and**
- **Number of sales.**

This company tracks a percentage of target for all three measures. They award a "Salesperson of the Month" based on the average of all three parameters. This makes it very clear to the salespeople that you believe all of these stages are really important.

Make sure that you limit your efforts to parameters that are meaningful. Measuring too many things is a common problem. As long as you focus on important parameters, the measurement process and management attention will make everyone aware that these statistics are really important, and that is what this effort is all about. Once the sales people understand that this is a better way to manage their business, they will use that information to do a better job.

11. Sales Reps doing demos

Q. How many sales reps can demo their own product?

A. It depends upon the product, the market, and the software company in question. In general, we would be surprised if more than half the sales reps selling software can conduct even a mid-level demo.

There are a variety of levels of demos which might be required:

- **Management Demo** — There is the management-level demo which highlights the features and benefits of the product. If the sales rep can't conduct this demo after spending reasonable time with the product, you should consider firing them. How can a sales rep sell to management if they can't conduct a features\benefits demo?

- **End-User Demo** — The next level is the end-user demo. This involves demonstrating to an end-user how they will actually use the product in day-to-day operations. Most companies have sample data to show this type of operational demo. In our experience, while most sales reps can conduct this demo, they quickly are unable to answer questions. In most cases they need a technical person to help them field the questions. In too many cases, the technical person ends up

conducting this operational demo. We feel that it is better if a sales rep learns how to do these demos and handles more and more of the questions.

- **In-depth Demo** — The third level of demo is a technical demonstration. It will usually be given to a programmer or other technical person. In this case, the customer really wants to know how the product really works. Few sales people can conduct this type of demo, and it isn't a good use of their time.

12. Overselling

Q. How can we get our sales people to stick to the script? We have a problem with the sales people overselling our product?

A. The first question to ask yourself is, "Do they really know they are overselling the product?" We have seen a number of cases where a technical distinction which was very obvious to the president was totally lost on the sales people. If this is your problem, you must educate your sales people and develop better sales materials.

A more difficult issue is where the sales people are knowingly overselling. We have seen cases where the product had a major limitation which would disqualify it for large percentage of the prospects. Rather than being screened-out early in the sales-cycle, the sales people felt that it was better to hide the truth from the prospects and see if they could sell around this limitation. The sales people hoped that once the prospects had seen the product, the flaw wouldn't be as important.

Part of the problem was that if the sales people disqualified the prospects early on, they were worried that they wouldn't have enough prospects to deal with. If this is the problem, you must analyze the percentages on how many prospects you convert. By that, we mean how many prospects would have dropped out if you had fully disclosed the facts early on, eventually would have bought. The sales people really want to believe that this is high. You can resolve this by identifying the prospects they are knowingly failing to inform, and seeing how many of them actually buy.

The other side of the picture is that if you disqualify them early on, your sales people are free to identify new and better sales situations. Perhaps you should make this limitation very clear in your lead generation materials so that your sales people are only dealing with prospects who have passed this hurdle. In most cases, we have found that it is more effective to eliminate prospects as early as possible so you can focus on the likely prospects. While this might involve cold calling which isn't a lot of fun, it is good business.

13. Recruiting a Director of Marketing or Sales

Q. How should I recruit a Director of Marketing or Sales?

A. Approaches you should consider include putting the word out verbally, running ads in newspapers and trade magazines, and hiring a recruiter. A number of good recruiting and search firms specialize in software marketing and sales executives. With these resources, you should identify some good candidates.

If you can't find a good candidate with software sales experience and a knowledge of your market, you might consider someone who has been selling non-software products to your target market. You should insist that they have both industry experience and the appropriate marketing and/or sales management experience. If these bases are covered, you might be able to teach them about software and get them to be productive quickly.

14. Marketing and Sales Cooperation

Q. What can I do to get marketing and sales to be more cooperative?

A. First you must understand that marketing and sales groups in the same organization are inherently adverserial. Since each is responsible for steps in the sales cycle, each is bound to blame the other when problems occur. Upper management's attitude toward problems and problem resolution will strongly influence how groups work together when the going gets tough. If management simply yells at sales when sales are down, sales will turn around and yell at marketing. On the other hand, if management asks why sales are down and really digs into the issues, marketing and sales will find themselves working together to solve the problems.

If you have a problem with lack of cooperation between your departments, examine how you deal with these problems. Perhaps you, by your actions, can foster a more supportive and cooperative environment which will reduce the conflict between your departments.

15. Closing Sales

Q: We have lots of people interested in our software, but nothing ever seems to happen. How can we close sales?

A: This is one of the most common questions with fledgling software companies. There is no definative answer, of course. (If there was we'd have published a book about it and be living a life of ease on the Riveria.) There are a couple of good guidelines however, that we have been using with some success with our software clients.

The first suggestion is to buy a sales book wiht 101 closes and try the closing techniques in the book. In many cases, much of the problem is just sales technique. If your sales people aren't experienced and trained, they may not be asking for the order. Technical people in particular, are very prone to selling the features forever. They feel that it is unseemly to ask fo the order. "When the customer is ready to buy, they will say so." You can remedy this sales technique problem by training your sales people and/or hirng new sales people.

While there may problems with an individual sales rep's closing technique, we more often find that the sale is getting hung up somewhere in the process. Thus, there is a glich in the sales cycle. The best way to diagnose this problem is to recount a number of sales situations (both good and bad) in detail to see if you can find a pattern. In most cases, you can identify a common pattern. If you don't have enough information, you might call up the prospects and customers and ask them their prospective in the sales cycle. Ensure that the responsible sales person doesn't make this call, so the prospects and the customers will open up.

Once you have identified the bottleneck, you can develop marketing materials and sales techniques to deal with the problem. Here are some of the common closing problems that we encounter.

    * Product Understanding — If your prospects really don't understand your prod-

uct, you may need a better product brochure.

* **Product Benefits**—Your prospective customers, on the other hand, may understand your product's features, but they don't really understand the benefits. In this case, youmay need to prove your benefits and develop the materials and your story to explain these benefits.

* **Management's Understanding** — Another common situation is where you sell the potential user, but upper management rejects the proposal. In this case you must arm your advocate with a proposal which will sell upper management. You may also need to have a letter series to upper management to support your advocate.

As you can see, there are any number of ways that the sale can stall. Only by analyzing your sales cycle and refining your approach can you continue to expedite your sales cycle.

16. Selling to Management

Q: We have a very good technical product which our sales people find very easy to explain to technical people in prospect sites. The problem is that all too often out prospect's upper management (which isn't technical and doesn't appreciate our project) stalls or overturns the decision t purchase our software. How should we deal with this technical cs. upper management   situation?

A: Every sale hinges on selling the ultimate decision maker. It appears that upper-management is the decision maker in many situations for your product.

Selling to senior executives is often much tougher than selling to technical people. In many situations, the lower individuals are very happy to talk with you. They are technically interested in what you have to sell and they like the attention. Sadly, in many cases, they have very little idea of what it takes to sell your product within their own company. There are several steps that you can take to deal with this situation.

Starting at the top

The first and best step is try to start at the top. Initiate the contact at your prospect's company at the level where the decision is usually made. Introduce yourself and your company's product. While you'll usually be directed down to your technical contact, you will have gained visibility and recognition at a very important level. All other things being equal, this is the best solution if you can make it work.

Our hesitation is that we have seen many technical companies who were totally unable to make the initial management sell. There are a number of factors which may make this very difficult:

* Your company may be positioned as a technical product company which is of no interest to upper   management.

* Your sales people may not be able to sell to senior executives and may not really understand what is important at upper levels.

* Your marketing materials may not be directed to(or comprehensible by) upper management.

Evolving a management sell

Even if you decide that you will have to change a number of items before you can sell directly to upper management, you can start to evolve your approach. A number of these points will take significant time and effort to redirect your approach toward senior executives. You should start by talking to upper management within your existing customers. Interview them to understand what they saw in your product. Analyze how that differed from their technical person's perspective and how it differed from your own perceptions. Ask them for copies of their own internal justifications.

Develop a model of how and why upper management will buy your product. Once you have this model, you can begin to develop materials to support this strategy. Be sure to prepare documentation that will help your techie advocate sell to his management.

Getting management involved

Often getting upper management's early participation is a critical success factor. If this is the case, have your sales people explain this fact to the technical person. Suggest that you have found that odds of success improve if the upper manager has a chance to express his concerns to a sales person. If your technical champion isn't comfortable opening the dialog between the sales person and their boss, you might fall back to plan B:

* The sales person sends the techie a short brochure which contains an executive-level sales pitch.

* The champion reviews this document with the decision-maker.

* Your sales rep attempts to talk/meet with the executive decision maker.

Instruct your sales person to write off the prospect if your technical champion won't at lead talk with their own upper management. This last step is critical. If your sales requires executive approval, then you must have entre at the proper level. If you can't get the proper access, then move on. Your sales people will find it difficult to drop a prospect just because the technical evaluators won't involve upper management, but in many cases this is a critical prospect qualifier. They really aren't a good prospect is management doesn't get involved.

Continuing the management sell

Now that you have taken the first step to become more management oriented, you must lay out a plan to evolve your sales strategy. Identify the items which must be changed and develop marketing and sales programs to implement these changes. As you evolve, analyze your lost (or stalled) sales carefully. Increase the priority on programs that would have helped in these lost sales situations. While this isn't a quick-fix approach, you should be able to see early and steady improvements.

17. Marketing Add-On Products

Q. How should we market add on products (like report writers, batch programs, etc..) which can be used with our main program?

A. We assume that you have decided to market your add-ons as separately priced features. If you just bundle them in with your basic product, there is no issue.

There are two distinct situations that we would like to examine in some detail:

● New product sales

● Sales to the installed base.

New Product Sales

Selling new-product add-ons is just like selling your original product. These sales are the easiest unless you are selling to a price sensitive market. In most cases, your new customers will evaluate the add-ons and decide if they are interested. As long as you have good marketing materials, you should sell to most of the customers who are interested. In a very price sensitive market, you may not be able to introduce the possibility of the add-on because the prospects are so skittish about price. In this case, all of your customers must be sold as part of the installed base.

Selling to your installed Customer base

Selling add-on products turns out to be much more difficult than we ever would have imagined. Since add-ons usually sell at a much lower price than the basic package, it isn't cost effective to have your sales people sell them. Some companies have their customer support people sell the add-ons, but this isn't terribly effective either. Selling is selling and it is very difficult for customer support people to shift in and out of a sales role.

Direct mail turns out to be the most common approach for selling add-ons. Develop flyers and mail to your installed base. Get testimonials. Offer a 30 day free trial. Offer discounts in your off-season. This can become a significant revenue stream as your installed base grows and you have more add-ons to sell.

Once you get a number of add-ons, you might consider offering consecutive discounts for your add-ons: 10% off on #1, 20% off on #2, 30% off on #3, up to a maximum of 40% or 50% off. You should offer these add-on discounts to new customers at the time of initial purchase. You can also structure similar deals for your installed base (remember the seasonal sale.) We have also found it effective to offer introductory deals to your installed base to help build the installed base of the new add-on. Remember that you need the testimonials and the installed numbers to help this sales process.

18. Sales Cycles

Q. How does the sales cycle vary by product price and the type of product?

A. In our opinion, the two most important factors are:

1. Number of People – How many people are involved in the decision.

2. Impact — How important is this decision to the acquiring firm or entity.

There are a number of common situations:

One person, no big deal

Utility software costing less than $100 is a common example of this type of software. Individuals are typically buying it for their own use. If it doesn't turn out to be as useful as they thought, or if it doesn't work as represented, they won't lose any sleep over it. Thus this is your classic impulse buy. People call an 800 number give out their credit card number to get the software shipped today. This is as easy as it gets.

One person, a big deal

A spread-sheet or word-processor are good examples of this type of software. An individual will be using it on their own, but this will be a key part of their job. If they pick the wrong critical application software, it will be costly to reverse that decision. This is due in part to the fact that these packages typically cost more, but there is a conversion cost and delay if they have to move their work to a new package.

Because there is more potential impact, a prospect in this category usually worries about this decision. They gather data and talk to their friends. Reviews and references typically make the difference. Detailed product demos and literature can help, but often the prospects aren't knowledgeable enough to assess the product information. This sales cycle can go on for years because the prospect won't buy until they are comfortable, and they don't know how to get enough information to become comfortable.

A group, no big deal

Often this is utility software for a company. When one person is buying the product, is no big deal to change, but once a company standardizes on a particular set of software, change is very difficult. Usually companies appoint someone to review the software, and they have to present their findings to a committee. The good news is that the reviewer often has the skills to evaluate the software. The bad news is that the additional people involved really slows the process down. A two- to four-month sales cycle is common for small organizations, and it can

easily take six months or even longer in larger corporations.

A group, a big deal

As you can guess, this is tough-city. Any software which requires a change in behavior is big-deal software. This is especially true in companies where many people will be involved.

Just the evaluation cost to a corporation can be considerable. If we assume that 10 people are involved, and they spend 30 hours each learning about the big-deal software, then the evaluation cost can easily exceed $9,000. (Assuming that their average fully-burdened hourly cost is $30, the calculation goes like this: 10 people * 30 hours * $30/hour = $9,000.) Corporate evaluation costs are often two to three times the software cost. This is part of why companies are so careful before even seriously evaluating this type of software. In larger companies, the costs are astronomical. This sales cycle ranges from six to twelve months and beyond.

19. Selling Hardware

Q. Should small software companies sell hardware if it is likely to increase software sales?

A. This is a tough one. As you can see from the subscriber survey, our readers are more than five times as likely to only sell software.

We recommend selling hardware only if all else fails. The hardware margins are very low in many competitive markets. Finally, if you must sell hardware, make sure that you control your margins. Set rigid limits on how much you will discount. You are selling the hardware as a service. If your customer wants to buy hardware from you, they may have to pay slightly more than the cheapest alternative.

For example, if you are selling a PC vertical market package to prospects who don't have a PC, they might want you to sell them a packaged system. This is a case where you should sell more software by offering hardware. Make sure that you don't meet the lowest bid that they find from mail order suppliers. We have one client who charges a hardware integration fee if the customer buys the hardware elsewhere. They price the hardware with reasonable margins and are quite successful. They lose some customers who want the cheapest hardware available, but they feel that this business would have cost them money.

If you decide to sell hardware to help sell your software, make sure you keep a close eye on your margins and your costs. We have seen too many software companies who were losing their shirt on the hardware when they included their people costs. It is complex and very easy to mislead yourself. If you aggressively pursue this path, you will end up being a VAR as opposed to a software publisher. Think about what this means (hardware maintenance, spare parts, inventory) before you leap into it.

20. Making the Sale Happen

Q. We've developed a fine sales plan showing leads turning into demos (or trials) which eventually turn into sales. The problem is the sales don't seem to happen. Any suggestions?

A. You've made the first step in formulating a plan. Now the trick is to watch the plan in action and to make adjustments that will cause the plan to come true.

Weekly sales meeting

The first step we recommend to all our clients in your situation (and there are more than you'd think) is that they implement a **weekly sales meeting.** This is a regular, can't-miss-it meeting for all hands involved in sales. Lay out the tasks for each week with a clear assignment for everyone.

Your weekly sales meeting should focus on *specific, measurable objectives* (number of mailers sent out, number of leads generated, number of trials ordered, number of contracts signed, etc.). Everyone who has an assigned task or objective should report on what they said (last week) that they would do and what actually happened.

One of the most important things to focus on in your weekly meeting is how you are doing against plan and what you must do to compensate for short falls. We will give you some common problems and sample solutions.

Late mailings

If your primary lead generation mechanism is direct mail campaigns, late mailings can severely hamper your overall marketing effort. Almost all of the remedies cost (additional) money. If your piece was intended to be sent via bulk or 3rd class mail, you can gain several weeks if you send it via first-class.

Low response rate on the mailing

You can evaluate your mailing piece, and try to improve it. Often this can help improve the response rate, but this takes time. Short term you may have to start cold calling to generate the leads that you aren't producing by direct mail. Make this a top priority even though it isn't much fun. If you don't get the leads, it is very tough to generate sales at the level required. If you are lead-poor, we often find that software publishers spend too much time with poor quality leads which become poor quality trials and never buy. Make sure that you have an adequate supply of leads to work.

If you can afford the additional cost (and maybe even if you *can't* afford it) you might try using a professional, direct-mail advertising agency. See earlier issues on how to find and evaluate ad agencies.

Low lead to trial ratio within 30 days

There are several possible problems. It may just take your prospects more than 30 days to decide to proceed to a trial. If this is your problem, you might look at your marketing materials to see if you can expedite their decision process. If they have a technical person conduct a technical product evaluation, you might have one of your technical people take responsibility for managing the technical evaluation and speeding it through the process. If the sale is hanging up with the manager, your sales person may not be following up aggressively enough.

Finally, you may not be qualifying your leads well enough. You may be getting too many leads which aren't really ready to trial within 30 days. In this case you might look back at your lead generation process to see what you can do to improve the quality of your leads.

Lower trial to sale ratio within 30 days

This is where the rubber meets the road. Can you close the business? We have seen far to many cases where technical people aren't willing to push for the close. They sincerely feel that the customer will buy when they are ready. Often they will say, "I know when I am ready to buy and that is how I want to sell." That is OK if they decide often enough and quickly enough, but in many cases it isn't fast enough.

Look at where the sale is hanging up. Who isn't sure? What are his concerns? What can you do to help convince him? Often there is a technical advocate who is unable to convince his management. Perhaps he needs to prepare a cost justification. Write one for him. One of the easiest and most powerful sales tools is a simple cost justification of your product.

Ask your existing customers for samples of what they prepared for their management. Generalize these and send them to your trials as part of your formal proposal. Make it as easy as possible for your advocate to sell his management.

Q. Funding (1989)

1. Business Plan

Q: What is a "business plan"? How do you go about preparing and implementing one?

A: Glad you asked that one. A business plan is a written statement of the strategy and tactics that you are intending to use in developing and growing your business. We believe that every business should have a written plan which documents the real path that management intends for the company.

The importance of a written plan

We are sure that you have a verbal/mental business plan which you could relate to an interested party. But unless you **write it down,** you are going to be missing several important benefits:

* Focused Thought-process —

Perhaps the most important benefit of a written plan is that it forces you to review and think through your assumptions, your strategy, your marketplace, etc. Very often the mere process of preparing a business plan is a catalyst that will add an enormous boost to your plans and strategies.

* Easy Communication —

If your business is going to grow you must be able to communicate with a number of people — both inside and outside the company. If you don't have a

written plan, this communication must be verbal, a very time consuming process. If you do have one, you can simply pass it out as necessary. You can use a business plan as a communication vehicle for new or prospective employees, for your banker/financier, for important vendors, etc. Answering questions is always easier than explaining things from scratch.

* Drawing a line at the dirt —

Another drawback of verbal plans is that it is very difficult to remember what your plan was last year. You are so close to the daily business that you forgot many of the details. With a written plan you can track your progress much more objectively.

WRITING A BUSINESS PLAN

Rather than suggest that you launch immediately into writing a 100-page plan, we urge you to write a two-page plan first. List the objectives of the business and the major projects for the next year or two. Review this simple plan with everyone involved. Make sure that you all agree on the high level of objectives. We think you will be surprised at the amount of discussion that this review process generates.

Once you have the two-page objectives pinned down, you can write a 10-page version. Usually this addresses your product, marketplace, people, and contains a financial plan. In the product section you should summarize your product plans. The market section should identify your market and how you are going to sell your product. The people section should describe the current management as well as your staffing plans. (What key positions need to be filled, when?)

Your financial plan, often called a Pro Forma Plan should show both expected Profit & Loss as well as your Balance Sheet numbers. You should make these projections monthly for the first year and a quarterly for the second. Usually, we find that projections beyond two years are a waste of time for small companies. You won't be making many decisions which go beyond two years, so we believe it's better to focus on doing the best job possible on the shorter term financials rather than spending your time inventing financial data for 1995.

For most software companies a ten-page business plan is adequate. It gives you a working document which your managers can work off of, and it gives you something to show the bank. Unless you intend to raise venture capital, the additional effort to develop a longer, more formal business plan probably isn't worthwhile.

2. Limited Cash Marketing

Q. I am developing a software product with scarce financial resources. I am not terribly interested in the Venture Capital (VC) route. What are my best marketing resources with very limited cash resources?

A. The short answer is to focus on selling, and to only spend time and money on marketing which will support sales. If you have very limited financial resources, you can't afford to start marketing programs which will take years to pay off.

Finding out how long you can last.

The first step is to determine exactly what resources you have available. How long will your current nest-egg last? With founder-funded companies one of the major financial resources is the founder's ability to go without getting paid. Develop a budget for the next three to six months. Then develop a cash flow without assuming any cash from sales. This tells you how long you can last without any sales. It also tells you how much it costs to keep the doors open another month.

A typical example might be that you can go for three months and that it will cost you $20,000 per month if the founders draw no salaries, $30,000 per month if they draw minimal salaries, and $40,000 per month with the founders drawing acceptable salaries. The founders can go for three months with no salary, the next three months with minimal salaries, but after six months they all must have acceptable salaries. This implies that by month four you must have accumulated sales (cash receipts) of at least $30,000, $60,000 by month five, etc. Make sure that you account for the time it takes to receive the cash from your invoices. It is very possible to go Chapter 11 even though you have significant accounts receivable.

Controlling Expenses

A final point before we start to look at the sales and marketing issues is to carefully examine your expenses. Make very sure that you have trimmed all of your expenses to the bone. Once you complete your product and your documentation, you may have some people who are no longer necessary as technical resources. You may be able to convert them into sales and marketing resources, but make sure that you don't carry more expenses than are necessary during the sales ramp up stage. We realize that this sounds harsh, but if your business fails because you kept non-critical people you will have made a big mistake, and they'll be out looking for a job anyhow.

Now that you have scrubbed your expenses we must start to examine your sales and marketing side of the business. Where do you stand? How many prospects do you have and where are they in the sales cycle? How long is your sales cycle and what are your ratios as prospects develop into sales. If you haven't developed a track record, you will have to start off with a pro forma plan. You will refine this as you proceed and get more information, but you must have a starting point.

A Pro Forma Marketing/Sales Plan

We will develop a hypothetical pro forma plan for the situation we discussed earlier where we needed to be at $30,000 per month in sales (cash in) by month four. Lets assume a 30 days AR period so we need $30,000 in sales in month three. Lets also assume an average sale of $10,000 so we must sell three copies in month three.

Trial to sale

Let's assume a 50% win ratio on our prospects who trial the product. Lets also assume that it takes one month for trials to buy. Thus we need six trials in month two.

Lead to trial

Let's assume that 10% of our leads decide to trial the product within 30 days. This means that we need 60 leads in month one.

	Month 0	1	2	3	4	5	6	7
Mailing	600	800	1,000	1,200	1,400	1,600	1,800	2,000
Leads		60	80	100	120	140	160	180
Trials			6	8	10	12	14	16
Sales(#)				3	4	5	6	7
Sales ($)				$30K	$40K	$50K	$60K	$70K
Cash Receipts					$30K	$40K	$50K	$60K
Cumulative					$30K	$70K	$120K	$!80K
Requirement		$20K	$20K	$20K	$30K	$30K	$30	$40
Cum Req		$20K	$40K	$60K	$90K	$120K	$150K	$190K
Cash Req		$20K	$40K	$60K	$60K	$50K	$30K	$10K

Direct mail to lead

Let's assume that 1% of the letters we send respond within 30 days. Thus we need to send 600 letters in month zero.

This is all required to support the month three sales to get the month-four cash. We need to ramp up to twice this level by month six to provide the higher cash in, in month seven. We might lay out a plan like the one shown above in Table II.

Now you must go back to your expense budget and make sure that you budgeted adequate money to support this level of sales and marketing. We would add in additional ten to fifteen percent to cover unforseen expenses. If this increases your expenses, and your cash requirements you will have to reiterate. You should be able to develop a workable plan in a couple iterations.

Implementing the Plan

Now that you have developed your pro forma plan you must start to implement it and get the feedback. As you recall, we made a number of assumptions about when you were going to do things and what the results were going to be. It is critical that you track these as you progress and that you make the necessary corrections. You also should convert this plan into a weekly plan, so that you can have weekly status meetings. Lay out all of the tasks for each week with a clear assignment for everyone in the company.

As you can see, this isn't an easy problem. It can fall apart at so many points in the process. Your staff will have to wear many hats, and many of the tasks that they will be asked to do will be new and uncomfortable. It is very easy to lose track of your progress and fail to realize that you are in trouble until it is too late. It is also very easy to be overly optimistic and mislead yourself. Weekly review meetings are a good way to remain objective and keep everyone involved in making your company a success. Often you may find that people will volunteer to help each other out when they see that someone is having a problem.

3. Raising Venture Capital

Q. *Where can we get more information on raising venture capital?*

A. The *Arthur Young Guide to Raising Venture Capital*, was published by Blue Ridge Publishers, Summit PA 17294-0850, 252 pages, $24.95 in cloth.

Venture Capitalists take six steps in their decision to invest:

1. They review the executive summary to your business plan (you *do* have an executive summary, don't you?). Make sure that you tell your story in the first page or two.

2. Next they review the whole business plan to decide on whether they want to meet you.

3. The interview. They are looking to see what they think of you — what makes you tick, and why. Often proposals are rejected after this step. If this happens, call to find out why.

4. If the meeting is positive, they will start their due diligence. This means that they will question everything in your business plan: your assumptions, your contracts, your customers, everything. You must maintain an open door policy.

5. Once the VCs decide that they want to invest, they start to negotiate. This stage ends with a term sheet which outlines the terms of the deal.

6. The final step is to sign a contract.

Nationally, about 2 to 3 percent of all proposals for venture capital are funded.

If you are committed to raising venture capital, we urge you to read everything on the subject that you can find. Next you should talk to as many people as possible. We should warn you that many people who have raised venture money are tempted to gloss over the difficulties. If you are prepared, you can ask more detailed questions and get them to open up. It typically takes six months to a year to raise money, and you must dedicate the CEO for that year to the task of raising money. This is a real investment of time and money so make sure that you are well prepared before you take on the quest to raise venture capital.

4. Money, Anyone?

Dear Dave,

I noticed that 23% of your readers were interested in raising venture capital or going public. I wanted to let your readers know about USS. USS is a public company listed on NASDAQ and in the software publishing business as you know. We have a site license customer base that exceeds 150 corporations and a line of PC data protection software products.

We are actively searching for acquisition possibilities that would allow us to grow and expand the business. We feel we have an excellent fund raising capacity and are looking for a company or products that would justify further expansion. If I can supply any further information, please call me at the number [shown below].

Stephen M. Hicks
President
United Software Security
(703) 556-0007

If anyone is interested in discussing the subject of acquisition with Stephen, please contact him directly.

5. Grow from $5M to $10M Per Year

Q. How can I grow my business from $5 Million per year to $10 Million per year, with minimum risk and instability?

A. The first question that you must answer is "Can you achieve this growth with the products you have in the markets you are currently serving?" If you can, that is the safest way to grow. To increase your revenues, increase your marketing and sales budget. Uncertainty causes risk; this approach minimizes the uncertainty and thus minimizes the risk. Be aware that this approach does increase risk by keeping all of your eggs in one basket, but this is the business you know best.

If you can't meet your revenue objectives without introducing new products or opening new markets, you are faced with a much more difficult challenge. In my experience, introducing new products and opening new markets are very difficult, similar in fact to starting your company in the first place. If you conclude that this is the approach you must take, I urge you to be very careful. Don't underestimate the effort and the cost of launching these new businesses. Make sure that you have the capital and the management resources to support both the old and new businesses simultaneously. I have seen too many cases of companies failing in a new business and jeopardizing the basic business because of the costs of the failure.

It may be that you can't grow your business to $10 Million without taking major risks. If this is the case, consider whether you should stabilize the current business and turn it into a cash cow. Once this is done, you can take your cash and evaluate investing in new businesses. While you don't necessarily need to change your organization, you should think of it in these terms.

6. Venture Funding - Validate the Market

Bruce Da Costa of Iconnix called after reading the venture capital article. He felt that one point that I hadn't stressed was the mandatory requirement that entrepreneurs validate their markets before taking in money. In many cases it takes time to work out a successful sales formula. This includes, but isn't limited to: product features, product positioning, pricing, sales materials and strategy and marketing programs. Once you take in money from investors, they will pressure you to move much faster than you might otherwise want to. If you encounter any problems, there will be incredible pressure to bull your way through them. This can cause you to make mistakes and to proceed quite differently than you would without the money. As long as you are self-funded, you make your own decisions. Self-funding might take a little longer, but in many cases the additional pressure from investors can spell disaster for companies that might otherwise have worked out their formula had they just had more time.

I believe it is critical that entrepreneurs view raising money from the investor's point of view. Would you put your own money into this company? As an investor you are looking for situations in which money is the only missing ingredient. You can assure that this is the case by developing the formula using your own money, which will also help to increase your valuation.

7. Company Valuation

Q. How should I value my company for estate planning purposes?

A. All other things being equal, I would value a healthy software company at one-times annual revenues. The actual valuations vary from one-half to two times annual sales, but one-times is the most common valuation.

8. Software Company Valuations

Q. Can you give me any examples of software company valuations?

A. While the specifics of most software company acquisitions aren't disclosed, two recent Computer Associates acquisitions were disclosed in *Macintosh News*. These are as follows: Cricket Software was purchased for $5 million to $10 million; their 1988 revenues were $10 million and they have 60 employees. Bedford Software was purchased for $13.1 million; their revenues for the fiscal year ending May, 1989 were $7 million, and they have 60 employees.

Reference: Macintosh News July 3, 1989, page 8.

Cricket's valuation is 1/2 to 1 times last year's revenue, which is the low end of the valuation range. Bedford is 1.8 times the most recent year's revenues, which is significantly better. While Cricket's revenue per employee is a very respectable $165K, Bedford's $218K is substantially better. If you rank the top 10 software companies by revenue per employee (see table), only two are better than Bedford, and only three are better than Cricket. While there were other factors which affected these valuations, exceptional financial performance can make a dramatic difference.

9. Venture Capitalists

Q. How do venture capitalists view their business?

A. There was an article on investing in publicly traded venture capital firms. It mentioned, "since roughly one-third of such emerging companies fail, venture capitalists seek a high rate of return - 1,000% say. Greater Washington Investors, a venture capital fund, garnered its biggest payback ever when a software company in which the fund invested $250,000

Software Company Revenue per Employee

Company	Revenue Rank	$000/Employee
Microsoft	2	257
AshtonTate	5	247
Lotus	3	187
WordPerfect	10	162
Computer Associates	1	145
Oracle	4	142
MSA	6	105
Cullinet	8	107
Software AG	7	82
Dun & Bradstreet	9	62

Reference: Software Magazine; June 1989; page 24.

in 1969 was acquired for $13 million in 1983. This article gave a list of publicly traded funds:

- Greater Washington Investors 301-656-0626

- Infotechnology, Inc. 212-891-7500

- Rand Capital 716-853-0802

- Clarion Capital 216-953-0555

If you are serious about raising venture capital, you should acquire some stock in one of these firms to better understand their end of the world.

REFERENCE: "Here's How To Get In On The High-tech Ground Floor", *Executive Wealth Advisory*, July 3, 1989.

10. Risk Versus Stability

Q. We are having an ongoing debate internally about how much risk we should take in our company strategy. Should we push for high growth and high risk, or should we strive to build a safe and stable business? What do you advise?

A. The place to start is with the shareholders and principals in the company. What are your goals as individuals? Do you want to have a nice job with an adequate salary and have fun building good products, or do you want to gain fame and fortune and take a shot at the gold ring? I have had many clients who view this as a surprising question, but I believe that it is fundamental to answering your question.

Another parameter is your line of business. In some businesses it is very difficult to grow faster than the market because the competitors are all strong and entrenched. In this type of market, the risks of a high growth strategy are greater than normal. On the other hand, some markets are exploding and there is very little competition. If you don't grow as quickly as the market, you are inviting competition which could eventually crush you. In this situation a slow growth strategy entails the highest long term risk.

Once you have surveyed your management team's risk profile, as well as the risk reward factors for your market situation, you can make reasoned judgments. Ideally the team and the market match, although sometimes they don't. If this is the case, consider changing your market or your management team.

11. Raising Money/Companies in Related Fields

Q. How can we raise money from companies in related fields?

A. This is an appealing prospect, but it does have some problems. The appeal is that companies in a related field know your market and your business. While they certainly know your market, you may be surprised at the amount of educating you must do to teach them about the software business. Software is very different from more traditional businesses.

Assuming that you can identify a company and some of its executives who understand your market and are interested in investing, next look at why they might want to invest. They might, for instance, want to learn about another aspect of their market. Or they might want to start their own software company and sell into your common market; be sure to ask them about this. I would urge you to have them sign a non-competition agreement. Educating a competitor isn't what you want to achieve.

If their motivation is purely financial, you must address how they are going to financially benefit from their investment. Being a minority shareholder in a privately held company can be an illiquid investment with little or no return. If you have plans to go public or to sell the company, your stock might be a good investment. But this situation isn't all that common for small software companies. Most founding teams don't want to give up the control that either of these options require. Unless the founding team is committed to raising professional investment money, I would assume that the stock isn't liquid. In addition, the founders can benefit from high salaries and other perks which a passive minority shareholder can't take to the bank.

If this describes your situation, consider a marketing partnership arrangement where the investors provide money to be used for marketing. They receive a royalty from sales until they have gotten two to three times their money back. This makes it very clear how they "cash out." This arrangement can work, and your industry investors can readily gauge their exposure.

12. Venture Capital & Software Companies

We recently received a call from a local venture capitalist who wanted to remain anonymous. He called to say that his firm is willing to consider investing in companies whose five year projected revenues were in the $25 Million range rather than the more typical $100 Million range that most venture capitalists are looking for. He went on to mention that he isn't keen on financing development. In general he likes to see development either self funded or customer funded. He also likes to see the founders coming from the industry being served. He feels that solid

industry expertise is a key ingredient in a software company.

While that information was interesting, it wasn't the main reason for his call. He sees too many people trying to raise money without any regard for how their company will perform as an investment. Before you seek outside funds, ask yourself two questions:

1. Will this investment make me more money? In our consulting business we frequently see nice software companies which are producing $1 Million in sales and are growing at twenty to thirty percent per year without additional investment. In most cases these companies are privately owned by the founders. The founders think that they could grow fifty percent per year if they brought in $1 Million in venture capital. Even if the entrepreneur could talk the venture capitalist into making this investment, this investment isn't a good deal for the company or the entrepreneur.

If we assume that the software company valuation is 1 times revenue (a typical software company valuation metric, by the way), the venture capitalists receive ownership of 50% of the company for their $1 Million. At the end of the first year, the revenues are $1.5 Million and the valuation is $1.5 Million, and the founder's share is worth $750K. If they hadn't taken in the venture capital, the company revenue might have only been $1.2 Million, and the company would have had a lower valuation, but the founder's share would have been higher. It is possible that the founder's value could be higher if the growth rate was higher and was sustained for a number of year in the investment scenario.

2. Is my company a good investment? In the sometimes desperate search for money, software entrepreneurs often forget that there needs to be a way to repay the investors (hopefully in a handsome fashion).

Being Venture-financed

The venture capitalist asked that we discuss the tradeoffs involved in raising venture capital. His experience (which agrees with ours) is that there are some major changes when a software company receives a venture capital investment because entrepreneurs and venture capitalists have very different utility functions.

Entrepreneurs usually like the independence, and the lifestyle of being their own boss and having the luxury of setting their own direction. Very often we find that the founder of a software company is simply interested in having fun with software while being paid reasonably for his (usually immense) effort.

Venture capitalists, on the other hand, are very single-minded: they want to make money. If they can do this while accommodating the entrepreneur's lifestyle, great, but they won't hesitate to sacrifice the lifestyle to protect their investment. When a venture capitalist makes an investment in *any* start-up company (not just software) they usually secure a controlling interest in the company. If the company gets into trouble, the venture capitalists will do what it takes to protect their investment. Oftentimes this means firing the founding team and bringing outsiders to manage the investment. It isn't that they dislike the entrepreneurs, they are just watching out for their investment.

In our opinion, you should reflect very carefully on the realities of venture-backing before you embark on a quest for venture capital. Here are some additional questions that you should ask yourself:

Market Size

1. How big can my company get within 5 years?

Management Team

2. Can our current management team (including me) get us there?

Other Money Sources

3. What other sources of financing are available? Will they get us to the same end point?

Money Needs

4. Can our company really effectively utilize the venture capital so that this additional capital will create enough additional value that everyone is better off?

Being a "good investment"

The point that we are trying to make, is that rather than assuming that you are trying to "talk someone into giving you money" that you should make sure that you would make the investment if you were sitting in the investor's chair.

An introduction to Venture Capital

If, in spite of all this, you think that venture capital might be appropriate for your company, give us a call. We would like to discuss these issues with you in more depth. If you would like to proceed, we will be happy to give you the VC's phone number.

13. Software Company evaluations

Q: What is our company worth? What are the general guidelines for placing a value on software companies?

A: Most venture capitalists (who are by nature very interested in evaluations) will say that a software company is worth between one-half and twice the annual revenues. If your company had revenues of $1 million last year, for instance, its value should lie between $500,000 and $2,000,000.

There is additional variation depending upon whether you used last year's revenue or next year's revenue in calculation. Corporate and international valuations tend to be higher because they are often getting additional benefits. For example, a corporate investor may value the ability to influence your technology direction or learn about your technology. Often international investors are also acquiring marketing rights for their territory.

14. Equity Compensation

Q: How does a fledgling software company attract developers and marketeers without selling out the business with too much equity incentives.

A: In our experience, equity is vastly overrated as a carrot to attract employees. In the classical under-capitalized startup, the founders are asking new employees to sign on and work 60 to 70 hours per week for little or no money. Entrepreneurs are the only group crazy enough to think that this is a real opportunity. Unless the potential employee really values the equity, you aren't likely to attract employees at stage zero, no matter how much stock you offer.

Startup Equity

We have seen far too many cases where small companies try to buy employees by offering outrageous chunks of equity. A typical corporate employee will probably be scared of the risks in joining an unfunded startup. Usually these corporate employees don't want to admit that they're really not entrepreneurial so they make excessive equity demands. They really want the startup company to say "No" rather than having to admit that they don't want to give up their three weeks of paid vacation, and sundry other benefits.

Our experience is that during the initial startup stages, the only people crazy enough to join up are true entrepreneurs. These folks will accept a fair equity stake for the risk that they are taking.

Even at the initial startup stage, your company has both cash and stock to offer to prospective employees. The value of the stock to the founders is often much higher than to the corporate employees (which is why they are asking for so much stock). We urge you to examine carefully how the various people value the stock.

Often we find that the true entrepreneur will take half salary for the first six months to get twice as much stock. A diehard corporate employee will give up all of his stock for ten percent more money. Don't give someone something (equity) which is worth more to you than it is to them.

Mid-Level Equity

The next stage is where companies try to recruit key people is when they reach $1,000,000 in annual slaves. Often a company at this stage needs to recruit a Marketing, Sales and /or Management executive. In many cases, the company wants to bring in this person to facilitate a funding (e.g. bringing in venture capital).

Typically this person will either be CEO, COO, or VP of Marketing. Persons contemplating this type of position typically expect 5 to 10% of the company in stock options. In most cases they aren't prepared to invest their own money in the company. They are looking at this job from a corporate context: large corporations give employees stock options and employees aren't asked to invest in the company. If you need to raise a venture capital, and if you can find a senior executive who can help accomplish that, then giving them an option for 5 to 10% of the company over 4 or 5 years is a fair deal. If they only last for one year, they only get 1 to 2% of the equity.

The prospective executive, in this scenario, will typically insist on a higher salary (to support a lifestyle they have become accustomed to), and will want a severance package. Your company, on the other hand, won't want to give them a dime if they can't bring in the financing. Further, you really don't want them ending up with stock if you part on bad turns. Our experience is that close to 50% of the employees in this type of situation are fired or quit within a year. Even though you check references, hold extensive interviews, etc., bad chemistry can cause lots of explosion in this type of pressure-cooker environment.

We would recommend that you negotiate the following before you hire a senior executive:

1. Specify exactly what relocation expenses will be paid, if any.

2. Stipulate an exact start-date and delineate, in writing, exactly what their 3 and 6 month objectives are.

3. Enumerate exactly how much stock is available via options and what the vesting requirements will be. (Be sure there is no vesting for the first 3 or 6 months.)

4. Specify a compensation (in lieu of stock) if he is terminated at the end of the trial period.

Although these measures may sound draconian, they can help avoid serious misunderstanding on both sides.

R. Subscriber Survey (1989)

Every periodical needs to know who its readership is and **Software Success** is no different. Earlier this spring we sent out a questionnaire asking a few, essential questions. We received and tabulated the responses for almost 100 of these Subscriber Surveys. Although the survey was short (just one page), the answers were illuminating.

1. Company Type

The overwhelming majority of you, not surprisingly, are with a software company. The next largest group is companies that sell both hardware and software. *Only about 7% of our subscribers are not software vendors.*

2. Company Revenues & Marketing Budget

The median software revenues for our subscribers was just less than $1million/year. While the typical company spent about 10% of its revenues on market-

Company Type

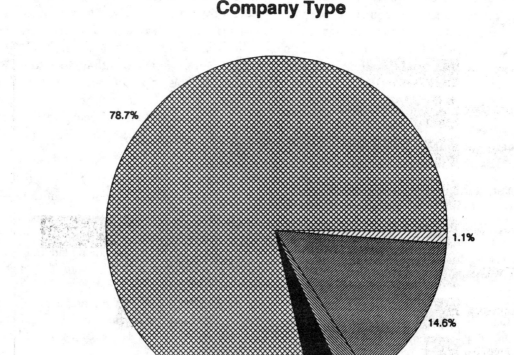

78.7% Software

1.1% Industry Observers

14.6% Distributor

2.2% Software & Hardware

3.4% Dealer/VAR

- ▨ Software
- ■ Dealer/VAR
- ▧ Distributor
- ▨ Software & Hardware
- ▨ Industry Observers

ing (not counting commissions and salaries) there was a marked trend towards decreased spending as the company size grew larger. The graph below uses data from only those respondents who provided both revenue and marketing budget information. The line is a least squares fit.

The median annual software revenues were less than $1 Million per year. The annual marketing budget was quite low. The median budget was less than $50K. The median marketing budget is only 4% of software revenues.

There is quite a variation in the size of the marketing budget, even for companies at the same revenue level. There is a fundamental dichotomy between growth and short term profits. If you want to grow your company you must invest in marketing. This is typical of companies with outside investors. On the other hand if you want to optimize profits so that you can pay high salaries, you will tend to hold down your marketing budget. This is more common in companies which are owned by the principals.

3. Software Type

Distribution of software by type was as follows:

Vertical	57%
Horizontal	27%
System Util	13%

4. Average Price/Unit

The most popular prices were $2.5K to $10K, and $25K to $100K. As you can see from the graph on the next page, most companies tended to sell more expensive software. We believe that this is due to the fact that most smaller companies have limited sales resources.

These sales limited companies find it easier to see a few copies of more expensive software than more copies of less expensive software. In many cases the software from the smaller firms is incomplete and many of the sales include some custom programming which increases the average price.

Average Price per Unit

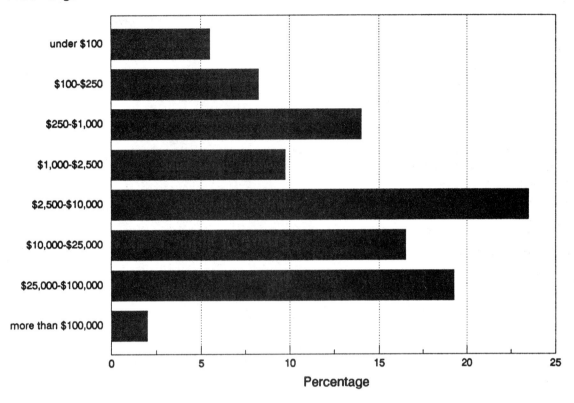

Sales by Computer Classification

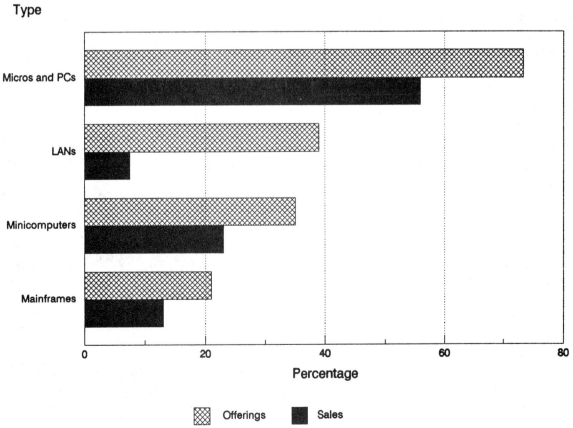

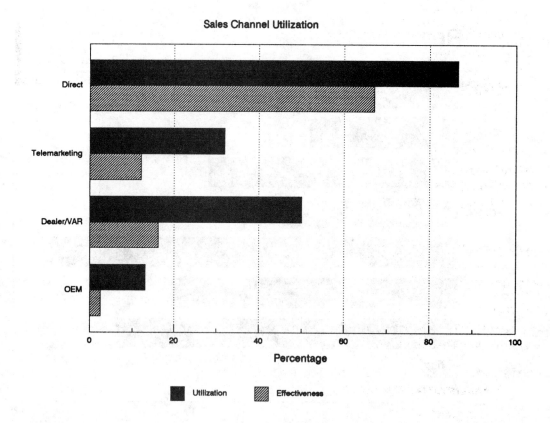

Sales Channel Utilization

5. Sales by Type

Micros were the most popular hardware platform and LANs were second Note that these percentages are greater than 100% because many companies were on more than one hardware platform.

While LANs are offered by almost 40% of the firms, they account for only 10% of the sales. It will be interesting to see if this changes over the next few years. If you look at the sales relative to the offerings, you see that Micro/PC has the highest ratio. We believe that this means that most of the micro companies are primarily micro companies. The low level of LAN sales indicate the immaturity of the LAN market. We were surprised that both the mini and mainframe sales were lower relative to the offering than we had expected. Looking at the surveys we found that these differences were due to micro companies who offered a mainframe version but who were focused primarily on the micro market. In many cases, it takes a distinct marketing program to sell your software on the different platforms.

Most of the companies who have Micro PC products get over 70% of their sales from the micro product. Lans were much less significant sales contributor in

that they only contribute 10 to 20 percent of sales for the companies who sell LANs. Minis are like micros in that most of the companies with Mini products get over 70% of their sales on minis. The same statistic is true for mainframes. For the smaller firms in the survey, they usually specialize on their primary platform. It is very difficult to sell a product in quantity of different platforms.

6. Sales Channel Utilization

Direct was the most popular channel, but VARS and Distributors were the second most popular channel. (Please note that this totals to more than 100% because most software firms use more than one sales channel.)

Most of the companies who sell direct sell more than 70% direct. Telemarketing ranged fairly evenly from 5 to 70 percent depending upon how the companies use it. The median company which specialized in telemarketing got 50% of its sales from telemarketing.

While distributors and VARs are very popular, they don't produce a lot of sales. Perhaps this helps account for the constant stream of questions on how to

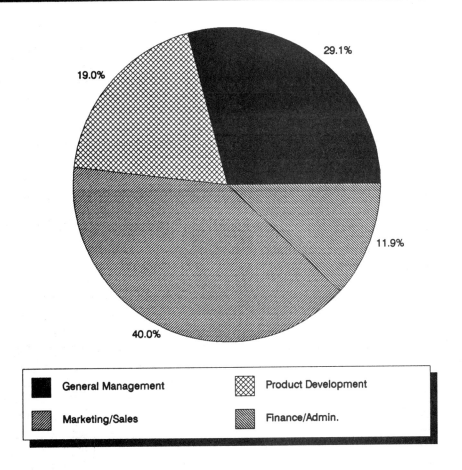

Respondents' Time by Function

29.1%

19.0%

11.9%

40.0%

Legend:
- General Management
- Product Development
- Marketing/Sales
- Finance/Admin.

sell through VARs and distributors. The median distributor sales were only 20%. The median OEM sales were also 20%

If you compare the effectiveness of the various channels relative to their utilization we can understand how the various channels actually work for companies.

Direct Sales is the primary channel. Most firms use it and they get most of their sales via direct sales. Direct sales are the basic first step. If you can't sell your product direct, you will probably find it very difficult to sell it via the other channels.

Telemarketing is third in utilization and second in effectiveness. If you make the investment in telemarketing it can become a dependable way to make sales. Many companies find that they have to invest in better marketing materials to make tele-

marketing work so there are some other factors which can undermine telemarketing.

Dealer/VARs are the disappointment of the last few years. The low level of effectiveness is especially disappointing given the level of investment required to recruit and train dealers and VARs.

OEM Sales isn't a very effective or widely used distribution channel, but once you have negotiated an OEM agreement it doesn't have a great deal of organizational impact. Thus the lower level of effectiveness for OEM deals feels OK. Our experience is that it takes time for most OEM deals to really pay off.

7. Company Age

The average company has been in business 5 years which is quite a bit longer than we would have guessed.

Years	Value
1	2%
2	4%
3	9%
4	9%
5	22%
7	17%
10	15%

8. Respondent's Time by Function

General Management

The distribution of general management time was bimodal. The working CEOs spend only ten to twenty percent of their time in general management, while the general managers in larger companies spend seventy percent or more.

Development

Development consumed ten to twenty percent of most CEOs time.

Marketing

Marketing was similar to general management in that most CEOs spent twenty to thirty percent of their time in Marketing and Sales, and the Marketing VPs, Managers and Directors usually spent over 70% in marketing and sales.

Finance

Finance and Administration typically consume ten to twenty percent of the President's time.

9. Company Headcount

As you might expect, there was quite a variation in company size. The average size of the responding companies was more than 30 people while the median was just over 10. Here are some sample headcounts:

Salaried marketing people	1-2
Sales	2-4
Development	2-4
Support	1-2
Administration	1-2
Total	5-10

S. Market Research (1989)

1. Home-grown Market Research

Q. We haven't ever done any Market Research. How much money should we budget for market research? Where should we use it and where not? What are low cost forms of research?

A. Market research is simply asking your customers and prospects for information to help you make better decisions. Stated this way, everyone does market research. Rather than setting budget levels for market research, we urge you to look at the decisions you are trying to make. When you identify a critical decision that you will have to make in the next six months, you might consider market research. Identify both the decisions you have to make and the questions you might ask your customers and prospects.

Create an in-house survey

Start very simply. Write a simple customer survey and send it to your customers. Future product features are a good place to start. Customers love to be involved in designing future releases of a product that they have already purchased: you can expect a good response rate from your customers. While customers might answer a two or three page questionnaire, keep it simple. Make it easy to complete. Send your draft questionnaire to several people outside of the company. Try a couple of your better customers if you are concerned about the questionnaire.

Questionnaires for prospects must be much shorter. One page is typically their limit. Again, make it very easy to complete. Start with the easy questions and work into the more difficult and sensitive ones. Put all the open ended questions at the end since the prospects may get side tracked, and may not complete any more of the questions. We have seen a number of companies who have used surveys as a lead generation and qualification mechanism. Often they offer the survey results to everyone who completes the survey. You might find that your cost per lead with the survey is as good as or better than your traditional lead generation.

Another aspect of surveys is that you can use them for a press release. Make sure that you include some public questions which you wouldn't mind publishing. Often these make very good early questions which get the prospect started answering your questionnaire.

Using College Talent

Local colleges and Universities can be a good way to get some basic market research conducted for little or no cost. In many business programs, students have to find local businesses to work with. Having them develop a business plan including conducting some basic research can be very useful. Don't expect fast results, and you shouldn't count on high quality results, but if you are patient you may get some excellent information.

Literature search

Literature search is something that you might get the students to do. They should be able to use their library and computer systems like Dialog to search all magazine articles which mention your target market or your competitors. While you may assume that you fully understand your market, you might be surprised at the data and competitive information this type of search can uncover.

Market research should be an adjunct to your marketing and business decision process. As you get some early results, you should gain the confidence and experience to do more. We believe that you will be surprised at the amount of information you can get for the money.

2. Low cost market surveys

Q. How can we conduct low cost market surveys?

A. The most important ingredient of your question is "low cost". You can find all kinds of high-priced market research from all sorts of places. If you want to be frugal, however, you must conduct the research yourself.

Do-it-Yourself Market Surveys

The first step is to define what questions are really important. This isn't as easy as it may sound. We often find that many questions that we come up with are difficult for the prospects to answer. Either they can misinterpret the question, or it just doesn't mean anything to them. As an example, we might

want to know the price elasticity of demand. If we ask a prospect, "What's your price elasticity of demand for Product X," most of them won't have a clue. On the other hand, they do know about their budget, and the highest price they would consider buying. You have to be very careful to ask them questions in terms that are easy for them to answer.

Testing your questions

Once you have some sample questions, you should try them out. Have employees and friends try the questionnaire. Listen carefully to their responses. Elicit their help to clarify the questionnaire. If you are still concerned, you might ask a couple of your customers to review it for you.

Once you have the questionnaire, you have to get people to fill it out. Send it to everyone who has requested information on your product. There are a number of alternatives to getting more data. You can hand them out at trade shows, and mail them to prospect lists.

Market Surveys as Lead Generation Tool

A market survey can be the most effective way to generate leads. This seems to be especially true when you are making a missionary sale. A questionnaire is a non-threatening way to get your prospects to think about the problem you are trying to solve. If you lead them through the cost analysis, they may come to their own conclusion that they could really use some help to solve this problem.

Finally there are a couple additional points which are worth remembering:

1. Make it Easy Keep the survey down to one page. Make it easy to answer. Give them boxes to check off. This is especially true if you are asking them to estimate numbers that they don't have exact data for. They may be very reluctant to write down a number, but they are happy to pick a range.

2. Make the Survey do double dutyInclude some interesting general questions which you can use in a press release. Make sure that you'd be happy to publish the answers. For example, you wouldn't want to publish budget numbers, but you might be happy to publish numbers about hardware acquisition plans, or number of employees per PC. This will allow you to publish a press release as a side benefit of your effort.

3. Low cost competitive intelligence

Q. How can I gain low-cost competitive intelligence?

A. The first step is to call your competitors up, and talk to them. If their product is low-cost, buy a copy. With higher-priced products you may want to get copies of the marketing materials.

Getting marketing materials

The simplest and most straightforward way is to simply call your counterpart in the competitive organization and offer to swap marketing materials. If you aren't comfortable with this approach, or there is a substantive reason for avoiding direct contact, you can resort to simple subterfuge.

Represent yourself as a prospect and ask them to send you information at home. You can also have a friend make the call. While this is a sensitive issue, we feel that as long as you only look at information which is in the public domain, it is OK.

Confidentiality

As long as the vendor is willing to send you marketing material without a signed confidentiality agreement, we feel that it is OK. The moment you sign a non-disclosure agreement or something else, we feel that we are dealing with a completely different issue. Everyone has to determine where they are comfortable in this grey area, and act accordingly.

Clipping Coupons

Another alternative is to search the trade magazines for articles about your competitors. In many cases, especially if you are competing with larger companies, you will find a literature search will turn up information you don't have. There is also financial information on large private companies and public companies.

Other Sources

If your competitor's stock is publicly traded, buy a share of their stock and get all the SEC information. You could even attend their annual Stockholder's Meeting. Private company information is available from D & B and Standard & Poors. None of these searches are very expensive and you just might learn some key information.

Info from Customers

The last and most important source of competitive information is from your customers. Each time you win a competitive bid, you should follow up with the customer and ask them what they liked the best about your product? Why they bought from you? What the competitor had that you didn't have? Gather this information and compile it. In our experience, this real-life customer's information is much more relevant that the paper information discussed above. We have seen cases where companies had documentation which was a year old, and the competitor had improved their product. They were competing with last year's competitor. The current competitive situation comes from your new customers. They will tell you what is happening in the here and now.

1992
Software Success
Reference Book

Chapter VI
Customer Support & Technical Issues

Chapter VI. Customer Support & Technical Issues

A. Support Survey (Jan 1991)

The support survey received 169 responses!! This almost doubled our previous high. I believe this shows, once again, the very high level of interest in support issues. Everyone with a software product has to deal with some support issues.

1. Company Revenues

The company revenues were pretty evenly spread under $5 million

Revenue	% Resp
<$250K	17.8%
$250K-$500K	14.2%
$500K-$1M	14.2%
$1M-$2M	24.9%
$2M-$5M	19.5%
>$5M	8.3%

2. Computer Type

The mix of computer types is similar to what we have seen in the past. I made one change in that I asked for the primary computer type. We got some multiple answers (197 responses from the 169 companies). So, there were people who were unable to pick just one computer type as primary.

Computer	% Resp
PC	67.5%
LAN	16.6%
Mini	13.0%
Workstation	8.9%
Mainframe	10.7%

3. Product Price

The product prices were also very evenly spread. People found it much easier to identify the primary product price (we had 171 responses).

Price	% Resp
<100	14.2%
<$1K	21.9%
$1K-$10K	28.4%
$10K-$25K	16.0%
$25K-$100K	18.3%
>$100K	2.4%

4. Number of Customers
We had a broad range of number of customers.

# Customers	% Resp
No reply	8.9%
<100	28.4%
100-500	20.1%
500-1K	8.3%
1K-5K	14.8%
>5K	19.5%

5. A Math Exercise
I thought it would be interesting to work through the median numbers and see how consistent they are. The median product price is $1,000 to $10,000, and the companies have 100 to 500 customers. Thus, the median company cumulative revenue is $100,000 to $5 million. The median revenue was $500,000 to $1 million. This is consistent with previous surveys showing that our median reader had been in business 5 years.

If I had to guess, I'd say the typical subscriber has sold 500 copies of a $5,000 product for a total of $2.5 million in cumulative revenue. Their new license revenue history might have been:

Year 1	$100K
Year 2	$200K
Year 3	$400K
Year 4	$800K
Year 5	$1,000K

With $2.5 million in installed sales, their maintenance revenues might be $375,000, which is 27 percent of total revenues (new license revenue plus maintenance fees). I have ignored two factors which probably offset each other. The first is that the maintenance potential for the installed sales is higher that I have indicated, since early customers paid less than the current list price for the product. If the price of the product has doubled over the five years, we would be getting 30 percent in maintenance from each dollar of first year sales that are still on maintenance.

The offsetting factor is that customers drop off maintenance. In particular, I have seen cases where early customers balk at paying 50 percent to 75 percent of their initial purchase price for a product. It just doesn't seem reasonable to them.

6. Free 800 Number

Slightly over half of the respondents have 800 numbers and half of them limit the 800 number to sales.

800#	% Resp
No one	48.5%
Sales only	27.2%
Everyone	23.7%

I was surprised that so few companies have an 800 number. There seems to be evidence that the 800 numbers encourage more calls, and the costs are quite low. Come to think of it, I don't have a 800 number for my ads. It isn't the money. In part, it just might be the fact that I haven't gotten around to getting an 800 number. I also am getting plenty of calls. I am not really sure that I will get more real buyers with an 800 number. I probably am concerned that I will encourage more curiosity seekers. I would be interested to hear from anyone who has implemented an 800 number, then dropped it.

7. Phone Support

Our respondents are pretty evenly split between free support and annual support with a fringe group offering hourly support. We had 186 total responses or 1.1 per respondent. Almost all of the hourly people also offered annual support, so it isn't a primary support offering for very many companies.

Support	% Resp
Free	46.7%
Hourly	9.5%
Annual	53.8%

I would have guessed that most of the free support people were in the PC world and that the mainframe and mini respondents would provide support on an annual contract. If you look at the table below, relatively more of the PC respondents offer free support, but a surprising number of mainframe vendors offer free support. This isn't the first time that we have reported this statistic. The last time was in the

newsletter I received a letter from a mainframe subscriber asking who was offering mainframe software with free maintenance. Since I don't know of any companies who fit this profile, I would like to hear from anyone with a mainframe product with free support.

The hourly support is consistently around ten percent. However, none of the mainframe respondents offered hourly support. I have experienced real problems trying to administer hourly support when dealing with small customers. I can't imagine trying to do this with large companies.

If you rank the respondents by degree of strictness, the LAN and mini vendors are the toughest. Then we have mainframe and workstations, with PCs offering the most free support. I would have expected the roles of the LAN and the workstation vendors to have been reversed. I guess the high level of support workload with LAN products have forced them to charge for support. The workstations are midway between the PC world and the mini world.

Table I Phone Support by Computer Type

Computer	Free	Hourly	Annual
PC	51%	9%	40%
LAN	20%	9%	71%
Mini	21%	8%	71%
Workstation	31%	12%	57%
Mainframe	37%	0%	63%

8. 900 Numbers

Only one respondent has implemented a 900 number. (Please let me know how it is doing.) Thirty percent of the respondents were considering using 900 numbers, and 6.5 percent didn't respond. The remaining 60 percent said that they would never use a 900 number. A number of them commented, "Never say never," but right now it appears that 900 numbers are facing real resistance. Later in this issue, there is a letter from a 900 number service provider who felt that I wasn't being fair to 900 numbers. I have talked to quite a few people who are quite closed to using 900 numbers, and these results support my subjective impression.

9. Training Location

On-site training is most popular. I was surprised at the number of firms which felt that training wasn't required, but offered it anyway. If the customers are willing to pay for training, they must think it is required.

Training	% Resp
No reply	3.6%
Not required	30.8%
On site	60.9%
Vendor location	36.1%

I believe that the disparity between offering training on site and at the vendor location can be attributed to several factors. The first is that the training may require customer data which is difficult to transport to the vendor location. Secondly, the customer hardware configuration may not be replicated at the vendor location. The third reason is that the customer may want to train a number of people and it is cheaper to have the trainer come to the people than vice-versa. Finally, the software vendor may not have a classroom facility.

While I realize that many customers like on-site training because of the convenience and the opportunity for help with installation and training, I think that many companies could benefit by offering regular vendor location training. If you offer training at your location, you may be able to get prospects to come to training before they have purchased your product. I have one client who sells a very technical product which is incredibly powerful, but requires training to harness this power. They offer pilot installations at no cost with on-site installation and training as part of a trial evaluation. They found that getting the prospect to send people to vendor training made a dramatic series of changes. A much higher percentage of the pilots purchased, and then a correspondingly high percentage of these companies renewed their support agreement. It appears that this was due to the increased management commitment in addition to the better training skills of the operators.

I also heard of another company which is using vendor location training as a sales tool. Both of these companies charge for this training ($250/day per person) so they are getting a real commitment. I also believe that offering regularly scheduled vendor location training adds credibility. If you don't have the facility to provide training you might be able to make an arrangement with a local PC store, hotel, or customer depending upon your requirements.

10. Hourly Support Charge

As an industry, we don't charge much for hourly support

Hourly rate	% Resp
No reply	47.9%
<$25	8.9%
$25-$50	6.5%
$50-$75	12.4%
$75-$100	13.6%
$100-$125	9.5%
>$125	1.8%.

The median hourly rate is $50 to $75 per hour, which is the common range for contract programmers. The only difference is that contract programmers often sell their time by the month and we are selling it by the hour (or even smaller units in most cases.)

11. On-Site Daily Rate

I asked for the on-site training daily rate not including expenses. It appears that the median daily rates of $500 to $600 correspond to the median hourly rates of $50 to $75. The only exception is that a significant 25 percent of the companies charge over $750 per day for on-site training. I noted that many of these $750 per day companies charged significantly less for their hourly support. My experience is that many companies provide a more skilled person for on-site training. In many cases, they are also providing consulting.

Daily rate	% Resp
No reply	32.5%
<$250	7.7%
$250-$400	10.1%
$400-$500	10.7%
$500-$600	8.3%
$600-$750	6.5%
>$750	25.4%

I am pleased to see companies offering higher level training and charging for it. At $400 per day, the business equation is pretty tough. My experience is that it is difficult for most companies to average ten days a month of billable training when the trainers have to travel. In most cases, there is a half day of prep and follow up for each day of training so that accounts for five more days a month. Then, if you add one day for sick leave (mental health days), one day of vacation, and one day of holiday, you have only one or two days left for training and administration.

Thus, the $400/day trainer will generate $4,000 a month in revenue. If I pay them $2,000 a month in salary, I probably break even with benefits, office space, computers, and administrative overhead. It is very difficult to find and retain people who are willing to travel, and are presentable in front of customers at this price level. I think that you are much better off to raise your rate and pay your trainers more. You can also attract better trainers with a higher wage rate. Finally, you will be able to provide better training if you have better trainers who are better

paid and who aren't burnt out because they are having to travel too much because their rates ar too low.

12. Percent of Licenses on Maintenance

If you look at the graph at the bottom of this page, you will see that most companies do quite a good job of keeping their customers on maintenance. I left out the 12.4 percent of the respondents who didn't reply to this question and the 18.3 percent who said that none of their licenses were on maintenance. Over half of the applicable firms have over 75 per-

Percentage of Licenses on Maintenance

(Excluding those answering "0%" and "No Reply")

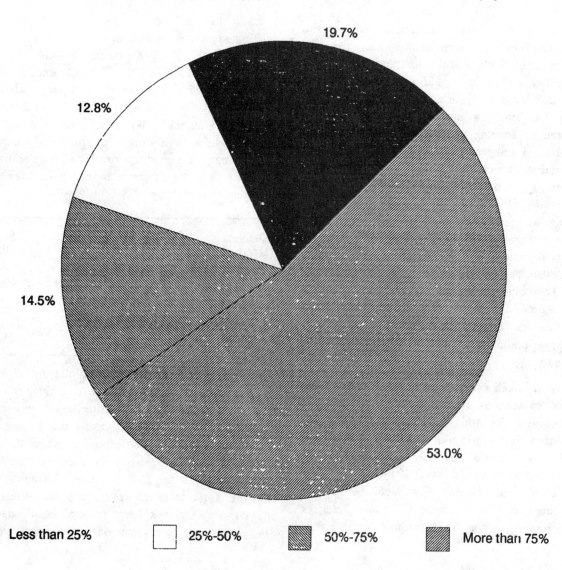

■ Less than 25%	□ 25%-50%	▨ 50%-75%	▨ More than 75%

Percentage of Revenue Coming from Support

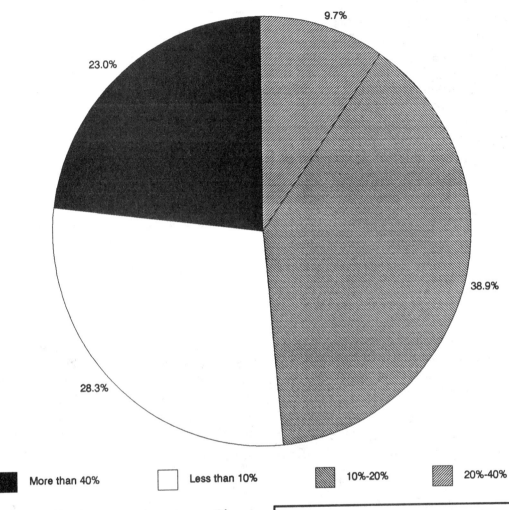

■ More than 40%	□ Less than 10%	▨ 10%-20% ▨ 20%-40%

cent of their software licenses on maintenance. Given the normal attrition that occurs with companies getting into financial difficulty and dropping old applications in favor of newer ones, this is very impressive.

13. Sales Commissions on Selling Maintenance

Typically, companies don't pay sales commissions on selling maintenance, but a few firms paid the same commissions as for their product and a few paid a reduced rate.

Commission on Maintenance	% Resp
No reply	15.4%
None	59.2%
Same	14.8%
Reduced	10.7%

Just to complete the set, there were a couple of respondents who paid higher commissions for maintenance. They both commented that getting customers on maintenance was critical to the success of their installation.

In retrospect, I think I should have asked if anyone else was paid a commission on maintenance. I have seen several cases where sales received a commission on maintenance that was sold with the initial license, and the support department was paid on license renewals. I believe that this will help focus the support department and the support manager on maintenance renewals. The percentage need not be high. One idea that occurs to me is to pay a commission on renewals and to deduct a penalty on non renewals. It seems to me that the penalty should be higher than the commission. I like the fact that this helps share the pain when a customer fails to renew their maintenance. My only hesitation is that some percentage of non renewal situations are beyond the control of the support staff. The company is consolidating data centers, the software has been replaced, there are no new releases to help justify staying on support. I would be interested in hearing from anyone who has tried this type of commission plan for the support department.

14. Percentage of Revenue from Support

If you look at the graph on the previous page, you will see that the median company is generating ten to twenty percent of its revenue from support. This is excluding the 33 percent of the companies who didn't reply or who answered that they received no revenue from support. I was pleased that this was close to the 31 percent who answered that they didn't have any licenses on maintenance.

I would have hoped that more than 9.7 percent of the companies would have gotten over 40 percent of their revenues from support, but that does take time.

15. Site License Multi-Copy Maintenance

Thirty-six percent of the companies didn't answer this question. (I assume that they don't offer or sell site licenses.) In fact, one respondent asked, "Does anyone sell site licenses or is it just a myth?" Well,

this question certainly shows that a lot of companies are selling site licenses. I have a number of client clients who sell a significant percentage of their product and revenue via site licenses.

Site license Maintenance	% Resp
No reply	36.1%
Same %	30.2%
X single	9.5%
One CPU	8.3%
Other	16.6%

If you can count on one point of contact, I believe you should charge the customer the same percentage of revenue for maintenance, but apply that to the then current site license fee. This allows the customer to hold down their maintenance fee by acting as a liaison and answering first-level questions within their site. If all of the licensees want to call your support organization directly, it is appropriate for each one of them to pay the single CPU price (this is the "X single" option).

I was disappointed to see companies providing support to a site for a single CPU support fee. They are not being fully compensated for the work they are doing. It also bothers me from an equity point of view. The single-CPU customers who are paying maintenance are subsidizing the site license customers.

The other category was "other" and it got a respectable showing. Given the new nature of site licenses and all of the variables, it is reasonable that many agreements will be negotiated and tailored to the specific situation.

16. Percentage of Licenses on Maintenance by Computer Type and Product Price

The PC respondents have the largest "0 percent" and "no reply" with 43 percent. These are probably the low priced retail type software companies. In my experience, it is difficult to charge for maintenance with products under $1,000. The second table below shows that product price has a very strong influence on the percentage of licenses on maintenance. Over 50 percent of the LAN, minicomputer, workstation and mainframe vendors have over 75 percent of their licenses on maintenance. Workstation vendors are similar to PC vendors. Only 26 percent of them have over 75 percent of their licenses on maintenance (this is even lower than the PC rate). On the other hand, only 12 percent of them didn't reply or have no customers on maintenance. At least they are trying to get their customers on support.

	No Response	0%	≤25%	25%-50%	50%-75%	>75%
PC	18%	25%	11%	8%	8%	29%
LAN	4%	7%	0%	11%	21%	57%
Mini	5%	5%	14%	14%	0%	63%
Work Station	6%	6%	20%	13%	27%	26%
Main-frame	5%	0%	22%	11%	11%	50%

The table below supports my experience that it is very difficult to get customers with low price products to sign up for support. I believe that this is partially due to the economics in that 15 percent of a $100 product is only $15 and at this price invoicing costs become significant. I think the more serious problem is that you only sign up for maintenance on products with which you are involved. If you view the product as a throw away, why would you sign up for maintenance.

Twenty-five percent of licenses on maintenance is the highest level for a product priced under $100 product. With prices under $1,000, a few brave souls have gotten maintenance up to the 50 percent to 75 percent level. There is a dramatic increase with prices over $1,000, and over $10,000, the maintenance levels are very impressive. One of the basic trade-offs in the software industry is between "quick and dirty" products that are easy to explain and easy to buy, and complex products that require sophisticated selling, education, training, and support. I have always realized that complex products offer barriers to entry which make them more valuable. In most cases, these more complex products are also more expensive. Their profitability should also be supported by higher percent of licenses on maintenance.

	No Response	0%	<25%	25%-50%	50%-75%	>75%
<$100	42%	46%	12%	0%	0%	0%
<$1K	22%	35%	16%	8%	8%	0%
$1K-$10K	4%	12%	12%	19%	12%	39%
>$10K	2%	6%	13%	5%	13%	68%

B. Support Survey (Nov. 1991)

This year's survey paints a portrait of a maturing field. No longer an infant, the software business is assuming many of the traits of an established industry. More than 65% of the respondents have been in business for more than five years, a doubling of the percentage reported just two years ago. And perhaps because of the recession, there was also a dramatic drop in the number of newborns (companies less than a year old), which were down from 9.3% in 1990 to just 1.7% in this year's survey.

But like gangly teenagers, many software firms are experiencing growing pains as they adjust to internal changes and a rapidly evolving environment. And like teenagers, many software vendors aren't fully conscious of all of the changes and challenges they'll face as they mature. In particular, relationships with customers, dealers, and employees need to evolve as the years pass, and nowhere are these changes more apparent or more awkward than in the complex relationships involved in supporting products. Thus, many companies are experiencing (or maybe are about to experience) the adolescent blues. We hope that you find our survey useful in helping you ride out the awkward stages on the way to a more successful future.

More than 65% of the respondents have been in business for more than five years, a doubling of the percentage reported just two years ago.

The recession also seems to have taken its toll. The responding companies were smaller than those of past surveys; most respondents' companies (69%)

had revenues of less than $1 million per year. In contrast, 46.2% of the respondents to the January, 1991 support survey worked at companies with revenues under $1 million.

1. Product Price

The recession may also be why more companies are selling products in the range of $1,000 to $10,000 this year (42.8%) than last year (28.4%). Conversely, fewer responding companies had flagship products in the $25,000 and above category this year (15.6%) than last year (20.7%). In general, the $1,000 to $10,000 price range seems to be ideal for many firms; smaller companies will buy products at this price, and larger companies require significantly less re-

view and approval for products costing less than $10,000. At most companies, orders for products costing more than this must usually be approved by several additional levels of management.

2. Maintenance as a percentage of total revenue

Perhaps because their product lines are maturing, about 13% of responding companies are reaping between thirty and forty percent of their revenues from support, and about 8% report that more than 40% of company revenues come from support.

Once again, the median company receives between 10 and 20 percent of its total revenue from mainte-

Maintenance Revenue as a Percentage of Total

Revenue

November, 1991

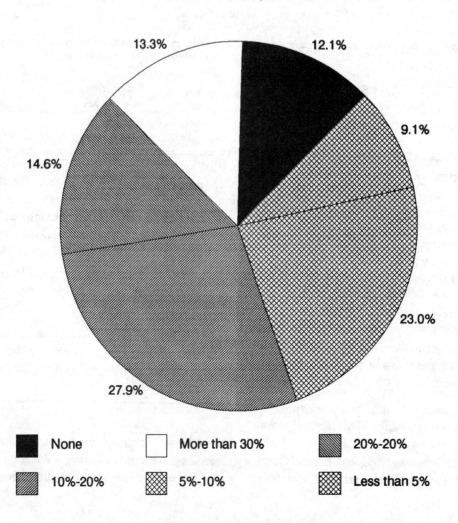

nance. This is consistent with earlier surveys, but it is a little higher.

In this year's survey on operating expenses (September, 1991), we found that companies receive, on average, 15.9% of their reved e f'om support. In comparison, our last support surv ((Ja'pa y, 1991) showed that the median maintenance revenue was 10 to 20 percent at companies that charge for support. The difference is that we now find the same median for all companies, including the ones who don't charge for support.

Thus, many maturing companies are generating significant maintenance revenue from a captive market: their own customer bases. I recently talked to a CEO of a company with very faithful customers. His company is making a limited number of new sales because they have almost saturated their market.

Surprisingly, his firm hasn't quit supporting its current product in a mad rush to create a new product line. Indeed, they are doing exactly the opposite: they are hard at work developing new features and capabilities for their existing product. They consider their maintenance contracts to be equivalent to selling their software on a subscription basis. As long as they continue to deliver a stream of good updates to their customers, they expect that their customers will reward them with continued patronage.

When companies compare the benefits of improving existing products to the risk of developing new ones, which they may not be able to sell to their current customers or to new markets, maintenance contracts look very attractive. In fact, customers who pay maintenance fees may represent one of the few markets where products are purchased on their technical merits alone, where sales and marketing are largely superfluous. What a "techie's" dream!

3. Maintenance as a percentage of total revenue vs. the number of years in business

As you would expect, there is a strong correlation between the number of years a company has been in business and the percentage of revenue coming from maintenance.

Of the 173 companies that responded, only one that had been in business less than a year had any maintenance revenue, which was only 5 to 10 percent of it's total gross revenue, indicating that the company

must have limited the free support period to a few months and has already begun to receive some maintenance renewals.

Only 15% of the companies that were between one and two years old had maintenance revenues ranging from 10 to 20 percent of their total revenue. The remainder received less than ten percent. This is understandable; if you sell twice as many copies of your product in the second year as in the first, and you charge 15% of your purchase price for maintenance, 7.5% of your total revenue will come from maintenance in the second year. I am very impressed that anyone can get 10 to 20 percent of their revenue from maintenance by the second year.

After companies have been in business for two years, 15 percent of them receive more than 30 percent of their revenues from support. There doesn't seem to be any clear path leading to even higher levels of support. When you work out the numbers, these long-term percentages depend upon many factors, including installation rates, price changes in the product, maintenance renewal rates, et

4. Number of customers

There is a wide va"ation in the number of customers, but the median seems to be about 250. In January, the median range was 100 to 500. Much of the variation stems from the equally broad range of product prices.

Number of Customers	% of Respondents
< 10	4.6%
10-50	16.8%
50-250	29.5%
250-1K	27.7%
1K-5K	13.3%
5K-10K	4.0%
10K-25K	2.3%
> 25K	1.7%

5. Number of new customers in the last year

The median number of new customers added last year was 50. This is a reasonable number of new customers if a company has been in business for five years and has 250 customers, but it indicates that many companies aren't dramatically increasing their sales to new customers. I also noticed that a significant number of companies had added very few new customers in the last year compared with their total customer base. If the continuing development of these companies' flagship products has slowed down, these products may no longer be competitive, and new sales may slow down. I worry that this is exactly what is happening to these companies.

Number of New Customers Last Year	% of Respondents
None	1.2%
< 10	8.5%
10-50	2.4%
50-250	24.3%
250-1K	15.6%
1K-5K	4.6%
5K-10K	1.2%
10K-25K	0.6%
> 25K	0.6%

Conversely, if you aren't adding about 17% more code each year to enhance your product, you aren't delivering enough added value to justify the money your customers pay for support, and your prospects won't be able to justify your new product price.

Is your company cannibalizing its current success? Several years ago, I read an article in one of the PC magazines that argued that the cost per kilobyte of object code in word processors had decreased 17% per year. This pleased me because hardware price performance has improved 15 to 20 percent each year since the 1950s, and it seems to me that software should experience roughly the same rate of technological improvement as hardware.

Indeed, many customers may never speak with anyone at your company but the support staff.

I suspect this is true, and that this phenomenon explains why few companies charge more than 15% annually for maintenance. If the vendor delivers 17% more code each year in updates, the customers should feel good about paying 15% of the purchase price for that code.

Conversely, if you aren't adding about 17% more code each year to enhance your product, you aren't delivering enough added value to justify the money your customers pay for support, and your prospects won't be able to justify your new product price. Eventually, you will either have to decrease the price of your product or suffer the consequences of not being competitive on a cost per kilobyte of compiled code.

Interestingly, 23.1% of the respondents to this year's survey charge more than 15% for annual maintenance. If these companies are going to remain competitive, they will have to include other services for this annual fee, provide very significant updates, or both.

6. Bonuses for Support

Ever since Tom Peters wrote his famous book, *In Search of Excellence*, everyone gives lip service to quality and great customer service. But few companies put their money where their excellence allegedly is. When asked whether they give bonuses for support, almost half picked the response, "Are you kidding?" And only a third of the responding companies include the support group in the bonus plan for the entire company.

Finally, a minuscule percentage of the respondents give the support staff special bonuses, which typically range from one to four percent. These support bonuses are small, but they're great morale-builders for the support team.

The pattern of responses indicates that many people still have unbelievably shortsighted attitudes toward their support staffs. Few managers seem to understand the crucial role that the support staff plays in determining their companies' reputations. Indeed, many customers may never speak with anyone at your company but the support staff. Do you really want someone who is demoralized, underpaid, and/or overloaded, to be your company's sole representative?

And if you're going to be getting anywhere from fifteen to thirty percent of your revenues from maintenance (and chances are you will, as your company becomes more established), you need to make sure that the people who provide support are top-notch people with friendly, helpful attitudes toward your customers. The attitude that support people are just glorified receptionists is just penny-wise and pound-foolish.

Bonuses for Support	% of Respondents
Not indicated	13.3%
Are you kidding?	48.6%
General company bonus	32.9%
Percentage of support fees	2.9%
	4.0%
Percentage of maintenance renewals	

7. First- and second-level support

It's important to understand that there are several different levels of support. First-level support includes answering questions based upon knowledge of a product's external features, such as the user-interface and existing documentation. This level of support also involves keeping track of reported bugs to advise clients of fixes or work-arounds that have already been discovered. Thus, first-level support includes knowing how the product should work, but not how to actually fix "broken" code.

Second-level support personnel work with the source code directly to make bug-fixes. Non-programmers provide most first-level support, while developers provide all second-level support.

In many cases, developers continue to provide support for new products until the software is stable. Interestingly, relatively few of the support people who are programmers but not developers have access to the source code. Companies seem to be drawing a sharp line separating support and development.

23.7%	Developers provide all support.
17.9%	Programmers who are not developers, provide first-level support. They don't have access to the code.
5.2%	Programmers who are not developers provide first level support. They do have access to the source code.
56.1%	Non-programmers provide first-level support.

These figures are similar to what we found last year. This year we asked whether the programmers (not developers) had access to the source code, and as you can see, only 22% of the programmers who aren't developers have access to the source code.

8. Support from dealers

As you can see, dealers aren't an important part of the support equation for most companies. A few companies use dealers to provide primary support, but it is difficult to recruit and train dealers for this role.

Support From Dealers	% of Respondents
Not relevant because we don't sell through dealers	50.9%
Dealers provide occasional support	23.7%
Our dealers don't provide support	15.0%
Dealers provide primary support	8.7%

9. Support managers

46.2% of the companies have a support manager. Last year we found the following breakout of titles in the support department:

Vice President	11.7%
Director	11.7%
Manager	23.3%
Total	46.7%

10. To whom does the support group report?

The president or CEO is the person most likely to manage support. The manager of the development group is the next most likely. Few companies have their support staffs report to people in the sales and marketing departments.

To Whom Does the Support Group Report?	% of Respondents
CEO	57.8%
Development	20.2%
Marketing	5.8%
Sales	2.9%

11. How many calls does each support person answer every month?

This is one of those basic parameters that every good support manager, even CEOs and development managers, should know. Almost 90% of the respondents knew the average number of calls each member of the support staff answers every month.

The median number of calls is 50 to 100 per person per month. That is less than five calls per day, and assuming that each call is less than thirty minutes each, this should leave the support people with time to fix problems, write documentation, or test new products. At the other end of the spectrum, support people who answer more than 500 calls per month may have little time to do anything else. The length of the average support call also affects this.

Calls Per Month Per Support Person	% of Respondents
Don't know	11.0%
< 10	12.1%
10-25	15.0%
25-50	10.4%
50-100	14.9%
100-250	19.7%
250-500	12.7%
> 500	2.9%

12. Cost per support call

Very few people, however, knew their cost per support call, and I believe that many of those who answered this question underestimated this figure. The following is a sample calculation:

Let's say that the monthly cost for a support person (fully burdened) is $3,000.

The median number of calls per support person is 75 calls per month.

The fully burdened cost per call is therefore $3,000/75 = $40.

I have talked to people who said, "We pay our support person $20 per hour, and our average call is less than 30 minutes. Thus, our cost per call is only $10." This line of reasoning is only correct, however, if your support staff has an endless queue of support calls.

The reality is that you can't fully load your support people and maintain adequate responsiveness, even if you drive them crazy. You must therefore include the cost of their time between calls in your calculation of the cost of the calls that they handle.

I think many of you have a cost per call of more than $100 because you have more expensive people (engineers and programmers) handling the calls, and they are spending more time on the calls than you realize.

Cost Per Support Call	% of Respondents
Don't know	59.5%
< $1	1.2%
$1-$5	9.8%
$5-$10	11.0%
$10-$15	4.0%
$15-$20	5.2%
$20-$25	2.9%
$25-$50	2.3%
> $50	1.2%

Money is the universal language, and knowing the cost per call allows you to translate support calls into a dollar cost.

I think that it is very important that you know your true cost per call so that you can decide which development activities are the most cost-effective ways to improve your product. For example, let's suppose that you received 20 calls in a month because your new installation manual is unclear. This may not sound like an emergency, but if each support call costs $100, you're losing $2,000 each month (or about two-thirds of the salary of a support person or technical writer) just because the instructions aren't clear. Once company managers realize this, it should be clear that the manual urgently needs to be fixed. Money is the universal language, and knowing the cost per call allows you to translate support calls into a dollar cost.

13. Average time to call back

Average time to Call Back	% of Respondents
No reply	1.7%
Try to answer all calls with very few call-backs	34.1%
90% of calls answered, 10 minutes to call back others	23.7%
30 minutes	12.7%
1 hour	12.1%
2 hours	9.2%
4 hours	7.5%
8 hours	1.7%
2 days	0.6%

I was really pleased with this incredible display of responsiveness. Only about 10% of the responding companies usually take more than two hours to call their customers back. In my experience, customers feel that vendors are being responsive as long the vendors call them back within two hours. Conversely, I don't know of a single case in which the average time to call back is more than two hours and the customers are happy with support.

Customer satisfaction with any company's support also depends upon the company's previous support record. I worked for a company that initially tried to answer all of the customers' questions while they were still on the phone because the firm didn't want to pay to return phone calls. But as sales grew, they had to institute a policy of calling back within 30 minutes. New customers were ecstatic to get answers so quickly, but the old customers remembered getting immediate answers and were unhappy that support was "slipping."

Our survey focused on average response time, but it's also important to plan for peaks in the demand for support. I worked with one company in which the support people averaged 20 to 30 calls per day (400 to 600 per month), which is a reasonable workload if each day's work is "average." But the firm sold an accounting package, and at the end of each month, customers had to wait eight hours or more for assistance because the customers, mostly accountants, were all trying to reconcile their books and write checks at the same time. Often, it took the support people more than a week to catch up.

Such poor planning for predictable surges in demand is inexcusable. It's unfair to your customers, and it's unfair expect to your support staff to face certain disaster every month. If you have such a problem, the first step you should take is to avoid scheduling vacations and training during the peak period. Next, you can assign other people, such as developers and managers, to help out with support during the worst part of the monthly crush of calls.

Finally, consider hiring part-time workers to help out with the extra load. In particular, parents who have left the company to stay home with their children might be willing to provide support during critical peaks because such work could fit in well with their lifestyle.

Once your support department falls behind, the problem often gets worse, because the longer you take to call customers back, the more likely they are to forget or leave out crucial information that could help you solve the problem.

Furthermore, the longer customers wait, the more they feel justified in asking all the questions they've saved up. If it takes a couple of days for the support staff to call back, many people feel that they'd better ask all of their questions at once, because they don't know how long it might take to get an answer the next time they call. In one case, this phenomenon increased the average length of a company's support calls from 20 minutes to more than 30 minutes.

Almost a quarter of the respondents, about 23%, say they don't give refunds under any circumstances.

14. Money-back guarantees

Our survey results point out what many firms have discovered the hard way: refund policies often pit your company against your customers, engendering bad feelings on both sides.

Almost a quarter of the respondents, about 23%, say they don't give refunds under any circumstances. Many of these companies (48%) sell their products for more than $10,000, which is a chunk of change few companies could easily refund. Conversely, none of the companies that sell their software for less than $500 refused to give refunds.

Product Price	% Giving No Funds
< $500	0%
$500-$10K	12%
> $10K	48%

But 22% gave refunds only during a limited time after the purchase of the product, which is likely to get your company into an argument with its customers about when the clock starts running. If your company sells its product directly and registers all users, this isn't a problem. If you sell your product through distribution channels, you don't have a clue as to when the customer bought your product. If you insist upon a copy of the purchase agreement, you can end up arguing bitterly with your customers, who can always claim they lost the receipt if the limited time period has expired.

About a sixth (17.3%) give refunds only if the product is technically flawed and therefore fails to work correctly. My experience is that this policy often invites arguments about what constitutes a failure. Customers think that the product failed if it didn't allow them to solve their problems. Technical support personnel take a much more narrow view of the problem; to them, if a product works as described in the documentation, it's not a flaw. I therefore worry that this policy ends up pitting your customers against your support people.

You may worry that you'll lose money if you offer a no-questions-asked refund, but most companies offering such a policy find that few people take advantage of the generosity of such an offer. For instance, I know a support technician who supported the first back-up software package. He received many calls from customers who couldn't install the software because of hard-disk controller problems. His approach was to offer callers the choice of either a refund or an attempt to fix the problem. He always said "If we can't fix your problem, you can always take the refund." In almost all cases, this offer defused an explosive situation. Very few customers took his initial offer of a refund; most of them wanted the product to work much more than they wanted their money back. Surprisingly, many of them were willing to do a lot of work to help him find and fix the problems. Some of them even waited days and weeks to get fixes for their problems. In a few cases, the problems were insurmountable, and customers were finally given a refund. If refunds are only given for product failure, I hope your support people have this type of non-confrontational attitude.

About a sixth of the respondents (15.6%) only gave refunds for a limited time and required the customer to give an explanation for the refund request. Again, this policy may generate customer animosity because customers and vendors disagree about when the clock starts ticking. It also introduces the need for an explanation, which can cause bad customer relations if you and your customers have different ideas about what constitutes a reasonable explanation. One of my clients who required an explanation was often told "I changed my mind. I don't have the time to learn how to use this product at this time." So what do you do in such cases? Tell the customer his explanation isn't reasonable and hope he takes your criticism well? Unless you insist that the product must fail before you issue a refund, little is gained by requiring an explanation. Indeed, you may even scare off prospective buyers by giving them reason to believe that you will try to weasel out of the refund.

A small minority of those responding (7.5%) impose no time limit, but require an explanation. Again, you should ask yourself what you gain by such a policy.

Only 6.4% offer a no-questions asked policy, which seems like the most sensible policy for most low-end software.

At the other extreme, 5.2% only give a refund if customers "really complain." Such a policy creates a "lose-lose" situation because it is essentially a "no-refund policy" with an exception made for those who complain bitterly. Indeed, many respondents who have such a policy say they have never given a refund. Not only are you rewarding people for behaving aggressively toward your own support people, who must deal with increasingly more irate customers, but you penalize all of the polite customers who feel they are entitled to a refund but are too nice to make a stink about it. Do you really want to create such negative feelings? Do you really want to withhold a refund until the customer is screaming through the phone at your support staff?

Why should you offer refunds? One of the common themes running through the comments we received in response to this question is the idea that refunds are a terrible thing, and your top priority is to minimize the amount of money that you have to refund. If you believe that, you're missing the point. The following are the best reasons why you should offer refunds:

1. Refunds increase the order rate.

When people are thinking about buying your product, a no-questions-asked refund often suppresses the part of the customer's brain that worries about all the things that could go wrong just long enough for the customer's speech center to kick into action and say, "I'll take it." Offering a money back guarantee reduces their risk and increases the orders you get from the fence-sitters; studies in almost all industries show that guarantees increase orders. This increase can be dramatic, and can sometimes amount to as much as ten percent.

2. Refunds keep unhappy buyers from hurting you.

A good reputation is hard to build but easy to ruin. A commonly cited rule of thumb is that one unhappy buyer will tell 20 people. I guess I would rather have the unhappy buyer tell me so I can refund his money and squelch further complaints. Furthermore, some people who buy your product probably shouldn't have. I believe that returning their money is much better than letting them damage your reputation.

Finally, if you have a good product, and your marketing and sales staffs present it honestly to the right prospects, your refund rate should be quite low, *less than two or three percent*. Most of the companies offering guarantees (even unlimited ones) refund less than two or three percent of their orders, which is less than they pay for credit-card processing.

If your refund rate is higher than this, something is probably wrong with your product or your marketing and sales efforts. One final note: If your customers pay by credit card, many of them already have a no-questions-asked, money-back guarantee. The credit card company will refund your customer's money and debit your account, no questions asked. Would you rather have potential customers feel good about you, or their credit-card companies?

15. Customer satisfaction surveys

Customer satisfaction is a hot topic in most circles these days, and here's what we found out when we asked about such surveys:

Customer Satisfaction Survey	% Respondents
Never have done one	40.5%
Do one every year	34.1%
Did one once, but didn't find it useful	4.6%
One included with product literature	4.0%

The most common answer to this question was that people had never done a customer satisfaction survey. Most of those who had done one continue to do them. Very few of the people who had conducted customer satisfaction surveys didn't find them useful. Including a survey with the product literature seems like an inexpensive way to gather some very useful information. The only problem with this approach is that your new customers have not actually used the product at the point when they get the survey, and therefore can't give you much useful feedback. They may intend to complete the survey later and set it aside with good intentions. However, your survey and other product literature, like many warranty cards, will probably be put back in the box and filed on a shelf, or thrown away.

16. Copy protection

Most vendors hate the idea of someone stealing their software, and customers hate the inconvenience of intrusive copy-protection schemes

Copy Protection	% of Respondents
None	30.6%
Hard-code name	29.4%
Check registration	25.4%
Software-based protection	23.6%
Software key	10.4%
Ask for information from the manual	1.1%

As you can see, the least intrusive approaches are the most popular; a third of the respondents say they use no copy protection at all. Hard-coding the customer's company name in the installed product may deter customers from giving a friend a copy of your product because many people don't want their names advertised on the first screen. Some people might help their friends steal software, but most don't want the entire world to know it. Of course, this scheme has its problems. For instance, many programs ask for the licensee's name and use the response to create the first screen. But because many people know this, many software screens display such licensee names as "Glargon of Zeldernon." Furthermore, many people copy the product diskettes to their hard disks, then run the installation program, so the original can be installed on any number of systems, and each "first screen" can display a different name.

Checking registration is another common method of copy protection. If you use this approach, you need some method of tracking the number of support calls for each registered user; if you get 100 calls from different people all using the same registration number, you can be fairly sure that it has been pirated.

The method of copy protection used seems to depend upon the hardware platform. Most workstation vendors (41%) reported using software-based techniques to thwart illegal copying. At the other end of the spectrum, none of the Macintosh vendors used software-based copy protection.

Some vendors (10.4%) are using software keys, hardware devices that look like the ends of cables and attach to the computer, often to one of the parallel or serial ports. The key contains a code, and software reads the code and confirms that the correct key is present. This is clearly the most secure approach because replicating the hardware is much more difficult than breaking a software copy-protection scheme. Hardware keys were used by 20.8% of the workstation companies and, surprisingly, by 14.2% of the companies that sell Macintosh products.

Policy	% of Respondents
We check registration and won't give them support un less they pay	31.2%
We check, but give support even if they haven't paid	21.4%
No reply	21.4%
Not applicable because we give free support	17.3%
We charge for support but don't enforece the rule	6.4%
We let the support person make the decision	3.5%

17. Customers who don't pay for support: What is your policy?

I feel that if you are going to charge for support, you should enforce the rules and refuse to provide support to customers who refuse to pay. It is unfair to the paying customers for the non-paying customers to get a free ride.

As an industry, we are getting tougher about forcing customers to pay for support. Last year, we found that only 25% of the companies charging for support screened the calls. Half gave support to everyone who called in, even those who refused to pay for support. About a sixth (16.7%) left the decision to their support people. This year, 52.6% of the respondents say they screen their calls, and only 21.4% provide it free of charge.

However, if you try to make customers pay for support, you will eventually have to decide what you'll do if someone who hasn't paid for support reports a problem with your product. I believe that you should resolve the problem, even though the customer hasn't paid for support. Why? I feel that your moral obligations under the basic warranty require you to fix such problems. Regardless of what the law says (and warranty rules vary from state to state), I believe that we owe our customers this level of support even if they haven't paid for maintenance. Also, most developers want to learn about all known bugs so that problems in the software can be corrected.

I believe that this dilemma is what makes it so difficult for many software companies to really hang tough and refuse to provide support when customers refuse to pay. (I am impressed with the industry's success in getting customers to pay for support.)

Some respondents commented that their companies do not allow customers using their product to drop support. I am not sure how they enforce this policy, but I have clients who sell support very aggressively and who have convinced most of their customers to continue paying for support.

Still, your company will eventually receive a call from someone who believes that they have found a bug, wants you to fix it, and is not about to pay you to fix bugs. Your choices are:

1. Ignore it and risk their wrath.

2. Give in and help them on the phone.

3. Come up with another approach.

The problem is that many of the worst complainers think they have found bugs, but have really only revealed their incompetence as users. (They didn't read the manual.) In these cases, customers have managed to get free support by complaining loudly and persistently. This just doesn't seem right.

Some companies tell customers who haven't paid for support that they must document their "bugs" in writing and submit the "bug" by fax or mail. These companies then try to fax or mail an answer to the customer within twenty-four hours. Many of the people who call with a "real problem" never send in their written descriptions because they solve their own problems when they try to document them. Conversely, when customers discover real bugs, you can use the detailed written data to figure out how to help them. If they fax you a legitimate problem, you can always call them up and work with them on the phone.

I like this approach because it makes it easier for your employees to handle sticky situations; it's easier to enforce your policy if there is a reasonable way to deal with the problem calls.

18. What does the annual support fee include?

Most of the companies who indicated having an annual support fee reported that the fee includes updates and phone support with the support fee. Very few companies provide phone support only.

What does the annual support fee include?	% of Respondents
Not applicable	20.8%
Includes updates and phone support	22.5%
Includes services other than phone support and updates	5.8%
Phone support only	4.0%
Not indicated	53.2%

19. Annual support fee as a percentage of product purchase price

This year, we found much greater diversity in annual support fees than we did in 1990. Although 15% is the nominal support fee, the median this year was between 12 and 15 percent.

Percentage of Price	% of Respondents
Not indicated	26.6%
<5%	5.2%
5-10%	6.4%
10-12%	15.0%
12-15%	13.3%
15% exactly	11.6%
15-20%	15.6%
20%	7.5%

The fees this year are significantly higher than they were last year. In particular, I am very pleased with the big decline in companies charging less than 10% and the corresponding increase in companies charging more than 15 percent.

20. Free Support Period

The most common free support period is 90 days. A year was the next most common free support period.

Support Period	% of Respondents
Not indicated	19.1%
Always free	16.8%
30 days	11.6%
90 days	31.2%
6 months	1.7%
1 year	22.0%

If one considers just those companies who responded and charge for support, about a third of this year's respondents provide one year of free support. Last year, 42% of the companies provided a year or more of free support.

Reducing the length of the free support period is a low-key way of increasing revenues. It appears that many of our readers have been doing this in the last year.

21. Policy for reinstating support for customers who have let support lapse and want it back

If you make it too easy to drop support and then reinstate it, your customers will drop support when it expires and pick it up again when you come out with a new release or update that has features they want.

I have a client whose customer base figured out that his company came out with a major release every two or three years. The percentage of customers on maintenance usually dropped by twenty to thirty percent during the time between releases. But when new releases were announced, customers rushed to pay for reinstatement of their support contracts. This company allowed the prodigal customers to reinstate support by simply paying the normal, one-year fee for a year of support. From the customer's point of view, this strategy made sense. They didn't usually

need phone support except for the period just after they had installed a new release. However, the company had trouble providing good support when its revenues varied so much, which was unfair to the good customers who always paid for support. In response, the company implemented a new policy. Customers who had dropped support had to pay all of the support fees that they would have paid if they had never dropped it. In addition, the company also required their prodigal customers to pay a penalty and pay for the next year in advance.

Policy	% of Respondents
Not indicated	26.6%
No problem, just pay the current support fee	34.1%
Pay for the time they were off support	23.1%
Pay a penalty for dropping support	12.7%
Pay for next year in advance	6.9%
Don't allow them to come back	0.6%

The firm explained its new policy at the same time it announced its next release. All of the customers who had dropped support were given 90 days to pay for support under the old terms, but after 90 days, the new rules would apply. A salesperson then called all the customers who hadn't yet signed up for support at the end of 30 days to insure that everyone understood the new rules. The company didn't want customers to claim they had never received the letter informing them of the new policy. The result of the new policy was that customers continuously paid for support, and the company had more money to pay for support staff and product development.

22. Making the transition from free to fee

I was really pleased to see that so few companies had encountered problems when they started charging for support. No one had changed to a fee-based system and gone back to offering free support. I was also surprised that the majority of companies had always charged for it. I feel that we are seeing a new generation of software companies who assume customers should pay for support.

Transition	% of Respondents
Not indicated	12.1%
Still free	8.5%
Always charged	52.0%
Changed to fee and back to free	0%
Changed to fee, lots of problems	0.6%
Moderate problems	6.4%
No problems	11.0%

23. Conclusion

Support can be very profitable and can provide the long-term basis for a solid business. It can also insulate you from month-to-month variations in sales.

However, support is also an area of the business that requires lots of attention. If you pay attention to your customers and take good care of them, your business will prosper in the long run.

C.   Miscellaneous   (1991)

1. 900 Numbers (Jan)

Dear Mr. Bowen:

I was greatly disappointed to see your brief "question and answer" on 900 numbers for customer support. The piece was so sketchy and incomplete that it, in my view, did more to confuse the reader than give a balanced appraisal of 900 services for user support. In my discussions with over 250 software companies, I have not had a single company raise a concern about a "porno association" with 900 numbers. There has been some concern about business blocking of 900 numbers, but no concern that their image would be tarnished as you indicate.

900 service may not be inexpensive. But compared to what? 800 service? POTS service constantly busy? The focus should properly be on what the technology company is trying to accomplish with 900 service

- to earn a profit, subsidize support, open new pay-per-call avenues of support (such as BBS/audiotext during non-business hours) which reduce overall demand for customer support, set up priority support for customers who need immediate support, and so on.

Contrary to your assertions in point 3 of your article, there are means available to address the concerns of an "irate" customer.Contrary to your Revlon example, I could provide dozens of other examples with radically different results. What does the Revlon promotional 900 service have to do with a business service over 900 for customer support? Just for starters, an entertainment based 900 program has its largest cost advertising. Is that true for software companies? No. I find the lack of effort put into this piece very disturbing.

Ben Greenspan
NexTel ,
(415) 931-3684

Dear Ben:

While no one has raised the "porno association" with you, I have had several clients and readers raise that issue. I suspect that most people would be reluctant to be that open with a vendor.

The business alternative that I see most companies considering is using 900 numbers as a billing alternative for support. Most companies have annual support fees which entitle customers to phone in for customer support. The problem comes up when customers don't pay the annual fee, but the call up for help. The alternatives include:

- * **Get a credit card number**
- * **No pay no talk**
- * **Bill them for the time**

Small companies and individuals have access to credit cards so the real collection problem is the larger companies where invoices without a purchase order can be a problem. It turns out that these same big companies block 900 numbers so using the 900 numbers to collect these hourly support fees may not be practical. The objective is to automatically collect the hourly support fees via 900 numbers.

I find it interesting that so many companies felt that they would never use a 900 number. This reaction seems to be fairly widespread. There was an article in the September/October 1990 issue of TeleProfessional on "Customer Service and 900 Numbers" by Carol Scovotti. Her conclusion was "Trend or not, 900-numbers have no place in business to business customer service."

I very much would like to interview any software companies who are using 900 numbers. Their real experience will tell more than our individual opinions. Please have any of your software company clients call me.

Thanks,
Dave

2. 900 Numbers = Better Quality Support (Jun)

(I received this letter in response to my comments in the January 1991 issue regarding my concern about using 900 numbers.)

Dear Dave,

I *CALL* my vendors' 900 numbers because I get immediate (usually high quality) answers, and this costs less than wasting my time waiting on the phone.

Leon Stevens
The Galt Company
618-548-3274

Dear Leon,

Thanks for the note. I have heard the same thing from a number of people. It appears that 900 numbers are gaining a positive image for immediate quality answers rather than the negative image I had worried about.

I am rather impressed that some of the vendors I have talked with are delaying offering a 900 number until they can provide top quality support. I talked to one company that has already implemented a 900 number and doubled their support staff. This company has been very pleased with the customer reaction to its 900 number. They offer free support to their dealers and end users must pay for support using the 900 number. They have been surprised that their dealers are actually calling the 900 number also because they feel that this higher quality support is worth the price. I have tried to talk this company into being interviewed for a feature article, but they seem reluctant. I suspect that it is because the

900 number is turning into a competitive advantage and they don't want their competitors to know the details of what they are doing.

At this time, my only concern with 900 numbers is economic. Empirically, it appears that 50% of the revenues go to someone other than the software vendor who is providing support. I have read and heard of a number of cases where the software companies are ending up recovering half of the costs of providing support. This isn't making money, but at least it is recovering some of the costs. I have talked to several people who claim that their approach isn't this expensive. I am following up on this and hope to have the details in the next few months.

The ideal scenario would be for 900 numbers to end up with a quality image, and for software companies be able to make money providing this support. We may be getting closer to this than I previously thought.

Thanks for the note.
Dave

3. Macintosh Developers (Jan)

Dear Dave:

I am responding to an article in the August issue of Software Success, "Whither the Macintosh Developers". You stated that the number of Macintosh developers dropped dramatically in 1990 and you did not know why. Well... did you know that the developers program was free of charge until 1990. Starting in 1990, Macintosh developers are charged $600.00 per year. This means that all the companies that had previous developer status were faced with a decision in 1990. (Was the $600.00 fee worth the benefits Apple was offering for their developers service). Many companies who were automatically renewing their developer status every year did not do so in 1990 for this reason. I thought twice about it myself but decided to keep my developer status. You must realize that you can be a Macintosh developer without actually having an Apple developer status. Therefore, there are a significant number of developers out there that do not show up in your stats. The benefits of being a certified developer or "Apple partner" are; frequent mailings of technical literature, CD roms with 500 megabytes of information, programming examples and upgrades to the operating system, Hypercard and much more. Developers also receive very substantial discounts on Apple hardware and free connect time to Applelink (Apple's on line developer service) and answers to technical questions.

Now, about Windows 3.0. Gee, I wonder where Microsoft got the idea for that? Did you know that Apple released the first windows machine in 1982 called the Lisa(Reg) which later became the Macintosh. I remember when it was released, I went down to my local Apple computer store and got a demo. I was extremely impressed. But the majority of people were saying that it was a toy. Who needs to use a mouse, icons, and windows anyway? Apple Computer (Reg) took a big chance introducing such a revolutionary concept. It wasn't long until other computers started showing up on the market with similar operating systems (Atari ST, Commodore Amiga and last but not least, IBM and clones).

The same thing is happening now with NeXT computers. The NeXT machines have true multitasking, run under Unix with a consistent and user friendly graphical user interface, have virtual memory, built in Ethernet networking, built in digital quality sound, 92 dots per inch screen resolution on a two page monitor, on screen Postscript, 400 DPI Laser Printer, read/write optical disk and more. Documents can be annotated with your voice input. A microphone is provided with every machine. It's the same old story. The general computer public is **very** slow to recognize the merits of new technology.

You can be sure that the Macintosh market is not dying as you seemed to imply. In fact, it is growing faster than the IBM market.

Sincerely,
Rich Love, President
Carnation Software,
(206) 333-4288

Dear Rich:

Thanks for the information about the changes in the Macintosh Developers program. I want to assure you that I think that the Mac is a great machine. The underlying reservations that I have are:

1. **Is the hardware really cost competitive for general purpose users?**
2. **Can software companies be competitive selling software on the Mac?**

I must admit that Apple made some steps with announcing the lower priced Macs in late 1990. I looked at this issue in early 1990 when my daughter needed to move up from her old Apple II. Her school used Macs, but I just couldn't justify the hardware cost difference for the Mac. An IBM clone and WordPerfect was a much cheaper and very effective solution.

The second question is much more difficult. There are two types of software products: ones which are bundled with hardware and ones which sell to current owners of hardware.

If you are selling a vertical market package which is a turnkey system, the customer will look at the total system cost including both the hardware and the software. If the hardware is much more expensive, the software vendor can end up with less net revenue if they can't pass along the higher costs. I had a client who found that the ended up eating 50 percent of the higher hardware cost. They were able to get some premium for the system on a Mac, but they had to eat some of the difference.

Another client was looking for a vertical package for his wife's business. He is very pro Mac, but he was concluding that he was probably going to end up with one of the PC solutions. The cost was a factor, but they had a larger installed base and had developed a more robust product. He still felt that the Mac looked better, but he wasn't sure that it was the best decision.

If you are selling add on software you want to have the largest base to sell to. That is why in the mainframe market why there are so many IBM software vendors and their are so few software vendors on the other mainframe hardware platforms.

As software vendors, we have to be very realistic about how we make money. The ideal hardware platform is free and universal. If we begin to identify with the hardware vendor it can cloud our business judgement. I worked with a number of minicomputer VARs in the middle 80s who were getting killed by the PC competition. They loved their hardware platform and found it very difficult to be objective. A lot of them went out of business because they couldn't go with the flow.

At the present time, I see this same attitude in the Mac and the VAX market. These are both very good technical systems, but they may or may not be good hardware platforms for software products. I have talked to other developers who wanted to develop new products for exotic (non mainstream but leading edge) hardware and software environments. In many of these case, they could build comparable products for more commercial platforms. It might be a lot more programming and it might not look quite as good, but they stood to make a lot more money. In half of these cases, the developers stay loyal to "their machine" knowing that their financial reward is likely to be less. That is fine as a personal decision, but I would be distressed if I owned stock in the company.

The AS/400 is an interesting example. It is less than exciting as far as mid range technology, but it was been a really successful platform for a lot of software companies. There are some really hot Unix boxes which have almost put a couple of my clients out of business.

As a software publisher, you must watch out for your own best interest. After all the rah rah dies down, you have to pay your bills. Your hardware vendor isn't likely to send you a check out of sincere gratitude. There are cases where new exotic technology can enable new applications and launch major new software companies. If that is your game plan, have at it, but please watch out for yourself.

Good luck
Dave

4. Low Volume Printing (Feb)

Dear Dave:

We print 20 manuals at a time (1 month supply) using HP Laserjet, WordPerfect, and Glyphix fonts. The cost is less than $0.03 per page with zero waste. To speed things up, we set the copies counter on the Laserjet front panel. The result looks very professional and allows us to evolve our product at low cost.

Andy Welch
Daedalian Systems Group
(416) 862-1401

P.S. Please show us examples of good/bad direct mail with your criticism. (Yes, I'd send you mine for evaluation.)

Dear Andy:

Thanks for the note. This is the kind of practical advice that helps all of us. I suspect that as your volumes increase that the low volume approach will begin to feel costly, but for now it seems like a good approach.

I have been thinking about how to evaluate direct mail packages. I would like people to send me two packages, the best and the worst, and I will try to see if I can find any general patterns in what makes direct mail packages succeed.

Thanks
Dave

5. Contract Writer (Mar)

Dear Dave:

I am now offering offsite technical writing and editing of user, technical, and design documentation, as well as marketing materials and publicity for software developers.

Applications experience includes inventory, order processing, purchasing and manufacturing; customer information; claims administration; and personal computer productivity and accounting for the manufacturing, public utility, insurance, and personal computer industries. Hardware and software experience includes IBM mini-computers and mainframes, XEDIT, Processmaster, Bookmaster, Wang text processing, and Macintosh.

For rates and information, contact:

Susan Bresler
PO Box 5495
Atlanta, GA 30307
(404) 371-9410

Dear Susan:

I just wanted to mention that you have worked for IBM, American Software, and GMD Systems International.

Dave

6. Telephone Support Software (May)

Dear Dave,

After reading the results of your Support Survey (Jan 91), it occurred to me that you might have run across a PC based software package to automate a telephone support department. Any suggestions?

We develop and sell AutoCAD-Based CAD applications, and have a client base of several thousand users worldwide. We are seeking a software package which can do these types of things:

* Maintain a data base of customer companies and contacts.

* Track support call information — date, time, nature of the problem, solution, support person who handled the call, etc.

* Assign tracking numbers to problems which cannot be answered in the initial call.

* Produce reports, such as:

  - Open (unanswered) problems

  - Call history for a particular customer or customer location.

  - Statistical counts of calls handled per time period, or per support person, or per product.

Any response to this fax would be appreciated, even if it is just your handwritten note of reply directly onto this letter.

Sincerely,
Stuart D Smolkin
President
Applications Development, Inc.
(504) 835-1627

Dear Stuart,

The one company I'm aware of with a product like you've described is:

BusinessWise
Steve Hartman
(408) 866-5960

I would be very interested to learn about anyone else with a product being used for support departments in software companies.

Dave

7. LAN Technical Support Experts (Jun)

Dear Sirs:

DPC&A is a software development firm that specializes in applications for the oil industry. Our particular expertise is in the area of petroleum economics. The company provides software products for mainframe, mini, and micro-computers. We have acquired expertise on all these platforms.

We have installed our software on several Local Area Networks, and generally the installations have been on a Novell network. Although our users have had good luck with our network installations, we do not feel we have the resources or expertise to adequately support these network users. We find ourselves spending more and more of our support resources supporting LAN work environments. These questions range from recommending what type of file server should be purchased, to specific questions regarding configuration problems, as well as questions regarding installation of additional network devices.

Our customers pay a support and upgrade fee for which they receive technical support regarding our software products. The questions regarding networks usually go beyond our expertise, and frequently take more time than we have allocated. For these reasons we would like to develop a relationship with several "network experts" to help our customers solve some of these network and hardware concerns.

We are exploring the possibilities of developing relationships with companies or individuals that would be able to help us support our more technical users in our key sales markets. This contract person would have to be familiar with DPC&A products so that the advice given to our customers, or prospective customers is accurate and of high quality. It is important to us that our products function efficiently on any network installation.

We are looking for such a person or company that could provide this network and hardware support resources on a contract basis. If Software Success is aware of such a company or person; or has available a list of network or hardware "experts" in Dallas, Houston, Denver, New Orleans, Oklahoma City or Tulsa markets, please forward this information or these names to us at the address below. We, in turn, will contact these individuals or companies about a possible relationship.

Thank you for your assistance.

Robert K. (Bob) Campbell
Manager of Technical Services
DPC&A
6510 Abrams Road, Suite 410
Dallas, TX 75231
(214) 349-6900

8. MicroComputer Trainer (Aug)

Dear Dave,

Software Publishers must become dedicated advocates of end user training. Why? A staggering number of corporate and governmental microcomputer training functions are being downsized and disbanded — even as these same organizations increase their purchases of highly complex software. This trend spells disaster for those companies in terms of end-user productivity and return on investment. It could also prove catastrophic for the software vendors whose products never seem to deliver on their promised benefits. Many upper managers, under fierce economic pressure, view end-user training as expendable overhead. These executives are buying into the exaggerated "ease-of-use" claims touted by some vendors.

What should software publishers do? Seize every opportunity to educate customers and prospects about what it really takes to train people to use your products. Here are three recommendations:

* Do you hold "executive education" seminars for customers or prospects? If so, emphasize the strategic importance, benefits, and probable costs of training.
* Clarify, in every medium from advertising to public speaking, what "ease-of-use" means. For example, the similarities between GUI (Graphical User Interface) products *do* reduce end-user training in certain "operations environment" skills (e.g., file handling, font selection). This is a real benefit that customers and prospects should understand. But the important features of most products — the ones that make them most valuable — frequently require a *lot* of training to master. Emphasize the productivity gains employees can achieve *if* they receive proper training.

* Your documentation should include estimates of the type and amount of training required. And, where feasible, suggest supplemental training materials, and/or authorized training vendors.

If my recommendations are implemented, the software publishing industry will gain enormous credibility — and increase the probability that its products are used to their full potential.

I welcome responses on this subject from your readers. To provide a forum for the discussion of training issues, I recently launched The Microcomputer Trainer. TMCT is a monthly newsletter directed specifically to the needs of corporate professionals who support and train end-users. We report on the most effective instructional techniques. Via in-depth case studies, we take our readers inside successful training operations. We review and evaluate instructional materials. And we supply trainers with management advice and hard-to-find statistical data they can use to win greater support within their organizations. If anyone wants more information about our publication, please contact us.

Sincerely,
Loretta Weiss-Morris
Editor and Publisher
The MicroComputer Trainer
TEL (201) 330-8923
FAX (201) 330-0163

Dear Loretta,

Thanks for the letter. A major challenge for software companies is to get their customers using their software productively. I have seen a number of cases where a significant number of customers never learned how to use the software they had paid for. This ended up being a major problem for the software vendor. The customers didn't renew their maintenance and it was difficult to find good references and testimonials. Over time, the word got out in the industry and it became harder to make new sales.

I think that software publishers must understand how to train their customers for very selfish reasons. If your customers aren't happy with your software, your business will not thrive. There are a number of things that software vendors can do to help their customers learn. They can educate them with written materials before and after the sale. They can provide good phone support. They can provide training a number of ways: tutorials, video tape, audio tape, on site training, vendor location training, and/or training the customer trainers. I've read your newsletter and feel that it provides insight into these issues.

Thanks,
Dave

9. Integrated Software for Software Companies (Aug)

Dear David:

1. **Suggestion: when you mention a product or service, include the supplier's FAX number. It's much easier to convey one's name and address by FAX than over the phone. (Don't have to wait on the line either.)**

2. **In addition to a product that manages the software support function, I'm interested in a complete, integrated software package for running all facets of a software company, e.g. customer and prospect data base, lead management, sales administration, accounting/invoicing, etc. In my experience, "off-the-shelf" products deal only with one of these areas, and none of them talks to the other. My goal is to maintain only one copy, of each data item, e.g. customer name and address — if there's more than one copy, then the laws of nature guarantee no two will be the same!**

Regards,

Dorian   Hausman
TBS Software
TEL (416) 940-9373
FAX (416) 940-9376

Dear Dorian,

I will try to implement suggestion number 1 and provide a FAX number if one is available. I find that I am using FAX much like I would use E-Mail. Instead of leaving a message for someone who isn't in, sometimes I write simple letters from my database and then FAX them. This way I am sure that they received the message correctly. Even with voice mail I am concerned about people transcribing numbers correctly.

I know of only one company who has a vertical package for software companies:

David Hearn
S.L.A.M.   Software
TEL (512) 834-8927
FAX (512) 467-9403

There are packages for doctors, dentists, retail stores, etc, but not for software companies. I am sure that our industry can benefit from specialized and integrated packages that are developed for our special needs.

The only concern that I would have in marketing a package such as this, is whether software companies would pay money to other software companies for software. I have had some experience with a company selling software for the support function in software companies and I know that they lost a number of sales because the software company prospects decided to develop their own custom software instead of buying a package.

I would be interested to hear from anyone who knows of other specialized accounting packages. Later in this issue you will find a list of software support packages.

Thanks,
Dave

10. Another Company Looking for Integrated Software (Aug)

Dear Dave,

In the short time, I've been a subscriber, I've already gotten considerable value from Software Success. I especially appreciate the down to earth answers you give ordinary people starting a business.

I am a partner in a new company developing niche software for engineering offices. We've had good initial success in test marketing our products mail order, and getting our leads from advertisements in trade journals. We're now ready to hit the big time. The only bottleneck we have is our accounting. We have three separate packages to handle order taking, customer records, and accounting. Each package works well individually, and each has fair ca-

pacity left, but they won't talk to each other. Information has to be transferred manually between them. While the volumes were low, it wasn't a real problem. However, if we don't come up with something better soon, maintaining our records is going to rob time from other more productive work.

We've been looking around for several months for a replacement but haven't found anything. We're prepared to spend some significant dollars, but none of the literature we've received gives us any confidence that they'll do what we want. We'd sure hate to spend the money and time only to end up in the same boat (only poorer).

Looking at other software developers, we can't see that we're all that unique (as far as records management goes). Surely we aren't the first with this problem. Surely somebody must have figured out a solution.

Our minimum requirements are:
1. Unlimited (or nearly so) invoices and customer records.
2. Creating an invoice automatically updates the appropriate ledger accounts.
3. Some kind of easy link between invoices and customer records. Either an automatic or semi-automatic export of invoice information to a separate program, or both use the same data base. As long as it's easy to use we don't care.
4. Made to be used by real people. i.e., easy way to identify and fix errors, plus, we don't want to pay mega$ for a consultant to set up our books.
5. Customizable invoices and packing slips.
6. Strong preference to real time posting rather than batch.

If you've heard of anything, we'd appreciate knowing about it. I thank you in advance for anything you can do to help us, and keep up the good work on your newsletter.

Yours Truly,
Gordon P Rachar
Sector Software, Inc.
TEL (403) 450-4906
FAX (403) 461-0602

11. Software for Software Support (Aug)

We have received information about a number of companies who provide Software for Software Sup-

port. Rather than trying to describe the products from their materials, I have decided to just provide the company names and phone numbers and FAX numbers where available.

AnswerSet Corporation	Omni Technical Service
TEL (408) 996-8683	TEL (509) 765-0579
FAX (408) 996-1852	
Business Wise	OPMS
TEL (408) 886-5960	TEL (404) 399-6099
FAX (408) 8667421	FAX (404) 364-0888
LYSIS Corporation	S.L.A.M. Software
TEL (404) 373-3359	TEL (512) 834-8927
FAX (404) 373-3619	FAX (512) 467-9403
Magic Solutions, Inc.	VoiceLink
TEL (201) 529-5533	TEL (708) 866-0404
FAX (201) 529-1808	FAX (708) 866-0412

12. Support for Custom Code (Sept)

Dear Dave,

I am an avid reader of your newsletter, Software Success, and have found it to address a number of issues which we have not considered or have applied limited resources to investigate.

XYZ, my company (not it's real name), is in the midst of negotiating a significant application contract. The monetary value of this new project is nearing the six digit figure and it is approximately four to five times larger than our largest contract thus far.

The application will be based upon Oracle in an SCO Unix environment running on a Compaq Systempro. The database is estimated to be approximately 3Gb in size. The client's annual revenue is approximately $12M and the client currently employs the services of a time sharing company for it's current application output. Approximately one half of the firm's revenue is a direct result of this application. They also plan on aggressively marketing the product which the application produces once the application is brought in-house.

I am interested in learning your opinion about the following:

Chapter VI. Customer Support & Technical Issues

We are being asked to provide an annual support agreement after installation and acceptance of the application by the client. Contractually, "support" is defined as being on call within a pre-agreed upon time period to resolve any problems that may surface which directly related to the software application. (Hardware and the operating environment are being handled by a separate agreement and are not to be considered in this discussion.)

Enhancements to the application requested by the client will be considered separately and priced accordingly. Once the enhancement has been accepted by the client and it becomes integrated into the application, due to the complexity of that particular enhancement or the number of combined enhancements which become part of the application, the cost of the support agreement may be increased.

The client is requesting support 24 hours/day, 7 days/week with a two hour response time from the moment their call is placed.

Up to this point in time, we have initiated a limited number of service contracts. These service contracts provide:

* A priority response to the customer

* The customer with the ability to budget expenses with greater accuracy as there are no additional invoices for service provided under the contract.

Most issues that we encounter:

* Can be remotely solved via modem;

* Rarely if ever is an on-site call required, and;

* Support never goes beyond 10-11PM.

Historically, we have found these contracts to be profitable but their cost has been in a lower stratosphere when compared against the situation that I am presenting to you.

Those clients which are not under a service contract are simply billed for time. Our hourly rates do not differentiate between support provided during regular business hours (i.e., 8AM-5PM, Monday thru Friday) and support provided outside of regular business hours. (As a side note, should our bill-ing structure provide a higher price for emergency support outside of the normal business hours?)

In speaking with similar firms here in my town, it is my understanding that most service contracts are written for support between 8AM-5PM, Monday through Friday and are priced at 20-30% of the initial development cost of the application. If the client desires service outside of those hours, the fee can be 30-40%.

Based on this information, here are my questions:

1) Is the support contract price of 20-30% reasonable and competitive as long as I deem to be able to meet our projected cost for this service plus a reasonable profit?

2) Should a premium price be attached to those estimated hours which are outside of the normal business hours? If so, as presented above, it is entirely possible that the support contract price might actually represent 30% or more of the initial development cost. How does this compare to the contracts which you are aware of?

I look forward to hearing from you.

Anonymous

Dear Anonymous,

We are talking about your company being the MIS department for your client. The ongoing development or maintenance of existing applications is often 70 or 80% of the MIS budget. This includes both resolving problems or bugs and enhancements.

My first concern is that it will be difficult to distinguish between problems and enhancements. Often, projects include some of each. If one category is free and the other is billed, you have an obvious area for disagreement. Over the years, it will be even more difficult to distinguish between the two.

I would hesitate to commit to a fixed price support contract for an extended period of time, because the customer can end up thinking that they should be getting limited enhancements along with their bug fixes. Later, I will outline some of the alternatives that we discussed.

I think it is critical to charge more for support hours used outside of normal business hours. Your employees will wise up and demand extra pay for off shift hours. It is important that the customer pay a premium for the off shift usage so they don't misuse your resources. I would consider a 25% premium for second shift and 50% for third shift and weekend time. You might check what the large service companies charge for off shift time. This type of off shift premium should also insure that your people only have to do emergency work in off shift hours. You will be amazed at how much can be deferred to prime time.

I would start with a 90 day warranty period where you will fix all reported bugs at no additional cost. This should be enough time for the customer to fully test the system and to report the bugs to you. You should be able to estimate this within the cost of the initial development. It also doesn't seem fair to charge the customer more for fixing bugs that were shipped with the system.

My next suggestion is to start with an hourly rate based on the shift. Then I would start with a support fee at 50% of the full contract price for the first year. This would give them a budget amount that they could pay. As you proceeded, you would actually track the billable hours for both bugs and enhancements.

If the customer uses less hours/money for bugs than budgeted, they can use the savings to pay for enhancements or they can have 50% of the savings rebated to them. This helps motivate the customer to hold down your support costs. I would hope that almost all of the true bugs could be found in the first 90 days, so I would expect that this long term bug fixing would take relatively little time.

If the bugs cost more than the 50% budget level, you have a real problem. You need a "stop loss" on your exposure here. You might say that you will cover excess bug fixing up to $10K, but over that, the customer will have to pay. If you get into this situation, you will have to renegotiate your agreement and you may be at great risk of not getting paid for the initial fees.

I hope that, with this structure, the customer will work with you to get the bugs fixed quickly and cheaply, and they will have the budget to get the minor enhancements and extensions that make software truly useful.

Good luck!
Dave

13. Freelance Technical Writer (Sept)

Dear Dave,

As a freelance technical writer and editor who specializes in user manuals and computer books, I'd like to call your readers' attention to the need for good documentation. Too often, user guides are written by programmers or sales/marketing people, who don't have the expertise–or the time–to produce useful, readable documentation. This shortcoming is especially apparent in the index, which is probably the most important part of a manual but the most difficult to create.

Can small companies afford to hire a professional like me to do this work? I don't see that they can afford *not* to, when you consider how much customer support time can be saved by a carefully written, well-indexed manual. In the end, your product is of little use if your customers can't figure out how to get the most from it.

Sincerely,
Mark Kmetzko
Oxford Communications Consulting
TEL (216) 321-0133

Dear Mark,

I agree that top quality documentation is critical to product quality. I also agree that the content and index are very important. I often find that companies are more concerned about how fancy their manuals are instead of how complete and useful they are.

One benefit which you didn't mention, is that documentation can play a critical role in the sales process. I often suspect that people spend more time reading the manuals as prospects than they do as customers. I have had clients who improved their documentation to facilitate their sales and were pleased with the results.

Good luck!
Dave

14. Usability Testing Services (Sept)

Dear David,

It was a pleasure speaking with you today, and many thanks for your time and interest in Usability Sciences Corporation.

As promised, please find enclosed a copy of Usability Sciences' news release on their Competitive Market Research offering, and company background information for your review. As I mentioned, Usability Sciences' Competitive Market Research service provides an objective method of comparing two or more competing software products from the user's perspective.

Usability Sciences provides usability testing services on PC software for ease-of-use and ease-of-learning from the target user's perspective. Several software companies have put their software to the test at Usability Sciences' labs including Lotus Development, Tandy, Borland, and NeXT.

I look forward to speaking with you again, soon.

Sincerely,
Hedi Zook
Account Executive
Capital Relations, Inc.
TEL (214) 907-9500
FAX (214) 437-5602

Dear Hedi,

While it appears that Usability Testing will become much more important as our industry matures, it seems like your focus is larger software publishers (you mentioned the top 750 software publishers).

I think that anyone who is setting up a QA function to provide internal testing should contact you and get more information on the services that you provide and the methodology you have developed.

Thanks for the information!
Dave

15. Releasing New Products (Oct)

Dear Dave,

I have just started subscribing to Software Success and have purchased the 1989 and 1990 reference books. I wish these had been available back in 1986, when we first started selling software by mail. We must have made every possible mistake. Since reading your reference books, we have really changed the way we are doing things.

We are a small software company that sells products to a scientific market niche. Our marketing is done almost entirely by direct mail and small ads in trade journals. We will soon be marketing three new products that will be selling for around $500 each. Some clients will buy just one of our new products. Others may buy two or three products.

Our big question is, How should we time the release of our new products? Should we advertise them all at the same time, or should we release them one at a time, perhaps a month or two apart? The advantage of the second method is that we could send out three sets of press releases, each announcing a new product. We hope this approach will get us a lot more free publicity. However, we don't want to annoy clients who want all three packages and would have to make a new order every month. Also, we are considering offering clients a discount if they purchase all three packages. I would appreciate any advice you or any of your readers have on this point.

Yours sincerely,
Evan Morris
President
EcoTech Research Ltd
TEL (306) 352-2468

Dear Evan,

The first point we discussed was the distinction between using a press release to announce your product's availability and letting your customers know that they will soon be able to buy it. Magazines generally don't run press releases announcing products before they are released. They want information on products that are available at press time. Because of this distinction, you can publicize your products to your customers before the product is announced to the world without jeopardizing your press releases.

I agree that you will get more publicity if you send three separate press releases instead of sending one release announcing all three products. One way to make these distinctions very clear is to send out a press release for each product once you have ten or twenty customers using that product.

Press releases can announce the "existence" of a product (vapor ware) or the fact that people are using it successfully. If you do the latter and editors ask why you didn't include it in an earlier press release, you can respond that your customers were still testing the product at the time of the previous press release.

My experience is that many alpha testers are more interested in learning about the product development process than actually using the product.

I prefer the following product release sequence:

1. Alpha testing

These are your first two or three customers. In many cases, they don't pay for the product because they are really an extension of your development group. My experience is that many alpha testers are more interested in learning about the product development process than actually using the product. It is very common for the individual who is doing the alpha testing to come to work for the developer. Because many alpha sites don't really use the product, they can only do functional testing, which merely determines whether the product meets the specs, not whether it really does the job.

2. Beta testing

These are real customers who are paying for the product because their businesses need it. In most cases, they have an existing connection with your company. They may have bought your previous products, or they may know the principals. They are customers, but they are in the "family." They will test the applications if they have the time to actually use the product. Because they plan to use the product in their business, they are very cautious about implementing the beta product. They will execute each step in the testing process very slowly. They want to help, but they don't want to risk damaging their business by depending on new software to carry out vital parts of their business before it is fully debugged.

As you plan your product release, you should decide the number of successfull beta sites necessary to trigger a general release.

The reluctance of beta sites to fully test the product as quickly as the vendor wishes is a very common situation. In far too many cases, vendors *assume* that the product is fine because they haven't heard from the beta sites. Call each site weekly to find out exactly how far your beta sites have progressed in their testing and implementation. If they aren't going to have time to test your product during your sched-

uled beta phase, ask them to remove the product from their system. This may seem harsh, but you're doing them a favor. Once the product is fully tested, it will be much easier for them to implement it. You are also avoiding a situation in which the beta site installs the original beta version months after you've finished all your other beta testing. In such cases, the tardy beta sites often encounter the bugs that previous testers have already reported and you have already fixed.

As you plan your product release, you should decide the number of successfull beta sites necessary to trigger a general release. Decide that you'll release the product when you have X sites that you can use as references, not before. (X is usually between 10 and 25, and depends upon both the product and the variety of customer environments in which the product will be used.)

3. Limited Availability

Limited availability means that a product is available to new prospects, but the company is limiting the number of customers who may implement the product at the same time. This is done so that the company can adequately support the product during this critical phase. This is an extra safeguard that can help to avoid a real disaster.

A common problem with beta sites selected by a vendor is that many of these sites may share most of the same characteristics. Therefore, the sites may not generate all of the situations that your product will encounter once it becomes generally available. I have seen many cases in which a product worked very well at beta sites, but the company was swamped with problems the moment the product was released to the public.

The objective of limiting availability is to insure that if problems do occur in this next wave of customers, then the company has the resources to deal with them. My rule of thumb is that the objective of limited availability is to double the number of installations completed in beta test.

...Pick companies that have had positive experiences with your company. This will help them deal with the emotional problems of encountering bugs in your product.

You can make many different announcements about product availability as you progress through this release process. The technical team and sales people usually contact previous alpha sites when looking for people to perform alpha testing of a new product. This phase is very controlled, and the announcement is made in strictest confidence to the potential alpha sites. Often, companies require the signing of nondisclosure agreements.

Beta testing is also somewhat controlled. You want only "friendly" sites to test your product, so pick companies that have had positive experiences with your company. This will help them deal with the emotional problems of encountering bugs in your product. It isn't usually a good idea to have cold prospects (companies that have never done business with your firm) beta test your product. For this reason, most companies selectively announce the beta test only to their good customers. Some companies send a letter to their best customers announcing the beta program and the expected date for limited availability.

Once you have enough successfully tested beta sites to use as references, it is appropriate to make a public announcement or press release. You should also send a copy of the press release to all of your customers and prospects. Please don't make a public announcement before you have happy customers. There is nothing more frustrating (or more humiliating) than getting a call from an editor who wants to talk to a happy customer and being unable to produce one.

The other issue you raised was whether to advertise all three products together and offer a package price on all three products before they are fully announced. I have seen ads for several products with banners on some of the new products which say, "Available in 1Q92." As long as your products aren't vaporware, you risk very little by pre-announcing them this way.

You indicated that a number of your prospects would like to buy all three products as a package. I question prospects' willingness to pay for products that they haven't received. Most vendors only take the customer's money when they ship the product. You might consider a program where they pay the regular price for the first product but will receive discounts on the second and third products once they are released. This works well if they pay by credit card or if you invoice them. However, if your customers work for large organizations, it may be easier for them to get authorization for one purchase and then receive the products as they become available.

Good luck!
Dave

16. Money-Back Guarantee (Oct)

Dear Dave,

We sell a product for between $50,000 and $100,000, and we have been asked about our money-back guarantee. I know that you believe in offering money-back guarantees with less expensive products, but should we offer one?

Anonymous

Dear Anonymous,

I believe very strongly that companies with inexpensive products should offer money-back guarantees, but at your price level, this doesn't make sense. I think that you should have a trial agreement giving the prospect a "reasonable acceptance and test period." At the end of the trial period, they sign an agreement stating that the product works and they accept it. After they've signed such an agreement, they have no basis for a refund.

Don't risk having a customer ask for a refund that you can't pay. I don't know anyone who offers guarantees on expensive products, and I suspect this is why.

Sometimes, however, when the vendor promises to provide future enhancements or bug-fixes to meet the acceptance test, the customers refuse to pay for the product until these enhancements or fixes are provided. If they are willing to pay, I would recommend that they withhold part of the payment until they get the enhancements. That way, you won't be asked to refund them $100,000, and we all know that very few small software comanies that receive $100,000 will be in a position to refund the money a month later. Don't risk having a customer ask for a refund that you can't pay. I don't know anyone who offeres guarantees on expensive products, and I suspect this is why.

17. Product Registration (Oct)

Dear Dave,

We have a family of products that range from $99 to $495. Our registration rate ranges from 10% on the $99 product to over 80% on our more expensive professional products. We are distressed at the low registration rate on the entry product because our marketing strategy for the $99 product was to sell it as a loss leader. We figured that even if we lost money on the $99 sale that we could convince them to buy the more expensive products. This strategy falls flat if fewer than 10% of the customers register their product.

Anonymous

Dear Anonymous,

I like the strategy of offering a $99 product, because the demographics of the people who buy this product match those of the people who buy the more expensive product. So, your strategy seems reasonable. The challenge is to get them to register the $99 product.

I have seen a number of ways used to get more people to register. I was paid $10 in cash by one vendor to send in my registration. I really like this. I have also seen some companies conduct drawings for free copies of other products.

In our phone discussion, you liked the idea of having a monthly drawing for a free copy of your $500 product. This should appeal to everyone who bought the $99 product. I also suggested that if they

register their purchase within 30 days, you should give them credit for $99 toward the $500 product if they ever decide to trade up.

We also talked about making the registration card big and pretty. Make sure that it is easy to spot and draws people's attention. Far too many registration cards are small and plain. This is a sales effort, and you have to pull out all the stops to get people to register. You might, therefore, consider providing envelopes with prepaid postage. Some companies even print the return address on the back of the registration card so that all the customer has to do is fold the card in half, tape or seal the bottom shut, and mail it.

Even if you provide free support, your customer list is one of the most significant assets of a software company. As you know, you can sell more products to these people. I am sure that if you make this a priority, you can improve your registration rate and, in turn, improve your long term sales.

Good Luck!
Dave

P.S. I would be interested in hearing from anyone who has had experience with programs aimed at improving product registration.

The twenty-five cent incentive still produces a significant increase in return rates.

D. Customer Relations (1990)

1. Is Customer Relations Really Important?

Given the fact that this is an issue about customer support, I guess this seems like an odd starting point. Almost everyone pays lip service to customer service or top quality support. The reason that I raise the question is that, as an industry, we don't behave as if customer support really matters.

I believe that most managers in software companies like the concept of good customer relations, but believe that in the best interests of the business they have to hold down costs.

Service First Corporation surveyed executives in charge of service at 200 companies and 57 percent rated "meeting customer needs" as their first priority. However, 73 percent also said that the only way to compete is on price.

REFERENCE: Business Marketing, November 1988.

Almost every business person I have met wants their customers to like them. This is just human nature. The corporate extension of this is the expression that we aim to provide top quality service. This is even true in companies which offer "no frills" services. They are offering the best inexpensive service that money can buy.

This isn't what I am asking. I assume that your support people want to help your customers. The question is: Have you made the conscious decision to invest in support? In the article by Davidow, Bruce D. Smith of Network Equipment Technologies, allocated $6 million for service, even if it meant cutting back on R&D! That is serious. In many business-to-business markets, the cost of acquiring a new customer is so high that you don't make a profit from new customers until the second year.

REFERENCE: The Service Factory Advantage, William H. Davidow, Business Marketing, October 1989.

Frankel & Company, a Chicago-based marketing services agency, conducted a survey of business marketers. They found that many companies felt that improving the value of existing customers was more important than getting more customers. (See the pie chart)

REFERENCE: New Marketing Trends Study: "Current Customer is King" Sales and Marketing Executive Report, October 11, 1989.

2. How Do We Develop a Service Orientation?

* You can do the following things right:

* Put the customer first

* Think from the customer point of view

* Review your support policies

* Ask your employees how they might improve customer satisfaction

* Develop an environment where your employees treat each other like customers

* Lead by example

* Keep in touch after the sale

What not to do!

* Don't give a damn

* Slam-dunk the customer

* Patronize your customers

* Hide behind the policy manual

* Encourage mechanized "thank-you-have-a-nice-day" customer interactions

In many businesses, the key to long-term profits is retaining the customers and keeping them coming back for more. Research on buyer-seller relationships conducted by Learning International revealed that the sales person can be critical in retaining or driving customers away.

3. Buyer Perceptions

A study of 210 Fortune 1300 and Canadian 450 firms found that buyers feel that sellers fall short in two critical areas: product quality and customer service. At the same time, they identified six predictors of customer satisfaction. Three of them carry 77 percent of the weight, and these depend most heavily on the sales person. The factors were:

Business Expertise and Image (29%)

This includes both the sales person and the organization.

Dedication to Customer (25%)

This is the credibility of the organization. Interestingly enough, competitive pricing is important in this area.

Account Sensitivity and Guidance (23%)

This stems from the sales person, the sales organization, and the product.

Product Performance and Quality (10%)

They want the quality to meet their expectations. Technical support after the sale applies here.

Service Department Excellence (9%)

This covers the interpersonal skills, reliability, and overall competence.

Confirmation Capabilities (4%)

This covers the sales person helping the advocate sell recommendations within the customer organization. It includes being realistic about the strengths and weaknesses of the product.

At the same time, if the sales person has a cavalier attitude or fails to communicate with the customer, they can cause the customer to stop doing business with a company.

REFERENCE: Service Management, Vince Caracio, Reseller Management, September 1989.

4. Strategies

The strategies for your sales people to support the long-term relationship can be viewed in terms of the following key factors.

Business Expertise & Image

This starts with projecting the proper image. Let your customers know that they are smart to do business with you. Project a leadership image for your company,

Dedication to Customer

Educate your customers, and give them ideas on how to improve their business operations. Communicate frequently with your customers via newsletters, calls and personalized letters.

Account Sensitivity and Guidance

Ask your customers for their opinions and make them feel important. In large key accounts you have to understand the politics of the situation. Finally, you must communicate with the top person. This will make your customer feel important.

REFERENCE: "With Customers, the Closer the Better", Kate Bertand, Business Marketing, July 1989.

5. Does This Stuff Really Work?

In 1987, Pacific Bell was losing 97 percent of its competitive Centrex bids. To make matters worse, they lost 60 percent of their top 20 customers in two years. They instituted a "priority panel" of top customers. The customers complained about a number of items:

* **The price was 40 percent higher than competitors.**

* **The system hadn't been enhanced.**

* **There were no custom contracts.**

* **The customers couldn't get one-stop shopping for the entire system.**

Pac Bell listened to its customers and made a number of changes to its product offering. In 1988, they won 93 percent of their competitive bids!!

REFERENCE: "To Buy or Not to Buy: Why Customers Keep Coming Back," Sales and Marketing Executive Report, September 13, 1989.

This is part of a growing trend where software companies are realizing that collaborating with their customers might be the best way to identify and create new product opportunities.

Rather than using traditional market research techniques like focus groups, companies are showing prospects and customers mock-ups. This helps the customer move beyond what they have worked with in the past and allows them to project themselves into the future.

Chapter VI. Customer Support and Technical Issues

I had very good luck using paper screen prototypes to show programmers detailed alternatives for a CASE tool. We mocked up alternative scenarios on paper and presented them to the customers. Initially, we thought that we would only use the paper for a limited period to time, and that we would eventually use rapid prototyping tools to present our alternatives.

I decided that having the paper screens was adequate to convey the alternatives that we were investigating, and that they encouraged discussion and new ideas. We were afraid that if we showed people screens on a PC the prospects would view it as more substantial and be reluctant to make suggestions.

One of the unexpected benefits of this process is that it involved the prospects in investigating the technical limitations that the product might have. In a number of cases, we were able to collectively resolve some of these limitations. In others, we were faced with hard trade offs, and we were more comfortable with the decisions that we made because we had involved more people in the process.

We found that the developers were quite uncomfortable having marketing and the customers involved in the design process. It was easy for the developers to reject this new source of input. We involved them in the customer discussions and I was surprised at how quickly the developers understood that this messy process was resulting in a better product.

We found that the developers were quite uncomfortable having marketing and the customers involved in the design process.

6. What Can My Company Do to Manage Customer Expectations and Build Satisfaction?

I believe this is critical. If the customer's expectations are different than your delivery commitments, you are going to have no end of trouble. In general, you can do the following:

* **Spell out simple messages.**

* **Match your customer expectations and your corporate strategy.**

* **Control your attitudes and incentives carefully.**

* **Meet your commitments regardless of cost.**

What Can I Do as a First Step?

The best solution to this came from a reader who sells a vertical market application which involves installation, training, and ongoing phone support. The VP of Support in this company wrote up a ten-page brochure which detailed exactly how things would work for each step of the process. It included both customer responsibilities and vendor responsibilities. It is not intended to be a legal document; it is a working document which facilitates effective communications.

I have also seen a number of newsletters which detail steps customers should take before they call customer support. In reviewing these lists from a customer viewpoint, I would be pleased with a checklist I could follow so that I was sure that I had done my job before I called. I would be interested to hear of any experience any of you have had with this type of customer support program.

Rather than dealing with a zero-sum game where you have to choose between product development and consulting, the consulting can carry its own weight.

Contract Programming

Custom or contract programming can be a major competitive advantage. It can also be a large swamp which sucks up energy and resources. In addition in-house consulting departments can be a major source of revenue.

The leading database software companies have started offering consulting services and the results can be impressive. Oracle reported $7.5 million in consulting service revenues in 1987. This constitutes ten percent of their annual U.S. revenues. They were predicting that the 1988 revenues would be $25 million or 20 percent.

Unify also sees consulting as critical to the bottom line. They also feel that the ability to provide the full service is critical to making the sale. At the present time Unify includes consulting in ten percent of its sales. Oracle hopes to eventually include consulting in 80 percent of its sales.

Another approach is to contract with a third party to provide consulting services. RTI uses a consulting group at Westinghouse Electric since they feel that they are in the business of providing data base products and not turnkey systems. Ashton Tate and Microrim are also keeping their focus on product development.

***

REFERENCE: Trend Toward Consulting Services is Burgeoning, Joshua Greenbaum Computer Systems News, October 5, 1987.

***

While I feel that consulting and contract programming involve a number of issues, I believe that they can be managed and this function can contribute to the bottom line.

I feel that if you manage it properly this function can contribute to the company and increase your ability to support R & D, marketing and sales. Thus, I feel that rather than dealing with a zero-sum game where you have to choose between product development and consulting, the consulting can carry its own weight.

***

REFERENCE: Manage Customers' Expectations, to Build Satisfaction, Milind M. Lele, Business Marketing, December 1988.

***

My own experience is that the most difficult issues center around support. As long as you are going to fold the custom code into your product, you don't have a major issue. If you plan to keep it separate you have to determine how to charge fairly for support. The ideal approach from the vendor's point of view is to charge time and materials.

Unless the vendor can control and oversee your people, this is difficult to sell. If the customer ends up with source code, this might be a reasonable approach since they could always take their support work elsewhere. If your modifications are linked to your product, this alternative is rarely seen as reasonable.

One approach I have seen is to offer support at 15 percent of the price of the contract work with a ten percent per year inflation charge. In this scenario, it is also reasonable to insist that the customer keep the base product on maintenance.

This will provide you with a reasonable maintenance stream. If your costs are much greater than this, you probably designed or coded your programs poorly, and you will end up paying for that.

7. Why Some Users Turn to Outside Firms

53%	Do not use
31%	Lack of expertise
6%	One-time project
5%	Lack of time
3%	Project size/complexity
2%	Political sensitivity
0%	Cost savings

When you are looking at contract programming, you should consider why companies turn to outside firms for programming services. The Ledgeway Group, Inc. in Lexington, Mass. conducted a survey of 178 Fortune 1000 IS managers. When they asked them why they used outside services they found:

The lack of staff expertise is especially relevant for projects which involve customizing your product. It is important to note that none of the users chose cost as a factor in turning to outside firms. You should take this into account when you are bidding this type of project. Of course your charges must be viewed as fair, but you don't have to cut your margins to the bone.

8. Pay Increases

Adapso conducted a survey of almost 100 companies which projected 1989 salary increases of 5.8 percent which was 0.2 percent less than last year.

***

REFERENCE: Pay Increases Level Off, Adapso Data, July 1989.

***

9. Support Resources

TSS/OL - Telephone Support System On Line.

Software package to help your customer support organization manage your support operation.

BusinessWise
(408) 866-5960

RTQ - The Remote Terminal Query System for CICS.
RTQ provides instant access to the contents of the remote user's terminal screen and displays the identical data on the requestor's screen.

On-Line   Documentation,
Inc. (714) 970-6124

Chapter VI. Customer Support and Technical Issues

=M=C=D= The Library BBS with Full-Text Indexed Databases

In addition to the typical BBS E-Mail capabilities, you could put your documentation, and technical tips on line.

FYI, Inc.
(512) 346-0133

"The Complete Guide to Customer Service"

Linda M. Lash,
John Wiley & Sons,
605 3rd Ave, NYC,NY
10158, $24.95

One Day Customer Service Seminars

[They offered them in December in Calif.]

(800) 258-7246
(913) 432-7757

The Help Desk Institute Bendata

(214) 823-2784

They have a newsletter, are conducting research, and have conducted symposiums.

Service Dealer's Newsletter

(800) 673-7808
(215) 657-3010

Lakewood Publications publishes a number of training and support books and newsletters.

(800) 328-4329
(612) 333-0471

"Service Wisdom: Creating and Maintaining the Customer Service Edge"

By Ron Zemke and Chip R. Bell,
Lakewood Publications,
50 S. 9th St.,
Minneapolis, MN 55402, $19.95

"How to Design, Implement and Manage a Superior Customer Service Program"

[This two day seminar was conducted in Calif in September 1989.]

National Management Center
(800) 648-0011
(914) 725-4402

Customer Service Manager's Letter.

This is a bi-weekly letter,
Prentice Hall, $9.95/month
Englewood Cliffs, NJ
07632-9940

Coping with Difficult Customers

A one-day seminar for $98,
Key Productivity Center
(800) 821-3919
(913) 345-2140

How to Build and Improve Customer Service

A one day workshop for $99,
Fred Pryor Seminars
(800) 255-6139
(913)384-6400

A 10-Step Anti-Stress Campaign for Customer Service Professionals,

(FREE)
Customer Service Institute,
(301) 585-0730

Consumer Complaint Handling in America Update

(FREE), Complaint Studies,
US Office of Consumer Affairs,
Washington, DC 20201

Customer Satisfaction Survey Software

[They also have a variety of videos and books],
Shamrock Press
(619) 272-3880

Software Support Conference

January 18-19, 1990 SFO,
Sponsored by the Association of Worldwide

Software Support Managers,
(800) 345-8016
(212) 883-1770

Customer Satisfaction Research

Held in February 1989
Dave Strickland, AMA
(312) 648-0536

P.S. There were a large number of one-day seminars. I just selected the first few from my file. I don't mean to leave anyone out, but...

10. In-House Training

Training really works, and people are beginning to believe it. Arthur Anderson conducted a study which found that the average person spends 100 to 125 hours to achieve competence on the typical software package. They also found that the same results could be achieved by taking an eight-hour seminar and practicing 16 hours. That is a savings of up to 100 hours.

Mentor is a provider of business-oriented training in personal computer software and hardware. They provide training on Time-slips. They have found the following from their seminars:

* **Seminar attendees use their product 50 percent more than before.**

* **Their satisfaction increased 40 percent.**

Mentor Technologies
700 Ackerman Road
Columbus, Ohio 43202
(800) 227-5502
(614) 262-8147

Training has achieved much greater acceptance in the last few years as companies have learned that training really does pay. The typical Fortune 500 company spends $2 million a year on training. In many companies, this feels like a risky investment because they haven't conducted a systematic analysis of training needs. In many companies, they merely circulate a menu of courses and let the managers choose.

Auditing a training program helps the training manager justify their budgets. The first thing that most training managers do is calculate their cost per

student day (keep this in mind when you are pricing your in-house training). The next thing is to plot the student critiques. These critiques may address the issue of the quality of training delivery, but they don't deal with relevance.

Ideally, you would like to analyze pre-training and post-training production. While this is a good idea, they are difficult to control and standardize.

A training audit involves interviewing students to see what they are doing with the material they were taught in class. If you can do this three to six months after the class, you will see what was relevant to the students and what wasn't.

I believe that every company which is offering training should conduct such an audit. You should gain some good statistics which can help you sell your training and at the same time you should learn how to make your training more effective. I believe that every company which is offering training should conduct such an audit.

Reference: Auditing Your Training Program, Bill Serbell, ComputerWorld, March 6, 1989.

Another approach to training your users is to teach your users how to troubleshoot their own problems. I bet you could come up with your ten most commonly asked questions, and the simple solutions to these problems. Another possibility is to divide a sheet into three columns.

At the same time you could write up guidelines to help guide people to solve their own problems. You could have your phone support people ask callers if they had followed the guidelines. If they hadn't they might decide to call back after they had tried them. You can have your phone support people monitor the calls and identify new problems to cover in the guidelines.

Another interesting concept was to train people how to handle what can go wrong and how to fix it. I really like this. Training is typically set up to create a controlled environment where nothing goes wrong. When the customer returns to their machine, and things go wrong, they are convinced that they have broken the system. Showing customers how

Chapter VI. Customer Support and Technical Issues

things break and how to fix it should really increase their confidence in dealing with problem situations.

REFERENCE: Offloading Troubleshooting, Naomi Karten, ComputerWorld, September 26, 1988.

11. What Customers are Looking for in Training

The following article suggested that customers ask vendors the following questions:

1. **What is the cost per person for training?**

2. **Are group rates available?**

3. **Can the training be customized to their needs?**

4. **Have the courses been tested?**

5. **What are the instructor's credentials?**

6. **Will the training be done on site?**

7. **Is a train-the-trainer class available?**

8. **What materials are available in the train-the-trainers class?**

REFERENCE: Third-Party Help Aids Learning, Sally Cusack, ComputerWorld, (date unknown).

Interestingly enough, people want better service, but only 25 percent said they would pay higher prices for better service.

12. Customer Support

In general, customers are dissatisfied with service. Opinion Research Corporation found that one third of consumers felt that the service they were receiving was unsatisfactory in four critical areas:

* **Providing prompt attention**

* **Solving problems that come up**

* **Providing detailed information**

* **Personalized attention**

Interestingly enough, people want better service, but only 25 percent said they would pay higher prices for better service.

REFERENCE: New Study Shows Consumers are Dissatisfied with Service Sales and Marketing Executive Report, April 26, 1989.

Customers are in the process of refining their definition of service as their sophistication increases. The Ledgeway Group asked 45 MIS Executives at Fortune 1,000 firms and found that responsiveness was far and away the most important MIS criteria for service vendors. The other responses were:

100%	Responsiveness
22%	Technical Ability
20%	Business Interest
16%	Product Commitment
14%	Price
14%	Relationships
14%	Flexibility
12%	Reputation
10%	Availability

REFERENCE: Service Redefined, Laura O'Connell, ComputerWorld, January 9, 1989.

At a more detailed level, the Ledgeway group conducted another survey of Software Support preferences.

How important are these support services to you?

Quality Documentation	4.3
Weekday Phone Support	4.0
Access to a Guru	3.9
On-site Support	2.7
Systems Design/ Planning	2.4
Bulletin Boards	2.3
Contract Programming	2.0

In general, companies prefer to have an annual contract for centralized services and expect to pay per incident for on-site training and consulting.

As an industry, we aren't meeting the customer's expectations for responsiveness. Fortunately, their internal staff isn't doing much better.

Average Time (hours)	Actual	Desired
To Get a Response:		
Vendor	5	2
In-house	2	1
To Resolve a Problem:		
Vendor	2	58
In-house	8	5

REFERENCE: Software Support, ComputerWorld, October 9, 1989.

In addition to training, companies have to deal with equipment failures. Over a twelve-month period, 70 percent of PC users experienced a hardware malfunction. The average repair cost $257.

Reference: Sales and Marketing Management August 1988.

13. Cost of Support and Creating a Profit Center

Typically, support costs are ten percent of revenue, and they can be over 30 percent of revenue. At the same time, companies are dealing with increases in salaries for customer service personnel.

According to Warren Blanding of the Customer Service Institute, salaries have increased from $12,000 to $20,000 for entry level people and from $20,000 to $40,000 for experienced personnel in the last few years. At the same time, Blanding is seeing more incentive and profit sharing programs in an effort to reduce the turnover rate.

Reference: Out of the Clerical Backwater, Sales and Marketing Management, November 1989.

Service Dealer Newsletter conducts an annual survey. Electronics/Computer Stores are one of their categories. These positions may be similar to some in your firm. The technicians were paid:

| $7.66 | Starting Average |
| $13.11 | High Average |

The labor charges to customers averaged $67.94 per hour. That is a much higher markup than most software companies that I see. In addition, 46.7% of the companies charge for estimates and 27.6% charge in advance for special part orders. Their net profit averaged 18.1 percent, which is quite good.

The average commission was ten percent and 44% of the technicians were receiving commissions.

REFERENCE: Service Dealer's Newsletter 1988 Survey,(800) 673-7808, or (215) 657-3010.

14. Customer Satisfaction Surveys

Many executives assume that customers who aren't happy will complain. This just isn't true. Technical Research Assistance Program (TARP) found that the best customers were most likely to complain. The primary sources of customer dissatisfaction were:

* Unfulfilled   expectations
* Company   policies
* Defective   products

The reasons that customers didn't complain were:

* They didn't believe that it was worth their time and trouble.

* They don't know how or where to complain.

* They don't believe that the company will do anything to remedy the situation.

Reference: Why Customers Don't Complain, The Competitive Advantage P.O. Box 10091, Portland, Oregon 97210.

Another survey by the U.S. Office of Consumer Affairs found that 96 percent of unhappy customers do not complain. For every complaint that is heard, there are six others that are equally serious, and 30 which are less serious. For these reasons, it really is important to encourage your customers to complain. Part of this is to educate your employees that getting a complaint out in the open is a good thing since you then have an opportunity to address the issue.

REFERENCE: Getting Customers to Complain: Believe It or Not, More is Better, Ed Crego and Ed Kazemek, Reseller Management, August 1989.

15. Customer Surveys

The reasons for conducting a customer survey include:

1. They can reveal the overall level of customer satisfaction.

2. They can give you a better understanding of customer needs.

3. They can address new product acceptance.

4. They can uncover good ideas for new products.

5. They can help you prioritize future enhancements

6. They can identify reference accounts.

7. They can generate qualified leads.

8. You will create good will with your customers.

9. You can profile your buyers to help focus your sales and marketing programs.

The Steps for Most Customer Surveys Include:

1. Define the objectives.

Chapter VI. Customer Support and Technical Issues

Put them in writing and discuss them internally.

2. Determine who will be surveyed.

Do you want to survey prospects who looked at your product and didn't buy? What about customers who are no longer using your product?

3. Select the sample size.

This isn't a problem unless you have a very large customer base.

4. Decide how the data will be collected

Personal interviews, phone calls or through the mail. Most companies use a mailed survey with phone follow up, if required.

5. Design the survey questionnaire.

Take real care to insure that the questions are clear and easy to read.

6. Decide if you will use an incentive to encourage participation.

While customers need less motivation to answer your survey, getting as many responses as possible is important. You can offer pre-minimum items like coffee cups, or you might consider a relevant book. You can also promote the survey through your newsletter.

7. Collect and tabulate the data.

There are a number of packages which will help with this.

8. Analyze the data and distribute the findings.

Make sure that you perform the analysis to find out what your customers are trying to tell you. It is also important to distribute the information internally.

9. Send a thank-you letter to respondents.

This will let them know that you heard them. You also should consider telling them a sample of your findings. I have also found that if you include some public questions that you can use these in a press release.

While customers need less motivation to answer your survey, getting as many responses as possible is important.

I agree that these are the reasonable steps to conduct a customer survey. I have found that it is typically more work than people anticipated because the analysis of the results is time-consuming. On the other hand, the benefits are much greater than anticipated.

Reference: Customer Surveys, Julia Donahue, SOURCEfile, September/October 1988.

If you are interested in the results of a customer survey, but don't have the resources to do it or are concerned that your customers won't talk to you, Specifics, Inc. specializes in customized studies exclusively for companies in the computer software and services industry. In addition to surveys on customer attitudes, they help clients:

Improve won/lost account ratios.

Design and price new products to meet real market needs.

Measure and increase advertising/promotional effectiveness.

Make the right acquisitions at the right price.

I have also worked with a number of clients on customer satisfaction surveys.

Reference: Pat Landry, Specifics, Inc., (203) 227-0735.

They also suggest that you survey your own employees and ask them to rate the internal service organization.

16. A Free Generic Survey

Serqual, a generic survey that assesses customer perceptions and expectations of service business is available free through the Marketing Science Institute (MSI), a nonprofit research center in Cambridge, Massachusetts (no phone number).

Serqual is a joint project between a team of academic researchers and a dozen marketers of business or consumer services. Met Life is one of the sponsors and has administered the survey by phone and by mail.

The first half of the survey evaluates customer expectations of service firms in a named industry. The second half focuses on the company conducting the research and keying the 22 general traits to the firm's abilities in that area.

The marketing professors suggest that marketers augment the 22 items with questions that relate specifically to their industry. They also suggest that you survey your own employees and ask them to rate the internal service organizations.

REFERENCE: Affordable Research that Works, Kate Bertrand, Business Marketing, April 1989

17. What Will My Customers Do if They are Mad?

No matter what you do, you will have unhappy customers. There are three basic actions that the customer can take:

1. They can complain to your employees with the hope that their problem will be addressed.

2. They can complain to prospects and other customers to get back at your company.

3. They can switch to another vendor and complain to them.

Given these alternatives, it is easy to see why you hope that your customers will complain to your company.

18. Developing a Support Strategy

Now that you have decided to conduct a customer satisfaction survey, I would like you to expand your scope and develop an overall support strategy.

The first step is to look at your competitors and determine the minimum service requirements. What is necessary to be in the business? If you don't provide these services you will lose the business, but you won't gain any extra points for providing them.

Value added services differentiate you from your competitors. They are above and beyond what is expected. This is often called "going the extra mile." You can receive a reward for offering these value added services.

This distinction is in the eyes of your customers. If there is any doubt in your mind about which ser-

vices are in which category, I would urge you to call your customers and ask them. You might also want to conduct a focus group to obtain this information. While a focus group sounds intimidating, it is just getting a group of customers and prospects together and talking to them about their perceptions. There are firms that facilitate this, but it shouldn't be too hard to organize.

REFERENCE: Creating an Effective Customer Satisfaction Program, Craig Cina, The Journal of Business and Industrial Marketing, Summer/Fall 1989.

While a focus group sounds intimidating, it is just getting a group of customers and prospects together and talking to them about their perceptions.

Topics for the Focus Group Would Be:

* Comparison of competitors.

* Identification of what is expected.

* Determination of the critical moments of truth when your employees have the opportunity to form a favorable long-lasting impression.

* Description of good and bad experiences.

* Identification of the key determinants in selecting a service provider.

* How poor service can cause the customer to switch vendors.

A Customer Survey Should Include:

* Use of support.

* Overall satisfaction with your service, and a comparison with other vendors they use.

* Verify the importance of each moment of truth as defined in the focus group.

How well do you stack up on these moments of truth compared to their other vendors?

You should also ask your support personnel to answer the same questions. How do they think they will be rated by your customers? Once you have the customer information, you can compare it with employee perceptions. This provides a very good forum for discussing the research findings.

The next step is to develop a service strategy to gain a competitive advantage in service. Determine what investments will have to be made and what changes you want to achieve. Determine the quantitative changes that you want to make.

For example, you might want to lower the average time to call back to two hours and the maximum time to call back to four hours. You might set up a procedure so that additional people man the phones when the time to call back exceeds three hours. You can pull developers and managers in to handle the calls.

REFERENCE: Creating an Effective Customer Satisfaction Program Craig Cina, The Journal of Business and Industrial Marketing, Summer/Fall 1989.

In simple English: If they don't make their customer satisfaction target, they don't get a bonus.

19. Incentive Compensation

I believe that if you are really serious about customer satisfaction you will measure it and link it to a bonus program. While I haven't seen this done at a smaller company, there are a number of cases where large companies have paid service management based on customer satisfaction.

BMW has set up a bonus pool for all non-union employees. It is based, in part, on customer satisfaction levels. Other factors like performance against budget and market penetration are also included.

At Xerox Corp., customer satisfaction levels can affect the annual bonuses of about 70 top executives. Ten percent of their bonus depends on customer satisfaction.

Even more importantly, customer satisfaction is a bonus qualifier for district managers. In simple English: If they don't make their customer satisfaction target, they don't get a bonus.

REFERENCE: Indexing Bonuses to Customer Satisfaction Sales and Marketing Management, October 1988.

If you are going to provide your support personnel with incentive compensation, there are a number of issues that you must address.

1. Who is eligible for this bonus?

This can be difficult if developers are pulled into support on occasion.

2. Exactly how are you going to measure customer satisfaction?

Is the entire bonus going to hinge on one measure or will you break it down to a number of smaller and more specific points like mean time to return calls, number of return calls over eight hours, etc.

3. How big will the incentive be?

My temptation would be to limit it to five to ten percent of annual compensation. This would make for a nice check, but you wouldn't have to cut salaries to afford it.

4. Trigger the incentive at 100 percent of target.

This avoids paying bonuses if you aren't really happy.

5. Keep it very simple.

20. Documentation

Documentation is a sore point with most customers. While I believe that, as an industry, that we have made less of a commitment to documentation than we should have, I believe that documentation is the fall guy for poor products. The customers are complaining about the documentation when their real complaint is with the software. This caveat aside, I would like to review what not do when developing manuals.

1. Avoid readability.
2. Conceal critical information.
3. Don't worry, be font happy.
4. Use jargon indiscriminately.
5. Bypass the obvious.
6. Seek to confuse.
7. Eliminate use of examples.
8. Aim for disorganization.
9. Include a useless index.
10. Store the manual in an awkward binder.
11. Do not test the manual.

Reference: Ten Steps to Terrible Manuals, ComputerWorld, October 16, 1989.

Using this list as a guide, I think we can identify a number of points that should be part of any documentation program.

1. **Make sure that someone is responsible for readability. This cannot be the programmer who wrote the product. Just as I need an editor for my newsletter, your programmers need an editor who will insure that it is readable.**

2. **Highlight critical information.**

If your programmers don't feel that the revised documentation highlights the important information, they should point this out to the editor.

3. Make it aesthetically pleasing.

An experienced editor should control the urge to use unlimited fonts.

4. **Cover the obvious.**

Have your editor work with the package and ensure that all the steps are there.

5. **Seek to keep it simple.**

6. **Use examples.**

Your editor can develop examples while working with the package.

7. Aim for organization.

This is one of the major skills that the editor will bring to this process.

8. **Make the index useful.**

The editor will provide this as part of their testing.

9. **Use a standard sized binder.**

This will help reduce your costs and will avoid the problems with unusual binders.

10. Test the manual.

It is a key part of the product. Send it to beta sites before you release it.

Once you have had a chance to work with the editor on documentation, you might let them work on some marketing and promotional writing.

21. Staffing

In most companies, you have to go outside to get an editor to help with your documentation. There are a number of alternatives which can be effective, depending upon your needs and the resources in your local area.

Hiring a contract editor is often a good first step. In most areas, (especially around universities), you can find independent editors. While it helps to find one who has some technical background, there are real benefits from having a novice user write your documentation.

Most companies start with a project to revise their documentation. They really don't know what the ongoing workload will be. In this situation, it is best to work with a contract writer. This allows both of you to test how well the chemistry works, and to really understand the ongoing workload.

Once you have had a chance to work with the editor on documentation, you might let them work on some marketing and promotional writing. Can they help you write articles and gain publicity for your company? You might find that you can create a meaningful full-time position with this expanded job description.

22. Implementing Second Level Support

One of the most difficult transitions for a support organization is to take the programmers off the phones. There comes a time when you can't continue with programmers covering the phones, making the modifications and developing new products. Usually, this comes about because the programmers are pulled in so many directions that they can't do justice to any of them.

There are three very distinct roles:

1. Customer Support

This is manning the phones and solving the problems which don't require programming. Customer support personnel don't have access to the source code.

2. Maintenance Programming

This group is responsible for fixing problems in the product and providing enhancements to address limitations in the product that aren't exactly bugs.

This group is responsible for keeping the installed base happy and protecting your support revenues.

3.   Development

Development builds new products and is driven by market demand as expressed by marketing and sales. This group is responsible for getting new customers and establishing new product lines.

Companies may use fancy titles, but I believe that these basic roles exist in all companies.

There comes a time when you can't continue with programmers covering the phones, making the modifications and developing new products.

In the beginning, one programmer fills all three roles. They like the involvement with the customers, and there is an economic imperative to get the bugs fixed and get the customer to pay. Many companies continue with this "one person does it all" philosophy for a number of years. The reasons for this are numerous:

* **Senior programmers require little direct management.**

* **The technical founders like the idea that programmers are providing support, since that is what they wanted when they were customers.**

* **The programmers are unwilling to admit that non-programmers might be able to handle the first level support better than they are doing it.**

If you want to implement a support group, you need a manager who can begin to document the most common questions and the correct answers. It is very important that you provide your support people with the correct answers for the technical questions that they answer. One side benefit of this process is that you will identify areas where your documentation is weak.

If you want to implement a support group, you need a manager who can begin to document the most common questions and the correct answers.

Take care in phasing in your support people. Make sure that they understand the product from a user point of view and that they really understand the documentation. If you manage this process, you will find that you will end up with non-programmers who make less than 50 percent of what your programmers make, and they will be providing better support!

E. Support Survey (1990)

As usual, we got a very good response to the support survey. The company type wasn't biased. The annual software revenues were also close to the reader survey as was the mix of type of software:

TYPE OF SOFTWARE	% RESP
Vertical	52.8%
Horizontal	19.4%
System Utilities	16.7%
Horizontal Micro	13.9%

We had a larger distribution of companies with products less that $1,000 than the reader survey.

UNIT PRICE	% RESP
<$1K	32.5%
$1K-$10K	25.6%
$10K-$25K	23.3%
$25K-$100K	16.3%
>$100K	2.3%

They are also close to the reader survey in the sales channels used.

SALES CHANNEL	% RESP
Direct	88.9%
Telemarketing	38.9%
VAR/ Dealer	52.8%
OEM	11.1%

There were slightly more mini and mainframe companies in this survey, which is consistent with the higher interest in support in these more mature markets.

CPU SUPPORTED	% RESP
Micro/ PC	80.6%
LANs	41.7%
Mini	41.7%
Mainframe	22.2%

There was a very great range in the number of customers.

NO. OF CUSTOMERS	% RESP
<100	33.3%
100-500	16.7%
500-1K	11.1%
1K-5K	22.2%
>5K	13.9%

Chapter VI. Customer Support and Technical Issues

The type of support offered was quite varied.

TYPE OF SUPPORT	% RESP
Free 800#	38.9%
Free Pay call	27.9%
Maintenance Cont	58.3%
Pay per call	11.1%

Pay-per-call was the only unpopular type of support. The effort to monitor and control the pay-per-call increases exponentially as the number of customers increase.

Maintenance agreements are the most popular type of support.

Some companies who have maintenance agreements provide 800 numbers while others still make the customers pay for the calls. Some companies have the customer call and leave their information, and the support rep calls back once they have done some research and have verified that the customer is current on support.

Most companies charge between ten and fifteen percent for support.

SUPPORT %$	% RESP
<10%	27.8%
10%-14%	30.6%
15%	16.7%
>15%	11.1%

In reviewing the surveys, it appears that these numbers understate the support fees for the companies who charge for updates separately. A number of the firms who charged less than ten percent for support mentioned that they also charge for updates, but they don't really know how much revenue that will produce.

Only eleven percent of the companies charge more than fifteen percent for support. I have found that many customers will complain if the support fees are greater than fifteen percent. I also know firms who have established a higher level (20 percent), but they also provide additional services and are committed to high service levels.

If you have competition, charging more than fifteen percent can be a real competitive issue. It isn't clear that charging less gains you a commensurate amount. It is just that customers feel that you are gouging at the higher level.

Companies often provide three months or one year of free maintenance.

FREE MAINT	% RESP
None	11.1%
<3 Months	38.9%
<1 Year	8.3%
=1 Year	25.0%
>1 Year	16.7%

I was surprised at the firms who offer no free maintenance. I have clients who insist that customers pay for the first year of support when they purchase the software, but offering no free support seems like pushing it to me.

I am also concerned about the firms who offer more than a year of free support. I suspect that many of them have committed to "unlimited free support." I worry about this type of open-ended commitment. I understand the marketing advantages of this, but your company will not be able to provide this free support if your sales ever slow down. You are precluding the possibility of supporting your company on maintenance revenues in the long term.

I am also concerned about the firms who offer more than a year of free support. I suspect that many of them have committed to "unlimited free support." I worry about this type of open ended commitment.

I was really impressed that most firms have non-programmers providing support.

1ST LEVEL	% RESP
Developers	19.4%
Support Prog.	30.6%
Non-Prog.	55.6%

Most companies give support to customers who aren't on support.

NON-SUPPORT CUST	% RESP
Give them	50.0%
Up to person	16.7%
Screened	25.0%

I assume that the companies who leave it up to the person really end up giving it away in most cases. It is very difficult for a support person to not give support. I must admit that I was surprised that 25 percent of the companies screened the calls. I was even more impressed that all of these firms provided no phone support if the customer wouldn't sign up for support. I really believe that you have to implement this type of tough policy if you want to get your customers to sign up for support. I am troubled by firms who ask their customers to pay for support, but let the deadbeats get free support. This just penalizes the customers who were stupid enough to pay for support. That is wrong.

Most of the companies who screen support calls offer FAX or mail support.

OPTION	% RESP
No Reply	30.6%
Telephone	55.6%
FAX	19.4%
Mail	22.2%

I have seen FAX become a viable alternative for non-support customers. It is a lower level of support than phone support, which is reserved for the paying customers. It forces them to write their problem down which removes some of the annoyance calls. Finally, it does allow you to identify and fix real problems.

The turnover rate was much lower than I would have guessed.

TURNOVER RATE	% RESP
<10%	72.2%
10%-15%	16.7%
>15%	11.1%

I must admit that I was surprised that 25 percent of the companies screened the calls. I was even more impressed that all of these firms provided no phone support if the customer wouldn't sign up for support. I really believe that you have to implement this type of tough policy if you want to get your customers to sign up for support.

Chapter VI. Customer Support and Technical Issues

1. Type of Support versus Number of Customers

The fewer customers you have, the more likely you are to offer maintenance contracts. If you have fewer than 100 customers, getting as much money as possible from each customer is important. There doesn't seem to be a pattern as far as 800 numbers, but companies with a large number of customers seem to be more inclined to let their customers pay for the phone call.

	Free 800#	Pay Call	Free Main- tenance	Pay per call
100	22%	11%	56%	11%
100-500	25%	13%	50%1	3%
500-1K	60%	0%	40%	0%
1K-5K	22%	44%	33%	0%
5K	29%	29%	29%	14%

2. Cost of Support versus Number of Customers

In general, the more customers you have, the less you charge for support. In fact, very few companies with more than 500 customers charge fifteen percent or more for support. I wonder if this is because companies get lots of customers because they don't charge a lot for support, or if companies with lots of customers have such great economies of scale that they don't have to charge as much. I wasn't surprised that 25 percent of the companies with fewer than 100 customers charge more than fifteen percent for support. Many young companies bundle other services with support so they feel justified charging more. The company with 1,000 to 5,000 customers which charges more than fifteen percent is a market leader and sells their support as very high quality.

	< 10%	10%-14%	15%	> 15%
< 100	25%	25%	25%	25%
100-500	17%	33%	50%	0%
500-1K	66%	33%	0%	0%
1K-5K	40%	40%	0%	20%

3. Free Maintenance versus CPUs Supported

Three months free support is standard for Micro/ PC and LANs. I was very surprised that anyone would offer a product on a LAN with more than a year of free support. I sure hope these products don't require much support. Mini and mainframe products offer either three months or one year of free support. If you can get away with cutting back to three months of free support, you have raised your purchase price twelve percent without drawing much attention to it. I am surprised at the number of companies who offer more than a year of free support.

	None	< 3 mo	< 1 Year	< 1 Year	< 1 Year
Micro/PC	11%	43%	7%	18%	21%
LAN	7%	53%	13%	7%	20%
Mini	0%	50%	6%	38%	6%
Mainframe	13%	38%	0%	38%	13%

4. First Line Support versus Annual Revenue

The shift from having developers provide support to having support programmers provide it, then having non-programmers provide it is one of increasing sophistication. If your product is very difficult to support, the developers may be the only ones who can provide first level support. As the product settles down, support programmers may be able to take over. They don't have to have the developer's knowledge of the product, but they still need to be able to look at the source code. The final step is to document the problems and the solutions well enough that non-programmers can provide effective first level support. There will still be problems which require a programmer to look at the source code, it just happens less often. The usage of non-programmers increases consistently as the company revenues increase. The very high level of developers supporting products in small companies is also consistent with this model.

	Developers	Support Program	Non-Programmers
<250K	40%	30%	30%
$250K-$1M	9%	36%	55%
>$1M	25%	25%	63%

5. Non Support Customers versus Unit Price

If a product sells for less than $1,000, companies tend to give customers free support even if they are supposed to pay for it. On the other hand, as the price increases, companies tend to screen their calls.

Fifteen percent of $25,000 is enough money that it is worth hassling the customer about paying for support.

	Give Them	Up to Person	Screened
<$1K	83%	8%	8%
$1K - $25K	33%	29%	38%
>$25K	33%	17%	50%

6. Options if They Refuse to Pay versus Unit Price

Very few of the companies with products over $25,000 allow the non- payer to talk to the support people. They let them mail or FAX their problem, but they can't talk to a support person.

	Phone	FAX	Mail
<$1K	59%	18%	24%
$1K - $25K	71%	12%	18%
>$25K	17%	33%	50%

I urge you to look at your support fees in two ways. First of all, you should look at it from your customer's point of view. What is normal in your marketplace? Unless it is very important, you probably shouldn't have to argue with your customers about your support fees. Look back to see what is normative for your situation. The second perspective is internal. Are you generating enough revenue to pay for the services you are providing?

7. Annual Turnover Rate versus Annual Software Revenues

If you look at the turnover rate by company revenue you find that small companies have very low turnover (all less than fifteen percent). Companies over $2 million are even more stable (their turnover is less than ten percent). In the mid range, there is more turmoil. My experience is that getting above $1 million in sales is a difficult transition for many companies. As a company goes from ten or fewer employees to twenty or more they go from no management structure (everyone reports to the boss) to a management team of four or five managers who run the company. This can impact some of the old-timers who remain individual contributors. They are used to dealing with the president, and they find it difficult to work through channels. Another problem is that too many companies fail to anticipate the support and training workload that an increase in sales will cause. It often takes three to six months to hire, and train new support people. The existing support people can get burned out before the new people are effective. If this happens, the new people get thrown into the battle too soon and burn out before their time.

8. Conclusion

Support is critical to the long-term success of most software business. First and foremost, you need the reference accounts. Long term, a good reputation is necessary (even if its isn't sufficient) for success in the software business. Financially, support fees can become 30 to 50 percent of your total revenues. This recurring revenue can provide the stability and can help fund research and development to keep your product alive and well. I urge you to look at your support fees two ways. First of all, you should look at it from your customer's point of view. What is normal in your market place? Unless it is very important, you probably shouldn't have to argue with your customers about your support fees. Look back to see what is normative for your situation. The second perspective is internal. Are you generating enough revenue to pay for the services you are providing? Early on, you may have to subsidize your support as part of the cost of building your business, but eventually you should make good money in your support business.

9. Documentation

We are in the process of updating our documentation and wonder if we could put all of our documentation into Readme files instead of paper documentation.

When customers buy a product the physical documentation is part of what they buy. Readme files aren't very visible so they don't help increase the customer perception of value. I find that most customers compare the physical package. You must insure that your product package compares well with your competitors. Once you have met the competitive requirement, I would look at the Readme file. Readme can't take the place of documentation.

10. Training: Your Place ...or Mine

We offer on-site training for our customers, but our trainers are frustrated at the low level of productivity because of the interruptions. We would like to get the customers to come to our location. What is your experience with getting customers to come to the vendor for training?

Customers like on-site training for a number of reasons. The primary reason is that it is customized for their situation. Secondly, the trainer can help with the installation and participate in getting the system operational. Having a trainer on site allows the trainer to complete part of the installation.

Another reason that companies like on-site training is that it allows them to get more people involved in the training. Usually, there are secondary operators who can benefit from small amounts of training. The trainer can also work with other groups who impact the system.

The final benefit is that they don't lose their key person. They can keep them involved in fighting fires so that everything doesn't come to a stop. (Recall that this is the other side of the vendor complaint.)

If you priced your training at time and materials, and the customer continued to be trained until they were proficient, you shouldn't care how inefficient they were. If they were only fifty percent effective, they would buy more training and you would make more money. It doesn't quite feel this way for several reasons. I would like to discuss these fundamentals before I discuss the solutions.

	≤ 10%	10%-15%	15%-30%	> 30%
< $250K	88%	13%	0%	0%
$250K-$500K	100%	0%	0%	0%
$500K-$2M	50%	28%	17%	6%
> $2M	100%	0%	0%	0%

The first problem is that many companies either give training away or underprice it. My experience is that a trainer is lucky to bill 10 days a month and that their fully-burdened cost (not counting travel) is two times their salary. Thus, if we paid a trainer $18,000 a year our fully-burdened cost would be $36,000.

If you divide this by 120 billable days a year, training costs us $300 a day to deliver. I suggest that you mark this cost up by at least fifty percent to $450 a day to provide some margin and cover other costs. If you are providing a more expensive trainer ($27,000), my suggested price would be $675.

I would suggest that you compare your trainer costs with your prices. I would be surprised if you aren't low. If you don't like that answer, you should compare your recent training revenues and training costs. Make sure that you include corporate allocations for management time and facilities including phone costs.

Even if you have a proper daily rate, you can still be giving training away. I have seen a number of vendors who specify a fixed number of training days as part of the initial contract. They assure the customer that they will be trained in three days or whatever the amount was. If the customer isn't trained in that length of time, the vendor provides additional training at no charge because they assume that the problem was theirs (either poor training or poor product). It is very easy for management and the developers to lay the blame on the less technical trainers.

The final way that the vendor can eat the cost of excess training is to provide it on the support line. At the end of the specified period of training, the customer is turned over to support. If the customer hasn't learned the product, the customer support people continue the training without any additional revenue.

If you look at these alternatives, it is very clear that there is very little pressure on customer management to ensure that their people put the time and effort into learning your product. I fundamentally believe that you must protect yourself so that you are indifferent, and allow your customers to make their own decision.

My Recommendations Are:

1. **Set your price for training high enough that you can make money assuming that you pay fair market value for good trainers. (Don't exploit your trainers to hold your prices down.)**

2. **Make it very clear to the customer that they are responsible for their own training. If they are prepared and can cover the material quickly, they can save time. On the other hand, if they have your trainer do everything for them, the time and the costs can increase dramatically.**

3. **Document the customer's responsibility to prepare for each stage in the training process. Notify them in writing before each training action. When you visit, review their preparation at the start of each visit. Note the areas that weren't done. If your trainer has to spend extra time because of lack of preparation, have the training manager call the person responsible for paying the bill. Explain that they were responsible for X and their people had done Y and this had taken an extra Z hours. Ask the responsible party if they would like to increase the budget allocation for training. I have found that if you start this dialogue with the responsible party early in the process that you can avoid a lot of unpleasantness later on. It is also useful to**

document all of the steps. If you don't document and confirm this information with your customer, you will end up eating these costs.

4. **The final approach is to offer alternative forms of training. You might offer the initial two days of training at your location in a monthly class. Assuming that you can train more than one customer, you should be able to offer a reduced rate. This is something that you can sell to the responsible   party.**

It also helps if you have a nice hotel (a suites hotel is a common solution) which is easy for your customers to use. In many cases, the people you are training aren't experienced travelers and anything you can do to make it easier for them will make them more willing to travel. Having breakfast included with the room may seem like a minor point, but I have clients who swear by it as a selling point for their training class.

If you put together this combination of the carrot (nice cheap vendor training) and the stick (additional charges if they require additional training), you should be able to move your customers to the balance of training which best suits their needs. If you have set your prices correctly, you should be indifferent to what options they chose. Ideally, they may chose more vendor training, but that may not be the case. (As an aside, I have seen very few cases of customers opting for vendor location training. I believe that it is due to their employees lack of travel experience. They would rather pay more for on-site training.)

A final option is to provide training in their city, but not at their location. I have had clients who rented a room at the hotel and provided training there. There are a number of problems with this. First of all, there is a cost involved in renting a room. This can be a real issue with the customer who feels that this is not necessary. Secondly, you must bring a portable computer and set it up in the motel. You have issues with security and having a printer available. Finally, the customer isn't working on their system. Minor differences will occur and will drive the customer crazy. They will also be frustrated that they aren't getting the trainer's help with their installation.

In conclusion, I find that if you exert economic pressure on the customer they will pay more attention to

training, and if they make the decision to use more of your time rather than managing their time, you should respect that. As long as you are getting paid fairly for the training, it is their decision.

11. Customer Service Schedule

We use SCO Xenix and when we call for support we have been informed that we will receive a call back at a specified time later in the day. When we receive the call, the SCO support person starts the conversation off by saying, I have 5 minutes to talk to you. I was really ... Do you know of anyone else doing this?

This is a new one to me. I understand what they are doing, but it sure goes against the basic concepts of friendly customer support people helping their users. Anyone else know of anyone scheduling support like this?

Dave

12. Channel Support Calls
a. Qualifying and Training Your Dealers

Last year we were very successful in recruiting a good number of dealers. We even got some international distributors. It took them a while to get started, but all of a sudden we are swamped with support calls. How can I get this back under control?

The tough answer is that the cat is out of the bag, and that it is going to take a great deal of work to put things right. I would like to run through the basics. Did you technically qualify your dealers and distributors to insure that they had the proper level of staff to sell and support your product? Did you train them to get them up to an initial level? How good are your materials and documentation to allow them to support themselves? How good are your support people at solving problems on the phone?

I will assume that you have good support people who are skilled at solving customer problems. I will also assume that your support people get frustrated with your dealers and start working with the customer/prospect a little sooner than they should. I find that most companies who start working with dealers and distributors are expecting sales without work.

The reality is that you have someone else selling and supporting your product. Initially this will require more effort on your part because you have to train the dealer. You could do the work yourself faster, but you are hoping for the long-term leverage of having others working for you. Thus the first thing that you must do is tell your staff that they should do everything possible to help your dealers on the phone. You might even have to send support people into the field to help fix problems that have gotten out of control.

Training the technical people at the dealer requires significant effort. In many cases, the dealers have less experienced and less technical support people than most vendors are used to working with. They also have horrendous turnover. It is important that you have classes and training materials so that new dealer support people can be trained. Make sure that your materials are designed so that the new support person can pick them up and learn how to provide first level support in a matter of days.

The next major area is training the dealer sales people. They need to understand who the potential buyers are for your product. I can just hear the guffaws. Some of you are saying that you should sell your product to anyone who can pay the bill. In all seriousness, that isn't right. There are customers that you shouldn't sell to. I have one client who has refused to sell to some prospects because he believed that there wasn't a good match and that he was concerned that the prospect would drive him crazy.

At first, this struck me as extreme, but I believe that it is really right. If you know that there are certain requirements to use your product successfully, you should make these very clear. In fact, you might try to disqualify prospects. This is difficult to teach your own sales people, and it is even more difficult to teach dealer sales people. Dealer sales people are likely to be more aggressive about getting sales and will pull in prospects who really shouldn't buy. You should work with the dealer and show them why these people shouldn't buy and help them close the ones who should.

If you institute this two-pronged approach of improving technical support and teaching the dealer sales people to disqualify poor prospects, your long term support should decline.

Supporting international distributors is much more of a challenge. In addition to the issues that I just discussed for the dealers, you have cultural differences which may have to be incorporated into your product and/or your materials. You should insist that the technical and sales people from the distributor visit your company to get trained. Then you should follow up with quarterly visits to keep them current, visit customers and prospects, and keep the distributor interested in your product. This is a complex relationship and you must be prepared to invest in it if you ever expect it to work.

13. PC LAN Service

We sell a LAN-based product and we wonder how other companies provide support of LAN-based products.

My experience is that most vendors who are selling LAN products end up offering support directly. In fact, LAN vendors were the only group of software companies who provided hardware installation support.

Finding VARs who can install and support LANs is difficult. It takes a great deal of both time and expertise to install and support a LAN, and that is both difficult to come up with and expensive.

I read the following article in Digital News which suggests that there may be another solution.

Mentor Market Research published a study which revealed that DEC, HP and IBM offer comprehensive LAN support even though they haven't marketed these services aggressively to date.

Customer service is the fastest growing segment of the PC LAN marketplace. While PC LAN hardware sales are only projected to grow five percent in 1990, companies plan to spend 21 percent more on PC LAN services.

Reference: "PC LAN Services: Best-Kept Secret in Town", Elizabeth Heichler Digital News, January 22, 1990.

14. BBS

My technical support manager wants to install a BBS. Is this common for non-PC software?

A BBS is an electronic bulletin board. BBS' started as an underground cult meeting place for PC hackers, but in recent years have become very respectable. Coca-Cola, Ashton-Tate, AST, and others are using BBS' to answer customer calls, and to disseminate information. The vendor staff can load files regarding new products, technical information, and so forth. Customers can then dial in and retrieve this information. Some systems even allow customers to place orders.

A recent application allows customers to send e-mail to customer support personnel. This can be more efficient than phone calls. Ashton-Tate's BBS handles 400 calls a day and AST handles 150,000 a year.

AST has a private section for dealers and will be offering a data base with almost every technical question they have been asked. Users will be able to call in and perform keyword searches. They expect this to cut down the live phone time considerably.

Coca-Cola implemented a BBS to communicate with its sales managers. They believe that it has saved them $300,000 in overnight courier charges.

A final reminder is that you must create the information that you will disseminate via the BBS. This will require that someone in your organization create and review the information.

Reference: "Is There a BBS in Your Future?", Ken Joy, Marketing Computers, December 1989.

Other resources mentioned in the article include the following BBS':

The Major BBS
(305) 583-5990

BBS-PC
(305) 790-0772

DLX, Inner Loop Systems
(213) 822-2800

FIDO BBS
(618) 251-2169

OPUS Private Oak Lawn
(214) 991-3381
(modem only)

PC Board
(801) 261-1686

RBBS-PC
(203) 268-8656

TBBS
(303) 699-6565

15. Support References

Dear Dave:

You have done an excellent job. This issue in particular addresses the future for all of us. I especially appreciate your reference notes. They will help me find full source on things that you summarized.

Thanks,

Bob Matthews
President/CEO
Matsch Systems

Dear Bob:

Thanks for the feedback. I like the reference sections for the same reason. If you run across other resources which you believe that others might find useful, I would appreciate it if you would send it to me.

Thanks,
Dave

16. Using 900 Numbers to Bill Support Customers

We have been talking about using a 900 number to automatically bill for support. What have you heard about companies doing this?

I have read about a couple of the larger software companies doing this, and I have talked to a lot of smaller companies who are considering doing it. It appears to me that there is a great deal of reluctance to actually implement 900 numbers. I have thought of several reasons that are causing the problem:

1. There is the porno association with 900 numbers. I think that this makes the companies reluctant to do this because of the risk to their image. I also think that they are

concerned that their customers won't call for the same reason.

2. It appears that one-third to one-half of the billed amount will go to the phone company and the 900 number provider. I have talked to several companies who have investigated 900 numbers, and they were put off by how little they would actually receive.

3. Customer support is a sensitive business and billing customers for support calls which are really product problems can be a real mistake. With the common practice of taking the credit card number or invoicing them, the support person can exercise some judgement. If the customer is irate, the support person may elect not to bill that customer. In fact it is this discretionary free support that is part of the motivation for 900 numbers. With 900 numbers the billing is automatically done by the phone company and the support person has no opportunity to not bill.

The other side of this is that most companies are uncomfortable with automatic billing. They think about a customer with a serious problem getting irate on the phone because they are going to be billed and the support rep can't reverse the bill.

Revlon launched a 900 number sweepstakes with 52 million free- standing inserts. They had expected a 1.8 percent response rate for the $2 calls. The callers would find out right away if they had won a $25,000 U.S. savings bond. They also promised to give a nickel of each call to charity.

The actual response was less than one tenth of one percent. Thus, they generated only 45,000 calls instead of the 936,000 they had expected.

It also turns out the Revlon had tried several other 900 number campaigns, and they found "the response rate was 'much greater' when its market of 14 to 21 year old females mailed their names and addresses on a piece of paper."

Reference: "Revlon 900 Campaign Was a Flop; Only $2,000 Raised for a Foundation", By Terry Brennan, DM News, August 6, 1990.

It appears that 900 numbers aren't here yet. I would certainly appreciate hearing from anyone who has tried using a 900 numbers (or is still using them).

17. Help Desk Institute

The Help Desk Institute "provides training classes, educational materials, and a networking forum for leaders in Help Desk Management."

I believe that much of the work they are doing would apply to software support centers. If you are interested, call or write them for a free copy of their newsletter, "Life Raft."

The membership benefits include:

Reduced rates at seminars

Subscription to "Life Raft"

Copy of The Guide to Help Desk

Problem   Management

Certificate of Membership

Directory of members

The cost is $395 for one year for an individual at one location. Additional members at the same site are $125.

Help Desk Institute
1755 Telstar Drive,
Suite 101
Colorado Springs, CO 80920
(800) 248-5667

18. Product Packaging
Cost Guidelines for Packaging a Typical Product

What are some standard cost figures that I can use for planning purposes for packaging my product?

John Hawkins interviewed Darrel Monda of Data Envelope, (800) 544-4417, and Darrel gave some standard costs for a generic binder with clear cover sleeve. He points out that you can print your promotional cover inexpensively in low quantities. The typical budget for 500 packages of a two-disk package are:

One time artist services - $200 to $2,000.

1,000 disks and duplication - $700.

1,000 printed disk labels - $150.

1,000 disk sleeves printed one color - $150.

500 generic vinyl folders - $1,000.

500 cover cards printed locally in two colors - $200.

This adds up to $3,000, not including the manual, or $6.00 per product. You should be able to print your manual for $0.50 to $1.00 depending on the size and the length of your print run.

Reference:"The Well Dressed Disk", By John L. Hawkins,Data Based Advisor, April 1990.

19. Enhancements vs. Maintenance vs. New Product

We are trying to balance how we allocate our R & D time on enhancements and maintenance versus new product development.

I feel that the top priority is to fix known bugs which keep the product from performing as advertised. If you can't or won't fix these bugs, you should first change your documentation. Next, you should offer a refund to any customer who has complained about this bug. Since that doesn't sound like fun, you should make fixing bugs top priority. Once the product is stabilized, this shouldn't be a major source of work.

The next topic is enhancements to the existing product. Usually they come from customer suggestions or from your support people. I have a number of clients who allow R & D to spend 25 percent of its time on these enhancements. You have to limit the time and prioritize them because there is a never-ending list of these enhancements.

The next area is technical housecleaning. This is work that the development group wants to do on the product to clean it up, make it easier to maintain, and facilitate future enhancements. Allocating 25 percent of the R & D budget to this category will help maintain the morale of your programmers and it keeps your product competitive. Many of these changes are fundamentally good, but they aren't appreciated by sales and marketing because they are too technical. It is also important to limit the effort

expended on these tasks because the programmers can spend endless time on them.

Enhancements are under the control of sales and marketing. They can decide if you need new or better features to fight the feature wars, or if you are better off with a new product. My experience is that most sales and marketing groups will focus on extending the features and fighting the competition. They will come up with an endless list of new and better features. This is fine as long as you are getting more sales out of this investment. At some point, the marginal return from this type of work drops dramatically. This is especially true if you dominate the niche. As long as you have active competitors who are adding features, you have to keep up with the Joneses.

If you get to the point where you don't believe that you are getting much marginal return from investing in additional features (or you don't believe that it will hurt you if you don't have new features), it is time to put your product into maintenance mode. Move some of your developers on to new product development, and just maintain enough capability to keep doing customer features and technical enhancements on your regular release schedule. You want to make sure that you sustain this minimum level so that you protect your maintenance revenues and allow sales to continue selling your product.

You should expect sales to decline over time with this strategy, and hope that new product revenues will more than compensate and that your total revenues will be better than if you had left your entire team on the old product.

20. Comp Time for Technical Support People?

Dear Dave:

What is your experience regarding comp time for technical support people? Along with this as a general issue, what about time such people spend on plans, in the evening, going to and coming from assignments? Is there a company size issue involved in whether or not people get comp time for travel time?

We have people would even consider that time spent away from home, be it in a hotel somewhere or at convention, or entertaining business clients

for dinner (company paid) should rack up as comp time. What's your advice?

Phil Jamieson
Software Partners 32, Inc.

Dear Phil:

Comp time can be a very emotional issue. In particular, I have seen it become a major sore point as companies made the transition from the small band of programmers trying to get the company going to a professional organization. You can also make matters worse when you hire young people with very naive ideas about what they should be paid for.

The first thing that I would like to distinguish is between salaried and hourly employees. Salaried employees shouldn't expect overtime except in very unusual situations. (More on this in a minute.) Hourly employees, on the other hand, work by the hour and should be paid for every hour that they work. In general, salaried employees are paid more than hourly employees (at least in terms of their base compensation) so this seems fair.

Comp time is based on the concept that if people are asked to perform above and beyond the call of duty that they should either be paid for this additional time or be allowed to take time off. I have been involved with a number of companies where R & D had to put critical project teams on extended hours. Management told the teams, "We have to really put a push on to get this project out and we would like all of you to put in longer hours." In most of the cases, management asked for 50 hours a week. If the employees agreed to work the longer hours, they were entitled to a combat bonus which would be 25 percent of their pay in this case. There was no time-and-a-half involved in the cases that I have dealt with. The overtime premium was a bonus for making the schedule, and it was greater than half the overtime pay, so we were paying more than time-and-a-half if the project made it.

I want to point out that this was a voluntary process. Management had to sell the team, and once the team was sold, there was a fair amount of peer pressure to step up to the commitment. **But not everyone could or was willing to work 50 hours a week, and that is okay.**

Most of the people who couldn't commit to the extra hours had personal situations (children, parents, and so forth) that prevented them from putting in the time on-site like the others. I feel very strongly that this type of program must be voluntary. This is an ethical position on my part, but I am sure that legally you could get yourself into real trouble if you fired a single parent who couldn't put in the hours because of their child care situation.

Interestingly enough, the teams that I was involved with reconciled their own deals with the players who couldn't work the straight 50 hours. The managers were given the freedom to modify the program to the individual's situation. For example, in one case, a single parent took a computer terminal home and was able to check on jobs at night for the other team members. This person wasn't putting in as many hours as the others, but everyone felt that they were making an equivalent contribution.

I would like to come back to the tech support situation that you mentioned. My experience is that support people and trainers in general identify with the customers and view the company as something of an adversary. Many of them feel that the company is exploiting them and that they have to stick up for their rights. I have seen situations that reminded me of movies about union organizers. In fact, I had one client where one of the trainers tried to organize a union in the tech support department (it had four employees.)

In most of these cases, I have found that the basic problem was economic. The company wasn't paying the tech support people enough. This is especially true in companies where management is technically-oriented. Very technical management tends to base value on technical excellence, so they usually underpay support people. If you adjust your pay scales and salaries to be competitive with your local marketplace, you should eliminate much of the problem.

At the same time, management must make it clear to the support people that development programmers will make more than support techs. It is a special skill, much like sales, which commands a special compensation. On the other hand, if a support tech is making a good competitive salary, they should be happy.

If you are paying your techs a fair salary and you aren't in a extraordinary crunch, we have to deal with what is normal for comp time. I will go through your list and give my opinions on the situations you listed.

Spending Time on Plans in the Evening.

I really don't think that people should be given comp time for spending a couple hours on plans at home. I am assuming that people who plan are at a managerial level and that we are only talking about a couple of hours. If we are talking about a day of off-site planning, comp time might become appropriate. If you have a manager who won't do their planning without comp time, I would think that you don't really have a good manager and I would be strongly inclined to demote them to an individual contributor.

Travel Time to and from Assignments.

My general feeling is that as long as people leave home at about the same time as normal, and they get home at roughly the same time, there is no need for comp time. They have to commute to the office, so commuting to a client location is equivalent. If they don't get home until midnight, it might be appropriate for them to take off early or come in late for the next few days.

General Travel Time

Travel time can be an extraordinary situation for some employees, and it may be appropriate to give them comp time before they travel. On the other hand, if travel is a regular part of the job, this should be understood before the person takes the job, and the salary that they accept should include this. I have seen many cases where trainers who travel eight to ten days a month are paid twenty percent more than support techs who don't travel. I don't mind paying a higher scale because the job includes travel, but I do hate getting hit up for comp time for this and comp time for that.

Convention Time

I sure wouldn't give someone comp time for being away from home.

Business Dinners

I can't recall a case where employees were given comp time for going to a business dinner.

In summary, as an employer I don't like comp time. It reminds me of employees who work for the state. If people really want that type of rigid accounting, they shouldn't work for a small software company. My experience is that employees in small companies work longer hours than employees in large companies, who work longer hours than government employees. It just comes with the turf. There are advantages of working in small companies: technical challenge, opportunity to grow, possible stock ownership, and flexibility.

I think it is important that management in small companies make sure that they don't burn out their employees, but you can't grow a small software company with employees who work thirty hours a week and complain about every demand on their time. If you have employees who have a big company mentality, I would sit down and figure out what you feel is fair. Write it down and get your management team to agree on a policy. Then present it to your employees. If some of them don't like the deal, they are probably best off going back to the state or the big company they worked for before.

One final note: You can head off this type of problem by raising the issue of long hours and extra demands during the interview process. I tend to be very blunt with big company employees that small companies are different, and they need to think long and hard about the demands of working in a small company. If you are really blunt during the interview process, you will run off some people who really shouldn't work in a small company. If they come to work, and then don't like the policy, at least you made the policy clear beforehand and you have made it much easier to terminate them if they can't live with the policy.

The one thing that you can't do is make exceptions to the policy. This makes it very painful for the people who are trying to live with the policy. If someone's situation changes, and they can't travel, you should try to change their job description to match their new situation. It might be appropriate to lower their salary if they are out of the range for the job they are moving into.

This is obviously a tough issue, but you must deal with it head on. Software companies are dependent on hard-working employees who are willing to go the extra mile to make things happen. One disgruntled employee can spread dissatisfaction through an entire company. My experience is that if you confront the disgruntled employee and say "you don't seem happy making the commitment that we expect of our employees and I think that you would be much happier working back at the state" that most times, they decide to resign and go back to a job more to their liking. This is really best for everyone.

21. Software Support Conference

Dear Dave,

I am writing to tell you about the Third Annual Conference on Software Support sponsored by the Institute for International Research. It will be held at the JW Marriott at Lenox in Atlanta, Georgia on January 24-25, 1991.

Topics to be covered include the latest in support automation, various approaches to providing support via the 900 number, third party suppliers, and consulting. There will also be several talks on dealing with the multivendor environment.

The speakers include representatives from Lotus Development, Ashton-Tate, Peachtree Software, IBM, WordPerfect, and Novell, among others.

Sincerely,

Audrey Wu, Vice President
Institute for International
437 Madison Ave
New York, NY 10022

Dear Audrey,

For more information, those interested should contact Audrey Wu at (212) 826-3340 ext 3053.

Dave

22. AWSSM

Dear Dave,

I tried to contact the AWSSM from the number that appeared in the January issue of Software Success. Unfortunately the number has changed. Do you have a new one?

John Parry
Flomerics
Kingston on Thames,
England

Dear John,

Ken Schotwell is the head of the AWSSM and he works at Triad. His number is 415-449-0606.

Dave

F. Miscellaneous Product Planning (1989)

1. Determining Market Size

Q. We market horizontal software (e.g., word processors, data base software, utilities) for the Amiga. Our sales have increased 50% from one release to the next, but we get most of our sales in the initial product roll-out. How can we determine the potential market size for our product categories?

A. This company markets business-oriented software for the Amiga. We've worked with this company and there's good news and bad news.

First, the good news. This company is doing a lot of things right. They are putting out good products which have received rave reviews. They are the market leader in the segments they serve.

The bad news is that even with thirty to forty percent of the sold market, their sales aren't adequate to provide a decent return on investment. It appears that the business market for the Amiga isn't adequate to support this company. There are two obvious choices:

- Move to a more lucrative hardware platform, or
- Establish a new software category.

Moving to a New Platform

Moving to a new hardware platform feels very risky to these individuals. They are technically comfortable with the Amiga, and they like being a big fish in a small pond. This move can easily put them out of business so it must be approached with care.

2. Repositioning Products

At the same time, it appeared that they could reposition their products and increase their market potential. Their major product is a very sophisticated database package, but 95% of their customers bought it to print mailing labels. Their ads stress the high-tech features. There are probably many mom and pop Amiga users will pay a lower price ($150) for a powerful mailing list manager which is also a real database. We think that this potential market might have been put-off by the high-tech ads.

If this repositioning doesn't work, we believe that they will either have to adapt to the Amiga market or move to other platforms.

3. Creating a new product Category

Q. We have a new product which is establishing a new category. We understand that this product will require missionary selling and extensive customer education. What methods work, and what should our expectations be?

A. A missionary product is one of the toughest sales and marketing challenges around. It's also one of the most rewarding and (potentially) lucrative.

Dark Clouds
The list of problems caused by being "first" can be daunting:

- **Unproven Market** — You don't *really* know if anyone will pay for your product, much less *how much* they'll pay.

- **No trails in the sand** — You don't have anyone to copy. As you develop your sales and marketing programs, you will be uncovering both successful and unsuccessful sales strategies. No one can tell you, in advance, if any given approach will work.

- **Longer Lead-times** — In general, establishing your vanguard position will take much longer than you expect, and you will measure progress in feet instead of miles. There probably are a dozen bottlenecks that you must work your way through before you have a production sales and marketing machine.

Silver Linings
All this hassle and effort can be worth it, however. The rewards for founding a new product category are substantial:

- **Market Leadership** — You have the benefits of market leadership. You set the prices. Competitors must react to *you*. Everyone (in the product category) knows your name.

- **Big Sales Potential** — With several exceptions, most of the larger software firms got their start with a new type of product. As the marketplace exploded, so did their sales. It can happen to you. It's better than winning the lottery because the tax-write-offs are more fun!

- **Public Recognition** — One of the real, but often overlooked benefits of pioneering software marketing is that you'll garner quite a bit of public or at least peer recognition. (Be careful that this isn't the *only* reward.)

Creating a Category

The first problem is to explain what you have and why your prospects should care. If you can't do this, you can't even start. We urge you to talk to as many prospects as possible as soon as possible. Write up a package which describes your product (a product brochure), get prospects to read it and ask them to tell you what they think you have and see if they are interested. Even if they don't like your materials, see if they will let you come in and demo your product. Find out if there is a real need for your product, and if so what the real benefits are. We realize that this sounds obvious, but we continue to be surprised at the number of new missionary products which haven't dealt with this fundamental question: *Is there really a market here?*

In many cases, the company is so in love with their technology that they don't want to take the risk that there may be no real need. This can be very sad because they might be able to reposition the technology or adapt it to solve some real problems and make a real contribution to the world.

One of the real advantages of having a missionary product is that you are unique. This will interest prospects once you know how to present it to them. It will also interest the media. They may help you with press releases and articles. Use PR to get the word out. Educational seminars can be effective because your prospects are curious. Often missionary products are implementing a new methodology. Offer to teach people about this new methodology and use your product to exemplify it.

Once you know what problem you can solve and you have identified a good prospect, you must determine how to sell your solution. Who should you approach? What are their hot buttons? Who can initiate the evaluation? Who will conduct the evaluation, and how are their needs different from the initiator? What materials will the evaluator need to sell the initiator? Look at what works and what doesn't work to discern the successful pattern. This is hard work, but it is rewarding. The final encouragement is that if you can establish your product as the leader in a new category, you can reap the benefits for many years. Good luck.

4. Entering an Established Product Category

Q. How can we enter an established product category with a new product?

A. Unless you have both a superior product and superior financial resources, don't attack the market leader head on. Remember Javelin! Once a product is positioned, it is difficult to knock it from that position. This is independent of whether or not the premises on which the positioning is based are accurate.

For instance, I commonly see market leaders who are positioned as the technical leader. While this may have been true when they entered the market, it is very likely that a new product is or can be technically superior. Attacking the market leader's technical position rarely works. On the other hand, you can focus on your area of technical superiority and use that to define your position.

For example, relational data base systems were initially unsuccessful in replacing established hierarchial data base products. Relational data base vendors subsequently determined that customers could develop applications more rapidly using their products. They then stressed these product attributes as positives. This approach seems more effective than focusing on the weaknesses of your competition.

5. Product Life-Cycle Planning

Q. How should we do product feature planning so that we can achieve an extended life cycle?

A. The first step is to do a competitive analysis. What features are your competitors offering? Don't forget the indirect competition. Look for alternative solutions to meet your prospect's needs. Often we find that manual systems often are very robust. In many cases they can do things that software systems can't.

The second step is to conduct a customer and prospect survey. Ask both your customers and your prospects what features they are interested in. Get them to help you set priorities. You also need to categorize features into the following categories:

- Must have to remain competitive (ASAP).

- Will need in the future.

- Customers will pay more for this.

- Nice to have but not really important.

The third step is to build the business case. Analyze the development cost for each feature. Estimate its revenue potential (including protecting the ongoing sales.) Protecting the maintenance revenue becomes important as products mature and the maintenance revenue builds. At this point you can prioritize the features based on their return.

The final decision is the most difficult. What level of resources should you commit to this feature development? There are several strategies which we have seen used:

1. **Hire all you canHire as many programmers as your maintenance revenue will support.**

2. **Defensive PloyStaff it from a defensive point of view. What is the minimum level to handle the features you absolutely must have? This approach typically leads to problems because companies usually underestimate the competition.**

3. **Balanced investmentInvest in development based on the expected payback. Develop a plan and manage your company so that you invest for some period of time, but you expect to break even in phase 2 and turn a profit by phase 3. This approach is more difficult, but if you have the resources it is the best way to manage your business.**

G. Documentation (1989)

1. Manuals as Marketing Tools

Q. We are having an internal debate about the wisdom of using our manuals as marketing tools. Our sales people don't want to send out the manuals too early in the sales cycle, but the technical founder feels that the manuals will make the sale in spite of the sales people. What do you recommend?

A. The first lesson in sales is to give the prospect enough information to agree to move to the next step in the sales cycle, but no more. Continuing to talk after you have made this "sub-sale" only risks undoing the decision just reached by the prospect. At the same time, the amount of information that people need to move ahead in the sales cycle varies from person to person.

I have seen companies send manuals to unqualified prospects who aren't even sure they have a business need for the software. If the prospect is currently trying to fully understand the business requirement, they typically don't need to know the technical details of the product. They can work from a simple understanding of the technical capabilities of the product, and focus on the business issues. On the other hand, if they clearly understand their business requirement, the only issue in their mind may be the technical capability of the product and its ability to solve their problem. The manuals, a demonstration or trial of the product, and/or technical discussions are all ways to address this latter type of problem.

In conclusion, I advise you to ask yourself why the prospect needs your manual, what use they will make of it, and if this is the best way to get them to take the next step. If sending the manuals is the best solution to these questions, by all means send it. Just make sure that you answer these questions.

2. Contracting Documentation

Q. *We would like to improve the quality of our manuals, but we can't afford to add full time employees. What do you suggest?*

A. We have seen companies have good luck with part time contractors. In most cities there are technical writers who are independent contractors. Check with your local college or university job placement office.

While the hourly rate for contractors may be higher than an equivalent hourly salary, you only pay them when they are working. The other benefit is that when the project is done you aren't carrying them on the payroll. In many cases you can get a pretty good estimate of the time and costs before you start on a project. This will help you evaluate the cost benefit tradeoffs with upgrading your documentation. Many mature contract writers (and we know of several who have been doing this for more than ten years) will give you a firm, fixed-price bid for your documentation.

3. On-line Documentation

Q. We produce our documentation on-line. Must we provide hard copy to our customers? How should we maintain our documentation?

A. Given the limitations of the current generation of computer displays, on-line documentation is more difficult to read than paper information. We don't know of anyone who only distributes their documentation on-line. While this may be partially due to the display limitations, we believe that it is also due to the fact that people feel better getting some heft when they buy a package. It makes them feel better about their purchase. We suggest that you print up some nice documentation for your customers. You'll feel great about it, and so will your customers.

4. Documentation Release(s)

Most companies release an update to the documentation with a software release. The only common exception is new software releases which have documentation which is so terrible that it must be updated. Usually the publisher makes an interim software release and distributes both the software and documentation at the same time.

5. Packaging

Darrell Monda is president of Data Envelope, company which specializes in packaging for software companies. While packaging is vital for products which sell at the retail level, Darrell feels it is equally important for non-retail products. Packaging conveys value, and all products must project the appropriate value.

I asked Darrell to describe how he would help a software publisher approach packaging. The first step is competitive analysis. What is your competition? Do they sell through distribution? What does their packaging look like?

The next step is to establish a price point for your product. He believes that you should attempt to limit your packaging cost to five to ten percent of the price at the wholesale distribution level. Thus, a $100 product might bring the publisher $40 from the distributor. This would give you a $2 to $4 target for the cost of your packaging.

In general terms, your packaging options depend upon quantity. If you are talking about less than 5,000 units, you must limit your-self to off-the-shelf packaging if you want to keep your costs within reasonable bounds. I asked Darrell to discuss the op-

tions for an initial 1,000 production run for various price points.

$29.95 = $12 to vendor

This is the first step in formal packaging. He suggested a clamshell which can hang on a rack. In addition, you have the diskette, the label, and the diskette sleeve. You might also include a header card which wraps around the disk and describes product features. The costs would be:

Disk + Dup	$0.50
Clamshell	$0.30
Header card	$0.05
Total	$0.85

This cost might go up another 10 to 15 cents if you include additional information. This is within our five to ten percent target range.

$49.95 = $20 to vendor

For this level, he recommends a billboard folder with custom printed identification pieces which slide into the front and into the pack. The billboard will cost $1.25 and your total cost will approach $2.00 when you include your printing, disk, and so forth. If you can order 5,000 units, you could go to a clear vacuum-form package where the cover is printed on the package. You can even have a window through which the diskette label is visible if you have multiple packages. This costs only $1.25 plus the disk and eliminates the cost of the printing. Just remember that you have to order 5,000 at one time.

$100 = $40 to vendor

A billboard vacuum-formed case is a good option at this price. It feels safe and holds up to a 100-page manual as well as both a 5-1/4 and 3-1/2 inch disk. He recommends this if you want to establish a retail presence. The case will cost $2.00 and the insides will cost another $1.00. This is under our 10% target.

$295 direct

At this price, you might be looking at lower quantities. Darrell suggests a slant box with a binder slipcase. The cost is less than $10, including the printing. As an example, he showed me a one-inch D-Ring, IBM standard size binder that had been silk screened in two colors on a nice grey cambric fabric.

The cost of the entire package, including warranty card, tabs, license agreement, and a 50-page manual was $10 in quantities of 500. Within the IBM standard format, you can vary the widths of the D-ring from 1", 1-1/2", and 2" without changing the costs dramatically. If you don't anticipate updating your documentation, you might include a perfect bound or sprial bound manual in a slant box. This would reduce the cost from $10 to $7.50.

If you want to go to the 8-1/2" x 11" format, the binder slipcase is 9" X 12". At low volumes, you can get a top quality binder for $13 to $14.

Demo disk mailers

One item that he was very proud of was a demo disk self-mailer. He prints both sides of the mailer with promotional materials. The instructions are inside. In quantities of 2,500 you can obtain the mailer with your disk inside.

Most common mistake/little guy makes?

Darrell felt that the little guy looked at his competitor's packaging and assumed that he had to match it. Since the large competitor is dealing with large quantities they can afford custom packaging. Custom packaging is very expensive in small quantities. Rather than finding what they can assemble from available pieces, the small guy wastes his money on custom packaging when the standard packaging would look as good.

If you are considering new packaging, you should call Darrell. He has a great deal of experience in software packaging, and can use the standard components that he has developed and assembled to help small software companies present their products professionally.

Reference: Darrell Monda, DataEnvelope, (408) 374-9720

---

6. Image Packaging

Q. How should I decide what type of marketing materials and packaging I need? What kind of image should we present?

A. The first step is to look at similarly priced products and competitive products. If you are selling a $25,000 system, it should look like other $25,000 systems. You sure don't want to lose the sale because your marketing materials and packaging don't look the part.

At the same time, you don't want to try to present yourself as more than you really are. We have seen a number of cases where startup companies who were competing with established companies hired ad agencies and developed very fancy marketing materials and ads. They looked like big companies. When their prospects found out that they were a small operation, the prospects felt mislead. Our experience is that young companies should focus on putting out attractive but low cost marketing materials. You can do a lot with laser printers and two color printing. Focus on the content — not how it looks.

a. Early Adapters

There is a certain category of software buyer who really likes to be the first kid on their block to buy the newest software. They are like people who really like to discover new restaurants before everyone else. If you try to look too mature, you will scare away these early adaptors, and you won't fool the followers.

b. Spending Smarter

Finally, you should really look at your sales cycle to identify the pressure points. Where in the cycle are your sales decisions becoming bogged down? What are the implications of a purchase decision for your prospects? What information do they need to make this decision? This is the real context to evaluate your needs for marketing materials. Your competitors may sell differently so they may have different needs. Make sure that you solve your own marketing problems rather than keeping up with the Jones.

H. Quality and Testing (1989)

1. QA & Testing

Q. Do you know of any references or ways we can train our new QA manager?

A. The Ninth National Conference on EDP/Quality Assurance and Risk will be held in Washington, DC on March 12-15, 1990.

The aim of this conference is to provide the entire EDP/QA community with:

* **Information exchange on workable, effective methods.**

* **Technology transferred to applications through selected QA and Test Technology sessions.**

* **Tutorial introduction sessions keyed to technical program tracks.**

* **Current information about managing software quality through standards and related topics.**

* **An opportunity to participate with others who have both management and technical concerns.**

Reference: US Professional Development Institute, 1734 Elton Road, Suite 221, Silver Springs, MD 20903, (301) 445-4400.

I. Product Quality Tradeoffs (1989)

Q. In order to make our product shipment deadlines, we are often faced with the need to take little short-cuts in developing our software. Do you have any recommendations on how to draw the line? How should we make trade offs between Software Quality and Programmer Productivity?

A. We always give software quality ten times more weight than programmer productivity. If you don't have a quality product, it really doesn't matter how quickly you created the product because it will be very difficult to sell. Even if you can make the sale, your programmers will be consumed by supporting customers and fixing bugs if you ship a low quality product. We believe that testing your product before you ship it will actually result in the best "life cycle" programmer productivity.

We have one item that we want to make clear, however: software quality is getting the agreed features to work as described. It does not mean adding in the 'bells and whistles' that every programmer comes up with.

Having firm specifications of the features to be included in the release is critical to producing a quality product. Negotiating this feature list involves sales, marketing, development, support as well as the CEO. Often development feels that sales and mar-

keting are intruding on their space, but we believe that it is critical to get everyone involved in this process.

While it is critical to define the major features in the next release it is equally important not to put development in a straight jacket. We have seen a number of companies who allow development a time budget of 20 to 25% of the project to add nice technical features. Usually these features have long term benefits in support or development but they have little meaning to sales and marketing. Development is free to add these features to the list up to a cutoff date. The cutoff-date is established to ensure that the product can be tested and documented by the scheduled completion date. After the cutoff-date, development cannot add additional features to this release; they can instead put them on the list for the next release. We urge you to look at you development cycle and see how you can rationalize it and hopefully cut down the wars between sales & marketing and development & support.

1. Software Quality Assurance

Q. What can we do to improve quality control? What about test suites?

A. We like "Quality Assurance" better than "Quality Control". You want to <u>assure</u> your customers of consistent high-quality software, not control it.

Building Test Suites

The basic objective with test suites is to compile test cases which have caused problems in the past. While the developers usually start by building their own set of test cases, our experience is that it is almost impossible for developers to anticipate all of the variations which will occur in the real world. In most cases, your customers will find the test cases which really shake out your product. Make sure that you capture these test cases so that you can fix them, and then insure that they remain fixed. We have been involved with a number of very complex products which have built up hundreds of test cases. The first challenge is to automate the process for your customers to submit the test cases. This is more complex than you might think. Often the problem is more than the specific commands that are given to your product. It may be part of the environment. In the past we were involved with a COBOL static analyzer. We found that many of our problems involved the compiler level, the copy libraries, and other system dependent code. Rather than just getting the source code, in many cases we had to get this additional information. If you can't recreate the problem with the first level information, determine what additional information may have contributed to the information. All of this information becomes part of your test suites.

Regression Testing

The next step is to develop a regression test so that you can verify that the test cases that you fixed previously haven't been broken by your latest changes. ("Yes, Jim that bug you fixed last summer is back.")

Most companies start by having their programmers manually compare the results. This is fine initially, but as your base of test suites grows this task can mushroom. We have seen situations where the manual regression test took twenty to forty hours. This can be a real burden and can slow down the process of getting new releases and fixes out.

Automatic verification involves more work than you probably anticipate. The first approach is to spool the output to disk and compare it with the "good" output. The number of very minor changes which aren't consequential are surprising. For example, if the date is on the report the compare program will flag this as different. Another situation is where a sort program may come up with the results in different order even though the answer is the same. You will have to make your compare smart to avoid flagging cosmetic changes as problems. You can do this by stripping your output file of secondary data. For example, you could strip out the date information. The sort type of problem is more difficult, and will depend upon the details of your situation. Eventually, these are all solvable technical problems.

Management Attention

The management issues can have more impact than you might think. You must make QA important in your company by your *actions*, not your words. Your commitment to quality will be tested as the promised release date draws near. You must insure that your programming team understands that running the test suites and doing the comparisons is critical. We have seen cases where development was under pressure to get fixes out to problem customers (sales was really pushing), and they cut the testing phase short. They didn't run all the test suites, or they didn't compare all the results because of time pressures. In these cases, management and sales had a false sense of security. They thought that all the test cases had been checked. The customers were very upset when old problems came back. Even though everyone found it easy to blame the programmers, we view this as a management issue because management hadn't insured that the resources were available to conduct adequate testing.

We would like to hear from software developers who have dealt with these issues. What tools have you found useful? While we are interested in hearing from vendors of these tools, we really want to hear from the actual users. Thanks

2. Quality Control Software

Q: Do you know of any statistics and quality control software which small software companies can actually use?

A: Not really. We know of companies who sell software testing tools, but we don't know of any case studies where these tools have been used in small companies. We would be very interested in learning of any cases.

3. Version Control

Q: How should I manage versions/releases, from making plans to keeping track of who does what?

A: First of all you should plan on an annual release which comes out on a regular schedule. This helps your customers participate when the release is coming. It helps them schedule their staff to install the new release. If you update your software much more frequently than this, it begins to feel like an imposition to your customers. The only exception to this is with software which has quality problems. If you need to put out a bug fix release, do it as soon as you have most of the known problems identified.

Making the version changeover

The best approach to getting your customers to convert to your new release it to sell them on the benefits. If you include some new functionality that your customers have been wanting, you should have little difficulty getting them to upgrade in a reasonable time. This ties in with the annual release because o annual timetable gives you enough time to get enough functionality into the new release to entice them.

Be sure to put a time limit on how long you will continue to support your old release. (Although it's our experience that most software firms end up supporting old releases forever.) It is very difficult to tell you customer that you won't take his maintenance fee and you won't help him with his problems. In our experience most software companies continue to provide limited support on old releases, and they depend on the support techs to sell their new release. As long as you realize that you have to sell your new releases, and you have something good to sell, you should be able to migrate your customers to the latest and greatest.

4. Improving Product Development Quality

Q. What can I do to improve the quality of the software that we develop?

A. Here's a short, unexpected answer: Control your marketing and sales staff!! (Not exactly the answer that you expected, was it? Maybe you expected an answer like this: hire better developers and to hold their feet to the fire.) The quality problem with most new products is that the company pushed them out the door before they were really done. There are a number of reasons:

1. **Money Talks The company needs the revenue.**
2. **Pre-announcement of the product We have a product intro ad running in six magazines next week.**
3. **Committed Shipment Date Twenty customers have already paid for it.**

A controlled introduction

Our guideline is that you should go through a boring, exhaustive product introduction process before you make your product generally available. (Alpha test at one site, Beta test at five to ten sites, and limited availability at ten to a hundred sites.) If you stick to this process you can limit the damage. New products always have problems which are found in customer sites. Avoiding this isn't possible in the real world. The challenge is to find the problems and fix them quickly with minimum customer impact. It is also important that your early installations understand where they are in the process and what the risks are. If you are completely open with your early installs, they will understand when problems come up and they will work with your technical people to diagnose the problems.

Reasons why not

The drawback of this approach is that there will be a delay from the time that you have got through the limited availability and when you start general marketing. Sales and marketing people can't wait, and they are very optimistic about when the product will be ready to roll. (I know because I have this basic problem myself.) In practice, there is very little lost opportunity. Once you are into the limited availability you will have a pretty good idea when you will be ready to enter general availability. You can start to make some plans, and you may have a one month delay in your advertising. In most cases, if you have good experience with the limited availability phase your sales people will be able to fill the early pipeline with customers or personal contacts. It appears to us that there is very little cost from being conservative about product introduction.

Benefits of controlled introduction

The benefits of this approach are numerous. You avoid swamping your support department with a wave of problems and upsetting your early installations. You also avoid losing the revenues from these early installations. On the sales and marketing side, you avoid demoralizing your sales people who have worked to bring customers in, only to have the product blow up and cost the sale.

Saving money for the _real_ introduction

Finally, you avoid shooting your marketing wad to generate leads that you can't convert into sales. One of our clients had a situation where they announced the product before it was ready. When the product finally settled down, the company didn't have any marketing money left to promote the product. They had also generated so much ill will that they had a very hard time getting anyone to install their product. A careful product introduction can minimize these problems.

5. Software Release Dates

Q: How do you suggest we handle software revision announcements? Should we announce a date when we have a firm date in mind? Or is it better not to say anything until it, the new version, is absolutely ready?

A: The answer to that question depends upon your customer base and your position in the industry. It doesn't make any sense to us to make a public announcement of a future release date unless you are a major vendor. (And there are real risks even if you are a major vendor.) On the other hand, you have to let your customers and prospects know that your programmers are working on the next release. This is often essential to make new sales and to keep youir customers paying for maintenance.

Our strategy about release dates is to be as vague as possible for as long as possible. For example, if your schedule is for an October release, we would initially tell customers that we are looking at a "year-end release". This type of date should be adequate for their planning needs. When they try to pin you down, you should respond that in the time-honored tradition of software houses: "Given the difficulty in predicting software schedules, we don't feel that is is useful for anyone to get more specific this early in the process." As you get closer to the actual date you might become more specific: "We expect the product to go into Beta Testing in September/October but we won't really know the date for general availability until we get into Beta."

J. Technology (1989)

1. To Port or not To Port?

Q. We developed our software for a specific mini running UNIX V. Should I keep my software on that one hardware platform or port it to as many hardware platforms as possible? How about porting to PCs?

A. Your first job is to make your software as competitive as possible on the base machine. If you aren't winning at least 50% of your competitive situations, you shouldn't even consider another hardware platform. Assuming that you are in good shape on your primary platform, you are faced with a choice of vertical versus horizontal growth. Vertical growth is to develop more modules to sell along with your basic package. This will generate revenue by selling to both your installed base and selling the new modules along with new system sales.

Additional hardware platforms provide horizontal growth in that you can sell to additional customers by being available on the new hardware. If you are losing prospects because they want either a larger or a smaller hardware platform, you might consider porting to other hardware platforms in order to satisfy these prospects. We urge you to take a very hard look at these other niches. Look at their requirements and what they are buying. We commonly find that these other niches have very distinct needs that can't be met by a simple port. Time and time again we see vendors port their software to other platforms only to find that their software won't be competitive on the new hardware without significant development. There are a couple of examples that come to mind that illustrate the point: 1-2-3 on a MacIntosh; and a mini system which looks really ugly as a PC product.

There's another thing to think about before you attempt to port your software: you'll need a marketing program to support this new niche. Prospects in the new environment may read different magazines, etc. You will probably have to develop new marketing materials for your new product. All of these costs indicate that you are launching a new product and that the programming costs might be the smallest part of the equation. As long as you anticipate the costs and do it well, going to a new platform can dramatically increase your business, but please don't underestimate the total effort that it will require.

2. Changing Platforms

Q. Our company has a leading edge software product that runs under Digital's VAX/VMS system. We would now like to support a UNIX environment for this product but find the task difficult due to a lack of programming tools, i.e. a forms package, an indexable file handler, etc. Have you helped other companies with similar problems? How?

A. The very first step is to look in a software directory like *Data Sources*. While you may have to spend some time understanding how they index their book, this simple research is often a very easy way to solve this problem.

Searching Directories

Our approach goes like this: Find products with similar functionality to products you are already using. Look for products that you already know that have been ported to UNIX. See what alternative products are listed in the same categories as known products. Call all of the UNIX vendors who are listed in these categories. You may not be able to identify tools from the directory listings, but you should be able to identify major vendors.

Interviewing Experts

If this fails, you can approach this problem on several other levels. The first is to make sure that you have the right people for the job. Part of your problem is probably due to the fact that your programmers know the VAX/VMS much better than they know UNIX. As part of this knowledge, they know the available tools for VAX/VMS much better than they know the UNIX tools. You should start interviewing UNIX programmers. Ask them about the tools problem as part of the interview process. They may have developed some home grown tools or they may know of available tools which can help address your problems.

Talking to Hardware Vendors

Another approach is to talk to the UNIX hardware vendors. Ask their software support people about what tools they know about. You should also ask them about other software vendors who are developing similar but non competitive products. These companies may know of tools which can help.

Calling the Trade Press

The final approach is to call the UNIX trade magazines. Ask their technical writers and editors if they know of tools that you should investigate. If you conduct this search you should have a very good idea of what is available and how people approach the category of problems that you are dealing with. Please keep in mind that different tools may be appropriate on a different operating system because of architectural differences. Often the real answer to the search is that you architect your product differently on this different system and you really need a different tool to solve the problems implicit in that approach. Don't forget, "When in Rome..."

3. X Windows and Portability

Q. What experience have other firms had with X Windows and other technologies which intend to make it easier to port software?

A. I have no first-hand knowledge of X Windows. I have several clients who are considering X Windows, so the technology appears promising. On the other hand, I have some clients who have been using 4 GLs to provide similar portability.

These companies have found that the 4 GL reduces the amount of time to complete the programming phase of the port. At the same time, they still have to get a target machine and test it out. There seem to be enough differences in target machines that this testing is mandatory.

I have also observed a common phenomenon which you should consider. Many companies start to offer their software on almost any hardware that their customers would like to consider, once they achieve that freedom. The freedom is exhilirating. After having been limited to one platform for years, it is great to be able to say "yes." This is phase lasts for six to twelve months.

Eventually, the sales people tire of costing, pricing, then bidding a new system every week. The support people continue to find quirks in the different systems and management is less than thrilled with paying for a new test system every other month. At this point, the company decides to limit their offering to a couple of good platforms. They can handle the others on an ad hoc basis. This makes life much easier.

The reality is that the costs of dealing with a new platform are much greater than the programming. they include training your people on the quirks of each system and getting a test system for your programmers and your support people. If you don't have a test system, your staff will be spending time going to the vendor's location to test your product. This can be very expensive and tiresome.

The next stage is to substitute new platforms as the market dictates. You may become disenchanted with one of your current suppliers, or a new platform may get the attention of both your staff and your prospects. It is reasonable to substitute one vendor every six to twelve months. If you have three platforms, this is equivalent to a two to three product line, which is common.

4. Mainframe to Micro downsizing

Q. Should the micro version of a mainframe product have the same look and feel as the mainframe product?

A. This is difficult because you want both products to be viewed as the same, but you shouldn't compromise the more robust environment. We have worked with a number of mini and mainframe vendors who ported their products to the PC without taking advantage of the PC environment. When PC prospects looked at these ported products they screamed "ugly". The vendors sold very few copies of these ported PC products. They managed to sell some PC copies to their mainframe and/or mini clients who wanted a compatible PC version.

Rather than handicapping the PC version, we urge you to improve both versions to a new, higher level. This way you can announce the PC version along with the new release of the mini and/or mainframe product. This is the best solution, but if you can't upgrade your mini and/or mainframe product I would come out with the best PC product possible and hope that the mini and/or mainframe product could catch up in the future.

5. 4GL-based Software Products

Q. *I am considering using a 4GL for our next development project. What are your thoughts on using a 4GL.*

A. The benefits of a good 4GL can be very impressive, but there are a number of longer term issues that must be considered. The first is the 4GL vendor's commitment to the business. You are hooking your wagon to their star so make sure that they are a long term player. Are they financially viable? What are their long term development plans? Do they have a strong marketing plan to gain widespread recognition for their product so it will help you sell your product? How is their support? What about their fees? Development systems? Run time systems? Will you be able to compete with their fees built into your product costs? What hardware platforms to the support today? What are their future plans?

6. The Ultimate Notebook Computer

As your classical traveling consultant and newsletter publisher, I have been an avid user of portable computers. I used the NEC version of the Tandy 100 and subsequently upgraded to a Toshiba 1200. I have been eyeing the NEC Ultralite for the last year, but even though its weight is great its limitations are significant. Then I read an article saying that cellular phones were the next option to be added to laptop computers.

My initial reaction was that this was nice, but not really significant. I have been mulling this over and have come to the conclusion that this might be the new hardware that will generate the next "killer application". Just for fun, I would like to hypothesize about my Ultimate Notebook Computer (UNC) and its software connection. The starting point is a 386 desktop system so that the UNC with a 386SX can run the same software as the desktop. In many ways it would look like the Ultralite: small, nice screen and keyboard. Inside it should have 4 or 8 megs of memory so that you could run the same software that you run on the desktop. It also should have a couple of megs of RAM disk and both a modem and a cellular phone. You might be surprised that I didn't ask for a larger RAM disk. That is key to this machine, as we will see below.

The first application would be that of a contact manager who manages lead and contact databases and generates letters and memos. The cellular phone could be used to send reports/letters to other computers including public E-Mail systems. It would be nice if you could also send directly to FAX machines. This first application is nice, but nothing special since you can use a standard modem to connect to a public E-Mail system. The built-in cellular phone simply adds the convenience of not having to connect to a hotel phone line.

The second application involves using your system as a cellular phone. With the addition of a headset you could have your system dial a number and act as your phone on the go. Again this is nice, but not great.

The great utility of such a device is its ability to send and retrieve files from the desktop machine in your office. The moment that you finish a report, your system could file it on your desktop machine. At the same time, you could retrieve any file or report that you need from your desktop. This is why you don't need a very large RAM disk. If you don't have a copy of the file with you, your system could dial up your desktop and retrieve it for you. In addition, each time you finish with a file your portable system could file it back on the desktop.

The benefits of this system for travelers like myself are obvious, but we aren't a mass market. I believe that this system could also be useful for managers in large corporations. If people could accept a notebook-sized computer as something to be used in meetings then, like a notebook, one would use it to take notes at the meeting. The notes could later be sent to your secretary for distribution, or from your desktop computer to the desktops of other meeting attendees. Urgent messages could be sent to their notebook computer.

Another application of this technology could be retrieval of reports from your desktop computer while in a meeting. I can't possibly count the number of times meetings I have attended were held up while someone retrieved a copy of a report.

And finally, the system would allow your secretary and staff to remain in contact with you while you are out of the office. This is my bright idea for the next great advance in computing. I would enjoy hearing your thoughts and reactions.

7. Prima Donna Employees

Q. How can we handle necessary, but "prima donna" employees?

A. We run into this all the time. There is a certain employee, usually a talented development-type, who is just a pain. They remind us of certain teen-agers we have known.

There are a number of tactical things that you can do to rein in "prima donna" employees (PDE), but in most cases you must reconcile yourself to the fact that you will have to set limits and that eventually the PDE will have to leave if they can't live with these boundaries. At the same time, you should begin to identify and nurture alternatives. As long as the PDE feels that you don't have any choice, but to give in to their demands, there is no reason for them to discipline themselves. The moment that you hire a possible replacement, they will hit the ceiling. They will realize that the free ride is over, but they will play it for all it is worth. Fundamentally, you

have to tell them that you want them to remain a player with the company, but they have to abide by certain limits. If they aren't willing to do this, they should consider looking elsewhere.

The tactical management of a PDE is tough. You must be very explicit about your limits. Let them know very clearly what is not allowed. They will exploit ambiguity to the max so you must clarify everything. At the same time, you must be very careful not to impose bureaucratic demands which aren't really necessary. Don't impose limits which you really aren't willing to stick by. Managing a PDE is much like raising a small child. Consistency is critical. Don't reverse your position without serious consideration. If the PDE learns that you really don't mean it, they will test all of your rules.

The final dimension is to view the PDE as a diamond in the rough. Help them understand how their behavior is undermining their effectiveness. Spend the time with them on a regular basis to help them become more effective. This type of positive effort can be very effective and can minimize the number of negative encounter sessions.

K. Support Issues (1989)

1. Providing Phone Support at No Charge

Q. We recently started charging for phone support after the initial 90 days. Our new customers understand that they have to pay for calls if they haven't purchased support, but our older customers feel that we should continue to answer their questions at no charge. Our support people are unable to say no. What do you suggest?

A. To begin with, you must accept the reality that your support people won't be able to refuse to help the customer. It isn't that they want to undermine the company; they simply are motivated to help the customer. I have seen a couple of approaches that work in this situation. The first is to have customers call in and leave their requests for information on a voice mail system. A manager answers the voice mail, and checks to see if each customer requesting support has purchased it. If not, the manager can call the customer to arrange for payment. This works reasonably well since the manager understands that the company can't continue to provide support unless customers are willing to pay for it.

An alternative is to offer FAX-based support for non-maintenance-contract customers. Those who aren't willing to pay for maintenance because they feel that the problem is a bug in the program can send their problem description(s) to you via FAX. Your company responds by FAX within 24 hours. This allows you to provide some support for the non-maintenance-contract customers, but it clearly offers customers who have purchased maintenance a higher level of service. I would be interested in hearing about other solutions to this problem.

2. Pricing for custom programming & training

Q. Our customers frequently ask us for custom, after-market programming. They want extensive on-site training as well. What are the competitive factors in pricing custom software and training?

A. Once you have sold your product to a customer, you have an advantage: you don't have to be the low-priced bidder. You can't gouge your customers, but you can charge them a fair price.

Fair is a function of what similar companies charge for these types of services, *in their locale, not yours*. If the cost of living in your area is low, but your customers are all in the big city (where costs tend to be high) what is *fair* or *high-priced* may be dramatically different from your local economy.

An Example: We have a client in the Midwest where $55 per hour is the going rate for contract programming. They set their rates at $75 per hour because of their specialized expertise. When they bid to New York City clients, they bid $100/hr. Far from objecting, their NYC clients thank them for being so reasonable!

Services Pricing

Generally, pricing services is different than pricing your software. In any particular situation, the incremental gross margin on a software sale is 70 or 80 percent, since your development costs are fixed costs. You can afford to discount to get the incremental sale. In dealing with services your costs are much higher and you can't afford to discount. Service pricing is much more cost-based than what you are used to with software.

Another example: If you are paying your trainers $2,000 per month, we would charge $500 per day plus expenses for on-site training. If your trainers bill only 4 days per month you break even, and you have an opportunity to make some money. Your training department should generate revenues which are twice its direct costs including salaries, benefits, travel, etc. If your training department bills at that rate, you are probably making enough money to cover your overhead costs and provide a reasonable return for your bottom line. If the department can't reasonably reach that level most months, it may actually be costing you to support that function.

3. Training Department Compensation

Q. How should I pay my trainers and training manager? What about extra compensation?

A. We see a lot of companies who start offering training by using contractors. This allows you to avoid the fixed costs of an employee while you test the market to see if there is a real demand for training in your customer base. The disadvantage of this approach is that you make very little money when you use contractors. You may receive $500 per day and pay your contractor $400, which leaves you only $100 for marketing expenxes and overhead — not a very profitable endeavor! You also are left with the accounts receivable risk. If you are in this boat (or are about to enter the boat) make sure that you don't have to pay the contractor until you receive the cash.

Training Staff

If this first stage is successful, you will probably consider hiring a full time person. In many cases you may consider hiring your contractor full-time, but this is often made difficult because their salary requirements are higher than the general market. While there are local variations, the salary for a trainer with a technical education and several years of experience ranges from $18,000 to the high 20's. Ideally you should try to keep their base low and give them a good commission. Pay them a comission only after their revenues have covered their costs, including overhead. As an example, if the trainer was paid $2,000 per month and we assumed 100% burden, they would have to bill 8 days per month at $500 per day to "cover" their costs. A 10-20% commission on revenues over $4,000 per month would probably be an effective motivator in this case. *Make sure that this policy is applied uniformly to all eligible staff-members.*

Training Manager Compensation

The training manager is a different situation. You need a mature manager because a training department is a management challenge. In addition you need someone with enough technical expertise to pitch in and cover for one of their people. We find that these skills usually command salaries in the $30K-$40K range, depending upon your location.

A Training Manager is critical to the success of this department so we urge you to hire some with strong management skills. If you have a weak manager you will be faced with a choice of letting the training department lose money or spending senior management time to keep it under control.

Training benefits

There are a number of non-financial benefits from having a strong training program: increased customer satisfaction, enhanced product reputation, fewer support calls, etc. We therefore urge you to explore ways to increase your training presence. Who knows, with a little time, care, and management attention, you might even make money at it!

4. Selling Hardware

Q. Should small software companies sell hardware if it is likely to increase software sales?

A. This is a tough one. As you can see from the subscriber survey, our readers are more than five times as likely to only sell software.

We recommend selling hardware only if all else fails. The hardware margins are very low in many competitive markets. Finally, if you must sell hardware, make sure that you control your margins. Set rigid limits on how much you will discount. You are selling the hardware as a service. If your customer wants to buy hardware from you, they may have to pay slightly more than the cheapest alternative.

For example, if you are selling a PC vertical market package to prospects who don't have a PC, they might want you to sell them a packaged system. This is a case where you should sell more software

by offering hardware. Make sure that you don't meet the lowest bid that they find from mail order suppliers. We have one client who charges a hardware integration fee if the customer buys the hardware elsewhere. They price the hardware with reasonable margins and are quite successful. They lose some customers who want the cheapest hardware available, but they feel that this business would have cost them money.

If you decide to sell hardware to help sell your software, make sure you keep a close eye on your margins and your costs. We have seen too many software companies who were losing their shirt on the hardware when they included their people costs. It is complex and very easy to mislead yourself. If you aggressively pursue this path, you will end up being a VAR as opposed to a software publisher. Think about what this means (hardware maintenance, spare parts, inventory) before you leap into it.

5. Tracking Tech Support Calls

Q. What do you advise as far as support call tracking?

A. The requirements for support call tracking depends on the complexity of your problems and the complexity of resolution.

If all of your support calls are handled in one call by one person, you can probably get by with an on-line log by customer. This will give you a simple indication of how many problems a particular customer has had. You can also search the on-line logs to see if anyone else has had the same problem.

If you have complex problems where multiple support people are working on aspects of the customer's problem, the on-line log will break down and you should consider a problem tracking package.

6. Keeping Trainers Fresh

Q. Our trainers are very good, but we have a real problem keeping them fresh? They tend to burn out quickly. What can you advise?

A. There are a number of sources of stress for trainers which you should try to minimize.

Define Responsibilities
The first and most obvious area if potential improvement is to formalize the expectations you have for

your customers with regard to training and installation. In most organizations, there are some guidelines in the proposal which outline what the customer has to do before training starts. This isn't communicated to the operating personnel who must learn the system and make it work. As a consequence, the trainer is thrown into a situation where they must perform magical feats of training just to be considered merely competent.

Controlling Expectations
We have a client whose VP of Support put together a training and support brochure. It describes all of the training classes, what the customer must do before each class, and what they will learn in the class. It also details the support policies and what training is bundled with the sale and what is charged separately. The VP of Support send this to the operations contact once the contract is signed and introduces himself. By opening the dialogue and documenting how they do business, the training and support people aren't put in the position where there they are stuck between the customer and the company. Everyone knows what the policies are and the trainer on the spot isn't the bad guy.

Allowing Adequate Preparation Time
Another area where we have seen trainers get burned-out is when their companies don't allow for preparation time and post-training follow-up time. In every case we have seen, there is a certain amount of preparation time before the class. This may include some brushing up on the materials as well as just getting the materials boxed up. The trainer has to call the customer and make sure that the customer has done their preparation. After the class, the trainer may have to research issues and problems that came up. They must have time to document the customer status. It is important to have a record of the visit and a short report on who the people were, what they had trouble with and any specific information about the site that could be useful in the future. There also may be an opportunity to sell them additional features or options, and this requires time to follow up.

Make sure that you understand these times and build them into your pricing and your schedules. In one case we saw, there was a half day of preparation and a half day of follow up for a two day class. This

meant that we were dealing with a 1.5 times factor where training days had to be billed at 1.5 times the cost for these same people on support. This additional time is very real. Make sure that you account for it.

Planning for the Overhead Factor
The next factor that you must analyze is how many billable days can you plan on in a month. When you take out vacations, holidays, sick days, and education, we have found that you are lucky to get 80% or 16 training days per month. After you divide this by 1.5, you end up with only 10 billable training days per month. If you are paying your trainers $2K per month, and your fully burdened costs are two-times salary, your cost per training day is $400 per day. This gives you no profit margin. At $600 per day you have a decent margin. If you have to pay more for your trainers, you will have to adjust your training fees accordingly. The purpose for this discussion is to make sure that you are charging enough for your trainers so that they can live with the workload and yet generate adequate revenue for the company. We have seen too many cases where the company didn't charge enough for training so they had to push their trainers very hard. The trainers kept quitting and the customers weren't getting the quality of training that they wanted and deserved. It was a vicious circle.

Allocate Improvement Time
If you have done all of these things right and you are managing your training business professionally, you should begin to encourage your trainers to watch each other teach their classes. Remember the education time. Give them the time to improve their materials. Let them do a good job. If they feel really good about the job that they are doing, they will get more satisfaction out of their work, and they will suffer less burnout.

Your customers want top quality training, and in our experience they are willing to pay for it. Make sure that you provide an atmosphere where your trainers can provide the best training they can, and make money for the company.

REFERENCE: "Keeping Training Fresh", by Bob Pike, *Creative Training Techniques* (800) 328-4329.

1992
Software Success
Reference Book

Chapter VII
Feature Articles and Case Studies

A. MBI Business Software (Jan 1991)

Danna Munley and her partner founded MBI Business Software in 1985 after they sold their prior company. The prior business had been a delivery service and they had spent a lot of time in court.

They hoped to build on this experience by consulting in the area of human resources. They helped companies set up plans, document their systems, and complete the paperwork. This business wasn't successful. They even developed a product to automate this.

In 1987, they moved from consulting to contract programming and developed nine or ten small business programs. In 1988, they picked three areas and came up with three software products: service, manufacturing, and locksmiths. All three were for small businesses.

In 1989 they started marketing all three equally with newspaper ads, trade shows (computer shows) and public relations. They pushed the service package, but they found that was really a generic package.

In 1990 they really started to sell when Danna realized that they were actually selling a service. This was something she knew how to do. They found a distributor back east to sell the HR package so they could focus on the others. In late 1990 they realized that the locksmith package was generating the revenue so they made the decision to focus 90 percent on it in 1991.

They sell the starter system for $499 with a limited number of records. Within a year most buyers trade up to the unlimited system for another $1,500. Often they also buy dispatch for another $299.

One interesting fact for the locksmith market is that most locksmiths have already bought computers for their key systems and for ordering from their suppliers. They are also technically knowledgeable enough that they aren't afraid of computers.

Danna has come up with a unique way to move leads to serious trials. She will send them the full program with a $100 deposit. She and her partner invest a couple hours with on line support (they use PC Anywhere) to get the system implemented. This system works. They have never gotten a system back.

It turns out that once the locksmiths are on the system, they don't require additional support. MBI offers a wide range of support options. Most customers select one hour of free support a month for $17.50 and free upgrades. Right now, ten percent of their 100 customers are on support, but they expect this to increase with the next update.

They are very successful converting leads to trials (30 percent) and so far 100 percent of the trials have bought. Thus, the current emphasis is on generating leads. They are planning on attending four trade shows in 1991, advertising in trade journals and newspapers, and direct mail.

They had very good luck with a recent trade show with eight sales for a $100 booth and a two-day show.

There are over 500,000 locksmiths so once they get the direct mail formula they can really roll it out.

Danna has been getting an article a month published in magazines and this is also generating lots of good leads.

Their objectives are:

1. **Produce a steady income.**
2. **Grow the business to $3 - $4 million and sell it like they did with their previous business.**

Their 1990 revenue is expected to be $50,000 and they expect 1991 to be at least $150,000 with 75 percent of their energy on the locksmith market.

Questions

Should we display the price of our system at trade shows? Our competitor is much more expensive, and several people have commented that they thought they couldn't afford us, but when they found out that our prices start at $499 they were very interested.

I don't have a problem with showing your price. It is important to let people know that they can afford your product.

Our brochures are pretty basic. Should we invest the money in glossy four color brochures?

I would start by looking at other materials that your prospects receive from other companies they do business with. I have had clients who marketed to companies who received lots of glossy sales materials and they had to spend the money to look good on the prospect's desk. You mentioned that your materials were a couple steps up from the key suppliers. Based on this I wouldn't invest much more in this area.

How do companies set their prices? We know that we will raise our prices, but we don't know when and how much?

I would start by conducting a survey asking prospects how much they would pay for this type of package. You can use this to generate a demand curve and determine the optimal price range. Since you want to get market share, you would select the low end of the profitable range.

While you are at it, you might as well ask some questions to help your programmer (how many records? Disk Size? or whatever). I would also include some public questions that could be turned into articles and or press releases. Examples of these might be: What percent of locksmiths have computers? Are they looking for additional software? etc. Ask your editors about issues and questions they are interested in.

Conclusion

MBI seems like a very promising business with a really large market. Now that they have determined that there is a market for their product, the question is how to roll it out and make some money.

If you reinvest your 1991 revenues in your marketing programs you should be able to grow to a level which will support the business. The biggest long term issue is can you meet your revenue objectives within the locksmith market.

B. XYPRO (Jan 1991)

XYPRO has a very nice press kit, or company backgrounder. It includes:

* **Company history and philosophy**
* **Services and benefits**
* **Professional biography and sheets on their products**

The company was founded in 1983 by Dale Blommendahl and Edwin Dobies to provide consulting services for Tandem users. They quickly decided that they couldn't build a large company based on

consulting so they focused their consulting on projects that would lead to products.

The company has both horizontal and vertical products. The vertical products are banking back office automation products. They developed the horizontal products at the demand of various customers. They needed better tools to help them develop their applications.

The horizontal products sell for $20,000 and the vertical applications start at $150,000. They often find that the initial sale of the horizontal product leads to technical consulting. The credibility they achieve with the horizontal products opens the door for the vertical products.

Dale estimated that 40 percent of the 1990 revenues of $1.2 million were from direct product sales. 30 percent were from consulting to enhance the products and the final 30 percent is from straight consulting.

XYPRO has done a very good job of going from consulting to product sales. I asked Dale how they had done this. He said that the key was to turn down consulting that wasn't related to the product direction to which they have committed themselves. This is a difficult given the immediate cash flow characteristics of consulting versus the much longer time frames for product sales.

XYPRO uses a number of marketing programs. They have just started using telemarketing to generate leads for their horizontal product. They have been using full page ads in the trade magazines every two or three months. They found that advertising every month wasn't cost justified. They are generating some immediate leads but for the most part they are building long term awareness.

The theory advanced by the advertising professionals is that you should advertise consistently. This is the only case that I know of where someone has found that consistently advertising every couple months was even more effective than smaller ads monthly. I would be very interested to hear from anyone who has experimented with frequency in advertising.

They can't use direct mail with their vertical product because it is too hard to find the right person. They have had good luck with direct mail for the horizontal package. They can get a list of Tandem sites from the Tandem Users Group.

Dale felt that ad leads were more urgent. Direct mail generated more leads, but they were less immediate. In his mind, the results were equivalent, but different. My own bias is that if you can set up an automatic lead follow up system that direct mail will produce more sales per year for the same dollars of marketing budget. There is a lag while the direct mail leads are warming up, but they offer greater sustained throughput. On the other hand, getting hot calls is really nice for everyone in the company. I also believe that using different media can positively reinforce your results. People may see your ad and then respond to your direct mail package or vice versa.

Trade shows work very well for the vertical package (they go to banking shows). They find that it is a great opportunity to meet the decision makers or the people who work for the decision makers. This last year has been poor for trade shows, since the attendance has been down. Perhaps this is due to the downturn in the economy.

They go the Tandem users group for the horizontal products. They generate leads and sales from this show.

I asked Dale what his greatest mistake had been. He said that this was difficult since he had made so many, but he said it was his naive belief that you could work deals with large companies without putting the time into it. He has found that it takes lots of time, even if your advocate is really enthusiastic.

In one of the cases, he had a letter from the customer saying they wanted to do something by a certain date. He had started programming on the project before the agreement was signed. The customer used this leverage to squeeze the deal once he was out on a limb. He had been used to working with other companies on a verbal deal and this had worked very well. He hadn't appreciated the fact that in certain companies, no one wanted to be responsible for decisions. He also had found that big companies want to do business with other big companies. In many of these cases, the fact that XYPRO was a small company frightened some of the people involved in the decision and delayed the decision.

There isn't much competition for the horizontal products. The challenge here is to find someone with the budget for tools. There is stiff competition for the vertical packages. His system's five year cost of ownership is 30 percent to 40 percent less than his competition. This is partly due to the lower product cost, and the correspondingly lower maintenance cost. The other factor is the lower cost of the Tandem hardware versus IBM hardware. The Tandem hardware cost advantage is offset by having to sell the prospect on buying non-IBM hardware.

Dale said that they hadn't done much PR. No one notices their press releases. On the other hand, they have published one article per year. He feels that an article per quarter would be much more impressive, but doesn't have the staff to support this.

Right now, they are in the process of raising capital. Part of this is coming from a distribution partner, but they are expecting to raise venture capital. Dale expects the company to grow to $5 million within three years, and the investors want even faster growth. Dale is concerned that rapid growth will jeopardize the technical quality of the product and the support and that this might seriously damage the company.

I asked Dale if he could go back and change one thing, what would have the greatest impact on the company. He immediately answered that he wished that he had raised money five years ago. He had previously looked for money twice (five years ago and two and one half years ago). Both times he had invested six to eight months of his time searching for money. He had found it to be a very frustrating experience.

This is an interesting thought. Most software companies can do very well without outside capital once they are up and running, but there are a few companies which need the capital to fully exploit a major opportunity. The nice part is that the investors can see how to recoup their investment given the magnitude of the investment. The reality is that raising money is hard, and it may be that you can't find an investor willing to help you grow the company. In retrospect, it is impossible to know if XYPRO could have raised money five years ago. I have been involved in a number of situations where I felt that the founders were reacting unreasonably to the investor demands. It wasn't that the investors weren't making extreme demands, it is just that is how it is done. If you look at any professional venture capital deal, the entrepreneur has given up control of his company.   The entrepreneur has to decide that the company's need for capital is more important this his personal need for control.   Negotiating the details of this with investors is tough.

It seems that XYPRO has built a strong product line for a good market. Getting over a million dollars a year in sales without a full time sales person is impressive. Raising capital will put additional pressure on the company as they try to build their distribution and sales capabilities, but the money should allow them to cut some corners and to survive some mistakes. I wish them well.

C. Sierra Micro Applications (Feb 1991)

Marketing Accounting Systems for Unions

I interviewed Mike Delaney, one of the partners of Sierra Micro Applications. Three of them started the company in 1985 right out of school. They needed a project for a college class and one of the members of the team was a member of a local union. He approached his union and developed a dues accounting system. They decided to offer this as a product and introduced this product in 1986.   Then they went to a conference and learned about training offices and apprentice programs. They developed ATIS: "The Apprentice Training Information System." ATIS sells for $2,850 and includes one year of phone support. ATIS manages the apprentice program, produces the affirmative action reports, and schedules classes.

In general, this is a very tough market. The buyers don't have a profit and loss orientation, so cost reduction arguments aren't meaningful. Sometimes unions decide to buy because it is a "neat toy" and makes them feel more powerful and impressive. It is fairly easy for the company to impress the training coordinators (TCs), but the TC has to go talk to the board. Outsiders aren't allowed to talk directly to the board, so Sierra is providing the TC or materials for the board.

TCs are paid $45,000 to $50,000, so you would think that their time would be considered valuable.   In many cases, the TC doesn't have clerical support so they are maintaining the apprentice records manually. If they have developed their own software, they think that the software is very inexpensive, but

if they are coming from ledger cards, they think it is way overpriced.

In the smaller unions, a TC might have 150 apprentices and the board might object to spending money so that the TC won't have to work as hard. In larger offices, you can have four managers and five administrative people. The sale is quite straightforward in these larger offices. If they don't have a system they like, they will buy ATIS. These large offices are much closer to economic buyers because they are spending very marginal dollars on getting the job done. They are also at the point where they know that they can't do the job manually.

Sierra's sales have been flat at nine or ten units a year for the last few years. In the middle of 1990, they decided to lower the price from $2,850 to $989 at a conference to see if they could generate a lot more demand. They found that there was no real change in the level of demand. They made four sales at this price, but two of them would have bought at the old price. They then raised the price back to the $2,850 level, which is where it is now.

The thing that seems to motivate people to buy this software is wanting a computer in the office. If they make the decision to get a computer, ATIS makes the computer look good even if they can't make the hard justification. Michael pointed out that the big operations are an exception to this because they have maxed out with the manual ledger system. They have no choice but to computerize. The computer is the only way that they can maintain their standards as they grow.

The problem is that they aren't making much money. In 1990, they grossed $100,000 with costs of $69,000.   Michael and his partner earned $16,000 which is low even for Fair Oaks, California. My guess is that they could easily double their income if they just worked as programmers. I asked Michael why they didn't just quit. He said that they believed that things would get better.

I asked Michael how their support/maintenance economics were. They charge $450 per year for support and updates. This is fifteen percent of the new purchase price, which is standard. The bad news is that only eight out of their thirty customers have renewed their support. Perhaps another five will sign up for support next year. All in all, it looks like 50 percent of their customers will pay for support. This is lower than desired, and makes it more difficult to build up support as a profit center.

Contract programming accounts for 25 percent of their revenue. They get a significant amount of contract programming with many of their ATIS customers who want extensions to the system. They are also doing local contract programming to help pay the bills.

The real issue is how much more they should invest in ATIS at this point in time. It appears that there may only be 60 unions in the industries that Sierra works with that have over 500 apprentices (the easy logical sale). Getting more than ten sales a year with this very small market probably isn't a reasonable expectation. Sierra wouldn't drop ATIS. They would continue to support and sell it, they just wouldn't invest time or money in this market. They have developed several other products which might have a much greater potential. (One example was modifying ATIS for training for companies which handle toxic wastes. These companies have to provide reports for the EPA and can pay very significant penalties if they screw up.)

Michael and I discussed sending a survey letter to the union training coordinators as a parting shot (the final marketing program). He has surveyed his customers about their time to do various tasks before and after getting ATIS. Thus, we can develop a worksheet to show the prospects how much time ATIS might save them. (Typically they talk about hours per month per apprentice. As an example, a new customer just created a pay raise report in one hour. It normally took her two to three days. She called yesterday to say "thank you.") While we are at it, we could ask them if they have a computer or are planning to get a computer, and what software they would use if they got one. This survey has two purposes. The first is that it should generate some leads. The second is that it should provide some information about the true potential for this market for the next few years. This can be the basis of the decision to focus on other markets or not. They also have five other systems, but they have not yet marketed any of them. Thus they do have realistic alternatives.

Observation

The situation that Sierra has gotten into isn't all that unusual in my experience. The developers find a problem in which they are interested. The customers who buy the product give the company lots of great feedback. At the same time, the company is generating leads and making some sales. The problem is that at the end of the year the company isn't making enough money to provide the principals income commensurate with their level of skill and effort. This is an example of reaching a point where you can't see the forest for the trees.

I think every small business needs an interested outsider who can meet with management on a regular basis, review their progress, and give them feedback. This outside perspective is one of the really positive things that you can get out of a venture investment. If you don't have investors, I urge you to find someone to meet with you at least quarterly to review your progress. I promise you that you will benefit from this outside perspective.

D. CSE Corporation (Feb 1991)

Growing a Software Company

I talked to Bob Brayton, Vice-President of Operations of the CSE software products business. CSE came out of a mining business. The parent company manufactures gas detection and emergency breathing equipment. The owners made a decision in the 80s to diversify their business to reduce their dependence on the U.S. mining business. In 1985 there was a U.S. mineworkers strike. They expanded to Poland, China and South Africa. At the same time, they wanted to look for a business outside of mining.

Software development sounded like a good idea and they started development in Poland. There was a fairly large pool of top flight Polish programmers. At that point, all companies doing business in Poland had to work with a trading company. CSE and a Polish trading company jointly funded the development of a 3D CAD Product (Protocol).

By early 1989, they had a product and started running small ads, hired their first software marketing people, and got a dozen good customers. They got a good number of customers through trade shows. At the same time they made several OEM/private label deals.

By 1990, the company had grown to six people (Bob, three programmers, the sales person, and an administrator), with revenues of approximately $100,000.

CSE has decided that VARs are one good way to sell this product. It requires a local presence for training and support. They are looking for the top 50 to 100 VARs in the country. These are larger VARs with revenues over $2.5 million. They also have to specialize in CAD and be carrying other CAD products. Bob feels that it isn't very hard to find these top VARs, but it is difficult to recruit them without a major advertising budget.

CSE has found that it takes one to two man months per VAR to get them up and running. They invest $5,000 to $10,000 in each VAR. This heavy level of investment has taught CSE to be very selective about the VARs that they take on. CSE provides full support to these big select VARs. He gives them an effective exclusive for a territory which extends a one hour drive from their office as long as they sell four products a month. The 386 product (computer plus software) sells for $10,000 so selling four a month will support a sales person for the VAR.

I asked Bob how they dealt with dealers who didn't meet their specs who approached them. He said that they didn't go through the big program with these second-tier dealers and that they wouldn't give them an exclusive on the territory.

Last summer, the owners decided that the business needed another $3 million to support the advertising and marketing program, and that they had to raise this capital from outside investors. It took six months to work the plan and get their thoughts straight. Discussions are currently being held with various investor groups.

This is a good example of a technically driven company which has anticipated the funding required to develop the product. The ability to raise the capital on reasonable terms depends upon how much of a track record the company and product has established. Investors are looking for situations where all you have to do is add money.

At this point, CSE has established that they have a good product that people will buy. They also have had some success getting a limited number of VARs effectively selling this product. The big gamble is that the infusion of money for the advertising will pull in both the customers and the select VARs.

Given the track record this seems like a reasonable risk.

As an aside, Bob's personal story is worth a footnote. He graduated in 1972 as a chemical engineer. He moved into new projects and new ventures on the mining side of the business. He really enjoys the software business. He has decided that he will stay in the software industry. He really likes the growth opportunities and the future opportunities for sweat equity.

Greed and Fear

My experience is that it takes one person full time for a year or more to raise capital. In addition, the person responsible for raising the money has to have the support of other people to develop a quality plan. The six months to get the thoughts straight seems about right. Once you have a good plan, in most cases it takes another six to twelve months to actually close the money.

Most software companies are small and can reasonably grow via self funding. You can bootstrap your way into the business. Most of these businesses may not grow more than $5 million a year in revenue but they are really nice businesses for the owners/principals. There are only a few software companies which have the potential to grow really large (over $25 million in sales). Some people are able to bootstrap a small business into large business by being at the right place at the right time, having great products, and excellent business instincts.

The potentially large software companies often lose a lot of money in the early stages. You have to invest a lot of money in R & D to develop a best of class product. The marketing investments in promotion and lead generation also add up. For all of these reasons, the potentially large companies look terrible financially during this adolescent stage. They are investing for their maturity so that their short-term results are deliberately depressed. As an investor, I find myself wondering if this business really takes this level of investment to achieve critical mass, or is there something wrong with the product/market/people. While investors do their "due diligence" to try to reduce their risks, in many cases the only way to find out is to try.

I have seen several cases where the investors tried to minimize their risk by handing the money out in chunks based on meeting milestones. I talked to one CEO who had self-funded his business this way, and then had brought in another investor who had done the same piecemeal investing. The CEO told me that he felt this funding approach had been instrumental in the failure of the business. He had spent so much time winning the battles to lock in the next round of funding that he felt that he hadn't really focused on winning the war and building the long-term business.

This same dilemma applies to the small bootstrap companies. In these cases, the financial objective is to generate enough cash to cover the next payroll. It is very common to see companies that are going from payroll to payroll and are never taking the chances that will allow them to break out of the trap.

It is very common that this type of company will have two options. The current path offers a 99 percent probability of survival with very little chance of economic return. The other path might have a 50 percent chance of great success, 40 percent chance of survival, and 10 percent chance of failure. As an investor, I want the company to follow path number two. I have a positive expected value even if there is some chance that the company will go out of business. At least there is an upside. That is why investors are drawn to deals like CSE, there is a chance that it could be a home run. At the same time there is a chance that it will crash and burn. All investors battle fear and greed, and I haven't seen a good investment that hasn't had significant parts of both of these.

E. S.O.A.P Notes (Mar 1991)

I interviewed Dave Hamilton, President of SOAP Notes. His phone number is (800) 635-2481. SOAP Notes has developed a computerized way for doctors to keep case notes. It is based on a bar code chart and a wireless bar code reader. The doctor scans the bar codes on the wall chart and the report is kept in the wand. The wand is the size of a credit card. At the end of the day, the wand is placed in the downloader, and documentation is automatically produced. The system replaces dictation, writing, or remembering.

I love the origins of this system. The company was in the custom software business and was working on a contract for a lawn service business. The lawn service business owner decided that he didn't want to pay for the development, but a chiropractic consultant in the same building got interested in applying this concept to his industry. The initial application was developed for $8,000 and in the first month they sold 71 systems at $1,500 each. They sold 1,200 systems in the first year and had first year revenues of $1.3 million in 1989.

This is less than full revenue because dealers embraced this product quickly. Initially they were selling direct, but now 70 percent of their sales are through dealers. Last year's sales were $850,000 because the unit volume declined a little over 1989 because of competition, but more importantly the prices dropped because the sales went through dealers. The immediate competitor copied the system and took some sales away, especially in their home state of Florida.

I think that it is important to note that dealers do want some products. This is a relatively low priced product which requires very little training. It sells to a fairly large vertical market and initially had no competition. This is fairly close to the ideal profile for a dealer product that we found in last year's survey.

For 1991, they have modified the product for two additional markets: physical therapy and podiatry. It appears that this product only appeals to part of the market. The larger clinics have a very easy economic rationale. They had one customer who eliminated a second shift which was typing up dictation reports. There is less motivation for the smaller practitioners. They also must be computerized, which eliminates some part of the market. There are 40,000 chiropractors in the U.S. and sales have leveled out at 1,000 units per year. Dave believed that 20,000 of these chiropractors are computerized, so we are getting five percent of the target market per year. This may be the maximum absorption rate. Thinking about it, I don't know of any cases that were much faster than this. I would be interested in hearing from any of you with comparable numbers.

The marketing program is to advertise in national journals which are read by everyone in the profession. They run four or five full-page, four-color ads each month. These ads cost $1,000 to $1,300 each and they generate a steady stream of bingo card leads. They just tried a card deck and felt that it was a great success. The offered the video tape and generated lots of responses. The card had a circulation of 31,000 and they had generated 112 responses within 30 days for only $10 per lead. This is significantly cheaper than the ad leads. They don't know if the conversion rate and quality for card decks is comparable, but right now it looks good. The magazine ad leads start at 60 to 90 leads or $15 to $17 per response. After a year of consistently advertising, the cost per lead climbs to $27 per response. It is getting more difficult to track leads since they have been in the top five magazines every month for the last two years.

The lead-to-sale conversion rate ranges from 17 to 23 percent. They are hoping to get enough data to determine this by magazine, but they haven't done that yet. This combination of low cost per lead ($20 per response) and a 20 percent conversion rate means that their cost per sale is $100, which is 6.6 percent of retail or eleven percent of the dealer cost. You can see that holding the cost per lead down is important for SOAP to maintain its profitability. Thus, I am pleased that they are experimenting with card decks.

They developed the video six months ago. They found that people received their information pack and still wanted more information. This product is a new concept, and they felt that a video would be a good way to help people visualize it. The image of the doctor using the wand on the wall chart really helped me understand how easy it was to use the product.

They developed the video in house with some help from a local mixer. They used a computer animator for some very nice graphics. They also hired an actress to present the product. The video is ten minutes long and cost $1,000. I must admit that I was surprised. I would have guessed that the video cost $10,000. It looked very professional.

I asked Dave if they had tried to sell the video. He said that they had tried to sell it for $10 (their cost is $4 per video in quantities of 100). This lasted for almost three months, and only three people had paid for it. The rest had demanded to get it for free. The reality is that at $4 per video it doesn't cost much more than a four-color brochure, and no one would consider charging for a brochure. They provide dealers with videos, but the dealers have to pay for them (at cost).

Right now they are averaging 200 videos per month. The sales cycle is to send the bingo card leads an information packet. They receive a call at one week to qualify them. If they pass the qualification stage, they send them packet number two, which includes the video. These leads are then turned over to the dealers. Dave didn't feel that the video had helped him recruit dealers. The dealers liked the fact that the prospects knew what the product did, but they hadn't demanded the video.

They also developed a training video which is 70 minutes long. They used the actress, and someone in the company did the voice overs on the screen shots. They got access to some editing equipment, and they are able to update the video as the software changes. I think that this is an important point. My experience with videos, from several years ago, was that you had to work with the production house and that once the video was done it was "in the can." It was so expensive to create the video that it never occurred to me that you could edit your video. SOAP has made a real investment in learning the video technology and is benefitting from this expertise.

Their dealer program consists of 40 active dealers who have sold products in the last couple of months. Another 40 have sold products in the last year. Most of the active dealers have sold four or five products in the last year. Then they have two top dealers who have sold 95 and 83 units respectively in the last year. These are both large organizations with a very strong presence in the chiropractic market. They are selling a broad range of products and were geared up to take on another product. The general VARs don't know this market and haven't been successful.

There are two development efforts. The first is to make the product more attractive. They pick up a steady stream of customers by removing objections. They also have clusters of users by town. This is how they hope to keep selling their 1,000 units per year to chiropractors.

The next effort is to develop the charts for new specialties. Dave felt that it was important to find two or three experts in the field. He stressed that you shouldn't let one person dominate the product development. One of his products had to go back into development because the doctor who dominated it had an unusual point of view. This strategy should allow SOAP to grow even if the individual products top out quickly.

I asked Dave where he was going with the company. He is 37 and is having fun. He said that he had a lot of potential buyers during the first year. In retrospect, that was when he should have sold, if he had wanted the quick buck. I don't think that money was anywhere near the top of his list of priorities. He talked about pen-based computing, touch screens, and linking billing to the SOAP notes. He is happy with his business. It is a good place to work, and everyone is making money. No one is rich, but they are enjoying themselves.

Right now, no one knows the long-term product cycle. If you can develop a niche product and then sell 1,000 copies a year for the next ten years, you have a great business. On the other hand, if sales dry up after two or three years your R & D as a percentage of revenue will be much higher and your profitability will be much lower. Dave is trying to introduce multiple specialized products each year. If he can get ten to fifteen products all doing close to $1 million a year, this will be a fantastic business.

This is the next challenge for this company. If Dave is able to grow the business, then he was smart not to sell. On the other hand, if it stays at $1 million in sales and he isn't able to grow it he should have sold out when he could. This is one of the interesting dilemmas for entrepreneurs. Most of us start companies to sell them, but it is easy for us to feel that they are always worth more than anyone would pay us for them. My own experience with my clients is that if you want to sell, you should determine your walking away price. Once you can get that much, sell. Don't listen to yourself about how great next year will be. I have watched several deals where investors and/or buyers were rebuffed because the entrepreneur believed his own story. The company or the founders didn't get the cash that they needed and deserved. This is just being greedy. The other motivation is that some people just love to run their companies. They can't imagine doing anything else. They don't want to sell the business since they just would have to go start another. This is fine. I just hope that you can sort this out clearly for yourself. This is a complex issue and is critical to making starting a company work for you. When you start a company and put your capital (personal and financial) at risk, you should get your reward. You may take part of this out in cash and part in psychological rewards. Everyone has their own balance. It is very important to get the right mix to end up happy. Good luck to all of you.

1. Free Advice for SOAP Notes (May)

Dear David,

I read with interest the interview with Dave Hamilton of SOAP Notes. Sounds like an intriguing product with many potential applications. You mentioned that they run four or five full page, full color ads each month, and that these ads generate "bingo card" leads.

First, I wonder why they're relying (if they are) on bingo card leads from full page ads. Why not run a coupon or feature an 800 number and get their leads directly? Direct leads are usually much more highly qualified than bingo card leads, and would probably convert better.

Second, I wonder why they feel the need for full page, full color ads in the first place. In lead generation, the quality of the lead is often inversely related to the size of the ad, i.e., the smaller the ad, the better qualified the lead (though with a lower quantity) and the larger the ad, the less qualified the lead. Also, why do they need four-color? I don't see anything in this product that demands color. I suspect all they're doing with the color is attracting a higher percentage of tire kickers.

Their experience with the card deck would seem to bear this out. A 3" X 5" one-color (maybe two) card delivered leads at 50% lower cost. Basically, I think they're spending too much for advertising. The enclosed article touches on the "Quality/Quantity" in lead generation and addresses some ways to fine tune an offer for maximum lead quantity. Feel free to quote from it if you think it would interest your readers.

I also wonder if a video tape is the best offer. Everyone likes videos, and everyone can play one ... whether their practice is automated or not. Note, however, that almost no one was willing to pay for it. More tire kickers. A demo disk might better separate the video buffs from the more computer-oriented doers. I still would include the video in the fulfillment package (it probably helps sell the product), but not advertise it.

Continued success with the newsletter.

Sincerely,
George Duncan
Duncan Direct
(603) 924-3121

Dear George,

Thanks for the letter. I agree with your advice. I have often wondered if I was just being stingy. I keep advising my clients to start with small ads. I happen to like classified ads. They have been very effective for selling my books. In many cases, display ads cost significantly more per square inch than the smaller classified ads.

I think that many people shy away from classified ads and toward the full page four color ads because they fear that they will tarnish the reputation of the product and their company. I think this is the real reason many people go with fancy advertising.

I read an article a while back that said direct marketing people were like the Skinner School of Psychology and that advertising people were like the Freudian School. Direct marketing people believe that the numbers tell the truth. Cost per lead and cost per sale are 99% of what matters. Advertising people believe that company image is the most important objective. Thus they really focus on how good the ads look.

I am very much in the direct marketing camp. I still remember a call from a CEO who was told by his Chairman, "You spent $1.5 Million on that ad campaign, won a Clio for the ad agency and didn't generate a single sale. You're fired."

If any of my readers would like to get a copy of your article and brochure, I suggest that they give you a call.

Thanks for the ideas.
Dave

F. DENEB (Apr 1991)

I spoke with Ken Lykins, Vice President and co-founder of DENEB Systems in Dayton, Ohio. Ken is the partner with the industry experience and Norm Suda is the computer expert. This is a very complementary partnership which I have seen in a number of successful small companies.

DENEB offers software to the construction industry and focuses on job shop cost accounting and estimat-

ing. They have switched to dealer sales since they found that direct marketing was too expensive. This decision was also influenced by Ken's experience as a customer. He insisted on dealing with companies with a local presence, and he wanted to be sure that he offered the same level of service to his own customers.

DENEB has 800 installations and over 60 percent of them are multi-user facilities. They use a wide variety of marketing programs: trade shows, videos, articles, a dealer newsletter, an end user newsletter, a demo disk, and so forthKen sent me DENEB's video for review. It was quite well done. It started off with three actors playing prospects who were discussing their problems and asking if a computer could really help. My only negative thought is that this video would be significantly more effective with real customers rather than actors. With 800 installations there should be no problem getting volunteers. This will increase the cost (travelling to customers sites, production costs, and so forth), but I think that it would be much more effective. I have seen a couple of videos with real customers and they seemed very credible.

The second phase of the video was titled "IBM and DENEB - Partners Providing Solutions for the Construction Industry". This portion pushed the RS/6000. To be honest, I was a bit surprised at the how much the video emphasized IBM and the RS/6000. Ken said that this was done deliberately as part of the early marketing strategy to establish DENEB's reputation and credibility. DENEB's prospects are conservative and this safety net helps bring them in.

The third phase was "People Who Know Business." Customer quotes were written on the screen with voice overs and a DENEB spokesperson then talked about the company's relationship with IBM and its experience in the industry. The video closed with the message "Call us or IBM."

I think this video should be quite good at opening the door and establishing DENEB as a legitimate player. If I was considering buying software in the construction industry, this video would get me to take the next step and call.

I also looked at the demo disk. One nice point with the demo disk was that the instructions were on the label and were easy to follow (which isn't always the

Chapter VII. Feature Articles and Case Studies

case). They use IBM Story Teller software using a story line "a system designed to meet needs." The good news is that it looked pretty on my VGA monitor. The bad news is, it was slow on my 386. I also didn't like being a passive observer. I find that far too many demo disks take a very simplistic and overly thorough approach. They seem to feel obliged to take me through every possible menu item. I would prefer that a demo show me the top five choices, then walk me through all the rest. I lost interest after about five minutes, but I have a short attention span. Technical evaluators might like this demo disk, but they wouldn't prefer to read the manual instead. The objective for the demo disk wasn't clear to me. According to Ken, it is used primarily as an attention-getter at trade shows. I think that it is very effective in this role.

Ken started in the construction industry in 1962, and he used early software products in the 1970s. In 1988 he went to a Reynolds and Reynolds division which was in the software product business for construction companies. Ken felt that this experience was very important because, even though he didn't like the big Company politics, he felt that he learned alot about marketing and business. In the meantime, he and Norm Suda had become acquainted through a number of contacts. Norm had built a software product for a software publishing company and then left. When this company decided to get out of the product business, Norm and Ken approached the owners and bought the product.

There are some parts to this story that are very common. The industry experience and working for larger companies are things that I see quite often. Buying the product for very little cash is also another common requirement. Most software products are developed for "free." This may involve getting the customers to pay for the development on a contract basis, programming it nights and weekends while working at a daytime job, or programming full time and not drawing a salary.

This is a "sweat equity" business and you can't afford to invest your cash in creating the product. You are going to need all the cash that you can muster for the marketing and sales, so keep your powder dry. Just so I don't get calls, I will acknowledge that there are products that do require development capital. These products have the positive aspect that they are so complex that they have a real barrier to

entry and future competitive advantages. The bad news is that it is very, very hard to raise money for these products. It can be done, and when it all works these companies are great successes.

DENEB spent its first year selling direct to reference accounts in Dayton. Then, in late 1984, Ken and Norm decided to sell exclusively through dealers. They signed up their first local dealer, turning over all their local sales and prospects to the local dealer.

This was a tough decision for Ken, but I agree that it was the right one. Ken said, "Once you get accustomed to selling direct and receiving full revenues, it is tough to give it up." But as he pointed out, you cannot afford two marketing programs. This point really emphasizes the need to commit to one and only one marketing program, if you really want it to work.

This is probably the most pragmatic reason to fully commit to dealers if you want it to work. If you split your marketing and sales dollars between your dealer program and your direct sales, neither program is getting its full attention. The other obvious fact is the direct marketing and sales programs will probably get higher priority since they are managed from your office. Failing to support remote dealers isn't nearly as upsetting as facing your own company employees who aren't generating leads (and therefore aren't making the sales commissions).

Back to DENEB. Ken said, "We have too many leads to worry about whether the dealers are really following up, but occasionally we will audit a dealer to see if the dealer is doing a good job." This is a much more mature attitude than I have generally observed. I have seen so many cases where the vendors are obsessed with how well their dealers are following up on the leads. I think that this undermines the basic relationship.

If you are really committed to dealers, you have to trust that they will use your leads to make the sales for their own benefit. Audits will weed out bad dealers, but you have to trust the good ones to operate appropriately.

The dealer discounts with DENEB start at 30 percent to 40 percent and the best discount is 55 percent. The discount is based on cumulative sales. They also have both source code and object code dealers.

I was surprised that DENEB's updates are also sold through the dealers. DENEB looks to the dealers to provide ongoing direct support, so it makes sense for them to share in the update and support revenues.

I asked Ken how he deals with an unregistered dealer who wants a discount and has a customer ready to buy. I was expecting to hear "We end up giving them the minimum discount of 30 percent, but we resent it." Instead, Ken tells them, "You can't sell our product at this time since you aren't trained. Please turn this sale over to our existing local dealer." DENEB is willing to risk losing the sale knowing that the non-dealer may turn the sale over to a competitor.

The reason that Ken takes such a hard line is because he doesn't want to undermine his own dealers. He has found, in many cases, the customer has decided to buy DENEB's product and is just shopping around for price. If DENEB allows the new or non-dealer to make the sale, an established dealer has lost a sale which he deserves, and a customer has purchased a product from a dealer who can't really provide support. Ken summarized his position as, "It is more important to minimize price shopping than to maximize incremental sales."

DENEB has 100 to 125 dealers who have made a sale in the last three or four years. Many of these dealers are active in that they are supporting their customers even if they aren't making new sales. DENEB is selling 150 systems per year and has some vertical market dealers who are selling ten systems per year. (Here is where the old 80/20 rule applies.) If a dealer doesn't take care of his customers, he won't be re-authorized.

I asked Ken how DENEB had become allied with IBM in the "Cooperative Software Program (CSP)." DENEB had become familiar with Altos, AT & T, and IBM through UNIX Expo. DENEB ported to the IBM RT in 1987, and was able to use its relationship with the people at IBM to get into the CSP. DENEB ported to the RS/6000 when it was released in February, 1990. Ken stressed how difficult it was getting accepted for the CSP. For example, prior to the CSP, less than ten percent of DENEB's sales were with IBM. Now over 30 percent of DENEB's sales are with IBM. This is good, but it has taken a number of

years. He also mentioned that it took two years to get IBM to develop and approve the video.

He said, "We had to spend big bucks to get to the point where IBM would respect us." This is a real problem that I see over and over. I see small companies who want to get the relationship with a company like IBM, but want to find the shortcut. They don't want to make the investment. They want to get the distribution/sales partner to make the investment for them. This just doesn't work. The distribution/sales partner has to be sold.

The good news is, if you actually make the sale, you can get some real benefits. In this case, IBM financed the video, the demo disk, and paid for a 100,000 piece mailing. There was an AIX marketing budget and DENEB "just got lucky and tapped into the money." This isn't luck, it is just the reward for the investment they made in impressing IBM.

DENEB also continued its investment in IBM last year. They visited the local branches and went to joint trade shows with IBM. I asked Ken how much he thought they had invested in the IBM relationship. He said that it was at least $250,000 and was probably quite a bit more if you factored in the time for everyone who was involved.

I asked Ken about IBM's CSP program. There is no sharing of hardware dollars, but DENEB shares 25 percent of the software sale with IBM. When he was offering his product on the IBM RT, IBM offered him a 60 percent discount on the RT. He declined this for a couple of reasons. The first is, the hardware vendor can always change the rules. If the software vendor becomes dependent upon these hardware dollars, he becomes dominated by the hardware vendor. The second reason is that the hardware vendor is also free to increase your quota almost on a whim.

This is an argument that I have with a number of my clients. I worry that if you start paying too much attention to the hardware dollars, you become less of a software company. It takes all of the time and energy you can muster to succeed in the software business. You really cannot afford to split your energies. (This is much like Ken's position on being fully committed to dealer sales.) Focus is critical to success with any business, and it is especially critical to small business. There are lots of temptations, but if you weaken and start to chase the rainbows, you don't get your garden planted.

Ken stated that DENEB generates over 3,000 leads a year or 250 per month, which puts them in the top twenty percent of our respondents in last year's survey. They attend six to eight trade shows or conferences and advertise in a dozen trade magazines off and on. They have done direct mail in the past and aren't sure if it paid off because they didn't track it well. They are now watching the 100,000 IBM direct mail effort sent in February to see if it pays off.

I asked Ken what percent of his people and budget are in marketing and sales. Fifty percent of DENEB's people are in marketing and sales, but they spend 70 percent of their budget in marketing and sales, including salaries and direct expenses. This is really key to their success. I see so many technology- driven companies where the development group gets 70 percent of the budget and 80 percent of the people. The management in these companies is almost always technical and they are surprised that their products aren't well-received in the market. I think these managers really believe that if you build a better mousetrap, the world will beat a path to your door. (But remember, they have to hear about the mousetrap first!)

As far as his personal objectives, Ken says he is not interested in selling the company since DENEB doesn't have the right numbers yet to get the valuation that he and Norm would like. They are also both having fun running the company. My guess is, once they get the company revenues up to $5 million a year and have a valuation in the $5 million to $10 million range, they might be tempted. Who knows? Right now they are building up their company and that is their current objective. I think their heavy marketing investment will end up paying off in future sales and will bring the good valuation they are looking for, but it does take time.

Ken Lykins can be reached at (513) 223-4849.

G. New Ideas (Apr 1991)

Frank Koranda is the founder of New Ideas. His experience is fairly typical in our industry. After graduating from college in 1984 with a degree in Computer Science, he worked for a couple of companies developing in-house applications. Then, he went to work for a company that developed commercial accounting software tailored for grocery stores. In 1989, he went out on his own, starting his own software development and consulting company.

He has mainly worked on custom software for other businesses, but along the way he developed a program called Disk Directory. This is a product to help a LAN manager manage the files. His product identifies inactive files and archives them, deletes or transfers an entire category of file types, identifies duplicate files and determines disk space usage based on user-defined file categories.

Frank's immediate delay is documentation, which probably requires a couple of weeks of hard work. He is reluctant to sell to his contacts without at least finishing the documentation.

Frank is aware of only one other product similar to his and it involves laboriously tagging each file. With Disk Directory, you simply set up your criteria and run batch jobs. His approach is more like a production concept. It occurs to me that with his product, people will actually be able to manage their files and slow down the rate of adding new disks. Without automatic tools, the hardware vendors just get rich.

The competitor's product sells for $300, but Frank is thinking of pricing Disk Directory at $149. I am worried that a $149 price tag gives the wrong message. It tends to categorize the product as an individual tool. I would initially price it at least $295. This is priced more like an MIS tool. One of the beta sites reduced the disk maintenance from one hour a week to five to ten minutes. This is worth real money to a LAN manager. Within a year or two, I would expect the price to go to $995 as the product matures and adds more features.

I think that this product could be advertised in the classified ads in LAN magazines. The classified ads in magazines of this type aren't very expensive, and a good percentage of the readers should be qualified prospects. These ads have about a two- month lead time, so I urged Frank to place the ad and use the two months to complete the documentation. This approach commits him to complete the documentation and packaging.

Placing the ads is a much bigger commitment than spending some time writing documentation. It is a commitment to starting a new business, and this isn't an easy decision to make. I have seen far too many people who have invested tens of thousands of their own dollars in publishing their own products, and finally realize that they don't have a real business. I see too much money spent on fancy brochures, packaging, and expensive ads before it is really clear that there is a real demand for the product.

Frank is facing the transition from contract programmer to software publisher and it is a difficult one. In the contract programming business, you make money by finding work and keeping busy and keeping your overhead low. Considering the state of mind of the typical programmer or manager, many of the up-front costs associated with producing a product "just don't feel right." These include documentation, packaging, marketing, and so forth. I have even observed this phenomena in very large organizations.

My advice is to proceed with caution. Develop some minimal documentation and packaging with an eye to holding down the costs. Set yourself a marketing budget and place some inexpensive ads. If you have a good concept, you should generate enough sales to pay for the next ads. You may not make enough money to quit your day job, but at least you aren't putting your life savings into it. This reminds me of the vanity book press. Very few people make money with self-publishing, and it is very easy to blow your money. My approach is to test the waters knowing how much money you are willing to invest.

If you get the business going with a positive cash flow, since you are working for free, you have to decide if you can grow the business to support you full time. Fundamentally, this requires that you be able to generate the volume and thus the revenues to have the profits to pay yourself a salary.

There are some nice situations which don't have this potential. I had one client who had a nice little product with a limited market. This fellow found out that a small ad in one magazine would generate $500 per month in profits, but larger ads lost money and he couldn't find any other profitable magazines. In this case, this person decided to shut the product down since the hassle of dealing with this product wasn't worth the $500 per month. (He was a doctor earning almost $200,000 per year in his practice.)

It seems to me that you should be able to determine ahead of time how big the market is, but my experience shows it is really difficult to determine the breadth of appeal of a new product. If there are existing similar products, you can use their sales to gauge your probable success.

Frank Koranda can be reached at (402) 443-5460.

H. JIAN/Tools for Sale (May 1991)

Burke Franklin is the President and Founder of Jian/ Tools for Sale (415) 941-9191. Biz Plan Builder, Jian's first product and flagship, was introduced in February 1988 at $79 and now sells for $129. Over 42,000 copies of Biz Plan Builder have been sold.

Originally, Burke was a field sales rep and had become frustrated dealing with questions that the marketing materials should have answered. So, he started a business creating brochures, marketing materials, catalogs, etc. to help people sell their products more effectively.

Burke also understood that there were multiple audiences for the marketing materials. The sales person was working directly with the technical contact, but the purchasing agent or financial person also had to be sold. In many cases, the marketing materials presented the case to these secondary approvers. Burke felt that it was important to make the case for these secondary people in the marketing materials because the technical people often had difficulty talking to the financial people.

As part of his consulting practice, Burke worked with several of his clients on business plans. After completing five business plans, he found that when he started on number six, there was very little that was unique or new. He then read nine books and all the articles he could find on writing business plans.

Burke realized that some day he would need a business plan of his own, especially if he started his own company or worked as VP of Marketing for another company. In 1987, over the Christmas holidays, he began to assemble a folder of everything necessary to write a business plan. He thought maybe he might sell an outline of a business plan for $29. (He was on his way to writing yet another book on how to write a business plan.) As he worked on the outline, he kept going to his folder and adding more information.

At this point, Burke realized that business plans were really a selling piece to get money and manage a business. Plans had many purposes, but they all looked alike. Burke then decided he would give people a super deluxe business plan, with everything a business plan needs. By this time, he was seeing this as a software product where he could add a lot of information very cost effectively. He wanted to make this an extraordinary deal, giving people $1,000 worth of information for only $69. He felt that by offering such a great deal, he could build sales quickly.

Burke strongly believes it is very important to maximize every opportunity to "get in front of people and show your stuff." On February 6, 1988, his product was finally ready to sell, so he took his "ugly little package with a goldenrod colored cover" with him to a meeting at the Silicon Valley Entrepreneurs Club. He gave a five minute sales pitch to the club members and that night, after the meeting, he closed his first sale.

He then contacted a distributor who advised raising the price to $79. Burke feels, most engineers hold their cards too tightly to their chest. The benefits of telling others and getting the feedback outweigh the risks that someone will steal your ideas. Burke also feels that if a possible competitor hears about your product, he may actually be less likely to develop one that will compete with yours. They may reposition their own product to avoid competing or they may focus their energies on an alternative product.

Burke did acknowledge that he didn't show the product to other software companies. He showed it to users, dealers and distributors from whom he received lots of feedback on pricing, packaging, production houses, etc. One key philosophy that Burke expressed over and over was, "Get as much feedback as possible, as quickly as possible."

People love to give advice, and there is a benefit in telling them later, "I took your advice. What should I do next?" This is music to their ears. If you involve people who can help you down the road and take their advice, they will begin to buy in and this will create future opportunities.

Jian's first ads were classified ads in popular computer magazines like MacWorld and PC Magazine. Burke advertised in all of the popular magazines that would give him 30 day terms. This allowed him to bootstrap the ads, and he made money on the ads right away. He was advertising the product as a "Business Plan on Diskette", for $79.

By chance, Burke was introduced to a guy in Palo Alto who specialized in color analysis, and who had done a great deal of work for a number of large companies. Burke showed this color analyst his "goldenrod package" and was told that yellow was a "universally disliked color", and that the package should sell the product. People should be able to turn it over and see what it does. Burke took the guy's advice and changed the package to a conservative photo of papers on a desktop, tasteful but not too eye-catching. (At this point I'd like to make a comment. I have seen some research showing that the color yellow can actually be one of the most eye-catching and effective colors for packaging. I've used goldenrod paper lots of times in my materials with great results. The good news is that Burke ended up with a package that he liked and had confidence in.)

Sometime after, Burke went to a large software retailer with several of his employees and his graphic artist. They wanted to see how Biz Plan Builder looked on the shelf compared to other companies' packages. It was really obvious that Biz Plan Builder didn't jump off the shelf, so further changes were made to make the package more eye-catching.

Burke explained that he believed in an evolutionary approach, and accepted the fact that he would make mistakes. He didn't put too much money into materials early on, and only had 100 copies with the goldenrod cover when he decided to change it. He just printed new covers and threw away the old ones.

During Jian's early stages, the classified ads were generating three or four sales per day. This was enough to continue to fund the business, but Burke was still consulting to pay the rent. At the same time, he was able to use contacts he'd made through consulting to set up payment terms for Jian.

Burke mentioned one creative trade that I really liked. He developed a brochure for a disk copying firm in return for an initial run of disks. This was a barter deal that worked for everyone. I would think that many small software companies might find an occasional opportunity for barter. The key point is to keep your mind open and explore the opportunities. Ask people if they might consider. ... Occasionally they might say yes.

Because of the two month lead time for national magazines, Burke placed some ads in local daily and weekly newspapers. This also began to generate sales.

Burke made a very strong point that he kept or dropped the ads based on their sales (not leads as the ad reps like to talk about!). He had a simple spreadsheet for the magazines that tracked the sales, costs, profit or loss and the ROI. He stopped the bad ones and continued with the good ones as long as they worked. Over time he found more magazines that worked until he was advertising in more than 20 magazines.

I asked him why he didn't try full page, four color ads. (See the letter later in this issue by George Duncan on this same issue.) Burke said he looked upon the classified ads as a reference section. People look in the classified ads for offbeat products. Burke was worried that big ads would get lost with all of the big hardware company ads.

Another key part of his advertising strategy was the use of a toll free 800 number. He started this six months after placing his first ads, and recalls that it did increase the response rate. He says it is easy to get an 800 number. Just call the phone company. They want to sell you the service, so they make it easy for you to buy.

He also developed a flyer describing his product to send to people who requested information. He never mailed his flyer to cold lists.

Developing phone scripts was another key approach which allowed him to expand the business and bring new people into the sales role with minimum training cost.

He listened to himself explain the product over the phone. He wrote it down and used it as his phone script. He wrote it as he would say it — contractions and all. He found that the scripts helped if his mind was on something else. He was surprised that half way through the script, people would say, "Will you take Visa ..." and the sale was made.

Getting credit card authorization was critical to helping people buy over the phone. If you asked them to send a check, a number of people would never buy. At that time banks didn't want to give credit card privileges to mail order companies or companies that operated out of the person's home, and Jian met both of these criteria (In fact, Burke felt that it wasn't even worth it to contact the banks.) Instead, he found someone who was an agent. This agent got a commission on the credit card sales. (It wasn't really clear to me how this relationship worked, but Burke did manage to get credit card privileges.)

Burke also felt that 30 day return privileges were important. He didn't want unhappy customers out there complaining about his product. His return rate has been about 2.3% which is less than the American Express fee of 3%. He views this as part of the cost of doing business. I couldn't agree more. I am very sure that the increased sales, because of the guarantee, are much greater than the refunds that you end up giving. (I mentioned this to Burke and he immediately responded that American Express was expensive, but worth it. I have been surprised at the number of AMEX charges we get for the newsletter from small companies. It is clear that AMEX has the corporate market locked up, so if you are selling to small businesses, AMEX could be significant to your sales.)

I asked Burke about his early sales to dealers. First, he got some standard invoice forms at a stationary store, then went around and talked to the dealers. He offered them a 3 for 1 deal on their initial order and agreed to invoice them, basically handing them 3 products and an invoice. He felt that it was important to do business on their terms, and this approach has built up Jian's dealer sales, but they still have found it difficult to get into broad distribution.

Burke really believes in press releases and is surprised that some software companies don't even bother to send them. He is very convinced that press releases lead directly to sales. Early on, Jian's press releases even lead to some articles being published, which in return, lead to a great flurry of sales activity.

Burke had an interesting insight about interviews with the press. He has seen cases where someone makes a negative comment while being interviewed and then they are surprised when that comment ends up with a prominent role in the interview or article. He feels that most reporters feel a need to publish a "balanced" article (with both positive and negative comments). Thus, Burke feels you should design in some small bad news that is actually positive. For example, you might say that you have some customers who have been upset because it took you several weeks to fill their orders because you were swamped with orders and ran out of product.

Burke also felt that it was important to have a good answer for the "Who are your competitors?" question. He spent time trying to develop answers to some of these common questions in terms which the editors could relate to. For example, he would explain that his major competitors are people who write their own plans from scratch. The problem with this, as any writer knows, is that you can stare at a blank sheet of paper. Editing a plan and filling in your specific information is much easier. The editors were able to relate to this and he felt that it helped them understand his product much better.

When asked what he would have done differently, Burke answered that he knows he had to experience all of the steps and make the mistakes that he did. It just would have been nice if he could have done it quicker. He mentioned once again that getting the product out into customers' hands as soon as possible and getting the feedback was fundamental to the whole process. Get going in a positive direction, and don't worry about getting ripped off.

Burke also feels that if he had received a big cash investment for Jian, his mistakes would only have been bigger and more painful. He says, "With a lot of money to spend, you can get sloppy. Having little makes you creative. That creativity continues as income increases!"

I asked Burke where he is going with the business and what he wants from it. He mentioned that the growth and profits are important. They are a necessary condition. You need them to support the business, but they aren't the end goal. He really likes getting feedback from customers who have used his products to improve their businesses. I find the same thing is true in my business. The feedback from a reader about how I have helped is really important. I think that most entrepreneurs really want to create something. The money is secondary.

I. Bradley Company (May 1991)

I interviewed John Zitzner President and Founder of Bradley Company. In 1983, John began consulting, after leaving a large business forms company where he had sold forms management programs.

By 1984, PCs were the new kids on the block, and John was using a Radio Shack PC for word processing. The business forms company had used a Data General minicomputer at headquarters with batch programs providing information to customers. The information was good, but it was out of date by the time it was shipped to headquarters, processed, and then shipped as reports back to the customer. John thought a PC could offer some major advantages by being more responsive. This would help make customers be more independent.

At this point, John started looking for custom software houses to develop his idea. His first experience with a custom software house was a flop, but the second worked out well. John was able to negotiate a good deal where he only had to pay $7.50 per hour up front. Another $7.50 per hour was paid out of future sales. Finally, the software house got 25% of the gross profits for the first three years. While these are 1984 rates (and very low rates even for 1984!) I have seen a number of deals structured along these lines.

Development took a little over a year and the first installation was in 1985. The software was decent, and was good enough to generate some sales. This was OK since John had kept the overhead down. He worked out of an office at home until the end of 1984, then in 1985 he moved into a 150 square foot office, once he began generating sales. Bradley company has grown from the original 2 employees to 14 today, and now operates from a 3,500 square foot location. At the same time, the company grew 980% in its first five years from 1985 to 1990 (with revenues going from $100K to $1.2M.). In 1990 they made the INC 500.

I asked John how he was able to sell to very big companies right from the start. He felt he'd had breaks all along the way. If his prospects liked his concept, they really didn't have any serious alternatives. There were some general purpose mainframe packages, but they were expensive and didn't provide the semi custom solution that his product offered. The other alternative was the Minicomputer solution from the forms companies. This didn't offer the immediate capabilities that the PC solution did and it involved the tie in with the forms company. Finally, John felt that his background, along with his sales skills was a major factor in his success. Initially, he sold the first copy to Home Life for $8K. Today the network version is $45K.

The company lost money in fiscal years 1984 and 1985, but broke even in 1986 and finally made a profit in 1987.

When asked how he had financed the business, John said that he and his wife had saved a major part of his salary from the business forms company. He felt that there was more to life than working for someone else. He gave it all he had while he worked there, but once he stopped learning, he knew that his long term future success would depend on his own hard work.

Living well below his means gave him the nest egg to get through the first two years of losses. At the same time, he was able to do some consulting to help pay the bills. He began drawing a salary in 1986 when the financials improved, but drew less than a full salary because he wanted the company to show a small positive profit.

I asked John how he managed to afford the airfare to visit prospects while he was selling a low priced product. Once again he felt he'd received a lot of very good breaks. He flew on People's Express from Cleveland to New York for $29. Today this same trip costs him over $500. He jokingly said that People's Express made it possible for him to travel and he didn't know if it would be possible to start the business today with the higher airfares. John also mentioned that about 30% of the time his customers and prospects would pay for his travel expenses. As he said, "Every little bit helps when you are bootstrapping a business". John wondered out loud if this could be done in 1991. I suggested it had more to do with the state of his business than the outside world. I have seen a number of cases where big companies are willing to go out of their way to help small companies that are developing unique products, but this charity disappears the moment there are alternative products or the small company gets underway financially. I almost think that some big companies view these types of relationships as their R & D.

The development relationship evolved in late 1986 when the contract with the custom software company expired. John hired a third employee, a recent computer science graduate, who had studied COBOL, the language of John's product. This person is now the Technical Director and has grown up with the company.

In March of 1986, John took on a partner who became the Executive VP. The company didn't have money for any big salaries at that point, since 1986 was the breakeven year. This new Executive VP helped keep the company moving and earned his sweat equity by taking a low salary. He now heads up software development, installation/training and the marketing area.

The Director of Marketing and Sales was hired in 1987. He was an ex-entrepreneur who had decided he wanted to work for a small company. He also knew that he didn't want to run his own company. This Marketing Director really turned around the company's image with its Fortune 500 customers.

The company financing was "classic bootstrap". The company received some early loans from family members, and in 1988 sold a little stock to employees and a few outsiders. They only raised $20K to $30K, but John stressed that this was a significant addition to their working capital. This is an important point to make. If your company is growing and profitable, you shouldn't require large investments. I really believe that your business will be stronger because you have to make careful decisions as you husband your cash. My experience is that you make more mistakes by acting too quickly than by acting too slowly. In many cases, you'll think things through more carefully, and as more information becomes available you'll make better decisions. For this reason, I believe that bootstrapping a business can contribute to its strength. However, I understand, first hand, the grief inherent to managing a "cash-poor" business.

The only significant outside funding for Bradley was a line of credit backed by its accounts receivables. John understood you have to sell the bank in much the same way you sell your customers. You have to develop a plan. Bradley's Director of Finance & Administration, who rounds out the five person planning team, began by interviewing a number of banks. Most banks wanted personal guarantees, but one of them didn't. Since Bradley sold to the Fortune 100, its AR was quite low risk. The initial line of credit was for $50K and has grown significantly more with its rate at 1% over prime. This line is backed by the AR since Bradley doesn't have any real assets to borrow against. John expressed his conviction that it is very important to do what you say you are going to do. The bank has asked for financial statements every month, and the Finance Director has made sure that these are delivered like clock work, along with updated copies of the marketing materials.

Bradley's marketing and sales cycle is a little longer than average, and involves three people at different stages and levels. Marketing starts off by getting the leads and reports on the lead production every month. The sales people then follow up and develop a relationship with each prospect. The average sales cycle is one year, with the minimum being three months and the maximum three years. The sales person's objective is to insure that when a prospect decides to buy, Bradley will be on the list of products being seriously considered. Bradley sells a demo copy of the product for $95, and Bradley considers prospects 80% sold at this stage.

Once a prospect has bought the demo, the Director of Marketing and Sales takes over. His job is to expand the relationship and he recently began using a very effective contact management package to track this relationship development process. The next critical point comes when the prospect has narrowed his list down to the couple of products to seriously consider. Once Bradley's on this list, they consider themselves to be 95% sold. John gets involved at this stage and makes the final sales call.

Bradley's objective is to get 33% of marketshare, including all those deals which were won by competitors and for which Bradley was not even considered. John feels that he is accomplishing this since he is closing over 50% of the deals where he makes the final sales call. This is the first time I have seen anyone set such a clear market share objective. On the other hand, if your objective is to dominate a niche long term, you then have to be very aware of market share. This is difficult to measure, but I feel that Bradley is doing a good job of understanding its market share.

Recently Bradley has started looking at additional products to sell to its customers. John considered either selling the same product to a new market or finding new products for the same market. He has opted to find new products since he liked the market he is in now.

The first new product chosen was an in-house print shop management product. Forms are printed by the in house print shop and are used by the same people who buy the forms management product. Bradley contacted a Canadian company with this product and got an exclusive for the insurance industry (the core of Bradley's business). This was a very pragmatic decision and I think Bradley will do very well selling this product to the insurance market. By focusing exclusively on the insurance market, no energy will be wasted selling to low return markets.

The second product was developed by a local company to manage boxes of used documents. Companies have to keep records for seven years and storing and finding records is a real problem. Bradley learned of this product through a customer and approached the company with an offer. This product met Bradley's criteria to pick up new products with a sales price over $10K.

In my experience, it is really important to start out with very specific selection criteria and to stick to them. I have seen too many cases where companies have started out with selection criteria and have changed them the moment they saw an interesting opportunity. Selling the in house print shop management package outside the insurance industry is an example of this temptation. When John was describing this product, I was really afraid that he was going to explain how he had decided to sell it to everyone in the US, since this was a reasonable extension of his market. My experience has shown that this kind of diversion rarely works out for the best and, in most cases, it wastes time and money.

Bradley is also looking at adding on services and has doubled its consulting services since 50% of its customers have expressed an interest in on site consulting. This is an excellent way to leverage the customer base.

When asked about his personal objectives, John said he wants to keep the company growing, and keep the employees and customers happy. He believes if you focus on these key issues, then everything else will take care of itself. He has no plans to sell the company and is convinced that in five years "something great" will happen if he stays on this track.

J. Fisher Idea Systems (Jun 1991)

In writing these monthly "feature articles" about various software companies and how they came to be, I have begun to realize something about the people I interview. I have found that each of these people is a true entrepreneur, really dedicated and committed to his or her "mission". They each have an idea of how they can make the world better and they set out, with a passion, to find or develop the products to do this. The key word here is "passion", a common trait that I see more and more in my clients and readers.

Without this passion, a venture becomes just another business, doomed to mediocrity or failure down the road.

For years, my daughter has kept a little sign over her desk that reads, "Part of being smart, is knowing what you're dumb at" — not to say my readers are dumb! Quite the contrary! The point I'm trying to make here is this: the more of you I meet and talk with, the more impressed I am with your ongoing sense of adventure and pursuit of new knowledge to make your companies the best they can be!

So many of you possess that "passion" of the true entrepreneur. So, give yourselves a pat on the back and I'll move on!

For this month's feature article, .I interviewed Marsh Fisher, Founder and CEO of Fisher Idea Systems, (714) 474-8111. Marsh is indeed one of these true entrepreneurs I just spoke of. As early as 1964, he imagined a software product to help with word association, a technique he often used in his hobby of writing comedy. At that point though, he was busy working as one of the founders of Century 21 Real Estate, and had neither the time nor the money to invest in his idea.

By 1977, he had both, so he retired to Hawaii to write comedy and begin working on a word association "thesaurus".

As he thought about the concept of word association, Marsh decided what he really wanted was a thesaurus for his own use. At the same time, he was learning about and becoming interested in a new academic discipline, Cognitive Science. This discipline explores and studies how the human mind really thinks. Over the years, Marsh has collected over 300 books on Cognitive Science and is really excited that 250 Universities and Colleges throughout the world now teach classes in Cognitive Science. The University of Buffalo offers a Masters Degree and the University of Massachusetts offers a Phd.

Marsh feels very strongly that creativity is a skill which can be built on and improved. It is a process that can be learned and cultivated. To be competitive, our society must make problem solving and ideas a part of our culture. Marsh predicts that by the year 2000, "Thinking 101, 102, ... " will be taught in every school. (I hope he's right!)

Marsh invested $4 Million in launching his business and developing his product (Idea Fisher). This wasn't a Venture Capital/Business Plan scenario. Instead, it was more of a glimmer of an idea, then a hobby, then a serious business type of scenario. The first five years (1977-1983) were the hobby/research phase. Marsh had no idea just how to develop his idea, and at one point he threw out two years of work and started over.

At any given time, Marsh had 10 to 20 people working on different parts and eventually had input from over 250 people. He hired librarians, admirals, art directors, and people from all sorts of fields. His challenge was to find people who represented a solid cross section of Americana. These people had to be able to work at the High School level and up. He developed editorial guidelines for his researchers, and took two years to train each one so they could work independently.

Marsh describes his product, Idea Fisher, as an "idea thesaurus". PC Magazine reviewed it as a Brainstorming package and named it as Editor's Choice, and had this to say about Idea Fisher: "Designed to mimic the creative thought processes of the human mind, it makes connections between word clusters to help you free associate new ideas."

I find it interesting that Marsh took the raw, brute force approach to developing the connections between word clusters. He had people from each area of expertise think, research, and then document the linkages. There are 500,000 words in the English language and that number is growing daily. There are 150,000 words in Websters dictionary, and you can cut that down to 61,000 by eliminating synonyms. Thus, the task was to fill out a 61K by 61K matrix (or 3.6 Billion cells). Idea Fisher ended up with 700,000 connections or 20% of the words related. (There is a formal procedure involved here, but it was beyond the scope of this article.) The large number of connections explains why the product takes over 7 MB of disk space!

Marsh said he felt his venture turned into a serious business in 1983 when he began hiring people. At that point, he thought it would only take a couple of years and $1 Million to produce Idea Fisher. At each stage, it seemed the product was getting better and better. People from the University of Hawaii helped with the research. Plus, the growth and acceptance of Cognitive Science reinforced Marsh's decision and the direction he was taking. The more he did, the more he believed, and fortunately he had the money to carry Idea Fisher forward and develop it to its fullest potential.

In 1989 Marsh began testing. He thought his target market was large ad agencies, so he set the initial price at $10,000. This turned out to be a hard sell because the ad agencies didn't have money to spend.

The price was reduced to $595 for the general PC marketplace. Marsh feels that $595 is the upper limit for individuals using Idea Fisher. He also sells site licenses for $10K to $100K including training. In this role, the company really becomes a consultant on creativity.

Since August 1989, Marsh's company and product have been featured in over 200 magazine articles. In addition to computer magazines, Idea Fisher has been featured in articles in Omni Magazine and Fortune. The company's only advertising has been through PR done by Marlee Parker of Parker Chandler Public Relations (714) 364-0191.

On the sales front, Idea Fisher has a sales rep on the East coast who sells site licenses and consulting to the Fortune 1000. Idea Fisher is also in the Egghead catalog.

Marsh has kept his company very small, with only 6 full time people in fulfillment. Everyone else is on a contract basis: programming, editing, PR, etc..

Marsh has moved very slowly and very carefully with marketing because he wanted to avoid making a lot of mistakes. He mentioned that his marketing has been "trial and error". This certainly matches my experience. You can study your market, and make your best guess, but time after time reality surprises me.

One of the reasons Marsh decided to go with the PR approach is because it provides very broad exposure. After his initial bad experience with trying to sell to the ad agencies, Marsh concluded that he really didn't know just who wanted his product. He decided to look at the profiles of the people who responded to the PR and use this information to focus his marketing. He found that the majority of his customers were "idea" people. Many of them were in areas such as new product development or planning (a company's movers and shakers). They were looking for new ways to look at something, without digging through mountains of paper in the library. They wanted to generate the maximum number of new ideas per hour with a minimum of effort.

Idea Fisher's market and acceptance has grown and it is now being used in many schools, including a version to be used by community colleges throughout the USA.

I find myself intrigued by this type of product, company, and founder. Idea Fisher is a perfect example of a pure R & D driven company in which the founder builds a product that he himself would love to have. The positive aspect of this approach is that the product is usually excellent. The bad news is that the market is determined in real time. I have seen a number of excellent products which had markets too small to support the business. It really was a shame that the founder had invested all this time and money to build a product with limited appeal and one which might never return his investment.

On the other hand, sometimes the magic works, and the R & D guy gets lucky. He really has his finger on the pulse of the market and comes up with a hot new product that gains wide acceptance. I believe that Idea Fisher stands a good chance of establishing a major new product category, and if that happens, Marsh Fisher's investment will be paid back many times over. Good luck, Marsh!

K. A tangled tale and a marketing challenge (Nov 1991)

Dear Dave,

In 1982, I was working for a local computer programming firm that programmed IBM mini-computer systems that sold for $10,000 to $25,000. This company went out of business, and I went home jobless.

A few weeks later, I was contacted by representatives of two of the accounts of my previous company. They each complemented me on my talents and abilities, and then asked me whether I was interested in providing additional services at an hourly rate. Because I was out of work at the time, I decided to give it a try. Nothing ventured, nothing gained.

Right? Little did I know that I had just put myself "in business for myself."

One of the two companies was a small, specialized, multi-attorney law firm located downtown. This company was founded and run by an attorney who offered me the chance to develop a software package for this specialized type of law and then market the package with his and his office manager's help. We were going to split the profits three ways.

Over the next several years, I spent an extensive amount of my time at a greatly reduced rate ($20/hour) to develop a software package for this type of law. I worked overtime for regular rates and was loyal to the cause as I continued to chase a rainbow.

As I was developing this package, my company also grew. Business was good. We began attending one or two trade shows a year. There was enough contract programming work to keep us going.

Several years ago, the firm I was contracting with merged with a larger local firm, primarily because the larger firm did not have its own specialized group. The attorney with whom I had worked became a partner in the new firm, and several of his people were dismissed because of the merger. The new firm also had its own computer system, but it could not do what my system could do. Therefore, they kept the old IBM minicomputer going just for the newly founded "specialized department." No further development of the old package was requested because my attorney friend no longer had any say in the spending of R&D dollars and now worked for someone else.

About this time, I began developing a new package, which could be integrated with other functions. This was primarily because many of our current customers were looking for faster software that was easier to learn and use. It was PC-based and compatible with Novell networking software.

In 1989 and 1990, business began to drop off. I set out to produce a 'software package' that I could market. This would be the way of the future, I felt, replacing all of the headaches of contract programming. On my own time and at my own expense, I developed another set of programs for this specialty. These programs were also compatible with the PC-based product described in the preceding paragraph. I gave the new package a name and obtained a

trademark that still hangs on my wall today But I didn't have the know-how to effectively market the package, so I did nothing with it.

Later, I developed a smaller system for another vertical market. The system simply tracked customers and commissions due. I thought that the package could be sold for around $1,000, so I decided to test the waters and take the marketing plunge. I decided to try a direct-mail marketing approach.

We bought a list of prospects in the local area from a well-established list broker. Next, we purchased IBM's Storyboard and spent an uncountable number of hours learning the product and developing a "presentation disk" of our product. We purchased a thousand five-and-a-quarter-inch floppies with our logo screened on the sleeves. We had our printer create offset-printed diskette labels, a personalized letter, a reply card, reply envelopes, and outer five-inch by eight-inch envelopes. The total cost of the mailing was about $1,000.

We decided to first mail out about 200-250 copies to track our response ratio. We duplicated the presentation disks and purchased a business reply mail (BRM) permit. Our mailing went out with first class postage on it. It failed miserably.

While the response rate was over 5% from the first mailing, all of the responses told us that the software was the wrong media type for their computer, or they were looking for a somewhat larger, in-depth package. So much for our first direct mail experience.

Back to our attorney friend... Earlier this year, the large law firm was looking for PC-based, specialized software to replace the now archaic minicomputer that was running the old software that I had developed. I was invited to show them my new package. My attorney friend got wind of the new development and immediately made a claim to owning a portion of the new package that I had labored long and hard to port to the DOS and Novell environment.

Although I did not feel that he had any claim to the package, I decided to hear him out. He offered to invest some money in the promotion and marketing of the package in exchange for a percentage of revenues (10%). This would solve several problems. First, he would relinquish his claim to owning any of the code. Second, it would give me marketing and promotional money. Finally, it would allow me another chance to market a vertical software package directly, this time with a higher price-tag.

Since then, I have hired a business planner, contacted my attorney to cut the deal, opened a new checking account for the new company, and begun re-creating another presentation disk, this time for the specialized package. My attorney friend had located a list of specialized firms that could benefit by using the software package and has offered many insights into how to properly address the market. He feels that we should charge $20,000 to $25,000 for all the software, selling it as an integrated solution. I think that $5,000 to $10,000 would be more appropriate.

After ten years of contract programming, I would very much like to change the way we do business and get started marketing one or more vertical solutions. This is the way to go, if I could only get started.

Dave, I have several questions for you, now that you understand my position:

1. Do you feel that we are spending too much by mailing out a presentation disk right off the bat? It costs us $2-3 per piece to do this.

Answer : I would send out a much simpler, less expensive mailer offering your prospects your presentation disk. In my experience, the low-tech prospects aren't nearly as enamored with demonstration disks as the software companies sending them out. The fact that so many of your prospects had problems with the disk format really bothers me. I would probably develop a brochure to describe the product.

2. Our printer murdered our letters by printing them black-on-white with no headings. How do we send out personalized letters without signing all of them by hand? We have a laser printer and word-processing software.

Answer : The only practical answer is probably to sign them by hand. You can have your signature printed in blue on the letters, but it doesn't look like a real signature. I sign at least 2,000 letters each month. I've found that the best time to do this is late at night, while I'm listening to the blues. Cold beer helps, too, and wrapping bandages on your fingers helps to prevent callouses.

3. How do we overcome the media dilemma that we had with the prior disks?

Answer : When your prospects request the demo disk, ask them to specify the format.

4. We now employ one full-time programmer other than myself, and a secretary/receptionist/office manager who can help with the mailings. How do we "phase-in" a sales force and/or a marketing staff gradually, so that we can afford them and still get the ball rolling?

Answer : In the short term, you will have to learn to do the marketing. You can use outside experts, but you can't afford a full-time person for marketing. On the other hand, I believe that hiring a full-time salesperson should be your top priority. I have seen people have very good luck hiring someone from the industry who wants to make more money. In the early stages, these application specialists can make the technical sale. You might consider hiring a paralegal and teaching him or her to sell.

Another approach is to find a salesperson who has some understanding of your market. You will still have to provide the applications expertise, but they should already know how to sell.

5. How do we market our package once we have a hot lead? Do we sell them a demo copy for $99 as we are hoping to do, or do we hop on a plane and fly to who-knows-where to do an on-site presentation of our package? This can become very expensive.

Answer: You cannot afford to fly to present your product at the drop of a hat. Your salesperson must qualify each prospect and get him to try the demonstration copy. I have seen many companies lose money on each sale because the cost of the sales calls eat up any profits.

Any good salesperson will know how to qualify your prospects before you proceed to the presentation stage. Thus, if you plan to continue making on-site presentations, you will at least be limiting these visits to serious prospects. Your salesperson may even be able to get your prospects to pay for your expenses to visit them.

I also strongly recommend that you consider doing remote tele-demos. A tele-demo is conducted via modem with software, so that prospects can see the software on their machines. I have had several clients who have purchased pairs of 9600-baud, error-correcting modems for these tele-demos. The company sends the modem and the remote-control software to the prospect. The prospect must then get a conference room with two phone lines and must install the modem and software. Then you can conduct the demonstration without visiting the prospect. I have found that if you use this approach, when the prospect asks very specific questions, you can quickly get the expert at your company to answer the question by telephone. However, if salespeople are making the presentation alone, they often try to answer very specific questions and therefore give mediocre (or even wrong) answers.

A pair of such modems costs around $1,000. To get the most mileage out of your modems, you can send them to prospects via express mail, and customers can send them back the same way. Usually, technical people can set up the demonstration in an hour or two, and it's wise to have them set things up the day before the demo to avoid embarrassment when you're giving your presentation.

The other approach is to sell or give them the demo copy of your product. I have a number of clients who try to sell the demo copies, but if your sales people get a commission on selling the demo copy, it seems to me that they may focus more on selling the demo than on selling the product. The same thing can happen to the prospect. If you set the price of the demo too high, the prospect can spend too much energy trying to justify the purchase of the demonstration disk to their management. This is the last thing that you want to happen.

The whole justification of charging for the demo is that you want to qualify the prospects who receive the demo and recover the cost of the demonstration. No one is going to get rich selling demo systems. Your salespeople will need to be able to waive the cost of the demo system if that is appropriate. I therefore don't recommend selling the demo for $99; I would set the price of the demo system at its cost. Most companies credit the cost of the demo if the customer buys the product.

My other concern is that your prospects might not install the demo disks. My experience has shown that prospects in many non-technical markets are intimidated by demo disks, and getting the prospects to install and use the demo is difficult. In many cases, a good brochure has been much more effective

in selling the product than a demo disk. The programmers who create the product and the demo disks are often excited about the demo disk, but the idea of installing and using the demo often intimidates the non-programmer prospects who evaluate the product. Please make sure that the demo disk is truly helping you make sales. This is what really matters.

6. My attorney friend is willing to contribute $10,000 to help us get started. He wants me to use this money for the initial costs of selling the package. He feels that if our presentation disk is good enough, prospects will hop on a plane to come see it first-hand here. We will then use some of his money to pick up the prospect at the airport in a limousine and provide an all-day presentation. We would provide a catered lunch at our cost. Is this a sound approach?

Answer: It would be really nice if a demo disk were good enough to convince prospects to spend their money to come visit you, but I wouldn't count on it. I haven't seen this work for anyone as well as you envision it. I have seen people impressed enough by a new product that they were willing to pay for the vendor's airfare and motel expenses.

Even if it is possible to get half of the most serious prospects to pay for the airfare, you will still have some significant selling expenses. The more I think about it, the more I am convinced that you need a good salesperson. This should be your top priority. And your second priority should be the tele-demo. If you can avoid personal sales calls, you will dramatically reduce wasted resources.

One thing we discussed by phone was targeting your local market. You have a significant market within driving distance. I would develop a simple mailing, maybe just a letter, and buy mailing lists in your local market. You can refine the sales pitch and make your sales calls in your own backyard, where it doesn't cost you air fare.

You also mentioned that your "attorney friend" wanted a 10% royalty on all revenues until he had received a maximum of $2 million. This would probably kill the business. Even if he were investing enough to launch the marketing, it is very difficult for a software company to pay 10% off the top to its investor. In our recent article, "Operating Expenses Survey," (September, 1991), we found that the average profit before taxes was 11%. A 10% royalty would take the lion's share of these profits and would cripple the business. At the very least, you should accrue the royalties so that the company can use the cash. I would probably drop the idea for this business entirely if your "attorney friend" continues to claim an interest in the product and insists on his own royalty approach. You could, however, offer to sell him stock in the new company rather than give him royalties.

7. Should I seek out other investors?

Answer : You need investors, and it will probably take $250,000 in outside funding to launch this product unless it is particularly well received. In spite of the need, I advise you to wait.

You have very little to show a potential investor now, so you need to complete the product, make some sales and develop your sales and marketing strategy based on results. Once you have done these things and have some revenues, you might be able to attract other private investors.

8. How do I determine what price to ask for the package?

Answer : I would start somewhat low. You need to get ten reference customers. I would tell your prospects that the price of the product is $20,000, but you are looking for reference customers, and you are therefore selling it for $10,000 to the first ten customers who installed the product.

On the phone, you indicated that $10,000 is probably an acceptable price. If you are selling well at $10,000, you can consider moving the price up to $20,000 later. Let the market guide you on this decision.

Postscript

After further discussion, the company founder decided to send out a simple survey letter to local prospects in his market to determine the potential for his product and to generate some leads. In the first week, his response rate was higher than four percent, and it appears that he is well on his way to making his first installations.

1992
Software Success
Reference Book

Chapter VIII
Sales Cycle

A. Demonstration Survey (Feb 1991)

We set yet another record with 179 responses. This is slightly more than the lead survey, but this survey required more data and a number of readers sent the survey back empty because they don't have the information at this time. (I hope they capture the information as they proceed.)

1. Number of Leads per Month by Product Price

Product Price	% Responses
No Reply	1.1%
<$100	12.3%
<$1K	24.0%
$1K-$10K	31.3%
$10K-$25K	14.0%
$25K-$100K	17.3%
>$100K	3.9%

2. Product Price (Primary)

The distribution of product price is similar to what we have previously found, but this time we have a little more detail. The most popular price point is $1,000 to $10,000. This is common for both vertical market packages and tools and utilities sold on minis and mainframes to corporate customers.

The under $1,000 price range was next, and there was something of a dip between $10,000 and $25,000 (e.g. there were slightly more products in the $25,000 to $100,000 range than the $10,000 to $25,000 range.) I think this is due in part to the awkward nature of the $10,000 to $25,000 price range. For a corporate product, it is high enough to require senior management review and yet it is really too low to pay for on-site sales calls.

I have seen a number of companies raise the price of corporate products above $25,000 to cover the cost of sales calls and on-site support. In a few cases, the prices didn't hold because the value wasn't there and the companies had to drop the price. However, in most cases (with very high-value applications) there was very little price resistance.

The same strategy is much more difficult with software which sells to smaller companies. In these smaller companies, they are much quicker to react to higher prices. Price increases can be done, but you

may have to provide more value in the way of support, and service.

One final comment: I was surprised at the relatively large number of companies with products under $100. My experience is that it is difficult to build a company with a product priced under $100. You can't count on distribution for the initial sales push, so you have to make direct sales. It takes a pretty "hot" product to get the response rate to make money during this critical stage.

3. Number of Leads per Month

Once again, the number of leads per month seems pretty low to me. (See the graph on the next page for the distribution.) The median is close to 50. This is quite a bit lower than I would like. The distribution is quite similar to what we found in the lead generation survey last year. Once again, 25 to 50 leads per month is the most common range.

My experience is that most small software companies can improve their revenues and profitability by generating more leads. Sometimes I get the feeling that I am dealing with guilds from the middle ages. People really believe that they have to hand craft the leads. It is expensive, but they are really good leads.

In many cases, the battle that I end up waging is to automate the lead generation process. This usually entails some reduction in quality (fewer personal letters to less qualified lists), but there are also significant cost reductions.

It is common for small volume personalized letters to cost as much as $2.00 per letter for batches of 100. It is common to lower this to $1.00 per letter with batches of 1,000 and you can get it down to $0.50 for batches of 5,000. Lowering the cost per unit by a factor of four can result in a significant reduction in the cost per lead even if the mass production mailing is slightly less effective.

4. Percentage of Leads that Buy within Six Months

The graph is at the top of the page 8-4. The median is that five percent to ten percent of the leads buy within six months. This is pretty good. I commonly find that ten percent to fifteen percent eventually buy, but that can take years. Very long sales cycles are the bane of many software companies. This is especially true for companies which are selling software which changes how people work. If you are going to change people's behavior, it is going to take a significant amount of time for the prospect to in-

In one case, there had been a very expensive minicomputer software product. My client improved the response by highlighting their price in their marketing materials.

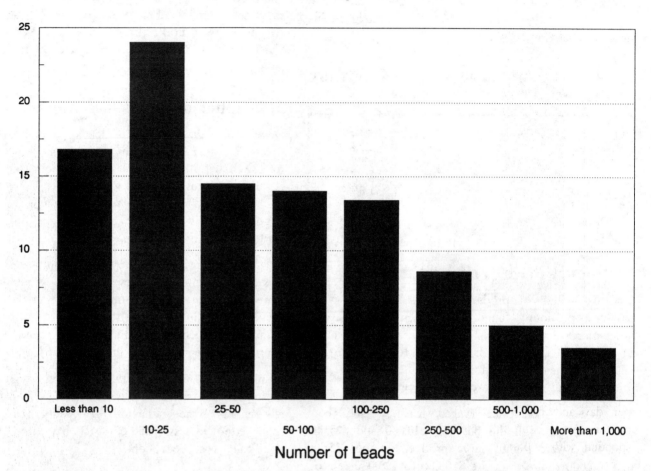

Number of Leads per Month

Number of Leads

sure that the product will really work in their environment.

I was bothered by the less than one percent response. If you are really converting less than one percent of your leads to sales, you are doing something wrong. Are you communicating what your product does? What about your qualifying criteria? I actually believe that you should try to describe your qualifying criteria in your marketing materials. Let people know who should buy your product and who shouldn't.

The only exception is when you aren't generating enough leads and you want more. I have worked with products where our prospects just assumed that they couldn't buy the product we were selling.

In another case, prospects had disqualified themselves when we included the purchase price. Our response rate had improved when we didn't mention the price, but it improved even further when we featured a monthly lease price for the entire system.

As you can see, we are trying to optimize total sales from our sales resource. Depending upon the situation, the right thing to do may be to generate more (less qualified) leads which are less likely to buy, or to generate fewer "good" leads. If your sales people don't have enough to do, or are spending too much time chasing too few leads, you should generate more leads. In other cases, it may be appropriate to have marketing qualify the leads for sales. Marketing can do this in the initial lead qualification process by making a hard sale (e.g., "This system

Percentage of Leads Buying Within Six Months

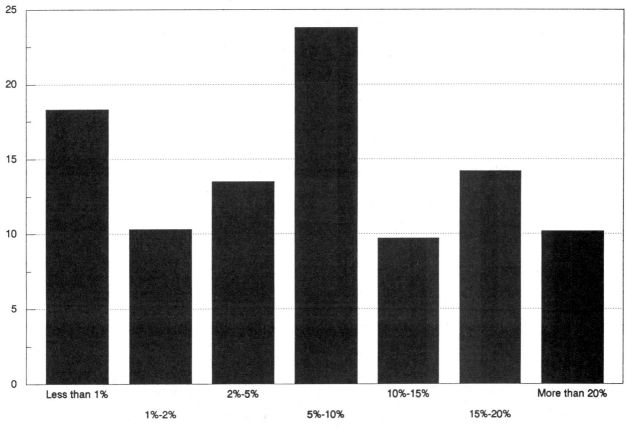

Percentage of Leads Buying

will produce savings if you process over 1,000 orders per day and can afford a $20,000 system."), or you can further qualify the leads once they have responded with follow up letters.

One of my pet peeves is companies who spend lots of money generating leads, then don't follow up. My experience is that a good follow up program of twelve monthly letters which might cost $5 can double or triple the number of prospects who buy from $50 leads. This can cut your cost per sale by more than half and this is the number that really matters.

5. Number of Trials/Demos per Month per Sales Person

The most common level of activity is two to five trials or demos per month. The median is five to ten. I realize now that I should have made more of a distinction between demos and trials. There is very little time investment in mailing out a demo disk, but traveling to a prospect site to demo your product can involve a considerable effort. Trials can also take a significant amount of time.

My experience is that getting five trials or serious demos per month is an aggressive target for a sales person. I view serious trials or demos as ones which turn into sales more than 50 percent of the time. Most of the companies that I work with have a sales cycle which starts with sending information. The next step is some form of low investment demo (this might be a demo disk or tele demo). This low investment demo is used to qualify the prospects who are really worth the full demo or trial. The percentage of low investment demos that move to the serious stage has ranged from 10 percent to 80 percent.

The ten percent case was a company that offered a demo disk in its ads. They received lots of requests for a demo disk, but very few prospects actually looked at the demo. The company started following up the demo mailing with a support call to see if the prospect had looked at the demo. They offered to walk through the demo with the prospect. It was almost as if we were qualifying our prospects after we had sent them the demo disk. The follow up process managed to improve to conversion rate, but it was pretty expensive. In retrospect, I think that this company would have been better off doing more qualification before sending the demo disk.

At the other end of the spectrum, a company started offering a teledemo. Historically, they had offered free trials of their mainframe product. Initially, they were very selective about the teledemo because they were apprehensive about the effort. Over 80 percent of the early teledemos ended up buying. It was apparent that they had been overly selective in scheduling the teledemos. Given their effectiveness, they decided to increase their capacity to conduct the teledemos. They hired a technical support person to work with sales to provide the teledemos. As they increased the number of teledemos, the conversion rate declined, but the absolute level of sales increased. They were using the teledemo to help qualify some of the softer leads. In this way, they pulled some prospects forward who might never have gone ahead with a trial.

6. How do you show your prospects your products before they buy?

Visiting the prospect and conducting a demo was the most popular approach, with a 55 percent response rate. Sending a demo was the next most popular approach.

How Shown	% Response
No Reply	1.1%
We Don't	10.6%
Full System	30.2%
Visist\Demo	55.3%
Send Demo	48.0%
Video	6.1%
Dial in	8.9%
Demo HW	15.6%
Dealer	19.6%

I was surprised that sending the full system was this popular (30 percent). My experience is that if you get the prospect to sign a legal trial agreement before you send the full system, you can minimize your risk as long as you are selling to medium or larger businesses. There is some risk with small companies and individuals that they will keep your software and not pay. My feeling is that as long as you take

reasonable precautions to protect your product, the risk is worth the additional exposure and sales. I suspect that very few of the thieves would ever have purchased the software that they steal. Thus, we aren't losing money, but it does hurt to know that we are being ripped off.

Dealer demos were significantly higher than I would have ever guessed (19 percent). For all of the complaints that we have as an industry about dealers, we are getting some coverage. I am sure that there are some problems with the quality and the quantity of the demos, but a number of companies are getting some coverage.

# trials/mo/person	% Response
No Reply	9.5%
One or less	13.4%
2-5	36.9%
5-10	19.0%
10-25	11.2%
25-50	5.0%
More than 50	5.6%

The hardware vendors are also providing more support (15 percent) than I would have guessed. Being able to use the hardware vendor's facility for a demo can be a real advantage if your software runs on mini or mainframe computers.

Dial-in demos (8.9 percent) are growing in popularity. There were a number of comments about how successful the dial-in demos had been. One account that wanted to encourage dial-in demos purchased a pair of 9600 baud error-correcting modems. They used the modems to pin down dial in demos. They offered to fedex the modems to a prospect if the decision maker would attend the demo. With normal modems the speed was slow and errors will disrupt the demo. It is difficult for the prospect not to think poorly of your product even if they know that it is a modem limitation.

Videos were used by only six percent of the companies. I think this is due to a number of reasons. The first is that a video tape can be costly. The second and perhaps more difficult issue is that you have to be very sure that you have the right message before you produce a video. Given the high fixed costs, you don't want to be changing your mind. Demo disks are cheap to produce and easy to change, so there is less penalty for not having the right message.

The "we don't" response are companies who make a one-step sale. They are expecting prospects to buy based on seeing an ad or literature. At lower prices, it isn't cost effective to spend money sending out a demo disk. This barrier may be more psychological than financial, since the cost of a demo disk is equivalent to the cost of a brochure. It seems to me that almost all software companies have to show their prospects what they are buying. You can do this on paper or on disk, but most people want this information.

7. On-Site Demo

As you can see, most companies do on-site demos, but 35 percent don't. A hardy seven percent get the prospect to pay for travel. I have worked with several clients who have done this and it was a great deal of trouble. I felt like we were making the travel payment the issue rather than the purchase of the software. Both of these clients implemented tele demos as a way of qualifying the prospects. This seemed to deal with the risk of visiting unqualified prospects without making an issue of the travel expense. Once they had conducted the tele demo, they were much more willing to incur the travel expenses.

On-Site Demo	% Response
No Reply	1.7%
We Don't	35.2%
Pay Travel	7.3%
We Do	58.7%

8. Demo Disk

I was pleased to see that demo disks had such a low failure rate. Only 6.7 percent of the respondents felt that their demo disk was a failure, and 37.4 percent felt that it had been successful (5.6 times more likely to succeed than to fail). The area for improvement is the "tried but OK." Most of the people I have worked with who have been pleased with their demo disks have gone through several iterations of improvement. I think of the demo disks as a direct mail package which must be refined over time.

9. Demo Disk Type

The crippled system which has limited functionality is the most popular approach. This balances the tradeoff of offering the most information and the

risk of losing it all. A significant number of people use the full system (17 percent).

Demo Disk	% Response
No Reply	1.7%
Never Tried	28.5%
Tried, Failed	6.7%
Succeeded	37.4%
Tried, OK	26.8%

The second most popular approach is to use a storyboard demo. You can use graphics, sound, and so forth to tell your story. I think of this type of demo as a brochure on disk. This requires a great deal of creativity. It is very possible to have a disaster with this type of demo disk. As with most creative projects, the small differences make a world of difference. I have also seen cases where involving outside people can result in a much more effective demo disk. This type of demo is part way toward the video as far as the creative demands and the costs involved.

Demo Disk Type	% Response
Storyboard	26.3%
Hit Key, limited	8.9%
Crippled	35.8%
Full System	17.3%

The hit key limited system is the least popular approach. I think that this type of demo is very demeaning and unsatisfactory to the prospect. It is also more work than the crippled system approach. I haven't seen many "hit the key" demos lately, and I believe that they don't work.

10. Videotape

Only fourteen percent of the respondents have used a videotape compared with 72 percent who have tried demo disks. The table above compares the distribution of companies failing, succeeding and doing okay for both demo disks and videotapes. I limited the analysis to the companies who had tried using either the demo disk or videotape. The failure rate was the same for both programs (nine percent). The success rate for the videotapes was slightly higher than the rate for the demo disks. I was pleased to see this. If you don't have much of an investment in a demo disk, it is okay if you only get okay results. On the other hand, if you are investing the big bucks (and big energy) in a videotape, it is a real let down if your results are only okay. This is much like using display advertising as promotion.

Videotape	% Response
No Reply	2.2%
Never Tried	86.0%
Tried, Failed	1.1%
Succeeded	7.3%
OK	3.4%

Success	Disk	Video
Failed	9.4%	9.5%
Succeeded	52.7%	61.9%
OK	37.8%	28.5%

Videotape Cost

Software companies sure know how to pinch their pennies. These costs are quite a bit lower than I have seen in my consulting work. If you hire a professional firm, the costs will be between $10,000 and $20,000, which is what 44 percent of our respondents spent. My experience is that if you get a video for less than $10,000 you are doing it on an ad hoc basis. I have talked to companies who have used local universities and TV stations to do their video tapes. These low- budget tapes are working so don't let the lack of budget keep you from trying videotape.

Cost	% Response
<$1K	20%
$1K-$5K	20%
$5K-$10K	16%
$10K-$15K	20%
>$15K	24%

11. Cost of Trial or Demo

There was quite a range in the cost for the trial or demo. I think that this question suffers from the fact that I didn't distinguish between demos and trails. If you have to visit the prospect for the demo or trial all of a sudden, the travel costs will overwhelm the materials cost for the software.

The under $5 cost will get you a demo disk and a simple brochure in the mail. Software packages with multiple disks and large manuals can cost up to $50. This is especially true if the manuals are reproduced in small volumes. A 300-page manual with a two binders might easily cost $30. If you are sending out

your full system (crippled or not), your costs might be $50 when you include postage. You will probably think twice before you send out a $50 demo system. On the other hand, if you require that the prospect pay $50 to $100, you worry that you are discouraging serious prospects.

Cost of Demo	% Response
<$5	27.9%
$5-$10	11.7%
$10-$50	12.8%
$50-$100	7.8%
$100-$250	2.2%
$500-$1K	6.1%
>$1K	6.7%

If you print a perfect-bound book of 300 pages in quantity of 1,000 your costs might be under $5 each. All of a sudden, it is much cheaper to send out a demo. Your costs are probably under $10 for the book, the disks, and postage (the book weighs less than the binder so it costs less to mail). If you have a new release where you will be sending out a new set of documentation, you might find that printing your documentation as a book will save you money, and you get the extra books for demos and prospects as a bonus. The drawback is that your programmers can't change the documentation on a weekly basis (irony). I personally like forcing development into formal releases with documentation that will be published and have a shelf life.

12. Cost of Demos as a Percent of Revenue

We received a fairly low response to this question and a fair number of complaints about the formula. The idea was to determine how significant demos were relative to the revenue. For example, if I were selling a $100 product, my demo cost $3, and ten percent of my demos purchased: it would cost $30 in demos for each purchase. This would be 30 percent of revenue, which is very significant. I have seen a couple of situations where the combination of high demo cost and low demo-to-sale conversion rates made demos a very significant percentage of revenue. In one case, demos were almost 20 percent of revenue, which was a major factor in the company losing money. We were able to lower it to ten percent of revenue by both lowering the cost and improving the conversion rate. This pushed the company into profitability.

% Revenue	% Response
No Reply	60.9%
Don't Know	0.6%
1%	11.7%
1-5%	10.1%
5-10%	8.4%
10-20%	5.6%
20-30%	2.8%
30-40%	0.6%

I suspect that the one percent responses are selling more expensive products. For example, if my product cost $10,000, my demo cost $10, and ten percent of my demos bought, my demo cost per sale would be $100 or one percent of revenue. With lower priced products demo cost and efficiency is very important. Nine percent of the respondents or 22.5 percent of the people who answered this question spend over 10 percent of revenue on demos. This can be an important cost center.

13. Number of Leads as a Function of Product Price

I find myself thinking about the low number of leads that the companies in the survey are generating.

As you can see, there is some relationship between product price and the median number of leads. I

Product Price	Median #Leads
<$100K	50-100
<$1K	100-250
$1K-$10K	25-50
$10K-$25K	10-25
$25K-$100K	10-25
>$100K	10-25

would have expected lower priced products to have more leads. This is true except for the slightly lower number of leads for products under $100. I would sure like to do a feature article on anyone starting a company with a product priced under $100.

If you multiply the product price times the number of leads times the percentage of leads that buy, you have the expected revenues. If we assume that ten percent of the leads buy, our expected monthly revenues would be $1,000 per month for products under $100 ($100 * 100 leads * 10%), and at least $100K for products over $100K ($100K * 10 leads * 10%).

I am beginning to think that the price of the product represents the value of the asset that has been created. The revenues are a return on the asset so the greater the asset the greater the revenues. There are all sorts of exceptions to this observation, but I find it to be an interesting concept.

B. Telemarketing Survey (April 1991)

We had 186 replies to this survey. This isn't a record, but it is very good. I had anticipated a somewhat lower response because only 30 percent of our subscribers sell via telemarketing. I tried to make this survey more general to cover more uses of telemarketing than just selling. At any rate, I am pleased with the response.

1. Company Revenue

The revenues were much like the previous surveys. I must admit that I had anticipated that this survey would be made up of smaller companies. This is based on my perception that telemarketing has gained acceptance over the last ten years. Thus, I had expected that companies which were started ten years ago (and which would be larger on average) would have made less use of telemarketing. The converse is that the new and smaller companies would be making more use of telemarketing.

I am very pleased that we didn't find this in the survey results. I think this indicates that the larger and more established companies are being just as innovative as the new companies.

Company Revenue	% Respondents
<$250K	18.3%
$250K-$500K	14.0%
$500K-$1M	18.8%
$1M-$2M	23.1%
$2M-$5M	16.1%
>$5M	9.7%

2. Product Price

I had anticipated that the product price would be significantly lower for this survey. This is due to the common perception that telesales is limited to lower-priced products. While I am very sure that most customers want to see a person face-to-face before they buy a $100,000 plus product, I have several clients selling software over $20,000 without ever visiting the prospect.

Because of my preconception, I combined all of the upper price ranges into over $10,000. We had 28.5 percent of the respondents with products over $10,000. Of the demo survey respondents, 32.5 percent were selling products over $10,000. Thus, we have somewhat lower priced products. What I don't know is where the drop off was. It might be that we lost all of the over $100,000 product respondents in this survey. (3.9 percent of the respondents to the demo survey had products over $100,000.)

Product Price	% Respondents
<$100	6.5%
$100-$500	15.1%
$500-$1K	11.8%
$1K-$5K	30.1%
$5K-$10K	8.1%
>$10K	28.5%

The $1,000 to $5,000 price range is very popular. This can either be a vertical market package or a tool for large companies.

Comparing these results with the demo survey we find:

Product Price	Demo	Telemktg
<$100	12.3%	6.5%
<$1K	24.0%	26.9%
$1K-$10K	31.3%	38.2%
>$10K	35.2%	28.5%

As you can see, telemarketing is more common with products with mid-level pricing. It is really tough to make money selling products under $100 on the phone, and it is also more difficult to sell products over $10,000 via telemarketing.

3. Computer Type

The profile was very similar to previous surveys. The only difference was that we had somewhat fewer mainframe respondents (6.5% versus 10% or more in earlier surveys).

Computer Type	% Respondents
PC	67.2%
LAN	15.6%
Mini	16.7%
Workstation	8.6%
Mainframe	6.5%

4. Sales Quota

There are two ways to look at the following table. The first is to focus on the people who don't have sales quotas. If you combine the companies with no quota and those with no sales people you have 46.8 percent of the respondents. I really am bothered by this. What people are saying is that they don't have a planned target for sales. It really doesn't matter who is selling. Someone is responsible for sales, and they should have a quota or target. This is true no matter who is making the sales.

The second perspective is to look at the companies who have quotas. The median quota is $400,000 to $600,000. This matches a number of other surveys on this subject. We found very few companies with quotas over $1 million per year.

Sales Quota	% Respondents
None	30.1%
No sales people	16.7%
<$100K	7.5%
$100K-$200K	7.0%
$200K-$400K	10.2%
$400K-$600K	14.2%
$600K-$800K	6.5%
$800K-$1M	3.8%
>$1M	3.2%

5. Level of Competition

Number of Leads per Month

I had expected that the companies doing telemarketing would generate more leads. When I compared

Level of Competition	% Respondents
Low	22.0%
Medium	44.1%
High	30.!%

Frequency of Telemarketing

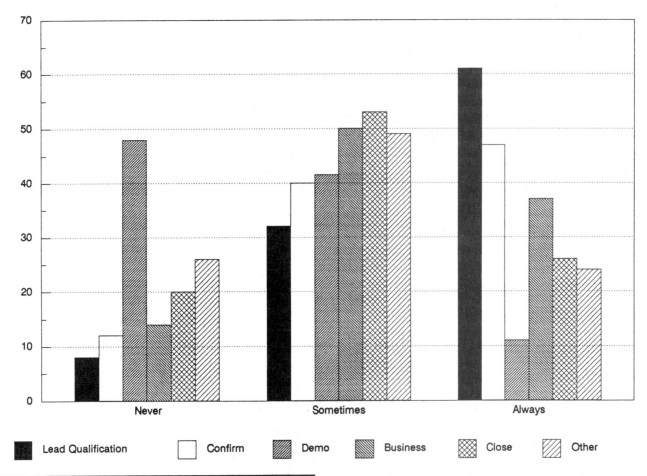

Leads/ month	% Respondents
Don't know	6.5%
<10	11.8%
10-25	24.2%
25-50	14.5%
50-100	12.9%
100-250	13.4%
250-500	7.5%
500-1K	2.7%
>1K	4.8%

the results of this survey with last year's lead generation survey, there were no consistent differences.

6. Frequency of Telemarketing

The first observation on the graph above is that there is a fair amount of consistency among the various types of telemarketing and phone follow up. An average of 22 percent of the respondents never follow up, 46 percent sometimes follow up and 32 percent always follow up. These are the averages for all of the categories in the graph on the next page.

The second observation is that there is a steady decline in telemarketing usage the further you get into the sales cycle. This makes sense. Even for companies who make their sales with direct sales calls, telemarketing can be useful early in the sales cycle. Direct sales companies often use telemarketing to qualify leads, confirm that prospects received the information, and schedule meetings.

If you look at it from this point of view, everyone is using telesales/telemarketing. Even the most die-hard direct sales organizations make use of telemarketing. The question is how much use you make of telemarketing. Where do you use telemarketing and where do you start to use more direct involvement?

This is a very fundamental decision. I actually think that you should make this decision before you develop the product. (I realize this is an extreme marketing perspective, but I hope that you will bear with me.) My approach is that when you are talking to customers and developing your product concepts for a product you think about the benefits. What will sell the product and how you will demonstrate these benefits to your prospects? I have worked with developers in the design stage on screens that will help sell the product. It turned out that these screens also appeared to make the product easier to use and provided better results, but that was a by-product.

When you are developing a product that is to be sold without a direct sales presence, there is much more pressure on the product to jump out and hit the customer in the face.

The other side of the coin is that it is often difficult to convert direct sales products into telemarketing products. I have seen a number of cases where products which had been successful when sold via direct sales could not be sold by telemarketing. There were a number of factors which were involved, and I don't know the relative importance of these factors.

The first category of problems were cultural. The sales and marketing people had experience selling direct products. They knew how to do this, and they understood how this would affect their personal careers. They viewed the changes implicit in telemarketing as threatening. One example was the sales manager who really liked managing high-level direct sales people. He felt that managing low-level (his perspective) telemarketing people was demeaning. He viewed it as a demotion! My experience is that you need to bring in telemarketing expertise if you want to change your sales approach. In most cases, it has really helped to hire a telemarketing sales manager who is on the same level as the direct sales manager.

The next category of problems are pre-sales and marketing materials. When you are planning on having sales people visit the prospects, there is much less pressure on the marketing materials to tell the story. The marketing materials become much more of a "leave behind." They need to be something that the prospect will be pleased to receive. The image projected by the materials is very important in this situation. Since they have met with your people, it is much less important that the marketing materials contain product-specific details. My experience is that new people need to re-do the marketing materi-

als if you want to change from direct sales to telesales. It is almost impossible for the people who created the marketing materials for direct sales to take a fresh look at them and reconsider what will be required to support a telesales effort.

7. Lead Qualification

Almost everyone calls to make the initial lead qualification. Only eight percent of our respondents never call. Of these calls, 79 percent were made by sales. When you consider that 17 percent of the respondents had no sales people, this is 95 percent of the companies who have sales people.

I continue to be surprised that companies don't have non-sales people qualify the leads. It seems to me that you could easily have an administrative person call the prospect and ask the basic qualifying questions. The only cases where I have been able to get this implemented was where there were no sales people. If the company has sales people, the sales people want to make the initial call. They don't want someone else talking to their prospect. The fact that this is so consistent makes me believe that having the sales people call is really the best way to qualify the leads.

8. Confirming Information Received

Forty-eight percent of the companies always confirm that the information was received. This is the point where I find it easiest to ask the qualifying questions. The call starts with asking if they received the information. It is fairly easy to ask a few questions. I think the prospect would be a little more willing to answer the qualifying questions since the company has given them the information that they requested. Seventy-four percent of these calls were made by the sales people.

I think one of the reasons the sales people are so likely to make these calls is that they are pleasant calls. There is very little pressure, and there should be almost no rejection. Given all of the other opportunities for rejection, it is reasonable that sales people would want to make these calls.

9. Business Need

Slightly more companies (37%) establish the business need via telemarketing and sales people make these calls 82 percent of the time (this is the highest percentage for sales follow up).

I am a little confused about why companies are more likely to establish the business need than to go through the demo. If the demo is so great that the prospects don't need any help with it, this makes sense. Another reason is that a good number of companies visit the prospect in person to demo their product. One scenario that I often see is that the sales person establishes the business need with the prospect before the demo visit. The approach is to insure that "if our product does what we claim, will it make good business sense for you to buy it?" If you can establish the business need, you should have a high closure rate when you demo the product.

10. Closing the Sale

Twenty-seven percent of the respondents close the sale over the phone and 81 percent of these calls are made by the sales people. This is 97 percent of the companies with sales people. I will look at which companies are most likely to close sales over the phone later in this newsletter.

11. Other Products

Only six percent of the respondent sell other products over the phone. Time and time again, I see companies with a major product and a number of smaller add-on products. Sometimes, the sales person can bundle these other products into the initial sale.

If that doesn't happen, it is difficult to go back to the customers and sell these other products. The sales people who are selling the primary product can't justify spending their time selling the other products because they can make more money selling the primary product. I thought you could hire junior sales people to sell these other products, but that seems to be difficult because the commissions would be so low. The company would have to subsidize these junior sales people. This is probably why these other products are sold via telemarketing.

My best results selling these other products is to use direct mail to offer customers special deals on them. Often this is done in the off season when sales of the primary product to new prospects are down. The customers like getting a deal and are willing to purchase in the off season.

12. Selling Training

Only 24 percent of the respondents sell training via telemarketing. Of these calls, 57 percent were made by the sales people. This was higher than I would have expected since I would have thought that the support manager or training manager would be making these calls. I have had very good luck with making the training manager responsible for selling training. Once they know that they are going to be measured on this, and that they can get a bonus if they actually sell training, they will figure out how to sell it.

My best experiences with selling training have involved a combination of direct mail and telemarketing. We developed letters that we sent to all customers describing the training available, and we talked to the customers who responded. The other approach is to call customers who are making too many support calls. I have found that it is effective for the support manager to call the business contact at the customer and say "Your people have been making alot of calls to our support people. It looks like you need some re-training in the following area. I think that you should schedule this to reduce the confusion and wasted time for your people."

13. Which Companies Close over the Phone?

Product Price

Companies with products from $1,000 to $10,000 are most likely to close over the phone, while companies over $10,000 are much less likely to close over the phone. It also appears that the $500 to $1,000 range is difficult. It requires a significant amount of selling, since it isn't an impulse decision like the very low-priced products. Yet it doesn't have the commissions to reward the sales person for following up.

Product Price	% Always Close by Phone
<$100	33%
$100-$500	25%
$500-$1K	14%
$1K-$5K	42%
$5K-$10K	43%
>$10K	17%

Computer Type

Workstation software companies are most likely to close sales over the phone. Minicomputer and main-frame companies are least likely.

Computer Type	% Always Close by Phone
PC	28%
LAN	21%
Minicomputer	16%
Workstation	37%
Mainframe	17%

Sales Quota

If there is no quota or no sales person, companies aren't likely to close sales via telemarketing. Closing sales over the phone does require good sales skills. It looks like most companies with quotas up to $600,000 can sell via telemarketing. The percentage selling via telemarketing drops for $600,000 to $1 million, but 60 percent of the companies with quotas over $1 million sell via telemarketing. The sample for companies over $1 million is pretty small, so the statistics are questionable for this extreme upper range. I know of several companies whose quotas are over $1 million which sell exclusively over the phone. They even conduct their demos with their support people calling the prospects and walking them through the demo. It can be done, but it does require that everything be right.

Sales Quota	% Always Close by Phone
No Quota	15%
No sales people	20%
<$100K	43%
$100K-$200K	47%
$200K-$400K	26%
$400K-$600K	48%
$600K-$800K	17%
$800K-$1M	0%
>$1M	60%

14. Real Life Telemarketing

Dear Dave,

I noticed your next newsletter (last month 4/91) will be dealing with telemarketing. I thought I'd relay our experiences, since we're in the middle of a telemarketing program right now.

Although we've attempted in-house telemarketing in the past, we've never had the discipline necessary to do it properly. As a result, this has been ignored by us as a source of lead generation. However, I recently discovered a company that specializes in TM for hardware and software firms. After some investigation, we decided to give it another try.

My firm had to provide the call list, and the questionnaire was developed jointly between their staff and ours. Since all I was trying to identify were companies in my market niche which were actively looking for our kind of product (Purchasing and materials management automation), I didn't need an extensive questionnaire — it ended up with four questions.

We purchased 100 hours of TM as a trial. The TM firm felt that they could get about 5-7 interviews per hour, or 500-700 interviews. They also predicted 10% of those would qualify as "hot leads" (based on our definition), thus, in theory, giving us 50-70 hot leads. The cost per hot lead, based on the cost of the TM plus the call list from a list house, was expected to be $75-$106. This compares to our experience of about $150 per lead with direct mail.

In actuality, the TM firm has hit almost exactly 5 interviews per hour, and 10% of those were highly qualified hot leads, with an additional 16% falling into the "warm" lead category. (Two weeks after I received this letter, I talked to Jerry and the hot leads had grown to 16% of the interviews. —Dave)

Our average product sale is in the $60,000 range, and we can typically close 20% of our hot leads within a year. This should thus be very cost effective for us.

I see TM as an essential part, but not the only part, of our lead generation efforts. What TM doesn't do is get exposure for our products (we opted to have the TM staff keep our anonymity, posing the questions as being part of a market survey.) We expected our direct mail efforts will give us product exposure as well as a supplemental stream of leads (advertising has only limited value for us, since there is no trade journal that hits any measurable percentage of our target market.)

A major benefit I see with TM is it can rapidly fill up a sales lead pipeline. Our effort took less than four weeks to complete, including script design, call list acquisition, and all the calling.

The firm I used was exceptional in their business style. I received pie charts of lead generation ratios during the call process, they fax'ed hot leads to me immediately, and they were very quick to respond to questions. If anyone is considering TM, they should definitely talk to these people. They are Hancock Information Group in Longwood, FL (407) 682-1556.

Keep up the good work with your newsletter. I hope we see an upcoming issue that covers Operating Ratios (revenue per employee, active customers per Customer Support employee, maintenance revenue per Customer Support employee, etc.)

Sincerely,
Jerry O'Connell
CEO
Structured Computer Systems
(203) 677-0222

Dear Jerry,

Thanks for the letter. This is the kind of reality based information that really helps all of us. I urge people to set aside 10% of their lead generation budget for experiments. I expect less than half of the experiments to work out, but when they do work out they more than cover the experiments that didn't work out.

The last time I asked people about lead generation sources I found that telemarketing was the primary lead generation technique in only 12.2 percent of the companies. Very few companies generate more than ten percent of their leads with telemarketing. At the same time, 6.1% of the companies were generating over fifty percent of their leads via telemarketing.

This corresponded to the same 6.1% of the companies who were expending a high level of effort on telemarketing.

Level of Effort	% Respondents
High	6.1%
Medium	2.0%
Low	10.2%

For each budget dollar spent, telemarketing generates more leads than other methods used. Thus, it appears that telemarketing is a cost effective way to generate leads.

Percent of Budget	% Respondents
0%	46.9%
< 10%	10.2%
> 50%	4.1%

The trend toward telemarketing is fairly strong (the number of companies increasing is three times larger than those who are decreasing.)

Trend in Usage	% Respondents
Increasing	12.2%
No change	4.1%
Decreasing	4.1%

When I looked back over the April 1991 issue on Telemarketing and the survey that I sent out, I was surprised that I didn't ask about using telemarketing to generate leads. Based on my experience, I had just assumed that people weren't doing it because it was too hard (even if it was cost effective). This is a very good example of closing your mind to alternatives that "aren't practical". Thanks for reminding me that sometimes they can be very practical. It just takes the courage to step out and find the resources to make it real.

Thanks again for the letter
Dave

Last minute update

I received a call from Jerry O'Connell with his updated numbers just as this issue was going to my editor. The TM reps called for 133 hours and conducted 617 interviews. This is 4.5 calls per hour which is a little less than the 5 calls per hour anticipated. The interview for Structured Computer Systems was shorter than the average interview used by the TM firm (it only had four questions). Thus the TM firm's estimate was slightly off.

The good news is that 19% of the leads were "hot" leads. (These leads met the criteria they had initially set up as "hot".) This is almost twice the expected rate of 10%. In addition to the hot leads, they also found 15% were "warm" leads which generated a very good supply of leads for the sales people to follow up on.

The TM firm charged $50 per hour, including phone calls and consulting time setting up the questionnaire. Thus, the hot leads cost $55 each which was significantly lower than the $150 per lead they had achieved with direct mail. They also felt that these were better leads since people tend to be more honest with an impartial person. Bottom line, this program was a great success.

C. Miscellaneous (1991)

1. How to Get Your Name in Front of the Top Guy (Mar)

Dear Mr. Bowen:

We enjoy your newsletter each month. It is nice to read about other software companies that have similar problems and interesting ideas. The surveys are always popular.

Summit Software markets PC-based cost accounting software to the financial services industry. The company is eight years old and has a large and active user group. We sell into the financial reporting or accounting area of the bank dealing with the controller or CFO. While upper management may use the reports and data, our systems have no identification with the user's boss. Upper management may make major decisions based on the results Summit helps to provide. The same group are speakers at meetings

interviewed for articles. We feel our name recognition by this important group could be beneficial.

Our question is: How would you suggest we address getting our name in front of the top guy?

Thank you
Jeannine D. Owens, Vice President
Summit Software, Inc.,
(214) 239-3426

Dear Jeannine:

There are a number of approaches. I will start with the most direct and then go to less direct approaches. The most direct approach is to call the CEO. While this is a nice simplistic solution to your problem, it probably isn't reasonable. If you don't have a reasonable pretext for contacting the CEO, you risk offending your CFO contact. Another idea would be to send a letter to the CEO. This isn't as likely to upset the CFO but it still has some risk of offending the CFO. You might send the CEO a survey asking for their feedback on your product and how they see its current and future applications. If you also send a similar survey to the CFO, you should have minimal risk of upsetting everyone. Another approach would be to send a letter with an article reprint. If you don't have an article, you might contact your CFOs and say that you would like to do an article on a CFO/CEO and how they both use your system. Then you could mail this article to the CEOs. (I should note that you could use this type of article in a lead generation where you mail letters to both the CEO and CFO with the reprint attached.) The article itself should get you some publicity in the CEO's world. This is the next approach. You could get press releases and articles in magazines that your CEOs read.

It occurs to me that I haven't suggested asking the CFO to introduce us to the CEO. I had one client that had some success in this area. They developed a presentation that the business contacts could use to gain entry with senior management. This helped the business contacts get a forum with senior management while it also increased our visibility with them. If you did the survey that I mentioned at the start, you could summarize the results in a presentation or report. You could let the CFO present this to the CEO or you could mail it directly to the CEO. My temptation would be to mail it back to the CEO if they had responded to the survey. If they didn't, I might involve the CFO.

You didn't say if you had a users group. If you did, you might explore having a day for CEOs. Presenting your survey results and having a round table discussion on the future of financial reporting from the CEO's point of view might draw in CEOs.

As you can see, there are any number of ways that you can promote yourself to the CEOs. If you are serious about increasing your visibility with them, you will probably have to explore many of these and come up with your own list of approaches. This type of program can take years to fully unfold, but the impact can be dramatic. I wish you good luck in this phase of your growth.

Dave

2. Sales Success Profile (April)

I received a card from a reader advertising a sales skills test. It is the $ales $uccess Profile and the points were:

50 question multiple choice sales skills test, measuring 12 sales skill areas.

PC compatible scoring software provided for instantaneous results.

Originally developed for a Fortune 500 Company

Validated against over 11,000 salespeople, accurate and legal to use.

Only $199.

Lousig-Nont & Associates, Inc.
3740 S Royal Crest Street
Las Vegas, NV 89119-7010
(702) 732-8000

I don't have any experience or know of anyone using this test. I have had a couple of clients who used this type of sales tests and a number of times the sales managers swore by the test that they liked. All of the managers who really used these tests had made a real investment in understanding the test

and then calibrating their sales people. It takes time to really get the results from this type of effort.

The people I know who have used this type of product have used services offered by consultants. They received tests from the consultant, and mailed the tests back to the consultant. It often took a week or two to get the results back. All other things being equal, getting the results instantaneously would be a real advantage. Louise-Nont offers a 30-day money back guarantee, so it might be Worth a try if you are looking for a test to help you hire better sales people.

3. Selling to the Federal Government (May)

Dear Dave,

I thought you might be interested in learning about PRAXIS. As the enclosed materials describe, PRAXIS is a federal software sales and marketing firm specializing in penetrating the government market. Our client companies are independent software companies with sales of $10 to $50 Million.

Thanks for your assistance.

Sincerely,
H Bailey Spencer
President
PRAXIS
(703) 739-8400

Dear Bailey,

The federal government is one of those markets that most small software companies don't go after. Your $10 Million threshold cuts out over 90% of the Software Success readers, but I would urge any readers who think they are ready to approach the federal marketplace to contact you. Your materials are very impressive and it looks like you are well positioned to sell to the federal marketplace.

Thanks,
Dave

1992
Software Success
Reference Book

Chapter IX
Index

IX. Index

A. Promotion

B. Lead Genration

Index

Index

Index

C. Pricing

Index

Index

D.   Distribution

Index

Index

E. Management Issues

Index

Index

F. Customer Support & Technical Issues

Index

Index

Index

G. Feature Articles

Index

H. Sales Cycle

Index